THE NEW HISTORICISM: STUDIES IN CULTURAL POETICS

General Editor, Stephen Greenblatt

HOLY FEAST AND HOLY FAST

FRONTISPIECE. In this Flemish retable of the Kinship of St. Anne from about 1500 we find feeding themes associated with Jesus' female relatives. In the center Mary presents her child to Anne, who offers him grapes (a eucharistic symbol), while in the lower left another woman nurses a baby. (Anne's left hand and the grapes have been restored.) Worshipers at mass would have seen a priest elevating the host just in front of this depiction of holy women offering food: both grapes (wine or blood) and Christ himself (bread or flesh). Musée du Parc du Cinquantenaire, Brussels. Copyright A.C.L., Brussels.

❖ *Holy Feast and Holy Fast*

THE RELIGIOUS SIGNIFICANCE
OF FOOD TO MEDIEVAL WOMEN

♦ CAROLINE WALKER BYNUM ♦

University of California Press ♦ BERKELEY LOS ANGELES LONDON

University of California Press
Berkeley and Los Angeles, California
University of California Press, Ltd.
London, England
© 1987 by
The Regents of the University of California
First paperback printing 1988

Library of Congress Cataloging-in-Publication Data
Bynum, Caroline Walker.
  Holy feast and holy fast.

  Includes indexes.
  1. Food—Religious aspects—Christianity. 2. Women—
History—Middle Ages, 500–1500. 3. Food habits—History.
I. Title.
BR253.B96 1987   248.4'6   85–28896
ISBN 978-0-520-06329-7 (alk. paper)
Printed in the United States of America

13 12 11 10 09 08 07 06
17 16 15 14 13 12 11 10

To the memory of
Merle Bernice Grubbs Walker
(1911–1979)

CONTENTS

LIST OF PLATES

Viterbo), by Benozzo di Lese, called Gozzoli. Museo di S. Francesco, Montefalco. Courtesy Alinari/Art Resource, N.Y.

10. Woodcut from John Brugman's *Vita alme Virginis de Sciedam*, 1498. Museum of the Catherineconvent, Utrecht. Copyright Stichting Het Catharijneconvent.

11. Three miniatures from a Life of Colette made by Master Jehan Boniface between 1468 and 1477 for Margaret of York. Manuscript 8, fols. 34r, 68v, 75v, of the Convent of Clares at Ghent.

12. Miniature of *imago muliebris*, from part 2, vision 6, of Hildegard of Bingen's *Scivias*. Plate 15 in Hildegard of Bingen, *Scivias*, ed. Adelgundis Führkötter and A. Carlevaris, Corpus christianorum: continuatio mediaevalis 43, 2 vols. (Turnhout: Brepols, 1978), 1: 228ff. Made from a hand-colored photocopy (1927–1933) of the lost original. Courtesy Brepols.

13. *Vierge ouvrante*, closed and open. The Metropolitan Museum of Art, gift of J. Pierpont Morgan, 1917.

14. *Madonna and Child before a Firescreen*, by Robert Campin. The National Gallery, London. Courtesy the Trustees, The National Gallery, London.

15. *Charity*, by Lucas Cranach the Elder. Musée d'Histoire et d'Art, Luxembourg.

16. Fountain of the Virtues, Nürnberg. Photograph by author.

17. *Ecclesia lactans* standing over the cardinal virtues, by Giovanni Pisano. Detail from a pulpit. The Cathedral, Pisa.

18. Detail of the Retable of St. Bernard by the Master of Palma. Sociedad Arqueológica Luliana, Palma de Mallorca.

19. Detail of the Retable of St. Ildefonso by the Master of Osma. The Cathedral, El Burgo de Osma, Soria.

20. *The Rest on the Flight into Egypt*, by Gerard David. National Gallery of Art, Washington, Andrew W. Mellon Collection. Copyright National Gallery of Art.

21. *Virgin and Child in a Landscape*, by Jan van Hemessen. National Museum, Stockholm. Courtesy National Museum, Stockholm.

22. *The Holy Kinship*, by Maerten de Vos. Museum of Fine Arts, Ghent.

23. *Virgin and Child, Heures de Milan*, fol. 120r. Museo Civico, Turin. Copyright Museo Civico di Torino; courtesy Agent Foto, Turin.

PREFACE

Part of this book was written in a pleasant office on the top floor of the Bunting Institute of Radcliffe College in Cambridge, Massachusetts. I am grateful to my colleagues at the Bunting, many of whom read portions of the manuscript or argued with me about my ideas. I would especially like to thank Linda Gordon, Ellen Bassuk, Nancy Miller, Eve Sedgwick, Marilyn Massey, Martha Ackelsberg, Bettina Friedl, Ann Bookman, and Debbie McDowell, who cared deeply about my work but never let me forget that the medieval women I studied sounded decidedly peculiar to modern ears. I would also like to thank the National Endowment for the Humanities for a Fellowship for Advanced Study and Research and the University of Washington for sabbatical leave in 1983–1984.

Not all of this book was written in the scholarly leisure of the Bunting Institute nor amid the riches of Harvard University's Widener Library. Much of it was composed in a cubbyhole on the top floor of Suzzallo Library at the University of Washington. Others who have struggled with the inevitably limited library resources of a relatively new institution will understand how much I owe to librarians for making my research possible. Kristi Greenfield of Suzzallo Acquisitions and Ruth Kirk and Anna McCausland of Interlibrary Borrowing Services found books for me, over and over again, with an enthusiasm that went beyond pride in a job well done and became pride in scholarship itself. Without them, this book would not exist.

The colleagues, former teachers, and friends who have influenced my ideas on the history of spirituality are a far-flung network. I would especially like to thank Giles Constable, John Boswell, Natalie Z. Davis, Lester Little, Elizabeth A. R. Brown, Richard Kieckhefer, Paul Meyvaert, Ann Freeman, Charles T. Wood, and Mark R. Silk for their inspiration and their help. Joan Jacobs Brumberg and Rachel Jacoff have

xiii

generously assisted with translations and citations. David Pinkney, Ruth Mellinkoff, Patricia Fortini Brown, Walter Cahn, and Anna Kartsonis taught me how to track down art historical information. Mary Martin McLaughlin, whose work has long been an example and an inspiration to me, read the entire manuscript and offered advice in both small matters of detail and large matters of interpretation. Ken Rose typed with care and enthusiasm. Elizabeth Goolian and my editor, Sheila Levine, not only helped me put the book together but also, in the process of doing so, offered me intellectual stimulation and friendship.

My deepest thanks go to three people: Judith Van Herik; my husband, Guenther Roth; and Peter Brown. Judith Van Herik helped me work out my positions both in relation to the several currents of recent feminist theory and in relation to psychoanalytic interpretations of food. Guenther Roth spotted iconographical evidence for me in museums, argued with me about what I mean by "cause," and saved me from my worst instincts in the matter of adjectives. Peter Brown is partly responsible for the fact that this study exists at all. Not only did he urge me to let it become a book when I was struggling to force it into the compass of a fifty-page article; he also started me on the search for a convincing interpretation of medieval asceticism when he asked me, more than five years ago, a telling question about the nuns of Helfta.

While I was at work on this book, Rudolph M. Bell of Rutgers University was investigating a similar topic. It was fairly late in the process of our respective researches that we each learned of the other's labors. When we did exchange portions of our manuscripts, we discovered how different our approaches were. Professor Bell's book, *Holy Anorexia* (Chicago: University of Chicago Press, 1985), covers a more limited geographical area and a longer time period. His subject is abstinence, treated without reference to the positive significance of food in Christian practice. His research is more quantitative than mine. His explanatory model is psychological. Whereas Bell has been interested in women's fasting behavior, putting it into a psychological context, I have concentrated on women's use of food as symbol, putting it into a cultural context. It is my hope, as it is Professor Bell's, that readers of our books will find our work complementary. *Holy Anorexia*, with its sophisticated statistical comparisons, strengthens my argument that food practices and food symbols characterized women's experience more than men's. I am grateful to a generous and lively fellow scholar who, rather than warning me off his territory, shared his manuscript and his ideas.

The method and the pace of this book also require some prefatory comment. In method the book is an interpretative essay in social and religious history. Although it makes extensive use of hagiographical material, it is not a technical contribution to the long-established field of hagiography. Where possible I have used the best editions of medieval texts and investigated the most pressing problems relating to the reliability of hagiographical accounts. But I have deliberately chosen not to provide exhaustive bibliographies on the women treated here or to follow every scholarly debate concerning either events or texts down the twisting byways of recent literature. In some instances I have even cited older editions alongside new ones to aid scholars who do not have ready access to the largest and finest libraries.

Concerning pace, it seems worth noting that this book unfolds slowly. The two background chapters are leisurely in their development. The long middle chapters—chapters 4 and 5—tell many stories and refer to many names and places. Though the tempo quickens in the final chapters, as the analysis becomes ever more complicated, I repeatedly break the flow by citing examples. There are two reasons for this pattern of exposition. The first is simply that I am committed, as a historian, to proving rather than merely illustrating my case. To convince modern readers of the decidedly bizarre behavior of some medieval women, it is necessary to give the evidence. But readers who are interested only in my explanation of that behavior might do well to start with chapter 6. The second reason for my deliberate pace, especially in the first half of the book, is the breadth and complexity of the analysis in the second half. Not only do I move, in the last five chapters, on several analytical levels; I also advance theories about the nature of asceticism and about women's use of symbols that are far-reaching in their implications for women's history and for the history of religions. Both to knowledgeable medievalists and to committed feminists—although for different reasons—these theories will seem to be audacious reversals of received wisdom. Such theories cannot be convincing—indeed, *should* not be convincing—unless they explain individual lives without violating their specificity. Thus, before sifting medieval experience through the fine mesh of my analytical sieve, I have tried to let particular women—such as Beatrice of Nazareth, Elizabeth of Hungary, Angela of Foligno, Lidwina of Schiedam, Dorothy of Montau, and Catherine of Siena—have a few paragraphs or even a few pages in which to tell their stories.

This book is dedicated to the memory of my mother, Merle Walker. A brilliant philosopher, poet, scholar, and teacher, she was as circumscribed as any fourteenth-century woman by her society's assumptions about female nurturing and self-sacrifice. Only those who knew her will understand fully the ways in which this book is a tribute to her and an exploration of the pain and triumph of her life. But this book is more. For the books my mother might have written never appeared. My act of writing is therefore my pledge to her granddaughter, Antonia Walker, and to her granddaughter's generation that women's creativity shall not in the future be silenced. It is also an expression of hope that those future generations of women will not lose the compassion, the altruism, and the moral courage that made Merle Walker's life not a tragedy of self-abnegation but a triumph over meaninglessness and suffering.

INTRODUCTION

*St. Bernard compared this Sacrament [the eucharist] with the human
processes of eating, when he used the similes of chewing, swallowing,
assimilation, and digestion. To some people this will seem crude, but
let such refined persons beware of pride, which comes from the devil;
a humble spirit will not take offense at simple things.*

JOHN TAULER
(FOURTEENTH CENTURY)[1]

Recent studies of thirteenth- and fourteenth-century spirituality have
focused on poverty and chastity as the basic motifs of religious life. Over
the past fifty years, poverty has been studied not only as the doctrinal
issue that split the Franciscan order apart but also as the essential ingre-
dient in literal "imitation of Christ" and as the basic metaphor for the
renunciation of wealth and power practiced by the upper and middle
classes of medieval Europe.[2] Chastity has been emphasized as the sine
qua non of religious status, as the reflection on earth of the life of the
angels, and as a requirement that laid a heavy burden of self-hatred on
those individuals—especially women—who were unable to assert control over their own lives.[3]

Sex and money . . . again and again modern scholars have emphasized
the guilt engendered by their seductiveness, the awesome heroism required for their renunciation. Yet this modern focus may tell us more
about the twentieth century than about the late Middle Ages. In our
industrialized corner of the globe, where food supplies do not fail, we
scarcely notice grain or milk, ever-present supports of life, and yearn
rather after money or sexual favors as signs of power and of success. But
even in today's world, it is not everywhere so. For the hungry, food forces
itself forward as an insistent fact, an insistent symbol. Guided by our
knowledge of impoverished modern countries, we should not really be
surprised to find that food was, in medieval Europe, a fundamental

I

economic—and religious—concern. Medieval people often saw gluttony as the major form of lust, fasting as the most painful renunciation, and eating as the most basic and literal way of encountering God. Peter Brown has commented that even though Paul discounted the importance of food and food practices for Christians (Rom. 14:17), "in the straitened Mediterranean [world], the kingdom of heaven had to have something to do with food and drink."[4]

In the Europe of the later thirteenth and fourteenth centuries famine was on the increase again, after several centuries of agricultural growth and relative plenty.[5] Vicious stories—of food-hoarding merchants, of cannibalism, of infanticide, of sick adolescents left to die when they could no longer work—survive in the sources, suggesting a world in which hunger and even starvation were not uncommon.[6] The possibility of over-eating and of giving away food to the unfortunate was a mark of privilege, of aristocratic or patrician status—a particularly visible form of what we call conspicuous consumption, what medieval people called magnanimity or largesse.[7] Small wonder, then, that gorging and vomiting, luxuriating in food until food and body were almost synonymous, became in folk literature an image of unbridled sensual pleasure;[8] that magic vessels forever brimming over with food and drink were staples of European fairy tales; that one of the most common charities enjoined on religious orders was to feed the poor and ill, pilgrims and wanderers; or that sharing one's own meager food with a stranger (who might turn out to be an angel, a fairy, a god, or Christ himself) was, in hagiography and folktale alike, a standard indication of heroic or saintly generosity.[9] Small wonder, too, that self-starvation, the deliberate and extreme renunciation of food and drink, seemed to medieval people the most basic asceticism, requiring the kind of courage and holy foolishness that marked the saints. To repress eating and hunger was to control the body in a discipline far more basic than any achieved by shedding the less frequent and essential gratifications of sex or money. As Christ supposedly said in a vision granted to Margaret of Cortona (d. 1297): "In this life, Christians cannot be perfect unless they restrain their appetites from vices, for without abstinence from food and drink the war of the flesh will never end; and they feel and suffer most from the rebellion of the flesh who refuse this saving remedy."[10] Or as Gunther of Pairis, the Cistercian historian and poet, said in a treatise on prayer and fasting written about 1200: "Fasting is useful for expelling demons, excluding evil thoughts, remitting sins, mortifying vices, giving certain hope of future goods and a foretaste [*perceptio*] of celestial joys."[11] In the late fourteenth century, Catherine of Sweden's hagiographer attributed to her the opinion that "abstinence prolongs life, preserves chastity, pleases God, repulses demons, illumines the intellect, strengthens the mind, overcomes vices, overpowers the flesh, and stirs and inflames the heart with love of God."[12] An anonymous satire on hypocritical monks, probably from the high Middle Ages, states explicitly that food and drink are harder to renounce than sex: "Many who are not lured by more serious faults are cast down by overindulgence in food and drink. . . . Indeed, thinned by fasting or vigils and repeated prayers, the stomach thinks not of a woman but of food; it meditates not on lust but on sleep."[13]

Eating in late medieval Europe was not simply an activity that marked off fine calibrations of social status and a source of pleasure so intense and sensual that the renunciation of it was at the core of religious world-denial. Eating was also an occasion for union with one's fellows and one's God, a commensality given particular intensity by the prototypical meal, the eucharist, which seemed to hover in the background of any banquet.[14] Because Jesus had fed the faithful not merely as servant and waiter, preparer and multiplier of loaves and fishes, but as the very bread and wine itself, *to eat* was a powerful verb. It meant to consume, to assimilate, to become God. To eat God in the eucharist was a kind of audacious deification, a becoming of the flesh that, in its agony, fed and saved the world. Thus, to religious men and women, renunciation of ordinary food prepared the way for consuming (i.e., becoming) Christ, in eucharist and in mystical union. Mechtild of Magdeburg (d. 1282?), who spoke of ecstatic experiences as "eating God," said of the mass:

> Yet I, least of all souls,
> Take Him in my hand
> Eat Him and drink Him
> And do with Him what I will![15]

The thirteenth-century Flemish mystic Hadewijch wrote:

> In the anguish or the repose or the madness of Love,
> . . . .
> The heart of each devours the other's heart.
> . . . .

3

> As he who is Love itself showed us
> When he gave us himself to eat
> . . . .
> . . . love's most intimate union
> Is through eating, tasting, and seeing interiorly.[16]

John Tauler, preaching on John 6:56 ("For my flesh is meat indeed"), said:

> There is no kind of matter which is so close to a man and becomes so much a part of him as the food and drink he puts into his mouth; and so God has found this wonderful way of uniting Himself with us as closely as possible and becoming part of us.[17]

And William of St. Thierry (d. ca. 1148) spoke thus of the meaning of the Incarnation:

> It is your breasts, O eternal Wisdom, that nourish the holy infancy of your little ones.[18]

> It was not the least of the chief reasons for your incarnation that your babes in the church, who still needed your milk rather than solid food, . . . might find in you a form not unfamiliar to themselves.[19]

Not only was food a more significant motif in late medieval spirituality than most historians have recognized, food was also a more important motif in women's piety than in men's. For certain late medieval women, fasting became an obsession so overwhelming that modern historians have sometimes thought their stories preserve the earliest documentable cases of anorexia nervosa. Women all over Europe served Christ by feeding others, donating to the poor the food that husbands and fathers felt proud to be able to save and consume. The eucharist and related devotions, such as those to the body, wounds, heart, and blood of Christ, were at the very center of women's piety. Eating God in the host was both a sweet tasting that focused and transcended all hunger and an occasion for paramystical phenomena of the most bizarre and exuberant sort.

In this book I explore the implications of food-related religious practices and of food images in the piety of medieval women. Although I have tried to cite enough cases to demonstrate the centrality of food in both practice and texts, my concern has been less to collect metaphors or to count cases of food asceticism, eucharistic devotion, or feeding miracles than it has been to show the manifold meanings of food and its pervasiveness in religious symbolism. Rather than mention every woman who fasted or saw visions of the Christ child in the chalice, I have concentrated on women whose life stories and writings survive in sufficient detail for us to trace, across the distance created by many centuries and by vastly different modern assumptions, the rich and paradoxical meanings of eating and not eating. Although I am aware of modern clinical definitions of food obsession, I have avoided using them, at least initially, because I find that medieval attitudes toward food are far more diverse than those implied by the modern concepts of anorexia nervosa and hysteria. To religious women food was a way of controlling as well as renouncing both self and environment. But it was more. Food was flesh, and flesh was suffering and fertility. In renouncing ordinary food and directing their being toward the food that is Christ, women moved to God not merely by abandoning their flawed physicality but also by becoming the suffering and feeding humanity of the body on the cross, the food on the altar. However absurd or vulgar some medieval practices and language may seem to casual modern observers, we do well to heed Tauler's warning (quoted above) not to take offense. Deeper study of these "simple things" suggests that food and body can be powerful ways of encountering suffering and fecundity—aspects of the human condition from which even we in the twentieth century cannnot hide completely.

Because I intend this book both for medievalists and for readers with a general interest in the history of women or the history of Christianity, I have provided background material for both groups. The first chapter is a brief account of the religious options available to medieval women; the second explains the major food practices of medieval Christians—fasting and eucharistic devotion—with attention to their roots in early Christianity. Both chapters contain much material that will be familiar to specialists, although I have presented it in a new way. The third chapter, which discusses the nature of the evidence, is provided primarily for scholars. It examines some of the problems raised by the use of hagiographical material; it also gives a close reading of several male figures to strengthen the case for characterizing food practices and metaphors as "female." The fourth and fifth chapters present the stories about women and the writings by them on which this book is based. I have chosen to tell some of these stories as *stories* before turning to a more analytical discussion because it is only by recounting the stories themselves that I can demonstrate to—and evoke for—readers the extent to which many food motifs tend to be woven into a single life. The last five chapters are the heart of the argument. In them I provide what might be called, respectively, a functionalist and a phenomenological explanation of the prominence of food metaphors and food practices in women's piety. In other words, I show, first, how women were able to use food practices to shape their experience and their place in both family and community and, second, what food-related behavior and symbols actually meant to medieval women. In doing this, I suggest both a new interpretation of late medieval asceticism and a new understanding of the significance of gender in medieval religion.

The last five chapters indeed become a complex refutation of the standard interpretation of asceticism as world-rejection or as practical dualism and of the standard picture of medieval women as constrained on every side by a misogyny they internalized as self-hatred or masochism. Rather, I argue that medieval efforts to discipline and manipulate the body should be interpreted more as elaborate changes rung upon the *possibilities* provided by fleshliness than as flights from physicality. I also demonstrate the extent to which religious women derived their basic symbols from such ordinary biological and social experiences as giving birth, lactating, suffering, and preparing and distributing food. The identification of this characteristic of women's symbols—which contrasts sharply with the enthusiasm contemporary males felt for symbols of reversal (especially the renunciation of wealth and power)—enables me to raise fundamental questions about differences in male and female religiosity.

Three introductory comments may be helpful. The first concerns chronology. Despite the fact that some of the most spectacular cases of fasting or eucharistic frenzy discussed below come from the fifteenth century, I have limited the bulk of my analysis to, and taken most of my examples from, the thirteenth and fourteenth centuries. I have chosen this chronological focus because my goal is to explain the origins of a particular emphasis within women's piety. I have not tried to follow that piety down into the sixteenth and seventeenth centuries, although one could argue that it persisted that long (and even longer) in Europe, especially rural, Catholic Europe. I shall, however, leave the subsequent history to others. My purpose is to put the inception of that piety into as broad a context as possible, to show that topics such as eucharistic devotion, fasting, and miraculous bodily changes should not be discussed in isolation from each other. To demonstrate the interconnection of devotional practices and symbols in one period, I had to avoid carrying the history of any of them too far forward in time. I have also concentrated more on delineating the overall pattern of symbols within the culture than on ferreting out chronological change. I have felt this to be necessary in order to make the pattern clear, but I hope I have not ignored change entirely.

Second, I am fully aware that most of the women I am discussing are exceptional. Mary of Oignies (d. 1213) and Catherine of Siena (d. 1380) are no more typical of religious women (or of women generally) than *The Canterbury Tales* and *The Divine Comedy* are typical of medieval literature or of medieval life. Indeed, medieval hagiographers pointed out repeatedly that saints are not even primarily "models" for ordinary mortals; the saints are far too dangerous for that. Like Christ himself, they could not and should not be imitated in their full extravagance and power. Rather (so their admirers say), they should be loved, venerated, and meditated upon as moments in which the other that is God breaks through into the mundane world, saturating it with meaning. And yet, in the discussion that follows, I move from these particular, exceptional women to their religious and social worlds, explaining the women by their context and the context by the women. Two things, speaking very generally, justify this endeavor. The first is that the evidence we can garner from chronicles, law codes, sermons, and so on suggests that some of the practices of exceptional women—their fasting, food distribution, psychosomatic changes, etc.—were found in ordinary religious women as well. The behavior of saints such as Elizabeth of Hungary (d. 1231) or Catherine of Genoa finds dozens of mundane parallels in women such as the mother of Peter of Luxembourg (d. 1387), the fourteenth-century laywoman Margery Kempe (d. after 1438), and the fasting girls noticed in passing by sixteenth-century broadside writers. The second justification is that those holy women of whom we have records, especially those who were canonized or widely revered, were *chosen* by their contemporaries as heroines, mirrors, and lessons—as lenses through which God's power and human aspirations were focused toward each other. Like a poem or romance whose manuscript tradition attests that it was widely read, women such as Catherine of Siena reflect what at least some of their contemporaries found valuable and awe-inspiring. It is therefore not unwarranted to take the stories most commonly told about saintly women—however atypical or abnormal they may appear to medieval or modern common sense—as important evidence about the assumptions of the people who admired the saints.[20]

Finally, it should hardly be necessary to comment that I am not concerned with whether medieval accounts of phenomena such as stigmata, levitation, miraculous bodily changes, extended inedia, visions, and food-multiplication miracles are "true." As a phenomenologist would say, I "bracket" the question of cause, either natural or supernatural, for such events. I am interested in what medieval people experienced; and while I have a historian's skepticism about all evidence, I also, as a historian, prefer to start my study of the past with what people in the past said themselves. Medieval people had several different models for understanding phenomena such as eucharistic visions or extended and total abstinence. Where they themselves suggest that what some see as a miracle is fraud or demonic possession or illness, I am interested in their models; where they note the difference between meditation and vision, or between visions of the inner and the outer eyes, I am curious about why they found such distinctions important. But when they do not employ categories or explanations that modern people find necessary, I try to avoid such terminology. Thus when I say, for example, that a certain holy woman lived for years without eating, I do not mean to imply that this statement is true (or false) by twentieth-century standards of reporting or of scientific verification. I mean that such a story interested medieval people enough for them to record it and that it expressed a way of finding value and giving meaning that holy women, their chroniclers, and their admirers all shared.[21]

My work has implications for modern problems and obsessions that will not be lost on many of its readers. I have touched on these in my epilogue. I have, moreover, tried to write in a manner that is accessible to those who are not medievalists. This is nonetheless a scholarly, not a popular, book.[22] It is a book about then, not about now. It is animated most fundamentally neither by horror at the problems of women in the modern world nor by delight at their advances, whatever I may feel of both emotions. My commitment, vision, and method are historical; I intend to reveal the past in its strangeness as well as its familiarity. My point is to argue that women's behavior and women's writing must be understood in the context of social, economic, and ecclesiastical structures, theological and devotional traditions, very different from our own. If readers leave this book simply condemning the past as peculiar, I shall have failed. But I shall have failed just as profoundly if readers draw direct answers to modern problems from the lives I chronicle.

I

The background

RELIGIOUS WOMEN
IN THE LATER MIDDLE AGES

Some of these women dissolved with such a particular and marvelous love toward God that they languished with desire and for years had rarely been able to rise from their beds. They had no other infirmity, save that their souls were melted with desire of him, and, sweetly resting with the Lord, as they were comforted in spirit they were weakened in body. . . . The cheeks of one were seen to waste away, while her soul was liquified with the greatness of her love. Many had the taste of honey sensibly in their mouths because of the gift of spiritual sweetness in their hearts. . . . Another's flow of tears had made visible furrows down her face. . . . Others were drawn with such intoxication of spirit that in sacred silence they would remain quiet a whole day. . . . so that they could not be roused by clamor or feel a blow. . . . Some in receiving the bread of him who came down from heaven obtained not only refreshment in their hearts but a palpable consolation in their mouths sweeter than honey and the honeycomb. . . . [They] languished with such desire for the sacrament that they could not be sustained . . . unless their souls were frequently refreshed by the sweetness of this food. Let the infidel heretics blush, who do not partake of this food either by faith or by love.

JAMES OF VITRY
(EARLY THIRTEENTH CENTURY)[1]

THE LATER Middle Ages, especially the period from the late twelfth to the early fourteenth century, witnessed a significant proliferation of opportunities for women to participate in specialized religious roles and of the type of roles available. The number of female saints, including married women saints, increased. Women's piety—whether monastic or lay—took on certain distinctive characteristics that powerful males, both secular and clerical, noted, sometimes with awe and sometimes with suspicion. Indeed, for the first time in Christian history, we can identify a women's movement (the beguines) and can speak of specifically female influences on the development of piety. If we are to grasp the significance of food as an underlying theme in women's spirituality, we need to understand the general changes in women's religious experience throughout the period.[2]

♦ New Opportunities

Being a nun was almost the only specialized religious role available to women in the early Middle Ages. (Canonesses, who appeared in the Carolingian period, were similar to nuns but took less strict vows of poverty.) The history of early medieval nuns is a complex one, and recent research suggests that there was more variation over time than earlier historians noticed, both in the influence of nunneries (and abbesses) on the surrounding society and in society's respect for the piety of married laywomen.[3] But however powerful certain early medieval ladies may have been either as abbesses or as saintly queens, specialized religious roles for women were usually restricted to the high aristocracy. In the tenth and early eleventh centuries—a grim period of war and hardship for western Europe—few female monasteries were founded, and religious leaders showed little concern for encouraging women's religiosity. The major monastic reform of the period, Cluny, founded scores of male monasteries but only one house for nuns before 1100, and its purpose was to provide a retreat for women whose husbands wished to become Cluniac monks.[4] Although we have no idea what proportion of the population of medieval Europe belonged to religious houses (or, indeed, what the size of the European population was), we are certain that before 1200, monks vastly outnumbered nuns.[5] Over the course of the twelfth and thirteenth centuries, especially in the Rhineland and Low Countries, this ratio began to change.[6]

The proliferation in the late eleventh and twelfth centuries of wandering preachers who attracted bands of followers determined to "imitate the apostolic life" in poverty and penitence had such a significant impact on women that contemporary chroniclers commented on the phenomenon, with as much trepidation as admiration.[7] Women flocked after wandering evangelists such as Norbert of Xanten (d. 1134) and Robert of Arbrissel (d. 1116–1117), and these preachers—ambivalent about itinerant preaching even for themselves and clearly hostile to it as a form of female piety—founded monasteries for them. So-called double monasteries (i.e., communities with both male and female houses, often side by side) emerged again in England, where there was also a significant increase in the number of female recluses (women who vowed themselves to a life of withdrawal in little cells attached to churches). On the continent, two of the most prestigious new orders of the twelfth century, the Premonstratensians and the Cistercians, found the number of women's houses in their ranks growing at an alarming rate. The story of female enthusiasm institutionalized as strict monasticism repeated itself in the early thirteenth century, when Clare of Assisi (d. 1253) tried to follow Francis in the mendicant (i.e., begging) life but was forced to accept a strictly cloistered role.

Women were not only followers, manipulated and circumscribed in their religious ideals by powerful clerics, they were also leaders and reformers. In the thirteenth century, when Benedictine monasticism for men was eclipsed by the mendicant movement (i.e., the friars), an Italian woman, Santuccia Carabotti, founded a convent near Gubbio, enforced a strict interpretation of the Benedictine Rule there, and later reformed and supervised twenty-four other monasteries, taking them under her direction.[8] In the early fifteenth century Colette of Corbie (d. 1447), who began her religious life as a hermit, reformed many convents of Poor Clares in France and Flanders and founded others.[9]

The rapid growth of women's houses strained the resources of the new orders, which had to provide clergy for the women's spiritual direction and sacramental needs. The Premonstratensians were the first to pass legislation curtailing women's monasteries; the Cistercians followed. As R. W. Southern has made us aware, misogyny—a male fear of female sexuality that was a projection of male fear of male sexuality—was sometimes the articulated motive for such repression. The notorious opinion, attributed to the Premonstratensian abbot Conrad of Marchtal, that "the wickedness of women is greater than all other wickedness of the world and . . . the poison of asps and dragons is more curable and less dangerous to men than the familiarity of women" may be spurious. But a number of twelfth-century monastic leaders feared that celibate males would be contaminated by women and were willing to limit women's religious opportunities in order to protect fragile male virtue. Bernard of Clairvaux (d. 1153) warned his monks: "To be always with a woman and not to have sexual relations with her is more difficult than to raise the dead. You cannot do the less difficult; do you think I will believe that you can do what is more difficult?"[10]

Recent research has, however, shown that male reluctance and opposition did little to slow the growth of women's religious life.[11] In eastern areas (such as Franconia and Bavaria), women even continued to attach themselves to the Premonstratensian order.[12] The Cistercian decree of 1228 forbidding the incorporation of any more convents remained a dead letter, and throughout the thirteenth century Cistercian nunneries proliferated (often with support from local Dominicans) in the Low Countries and the lower Rhineland. Although some monks, canons, and friars did resist taking responsibility for the pastoral care of nuns, some religious authorities, from popes to local clergy, and some prominent laymen supported and endowed women's houses.[13] Both Santuccia and Colette received significant support from popes and papal legates. In the thirteenth and early fourteenth centuries, these women's monasteries formed influential spiritual networks among themselves and produced collections of the sisters' lives and visions that were often read in both female and male houses as a form of spiritual instruction.[14] In some parts of Europe, where male houses declined fairly steadily both in economic base and in religious fervor, nuns were a majority of the cloistered religious by the fifteenth century.[15]

In the twelfth and thirteenth centuries new forms of religious life for women appeared alongside the old Benedictine nunneries and the female monasteries of the new orders. Some of these religious opportunities were heterodox, and historians are still debating the extent to which women were proportionately over-represented in the major heresies of the twelfth through the fourteenth century.[16] Although these heresies shared many characteristics, scholars usually divide them into three groups: dualists, antisacerdotal reformers, and aberrant mystics. The first group, known as Cathars or Albigensians, appeared primarily in the south of Europe and rapidly came to follow an independent and alternative religion based on a theology of absolute dualism. In contrast to the monism of orthodox Christian theology, Cathars believed there was a war in the cosmos between good and evil and a parallel war in the individual between spirit and flesh. The second group, which included such movements as the Waldensians, the Humiliati, the New Apostles of Gerard Segarelli, and later the Lollards, were reformers whose puritanical zeal became anticlericalism and then, under the pressure of persecution, denial of the sacraments.[17] The third group, which emerged as a threat in the early fourteenth century, was known as the Free Spirit.[18] These individuals carried personal mystical experience to the point of antinomianism (the rejection of all rules and external religious practices) and self-deification. But the contemporary notion that they were a formal movement, a kind of conspiracy, may have been in large part a fantasy generated by orthodox fear of the implications of mysticism.

It seems clear that women were powerfully drawn to such movements, at least until they too developed hierarchical structures that tended to exclude female leadership. But it also seems clear that these movements—which were often initially labeled heresies for reasons of ecclesiastical politics, not doctrine—expressed many of the basic themes found in women's religiosity in its orthodox forms: a concern for affective religious response, an extreme form of penitential asceticism, an emphasis both on Christ's humanity and on the inspiration of the spirit, and a bypassing of clerical authority.[19] Thus women may have flocked to the heresies not (as some have argued) because they felt neglected by or alienated from the church but because certain spiritual impulses that characterized both heterodox and orthodox movements appealed especially to women and were generated in significant part by them.

Indeed, the same impulses that issued in the various heretical movements were the source of new quasi-religious roles for women within the church—roles that were not so much novel institutional arrangements as simply ways of giving religious significance to women's ordinary lives. In the north of Europe (especially northern France, the Low Countries, Switzerland, and the Rhineland), we find women called *beguines*. (The etymology of the word is debated; but it may be a slur, derived from *Albigensian*, i.e., heretic.) These women set themselves apart from the world by living austere, poor, chaste lives in which manual labor and charitable service were joined to worship (which was not, however, rigidly prescribed as it was in convents). Initially, at least, their practice contrasted sharply with traditional monasticism, since they took no vows and had no complex organization and rules, no order linking the houses, no hierarchy of officials, no wealthy founders or leaders. In the south of Europe (especially Italy), we find, paralleling the beguines, the *tertiaries*—individuals who lived in the world but were affiliated with one of the great mendicant orders (usually Franciscan or Dominican) and followed a life of penitential asceticism, charitable activity, and prayer. In Spain, women in such quasi-religious statuses were known as *beatas*. And, all over Europe, even ordinary laywomen sometimes found, through pilgrimage, a way of temporarily setting themselves off from the demands of the world in a special religious role of devotion, service, and penitence.[20] Although there is no way of estimating the number of women in Europe who adopted such quasi-religious status, statistics for a few northern cities suggest how popular the vocation was. The thousand women living in beguine communities in Cologne in 1320 accounted for about 15 percent of the adult female population (and this figure excludes beguines living alone). In Strasbourg and Basel, other centers of the movement, beguines accounted for about 2.5 percent of the total population in the same period.[21]

Early in our own century, some historians argued that the wandering evangelists of the twelfth century (heterodox and orthodox) and the mendicants, tertiaries, beguines, and Free Spirits of the thirteenth and fourteenth centuries represented movements of protest by the new urban lower classes.[22] These historians saw tertiary and beguine groups as female guilds, with essentially economic functions. More recently, scholars have taken the religious nature of such movements seriously and have disproved the claims of predominantly lower-class membership. But it seems clear that the new groups can be associated with specific social statuses. Although the new orders and movements of the twelfth century began with aristocratic clerics and recruited from both town and countryside, thirteenth-century beguines, tertiaries, and even to some extent Cistercian nuns tended to be drawn from the new bourgeoisie or from a lower nobility associated with the towns. Thus women who joined the new types of religious life available in the thirteenth and fourteenth centuries often came from social groups that were rising and can be shown to have felt anxiety about their new wealth and status. Their ideal—as their most distinguished historian, Herbert Grundmann, pointed out years ago—was not simply austerity but, rather, *renunciation* of comfort and wealth. Women from the old nobility were apt to join traditional monastic establishments (Benedictine nunneries or houses of canonesses), which required large dowries from entrants.[23]

Two explanations for the emergence of new types of female religious life have recently been popular. One suggests demographic causes: religious women were the daughters for whom no husbands could be found.[24] The other explanation argues that the women who became beguines, tertiaries, or heretics were simply a religious surplus, left on the fringes to attempt some kind of quasi-religious life after Cistercian and Premonstratensian doors closed and the friars showed reluctance to expand their pastorate to large numbers of nuns.[25] Both explanations are plausible. Demographic factors in fact lay behind all late medieval religious movements. The structure of the medieval family and of inheritance patterns necessitated alternatives to the role of marriage and procreation for a large portion of the population. And in the thirteenth and fourteenth centuries the value of dowries went up sharply, making the marriage of daughters (or even the endowing of a place for them in one of the traditional monasteries) sometimes prohibitively expensive. Contemporaries themselves were aware of such social motives. A document from early fourteenth-century Ghent states that, a hundred years earlier,

> Jeanne and her sister Margaret, successive countesses of Flanders and Hainault, observed that these counties teemed with women who were denied suitable marriages because of their own situation or that of their friends, and that daughters of respectable men, of both noble and ordinary birth, desired to live chastely in monasteries but, on account of the numbers of them or of the poverty of their parents, were unable to do so easily. Furthermore, respectable demoiselles and impoverished noblewomen had to beg or pursue a life embarrassing to themselves and their kin unless a proper remedy was provided. Thus, under divine inspiration, or so it is piously believed, they founded in various parts of Flanders, having first sought the counsel and approval of diocesan and other worthy authorities, spacious places called beguinages [*que vocantur Beghinarum curie*]. Here these women, girls, or demoiselles were received to preserve their chastity by vow or without vow and to provide themselves with food and clothing without embarrassment to themselves or the contriving of their friends.[26]

Moreover, the male resistance to the pastoral care of religious women that is reflected in the Premonstratensian and Cistercian decrees referred to above continued in the fourteenth and fifteenth centuries.[27]

Yet it seems wrong to interpret the beguines, tertiaries, and female heretics of the later Middle Ages as surplus women, settling for quasi-religious roles because neither husbands nor monasteries could be found. On the contrary, saints' lives include many cases where noblewomen who could have afforded to enter monasteries instead chose beguine or tertiary status. The recent research of John Freed has demonstrated that, far from inhibiting the growth of nunneries, friars and local clergy often encouraged them. It is not clear that there was a great shortage of places, at least in Cistercian convents.[28] It thus appears that the beguines were less an unintended result of pastoral negligence than a new and attractive alternative to traditional cloistered life. Moreover, for many girls, it was the presence, not the absence, of a prospective bridegroom that activated desire for perpetual chastity. Although some young women unquestionably desired to leave monasteries to which they had been given, there were also many daughters forced into marriage or threatened with it who saw the convent as an escape. The dangers of childbirth and the brutality of many marriages—disadvantages pointed out by medieval moralists—led some women to prefer celibacy.

Virginity was not, however, merely a means of escape from family. It was seen by both men and women as a positive and compelling religious ideal.[29] Set apart from the world by intact boundaries, her flesh untouched by ordinary flesh, the virgin (like Christ's mother, the perpetual virgin) was also a bride, destined for a higher consummation. She scintillated with fertility and power. Into her body, as into the eucharistic bread on the altar, poured the inspiration of the spirit and the fullness of the humanity of Christ.

The period from 1100 to 1400 saw not only the creation of new types of religious life for women but also an increase in the number of female saints—a clear indication of the growing prominence of women both in reflecting and in creating piety. Of course, there was always resistance on the part of church authorities to the canonization of women. Although the number of canonization inquiries for women rose, a consistently smaller percentage of females than of males considered for canonization actually achieved it.[30] Nonetheless, recent scholarly investigations, both of actually canonized saints and of those who were simply popularly revered, suggest that the proportion of female saints rose from less than 10 percent in the eleventh century to about 28 percent in the fifteenth. According to Weinstein and Bell, the big rise came between the twelfth and thirteenth centuries, when the percentage of female saints almost doubled (from 11.8 to 22.6 percent). The trend peaked in the fifteenth century (at 27.7 percent), despite the fact that the total number of saints declined. In the sixteenth and seventeenth centuries, when the total number of saints turned slightly upward, the percentage of women dropped sharply (to 18 percent in the sixteenth century, 14.4 percent in the seventeenth).[31]

Not only did the percentage of female saints climb between the twelfth and thirteenth centuries; the percentage of married saints rose as well.[32] Throughout the period, women represented a consistently higher percentage of the married saints than did men, although Weinstein, Bell, and Vauchez suggest, on the basis of qualitative evidence, that a new ambivalence about marriage emerged in the fifteenth century.[33] The rise in the number and percentage of women saints correlates also with a broadening of the class base of saints (although a higher percentage of saintly women than of saintly men were upper class) and with an increase in the percentages both of saints from urban areas and of saints affiliated with mendicant orders (although the canonization of mendicant women always met with stiff resistance).[34]

The rise of the woman saint correlates most dramatically, however, with the rise of the lay saint. Indeed, by the end of the Middle Ages the lay male saint had virtually disappeared. Nuns (the only "non-lay" female role) continued, of course, to be canonized; but by the sixteenth century almost all the males canonized were clerics, and the model of holy behavior offered to the Catholic laity was almost exclusively female. According to Vauchez, 50 percent of the laity canonized in the thirteenth century, and 71.4 percent of those canonized after 1305, were female.[35]

Connected to the emergence of new quasi-religious opportunities for laywomen and to the increasing veneration of certain laywomen as holy were two other trends: the decline and disappearance of quasi-clerical roles for women, and the increased suspicion, from the early fourteenth century on, of exactly those prophetic and visionary powers of holy women that contrasted most sharply with male clerical authority, based as it was on ordination.[36] In the church of the tenth to the twelfth century, women did exercise some "clerical" roles: preaching, hearing confessions from nuns under them, bestowing blessings, and sometimes administering communion to themselves in rituals known as "masses without priests."[37] But such things were increasingly criticized and suppressed. The decretalist Bernard of Parma, in his commentary (ca. 1245), argued that whatever might be found in earlier practice women could not teach or preach, touch sacred vessels, veil or absolve nuns, or exercise judgment and that "in general, the office of a man is forbidden to women."[38] The powerful abbesses of the early Middle Ages are seldom found in the later period. Those double monasteries over which women ruled had mostly been eliminated by the thirteenth century. Although women in the world who were revered as saints were more likely than saintly men to come from the highest social ranks, those revered within monasteries or beguinages were often not abbesses or prioresses but, rather, ordinary sisters blessed with paramystical and visionary experiences.[39]

Thus, from the thirteenth century on, we find religious women losing roles that paralleled or aped male clerical leadership but gaining both the possibility of shaping their own religious experiences in lay communities and a clear alternative—the prophetic alternative—to the male role based on the power of office. It is worth noting that such a trend parallels secular developments in the same period. Between the twelfth and fourteenth centuries, aristocratic women's ability to manage large estates and to rule declined while ordinary women clearly gained opportunities for independence and economic profit in the small crafts, shops, and businesses of the new towns.[40] Such complex changes in the *kinds* of opportunities and sources of authority available to women, as well as in the kinds of women for whom opportunities were available, make generalizations about "*the* status of women"—statements to which historians have sometimes been tempted—presumptuous and ill-advised.[41]

The female religious role had only to become clear, however, to be met with suspicion. After the early fourteenth century, the forms and themes of women's religiosity aroused increased hostility. In 1310 a woman mystic, Margaret Porete, was accused of the Free Spirit heresy and burned in Paris. The beguines were suppressed by the Council of Vienne in 1311–1312, although the decree remained unenforced for several years and, after mid-century, the women's movement (in a far more "monasticized"—i.e., institutionalized—form) was once again permitted. The spiritual friendships and networks of thirteenth- and early fourteenth-century women attenuated as the fourteenth century wore on. Collective biographies of women by women disappeared.[42] Fewer holy women wrote. Male suspicion of visionary women was articulated in a series of influential works, by John Gerson and others, on the testing of spirits.[43] In late-fourteenth- and fifteenth-century hagiography, holy women appear more and more isolated and male-oriented. Their stories are now usually told by their confessors, whom they dominate as spiritual mothers and cling to as vulnerable advisees, needful of a guarantee of orthodoxy. Although holy women were, by the fourteenth and fifteenth centuries, more likely to be lay and married, to reside in the world, and to have opportunities for significant geographical mobility through pilgrimage, they were also more subject to male scrutiny and in greater danger of being accused of heresy or witchcraft. By the time of Catherine of Siena, Bridget of Sweden, and Joan of Arc the influence—even the survival—of pious women depended almost wholly on the success, in ecclesiastical and secular politics, of their male adherents.[44]

Suspicion of prophetic women reflected the general fourteenth-century suspicion of popular religious movements and of mysticism. The period was one of deep hostility to visionary and mystical males as well. But the ambivalence of church authorities and theologians about women mystics also reflected virulent misogyny—a misogyny that issued both in the actual witch accusations and in the witch-hunting theology of the fifteenth century. By 1500, indeed, the model of the female saint, expressed both in popular veneration and in official canonizations, was in many ways the mirror image of society's notion of the witch.[45] Each was thought to be possessed, whether by God or by Satan; each seemed able to read the minds and hearts of others with uncanny shrewdness; each was suspected of flying through the air, whether in saintly levitation or bilocation, or in a witches' Sabbath. Moreover, each bore mysterious wounds, whether stigmata or the marks of incubi, on her body. The similarity of witch and saint—at least in the eyes of the theologians, canon lawyers, inquisitors, and male hagiographers who are, by the fifteenth century, almost our only sources for their lives—suggests how threatening both were to clerical authorities.[46] Woman's religious role as inspired vessel had come to seem utterly different from man's role as priest, preacher, and leader by virtue of clerical office. And because it seemed so different, it titillated—and was both encouraged and feared.

◆ Female Spirituality: Diversities and Unity

Canonesses, nuns of old and new orders, beguines, tertiaries, recluses, Cathars, Waldensians, pilgrims, ordinary laywomen in shops and kitchens—there were many kinds of pious women in later medieval Europe. Yet the increasingly sharp contrast between lay female saint and clerical male saint suggests that behind the wide variety of women's roles a unity can be found. And we can in fact delineate some consistent differences between male and female religious experiences.[47]

At least some of women's forms of life (e.g., tertiaries' and beguines') were less institutionalized than men's. Indeed, the tendency of later historians to identify pious women with a particular order has obscured the extent to which, especially in the thirteenth century, institutional affiliation and structure were, to women, unimportant or constantly changing.[48] The thirteenth-century saint Juliana of Cornillon, for example, wandered from religious house to religious house; her contemporary, Christina the Astonishing (Christina Mirabilis)—despite later efforts to claim her as Benedictine, Cistercian, or Premonstratensian—was simply a laywoman seeking to follow Christ and the saints; Margaret of Ypres (d. 1237), although on the edge of Dominican circles, sought not a particular order with its articulated goals but a male protector whom she could love.[49] The very fact that male chroniclers felt they ought to tell the story of the founding of the beguines as if the "order" had a leader and a rule like those of contemporary monastic or mendicant orders suggests that women's more informal arrangements for giving religious significance to ordinary life seemed odd and dangerous to male sensibilities.

Moreover, the life patterns of holy women show basic differences from those of men. In their recent quantitative study of saints' lives, Weinstein and Bell have demonstrated that in general, women's saintly vocations grew slowly through childhood and into adolescence; a disproportionate percentage of female saints were certain of their commitment to virginity before age eight. Despite the fact that both chastity and marital status were more prominent themes in the *vitae* (written lives) of women than of men, male saints were more likely to undergo abrupt adolescent conversions, involving renunciation of wealth, power, marriage, and sexuality. Crisis and decisive change were more significant motifs in male than in female *vitae* throughout the later Middle Ages,[50] in part because medieval men had more power than women to determine the shape of their lives. For example, Mary of Oignies and Clare of Assisi, wishing to renounce property, were virtually forced to retain income and servants; Margaret of Cortona, Umiliana dei Cerchi (d. 1246), and Angela of Foligno (d. 1309) had to wait for their husbands or lovers to die before they could espouse chastity; the visionary Juliana of Cornillon and the holy invalid Lidwina of Schiedam (d. 1433) were as cruelly persecuted and neglected at the end of their lives as during the childhood and adolescent stirrings of their vocations.[51] Indeed, hagiographers operated with a somewhat inconsistent double model of the female adolescent. The virtuous girl might demonstrate her virtue either by heroically insisting on chastity (and thereby rebelling against her family) or by obediently marrying at her parent's command (and thereby retreating from what the church argued to be a higher good). Frequently, in saints' lives, she did both—with no explanation of what the change from one behavior to the other meant to her or cost her.[52]

It is because women lacked control over their wealth and marital status that their life stories show fewer heroic gestures of casting aside money, property, and family. But women's lives also seem to be characterized by earlier vocations—by continuity rather than change—because, as we shall see below, men and women tended to tell stories, to use symbols, and to understand inner development according to different models. Men were inclined to tell stories with turning points, to use symbols of reversal and inversion, and to externalize motives in events (particularly when talking about men). Women more often used their ordinary experiences (of powerlessness, of service and nurturing, of disease, etc.) as symbols into which they poured ever deeper and more paradoxical meanings. Women tended to tell stories and develop personal models without crises or turning points.[53] And both men and women saw female saints as models of suffering and inner spirituality, male saints as models of action.[54]

When we compare the writings as well as the *vitae* of men and women, we find no pious practices or devotional themes that are exclusively female or exclusively male, although there are certain miracles that occur only to priests (because they are connected to sacerdotal functions) and certain miracles (e.g., stigmata or bodily elongation) that occur far more frequently to women.[55] Men and women often thought in the same metaphors—since they read the same Scriptures and spiritual treatises and often heard the same sermons—and even spiritual themes that modern commentators have assumed to be gender-specific are found in the visions and writings of both sexes in the Middle Ages. For example, if women more often had visions of nursing the Christ child, there is at least one monk who received the baby at his breast; if men more often nursed from the Virgin, some women too were fed with Mary's milk.[56]

But recent comparative study of vision literature, saints' lives, and mystical treatises by women and men suggests that the patterns of male piety differ from those of female piety.

Mysticism was more prominent in women's religiosity and claims to sanctity than in men's; and paramystical phenomena (trances, levitation, stigmata, etc.) were far more common in women's mysticism. The reputations of holy women were more often based on supernatural, charismatic authority, especially visions and supernatural signs. Women's devotion was more characterized by penitential asceticism, particularly self-inflicted suffering. Women's writing was, in general, more affective, although male writing too brims over with tears and sensibility; erotic, nuptial themes, which were first articulated by men, were most fully elaborated in women's poetry. And certain devotional emphases, particularly devotion to Christ's suffering humanity and to the eucharist (although not, as is often said, to the Virgin), were characteristic of women's practices and women's words.[57] (Some of these differences become important in the chapters that follow.)

Indeed, recent scholarship suggests that differences between the sexes over-ride all other factors (such as chronology or social and economic status) in shaping women's piety. A pious peasant woman and a pious noble one were more like each other in religiosity than either was like the male saint of equal social status.[58] But differences among women can also be delineated. Recent work, for example, suggests certain regional patterns. Scholars such as Weinstein, Bell, Vauchez, and Kieckhefer agree that women saints in the north of Europe were more aristocratic and contemplative, more likely to be nuns or recluses and to find a basis for their sanctity in withdrawal and prayer. Female saints in the south of Europe, particularly Italy (which accounted for about a third of the saints of the later Middle Ages), tended to be urban, middle class, and more active in works of charity. Recluses were more common in England; mystical communities in which many nuns experienced the same or similar visions were more common in the Rhineland (especially in the thirteenth century); charitable service, particularly care of the poor and sick, was especially common among Italian women affiliated with the Dominican and Franciscan orders.[59]

Moreover, there were differences in women's spirituality that stemmed from their different religious statuses and life experiences. A study of women's own writings suggests that women who lived *in* the world (either as tertiaries and beguines or as laywomen) and women who converted as adults differed from nuns raised in convents by having a sharper sense of male/female differences, a sense of "the female" closer to the negative stereotype found in the misogynist clerical tradition, and a less intense sense of community. They were more aware of the prohibition of sacramental functions and teaching to women, more likely to see the female as weak and vulnerable, more male-oriented (i.e., more dependent on confessors or powerful male religious leaders, not to mention husbands and fathers), and more concerned with male power and male roles (although the concern was often a critique). For example, the thirteenth-century Italian tertiary Angela of Foligno spoke far more frequently of her spiritual "sons" than of any female companions. Converted as an adult after the deaths of her mother, husband, and children, Angela channeled her maternal and spiritual impulses into criticizing and advising local friars. The German beguine Mechtild of Magdeburg, who fled her family and friends in young adulthood, directed her considerable rhetorical abilities toward castigating the local diocesan clergy and friars. The twelfth-century recluse Christina of Markyate, who ran away on her wedding night, received most of her visions and prophecies for the benefit of powerful males. And in the fourteenth and fifteenth centuries, the tertiary Catherine of Siena and laywomen as different as Bridget of Sweden (later a nun) and Joan of Arc were advisers and leaders of men.[60]

In contrast, women in convents and beguinages, especially those who had been raised there, had a strong sense of spiritual networks or families of women. Michael Goodich has pointed out that mystical women in the thirteenth and early fourteenth centuries, especially in Germany and the Low Countries, existed in clusters, whereas male mystics were more often isolated and less influential. So common had the clustering of mystical women become by the early fourteenth century that contemporaries tended to revere houses, like Töss and Engelthal, rather than individuals.[61] For those who had experienced such community, like the Flemish beguine Hadewijch, who was evicted from her beguinage, the grieving for former companions was intense and never healed.[62]

We should not, however, make too much of regional diversity, of contrasts between nuns and quasi-religious, or of differences between child oblates and adult converts. Certain towns of the thirteenth-century Low Countries and Rhineland produced a piety more like that of the

Italian female tertiaries than the work of Vauchez, Weinstein, and Bell suggests.[63] The sharp contrast between a more contemplative and mystical life for northern women and the more active charity practiced in the south blurs when we read women's own words and find that a stress on service *and* ecstatic encounter underlies both kinds of lives.[64] Moreover, however querulous and apologetic some medieval women occasionally seem (and this quality becomes more pronounced in the fifteenth and sixteenth centuries), they differed from one another relatively little in self-image, and their vulnerability seldom inhibited the confidence with which they approached God. Cloistered women were as likely as women in the world to use graphic domestic images for self and God.[65] Women such as Gertrude of Helfta (d. 1301 or 1302) who entered the convent as tiny girls equaled women in the world, such as Gertrude van Oosten (d. 1358) or Margery Kempe, in their maternal tenderness toward the baby Jesus and their erotic yearnings toward the beautiful young Christ.[66] And, while it is true that nuns were more likely to use imagery androgynously and to advise others with self-confidence, tertiaries and laywomen in fact castigated, counseled, and comforted others just as eagerly and effectively. Moreover, whatever their status or degree of vulnerability, religious women felt no necessity to acquire metaphorical maleness in the course of their spiritual journey.[67] Male biographers frequently praised women for spiritual "virility," and women such as Catherine of Siena sometimes urged other women (and men) to behave "manfully."[68] But women's most elaborate self-images were either female ("mother" to spiritual children, "bride" of Christ) or androgynous ("child" to a God who was mother as well as father, "judge" and "nurse" to the souls in their keeping).

Most of our information on late medieval women comes from male biographers and chroniclers. The problem of perspective is thus acute. Some of the stories men loved to tell about women reflected not so much what women did as what men admired or abhorred. For example, Caesarius of Heisterbach, writing in the thirteenth century for male Cistercians, presented a collection of exempla (moral tales) organized according to types of Christian vocation. Writing about confessors, Caesarius simply explained what experiences, especially miracles and visions, happened to confessors (all of whom were male). But when he turned to "the order of virgins" (by which he meant female virgins), his account took a curious turn. Apparently unconsciously, he slipped into writing not about the visions and miracles that had occurred to the virgins (only two stories out of nine) but about virgins who had appeared in visions to men (the remaining seven stories). It is almost as if Caesarius could not imagine the women or their virginity being important to themselves.[69]

Male biographers romanticized and sentimentalized female virtue far more than male, especially by describing it (as does James of Vitry in the passage quoted above as epigraph) in heightened and erotic imagery.[70] They were also far more likely to attribute sexual or bodily temptation to female nature than to male (men's sexual yearnings could always be blamed on the presence of women as temptresses) and to see women struggling unsuccessfully to overcome the flesh.[71] For example, as John Anson has argued, the common story of the woman who masquerades as a man in order to enter a monastery appears to reflect male anxiety more frequently than it does historical reality.[72] It is therefore crucial not to take as women's own self-image the sentimentalizing or the castigating of the female in which medieval men indulged. If we wish to understand what it meant to medieval women to be "brides of Christ" or symbols of either mercy or fleshliness, we must pay particular attention to what women said and did, avoiding the assumption that they simply internalized the rhetoric of theologians, confessors, or husbands.

Sorting out the images of "woman" and the experiences of women in late medieval religion, with appropriate attention to the differing vantage points from which men and women viewed these matters, is far from easy. But recent research has done much to retrieve stories of women and to describe women's piety. It has, however, tended to focus on the renunciation of wealth, privilege, and sexuality in women's religiosity as in men's, largely because it has proceeded from two perspectives—that of the feminist and that of the traditional medievalist. Feminist scholarship has tended to concentrate on the negative stereotyping of women's sexuality and on women's lack of worldly power and sacerdotal authority.[73] It has done so because these issues are of such pressing modern concern. Traditional medievalists, although attempting to start from the vantage point of medieval people themselves, have in fact tended to use male religiosity as a model. When studying women, they have tended to look simply for women's answers to questions that have always been asked about men—questions generated in the first place by observing male religiosity.[74] Because medieval men were deeply concerned, for themselves and for women, with the renunciation of sexual gratification and of economic and political power, medievalists have seen these same renunciations as central in women's piety. Thus recent work on medieval women has tended to have either presentist issues or male models built in. Food has been ignored—chiefly because it is not, in modern eyes, a primary concern, but also because, to medieval men, it was one among many religious symbols and pious renunciations.

Yet food was crucial to the religious experience of medieval women, in ways so rich and complicated that it will take me a whole book to explain them. For food was a powerful symbol. Like body, food must be broken and spilled forth in order to give life. Macerated by teeth before it can be assimilated to sustain life, food mirrors and recapitulates both suffering and fertility. Thus food, by what it is, seems to symbolize sacrifice and service.[75] And, in Christian doctrine, the suffering, broken, crucified body on the cross, from which springs humankind's salvation, *is* food. But food was not merely a powerful symbol. It was also a particularly obvious and accessible symbol to women, who were more intimately involved than men in the preparation and distribution of food. Women's bodies, in the acts of lactation and of giving birth, were analogous both to ordinary food and to the body of Christ, as it died on the cross and gave birth to salvation.

Food is, of course, only one thread in the skein of women's spirituality, but by following it we touch on many aspects of women's experiences. Moreover, by studying the food practices and images of medieval women, we begin to consider their piety not by asking how it answers questions posed by presentist concerns or male perspectives but by allowing the women themselves to generate questions as well as answers.

FAST AND FEAST:
THE HISTORICAL BACKGROUND

*We order to you this fast of December . . . because it conforms to
piety and to justice to render thanks to God after having received the
fruits of the earth and to offer him the sacrifice of mercy with the
immolation of fast. Let each one rejoice in the copiousness of the harvest . . . but in such a way that even the poor rejoice in its abundance. . . . Let all make account of their riches and those who have
more give more. Let the abstinence of the faithful become the nourishment of the poor and let the indigent receive that which others
give up.*   POPE LEO THE GREAT
                                               (FIFTH CENTURY)[1]

FOOD SYMBOLIZED many things to medieval Christians. But the most
important Christian food practices were fasting and eucharist. Christians
male and female paid tribute to God's power and acknowledged their
own sinfulness by renouncing food. And Christians male and female
received their God most intimately in that holy meal in which he became
bread and wine.

The roots of late medieval eucharistic piety and food asceticism lie in
the early church. When the medieval authors Bernard of Clairvaux,
Mechtild of Magdeburg, Hadewijch, and John Tauler spoke of eating
and being eaten by God,[2] their language echoed words voiced centuries
before. Augustine of Hippo (d. 430) and Hilary of Poitiers (d. 367) had
said that we are all present in the sacrifice and Resurrection of the cross,
that Christ, in dying, digests and assimilates us, making us new flesh in
his flesh.[3] When Alan of Lille (d. 1203) wrote in his *Summa* for preachers that a faster "must take little food at meals so that part can go to the
needs of his neighbor," he was repeating in less resonant and expansive
language Leo the Great's exhortation to Christians (quoted above) to
couple abstinence with almsgiving.[4] When Thomas Aquinas (d. 1274)

31

discussed fasting and abstinence in his *Summa theologiae*, he carefully examined the patristic notion that humankind fell from paradise through the sin of gluttony.[5] There is at least superficial similarity between the food metaphors employed by patristic poets and those of late medieval eucharistic hymns. The hymn used for Monday Lauds and attributed to Ambrose (d. 397) reads:

> Christusque nobis sit cibus,
> potusque noster sit fides;
> laeti bibamus sobriam
> ebrietatem Spiritus.

(Let Christ be our food and faith our drink; let us happily drink the sober inebriation of the spirit.)[6]

The great eucharistic hymn once attributed to Innocent IV (d. 1254), the *Ave verum corpus*, echoes such imagery:

> Ave verum corpus, natum / ex Maria virgine,
> Vere passum, immolatum / in cruce pro homine,
> Cujus latus perforatum / vero fluxit sanguine,
> Esto nobis praegustatum / mortis in examine.

(Hail true body, born of Mary the Virgin, that truly suffered and was offered as sacrifice on the cross for humankind, and from whose pierced side poured forth real blood. Be to us in the extremity of death a foretaste [of heaven].)[7]

Down through the centuries, eating and fasting have been to Christians complex symbols and complex acts.

Yet the religious significance of fast and food changed greatly between the days of the early church and the later Middle Ages. By the fourteenth century the great fasts that in the early days had bound the church into a community became matters for attenuation and dispensation. Communion, once a communal meal and the heart of the mass, became separated from consecration; devotion pivoted increasingly not around eating the host but around the moment at which the elements of bread and wine became, in the hands of the priest, Christ's body and blood. Christ's fast in the garden and his sacrifice on the cross were spoken of less as part of a cosmic drama in which hell was forced to vomit forth the indigestible bread of Christ than as moments of terrible suffering that gave significance to all human experience because the man who suffered was God. Abstinence was seen less as self-control, offered to God in propitiation for Adam's sin of greed and disobedience, than as a never-sated physical hunger that mirrors and recapitulates in bodily agony both Christ's suffering on the cross and the soul's unquenchable thirst for mystical union. The bread of heaven, which to Cyprian (d. 258) symbolized the church,[8] was replaced in late medieval hymns, poems, and paintings by the flesh of Christ, ripped open and spilling forth pulsating streams of insistent, scarlet blood, to wash and feed the individual hungry soul.

In order to understand why food was so important a symbol to late medieval women, we must first look at how the religious significance of food changed for all Western Christians in the high Middle Ages. We must examine how fasting changed in meaning and context and how both the ritual of the mass and the theology of the eucharist altered as well.

♦ Fasting in Antiquity and the High Middle Ages

To a Christian of the Mediterranean world in the fourth century, feast and fast defined the church. Fasting and Sunday eucharist were what everyone had in common. To receive the bread and wine of communion was not only to be mystically and individually fed with the bread of heaven, it was also to be present at a sacrifice that was the victory and triumph of the church, a death that was simultaneously glory and resurrection. It was, in Cyprian's words, to be united with one's fellow Christians as the grains of wheat are united in the loaf of bread. To fast—either in preparation for this Sunday meal, in Lenten anticipation of the coming of the bridegroom, or in seasonal response to the harvest—was to join with scarcity in order that plenty might come. To fast was, as Gregory the Great explained, to offer to God a tithe of the year.[9] It was to embrace hunger, to join with the vulnerability to famine that threatened all living things, in order to induce from the creator and provider of blessings the gifts of fertility, plenty, and salvation. It was even, as Leo the Great stressed, to join oneself with the charity and fertility of God: fasting provided the alms that fed one's neighbor. Indeed, in fasting, "Christ is fed" (as both Leo and John Chrysostom said), for what one denied to oneself in fast was given to Christ's own body, his church.[10] Thus fast and feast not only joined Christian to Christian; they joined Christian to the rhythm of nature as well.

Fast and feast, in this sense, are found in many religions. Anthropologists and students of comparative religion, who once looked for a single cause or motive for religious responses, are now content to see many complex strands in fasting behavior. But it seems clear that in pre-industrial societies, where resources are limited, men and women frequently respond to the rhythm of plenty and scarcity, harvest and famine, by deciding to control it through voluntary fasting and believe that they can in this way coerce from the gods dreams and visions, health, good fortune, or fertility.[11] The earliest forms of fasting were often connected with fertility cults, with goddesses, and with women's physiological processes.[12] Penitential or propitiatory fasting seems to arise from this sense of nature's rhythm: if nature erratically and unpredictably humbles one through hunger, one may punish or humiliate oneself before God through similar humbling. This sense of food as a sign of vulnerability, a reminder (through flatulence and hunger pangs) of the toll the body can exact, can lead to the ascetic impulse—the desire to defy corporeal limits by denying bodily needs. Such an understanding of food abstention as inducement of fertility, as penitence, and as flight from matter was present in the Mediterranean world before the coming of Christianity.[13] Nor is the sense of fast as an activity that binds people to one another and to nature surprising in a world whose life rhythms were still determined by the seasonal rhythms of the earth. No matter how large and cosmopolitan some ancient cities became, they were less producers of wealth through commerce and industry than gigantic parasites on the countryside, as dependent on the harvest as any country village.

There are references to fasting in early Christian texts. The Scriptures themselves, both Old and New Testaments, provided some models. But fasting as an important religious behavior, defining the Christian community and signaling the individual's purity of heart before God, did not emerge clearly until the late third and early fourth centuries.[14] In early references to both individual and corporate fasts, many motives intermingle. Fasting (e.g., the fast before baptism) could be religious preparation; it could be purification or exorcism of evil spirits; it could express mourning for the departure of the bridegroom (as, e.g., in the fast of two or three days before Easter). It was also a meritorious work for God and neighbor. Moreover, fasting could be penitential. As it had been for the ancient Hebrews, food abstention was an expression of grief and repentance, a plea for deliverance from some test or chastisement, a sign of confidence in God's mercy, an intercession and a preparation for meeting God. As such, fasting was intensely corporate, a companion to prayer and almsgiving, a recapitulation of as well as a preparation for the eucharistic sacrifice. By fasting, the Christian joined with Christ, who, in the garden and on the cross, kept the rule of abstinence that Adam had violated in paradise and became himself sacrificial food, propitiating God and saving sinners. Augustine wrote in a Lenten sermon:

> Alms, in Greek, is the same as the word for mercy. And can one conceive of a greater mercy than that which came down from the sky . . . ? Equal to the Father in eternity, he made himself equal with us in mortality. . . . Bread himself, he experienced hunger; totally satisfied, he experienced thirst; health itself, he made himself weak . . . and all this to nourish our hunger, irrigate our dryness, succor our infirmity. . . . So he commands us, through alms, to give bread to those who hunger . . . to receive the stranger, although he [Christ] came to us and we did not receive him. . . . And so let our souls praise him . . . let us give alms often.[15]

Connecting fasting explicitly to charity, Augustine also exhorted his readers:

> Above all be mindful of the poor so that you lay up in the heavenly treasury what you withhold from yourselves by a more frugal mode of life. The hungry Christ will receive that from which the fasting Christian abstains.[16]

Augustine's contemporary Maximus of Turin (d. ca. 420) wrote: "What the first man lost by eating, the second Adam recovered by fasting. And he kept in the desert the law of abstinence given in paradise."[17] Hymns attributed to Gregory the Great (d. 604) and still used by the Roman Catholic church during Lent express this sense of "fruitful fast," of fast as self-control that enables one to propitiate God and aid one's neighbor:

> Sic corpus extra conteri
> dona per abstinentiam,
> ieiunet ut mens sobria
> a labe prorsus criminum.
>
> Praesta, beata Trinitas,
> concede, simplex unitas,

35

ut fructuosa sint tuis
ieiuniorum munera.

(Thus grant that the body be subjected from without by abstinence in
order that the sober mind may fast completely from the stain of sin.
Grant, blessed Trinity and undivided Unity, that the sacrifice of fasts
may be fruitful to your servants.)[18]

In the seventh century, Isidore of Seville, who summarized much of
patristic tradition, spoke of fasting as union with the angels: "Fast is a
holy thing, a heavenly work, the doorway to the kingdom, the form of
the future, for he who carries it out in a holy way is united to God,
exiled from the world, and made spiritual."[19]

As the passage from Isidore suggests, the fast of the early church was
not merely the fast of mourning, propitiation, purification, and penitence. It was not merely a shadow of the community of heaven. It was
also ascetic. Patristic writers themselves cited not only the Old Testament
models of David, Esther, and Judith, who by fasting offered pure hearts
to God, but also classical stories of the wondrous abstentions of Epi-
menides and Pythagoras. As Rudolph Arbesmann has said: "In the background there always [loomed] the vision of an ideal world in which man
would be able to live without any earthly food."[20] Christian writers drew
support for fasting from pagan writers, who had stressed hygienic, social,
and utilitarian motives. Behind the Christian praise of fasting as a way
of moderating lust, cleansing the brain and body, and preparing the soul
for God's inspiration lay a Pythagorean and neo-Platonic desire to escape
the body that dragged the spirit ever downward. In the words of Clement of Alexandria (d. ca. 215): "Fasting empties the soul of matter and
makes it, with the body, clear and light for the reception of divine
truth."[21] A work attributed to abbot Nilus (d. 430) adds to the idea that
Adam's sin was gluttony the notion that matter weighs down spirit:

It was the desire of food that spawned disobedience; it was the pleasure
of taste that drove us from Paradise. Luxury in food delights the gullet,
but it breeds the worm of license that sleepeth not. An empty stomach
prepares one for watching and prayer; the full one induces sleep.[22]

A mid-fourth-century treatise for virgins by the author we call pseudo-
Athanasius argues: "Fasting . . . cures disease, dries up the bodily humors,
puts demons to flight, gets rid of impure thoughts, makes the mind

clearer and the heart purer, the body sanctified, and raises man to the throne of God."[23] Many patristic writers associated food with lust and urged abstinence as a method of curbing sexual desire.[24] John Cassian, writing for monks in the early fifth century, said: "It is impossible to extinguish the fires of concupiscence without restraining the desires of the stomach."[25] And that indefatigable propagandist for asceticism, Jerome (d. 420), in a letter of advice to a widow, summed up the matter by quoting Terence: "Sine Cerere et Libero friget Venus."[26]

From such precedents and beliefs came the great corporate fasts of the church. Modeled on the Jewish fasts of Monday and Thursday, the so-called stations (the Wednesday and Friday fasts) emerged very early, perhaps before the second century. Later, in the West, Saturday was added to Friday as an extra fast (or *superpositio*) and Wednesday often dropped out. The fast of several days before Easter, a fast of mourning for those hours "in which the spouse was taken away," also developed as early as the second century. Lent, or *quadragesima*, distinct from this Easter fast and seen as a time of purification, emerged in the fourth century; during the seventh century, in the West, it was expanded from thirty-six to forty days. A second Lent (the Lent of Pentecost, ending on Peter and Paul's day, June 29) emerged in the East in the fourth century. A third period of fast, beginning November 14, also developed, although at first it was not a period of anticipation or Advent, as we know it, but rather an expression of penitence offered at the year's end.[27] Fasting was early prescribed as a preparation for baptism and holy communion as well, but direct evidence for this usage comes only from the late fourth century. The so-called quarter days (*quattuor tempora*)—later called in English Ember Days—were probably added to the calendar to counteract and replace pagan harvest festivals; they appeared in the West in Rome and spread slowly during the seventh century.[28] Special litanies and fasts appeared in various localities, and gradually the idea spread that the great feasts of the church should be preceded by fasts.

Strictly speaking, to fast meant to refrain from eating, and there are stories in the early church of monks such as Simeon Stylites going without food for all of Lent.[29] But early Christian food asceticism was extremely diverse. Fasting usually meant abstaining entirely from certain foods (the list could vary greatly) and limiting oneself to a single meal each day, taken after Vespers. Abstinence from particular foods thus tended to fuse with fasting (i.e., not eating) into a single concept.

37

Abstinence, strictly interpreted, meant so-called dry eating—i.e., taking only bread, salt, and water, though vegetables and fruits were sometimes permitted. Some monastic groups practiced more or less permanent abstinence of this type. The monks of Pachomius's monasteries, for example, abstained from meat, wine, and fish throughout the year. Some individuals, particularly hermits, practiced raw eating—i.e., they ate no cooked food. Strict dry or raw eating never became an element of ordinary Christian fasting in the West, however; and Western monastic rules (with the exception of Irish ones) were generally less austere than Eastern.[30] The Benedictine Rule, for example, permitted a moderate amount of wine and prohibited only the meat of four-legged animals, although the monks ate only one meal a day for more than half the year.[31]

The third and fourth centuries thus witnessed the emergence of fasting and abstinence as extensive corporate practices among Christians. Both in the periods of temporary food renunciation urged by popes and bishops on all believers and in the lives of permanent self-denial undertaken by monks, food abstention was a group practice. But the same centuries also saw the beginnings of virtuoso performances by individual ascetics. Leaders of cenobitical or hermit groups (for example, Basil) sometimes practiced far greater austerity than they legislated for their followers.[32] The very notion of *superpositio* (the added-on fast) suggests that individuals could multiply merit by multiplying their austerities. Preachers might continue to insist, as John Chrysostom did, that fasting is abstinence not from food alone but also from sin and that "Christ did not say: 'Come to me because I fasted . . . ,' but 'because I am meek and humble of heart.'"[33] Still, particularly within the monastic context, individuals were increasingly determined to root out the pleasure of food by any means. Gregory of Nyssa (d. 395) described taste as "the mother of all vice."[34] Origen, Cyril, and Basil all suggested that one should inflict pain on oneself in order to destroy pleasure and to force the body toward virtue.[35] In some quarters, particularly Egypt and Syria and, later, Ireland, competitive asceticism developed. In Palladius's *Historia Lausiaca*—which is more a historical novel than a factual account but for exactly that reason an excellent reflection of what non-ascetics admired in their ascetic heroes and heroines—we learn, for example, of one Macarius of Alexandria. When he heard that the monks of Tabennisi ate no cooked food for all of Lent, he lived on raw food for seven years. When he heard that a certain ascetic ate only a pound of bread a day, he put his bread into a narrow-mouthed jar and lived on what he could pull out in a single handful. And finally, when he heard of the severe fasting of the hermits in the Thebaid, he decided to eat only a few cabbage leaves on Sundays.[36] Female ascetics also practiced heroic austerities. John Chrysostom describes women "who even at a tender age go without food and sleep and drink, mortifying their bodies, crucifying their flesh, sleeping on the ground, wearing sackcloth, locked in narrow cells, sprinkling themselves with ashes and wearing chains."[37]

But for all the individualism, competition, and spiritual athleticism of certain late antique men and women, we must not forget that fasting was most basically something that brought Christians together—in gratitude for God's gift of the harvest; in obedience to God's command of abstinence, violated in the Garden of Eden but fulfilled on the cross; in charity toward the neighbors who would benefit from alms; and in foretaste of union with the saints in heaven. It is this sense of fasting and of food that we find in Romanos the Melodist's remarkable collection of hymns written for lay gatherings at the end of the fifth or the beginning of the sixth century.

Behind these hymns lies the rhythm of the seasons, of scarcity followed by abundance. Writing of Elias and the widow (3 Kings 17), Romanos sees fast offered in reparation for disobedience.[38] Thus fast is a joining with famine, death, and hunger. It is a choosing of lack that induces God to send plenty: rain, harvest, and life. Hunger is less deprivation or suffering than vulnerability, and the implication is that God will respond to vulnerability, to man's chosen lack, with food. Writing of the three children in the fiery furnace, the poet sees abstinence as coercing self-denial from nature.[39] Thus fire forgets its accustomed role, becomes a "spring," "watering the children instead of consuming them," "keeping them like a vine her harvest."[40] Man's choice of hunger is a choice of self-control, and it arouses in nature an answering self-control. The angel says:

> Holy children, hear my words. I do as I have been ordered, you do as you have been taught. As I hold back the flame, you hold back your tongues. . . . Do not fear. The fire will do you no evil; it will turn on your enemies. I have given the order that it fast as you have fasted and that it devour greedily the gluttons who do not sing with you.[41]

Hymning the miracle of the loaves and fishes, Romanos begins with a prayer for delivery from famine, pictures the assembled crowd fasting in expectation of the bread of angels, and then describes the multiplication itself as a type of the Incarnation. As the Virgin gave birth to new flesh, so the five loaves miraculously give birth to new bread.[42] In sharp contrast to the late medieval emphasis on Christ's body as broken and bleeding, Romanos writes of the Incarnation as fresh bread that feeds the hungry people of God.

When Romanos speaks of the Crucifixion and Resurrection, his image is, once again, of bread. In graphically physical language, he speaks of Adam waiting in hell "as the earth waits for rain," while hell exults that it has devoured Christ as it earlier devoured sinful humanity.[43] But Adam answers:

> He endured my punishment for me, bearing my flesh. He whom the cherubim did not dare to look at was pierced for me in the side and the water that poured down put out my torment. He whom you believe you will hold because he is a man you will devour because he is mortal; but as he is God you will vomit him up after three days.[44]

The food metaphors in Romanos are an expression of cosmic drama. Jesus is the "celestial bread" that hell "cannot digest." (In another hymn, Jesus forces hell to empty its bowels when he raises Lazarus from the dead.)[45] Insatiable, devouring hunger is evil, desire run out of control, the greed characteristic of hell and Satan. But if human hunger is controlled, it will be met with the bread of heaven, new flesh to redeem the flesh of Adam. There is here none of the late medieval sense that man imitates the cross in suffering, no sense of limitless hunger as a metaphor for the Christian desire for God. But around the fast of the individual worshiper circles a fasting community, a natural order with its own cycles of want and plenty, and even a cosmic drama in which the bread that Christ became at the Last Supper and on the cross purges hell itself.[46] It is this natural, corporate, and cosmic context that fell away from fasting in the later Middle Ages, leaving the food asceticism of heroic individuals to become more and more extreme.

Throughout the Middle Ages, the Lenten fasts and weekly fast days, especially Fridays, remained basic marks of the Christian.[47] In the thirteenth and fourteenth centuries a Christian was, as a minimal definition, someone who received yearly communion, fasted on Fridays and in Lent, paid tithes, and had his or her children baptized. In the following story from a twelfth-century chronicle, we can see the way in which food practices defined the Christian. One of the bastard sons of Arnold the Elder, founder of the line of Ardres, became a "Saracen" in the East.

He was, however, accepted back into his father's house when he returned. It was only when he insisted on eating meat on Friday that the full impact of his apostasy was brought home, and the family kicked him out. To violate the Friday fast was the clearest, most visible way of rejecting the faith.[48]

Medieval cookbooks suggest that the aristocracy observed fasting strictly, if legalistically. Meat-day and fish-day recipes were not separated in medieval recipe collections, as they were in later, better-organized cookbooks. But the most basic dishes were given in fast-day as well as ordinary-day versions. For example, a thin split-pea purée, sometimes enriched with fish stock or almond milk (produced by simmering ground almonds in water), replaced meat broth on fast days; and almond milk was a general (and expensive) substitute for cow's milk.[49]

By the thirteenth century, however, the understanding of fast and abstinence put forward by canon lawyers and theologians was a much-attenuated version of the ideals of the ancient writers.[50] The Lenten fast was now understood to terminate not at Vespers but at None; by the fourteenth century it terminated at midday, and a small evening meal was permitted. Abstinence was sometimes understood as simply abstinence from meat, although it usually included certain animal products (especially milk and eggs) as well. Authorities discussed which categories of Christians were exempt from fasting. Thomas Aquinas, for example, exempted children, the old, pilgrims, workers, and beggars, but not the poor who had roofs over their heads.[51] Dispensations for certain groups and under certain circumstances became common. Medieval cookbooks suggest that the aristocracy dined sumptuously on the fish permitted in Lent. "Fish" indeed included whale, dolphin, porpoise, and also beaver's tail and barnacle goose (because beavers and geese were thought to stay most of the time in water). Cooks concocted imitation eggs from fish roe and made "ham" or "bacon" slices from different types of ground or shredded fish.[52] The food in some Benedictine monasteries became very lavish. Whereas the average twelfth- or thirteenth-century aristocrat ate meals of four or five courses, some black monks enjoyed as many as thirteen to sixteen courses on major feast days.[53] Aware of such legalistic observance, Thomas Aquinas clearly feared that gluttony might taint the abstinence of some Christians. Greed, he observed, included eating rich, expensive dishes as well as eating too much food or food prohibited by the church.[54]

While the fasting requirements for ordinary Christians and Benedictine monks grew less stringent, however, some new monasteries adopted extraordinary rigor. Monastic fasting had almost disappeared in the central Middle Ages, with the addition of many feast days to the calendar, but the new orders of the eleventh and twelfth centuries turned to increased austerities.[55] The food asceticism of eleventh-century Italian hermits, for example, imitated and equaled that of the early monks of Syria, and propagandists such as Peter Damian spread their fame. The new orders not only practiced greater austerity, they also defined and differentiated themselves in part by their particular rules of abstinence. The Cistercians, for example, added to the Benedictine Rule a fast of bread and water on Fridays in Lent. The Carthusians, who fasted three times a week on bread, water, and salt (with permission), came over time to define their perpetual abstinence from meat (even for the sick) as so crucial a characteristic of the order that violation of this prohibition meant expulsion. But the early austerity of many orders, such as the Premonstratensians and Dominicans, was later relaxed, sometimes to be followed after hundreds of years by reform movements that returned to the earlier strictness. (The Trappists who reformed the Cistercians in the seventeenth century, for example, rejected the fourteenth-century relaxation.)[56]

What changed most over the long period from the sixth to the twelfth century was the tone of the discussion by preachers, lawyers, and theologians. As food became increasingly a matter of legislation and dispensation, concern with the *abuses* of legalism and literalism also grew. Thirteenth- and fourteenth-century writers, busy defining exactly who should fast when, urged spiritual more than physical abstinence. They stressed the need for moderation in observance.[57] And renunciation—whether of food or of vice—was invariably seen as more significant for the individual soul in its inmost recesses than for the community.

We find such an interpretation of food asceticism in one of the additions to the *Vitis mystica* (*The Mystical Vine*) of Bonaventure (d. 1274):

> The virtue of abstinence is in two parts. One is within, in the mind; the other without, in behavior. And that which is in the mind is to be observed always, but that which is in behavior is to be displayed according to circumstances. Indeed John, who was a pure man, practiced abstinence as much in mind as in body in order that he not be despised; but Jesus, who is truly our humanity [*homo noster verus*], who was incapable of sin,

used food and drink for a time. . . . Nor should you believe in any way that it is a greater virtue to abstain from food than to make use of food in moderation.[58]

The monastic writer Peter of Celle (d. 1183), in a sermon on fasting, also explained that one can fast from food and from evil. Abstinence from evil must never be relaxed, but abstinence from food can be. Fasting, he wrote, "is rightly done when it is done to wipe out vices; for the fullness of food heats up the body."[59] In a treatise for preachers, Peter the Chanter (d. 1197) explained:

> Paul the first hermit always fasted, and bread was sent to him from the skies. . . . And Jerome was content with mean vegetables, bread, and water. But this hardest fast we are not capable of because of our corruption. Let our observance be rational, for we do not want to be despoiled but, rather, clothed. For three things are necessary to the ass [i.e., the body]: food, that it be sustained; the rod, lest it be stubborn; burdens, that it may be useful to its master. Concerning the first, it is said: "No one hates his own body" [Eph. 5:29], for it is created by God, not by the devil, as Manichaeus said. . . . But concerning the second, the apostle said: "I chastise my body . . ."[1 Cor. 9:27]. And concerning the third, he said: "Bear one another's burdens" [Gal. 6:2].[60]

Fasting was at times almost completely allegorized or spiritualized. For example, the great monastic reformer Bernard of Clairvaux, who himself practiced severe abstinence, wrote in a Lenten sermon:

> How can one be, I shall not say a monk, but a Christian, who does not fast, when Christ gave us the practice? For if Christ fasted, it was to give us an example. . . . For Lent is a sacrament of all time [and fasting a sign of all abstinence]. If only the tongue sinned, then it only would fast, and that would suffice. But the other members sin. [So they must fast.] . . . The eyes should fast from curiosity . . . , the ears from tales and rumors, the tongue from detraction and murmuring and from vain and scurrilous words, . . . the hands from lazy signs and from all unnecessary busyness; but most of all, the soul from vices and the will from its own desire.[61]

Henry Suso, one of the most extravagantly ascetic of fourteenth-century saints, warned:

> In reading the lives of the ancient fathers our lukewarm blood curdles at the thought of their austerities, but we remain strangely unimpressed by

the essential point, namely, their determination to do God's will in all things, painful or pleasant. These men of fire thought it possible to do the impossible when helped by God. . . . However, we must not forget that some of these ancient fathers did not practice severe bodily austerities and nevertheless attained great holiness of life.[62]

Above all, we sense in the theologians of the twelfth to the fourteenth century an effort to give not only precision to rules but also dignity and spiritual significance to the practice of a wide spectrum of Christians. In the chapter on fasting in his *Summa* for preachers, Alan of Lille argued that abstinence must be inner and outer, that mere obedience to the law is not enough. Simply going without food, as the sick do, is morally indifferent. "Fast macerates the flesh, elevates the soul, restrains the spark of concupiscence, and excites reason. . . . For what can it profit if the mouth rejects food while the tongue lapses into mendacity?" Alan retains some sense that practice binds Christians together and has social significance. He argues that by fasting the Christian gains heaven, repairs the sins of his ancestors, prepares for eucharist, and gives alms to the poor. But Alan's emphasis is on personal devotion and individual observance:

> Fast is medicine to soul and body. It preserves the body from disease, the soul from sin. About its medicinal effects, earthly and heavenly philosophy agree. If Adam had fasted in paradise . . . , he would not have been exiled into damnation. If Esau had fasted . . . , he would not have lost his birthright. If Noah had fasted . . . , he would not have lost his modesty. Therefore, through fasting the body is purged that it may receive the eucharist sacramentally, and the spirit that it may receive it spiritually. . . . And three things should inform fasting: good intention, almsgiving, and love. . . . Oh man, consider the Fathers, who ate only once or twice a week. . . . But if you are not moved by ancient examples, be moved at least by the tale of St. Nicholas the baby, who took only one breast on the Wednesday and Friday fasts. And let not adults blush to fast when they see what children have done.[63]

Thomas Aquinas's extended treatment of abstinence in the *Summa theologiae*, written some years later, sounds a similar note. Stressing moderation, Thomas quotes Jerome, who said: "By eating and sleeping too little you are offering a sacrifice of stolen goods. . . . Rational man forfeits his dignity if he sets fasting before chastity, or night-watching be-

fore the well-being of his senses." And Thomas explains this by saying:
"Right reason does not refuse food to the extent of rendering us incapable of discharging our duties." The goal of fasting is to bridle lust
(which is particularly excited by meat), to make satisfaction for sin, and
to help the mind rise from earth to heaven. Like Alan, Thomas has some
sense of the social significance of fasting and of its corporate setting. But
in his discussion of the Ember Days (which Pope Leo I saw as a sacrifice
offered in return for an abundant harvest), we see how much the notion
of Christendom has changed. To Thomas, fasting is appointed on the
quarter days because they are times of ordination, at which "both the
ordainer and the candidates for ordination and even the whole people,
for whose good they are ordained," abstain in order to be ready.[64] Thus
the fast unites not a Christian community to the rhythms of nature but
a people to its leader, the priest. And this leader stands for the people—
in his eating as well as his not eating. Thomas Aquinas, like other thir-
teenth- and fourteenth-century theologians, saw the priest in the mass
as receiving for the people—an idea that became one among several
justifications for withdrawing the cup from the laity.[65]

This same sense of the significance of rules and of a Christian community subsumed in the priesthood reverberates in the great hymns for
Corpus Christi that are associated with Aquinas's name. Again and
again, the poet sings of a Christ who "obeys fully the law concerning
food [i.e., the Passover ritual] and gives himself as food with his own
hands," who "gave his brothers the lamb and the unleavened bread,
according to the law of our forefathers."[66] Again and again he stresses
the coming of the whole Christ to the individual Christian, who sees by
faith the body and blood in the fragment of bread. But even as he praises
the magnanimity of a God who gives himself into the hands and teeth
of the lowly, he underlines that the giving and the union come through
the power of priests:

> Sic sacrificium
> Istud instituit,
> Cujus officium
> Committi voluit
> Solis presbyteris,
> Quibus sic congruit
> Ut sumant et dent ceteris.

45

Panis angelicus
Fit panis hominum:
Dat panis caelicus
Figuris terminum:
O res mirabilis:
Manducat Dominum
Pauper, servus, et humilis.

(So he instituted the sacrifice and wished it to be performed only by priests, that priests receive it themselves and give it to others. The bread of heaven becomes man's bread; the bread of heaven puts an end to types [i.e., foreshadowings]. Oh what a marvelous thing! The poor man, the servant, the lowly person eats God.)[67]

A glance at twelfth- to fourteenth-century exempla—moral tales used by preachers to educate both monastic and lay audiences—tells the story of attenuating practice. Of thirteen exempla concerning abstinence listed in Tubach's recent index, five simply urge the practice, two are attacks on hypocrisy, and three urge moderation. Of thirty-three stories that concern fasting, only fifteen really advocate it or express admiration for ascetic feats (and several of these stories are merely repeated from patristic texts). Two tales stress the difficulty of fasting; seven urge the avoidance of hypocrisy or prefer an inner, spiritual response to legalistic observance; six advise moderation. There is a strong note of warning against not only excess but fraud and self-delusion as well. Abstinence is seen as a useful tool for conquering lust and, in one case, for converting or defeating heretics; but no tale places the practice within a cosmic drama, concerns a group fast (beyond one patristic story of a group of hermits), speaks of mourning or of the penitence of the Christian community, or suggests that fasting should issue in almsgiving. Practice is often allegorized or spiritualized. Gossiping is said to be worse than breaking fast; feeding the poor is better than observing it. We are even told of monks who break their fast out of charity in order not to scandalize their neighbors or tax them beyond their strength.

Among the exempla that deal with food, no clear pattern emerges. A few tales express abhorrence of stealing or hoarding food, see fasting as inducing miracles, or connect holiness and food multiplication. But when we listen to the voices of these preachers, we hear no insistent concern with eating—either as the act necessary for survival or as a metaphor for the way in which God is met.[68] As in treatises and hymns, so too in these moral tales for ordinary Christians, we seem to see a church straining to enforce minimum observance. Yet we also see an effort to give such observance a dignified meaning sensitive to the needs of individual lives and temperaments, so that hypocrisy and self-delusion may be avoided, spiritual growth may abound.

As in the third and fourth centuries, however, there were those in the later Middle Ages to whom such counsel seemed weakness. They responded to the pastoral concern of theologians and lawyers with a passionate conviction that evil was darker than the moderates supposed and could be rooted out only by drastic means. The majority of these new virtuosi were women. In some ways they may be seen as responding to a twelfth- and thirteenth-century "triumph of Christianity" as striking as the triumph of the fourth century. Like early ascetics, they found only compromise and failure in a church characterized by a new bureaucracy, a new definition of itself, a new pastoral policy, a new ability (through the requirement of yearly communion and confession) to touch ordinary Christians, and new, minimal requirements for observance. Words such as those of the *Vitis mystica*—"Nor should you believe in any way that it is a greater virtue to abstain from food than to make use of food in moderation"—must have annoyed some people even if they comforted others. Such Christians responded, as they had in the fourth century, with extravagant asceticism, a haunting sense of human evil and alienation, and a theology of sacrifice and self-sacrifice.[69] They revived ancient models, citing Jerome on the connection between food and lust, competing with the Desert Fathers in marathon fasts. They also struggled to recreate in their lives what they could not quite find in contemporary theology: the corporate sense of the early church. Although late medieval women remained individual—and often idiosyncratic—in their fasting behavior, they connected fast with feeding and abstinence with fertility as surely as Leo the Great had done, in a very different context.

But the food asceticism of late medieval people—especially women— was not merely a revival of the life of the desert or a frantic grasp at purity in the face of a church with moderate requirements. It was also imitation of the cross. The basic significance of Christ, and of Christ as food, had changed; and in the shadow of this change abstinence took on new meaning. In order to understand the new sense of Jesus as suffering flesh, we must consider the history of eucharistic devotion.

♦ A Medieval Change: From Bread of Heaven to the Body Broken

Although Christians evolved a fixed liturgy for their holy meal only very slowly, the eucharist was by 200 the central act of the church: a sacrifice of praise and a memorial of redemption. It is significant that a single meal—one consisting of the two basic elements of the Mediterranean diet, bread and wine—rose to prominence, for the older Mediterranean traditions of feasting lasted throughout the Middle Ages, in various forms of carnival.[70] Not all the Fathers agreed with Augustine, who tried to eliminate banquets and drunken revelry from the festivals of the martyrs.[71] The missionaries who carried Christianity to the northern lands permitted lavish meals on saints' days, as long as the meat was not sacrificed to the old gods.[72]

But the central Christian meal was not the carnival, not the bacchanal, not an exuberant revel expressing abundance and fertility.[73] The central meal, the central liturgical act, was a frugal repast, evoking less the luxurious, proliferating richness of the natural world than the human life it supported. Indeed, Christ had said it *was* human life, was body and blood. From the very beginning the eucharistic elements stood primarily not for nature, for grain and grape, but for human beings bound into community by commensality.

Early Christian writers saw the eucharist as spiritual refreshment and as a pledge of the church's unity, as the bread of heaven and the one body of Christ.[74] For example, the Syriac writer Ephrem of Nisibis (d. 373) linked the eucharist with the church not so much because he explicitly identified the church with Christ's body as because he saw the eucharist *in* the church uniting Christians:

> And because he [Christ] loved his Church greatly
> he did not give her the manna of her rival;
> He became the Bread of Life
> for her to eat him.

Like Cyprian earlier and Romanos the Melodist later, Ephrem saw in bread a powerful symbol of many (fragments, crumbs, loaves, etc.) united into one and a graphic pledge of the resurrection:

> His bread, beyond dispute,
> bears witness to our resurrection,

> for [if] he blessed the food,
>> how much more those who eat!
> In the twelve loaves
>> which he blessed and multiplied,
>>> he blessed and multiplied his Twelve.
> And he took bread and broke it,
>> another, only one [loaf],
> the symbol of the body,
>> the Only-begotten, [born] of Mary.[75]

The anthropologist Gillian Feeley-Harnik has recently pointed out that the early Christians not only took over Jewish notions of food as the embodiment of God's wisdom but also signaled an expansion of community by expanding commensality. From the Christian passover—no longer a private, domestic meal—none was excluded. Rich and poor, Jew and Gentile, coward and hero, all celebrated together. Eating Christ's body was an inclusive act, one that created community.[76]

For all the talk of sign and sacrament, type and symbol, no early writer doubted that a sacred reality lay behind the bread and wine; and in the third and fourth centuries increasing care was taken of the elements themselves as the "body of the Lord."[77] As an early Easter hymn (fourth to sixth century) expresses it:

> Ad cenam agni prouidi,
> . . . .
> Cuius sacrum corpusculum
> in ara crucis torridum;
> cruore cuius roseo
> gustando uiuimus Deo.
> . . . .
> iam pascha nostrum Christus est,
> qui inmolatus agnus est;
> sinceritatis azyma
> caro eius oblata est.

([We are] looking forward to the supper of the lamb . . . whose sacred body is roasted on the altar of the cross. By drinking his rosy blood, we live with God. . . . Now Christ is our passover, our sacrificial lamb; His flesh, the unleavened bread of sincerity, is offered up.)[78]

Or as a slightly later Irish hymn puts it:

49

Sancti uenite, Christi corpus sumite,
sanctum bibentes, quo redempti sanguinem.

saluati Christi corpore et sanguine,
a quo refecti laudes dicamus Deo.

hoc sacramento corporis et sanguinis
omnes exuti ab inferni faucibus.

. . . .

pro universis inmolatus Dominus
ipse sacerdos exstitit et hostia

. . . .

caelestem panem dat esurientibus,
de fonte uiuo praebet sitientibus.

(Come, holy people, eat the body of Christ, drinking the holy blood by
which you are redeemed. We have been saved by Christ's body and
blood; having feasted on it, let us give thanks to God. All have been
rescued from the jaws of hell by this sacrament of body and blood. . . .
The Lord, offered as sacrifice for us all, was both priest and victim. . . .
He gives the celestial bread to the hungry and offers drink from the
living fountain to the thirsty.)[79]

Exactly how Christ was present in the bread and wine was not a
question that animated early theologians. Between the ninth and twelfth
centuries, however, it became such a question. Preachers and schoolmen
argued over what sorts of metaphors were acceptable for expressing the
nature of God's presence.[80] The majority clearly favored language that
was frankly literal and physical. When the Fourth Lateran Council
(1215) stated—in phrases neither as scholastic nor as Aristotelian as they
might have been—that Christ is present in substance on the altar at the
consecration, it was merely making explicit what theologians and layfolk
had assumed for centuries:

There is one universal church of the faithful, outside which no one at all
is saved. In this church, Jesus Christ himself is both priest and sacrifice,
and his body and blood are really contained in the sacrament of the altar
under the species of bread and wine, the bread being transubstantiated
into the body and the wine into the blood by the power of God, so that
to carry out the mystery of unity we ourselves receive from him the body
he himself receives from us [accipiamus ipsi de suo, quod accepit ipse de
nostro].[81]

The proliferating eucharistic miracles of the twelfth and thirteenth centuries—in which the host, lying on the paten, shut away in the tabernacle, or raised on high in the priest's hands, turned visibly into Christ—were not (as some have argued) the result of the doctrine of transubstantiation. Rather, they were an expression of the sort of piety that made such doctrinal definition seem obviously true.[82] As Peter of Poitiers (d. 1205) put it: Christ is present beneath the veil of the species "like a hand in a glove." Peter the Chanter even went so far as to ask: "If we concede, without reservation, that the body of Christ is eaten, as Augustine says, why not say absolutely that one sees God?" (But Peter did not quite dare to answer that, yes, the faithful do literally see God through the elements as through a transparent veil.)[83]

The conviction that God was present in the eucharist more literally than in any other sacrament, that behind the veil of the "accidents" of "wine-redness" or "crumbliness" lay the substance of the body of God, raised certain problems for theologians. How could the *totus Christus* be present in physical elements so distressingly fluid or breakable? Would not the pious draw the risible conclusion—as they unquestionably did on occasion—that little bits of Jesus fell off if crumbs were spilled or that one hurt God by chewing the host? Desiring to avoid the implication, found in some eleventh- and twelfth-century supporters of the real presence, that the faithful do eat little pieces of God's flesh, theologians such as Aquinas affirmed that Christ's entire body was present in every particle. Thus his body was not physically broken in the fraction of the host. They also elaborated the doctrine of "concomitance"—the idea that both the body and the blood of Christ are present in each element. Faced with growing devotion to the bread and wine themselves, exactly because the crumbs and drops masked (thinly) the substance of Christ, theologians struggled to retain a firm emphasis on Christ's body as one, because one church and one humanity are saved in it.[84] In the Corpus Christi hymns associated with Aquinas, we hear echoing again and again not only the doctrine of transubstantiation but also the insistence on one Christ in two species. Only thus is total human nature (sensual as well as spiritual) saved:

> Verbum caro panem verum verbo carnem efficit
> Fitque sanguis Christi merum; et, si sensus deficit,
> Ad firmandum cor sincerum sola fides sufficit.

(The Word made flesh by a word changes true bread into flesh, and wine becomes the blood of Christ; and if sense is deficient [in perceiving the change], faith alone suffices to make the sincere heart firm [in believing it].)[85]

> Post agnum typicum, expletis epulis,
> Corpus dominicum datum discipulis,
> Sic totum omnibus, quod totum singulis,
> Ejus fatemur manibus.

(After [they had eaten] the lamb, which is a type [i.e., a foreshadowing], and when the meal was over, the body of the Lord was given to the disciples in such a way that the whole was given to all and the whole given to each, and this was done by his own hands.)[86]

> Quibus sub bina specie
> Carnem dedit et sanguinem
> Ut duplicis substantiae
> Totum cibaret hominem.

([To his disciples] he gave, under two species, his flesh and blood, so that it might feed the whole man, who is of twofold substance.)[87]

Sometimes the hymns become veritable theological tractates:

> Sub diversis speciebus,
> Signis tantum et non rebus,
>   Latent res eximiae.
> Caro cibus, sanguis potus,
> Manet tamen Christus totus
>   Sub utraque specie.
> . . . .
> Fracto demum sacramento
> Ne vacilles, sed memento
> Tantum esse sub fragmento
>   Quantum toto tegitur.

(Under the different species, which are only signs, not things [i.e., realities], lie hidden wonderful things. The flesh is food, the blood is drink, and yet the whole Christ remains under each species. . . . Finally, when the sacrament is broken, do not doubt, but remember: there is as much hidden in a fragment as in the whole.)[88]

The theological questions of transubstantiation and concomitance were not merely schoolroom problems. They arose from and had grave implications for Christian practice, as is demonstrated by a controversy that erupted in Paris in the later twelfth century—years before transubstantiation was defined. The question was whether Christ was present from the moment of the first words of institution: "Hoc est enim corpus meum." Since a body cannot exist without blood and since the blood was clearly not yet present, the wine not having been consecrated, Peter the Chanter concluded that the body could not be present until the words over the wine were said. Both elements were necessary for Christ to be present. Indeed, Peter held, both elements were necessary for the consecration of either to occur. If, during the mass, the priest discovered that he had forgotten to put wine in the chalice, he had to repeat the entire consecration.

Peter's argument met with outraged rebuttal in sermons, in theological analyses, and even in the glosses provided to accounts of miracles. It annoyed both learned and popular opinion, partly because it ran afoul of common liturgical practice (which was simply to fill up the empty chalice and go on) but mostly because, as Guy of Orchelles said, it made existing piety into idolatry. Priest and people alike had begun to practice adoration of the host from the moment of its consecration. If it was not yet Christ, then the faithful were worshiping flour. While no one involved denied that the elements were in some sense Christ's body and blood, the exact moment of the change mattered enormously because people were behaving as if Christ appeared, substantially and totally, in the wafer when the words "Hoc est corpus meum" were said.[89]

This rather minor theological debate reflects a great medieval change. By the thirteenth century the eucharist, once a communal meal that bound Christians together and fed them with the comfort of heaven, had become an object of adoration. The physical appearance of food on the altar was in fact a veil through which holy flesh was spiritually or mystically seen. Since Christ arrived at the moment of consecration, not of communion, he arrived in the hands of the priest before he appeared on the tongue of the individual believer. Whether or not one held or tasted the wafer, one could meet Christ at the moment of his descent into the elements—a descent that paralleled and recapitulated the Incarnation.

Despite the new focus on "seeing" rather than "receiving," on consecration rather than communion, medieval men and women did not lose their sense of the religious significance of food and hunger, both as facts and as metaphors. If anything, food became a yet more powerful and awe-ful symbol, for the bread and wine that lay on the altar were now even more graphically seen to be God. But the meaning of *food* and *hunger* changed. To patristic poets and theologians, the food on the altar had suggested that Christ himself came as bread to hungry humankind or that he "digested" Christians, binding them to him as his body—i.e., the church. Hunger meant human vulnerability, which God comforted with food, or it meant human self-control, adopted in an effort to keep God's commandments. In the sermon and song, theology and story, of the high Middle Ages, however, the food on the altar was the God who became man; it was bleeding and broken flesh. Hunger was unquenchable desire; it was suffering. To eat God, therefore, was finally to become suffering flesh with his suffering flesh; it was to imitate the cross.

Many changes in piety—some coming as early as the ninth century—foreshadowed, accompanied, and reflected the shift from communion to consecration as the focal point of devotion. Early medieval Christians had sometimes reserved the sacrament on the altar in a pyx (for carrying to the sick) and had combined it with or substituted it for relics in the consecration of churches. Perhaps as early as the eleventh century, at Bec and at Canterbury, they venerated it with genuflection, incense, and procession. But the cult of the sacrament, of devotion to the consecrated host itself, did not really begin until the twelfth century. It then developed rapidly. The pyxes and reliquaries in which the host was reserved became more and more elaborate, both to protect the host from profanation and to allow the faithful to adore it outside the mass. Lamps and candles were burned before it. Small, usually circular openings (*oculi*), were placed in the exterior walls of the apse, so that the pious could look directly into the eucharistic chest and venerate the host from outside the church.[90] From Germany come stories of knights and peasants galloping up on horseback so that the horses might adore God also, in a kind of equine communion known as the *Umritt*.[91] Perhaps as early as the ninth century, recluses had their cells in churches positioned so they could adore the host each day.[92] Visits to the host began in the twelfth century; some writers suggested that such visits might substitute for going on crusade.

The first evidence for the elevation of the host after consecration comes from Paris about 1200.[93] The practice spread rapidly, and with it the conviction that seeing the host had spiritual value—that it was a

54

"second sacrament," alongside receiving. Prayers were composed for the moment of seeing, which was honored by the ringing of bells, genuflection, and incense. By the thirteenth century we find stories of people attending mass only for the moment of elevation, racing from church to church to see as many consecrations as possible, and shouting at the priest to hold the host up higher.[94] An account even survives of guild members bringing charges against a priest for assigning them places in church from which they could not see the elevated host.[95] When John Marienwerder, Dorothy of Montau's confessor, wrote his account of her visions and teachings, he especially emphasized the saint's devotion to "seeing" Christ:

> The spouse [of Christ], compelled by the odor of this vivifying sacrament, had from her childhood to the end of her life the desire to see the blessed host. And if she managed to view it a hundred times in one day, as sometimes happened, she still retained the desire to view it more often.[96]

The cult of the eucharistic host was fully established by the late thirteenth century, with the institution in 1264 of the feast of Corpus Christi (revealed to Juliana of Cornillon and long worked for by Juliana and her friends Eva of St. Martin and Isabelle of Huy).[97] Despite the intense eucharistic enthusiasm of the area around Liège, Juliana's home, the feast made little headway at first, in part because some argued that a special festival for Christ's body might imply less reverence for it at every mass. But after the feast was re-promulgated in 1311/12, and again in 1317, it spread rapidly. In the fourteenth century, "showing" was separated entirely from the mass, with the introduction of the monstrance, a special vessel for displaying the consecrated wafer. The host was now carried uncovered in procession on Corpus Christi and left exposed on the altar for adoration, sometimes for the entire octave. By the fifteenth century certain feasts ended with the exposition and benediction of the blessed sacrament. Even before the promulgation of Corpus Christi, orders and confraternities appeared whose purpose was to promote the cult of the host and to make reparation for the sacrilege of heretics. One such confraternity, itself perhaps not the first, was the gray penitents of Avignon, founded in 1226.[98]

Elevation of the chalice emerged more slowly. The feasts of the Sacred Heart and of the Precious Blood were established only in modern times. But the roots of these festivals go back to the intense devotion to the heart of Jesus found among the Saxon nuns and Flemish holy women of the thirteenth century.[99] And as we shall see, late medieval spiritual texts were awash in references to the blood of the lamb.

In the mass itself, reception and consecration were increasingly separated, and the elements treated with increasing awe. More and more the rhythm of the service itself, the liturgical practices surrounding it, and even the architecture of churches suggested that God came "through" and even primarily "to" priests. In the early church the altar had been a simple table, and the priest had celebrated facing the people. By the twelfth century the altar stood against the wall of the apse and was often surmounted by a retable. A cross (usually not yet a crucifix) and candles adorned it. The priest celebrated with his back to the people, reciting the canon of the mass in an inaudible whisper, while the people engaged in all sorts of personal devotions (or daydreaming) loosely connected with the ceremony. Communion was given before, after, or completely apart from mass. Monks and nuns might go to the high altar; layfolk usually received at the side altar, where the sacrament was sometimes placed beforehand. Women had been prohibited since the days of the early church from receiving in their bare hands. From the ninth century, women and laymen usually received directly on the tongue. By the eleventh century only priests could take God in their hands.[100]

Moreover, changes in the physical elements themselves made them seem more awesome, magical, and remote. Since the ninth century the wafer had been made from unleavened bread, perhaps because it adhered more easily to the tongue than did leavened bread. In the early twelfth century the host began to be stamped with pictures of Christ rather than with the simple monograms common earlier.[101] In the twelfth and thirteenth centuries the chalice sometimes contained merely a drop of the precious blood mixed with unconsecrated wine (the so-called lay chalice). The cup was sometimes withheld entirely. In the thirteenth century the people were sometimes offered simply a cup of unconsecrated wine for cleansing the mouth after communion. The interchange of the various chalices often went unnoticed, and theologians argued over whether the faithful should be taught that they received the body and blood in the wafer and mere wine in the chalice, or whether the cup of the laity indeed held the blood of the Lord.[102] Thomas Aquinas justified the withholding of the cup by pointing out that the priest received both species.[103]

The theory that the priest received for the people was elaborated gradually. Otto of Bamberg (d. 1139) said that the converted Pomeranians should communicate through their priests if they could not receive themselves. Berthold of Regensburg (d. 1272) explained that the communicating priest "nourishes us all," for he is the mouth and we are the body. William Durandus the Elder (d. 1296) suggested that the faithful receive three times a year "because of sinfulness" but "priests [receive] daily for us all." Ludolf of Saxony (d. 1377) argued that the eucharist is called our daily bread because ministers receive it daily for the whole community.[104]

Not only was the priest the channel through which God descended, he was also seen as assimilated to Christ (or the Virgin Mary) in the act of consecration, as deified at the moment in which God arrived between his hands. "Oh revered dignity of priests, in whose hands the Son of God is incarnated as in the Virgin's womb," reads an often-cited twelfth-century text.[105] And the following lines have been attributed to the wandering preacher Norbert of Xanten, who founded an order of clerics:

> Priest, you are not you, because you are God.
> You are not yours, because you are Christ's servant and minister.
> You are not of yourself because you are nothing.
> What therefore are you, oh priest? Nothing and all things.[106]

In the early thirteenth century, Francis of Assisi expressed the same awe of priests:

> If it is right to honour the Blessed Virgin Mary because she bore him in her most holy womb; if St. John the Baptist trembled and was afraid even to touch Christ's sacred head; if the tomb where he lay for only a short time is so venerated; how holy, and virtuous, and worthy should not a priest be; he touches Christ with his own hands. . . . A priest receives him into his heart and mouth and offers him to others to be received.[107]

As the role of the priest was exalted, the gap between priest and people widened. By the late Middle Ages in northern Europe, elaborate screens were constructed to hide the priest and the altar.[108] Thus, at the pivotal moment of his coming, Christ was separated and hidden from the congregation in a sanctuary that enclosed together priest and God.

In such an atmosphere, deep ambivalence developed about the reception of communion.[109] On the one hand, theologians and canon lawyers encouraged frequent reception. The requirement of at least yearly confession and communion established at the Fourth Lateran Council (1215) was intended to set forth a minimum of observance. And a number of the new monastic orders required frequent communion. But, on the other hand, theologians feared that frequent reception might lead to loss of reverence, to carelessness, even to profanation of the elements. Familiarity might breed contempt. Albert the Great, for example, who supported the practice of daily communion, argued against it for women, fearing that frequent reception would trivialize response.[110] Theologians often asserted that abstaining out of awe was equal to receiving with confidence and joy. Quoting Augustine, they urged an interior seeing and feeding, which became the notion of "spiritual communion."[111]

Faced with such ambiguous advice, many pious people in the later Middle Ages developed, along with a frenzied hunger for the host, an intense fear of receiving it. Margaret of Cortona, for example, pled frantically with her confessor for frequent communion but, when given the privilege by Christ, abstained out of terror at her unworthiness.[112] Gertrude the Great expressed a sense of Christ and sacrament as truly awe-ful when she wrote:

> You, who are the splendor and the crown of celestial glory, you appeared to descend from the imperial throne of your majesty with a movement full of sweetness, and flooded the width of the sky with a sweet liquor so that the saints hastened to drink. . . .
>
> And you added this understanding [to the vision just recounted]: that one ought to approach the sacrament of your body and blood in such love for your communion (even beyond the love for your glory, if that is possible) that one would be willing to eat the sacrament to one's own condemnation.[113]

Gertrude took comfort for her own feelings of unworthiness from words that God supposedly sent to her when she tried to explain why a friend abstained: "I heard your [i.e., God's] blessed response: 'It is impossible that anyone receiving with such an intention [i.e., the intention to abstain from fear] could be irreverent.'"[114]

For all the terror the eucharist inspired, however, reception of God as food between one's lips remained a uniquely important mode of spiritual encounter. Late medieval saints, especially women, frequently received from confessors, or even the pope himself, the privilege of daily communion as an almost official recognition of their reputations for sanctity.[115] Religious superiors, bishops, and canon lawyers legislated against reception during ecstasy, in an effort to control the waves of frenzy for the eucharist that shook religious houses.[116] The deathbeds of pious people sometimes became the setting for bitter struggle between priest and recipient over how often the holy food could be taken.[117] Indeed, as the moment of consecration became increasingly fraught with meaning, as the power of priests grew ever more awesome, as the notion of eating God seemed more and more audacious and the drink of Christ's blood was permanently withdrawn, some of the devout found that their hunger, seasoned and impelled by fear, merely intensified.[118] The more church architecture, liturgical practice, and priestly power contrived to make the elements seem distant, the more some people luxuriated in them in private, ecstatic experiences. James of Vitry's description of the eucharistic piety of Mary of Oignies could be matched by dozens of similar descriptions from the next two hundred years:

> Thus [Mary] languished in exile. The sole and highest remedy was the manna of celestial bread, until she could come to the promised land [heaven]. In it, the anxiety and desire of her heart were tempered; in it, all her sorrows were appeased. . . . In the highest and most excellent sacrament, she patiently bore all the hardships of her enforced wandering. . . . The holy bread strengthened her heart; the holy wine inebriated her, rejoicing her mind; the holy body fattened her; the vitalizing blood purified her by washing. And she could not bear to abstain from such solace for long. For it was the same to her to live as to eat the body of Christ, and this it was to die, to be separated from the sacrament by having for a long time to abstain. . . . Indeed, she felt all delectation and all savor of sweetness in receiving it, not just within her soul but even in her mouth. . . . Sometimes she happily accepted her Lord under the appearance of a child, sometimes as a taste of honey, sometimes as a sweet smell, and sometimes in the pure and gorgeously embellished marriage bed of the heart. And when she was not able to bear any longer her thirst for the vivifying blood, sometimes after the mass was over she would remain for a long time contemplating the empty chalice on the altar.[119]

Despite the aura of majesty that surrounded the eucharist in the later Middle Ages, it seemed to the faithful to offer itself to their senses with astonishing familiarity.[120] It rang with the music of bells, glowed with light, dissolved on the tongue into honeycomb or bloody flesh, and announced its presence, when profaned or secreted away, by leaving a trail of blood. Christ appeared again and again on the paten and in the chalice as a baby, a glorious youth, or a bleeding and dying man.[121]

The changes in liturgy, theology, and even architecture discussed above help explain why so many visions of Christ came at mass. In an atmosphere where confessors and religious superiors controlled access to the eucharist and stressed scrupulous and awe-filled preparation, recipients naturally approached the elements in a spiritually and psychologically heightened state. When, after mumbling inaudibly, the priest suddenly and to the accompaniment of incense and bells raised on high a thin, shimmering wafer of unleavened bread embossed with the image of Christ, it is small wonder that the pious sometimes "saw" Jesus. When, after hours of self-examination and doubt, anxious nuns or laypeople took God on their tongues, it is small wonder that the bit of bread sometimes swelled "with marvelous sweetness" to choke them. Gazing aloft at a hanging pyx shaped in the form of a dove, some mystics thought they saw the Holy Spirit winging toward them, the wafer in his beak. Contemplating the new devotional object, the crucifix, in dim and damp churches, pious people sometimes thought it dripped blood because of their own private sins. Denied the cup or even the host by ecclesiastical regulation, many of the devout thought, when they at least obtained release from their inner distress and longing, that the comfort of Christ was in their mouths or hearts immediately—without the priest's enabling hands or words.

A glance at basic medieval attitudes toward food also helps us to understand certain aspects of eucharistic devotion. As culinary historians have recently observed, the characteristic medieval meal was the feast, and it was more an aesthetic and social event than a gastronomic one.[122] The feast was a banquet for all the senses; indeed, food was almost an excuse for indulging senses other than taste. Medieval chroniclers who describe feasts do not give menus, although they lavish attention on the entertainment provided. They describe the appearance of dishes, not the flavor; the sequence of events, not of courses. Medieval cookbooks make it clear that visual effects were more important to a medieval diner than taste and that vivid colors (for example, green dye from spinach or leeks, or gold- and silver-leaf garnish) were often applied at the expense of flavor. In some accounts of banquets, it is hard to tell whether the lavish pastry constructions, scenes, and puppet shows (known in English as "sotelties") displayed between courses were meant to be eaten or not. Medieval cookbooks provide detailed instructions on how to construct illusions or tricks for the eye, such as imitation meat concocted from fish, or roast fowl sewn back into its plumage in order to appear alive, or pies (like that in the nursery rhyme) with live birds baked inside.[123]

Given such assumptions about and expectations of food, it is small wonder that medieval mystics considered sounds and sights as crucial to the eucharistic banquet as eating, or that they sometimes felt they "ate" or "received" with their eyes or in their minds and hearts. It is no accident that Christ's feast involved all the senses, since secular banquets did so. Nor is it surprising that one taste (bread) changed easily into another (flesh, blood, meat, honey, etc.) in the mouth; for ordinary food, at its most sumptuous and exciting, was often illusion.

Even the legalism of medieval fasting practices might encourage the assumption—found both in cookbooks and in treatises on transubstantiation—that things were not really what they seemed. When an English diner in the 1460s had barnacle goose served to him as fish, he wrote that "we had to eat it as fish, but in my mouth it turned to meat."[124] His remark was presumably an ironic comment on hypocrisy or casuistry, but mystics used similar phrases simply and sincerely. When they "tasted" God's body, what they found was sometimes not what they anticipated, and they encountered it with more than the sense of taste. In a world where not only poets but ordinary folk as well treated the senses as far less discrete than we do and the items of the phenomenal world as more fluid in identity or significance, it is hardly surprising that those who ate God, like those who ate blackbird pie, were sometimes astonished, titillated, or disturbed by the experience.

Historians and theologians, both Protestant and Catholic, have customarily seen late medieval eucharistic piety as individualistic—as quietly but sometimes insidiously bypassing both priest and community.[125] Such interpretations have emphasized (and sometimes deplored) the loss of a liturgical context for devotion to the elements and the disappearance of any sense that Christians were united in a holy meal or in a communal sacrifice to God. But it is not quite true that late medieval eucharistic devotion lost all corporate elements, narrowing to simply the individual's inner experience of Christ. Exactly because the host became so insistently Christ's body—whose firm outlines had been violated by Roman (or

Jewish) spears and nails—it remained a powerful corporate symbol, a symbol of humankind, of Christendom, and of the church.

Two conservative theologians of the twelfth century, for example, described the eucharist as the salvation not merely of the individual who receives it but of all humanity, because it recapitulates the Incarnation. Hildegard of Bingen (d. 1179) received a vision in which Woman—as Eve, symbol of fallen humankind, and as the church, symbol of saved humanity—collects Christ's blood in a chalice and hears a voice saying: "Eat and drink the body and blood of my Son to abolish the prevarication of Eve and receive your true inheritance." Hildegard's vision was not a private, sensory experience but a theological statement. Her message is clear: Christians who eat God eat together, and it is humankind that is saved.[126] Expressing the same sensibility, Rupert of Deutz (d. 1135) wrote:

> To the one and only Son of God and Son of Man, as if to its head, all the members of the body are joined—all are received in the faith of his sacrament and the fullness of his charity—and thus one body, one person, one Christ, the head with all its members, ascends into the sky. . . . [And he shows himself to be] two in one flesh. A great sacrament is this! The flesh of Christ . . . thus satisfies [*implevit*] the whole world, so that it makes into one church all the elect who have been from the beginnings of the world or shall be until the end of time, joining God and man eternally.[127]

Moreover, some of the eucharistic visions seen by late medieval nuns, beguines, or laywomen have corporate elements or implications. For example, when Mechtild of Hackeborn (d. 1298 or 1299) received "the imprint of resemblance" to God in "the hour of communion," she received also Christ's heart in the form of a cup marvelously chiseled. "By my heart," she heard him say, "you will praise me always; go, offer to all the saints the drink of life from my heart that they may be happily inebriated with it."[128] Mechtild's sister nun Gertrude the Great received a vision in which those nuns who moved toward God holding the hands of others (i.e., trusting in the prayers of others for them) were the first to reach the splendors of light from Christ's heart.[129]

The host was a powerful symbol not just of humankind or of the monastic community but also of the church. William of St. Thierry explained that the body on the altar is Christ interceding for us: it is the physical body, born of Mary; it is also the mystical body, the church. Baldwin of Ford (d. 1190) stressed that communion unites us not only with Jesus but also with the whole church in community.[130] Arnold of Bonneval (d. after 1156), in one of the rare eucharistic prayers that survive from the period, expresses the identification of eucharist and church (although his emphasis is on the complex significance of the sacrament for the individual Christian):

> Christ calls this sacrament sometimes flesh and blood, sometimes bread, and sometimes his body. It is called bread because it is the nourishment of life, flesh and blood because of the truth of its nature, body because of its unity of substance. By his body he meant to indicate both himself and his church, of which he is the head, and which he unites by the communion of flesh and blood. And we indeed, when we eat the flesh and blood, will not be reformed in the corrupt and infirm nature of our body and soul nor returned to likeness with God unless a suitable poultice is placed on sin.[131]

Indeed, late medieval eucharistic devotion, paralleling the theological discussions of concomitance and of the *totus Christus* in every particle of bread, came to express an almost frantic sense of the wholeness, the inviolability, of Christ's body and a tremendous fear of rending and breaking. Tubach's index of exempla lists fifty-three miracles having to do with the host and only three concerning the chalice.[132] It is hard to avoid the conclusion that this emphasis on the host reflected a fear that the mystical body, the church, would be rent by its enemies.

Insistently the host forced itself onto the senses of believers as flesh with firm boundaries. The many miracles of consecrated wafers oozing or streaming drops of blood were understood to be announcing not just the sins of individual Christians but also attacks by outsiders, especially heretics and Jews. Miracles of bleeding hosts, which proliferate from the twelfth century on, sometimes have sinister overtones. The host becomes flesh to announce its violation; the bleeding is an accusation. When the nun Wilburgis (d. 1289) took the host to her enclosure to help her avoid sexual temptation, it revealed itself, in a quite common miracle, as a beautiful baby who spoke the words of the Song of Songs.[133] But when another nun hid a host that she dared not swallow because she was in mortal sin, it turned into flesh.[134] The second miracle sounds a threatening note not present in the first. Similarly, Peter Damian tells of a host that protested its abuse when used superstitiously: a woman who tried to conjure with it found that half of it turned into flesh.[135] Caesarius of Heisterbach reports that when another woman tried to use the consecrated wafer as a love charm and then guiltily hid it in a church wall, it turned to flesh and bled.[136] Beginning in the late thirteenth century, Jews were frequently charged with violating the host, which announced such violation by miraculous bleeding. Lionel Rothkrug has recently underlined the connection between eucharistic devotion and anti-Semitism. In the years before 1350 a number of Jews were murdered for alleged desecrations of the host.[137]

Moreover, eucharistic miracles were explicitly seen as vindications of orthodox doctrine. Eleventh-, twelfth-, and thirteenth-century preachers such as Peter Damian, Eckbert of Schönau, and Alan of Lille embellished their sermons against the Cathars with stories of bleeding hosts.[138] Several thirteenth-century theologians, such as the hagiographers James of Vitry and Thomas of Cantimpré, supported the increasing frenzy of women's eucharistic piety as a counter to the heretical denial that God could be present in matter.[139]

The abstinence of Lutgard of Aywières (d. 1246) reflects a similar fear that God's body might be breached by heresy. Lutgard both identified with Christ on the cross by fasting for seven years and, at the Virgin's command, offered her fast as a reparation to God for the depredations of the Albigensians.[140] When Gertrude the Great made the eucharistic host into many crumbs in her mouth, thinking that each particle stood for a soul in the flames of purgatory, she seemed to be equating the crumbliness of bread not with the unity of Christians (as did Augustine) but with their individualness, their separateness, their suffering. Gertrude, who often feared to take communion, was aware of the audacity of thus violating the integrity of the body of God.[141] A similar note of warning sounds in a vision of crumbs received by Francis of Assisi. When Francis was ordered to gather up the crumbs and make them into one host for the brethren, he also saw in vision that those brothers who did not receive the gift devoutly were afflicted with leprosy. The joining of "fine crumbs" into a host here symbolizes unity, but the host then stands for a Rule and those who observe it improperly are made ill by it. The symbol of unity excludes as surely as it joins.[142]

If bread/body/flesh, with its firm boundaries, symbolized spiritual refreshment and, at least to some extent, church, blood was an altogether more complex and ambivalent symbol. As the letters of Catherine of Siena suggest,[143] blood was life itself, coursing through Christ's veins, leaping forward from his violated side. It was food, both because blood itself feeds flesh and because blood (processed into milk, according to medieval physiological theory)[144] feeds the young. It was a purging bath. It was bloodshed, the palpable sign of attack on God. Gertrude the Great said the eucharist redeems "even blood," which she called "the most horrible of natural objects."[145] It is not surprising, therefore, that blood became a more common and insistent symbol as the fourteenth century wore on. The increased clerical determination to withhold the cup (the blood) from the laity may thus have a deeper reason than the one usually cited: fear of profanation through spilling. To associate the laity directly with such a powerful symbol of violation as well as of salvation may simply have been fraught with too much significance. Indeed, the demand of the Utraquists, who pushed for communion in both kinds (*sub utraque specie*), may have seemed not only a deliberate rejection of the doctrine of concomitance and a nationalist protest against the headship of the Roman church (which it certainly was) but also a dangerous democratization of an extraordinarily potent and complex symbol.

The corporate implications of late medieval eucharistic symbolism are thus at least partly defensive. Whereas Cyprian had seen the bread of heaven as a symbol of Christ's church precisely because the grains of wheat were gathered into a whole, later medieval theologians and visionaries saw in Christ as bleeding flesh not only the redemption of humankind but also an entity under attack. And however powerfully the entity sometimes suggested the Christian community, either united in love or violated by enemies, it was basically not a corporate symbol at all. The bread on the altar was the suffering flesh of the God-man who died; the blood and water that poured from the broken body fed and cleansed the individual Christian. In certain ways, the priest, not the eucharist, was the powerful corporate symbol. He was the "mouth" of the church, as Berthold of Regensburg said. But as Durandus implied, he also *was* the church; he received for all. Certain twelfth-century texts suggested that insofar as the priest was the "womb" within which Christ was consecrated, he stood for all humanity.

It is thus accurate to say that late medieval eucharistic piety was individualistic. The emphasis was increasingly on experience—on tasting, seeing, and meeting God. For the most part, the elements of cosmic drama fell away from eucharistic hymns and stories. And as encounter with the eucharist came to mean binding unto oneself either the inebriating joys of mystical union or the unspeakable pain of God's suffering, hunger became a powerful metaphor for desire. In early Christian hymns, *hunger* seems to mean human vulnerability (either inflicted by nature's rhythm of scarcity and plenty or espoused deliberately in fasting); the implication is, therefore, that the hungry will be satisfied. In the spirituality of eleventh- and twelfth-century Europe, however, hunger began to mean a craving that can never be filled. Thus the author of the famous hymn "Dulcis Jesu memoria" wrote:

> Dulcis Jesu memoria
> Dans vera cordi gaudia:
> Sed super mel et omnia
> Ejus dulcis praesentia.
> . . . .
>
> Qui te gustant, esuriunt,
> Qui bibunt, adhuc sitiunt;
> Desidare nesciunt
> Nisi Jesum quem diligunt.
> . . . .
>
> Jesus decus angelicum,
> In aure dulce canticum,
> In ore mel mirificum
> Corde pigmentum caelicum.

(Sweet is the remembrance of Jesus in the true joy of the heart. But his presence is sweet beyond honey and all things. . . . They who taste you [Jesus] still hunger, and they who drink you still thirst. They are not able to desire anything except Jesus, whom they love. . . . Jesus, glory of the angels, [you are] a sweet song in the ears, in the mouth wonderful honey, the spiced wine of heaven in the heart.)[146]

The *Letter to Severinus*, by a certain brother Ivo (late twelfth or early thirteenth century) expresses the same sensibility:

Thus loves a loving soul. . . . Its desire ever increases. For he can never be satiated whose desire is only to desire. Desire is the hunger of the soul. . . . God says: *They that eat me shall yet hunger* [Eccles. 24:29]. Oh God, to love you is to eat you. You refresh those who love you so that they hunger more, for are you not simultaneously food and hunger? He who does not taste you will not know at all how to hunger for you. For this only do you feed us, in order to make us hunger.[147]

In the thirteenth century, as the craving for experience of God intensified, Hadewijch spoke thus of love:

> To die of hunger for her [i.e., Love of God] is to feed and taste;
> Her despair is assurance;
> . . . .
> Her tender care enlarges our wounds;
> . . . .
> Her table is hunger.[148]

Thus, by the thirteenth and fourteenth centuries, the emphasis of hymn, sermon, and story was less on the bread of heaven than on flesh (i.e., meat) and blood. To eat God was to take into one's self the suffering flesh on the cross. To eat God was *imitatio crucis*. That which one ate was the physicality of the God-man. If the flesh was sweet as well as bitter, that was because all our humanness, including our fleshliness, was redeemed in the fact of the Incarnation. If the agony was also ecstasy, it was because our very hunger is union with Christ's limitless suffering, which is also limitless love.

This sense of God as food permeated spirituality outside as well as within the eucharistic context. Colette of Corbie, for example, received one night, as she prayed to the Virgin, a vision of

> a dish completely filled with carved-up flesh like that of a child. And she heard this reply: "This is what I request of my beloved on account of the horrible sins, injuries, and offenses that people do against him, offenses that tear him into smaller pieces than the flesh cut up upon this plate." And because of this vision she bore for a long time in her heart sadness and pain.[149]

Ida of Louvain (d. 1300?) supposedly tasted the Word as flesh on her tongue whenever she recited "Verbum caro factum est" (John 1:14).[150] In contrast to early medieval monastic texts, which frequently speak of reading and meditating as chewing the word of God but lay no claim to a physical experience,[151] Ida's biographer tells us that the Word she chewed was like honey, "not a phantasm but like any other kind of food."

The theme of God as food was also a common iconographic motif. For example, a fifteenth-century Swabian altarpiece depicting the so-called "mystical mill" shows Mary emptying sacks of wheat into a funnel, from which emerge both the Christ child and the host (see plate 1).[152] In paintings of the mass of St. Gregory (based on an early medieval story that gained popularity in later medieval art), Christ appears at the moment of consecration, sometimes bleeding graphically into the chalice to provide food and drink for Christians (see plate 3; see also plates 26, 27, and 30).[153] An even more stunning depiction, from the studio of Friedrich Herlin in 1469, shows Christ as a bleeding man of sorrows with a grain shoot (representing bread) and a vine (representing wine) growing out of the wounds in his feet and hands (see plate 4).[154]

Feast and fast, and the metaphors in which they were hymned and preached, thus changed between the time of the early church and the high Middle Ages. To early Christian preachers, fast and feast joined the believer to the rhythm of the seasons. Virtuoso ascetic performance was admired, but it was only a variation on the corporate practice of the church. The individual believer received the sweetness of God's body in concert with other believers, in a community symbolized qua community by the bread of heaven.[155] By the later Middle Ages, despite efforts to enforce a uniform, moderate observance, the setting given to fasting by preachers and theologians was less corporate and cosmic; the practice of some individuals was increasingly idiosyncratic and extreme. Devotion to God's body was also at least partly cut loose from a corporate setting. Not only did reception itself frequently occur after mass; the believer sometimes encountered the flesh and blood through private vision as well, at the moment of elevation or even completely apart from the liturgy.

Such changes may in part reflect the massive social and economic changes between antiquity and the medieval world. In the small, busy, merchant-dominated cities of the medieval urban revival, where the new eucharistic piety flourished, food was perhaps more a commodity, cut off from the rhythm of village life, than it ever was in the vast cities of the Roman Empire, so dependent on the countryside for grain. Thus it was easier for the daughters and sons of these merchants or urban aristocrats to think of food as an object to be manipulated rather than as a necessity of life so basic that it defined and was defined by community experience. Perhaps, then, it is not surprising that in a period of intense world rejection, this commodity obtruded itself as a privilege to be renounced. Nor is it surprising that virtuoso fasts grew more common as famine and malnourishment began, from the later thirteenth century, to be noticeable aspects of European life.

Whatever the connection between economic facts and religiosity, however (and there is certainly no direct correlation between the shifts in Christian piety and European economic conditions), these changes in sensibility and practice were large changes. They touched all Christians. Indeed, so crucial a facet of human experience as food could hardly have had significance for only one social group or one gender. But careful examination of the evidence suggests that in the later Middle Ages, both feast and fast were more central to women's spirituality than to men's. Against the background sketched here of food practices and metaphors in the high Middle Ages, and their roots in earlier tradition, I wish now to explore what food meant to pious women and why it meant what it did.

II

THE EVIDENCE

FOOD AS A FEMALE CONCERN:
THE COMPLEXITY
OF THE EVIDENCE

And blessed Mary said to [Alpaïs]: ". . . because, dear sister, you bore long starvation in humility and patience, in hunger and thirst, without any murmuring, I grant you now to be fattened with an angelic and spiritual food. And as long as you are in this little body, corporeal food and drink will not be necessary for the sustaining of your body, nor will you hunger for bread or any other food . . . because after you have once tasted the celestial bread and drunk of the living fountain you will remain fattened for eternity. . . ." And so it was. . . . But in order that the tumult of gossip be quieted, since some said she had a devil—she who neither ate nor drank—two or three times a week she was accustomed to accept some morsel. And she would roll it around for a time in her mouth . . . and then spit it back whole. . . . And I give this on my own testimony since I received in my own hand a little bit of masticated fish she spit out. . . . Thus, rejoicing as if possessed, she frequently vomited from too much food, as if her drunkenness and inebriation were increased by anything beyond a tiny bit. And this was how and of what sort her preservation was, how and of what nature were the beginnings of her conversion, and how God underlined her merits and virtues with miracles . . . by which miracles manifest signs are given to the readers [of this story].
LIFE OF ALPAÏS OF CUDOT (D. 1211)[1]

IN THE SPIRITUALITY of late medieval Europe, eating and not eating were powerful symbols. Both men and women fasted or adulterated what food they ate in order to destroy any pleasure they might experience in it. Both men and women adored Christ in the bread and wine on the altar, received eucharistic visions, and worked to propagate eucharistic piety. Both men and women gave alms and food to the poor. Men such as Dominic (d. 1221), Richard of Chicester (d. 1253), and Vincent Ferrer (d. 1419) and women such as Clare of Assisi, Agnes of Montepulciano (d. 1317), and Catherine of Siena were said to perform miracles in which they multiplied food for others or had their sanctity rewarded by manna sent from heaven.[2] Poets and exegetes built elaborate allegorical constructs around the themes of milk and meat, honey and the honeycomb, bread and wine, feeding or nursing. Visions in which instruction, comfort, grace, and salvation were seen as milk or blood pouring from the breasts of the Virgin, of Christ, or of religious leaders such as the apostle Paul or Francis of Assisi were received by both men and women between the thirteenth and fifteenth centuries.[3] But despite the pervasiveness of food as symbol, there is clear evidence that it was more important to women than to men.

It may seem surprising that this fact has not been noted before, especially since both the more bizarre cases of fasting girls[4] and the deep devotion of women to the eucharist have been fairly frequently discussed by scholars. In the late nineteenth and early twentieth centuries both medical doctors and Catholic theologians were deeply interested in the phenomenon of women (usually adolescent girls) who claimed to live without eating. This interest was foreshadowed in the eighteenth century when Pope Benedict XIV (d. 1758) commissioned an appendix for his great work on canonization to consider whether the extended fasts claimed for certain Catholic women, several of them stigmatics, could be natural.[5] By the late 1800s a number of Catholic scholars were fascinated by such phenomena,[6] and earlier in this century, Catholics—stimulated in part by the case of Theresa Neumann of Konnersreuth (d. 1962)—continued a fairly heated discussion of whether the ability to live without eating need be in any sense a result of supernatural power and, therefore, a sign of sanctity. (Given the strange behavior of certain fasting girls, many theologians wished to answer that it is not.)[7] Nineteenth-century doctors such as W. A. Hammond and Robert Fowler attacked the claims of fasting women with considerable bad temper;[8] and the interest of the medical profession in fasting led in the late nineteenth and early twentieth centuries to food fads and to scientific experiments, culminating in a test by the Carnegie Institute in 1912 to determine how long human beings could survive without food.[9] The early 1980s saw a flurry of interest both in the popular press and among doctors in so-called female eating disorders—without the least awareness of the religious context in which, until very recently, similar behaviors occurred.[10]

The role that thirteenth- and fourteenth-century women played in the propagation of eucharistic devotion has also been noted by scholars, often rather incidentally.[11] But historians have tended to correlate eucharistic concern with factors other than gender—for example, with religious order (particularly Cistercian or Dominican),[12] with region (particularly the Low Countries or southern Germany),[13] or with type of religious life (particularly monastic or anchoritic).[14] The overwhelming tendency among historians of spirituality, until recently, has been to study figures in the context of the orders with which they were affiliated, thus obscuring broader trends in the history of piety and sometimes leading to rather sterile debates over precedence.[15] The recent extensive work on medieval saints, some of it deeply interested in social context, has, with a few exceptions, been more concerned with class or regional differences than with gender.[16] It has, moreover, sometimes been so concerned with social or psychological issues as to lose any fine-grained sense of spiritual themes.[17] Thus the extent to which women of all life-styles and affiliations revered the eucharist—laywomen, recluses, tertiaries, beguines, nuns of all orders, and those women (especially common in the early thirteenth century) who wandered from one type of life to another—has been obscured, although the evidence has long been available.

Basically, however, women's concern with the religious significance of food has been ignored because phenomena such as eucharistic devotion, fasting, food multiplication miracles, and lactation visions have been treated in isolation from one another. Just as doctors and psychiatrists tend to treat fasting under such rubrics as fear of mutilation, rejection of the mother, and battle for control—forgetting that, whatever else it is, it is a food practice—so theologians and historians have failed to notice that food miracles, eucharistic piety, and abstinence are all food practices. Once one notices that eating and not eating are central themes in medieval European culture, as in many cultures, much of the long-available evidence on spirituality appears in new patterns, and new evidence begins to emerge. It is then that the religious significance of food for women becomes clear.

◆ *Quantitative and Fragmentary Evidence for Women's Concern with Food*

A number of recent works on sanctity provide quantitative evidence that food is a more important motif in women's piety than in men's. Donald Weinstein and Rudolph Bell, in their study of 864 saints from 1000 to 1700, demonstrate conclusively that all types of penitential asceticism, including fasting, are significantly more common in female religiosity. Although only 17.5 percent of those canonized or venerated as saints from 1000 to 1700 were women, women accounted for almost 29 percent of those saints who indulged in extreme austerities, such as fasting, flagellation, or sleep deprivation; 23.3 percent of those who died from such practices; and 53.2 percent of those in whose lives illness was the central factor in reputation for sanctity.[18] Richard Kieckhefer, in his examination of fasting by fourteenth-century saints, cites almost as many examples of women as of men, despite the fact that fewer than 30 percent of those revered as saints were women. Kieckhefer also finds that, in the period he has studied, Henry Suso is almost the only male to receive eucharistic visions.[19] André Vauchez, in his study of late medieval canonizations, suggests that fasting was important for only one type of male saint—the hermit (who was often a layman)—whereas it was a crucial component of the reputation of holy women.[20] The older work of Herbert Thurston, which attempts a "scientific" approach no longer fashionable, nonetheless assembles a wide range of cases. It is, therefore, worth noting that Thurston's discussion of "authentic" food multiplication miracles lists almost as many performed by women as by men.[21]

Peter Browe's work on the eucharist indicates, moreover, that the eucharistic miracle is almost entirely a female genre.[22] If one accepts Browe's categories (of twenty types of eucharistic miracle), only two types occur primarily to males, and both of these are associated with the act of consecration, which could be performed only by men. The two male types are the miracle of the spider in the chalice, traditionally told of priests, and the miracle of transformation at the moment of consecration, which was by definition limited to priests. At least eight types of eucharistic miracle, however, are predominantly or exclusively female. Four types occur almost exclusively to women: miracles in which the recipient becomes a crystal filled with light, miracles in which the recipient distinguishes consecrated and unconsecrated hosts, miracles in

76

which worthy and unworthy recipients and celebrants are distinguished, and miracles in which the eucharist has a special effect on the senses (smelling sweet, ringing with music, filling the mouth with honey, announcing its presence when hidden away or hoarded, etc.). Predominantly but not exclusively female are miracles in which the host or chalice changes into a beautiful baby—miracles that sometimes (but not always) have highly erotic overtones for both men and women. Most striking of all, there is only one male example (after the patristic period) of the common story of the saint who lives largely or entirely on the eucharist. There are very few male cases of the various distribution miracles, in which the eucharist is brought by doves or angels or flies by itself through the air, and these are mostly told of low-status males— lay brothers or altar boys. And there appears to be only one male case of the miracle in which Christ becomes the priest and offers himself as food—an act sometimes accomplished with frightening literalism, as when he tears off the flesh from the palm of his hand for Adelheid of Katharinental.[23] Not only are these patterns striking in themselves, it is also clear that the male miracles underline the power of the priest, whereas in at least half of the women's miracles it is the quality of the eucharist as food that is stressed.[24] The eucharist is offered as flesh or honeycomb; it affects the taste; it sustains life; it is vomited out if unconsecrated.

A cursory glance at the history of eucharistic piety indicates that women were prominent in the creation and spread of special devotions such as the feast of Corpus Christi (revealed to Juliana of Cornillon)[25] or the devotion to the Sacred Heart (found especially in the Flemish saint Lutgard of Aywières and the many visions of the nuns of the Saxon monastery of Helfta).[26] So important was the eucharist that some thirteenth-century women (e.g., Ida of Nivelles and the Viennese beguine Agnes Blannbekin) made vocational decisions or changed orders out of desire to receive it more frequently.[27] Stories of people levitating, experiencing ecstasy during the mass, or racing from church to church to attend as many eucharistic services as possible are usually told of women—for example, of Hedwig of Silesia (d. 1241), Douceline of Marseilles (d. 1274), and several of the Flemish holy women described by James of Vitry (see the epigraph to chapter 1 above).[28] The work of Imbert-Gourbeyre, despite its scanty documentation and notoriously uncritical stance, nonetheless provides a revealing idea of what the pious expected of religious heroes and heroines. Imbert-Gourbeyre culled from saints' lives nine cases of miraculous abstinence, all of them female, and fifty-two cases of miraculous communion (between the thirteenth and sixteenth centuries), of which forty-five are female.[29]

Even in accounts written by medieval males for male audiences, we find the eucharist and the attendant theme of the humanity of Christ associated especially with women. For example, Caesarius of Heisterbach, writing in the early thirteenth century for male novices and drawing on his own male world, in general told overwhelmingly male stories. In his treatment of dying, in the *Dialogue on Miracles*, he gives fifty-four stories about men and eight about women; on punishment of the dead, he gives forty-seven male stories and eight female; on such topics as lust and despair, he preserves a similar ratio. But we find as many cases of nuns as of monks receiving the infant Jesus in visions, and there are more than half as many appearances of the crucifix to women as to men. In the section on the eucharist, where he turns from celebrant (all male stories, of course) to recipient, we find almost as many miracles occurring to women as to men.[30] Although several early collections of exempla addressed to men (for example, Conrad of Eberbach's, Peter the Venerable's, and Gerald of Wales's) contain stories only about males,[31] both James of Vitry and Thomas of Cantimpré, writing in the thirteenth century, give female as well as male examples of eucharistic miracles and devotion.[32] Tubach's index of exempla lists thirty-two miracles concerning the host that occurred to men, twenty to women. Of the male miracles, twelve occurred to priests.[33]

Exempla about fasting or abstinence show a similar pattern. About 10 percent of the stories in Tubach's index concern women.[34] (The stories were, of course, told by preachers—i.e., by men.) Women, however, figure in a significantly higher percentage of the stories concerning food practices. Exempla about abstinence are few—fourteen cases, eleven of which tell of a man or woman practicing abstinence. Nonetheless, of the eleven, four (36 percent) are about women and seven about men.[35] Moreover, the four stories about women seem to express anxiety about female practice, for two urge moderation and two (the only two with this motif) show individuals tricked by the devil into or out of abstinence.[36] The thirty-three stories of fasting (twenty-six of which are about the food practices of individuals) are predominantly about men, although cases of females are 19 percent of the total (five out of twenty-six)—still above the percentage of women's stories generally.[37] When we look more closely at the cases of fasting, however, several interesting facts emerge. The longest fasts are those of women. (One lasted thirty years, another three, whereas the longest male fast was seventy-eight weeks).[38] Women provide both of the cases of fasting until death.[39] Furthermore, of the twenty-six stories about individuals, only nineteen are actually about fasting. (The others are about *failure* to fast.) Since all the female cases are about fasting, women account for 26 percent (five out of nineteen) of the stories of people who fast.

Not only did preachers tell a disproportionate number of stories about women and food practices; they also tended to advise women about both fast and feast. Even in the patristic period, writers who addressed women tended to associate food and lust and to devote an inordinate amount of the relatively little writing they directed toward women to these topics. Two of Jerome's most extensive discussions of food as incentive to licentiousness were addressed to women,[40] and Fulgentius of Ruspe (d. 533), a disciple of Augustine, wrote several letters on fasting to women, urging a fine balance between abstinence and moderation:

> We must practice such moderation in fasting that our body is not excited by the full satisfaction of the appetite or enfeebled by too much privation. It is necessary then that the fast of virgins be followed by eating such that the body is not drawn by the pleasures of eating nor excited by its fulfillment.[41]

Medieval preachers such as Peter the Chanter repeated Jerome's advice to women and cited patristic examples of female ascetics and fasters.[42]

In monastic circles in the high and later Middle Ages, we find some evidence that moralists associated food with men more than with women. But the food behavior especially associated with men was gluttony, not abstinence or food providing or eucharistic fervor. For example, a short but popular antimonastic parody from the later Middle Ages, the *De monachis carnalibus* (*On Worldly Monks*), survives in three versions, one an adaptation for nuns. Although the monks' versions present a fairly unpleasant picture of the monk who "asks no more than that his guts be filled," the nuns' version eliminates most of the food references, suggesting that vanity about looks and clothes is a greater temptation to women than meals.[43] This concern with greed as a vice of monks, which becomes a theme in medieval satire,[44] probably reflects the fact that some

79

late medieval monastic houses set lavish tables.[45] In general, male houses were both wealthier and larger than female houses, and gluttony was, in fact, a greater possibility and, therefore, temptation.[46]

Throughout the Middle Ages, however, preachers associated religious food practices—especially charitable food distribution, fasting, and eucharistic fervor—with women. In the thirteenth and fourteenth centuries, theologians such as Albert the Great, David of Augsburg, and John Gerson tended to worry about women's eucharistic piety and their food asceticism, although writers such as James of Vitry, Thomas of Cantimpré, John Tauler, and Gerson himself also found these aspects of women's spirituality useful in polemic against heretics or against the apathetic orthodox.[47] Gerson, who perhaps more than any other male writer stressed the eucharist as experiential reception of God, felt that Mary received mystical eucharistic experiences beyond those of all other mortals. Moreover, he described the ecstasies of both male and female mystics in striking feminine metaphors:

> In him [Christ] is the true vine, whose wine generates virgins and not only generates them but impregnates them. Let him give that wine, let him give the sober inebriation of the spirit as drink. He introduces me into the cellar of the vineyard. What do you want, oh my soul? A little while ago you said (after asking for the kiss of his mouth): thy breasts are sweeter than wine. . . . Why do you now seek wine? But I shall answer for you that he is both wine and milk to you. . . . He calls: Eat, my friend, and drink and be intoxicated. . . . He will be sweet fruit to your throat.[48]

Male theologians wrote much on the eucharist, and certain formal theological considerations of the sacrament were (like all scholastic theology) exclusively male genres. But it is striking how many important treatises on the eucharist or on the closely connected theme of the humanity of Christ were addressed by men to women. One thinks, for example, of the works of Jan van Ruysbroeck (d. 1381), Richard Rolle (d. 1349), Henry Suso, and Dionysius the Carthusian (d. 1471).[49] It is also noteworthy that many of the preachers who were central in elaborating eucharistic piety preached most often to women (for example, Guiard of Laon [d. 1248] and John Tauler).[50] Moreover, many of the earliest texts recommending frequent communion were directed to women, although, in general, little theological injunction was written for them. In the eleventh century, John of Fécamp, Peter Damian, and Pope Gregory VII all recommended to women eucharistic devotion and frequent reception.[51]

Iconographic evidence also suggests that medieval people of both sexes associated food and fasting with women. In particular, the eucharist was associated with female saints. The communion of the Virgin, of Mary Magdalen, and of Mary the Egyptian was a fairly common theme in painting.[52] The saints most frequently depicted on eucharistic tabernacles were the Virgin, the Magdalen, Christopher, and little Saint Barbara, as she was known from the *Golden Legend*.[53] Dumoutet comments that Barbara was probably the saint most frequently associated with the eucharist in iconography. (See plate 7 for a retable with saints Barbara and Catherine.) Popular wisdom held that Barbara's devotees would not die without a chance to receive the sacrament at the end.[54] Mary Magdalen was the saint most closely linked with fasting, owing to the version of her legend that circulated in the Middle Ages and attributed to her a fast of many years in the desert near Marseilles.[55] As the cult of the host grew in the later Middle Ages, tabernacles came to associate the consecration with the Incarnation, and therefore with the Virgin Mary. The Cistercians generally stressed the association of Mary with the sacrament, and at Cîteaux the pyx was held by an image of the Virgin.[56] The angel's words of salutation to Mary were sometimes reproduced on tabernacles.[57] In his explanation of the mass (1285–1291), William Durandus said that the pyx or tabernacle or reliquary in which the host is kept signifies Mary's body.[58] There is even an extant tabernacle that explicitly identifies the container with Mary. (It is surmounted by Anne, Mary's mother, and thus suggests that it is Mary herself.)[59] As retables developed, they also tended to link the moment of consecration (sometimes depicted as the Mystical Mill or the baby Christ in the chalice) with the Annunciation or some other scene suggesting the Incarnation or the reception of Christ—for example, the Virgin capturing the unicorn, meeting with her cousin Elizabeth, or nursing the Christ child (see frontispiece and plates 1, 6, and 7).[60] Depictions of the iconographic motifs of the Eucharistic Man of Sorrows or Christ in the Winepress (see plates 1, 5, 25, 26, and 30) often include nuns or other female figures (Mary or Caritas), not only as recipients of food but also as providers or celebrants.[61]

Quantitative patterns, therefore, suggest that food practices were more central to female spirituality than to male in the later Middle Ages. Quantitative evidence is, however, the least reliable type of evidence on

81

this matter. This is so not only because the total number of recorded eucharistic miracles, exempla, saints' lives, causes for canonization, retables and pyxes, and treatises on asceticism is sometimes too small for percentages to be trustworthy indices. It is also because the stories themselves are misleading. To say this is not to raise the question of whether the miracles reported in these writings "really happened." My point here is merely that the numerous passing references to eucharistic devotion and food asceticism in saints' *vitae* and other sources must be viewed with skepticism, because, if they are only passing references, there is a distinct possibility that the authors themselves may not have meant them literally. There is reason to suspect that fasting and visions were sometimes described or attributed where neither was experienced and, conversely, that they were sometimes discouraged in individuals who were driven obsessively toward them. Both these points deserve elaboration.

Among early Christian writers, both Jerome and Cassian had taught that meat and wine excited sexual lust and that gluttony was the basic source from which flowed other sins.[62] A number of the Desert Fathers (for example, Anthony, Hilarion, Simeon Stylites, and Gerasimus) were said to have practiced extreme food asceticism, combined with intense eucharistic piety.[63] Many hagiographers and saints from the eleventh to the fifteenth century bore this model in mind. Peter Damian told of Italian hermits who mimicked Paul and Anthony.[64] In the *vita* of Mary of Oignies, James of Vitry underlined the ways in which Mary imitated the Desert Fathers, and Raymond of Capua made the same point about Catherine of Siena.[65] Peter of Vaux claimed that Colette of Corbie surpassed the Fathers in her food asceticism.[66] Henry Suso posted the sayings of the Fathers on the walls of his cell, and a number of the aphorisms he chose dealt with fasting.[67]

By the high Middle Ages, fasting and eucharistic devotion were expected of saints, especially hermit saints and women.[68] Those, such as Richard Rolle, who were not able to maintain fasts were criticized for their failure; and a writer like Tauler who did not have the gift of food asceticism felt it necessary to apologize for the lack.[69] Witnesses in canonization proceedings regularly testified to the fasting of candidates for sanctity, although additional evidence sometimes suggests that the testimony was not true. Vauchez cites, for example, witnesses who deposed that Philip of Bourges (d. 1261) and Thomas of Cantilupe (d. 1282) practiced abstinence, although a cleric of Philip's diocese refused to believe in his sanctity because he "drank and ate normally," and several other witnesses testified that Thomas did not try to be better than other men.[70] At various points in Raymond of Capua's account of Catherine of Siena he tells us that "after this" she "ate nothing"; but later in the narrative there is clear evidence of eating—perhaps even of binge eating. For example, two witnesses recount that she once broke a fast of fifty-nine days by eating large amounts of food on the feast of the Ascension.[71] Alpaïs of Cudot's hagiographer reports simultaneously that she lived without corporeal food and that she sucked morsels of food three times a week to quell gossip.[72] "Eating nothing" in hagiographical accounts often means "not eating normally."[73]

Hagiographers were thus expected to include at least passing references to food abstention and eucharistic piety in their accounts of pious people. There is, moreover, some reason to think that women's *vitae* in the later Middle Ages were even more stereotypical than male *vitae*. In part this may be because women's lives were in fact less diverse and because women often learned patterns of piety from one another.[74] Michael Goodich has suggested that religious women, more than their male counterparts, tended to be associated in groups and to come from socially and geographically homogeneous backgrounds. In the thirteenth century, for example, several convents in the Low Countries (Aywières, Ramey, and Salzinnes in Namur), the monastery of Helfta in Saxony, and Clare's convent at San Damiano each contained a group of learned and mystical women. Indeed, in the thirteenth and fourteenth centuries the isolated woman ecstatic was rare; usually the sources show us several women—in a beguinage, convent, or hospital, or in a group surrounding a particularly saintly tertiary or recluse—learning mystical practices together and (albeit very hesitantly) sharing their visions. Simone Roisin has pointed out that in this period, the reputations of female mystics had more influence outside their cloisters than did the reputations of male mystics; their *vitae* were frequently read in male as well as female houses. Thus women's *vitae* and their daily lives borrowed patterns from each other. By the late thirteenth and fourteenth centuries, a number of collective biographies written in the Rhineland—the so-called *Nonnenbücher*—give dozens of vignettes of ecstatic, visionary, or pious women who bear a remarkable resemblance to one another. So standardized had the expectations become that in the fourteenth century the author of one of these books, Christina Ebner, commented that she was puzzled by the presence at her house, Engelthal, of a nun who did not have visions and ecstasies.[75] By the late fourteenth and fifteenth centuries, when holy women had become more isolated from each other and were increasingly dominated by their confessors, who were more and more frequently their biographers, a prototypical female *vita* (for example, that of Catherine of Siena) was often the model according to which biographers wrote and women lived.[76]

To holy people themselves, fasting, meditation, and eucharistic devotion were often merely steps toward God, part of the preparation for contemplation. To their adherents, however, abstinence or trances were signs and sources of supernatural power. Thus we sometimes find that the further an account of a saint is from the saint herself, the more her food asceticism or paramystical phenomena are emphasized. For example, the biographer of the peasant saint Alpaïs, who supposedly lived for forty years on the eucharist alone, devotes much attention to the saint's visions and spiritual teaching, whereas the contemporary chroniclers and collectors of exempla who picked up her story focused almost exclusively on the miraculous non-eating, including clinical details about her failure to excrete and the emptiness of her intestines.[77] In the second book of the *Herald of Divine Love*, Gertrude the Great strained to express an ultimately inexpressible union, more or less ignoring the paramystical phenomena that dominate the other four books, which she did not write.[78] Simone Roisin has found that in general, thirteenth-century saints' *vitae* written for the laity contain more miraculous elements, whereas those composed for the cloistered stress inner spiritual development and mystical union.[79] Culling references to fasts and eucharist from biographies of holy people thus tells us more about the stereotypes of holiness held by different audiences than about the exact distribution of ascetic or pious practices.

If adherents encouraged feats and miracles of abstinence, church authorities on the other hand were often suspicious, especially of the abstinence and piety of women. As I explained in chapter 2, the twelfth and thirteenth centuries saw the curious conjunction of a new wave of extreme ascetic practices with repeated exhortations to moderation. Spiritual writers such as Bernard of Clairvaux stressed inner rather than outward response, while theologians such as Peter the Chanter and Aquinas urged common sense and "rationality." These calls for reasonableness and interiority were clearly in part a response to such alarming austerities as wearing iron plates, mutilating one's flesh and rubbing lice into the wounds, or even jumping into ovens or hanging oneself.[80] But the austerities were in part a response to the injunctions to moderation. In such an environment, women's asceticism often came in for particular criticism.

The suspicion of ascetic practices or of marvels that we find in medieval texts sometimes merely reflects what Richard Kieckhefer has called the "imitation-wonderment" topos in saints' *vitae*.[81] Authors were fond of exhorting readers to admire (wonder at) rather than to emulate (imitate) saintly asceticism, or to imitate the virtues revealed in the deeds of the saints because the deeds themselves were beyond the limited abilities of ordinary folk. Thus James of Vitry urged readers not to copy but, rather, to venerate the saintly women whose stories he told.[82] The nun who compiled Gertrude the Great's visions reported that Christ himself refused Gertrude's prayer that a sister be given wonder-working powers; it was preferable, he explained, that the pious learn from the spiritual teaching of those who had "tasted the kingdom" in mystical union rather than that they be enticed and overwhelmed by signs and miracles.[83]

But hostility toward women's ascetic practices often went beyond the advice of preachers or hagiographers that the faithful should admire rather than imitate. Abelard in the twelfth century and Henry Suso in the fourteenth warned their beloved spiritual daughters that severe asceticism was unwise for the "weaker sex."[84] Suso wrote to Elsbet Stagel:

> Dear daughter . . . discontinue these excessive austerities which are unsuitable to your sex and unnecessary for your disposition. . . . The good Jesus did not say, "Take up my cross," but "Let every man [*mensch*] take up his cross." Consequently you should aim, not at imitating the austerities of the ancient fathers or of your spiritual father, but at crucifying your bad habits without detriment to your health.[85]

And Francis of Assisi intervened to get Clare to modify her fasts.[86] Thirteenth- and fourteenth-century theologians sometimes scoffed at women's eucharistic visions and curtailed their access to the eucharist. Albert the Great, for example, opposed daily communion for women because of their "levity" and commented that nuns' visions of suckling Jesus were "silly," although he defended them against the dangerous charge of heresy.[87] David of Augsburg suggested that some female visions were

merely indulgence of erotic "ticklings."[88] It is true that by the early fourteenth century certain mystical responses were dangerous for men as well
as for women and that men frequently urged or forced men to modify
their practices.[89] But thirteenth- and fourteenth-century literature of
spiritual counsel contains a specific and growing suspicion of female
asceticism and female ecstasies that reflects a general suspicion of female
character. Indeed, Weinstein and Bell suggest, on the basis of their survey of late medieval *vitae*, that female saints were depicted as the morally weaker sex generally and that hagiographers tended to attribute the
sins or lapses of women to inner faults, whereas male lapses were apt to
be attributed to "pernicious outside influences" (including, of course,
women).[90]

Women sometimes internalized such suspicion of their piety or evi-
denced a deep ambivalence about their own yearnings toward supernatural power or extraordinary penitential practices. Clare of Assisi, herself
a practitioner of extreme food deprivation, encouraged Agnes of Prague
to mildness and prudence in fasting.[91] Angela of Foligno called the idea
that she give up eating a "temptation."[92] Beatrice of Nazareth and Columba of Rieti feared that their eucharistic devotion and asceticism were
inspired by the devil.[93] Lutgard of Aywières was required by her own
abbess to omit frequent communion, and Catherine of Siena's fellow
tertiaries at one point urged that she be deprived of reception and ejected
from the church because of her exuberant ecstasies.[94] Margaret of Cortona, though repeatedly urged by Christ himself to daily communion,
went through agonies of uncertainty that led her repeatedly to abstain.[95]
Gertrude the Great worried about the dangers of private revelation; if
she introduced new prayers on the authority of visions alone, she rea-
soned, then the community would have no protection against false sisters
who claimed similar inspiration.[96]

Medieval people were, moreover, acutely attuned to the dangers of
confusing despair, pride, exhibitionism, or illness with piety. The biographers and inquisitors who investigated sanctity and provided glosses
on it stressed, for example, that food abstinence must be voluntary, a
means to self-abnegation. Taken alone, it was not necessarily good. It
might be disease, depression, or delusion. Catherine of Siena insisted
that her inability to eat was an infirmity, not an ascetic practice at all; in
a vision she heard Christ command her to return to the table and eat
with her family. (The "infirmity" had progressed so far that she was

unable to do so.)[97] Even Catherine's biographer, Raymond—who emphasized her fasting partly because he felt guilty about his own failure to fast, partly as propaganda for the Observant reform to which he was deeply committed—exhorted his readers that true merit lies not in fasts but in charity.[98] A witness in the canonization proceedings of an extreme ascetic, John the Good (d. 1249), testified that John sometimes, in the presence of all, "ate more than any other brother and more quickly," in order to prove that his abstinence was under his control.[99] Columba of Rieti, who was criticized both for abstinence and for frequent communion, defended herself by eating a grape before witnesses to squelch rumors that she lived only on the eucharist.[100] Thus, just as popular enthusiasm for feats of ascetic prowess and traditional assumptions about the hermit role may have led to the widespread presupposition that fasting and visions went with holiness, so clerical suspicion of ecstasies and extreme asceticism, particularly in women, may have induced many pious people to hide or even to modify self-mortifications to which they were drawn.

Tabulating references to piety in hagiographical literature can, therefore, be misleading. Allusions to fasting or eucharistic devotion were often simply clichés, and clichés can obscure as well as reveal devotional practices. Furthermore, as is well known, miracles told of one saint were often borrowed and told of others: as Gregory of Tours had said centuries earlier, the saints share one life in God.[101] Yet it is difficult to avoid the conclusion that abstinence from food and devotion to the eucharist were more important to saintly women than to saintly men. Indeed, the discussion above suggests that men's reputations for abstinence were more likely to be exaggerated than women's, whereas women were more apt to doubt their ascetic practices as pride or delusion. Moreover, hagiographical materials and chronicles frequently give us glimpses of the more ordinary folk who surrounded, admired, and doubted the saints. These glimpses support the argument that food asceticism, like charitable food distribution and performance of food-related miracles, was particularly the role of women in the high Middle Ages.

There is no evidence that mothers were generally more supportive of future saints than were fathers, and it can be demonstrated that daughters' vocations met with more parental opposition than sons'.[102] Nonetheless, a number of saints' *vitae* suggest that mothers or surrogate mothers taught their children fasting and eucharistic devotion. Aelred of Rievaulx (d. 1167) reports that King David of Scotland (d. 1153) learned fasting and eucharistic devotion from his mother, herself a saint.[103] Peter of Luxembourg, one of the few males who broke his health with fasting, had models of asceticism in both mother and father. But Peter's biographer tells us that his mother was more active in charity, providing meals for the needy three times a week and sending delicacies from her own table to women in childbirth. Peter later followed the example of both parents, giving money and food to the poor.[104] The author of the *vita* of Colette of Corbie implies a similar contrast between male and female practice when he notes that Colette's father gave money to the poor, especially reformed prostitutes, whereas her mother lived parsimoniously, undertook many penances, meditated every day on the life of Christ, and went to weekly confession and communion.[105] It appears to have been a cliché of hagiography that pious fathers gave alms while pious mothers gave (and gave up) food. Moreover, in praising the patience displayed by saintly girls toward unsympathetic mothers, hagiographers often reveal that the girls were carrying to extremes devout practices learned from other women. When little Dorothy of Montau wished to practice the severe fasting she saw her mother perform, conflict flared between mother and daughter.[106] Juliana of Cornillon, taught fasting by the religious woman who was caring for her, was punished while a child for taking the teaching too much to heart.[107] Elizabeth of Hungary may have found a model for her extreme fasting and compulsive food distribution in the behavior of her future mother-in-law Sophia, who raised her (although subsequent commentators suggest only that there was tension between Elizabeth and her surrogate mother).[108]

Other vignettes from chronicles and saints' *vitae* suggest that food abstinence frequently characterized women who were not considered saints. Catherine of Siena's fasting developed in the course of conflict with her parents about her religious vocation, but her biographer tells of another girl in the family whose self-starvation began in response to the dissolute behavior of her young husband.[109] The early fifteenth-century English laywoman Margery Kempe, upon Christ's advice, manipulated her husband into accepting continence by offering to give up the public fasts with which she was embarrassing him before the neighbors.[110]

Because medieval people loved marvels, chroniclers often preserved stories of strange eating behavior. Most of the surviving tales are about women. Ninth-century chronicles report, without much detail, two cases of twelve-year-old girls who refused to eat for three years.[111] In one of these stories, told by Einhard and picked up by a number of other chroniclers, the girl began her fast "first from bread and then from all food and drink" after receiving Easter communion from the priest. Readers are then told simply that, after three years, she "began to eat again."[112]

Far more interesting are two healing miracles recounted in the earliest *vita* of Walburga (d. 779), written by Wolfhard, priest of Eichstätt, about a hundred years after her death.[113] Many food-related themes cluster about Walburga's life. That she herself fasted and sometimes remained in the church after Vespers while the other nuns took supper in the refectory is one of the relatively few details we know about her own piety.[114] She was also one of the most famous myroblytes, or oil-producing saints, curing the afflicted for more than a thousand years after her death with an aromatic fluid that flowed from the stone on which her relics rested—some said from her breastbone.[115] The symbol of ears of corn with which she is associated iconographically seems to have been borrowed, along with other details, from an earlier fertility cult, that of Walborg or Walpurg, the earth goddess.[116] Not surprisingly, then, two of Walburga's early posthumous miracles were cures of what can quite accurately be called "eating disorders." Wolfhard recounts that a man named Irchinbald was in danger of becoming a glutton until he was suddenly seized with loathing for food. He then went for twenty-seven weeks without bread or meat, taking only a few vegetables or a little egg yolk. When he had become emaciated and extremely ill, he heard a voice telling him to go to Monheim (to which some of Walburga's relics had been translated), to pray to Walburga and to drink from the consecrated chalice that would be offered to him by three nuns standing near the altar. As soon as he drank, he felt hungry for bread. A similar story is told of a servant girl named Friderade. But, in her case, the self-starvation was not cured. Rather, it was elaborated into a miracle.[117]

Friderade, so the story goes, suffered from a voracious appetite; she ate until she grew enormous with gout or dropsy. When she visited Walburga's shrine her swollen feet were cured, but not her appetite. She then confessed to a sister Deithilda and received consecrated bread from the priest. After this she felt a loathing for all food except the eucharist. Deithilda, who worried about her, persuaded her to drink a little beer, but it merely gushed out again from her mouth and nose. Friderade subsequently passed three years without eating. A priest who observed her for the local bishop testified that she indeed survived without food. Thus, in these two ninth-century miracles, a man's loathing for food was cured by a sacred drink administered by nuns, whereas a woman's greed was cured by sacred bread administered by a priest. As the hagiographer tells the story, Irchinbald's transition from gluttony to starvation is natural; it is his return to eating that is the miraculous cure. In contrast, Friderade's loss of appetite is the miracle. The implication is that her subsequent return to eating needs no explanation.

By the twelfth century such reports were more common. One of the most interesting is found, like Walburga's cures, in a saint's life that has overtones of fertility cult. In the *vita* of Bridget of Kildare (d. ca. 525), food is a central theme. Bridget supposedly turned a stone into bread in time of famine. (But when two of her nuns were discontent, wanting meat, the bread turned into serpents.) She gave away butter. The cows she milked produced enormous amounts. She is associated iconographically with a cow and a large bowl.[118] Lawrence of Durham, writing a version of her life six hundred years after her death, found in the chapter on her babyhood an opportunity for inserting a contemporary marvel. Bridget, he notes, was allergic to cow's milk. Once she was weaned she could not keep milk down. But she grew anyway, as if she were eating.

Although her stomach was indignant and rejected all food . . . , nonetheless her body grew and was beautiful, as if she had food. And let no one be surprised because I know of such a thing from our own time. There was a virgin from the south of England who lived in her father's house for twenty years without accepting any food, with this exception that every Sunday she fed her body on the communion of the Lord's body and because the morsel could hardly pass down her throat she was accustomed to accept a little holy water to make this easier. And on feast days she only tasted the water but did not swallow, and through the course of these years she neither took food or drink nor did she have any appetite for food and drink. And her body thus destitute of strength, she lost the ability to grow, but her mind remained firm and her members well co-ordinated and she did not lose the ability to speak. And since this thing, which is more remarkable, is proved by more witnesses to its truth than there were inhabitants in the place where the girl lived, we should believe such a thing all the more of St. Bridget, since it is a lesser marvel.[119]

Similar stories are found in other lives and chronicles. Roger of Wendover and Matthew Paris reported for the year 1225:

In that same year in the city of Leicester a certain recluse died who, for seven years before her death, had never tasted food except that she received the body and blood of the Lord in communion on Sundays. When the bishop of Lincoln, Hugh of Lincoln, heard of this miracle, he did not believe it. Completely incredulous, he therefore had her strictly guarded for fifteen days by priests and clerics until it was found that she really took no nutriment for her body in all that time. And she always had a face whiter than a lily but with a rosy tint, as a sign of her virginal purity and modesty.[120]

James of Vitry coupled with his account of Alpaïs a reference to a recluse from Normandy who "for many years" "ate and drank nothing, nor from her mouth nor from any of the other natural organs did anything go out."[121] Caesarius of Heisterbach also told the story of Alpaïs alongside another account, this one of a woman who lived on Sunday communion alone "without bodily hunger" and passed the test of identifying an unconsecrated host.[122] A little later, Roger Bacon described a woman of the diocese of Norwich who

did not eat for twenty years; and she was fat and of good stature, emitting no excretion from her body, as the bishop proved by careful examination. Nor was this miraculous but, rather, a work of nature, for some balance [constellatio] was at that time able to reduce to a state of almost complete equilibrium the elements that were before that in her body; and because their mixture was from their proper nature suitable to a balance not found in other makeups, their alteration happened in her body as it does not in others.[123]

By the fifteenth century such cases served theological purposes and were carefully tested by the authorities, who occasionally unmasked frauds. Thomas Netter (d. 1430), in a treatise against the Lollards, told the story of Joan the Meatless as proof of the doctrine of the real presence:

If Elias could live on a little bread and water brought by angels for forty days, how much more can people live on the flesh and blood of Christ? . . . But if anyone does not believe this, I will cite a case from our own time and experience. In the northern part of England, called Norfolk, which is very rich in both temporal and spiritual things, there recently lived a devout Christian girl called in the vulgar tongue Joan the Meatless (that is, "without food"), because it was proven that she had not tasted food or drink for fifteen years, but only fed with the greatest joy every Sunday on the sacrament of the Lord's body. And what is even more remarkable, she could distinguish a consecrated host from unconsecrated ones among a thousand breads all alike and could not be deceived about the truth of the sacrament. And what many thought was more wonderful still, she did this not so much by divine inspiration but by a certain skill of her senses, since she had such a horror of all bodily food that she could not tolerate its taste or smell and turned from it even at a distance.[124]

Canonization inquiries for Colette of Corbie (d. 1447) uncovered not only the saint's own "miraculous" fasts but also stories of Colette herself rejecting a fraudulent faster and curing, with water from her relics, a nun who had not been able to eat for thirteen years.[125] There are at least seven cases of "fasting girls" in the sixteenth century; their self-starvation is reported both as evidence for canonization and as a scientific curiosity.[126] Also from the sixteenth century comes the first case in which the claims of a faster are unmasked, not as fraud but as disease. John Weyer (d. 1588), well-known for his skepticism about witchcraft, discovered that a ten-year-old crippled girl, Barbara Kremers, whose mother claimed that she neither ate nor excreted and whose marvelous abstinence had been certified authentic by her local town council, was being secretly fed by her twelve-year-old sister. After persuading Barbara to eat normally and to give up her crutches, Weyer sent her home under ducal protection. The outraged duke insisted, however, that all certificates and testimonials about the marvelous fasting be burned in the marketplace, and he reprimanded the town council.[127]

Between the early Middle Ages and the fifteenth century, when the illiterate Swiss hermit Nicholas of Flüe (d. 1487) became famous for living twenty years on the eucharist alone, such stories are not told of men.[128] Peter of Luxembourg and James Oldo (d. 1404), who began extreme fasts, resumed eating at the command of their superiors.[129] The male examples closest to these female cases of extended starvation are the case of a young monk in twelfth-century England, who went for more than a year "eating very little,"[130] the rather similar account of Aelred of Rievaulx,[131] and a passing chronicle reference to Facio of Cremona (d. 1272), who supposedly neither ate nor drank for seventy-two days, during which time he twice received communion.[132] There is, at St. Mary's in Bury St. Edmonds, the effigy and tomb of one John Baret (d. 1463), about whom tradition holds that he died from imitating Jesus' fast of forty days; and similar traditions have been attached to effigies in other churches. But these stories may have arisen simply from the emaciated appearance of the carved corpse.[133]

An impressive array of examples can thus be collected to show that fasting and eucharistic miracles were more prominent in women's religiosity than in men's. But my purpose in this book is not simply to count cases of male and female behavior. It is, rather, to demonstrate that food was an obsessive and overpowering concern in the lives and writings of religious women between the twelfth and the fifteenth century. It was women, not men, who were reputed to live for years on the eucharist alone or whose abstinence went so far that normal bodily functions such as excretion ceased. It was women who in story after story drank pus or filth from the sick they cared for, while abstaining from ordinary food. Moreover, it was women who developed eucharistic piety, including the cult of the Sacred Heart and the feast of Corpus Christi; women who in vision after vision saw Christ in the host or chalice; women who gave the food from their tables to the sick or the poor, frequently in defiance of husband or family; women whose miracles in life multiplied food for others and whose bodies after death exuded healing liquid. Finally, it was women who in their writings repeatedly used bread, blood, hunger, and eating as their dominant images for union with God and neighbor— language which appears in male writers but is never central to their piety.

Quantitative patterns are thus no more than the beginning of my inquiry. Indeed, such patterns obscure even while they elucidate. For, in order to be counted, phenomena must be cut apart from each other and put into countable categories. What is really important to an understanding of women's piety, however, is not the number of food miracles or fasts or the frequency of eucharistic ecstasies, but the way in which food as a polysemous symbol of suffering and fertility lies at the center of how women thought and how they survived. In the rest of this book, therefore, I shall be concerned with particular lives and particular texts, in all their complexity of lived and literary metaphor. I shall try to demonstrate, by exploring women's stories, that food was an overwhelming concern, that denial and devotion—fast and feast—were connected in basic and complex ways, and that the causes of women's piety lie deep within the structures of medieval assumptions and medieval society.

In order to demonstrate this, I shall first briefly examine the male piety to which women's religiosity must be compared.

◆ Men's Lives and Writings: A Comparison

The claim that food and food imagery are not central to male spirituality may seem odd, for, as chapter 2 makes clear, theories of fast and feast in the early church were formulated by men, and medieval traditions of food asceticism went back to the Desert Fathers of antiquity. Although medieval women sometimes took Mary Magdalen as a model of fasting or penitence and Catherine of Alexandria as a model of wisdom or of ecstatic union, confessors and hagiographers usually claimed that both pious men and pious women imitated male models.[134] All stories from the early church of individuals who survived on the eucharist alone were told of men. It was Clement of Alexandria who in the second century elaborated the explicitly eucharistic image of Christ as a mother feeding the soul from his breasts,[135] and the direct source in the later Middle Ages for such imagery was the writings of Anselm (d. 1109) and of several twelfth-century Cistercian monks, among them Bernard, Guerric of Igny, and William of St. Thierry.[136] As John Tauler implies (in the passage quoted as the epigraph to the Introduction above), the *locus classicus* of metaphors of tasting and devouring was Bernard of Clairvaux's commentary on the Song of Songs, which describes formation in the image of Christ as "being swallowed and digested by him."[137] What can it mean, therefore, to claim that food symbolism was more important to women than to men?

Clearly such a claim does not mean that food metaphors and food practices were the exclusive preserve of pious women. As Vauchez and Kieckhefer amply demonstrate, male saints practiced both food asceticism and passionate eucharistic devotion. Dodo of Hascha (d. 1231), Lawrence of Subiaco (d. 1243), John the Good of Mantua (d. 1249), the pious hermit who became Pope Celestine V (d. 1296), Peter of Luxembourg, and James Oldo are examples of devout men known for their food austerities.[138] But, as Vauchez has pointed out, fasts and ecstasies are characteristic only of the minority of male saints who are lay. And even males who belonged to this current of lay, often eremitical, piety barely approached either the eucharistic frenzy or the self-starvation of their female contemporaries. Men who used elaborate food metaphors in their eucharistic treatises and sermons did not carry those images over into their other spiritual writing as central metaphors for encounter with

God. It is in women's *vitae*, not men's, that eating/not eating sometimes becomes both the leitmotiv tying the story together and the underlying psychological theme. In order to understand this, we must explore the *vitae* and writings of a few late medieval men who did fast, display unusual eucharistic fervor, or develop food metaphors in a context of affective spirituality. Such an exploration shows very precisely that food is, at best, *a* theme, not *the* theme, in male lives and sensibilities. For example, Francis of Assisi, the most influential male saint of the later Middle Ages, insisted on retaining lay status and displayed an intensely affective piety; but neither feast nor fast was a central concern in his devotion. Despite Francis's repeated descriptions of himself and of the "good friar" as woman and mother,[139] he did not in fact display the concern with food metaphors so marked in the piety of thirteenth-century women.

The extensive material that survives on Francis and his early followers has given rise to scholarly controversies about the basic characteristics of his religiosity. It is clear, however, that fasting and abstinence were not central aspects of Francis's concern for "purity of heart." He did, of course, practice harsh food asceticism himself, but neither his own writings, the stories of the three companions, the *vitae* and miracle collections by Thomas of Celano, nor Bonaventure's *vitae* discuss it in much detail.[140] All these accounts agree that Francis rarely ate cooked food and, when he did, he mixed it with water or ashes to spoil its flavor[141] (a practice later imitated by other Franciscans such as Francis of Fabriano [d. 1322]).[142] He drank wine only when he was ill and even took little water. Passing references in the *vitae* indicate that he sometimes fasted to the point of weakness and probably permanently damaged his health by so doing.[143] Thomas of Celano, in the First Life, describes Francis pretending to eat but dropping the food into his lap.[144] But neither Francis's own writings nor the early biographies, which present him as an example for teaching others, suggest that food denial was an important practice to him. His Rule of 1223 says merely that the brothers are to fast on Fridays and in Advent and Lent but "are not bound to fast at other times." They *may* fast after Epiphany if they wish. But "in case of manifest necessity [they] are not bound to corporal fast."[145] The only references to food practices in his earliest Rule (1221) are an admonition to the sick not to feel hesitant about seeking medicines, an injunction to the brothers who practice greater rigor not to despise those who practice less, and the reminder that "in case of necessity, the friars, no matter where they are, can eat ordinary food."[146]

The message in Francis's own writings is clear—and far closer to the tone of the New Testament than to that of the Desert Fathers of the third and fourth centuries. Francis's deepest concern is with detachment, which he calls purity of heart, and with teaching by the example of one's own life. The good friar must be truly poor, as the new urban poor are poor; he must have no security, no guarantee for the morrow. The pattern of his life must comfort rather than scandalize; it must display Christ's love in the midst of the needy. Thus Francis's two Rules quote Romans 14:3, "Let not him that eateth despise him that eateth not; and he that eateth not, let him not judge him that eateth," and Luke 10:8, "Eat what is set before you."[147] These fragmentary Rules argue against carrying asceticism to extremes, lest the body be harmed, lest hypocrisy be encouraged, lest those who cannot bear great asceticism be made to feel inferior by those who can. Like the twelfth-century preachers of moderation, Francis himself links actual and metaphorical fasting; in his letter to the faithful he merely enjoins that "we are also bound to fast and avoid vice and sin, taking care not to give way to excess in food and drink."[148] Indeed, since Francis's central concern is for a poverty that means complete vulnerability to circumstance, it is not surprising that corporate or even individualistic food asceticism should have little importance to him. Periodic renunciation of certain foods or meals depends, after all, upon the regularity of the sustenance and commensality being renounced. In a tone that echoes Paul and Jesus, Francis denigrates not eating as a mark of religious commitment, substituting instead a vulnerability to want and hunger that joins the one who begs to the lowliest of the world.

In Francis's own words, therefore, food is not the chief symbol for the world one renounces, nor is hunger an image of detachment. Rather, the irregularity with which food comes to a beggar is one of the marks of the "poverty" and "nakedness" that are Francis's major images. Thus it is not surprising that despite Francis's personal abstinence, most of the early stories about his food practices deal with his *eating*. The material that probably derives from Brother Leo and was reworked in Thomas of Celano's and Bonaventure's *vitae* of Francis not only states explicitly that Francis was "prudent" with his friars yet "austere" himself,[149] it also instructs by his example, first, that we must never use our asceticism to censor others and, second, that we must always have faith that God will feed us in our need.

In one story a brother wakes in the night very hungry and Francis eats with him in order to show that "we are bound to beware of superfluity of food . . . but we must shun too great abstinence even more."[150] In another story Francis eats grapes in order to induce a sick brother to follow his example.[151] In yet another story the friars lay a very poor table for a visiting doctor but in response to Francis's trust in God a wealthy lady arrives with a feast for the assembled company.[152] When Francis himself is sick, we are told, fish, parsley, wine, and even marzipan miraculously appear.[153] Stories of food sent for the hungry brothers record not exactly feeding miracles performed by Francis but, rather, occasions on which he both predicts the future and offers his confidence in God as a model for others.

Sometimes Francis's eating is presented primarily as a warning against hypocrisy—again with an almost New Testament condemnation of pride in religious observance. On two occasions when Francis was very ill, for example, he ate the meat or lard he needed to survive. Once recovered, he confessed the eating in extravagant self-denigration—including stripping himself naked and asking a brother to lead him by a rope before the people. Such displays were intended, apparently, to give an example both of humility and of taking food in necessity.[154] Thomas of Celano says that Francis characterized hypocrites as people who "sell the pallor of the face of fasting for ruinous praises, that they may appear to be spiritual men," and that he explicitly enjoined superiors to take extra food if they needed it *in public*, not in private, so that others would not be "ashamed" to provide for their bodies.[155] Thomas even tells the odd story of a friar who worried about eating meat when Christmas fell on a Friday. But Francis urged the brothers not only to eat but even to smear the walls with meat so that the very building would feast on the day of the Lord's birth.[156]

In Bonaventure's later *vitae*, which gloss the material so as to minimize many of Francis's austerities, we find similar stories of Francis eating in order to encourage others to do so. The most extreme asceticism in the *Legenda maior* is that of someone Francis cures, not of Francis himself.[157] Moreover, food is not, in Bonaventure's account, a frequent or a powerful symbol. When Francis has a vision of himself feeding his brothers with crumbs, for example, the food is an image of something unrelated to nurture or sustenance; it stands for the Rule. The point of the story, as Bonaventure glosses it, is the wickedness of those who refuse to accept the Rule with reverence. When Bonaventure recounts an occasion on which food came as miraculous alms, his point is not to commend or comment upon the friars' fasting but, rather, to emphasize poverty and mendicancy.[158]

It thus seems clear that despite Francis's own abstinence, poverty was a far more basic value to him than fasting, and nakedness/clothing a more important metaphor. M. D. Lambert, Michel Mollat, Lester Little, and others have elaborated the complex ways in which voluntary poverty—that is, renunciation of ownership and money, and of the power money brings—were central practices and images in the spirituality of Francis and his followers.[159] As Thomas of Celano and Bonaventure described him, Francis not only married Lady Poverty, he *was* Lady Poverty.[160] And for the denuding of poverty, nakedness was a key metaphor. At the crucial turning points in Francis's life, he cast off his garments as a literal sign of renunciation of the world. When he rejected his earthly father, for example, he took off his clothes and his shoes and threw away his money. When he prepared for death, he again removed his clothes in order to meet his heavenly father naked.[161] The Leo material includes at least two other stories of Francis stripping himself as a sign of humility or penitence.[162] Thomas of Celano in the Second Life reports that Francis met a brother who begged him for his tunic (presumably as a relic); Francis gave it away at once, leaving himself naked in the cold.[163] Thomas's First Life of Francis lists thirty-six healing miracles, only one of which is performed with food;[164] but the Second Life lists at least seven occasions on which Francis gave his clothes to the poor.[165] When Francis served and kissed lepers, his crucial act was giving them alms and clothing them with his own garments, not drinking the pus of their sores (a favorite asceticism of later female tertiaries).[166] In the *Legenda maior*, Bonaventure suggests the centrality of denuding as an image of detachment and generosity when he says:

> Francis now developed a spirit of poverty. . . . He had never been able to stand the sight of lepers . . . but now in order to arrive at perfect self-contempt he served them devotedly . . . because the prophet Isaias tells us that Christ crucified was regarded as a leper and despised. He visited

their houses frequently and distributed alms among them generously, kissing their hands and lips with deep compassion. When he was approached by beggars, he was not content merely to give what he had—he wanted to give his whole self to them. At times he took off his clothes and gave them away, or ripped and tore pieces from them, if he had nothing else at hand.[167]

Although it may be impossible, as many have argued, to separate Francis himself from the colorful stories that circulated so early about him, what matters for my purposes is that the early friars did not see the man who called himself "mother" as one who fed them with his life's blood or closed his body off miraculously to food. Rather, they saw him as an image of the poor and naked Christ—as someone ever ready to give his ragged tunic to another, begging from meal to meal, trusting in the providence of God.

Nor, for all his deep reverence for the sacrament, was holy feast central to Francis's spirituality. His hagiographers assure us that he revered the Body of the Lord, communicated "frequently," and wanted to hear mass once a day.[168] In his own words there echoes a deep awe both before the eucharist and before priests who can hold God in their hands. But the eucharist was, to Francis as to many around 1200, more a revelation than a meal. He spoke, with profound reverence, not of receiving but of "seeing" the host. He was awestruck before God "come down" into a Virgin, "hiding under the form of a little bread."[169] He sent his friars from church to church with pyxes to "house" Christ (i.e., the consecrated wafer) reverently, just as he sent them to pick up and care for all books in which the name of Jesus might be inscribed or to repair the crumbling stones of any chapels in which God was worshiped.[170] Although his eucharistic fervor (which he may in part have copied from the devotion of contemporary women in the Low Countries)[171] was sincere and influenced later Franciscans, he seems to have revered the host, rather as he revered Bibles, as a relic of Christ. His concern to see God at the moment of incarnation in the hands of priests did not emphasize the quality of the eucharist as food, link feast and fast as practices, or flower into metaphors of eating, drinking, intoxication, or assimilation as ways of speaking about the soul's union with God.

Food was, however, central to Clare of Assisi, the woman who chose to follow Francis in asceticism and who fought unsuccessfully most of her life for the right to imitate his poverty. We have, of course, far less material about Clare, and her range of activity was far more constrained than Francis's.[172] But, in contrast to the evidence concerning Francis, the early evidence about Clare—Thomas of Celano's *vita*, the process for canonization, the bull of canonization itself, and even Thomas's descriptions of her and her sisters in the *vitae* of Francis—does not treat her food asceticism merely in passing or as part of a catalogue of austerities. Rather, Clare's food practices are central to the argument made for her holiness. Both Thomas's *vita* and the bull of canonization underline her devotion to the eucharist and her food asceticism. Thomas wrote:

> During these Lents [i.e., the forty days prior to Easter and the period from November 11 to Christmas], she took no food whatever on three days of the week, Monday, Wednesday, and Friday. Thus the days of her meager fare and the days of her strict mortification followed one upon the other in such wise that a vigil of perfect fast was ended by a feast of bread and water! It is not remarkable that such a severity maintained over a long period made Clare subject to infirmities, consumed her strength, and undermined her bodily vigor.

Thomas says that Francis himself and the bishop of Assisi finally forbade her practice of keeping three days of total fast and forced her to take an ounce and a half of bread of day.[173] The account thus makes it clear that Clare—unlike Francis, who desired to be indifferent to food and never made a point of eating nothing—found it important to keep a "perfect fast," that is, to close her body entirely to food.

Clare's advice to her sisters was harsher than Francis's. Her Rule does repeat Francis's admonition to moderation ("in times of manifest necessity sisters shall not be bound to corporal fasting"),[174] and in a letter to Agnes of Prague she did recall that Francis urged his followers to celebrate feasts by a change in food and to be lenient in recommending food practices for the weak and infirm.[175] Nonetheless she also stated unequivocally: "At all times the sisters are to fast [i.e., to take only one meal a day]"[176] and "we who are well and able [should] always eat Lenten food."[177] When she heard that Agnes had undertaken food austerities similar to her own, she felt compelled to recommend some relaxation (as Francis had done with her). "I ask and beg you," she wrote, "to refrain wisely and discreetly from any indiscreet and impossible austerity in the abstinence which I know you to have adopted."[178] But taken together, Clare's and Agnes's practices and Clare's own Rule suggest that food austerities had greater prominence in the daily lives of early Franciscan nuns than in the lives of the friars.

Other food motifs are important in Clare's story as well. She shed tears before the holy food of the eucharist and approached it with awe.[179] She once put an enemy to flight with the host.[180] Her iconographic motif is the monstrance. She is thus associated visually as well as in written evidence with the emerging cult of the consecrated host.[181] Furthermore, serving—especially feeding—others is a major theme in Clare's *vita*. Aside from a few miraculous cures, her major miracles during her lifetime were the multiplication of bread on one occasion and of oil on another.[182] She served the sisters at table and cleaned up the filth of the sick without complaint.[183] Part of her enthusiasm for holy poverty seems to have stemmed from the fact that begging brothers brought back mere crumbs for the sisters' meals; Thomas tells us she was "almost sorry" when begging produced "whole loaves."[184] On one occasion, when Pope Gregory IX issued a bull whose result would have been to provide less preaching to her convent, Clare seems to have threatened a kind of hunger strike. In any event—or so Thomas tells us—she drew an analogy between "food for the soul" (i.e., preaching) and earthly bread: if the pope forbade preachers to come, she said, the sisters would refuse to accept the mundane bread provided by the begging brothers.[185]

A final food motif in the Clare material appears in the process for canonization, where two witnesses recount a lactation miracle.[186] According to the fullest of the reports, Clare once saw Francis in a vision and took him a jug of hot water and a towel. When she reached him, he bared his breast and gave her suck, and the substance was "sweet and delightful" and "such pure shining gold that she saw her reflection in it." It is reasonable to think that this vision was influenced not only by the extensive use of nursing as a metaphor for instructing and counseling in twelfth-century spiritual literature but especially by Francis's own notion of himself and any good friar as "mother"—a notion found repeatedly in the earliest Francis material.[187] Nonetheless, the appearance of such a vision to Clare rather than to Francis's male followers, together with other evidence of Clare's emphasis on serving and feeding others while herself not eating, suggests that food was to Clare what clothing and money were to Francis: a basic symbol of both sacrifice and service.

This brief comparison of Clare and Francis suggests, far more vividly than do any statistics, the distinctive emphases of male and female pie-ties. Raised in the same small Italian city, tributary to the same spiritual currents, influenced by each other, Clare and Francis expressed the same craving for self-abnegation and world denial. But they expressed it in different behaviors and metaphors. Only to Clare was food crucial. Francis renounced wealth; Clare renounced food. Francis repaired churches, clothed the poor, begged, and preached in the streets of the town; Clare, both miraculously and prosaically, served and fed her sisters in the cloister. To Francis, "nakedness" was the symbol of the poverty and humility of Christ. Clare's most fervent denuding of self was abstinence.

Another piece of thirteenth-century evidence suggests that contemporaries recognized this contrast between Francis and his female disciples. An anonymous French Franciscan who transcribed a collection of materials on Elizabeth of Hungary cast Francis and Elizabeth in distinctive roles associated both with gender and with food. He wrote: "[Francis] was the father of the friars minor and [Elizabeth] was their mother. And he guarded them [*custodiebat eos*] like a father, she fed them [*nutriebat eos*] like a mother."[188] If we turn to those fourteenth-century men whose piety is at first glance most nearly parallel to that of fourteenth-century women—Henry Suso, John Tauler, Richard Rolle, and Jan van Ruysbroeck—we find clear evidence of the difference between male and female piety suggested by the anonymous Franciscan's comparison of father Francis and mother Elizabeth.

Henry Suso was both the most extreme food ascetic among fourteenth-century men and one of the few male saints of the period gifted with eucharistic visions.[189] He was deeply influenced by women; both his practices and his writings were very close to the female spirituality of his day. Yet Suso's fasting never became a food fixation or a denial of ordinary hunger sensations; hunger, eating, and food were not basic metaphors in his writing. Insofar as nursing was, for him, a fundamental motif, it expressed the centrality not so much of food as of women and mothers in his emotional world. A passage chosen almost at random from Suso's *Little Book of Wisdom* finds him describing patience in suffering (a basic fourteenth-century motif) as a living sacrifice, a sweet odor, a valiant knight in tournament, a cup of wholesome drink, and a glittering ruby.[190] Such a range of images is typical of Suso; eating and drinking are no more or less important here than elsewhere in his spiritual writing.

Suso's orientation was almost entirely toward women. He explicitly identified with his mother's piety rather than his father's worldliness;[191] he served as adviser to several communities of nuns; his *vita* (which was drafted in part by Elsbet Stagel, in part by someone else, perhaps also a nun)[192] makes it clear that he sought female followers, that more women than men came to him for advice, and that this popularity led to unpleasant gossip.[193] Moreover, despite his liking for chivalric metaphors, Suso often saw himself in female images. Although the earliest extant account of his life was compiled by women and therefore, presumably, colored by their choice of language, it is hard to avoid the conclusion that the feminine metaphors employed to describe Suso reflect his self-perception, since both the reported visions and his own prose in other works repeatedly cast him in female roles. He supposedly once said to God: "People call me the father of the poor . . . ; it is my policy to weep with the tearful and mourn with the sorrow-laden as a mother smoothes the ruffled brow of a feverish child."[194] Such language, in which others call Suso "father" but he himself claims a maternal responsibility, is typical of his *vita*. When God offered him a vision of himself as a knight, he tried to reject it.[195] In another work he wrote: "Lord, your treatment of me is puzzling: I look everywhere for your divinity but you show me only your humanity; I desire your sweetness but you offer me your bitterness; I want to suckle but you teach me to fight."[196] But he welcomed Jesus' description of him in a vision as a maiden picking roses.[197] Speaking for all souls, he wailed: "The heavenly Father created me more lovely than all mere creatures and chose me for his tender loving bride, but I ran away from him"; "formerly I was called his dear bride, but now, sad to say, I do not deserve to be called his poor laundress."[198] Moreover, Suso repeatedly described himself as a nursing baby.[199] The following lines from his *vita* are typical, and the metaphor may be his own: "When he enjoyed the familiar presence of Eternal Wisdom he felt like a smiling babe held securely on its mother's lap, hungrily nuzzling its head against her breast."[200] Sometimes his desire to suckle was expressed in more than metaphor. One night, after he had stepped aside for a poor woman because he "revered Mary in her," Mary appeared to him in a vision and let him drink liquid "flowing from her heart."[201]

Suso thus clearly identified with women and children and with female piety. Nonetheless, he discouraged women from exactly those austerities in which he gloried. His words to Elsbet Stagel reflect a feeling of superiority to pious women and a somewhat defensive pride in his own ascetic attainments: "Discontinue these excessive austerities which are unsuitable to your sex. . . . [Do not] aim . . . at imitating the austerities of . . . your spiritual father."[202] Moreover, although he frequently likened his own soul to maiden or mother, he sometimes used "woman" as an image of moral weakness (rather than humility) when addressing actual women.[203] To a spiritual daughter he wrote: "Know that you cannot teach yourself; you are weaker than Eve in paradise, and yet you want to lead others to God!"[204] And he urged her to act "virilely," to be a "knight" for God, and even likened himself, in teaching her, to a knight training a new squire.[205]

From age eighteen to forty, Suso practiced extreme austerity in the use of food and drink as part of a general program of bodily mortification, which included frequent scourgings, wearing a hair shirt, and carving the name of Jesus into his bare chest with a stylus.[206] Yet throughout his intense fasts and thirsts, he never lost his taste for food and drink.[207] Once, after having abstained from meat for many years, he gave in to a craving for it; as a result, he was attacked by demons and suffered a kind of lockjaw for three days.[208]

A charming story from chapter seven of his *vita* makes it clear that his food asceticism was merely one aspect of a general training in self-denial rather than the keystone of his ascetic vocation. Suso, so the story goes, loved fruit. In order to cure him of this craving, God sent a vision of an apple that said: "Eat me!" Suso replied, "No." But then, remembering that he always took an extra portion when fruit was served, he vowed to eat no fruit for two years. Because there was for several years a poor harvest, fruit was in any case scarce; yet when it became available, Suso still craved a double portion. At the point where hunger had almost conquered his will, he "made a bargain with God." If God wanted him to satisfy his craving, God would send him much fruit, Suso said to himself. It seemed an unlikely possibility, in view of the shortage, but early the next morning a stranger brought a sum of money to the monastery with the stipulation that it be spent for apples. Suso was delighted.[209]

Thus, despite Suso's identification with female piety and his pride in his extreme austerities, he never lost the desire for food—as so many ascetic women did. Even in his youth, fasting was not at the core of his determination to imitate Christ and to suffer in patience, as his mother had done. Nor was food a powerful image to him.[210] The eucharistic vision he received "many times" is surprisingly lacking in vivid detail, let alone food imagery. He merely saw rays emanating from the host, and his soul melted away, pierced with sweetness.[211] The description of his table manners, which so amused and annoyed the great historian Huizinga, makes it clear that to Suso, food practices frequently evoked other religious concerns, whereas other practices or symbols seldom evoked food. When Suso drank, for example, he swallowed five times for the wounds of Jesus. He ate the first and last morsels of each meal in honor of the heart of Jesus. He cut any large fruit into four parts, three for the Trinity and the fourth part for Mary; he left the fourth part unpeeled for Mary's baby, because children do not peel fruit.[212] In such practices the emphasis is on the body or the babyhood of Christ and not on the fact that self-discipline is achieved through food. Suso's only persistent and elaborated feeding or food image is nursing—which seems to express not a fixation on food but a profound need to be cared for, as a child is cared for by its mother.

Francis of Assisi and Henry Suso are probably the thirteenth- and fourteenth-century men whose piety is most "feminine"—if we use the term *feminine*, as historians of spirituality have done, to mean affective, exuberant, lyrical, and filled with images. It is, therefore, deeply significant that despite the austere asceticism and eucharistic fervor of these two saints, metaphors other than food and practices other than fasting dominate their piety. The spirituality of three other male writers—the English hermit Richard Rolle, John Tauler of the Rhineland, and Jan van Ruysbroeck from the Low Countries—was also, in this sense, "feminine." All three elaborated the devotion to Christ's humanity so central in women's piety. All three—Rolle most of all—voiced the emotional identification with the events of Christ's earthly life that characterized ecstatic women such as Mary of Oignies, Hadewijch, Elsbet Stagel, and Margery Kempe.[213] Ruysbroeck and Tauler were crucial figures in the development of eucharistic devotion, and all three were closely associated with cloistered women. Yet for none of the three was food asceticism a major religious practice; for none of them was food a fundamental metaphor for encounter with God or service of neighbor. None chose *hunger* as his basic synonym for *desire*, and to none was eating a major metaphor for becoming one with Christ's sufferings (as it was for Hadwijch), for the delights of mystical union (as it was for Mechtild of Magdeburg), or for the saving of souls (as it was for Catherine of Siena).

All three of these writers advised women, wrote for them, and were influenced by them. Rolle's *Form of Living*, like his other two English epistles, was written for a woman. Ruysbroeck's *Mirror of Eternal Salvation*, which contains a treatise on the eucharist, was probably composed for Margaret of Meerbeke, to whom he addressed his *Book of the Seven Cloisters*. And Ruysbroeck, like Suso, was deeply influenced by his mother, who figured prominently in the visions he received before he resolved his vocational crisis and entered the hermitage at Groenendael.[214] Most of Tauler's sermons were preached in German to nuns.[215]

On some level, however, Tauler and Rolle disliked women. Rolle was closely associated with a nunnery during his life as a hermit, and he symbolized his conversion by putting on a habit made of his sister's dresses. His *vita* was prepared by nuns, and he performed the great majority of his miracles for women.[216] Yet Rolle, possibly because of a deep attachment he had developed toward a woman who was totally ignorant of his feelings, judged women harshly. He saw them, in Knowles's words, as "a great danger . . . , an occasion of sin, deceitful, foolish, and weak in reasoning."[217] Tauler too, like his fellow Dominican and contemporary Suso, viewed the nuns he advised with a certain ambivalence. He saw women as created in God's image[218] and described Mary as the means by which humankind retrieved the likeness to God lost in Eden.[219] He recognized that eucharistic piety was a particular characteristic of women.[220] Nevertheless, he repeated negative stereotypes of the female:

> We are all women in our frailty, a man like me, no less than you women; giddy we are, and unstable. But I have been in countries where they act like men, showing great strength in their conversions, and great steadfastness. The word of God produces greater and finer fruits there in a single year than in ten whole years with us. Miracles and great grace are to be seen there among such blessed people. In other countries they all behave like women. Whatever their opportunities they make nothing of them. I know that you will not like to hear me speak in this way about women, but, my dear children, we must all become men and use our strength to turn to God, if we are to be of any use.[221]

Unlike Suso, Tauler felt no great need to describe himself or God in female images although, like all spiritual writers, he calls the soul "a bride."[222] To Tauler, tenderness as well as harshness and rigor was incorporated into the notion of the Godhead through the male images of "loving father" and "good shepherd."[223] But when he needed not only to symbolize utter self-abasement but also to urge it as the only path to God, he chose the Canaanite woman from Matthew 15:21–28 and told of a contemporary woman who offered to go to hell in order to debase herself before the Creator.[224]

Tauler and Rolle rejected severe asceticism as inappropriate attention to "works" and were slightly defensive about being themselves unable to practice it. Rolle's *vita* includes a passing reference to fasting:

> He spurned the world too with its riches, being content with only the bare necessities of life. . . . He mortified his flesh with many fasts, with frequent vigils, and repeated sobs and sighings, quitting all soft bedding . . . fixing his mind always on heaven, and desiring to depart to be with Christ, his most sweet Beloved.[225]

But Rolle's own words clearly indicate that he did not practice extraordinary food asceticism and that he was criticized by contemporaries for failing to fit the recognized hermit pattern.

In the *Melody of Love* Rolle claims that he has been attacked unfairly by some who attribute the mystical favors he receives to drunkenness or a full stomach. Although he describes himself as practicing penance, avoiding women, and macerating his flesh, he admits that he has found it necessary to eat and that "although I am gratified with the heavenly melody, some hold me for a man of nothing. These evil tongues say that, like the rich, I live well. And they wish to convince everyone that I am unworthy of God."[226] In the *Fire of Love* he comments that it is better to eat a little too much by mistake if it is done "with good intent to sustain nature" than to fast until one becomes too feeble to sing with love of God.

> Eaten have I and drunken of this that seemed best, not because I loved pleasantness but because nature must be sustained in the service of God. . . . I dare say with blessed Job: "Fools have despised me . . . ," nevertheless they shall be ashamed when they see me that have said that I would not abide but where I might be delicately fed.[227]

Rolle criticizes those who put away not merely superfluities but also necessities or who desire to please God by "too much abstinence and nakedness":

> And though paleness of face be the beauty of solitary man, nevertheless their service is not rightly ordered; for if they be bidden to chastise their bodies and bring them into the service of the spirit, yet ought they not to slay their bodies, but keep them for the honour of God.[228]

Like Francis of Assisi, Rolle seems to have conceived of true asceticism as the state of being at the mercy of others rather than as rigorous control and denial of self. Thus he stressed the irregularity of sustenance more than its absence, writing: "I freely praise the giver of the law . . . because in this life I am without power nor do I have anything when I hunger except what others give to me and I eat not when I will it but at the will of other men."[229]

Tauler, like Rolle, was both unable to fast and unimpressed with the spiritual value of extreme food asceticism. He advised the faithful to accept the suffering God sends rather than seek out more bitterness through self-imposed austerities or the "busyness" of "works":

> Set your heart at rest. Whether you have deserved it or not, take your suffering as coming from God, thank him for it and be at peace and at rest. . . . [But some people] want to take still more [bitterness] upon themselves. They make themselves ill and queer in the head, and it is all of no avail. The reason why they derive no grace from their efforts and make no progress is that the whole performance is self-determined, whether they are doing penance, fasting, praying or meditating. They expect God to fall in with their ideas.[230]

Tauler argued that the value of suffering lies in self-abnegation; therefore silence is the best austerity, more useful than fasting or vigils or self-flagellation.[231] He called the tendency to judge (or even to pay attention to) the ascetic practices of others a "murderer" and "thief" that robs God of proper honor and devotion,[232] and he warned that asceticism can lead to pride:

> Dear children, what are these delights and satisfactions that we have to be detached from? They are things like fasting, keeping vigils, praying, observing the Rule of the Order; these are the delights which it has not been our Lord's will for me to find in our Order.[233]

Tauler even advised the faithful to rejoice in God's creation so long as its beauties do not distract them from the higher beauties of God himself:

> Nor do I mean [that we should despise] those things which serve the needs of our nature. When we are hungry or thirsty we will naturally enjoy eating and drinking, a tired man will naturally look forward to a good rest. . . . Even so, if we desire these things greedily as mere sources of pleasure, and not because we need them or find them useful, they can hinder the birth of God in our souls.[234]

Urging an inner poverty, a repose beyond works and busyness, Tauler justified his own inability to practice asceticism as itself a scourge sent by God and at the same time argued for a deeper and higher surrender that went beyond all practices—even beyond discursive meditation on Christ's Passion:[235]

> But God . . . often breaks down whatever rests on such a foundation as this [i.e., pious practices] by frequently arranging things which run contrary to men's desires. If they want to keep vigil, they are obliged to sleep, against their will; if they like to fast, they are made to eat. . . . For just as worldly and sinful persons are seduced by sensual pleasures, so these people are held back by complacency in what they do or what they feel, and are thus hindered from an absolute and simple surrender to God.[236]

The Flemish mystic Ruysbroeck, anxious (like Tauler) to counter any suggestion of quietism or antinomianism, also made room for meditation on the Passion, for fasting and abstinence, and even for physical manifestations of likeness to Christ such as stigmata. But he preferred a higher and deeper union with Christ's divinity, beyond works and busyness and concern for practice.[237] In his *Book of the Seven Cloisters*, written for a nun, he praised the "poor convent," warned against excess in food and drink as the "root of all sins," and pointed out that Adam fell through greed although he was not hungry, whereas Christ, hungry and tempted by the devil, resisted food, saying "Man does not live by bread alone" (Matt. 4:4). But he also warned against eating too little and damaging the body, which should be our servant, and pointed out that wise religious leaders such as Augustine and Francis, while strict for themselves, were lenient toward the human needs of their followers.[238] Moreover, Henry Pomer, in his life of the saint, lays no stress whatsoever on food asceticism.[239] He even suggests that what was remarkable about Ruysbroeck's devotion to the eucharist was the fact that he did not treat it like food. Unlike other celebrants, Ruysbroeck seemed to absorb the host without opening his lips or chewing or rolling it on the tongue; rather, he was transported to God from the moment he touched the elements.[240]

Despite their profound devotion to the eucharist, neither Tauler, Rolle, nor Ruysbroeck uses food as a basic image. Ruysbroeck, although influenced by Hadewijch, to whom food imagery and eucharistic devotion were crucial,[241] makes little use of any image from animate nature, although his work is filled with metaphors of light and water, sun and sea.[242] Even in the little eucharistic treatise found in chapters 4 to 17 of the *Mirror of Eternal Salvation*, hunger and thirst, although occasionally metaphors for desire for God, are not the most common images. Ruysbroeck ranks them fourth among the seven blessings of those who attain union with God.[243] The only passage in which hunger becomes an image of insatiable, consuming desire is a discussion of Christ's devouring of *our* sins.[244] Only in the *Book of the Twelve Beguines* do we find repeated passages in which desire for God is treated as insatiable hunger, as hell itself,[245] and an occasional earthy image (like those so common in Ruysbroeck's contemporary, Catherine of Siena) of Christ as roasted meat and warm drink.[246] And the *Book of the Twelve Beguines* not only puts such images into the mouths of women, it is also sometimes directly imitated or even borrowed from Hadewijch.[247]

To Rolle, heat and melody are the dominant images, as the very titles of his works indicate.[248] Even where he quotes biblical passages that suggest images of eating or drinking, Rolle avoids elaborating them. Commenting, for example, on Psalm 77:25 ("Man has eaten the bread of angels"), Rolle writes: "The sound of praise is angels' food."[249]

Tauler's basic themes, often adopted from Eckhart, are of the soul's freedom from "works" and worldly concerns, its true "patience" before God, its final "illumination" and "transformation" into God. He uses traditional Bernardian language of "eating" and "being eaten" to describe the sacrament, but such imagery expresses not so much yearning as repose. Neither Christ's body, his flesh, his humanity as "food" nor our desire as "hunger" is central in these passages, but, rather, an Eckhartian sense of our deification:[250]

We feed upon our God [*Wir essent unsern Got*]. How wonderful and inexpressible is this love of His that found this marvelous way for Him to come to us.[251]

It is God Himself, and no intermediary. There is no difference between it and God. In this gift He gives Himself to us directly and not in any figurative way; He is united, simply and purely, with us. This is a feast indeed.[252]

All the other food we eat is a base and lifeless thing, deriving its worth only from the dignity of human life which it supports. But this noble food is living itself, and is the life of men. All those who are refreshed and nourished by it live eternally.[253]

Tauler, like Rolle and Ruysbroeck, allows biblical passages to suggest food metaphors to him. For example, when he preaches on John 7:37 ("If any man thirst, let him come to me and drink"), he says that the Holy Spirit gives us thirst for God and that once we shake off earthly things, we are jubilant and inebriated with God. But even here he weaves thirsting in among other images (such as that of hounds pursuing the hart), and he shies away from the sort of hunger images that delighted fourteenth-century women—images in which hunger is insatiable longing.[254] Rather, he speaks of taking the rich and tasty dishes of God prepared in the kitchen or of a workman stopping to eat in order to go on working.[255] Food is refreshment or respite; it is not a central image either of our craving for mystical union or of suffering in imitation of Christ. Aware of the eucharistic piety of the women of his day, he holds back a little from advocating its enthusiasms. In a Corpus Christi sermon on John 6:5 ("He that eats my flesh and drinks my blood abides in me"), he warns:

He does this [gives himself as bread] so that he may come into us, sink into us, become a part of us, so closely and intimately that even the senses can grasp and understand it. Had he wished, he could have done this in a much grander and more splendid way, illumining and transfiguring us. Indeed St. Hildegard wrote that this does happen every day, though invisibly. A sister of our Order up in the mountains had a vision of this very thing; she saw an amazing light surrounding the priest and the altar, a great host of angels and many lovely things. She saw all this with her bodily eyes; but this is not the way in which our Lord gives Himself to you and me.[256]

Men such as Francis of Assisi, Richard Rolle, and Henry Suso are often seen as the most extreme examples of the affective spirituality that characterized many late medieval women. And it is certainly true that their emotional identification with scenes from Christ's life, especially his Nativity and Crucifixion, was both literal and extravagant—although some medieval women, such as Mary of Oignies and Dorothy of Montau, exceed it in exuberance. In any case, there was nothing exclusively "feminine" about tears or ecstasies, about visions or poetry, in the later Middle Ages. Yet the men who displayed such characteristics were frequently advisers of women and closely influenced by them, and the characteristics were more often found in women's religiosity.[257] In discussing Francis, Suso, Tauler, Rolle, and Ruysbroeck, I have looked briefly at those thirteenth- and fourteenth-century men who were most influenced by women and whose piety most resembled theirs. It is thus significant that their devotion showed no marked interest in food, either as ascetic renunciation or as metaphor for encounter with God. It is also significant that they explicitly associated eucharistic devotion and fasting with their female followers and both admired and castigated in women the extravagant visionary and ascetic experiences they themselves found it impossible to achieve.[258]

FOOD IN THE LIVES OF WOMEN SAINTS

[A voice said:] "Believe, daughter, and you shall eat. And let no one put away from you the consolation of suffering for me, because you will not lack me; indeed, you have me now; and because you love me, now you have what you love. . . . Trust therefore, daughter, and hasten to Lukardis, your sister, and join yourself thus to her so that your mouth can receive breath from hers. . . ." [Agnes obeyed, and Lukardis blew in her mouth.] . . . In that moment, [Agnes] felt in her mouth as if she had the sacrament of the host given to her by the hand of a priest. Through this, she afterwards asserted, a great savor of the sweetness of divine grace penetrated her at this very hour . . . so that, her inner eye being illumined. . . , she saw openly many miraculous things worked within the servant of God, her sister, by God. And among many other things she saw celebrated in the heart of the handmaiden of Christ the delicious banquet of God. . . . There, if it is permitted to say it, she knew the holy Trinity in unity of essence as if it celebrated mass. . . . And each [sister] saw herself in the other as if in a mirror and knew there marvelous things in the light of divine understanding. LIFE OF LUKARDIS OF OBERWEIMAR (EARLY FOURTEENTH CENTURY)[1]

IN THE HIGH Middle Ages devout Christians fasted before communion and received their God as food. Because, in this one ritual moment, food actually became God, food was a powerful symbol. Mystics and preachers from Augustine and John Chrysostom to Bernard, Tauler, and Gerson used food as a metaphor for grace and inspiration, fast as a symbol of penance and preparation. Some holy women carried the religious significance of food much further. Not only did abstinence and eucharist lie at the heart of their practice, each took a more radical form, fast sometimes lengthening into years without eating, communion soaring into days of frenzy or trance. Moreover, as the passage from the Life of Lukardis suggests, eating and not eating became more than metaphors for grace and desire. They became actual modes of experiencing. And such experiencing was not limited to the context of the mass. To both Lukardis and Agnes, revelation and healing were given from nun to nun as food. Any grace might taste like the sacrament; any communion or sharing might be a banquet; any gift might be given by or into the mouth.

It is only through close analysis of a number of medieval stories that we can see the way in which food themes interact and interweave in women's lives. Such analysis indicates that women's ways of serving their fellow Christians and of uniting with God were closely tied to food, both symbolically and in fact. Medieval women fed others. They abstained in order to feed others. They fed others with their own bodies, which, as milk or oil, became food. They ate or drank the suffering of their fellow creatures by putting their mouths to putrifying sores. Moreover, women achieved ecstatic union by fusing with a God who became food on the altar. In a fierce imitation of the cross that included self-flagellation, self-starvation, and acute illness, women became the macerated body of the Savior, the bleeding meat they often saw in eucharistic visions. In erotic union with the adorable body of Jesus, they felt grace within as inebriating drink or as a melting honeycomb.

This association of the contemplative, the ascetic, and the charitable activities of women with food—both actual food, eaten and distributed, and food as a symbol of gift or flesh—runs throughout the *vitae* of women saints. Some of these *vitae*, particularly the collective lives known as *Nonnenbücher*, were written by women, though the majority of extant descriptions of holy women were composed by men. Thus it would seem that both men and women contributed to the tendency to describe women's experiences and women's bodies in food imagery. The guidance of confessors and preachers as well as of abbesses and spiritual friends lay behind the striking pattern of feeding miracles, eucharistic visions, and extended fasts that characterized women's lives. The analysis that follows demonstrates how important food was to women, both as symbol and as fact. It also suggests that the association of woman with food, especially the notion that woman's body *is* food, was important to both men and women from the thirteenth to the sixteenth century, and perhaps beyond.

◆ The Low Countries

The centrality of food in female spirituality first emerged in a remarkable group of Low Country women in the late twelfth and thirteenth centuries. Mostly the daughters of wealthy urban families, frequently suffering intense adolescent conflict over their parents' desire for them to marry, often of quasi-religious status rather than affiliated with any established order, these women combined a contemplative orientation with intense spiritual friendships.[2] They displayed a quiet sense of serving others through prayer and sometimes through more active charities. The most famous is the beguine Mary of Oignies, precursor in many devotional practices of Francis of Assisi. Numerous others emerge from the sources with distinctive personalities: the learned and accomplished writers Beatrice of Nazareth (d. 1268) and Hadewijch; Margaret of Ypres (d. 1237), who died young and never really found the spiritual adviser she craved; Ida of Nivelles (d. 1231), Ida of Louvain, and Ida of Léau (d. late thirteenth century), with their eucharistic fervor; the suffering leper Alice of Schaerbeke (d. 1250); Juliana of Cornillon, who wandered in search of a religious house, never finding adequate support for her great vision of the feast of Corpus Christi; Lutgard of Aywières, quiet, reclusive, but sought out by others as a reader of hearts; and Christina the Astonishing, whose *vita* is filled with some of the most vivid and improbable miracles of the thirteenth century. In their *vitae*—written by two remarkable clerical biographers, James of Vitry and Thomas of Cantimpré, and several less well known, sometimes even anonymous, authors—food metaphors are prominent. The male authors found extravagant eating imagery useful in describing the ecstatic experiences of their subjects; the women themselves—when we hear their voices recounting visions or delivering pithy opinions—used eating imagery not merely for the eucharist but for other spiritual experiences as well.[3]

Mary of Oignies, who frequently experienced the taste of honey in her mouth at mass, also received sensations of being full or of tasting sweetness when she heard words of spiritual advice.[4] When her biographer, James of Vitry, wondered why her frequent vigils, fasts, and effusions of tears did not cause headaches, Mary replied: "These tears are my feast [*refectio*]; they are my bread day and night; they . . . feed my mind; rather than emptying and afflicting my head, they bring satiety to my soul."[5] Lutgard of Aywières, harassed by suitors in her youth (one even attempted to abduct and rape her),[6] spoke thus to a prospective husband: "Go away from me, food of death, nutriment of villainy, since I am held back by another love."[7] As marriage was the food of death, so death, to Lutgard, was the food of life. Five years to the day before her death, upon hearing the gospel parable of a man who prepared a great feast, she told Sybil of Gages that on that very day she "would go to the meal of the spouse of the lamb."[8] Ida of Louvain, like Mary of Oignies, experienced bizarre sensations of eating when no food was present. She received the "food of spiritual reading" into her stomach, felt the eucharist slip down her throat like a fish, said to the other nuns before communion, "Let us go devour God," and found her mouth filled with honeycomb whenever she recited John 1:14: "Verbum caro factum est."[9] When one of her blood sisters called her to come away from prayer and smell the sweet wine her father offered for sale, Ida said, "Wine will provoke me to tears," but, said her hagiographer, she "did not mean material wine."[10] Juliana of Cornillon, who practiced extreme fasts and felt passionate craving for the eucharist during adolescence, was teased and disciplined for her excesses. When her nurse and sisters tore her away from prayer, calling her to eat, she told them in a jolly way, "I want better and more beautiful food," but she hid her real meaning from them.[11]

Such passages suggest that these women quite unself-consciously thought of God as food. Moreover, the biographers who repeated their comments persistently used extended food metaphors to elaborate the significance of women's practices. James repeatedly described Mary's ecstasies as inebriation, as hunger and fullness, as receiving "milk and honey from the lips of the spouse."[12] Thomas of Cantimpré spoke of Margaret of Ypres as accepting, chewing, and savoring God.[13] The anonymous author of Alice of Schaerbeke's vita described her as restored by liquid from the breasts of Christ, as inebriated with his sweetness.[14] He wrote thus of Alice's seclusion because of disease:

The first day she went into the [little house built to isolate her from the other sisters], the Lord appeared to her and took her in his arms with an embrace and said: "Welcome, daughter! I have long desired this tabernacle. As long as you are in this body, I will remain with you. And I will be your cellarer [the monastic official in charge of food] to provide you with what you need."[15]

The author of the brief *vita* of the beguine Gertrude van Oosten echoed James of Vitry's *vita* of Mary of Oignies when he said: "And so day after day tears were her food day and night, and if she took any corporeal food it was only a little and never without weeping and wailing."[16]

Food was not, however, merely a metaphor for interaction with the divine. It was at the heart of religious practice. The primary devotional emphasis in these Low Country *vitae* is the substitution of holy food (eucharist) for ordinary eating. Whether or not penitential asceticism in general characterized their lives, the women all fasted in order to prepare themselves for Christ's body and blood. Several of them were incapable of eating ordinary food when they experienced the filling of Christ. Mary of Oignies vomited out an unconsecrated host and compulsively washed her mouth to rid herself of the taste.[17] Ida of Léau repeatedly experienced fits and trances which she fought to control, because new legislation had been passed denying the cup to anyone suffering from frenzy.[18] While out of her senses she could not swallow ordinary food even if it was placed on her tongue, and even while in her senses she felt no normal hunger on days when she had the eucharist.[19] Margaret of Ypres could taste nothing except the eucharist during the last year of her life.[20] Ida of Louvain and Christina the Astonishing were both considered insane and were chained up by their families because of their eucharistic cravings.[21]

The mass (and/or reception of the eucharist) was frequently the occasion on which these women received ecstatic union with Christ. And the sweetness of ecstasy was often experienced as palpable food. When Ida of Louvain, for example, began to feel stronger and stronger desire for frequent communion, she was too modest either to bring the matter up with her confessor or to receive the eucharist without his permission. Thus, wrote her hagiographer:

> It frequently happened at that time that, when the priest received the holy communion at the altar, as the custom was, she, in the intensity of her desire, received with her mouth at the selfsame moment the most sacred pledge of the host of the Savior (brought, we believe, by a ministering angel) and discerned it with the sense of taste and even chewed it with her teeth.[22]

Unlike Francis, Suso, and Ruysbroeck—whose most intense eucharistic experiences were weeping at the "sight" of the Lord or experiencing the eucharist as "light" or as a vague sweetness within—Ida received her Lord as food between her lips.[23]

When religious superiors denied the cup or the host to women, sometimes in direct response to their extravagant behavior, Christ often fed them directly in visions. For example, Ida of Léau was denied the chalice because of frenzy and Alice because of leprosy.[24] Ida of Louvain was denied the cup because of nosebleeds and, at another time, was denied reception because of her status as novice.[25] Lutgard's abbess forbade her weekly communion, probably because of the jealousy of the other nuns.[26] In consequence, all were comforted, fed, and vindicated by Christ. Ida of Louvain and Lutgard had vivid experiences of nursing from Christ's breast.[27] Thomas tells us that once, when Lutgard stood before the crucifix during one of her illnesses, she suddenly "saw Christ with his wound all bleeding. And she sucked such sweetness with her mouth at his breast that she could feel no tribulation." On another occasion the figure on the crucifix leaned down and picked her up, holding her to his side to nurse. Yet another time Christ came as a lamb to her and sucked from her mouth a marvelously sweet song.[28] Thomas also describes a fourth vision in which Lutgard encountered God (or God's representative) in a graphically mouth-to-mouth embrace that brought comfort in deprivation. She saw John the Evangelist as an eagle sucking from Christ's breast; the eagle then flew to her, inserted his beak between her lips, and filled her soul with splendors.[29] The author of the *vita* of Ida of Léau makes it quite clear that God substitutes heavenly feeding when women's passionate devotion is denied by earthly authorities.

> And many grieved [when the ablutions cup was prohibited to nuns], thirsting with unquenchable thirst, . . . and they observed the sentence given because of the good of obedience, although they burned against it. . . . [But] listen to what the philosopher says: Who gives a law to lovers? Love *is* their paramount law. Therefore blessed Ida . . . , afflicted by a rigid sentence which was the way of the order, prostrate as much in body as in spirit, . . . lifted up her voice to God saying: "You know, oh Lord, that I dare not come to you but you can still come to me." Which things being said, the father of mercies . . . filled her desires lovingly and quickly. And . . . he visited her through the whole year on Sunday, giving her sweetness and savor more fully than she had had before when she had received the body of the Lord.[30]

The heavenly food these women craved was not only sweetness, inebriation, joy; it was also identification with the suffering of the cross.

118

Filled with Christ, the recipient was simultaneously crucified with his agony. Intensely literal in their *imitatio Christi*, desiring to fuse with the physical body of Christ that they chewed and consumed, these women provide some of the earliest examples of the novel miracle of stigmata. Mary of Oignies responded to her eucharistic craving and to guilt about eating after an illness by mutilating herself in the form of Christ's wounds.[31] Ida of Louvain received stigmata at the moment in her life that was the high point both of eucharistic frenzy and of conflict with her family; although she asked to have the outer signs removed, the inner pain remained.[32] The recluse Elizabeth of Spalbeek (or Herkenrode) (d. after 1274), who imitated the Passion of Christ in elaborate pantomime and self-torture, supposedly received in her body "very clearly . . . without any simulation or fraud" the five stigmata of the Lord as recent wounds, "which frequently, and especially on Fridays, emitted a stream of blood."[33] Moreover, like Christ's death on the cross itself, such imitation had evangelical overtones. Lutgard, Alice and others offered their excruciating hunger for Christ's body and blood in exchange for the salvation of the souls of their fellow Christians.[34]

Extreme fasting is a theme in every female *vita* from the Low Countries. When the women lived into old age, fasting was usually most intense in adolescence. It was often combined with sleeplessness and hyperactivity. The *vitae* of Mary of Oignies, Juliana of Cornillon, Ida of Louvain, Ida of Léau, Elizabeth of Spalbeek, and Margaret of Ypres make it clear that the women reached a point where they were unable to eat normally, where the smell and sight of food caused nausea and pain. Mary of Oignies, who mutilated her flesh out of guilt over eating, then embarked on a program of extended fast. She ate only once a day (at Vespers or at night); she took no wine and no meat; often she ate only coarse black bread that tore her throat and made it bleed. Once, after thirty-five days of total abstinence and silence, she "came back to herself" and tried to consume earthly food. But she could not bear its odor and could sip only wine from the ablutions cup. Ida of Louvain, who refused to accept anything from her merchant father except the room she lived in, worked at night to provide food for herself and for the poor who came to her for aid. She ate only moldy bread and, if food was served to her, she mixed it together in order to destroy any pleasant taste it might have. Once she went for eleven days eating only the little flowers of the lime tree. Juliana of Cornillon, who was punished for excessive fasting as a child, tried to hide her refusal to eat during adolescence, but she consumed so little that her sisters wondered how she lived.[35] When Lutgard, during one of her seven-year fasts, was commanded to eat, the food refused to pass down her throat.[36] Philip of Clairvaux reports that Elizabeth of Spalbeek ate almost nothing. She condescended, with obvious reluctance, to lap up a little milk, but she abhorred food. When relatives or companions put fruit, meat, or fish to her lips, she sucked a little juice but took in nothing of "the grosser matter." A dove consumed more in a single swallow, says Philip, than Elizabeth was willing to drink of the wine she was offered, and he remarks: "She ate and drank more to satisfy the will of others than because of her own will or even because of necessity."[37]

Such fasting was interpreted by biographers as renunciation of the world. Thomas of Cantimpré comments that Christina the Astonishing came from a family so poor that she had nothing to give up except food and drink.[38] But fasting was often specifically a response to guilt over the wealth and conspicuous consumption practiced by merchant families. Mary of Oignies, Lutgard, and Ida of Louvain (whose father sold wine) struggled to avoid the prosperous marriages planned for them. Juliana of Cornillon fasted as part of a battle with the superiors of her little monastic dependency, who were too lenient for her severe adolescent taste.

Fasting was seldom explicitly labeled, either by women or by their hagiographers, as an attack on the body, an exertion of control over it, or an effort to destroy its sensations or responses. Hagiographers occasionally praised women's ascetic feats and compared their subjects favorably to the Desert Fathers of antiquity.[39] But they almost never drew a dichotomy between flesh and spirit, nor did they justify fasting by reference to a connection between food and lust. Rather, they spoke of abstinence as preparatory to and simultaneous with true feeding by Christ. It was identification with Christ's suffering; it was affective, even erotic, union with Christ's adorable self. It was also service of others.

The hagiographers and the women themselves saw self-starvation and illness as extensions both of Christ's suffering on the cross and of the pains of purgatory. Purgatory was not primarily, to these women, a physical place somewhere, a logical complement to heaven and hell; it simply *was* suffering—redemptive suffering—which was simultaneously Christ's and the sinner's. Thus suffering on earth could replace suffering later, and by suffering one could redeem others as well as oneself. Margaret of Ypres desired the torments of her death to last until they consumed her time in purgatory, and Christ in a vision guaranteed that this had already happened.[40] Lutgard told a friend that Christ had promised her that her blindness, patiently accepted, would replace the pangs of purgatory.[41]

Such suffering also served one's neighbors. Alice of Schaerbeke offered up for specific goals the loss of various parts of her body to leprosy.[42] Lutgard, at the Virgin Mary's command, undertook three fasts of seven years each (on bread and beer) in order to relieve souls in purgatory and to quiet Christ's anger over heresy.[43] On a less universal note, Mary of Oignies fasted forty days to drive a demon out of an afflicted nun.[44] Speaking to a beloved companion after losing her right eye to leprosy, Alice of Schaerbeke voiced the notion of suffering that sustained many religious women: "Dear sister, do not grieve [for me]; and do not think that I suffer for or expiate my own sins; I suffer rather for those who are already dead and in the place of penitence [i.e., purgatory] and for the sins of the world."[45]

Fasting was not the only form of service these women practiced. They also cared directly for the sick and the poor, often by providing food. Mary of Oignies, who never achieved the complete poverty she wanted, gave her own goods to the poor, begged in order to feed them, and worked for their food and clothing.[46] Christina begged in order to share her food.[47] Even little Juliana of Cornillon fed her sisters by requesting the job of cowherd and producing more in milking the cows than anyone else had been able to do.[48]

A charming story from the life of Ida of Louvain illustrates not only Ida's commitment to feeding the poor but also her strange eating habits, her ecstasies, and her conflict with her father. Moreover, it shows the way in which such motifs tend to be woven together in these *vitae*. One day, so the story goes, Ida was snatched into ecstasy while returning from Vespers and saw Mary carrying Jesus on her breast. She fell down in the street as if dead and "a great wave of corpulence" invaded her body. She began to shake, alarming her companion. At this very moment, however, a poor man was being denied hospitality by Ida's father. When the pauper, muttering to himself, made his way past Ida in the street, she came back to herself, went to her father, and obtained alms for the beggar. She then returned to her room and dallied in spiritual delights for thirteen days. During this time she took material food only once, when bread lying beside her bed began to smell unnaturally sweet. Then she snatched it up and ate it "by divine purpose, that her body, which was taking no material bread, might be strengthened during these thirteen days."[49]

The religious women of the Low Countries fed others through miracles as well as by the work of their hands. Ida of Louvain cured the religious doubts of a young girl by changing beer into wine. On one occasion the bread on Ida's table grew rather than diminished during the course of the meal, in order to help the poor and sick to whom it was to be distributed.[50] Lutgard twice cured girls who felt a craving for meat, which Thomas in one instance labeled an "infirmity."[51] The fruit Juliana of Cornillon gave to a friend was subsequently discovered to have supernatural sweetness.[52]

Most remarkable of all, the women's bodies themselves became a source of food. They exuded oil, milk, or sweet saliva that had the power to cure others. Such extraordinary exuding was clearly predicated on unusual closure. Hagiographers connected failure to eat ordinary food or excrete ordinary fluids with exuding extraordinary liquids. Thomas of Cantimpré mentioned, for example, the moment at which Lutgard ceased to menstruate.[53] He also reported that Christ once commanded her to get up from a feverish sweat in which she was languishing and go directly to church. "Why are you lying there?" he asked. "You must do penance . . . not indulge in sweat." When, after this reprimand, she ran to Matins she saw Christ in the doorway of the church, and she nursed from his side.[54] Philip of Clairvaux combines with his discussion of Elizabeth of Spalbeek's inedia the information that "neither saliva nor sputum emanated from her mouth nor any mucus or other fluid from her nostrils."[55] It is exactly in those *vitae* that stress both women's exudings and the lactating Christ that unusual closure also comes in for special attention.

Exuding curing fluid is particularly a theme in Thomas of Cantimpré's writings.[56] He tells us, for example, that Christina the Astonishing fled into the remote desert, where she became very hungry. So she prayed, and God made her virgin breasts swell with milk, from which she fed herself for nine weeks. Later, when she was persecuted by sisters and friends who thought her mad and chained her in the cellar, her breasts filled again and ran with oil. When the oil proved a curing salve that healed, among other ills, the sores of one of her sisters, her tormentors released her from the cellar.[57]

Another of Thomas's heroines, Lutgard, also exuded oil, although in her case it came from the fingertips. The incident is presented as her response to the vision (discussed above) in which John the Evangelist drank from Christ's breast and then breathed into her mouth. Lutgard repeatedly nursed from Christ and saw others do so. On one occasion, after Christ (in the form of a lamb) sucked from her lips, her voice became more solemn and wise; on another occasion, after she had nursed from Christ's breast, her own saliva became sweet to the taste.[58] Her characteristic cures were performed by touch or saliva. "Those who had illness in hand or foot or other members were cured at once by contact with her hand or her saliva," Thomas says. "But this drew many people to her, and she asked God to take [the gift] away."[59]

James of Vitry's biography of Mary of Oignies reflects a similar concern with miraculous fluids. James recounts that Mary thought she saw milk (not oil) flowing from relics on an altar dedicated to Nicholas of Myra, the most famous medieval myroblyte.[60] A later beguine and stigmatic, Gertrude van Oosten—who displayed so fervent a devotion to the infant Jesus that the devil sometimes appeared to her as a crying child—found that her breasts filled with milk when she meditated on the Nativity.[61] Moreover, unusual bleeding (in contrast with the ordinary bleeding of menstruation) was a sign of holiness in many of these Low Country *vitae*. Ida of Louvain, Ida of Léau, Mary of Oignies, Lutgard, and Beatrice of Nazareth all suffered violent nosebleeds during eucharistic ecstasies, and their hagiographers saw the bleeding as a sign of mystical favors. Lutgard's various biographers report that even her hair dripped with blood when cut.[62] Not only do the hagiographers attribute stigmata to several of these women; they also claim, in the cases of Elizabeth of Spalbeek and Gertrude van Oosten, that the wounds bled in a periodic pattern.

Holy women continued to feed others miraculously from beyond the grave. Indeed, in death they sometimes achieved a quasi-sacerdotal feeding role denied to them in life. By the late twelfth century, women were prohibited not only from ordination but even from contact with altar vessels; by the late thirteenth century, lay people were denied the chalice. Yet after death holy women occasionally reappeared in visions to offer communion—and they appeared to men as well as to women. After Mary of Oignies's death she came to a Cistercian monk, and, James tells us, a golden chalice that issued from her mouth gave drink to two of the monk's friends.[63] Juliana of Cornillon was seen after her death assisting Christ with the cup at the altar. The woman who received this vision was cured of a great desire for food and drink "which the weakness of the flesh had given her" and felt herself "inebriated" with "spiritual refreshment" so that she did not need to drink wine.[64] Although male biographers may have overemphasized the importance of women saints to male followers, while neglecting their impact on other women,[65] such visions make it clear that holy women served both males and females by their fasting and by their feeding. The visions also demonstrate the extent to which both men and women in the thirteenth century associated women with feeding and with food.

Two hundred years after Mary of Oignies and more than a hundred years after the Flemish holy women Ida of Léau and Ida of Louvain, a poor laywoman in what is now Holland gained both respect and notoriety for a very similar type of female spirituality. In the story of Lidwina of Schiedam, who died in 1433 at the age of fifty-three, such themes as charitable food distribution, feeding miracles and visions, fast and illness, miraculously sweet bodily effluvia, and eucharistic devotion are tightly interwoven.[66] As in the lives of Mary of Oignies, Lutgard of Aywières, and Ida of Louvain, food is clearly the dominant fact and the dominant symbol in Lidwina's life.

Several hagiographical accounts of Lidwina exist, incorporating information provided by her confessors;[67] moreover, the town officials of Schiedam, who had her watched for three months, promulgated a document that survives. Suggesting that Lidwina's miraculous abstinence was the aspect of her life that most captured public attention, the document solemnly attests to her complete lack of food and sleep and to the sweet odor given off by the bits of skin, bone, and entrails she supposedly shed.[68] Her biographers also report that Philip of Burgundy's soldiers, while occupying the city, set a guard around Lidwina to test her fasts, which they then authenticated.[69] On another occasion four soldiers of the same Philip broke into her house, seriously injured her niece, and ridiculed and abused Lidwina, claiming that her swollen body was pregnant by the local priest.[70] The incident corroborates the impression that her prolonged survival in extreme illness and without eating was what most attracted contemporary admiration, making enemies of her city fear the power of her prayers.

The accounts of Lidwina's life suggest that there may have been early conflict between mother and daughter. When her terrible illness put a burden on the family's resources and patience, it took a miracle to convince her mother of her sanctity.[71] One of the few stories that survive from her childhood shows her mother annoyed with her childish dawdling. Lidwina, who was required to carry food to her brothers at school, slipped into church on the way home to say a prayer to the Virgin. The incident shows how girlish piety could provide a respite from household tasks—in this case, as in so many cases, the task of feeding men.[72] We also learn that Lidwina was upset to discover that she was pretty, that she threatened to pray for a deformity when plans were broached for her marriage (here her mother defended her), and that, after an illness at age fifteen, she grew weak and did not want to get up from her sickbed. The account thus suggests that she may have been cultivating illness—perhaps even rejecting food—before the skating accident some weeks later that produced severe internal injuries. In any event, Lidwina never recovered from her fall on the ice. Her hagiographers report that she was paralyzed except for her left hand. She burned with fever and vomited convulsively. Her body putrefied so that great pieces fell off. From mouth, ears, and nose she poured blood. And she stopped eating.[73]

Lidwina's hagiographers go into considerable detail about her abstinence. At first she supposedly ate a little piece of apple each day, although swallowing bread dipped into liquid caused her much pain. Then she reduced her intake to a bit of date and watered wine flavored with spices; later she survived on watered wine alone—only half a pint a week—and she preferred river water contaminated with salt from the tides. When she stopped taking any solid food, she also stopped sleeping. Finally she ceased to swallow anything at all.[74] Although Lidwina's biographers present her abstinence as evidence of saintliness, she was suspected by some during her lifetime of being possessed by a devil instead; she herself seems to have claimed that her fasting was natural. When people accused her of hypocrisy because she found joy in her illness, she replied that it is no sin to eat and therefore no glory to be incapable of eating.[75]

Fasting and illness were thus a single phenomenon to Lidwina. And since she perceived them as redemptive suffering, she urged both on others. We are told that a certain Gerard from Cologne, at her urging, became a hermit and lived in a tree, fed only on manna sent from God.[76] We are also told that Lidwina prayed for her twelve-year-old nephew to be afflicted with an illness so that he would be reminded of God's mercy. Not surprisingly, the illness itself then came from miraculous feeding. The nephew became sick after drinking several drops from a pitcher of new beer on a table by Lidwina's bedside—beer that had overnight become marvelously aromatic and sweet.[77]

Like the bodies of many other women saints (such as Christina the Astonishing and Lutgard), Lidwina's body was closed to ordinary intake and excretion but produced extraordinary effluvia.[78] The authenticating document from the town officials of Schiedam testifies that she shed skin, bones, and even portions of intestines, which her parents kept in a vase; and these gave off a sweet odor until Lidwina, worried by the gossip they excited, insisted that her mother bury them. Thus Lidwina's body shed holy pieces exactly as did the body of Christ, which once left behind a miraculous host after appearing in a vision.[79] Moreover, Lidwina's effluvia cured others. A man in England supposedly sent for the water she washed her hands in to cure his diseased leg.[80] The sweet smell from her left hand led one of her confessors to confess his own sins.[81]

Lidwina even nursed others, in an act that she herself explicitly saw as analogous to the Virgin's nursing of Christ.[82] One Christmas season, all her hagiographers tell us, a certain widow Catherine, who took care of her, had a vision that Lidwina's breasts would fill with milk, like Mary's, on the night of the Nativity. When she told Lidwina, Lidwina warned her to prepare herself. Then Lidwina saw a vision of Mary surrounded by a host of female virgins; and the breasts of Mary and of all the company filled with milk that poured out from their open tunics, filling the sky. When Catherine entered Lidwina's room, Lidwina rubbed her own breast and the milk came out; and Catherine drank three times and was satisfied (nor did she want any corporeal food for many days thereafter).[83] One of Lidwina's biographers adds that when the same grace was given to her again, she fed her confessor, John Walter;[84] but the other two hagiographical accounts say that the confessor was not there at the appointed hour and did not receive the gift.

Lidwina also fed others by charity and by food multiplication miracles. Although she did not herself eat, she charged the widow Catherine to buy fine fish and make fragrant sauces and to give these to the poor.

The meat and fish she gave as alms sometimes went much further than anyone had expected.[85] She gave water, wine, and money for beer to an epileptic burning with thirst; she sent a whole pork shoulder to a poor man's family; she regularly sent food to poor or sick children, forcing her servants to use for others money or food she would not herself consume.[86] When she shared the wine in her bedside jug, it seemed inexhaustible. So pleased was God with her charity that he sent her a vision of a heavenly banquet table laden with the food she had given away.[87]

Lidwina clearly felt that her suffering was service—that it was one with Christ's suffering and that it therefore substituted for the suffering of others, both their bodily ills and their time in purgatory. Indeed, according to at least one of her hagiographers, her body quite literally became Christ's macerated and saving flesh, for, like Ida of Louvain, she received stigmata.[88] John Brugman, in the *Vita posterior*, not only underlines the parallel between Lidwina's wounds and those on the miraculous bleeding host she received; he also states explicitly that in her stigmata, Christ "transformed his lover into his likeness."[89] Her hagiographers tell us that the fevers she suffered almost daily for many years before her death released souls from purgatory.[90] This notion of substitution is reflected quite clearly in the story of an evil man in whose stead Lidwina made confession; she then took upon herself his punishment to the increment of her own bodily anguish.[91] We see substitution of another kind in the story of Lidwina taking over the toothache of a woman who wailed outside her door.[92]

Thus, in Lidwina's story, fasting, illness, feeding, and suffering fuse. Lidwina becomes the food she rejects. Her body, closed to ordinary intake and excretion but spilling over in milk and sweet putrefaction, becomes the sustenance and the cure—both heavenly and earthly—of her followers.

But holy eating is a theme in Lidwina's life as well. The eucharist was at the core of her devotion. During her pathetic final years, when she was almost unable to swallow, she received frequent communion (as often as every two days). Her biographers emphasize that during this period, only the holy food kept her alive.[93] But for much of her life she was embroiled in conflict with the local clergy over her eucharistic visions and hunger. One incident in particular shows not only the importance of Christ's body as food in Lidwina's spirituality but also the way in which a woman's craving for the host, although it kept her under the control of the clergy, could seem to that same clergy a threat—both because it criticized their behavior and because if thwarted, it could bypass their power.[94]

Once an angel came to Lidwina and warned her that the next day the priest would bring her an unconsecrated host to test her. Then the priest came and pretended to adore the host, but Lidwina, when she received it, vomited it out, declaring that she could easily tell the Lord's body from unconsecrated bread. The priest swore that the host was consecrated, however, and returned angrily to the church. Lidwina then languished for a long time, craving communion but unable to receive it. About three and a half months later, Christ appeared to her, first as a baby, then as a bleeding and suffering youth. Angels appeared, bearing the instruments of the Passion, and then (according to one hagiographer) rays from Christ's wounded body pierced Lidwina with stigmata. When she subsequently asked for a sign, a host hovered over Christ's head and a napkin descended onto her bed, containing a miraculous host marked with drops of blood, which remained and was seen by many people for days thereafter.[95] The priest returned and ordered Lidwina to keep quiet about the miracle but finally agreed, at her insistence, to feed her the miraculous host as communion. Lidwina was convinced that it was truly Christ because she, who was usually stifled by food, ate this bread without pain. The next day the priest preached in church that Lidwina was deluded and that her host was a fraud of the devil. But, he claimed, Christ was present in the bread he offered because it was consecrated with all the majesty of the priesthood. Lidwina protested his interpretation of her host, but she agreed to accept a consecrated wafer from him and to pray for his sins. Subsequently the priest claimed that he had cured Lidwina from possession by the devil, while Lidwina's supporters called her host a miracle. Although Lidwina's hagiographers do not give the full details, they claim that the bishop came to investigate the matter, that he blessed the napkin for the service of the altar, and that the priest henceforth gave Lidwina the sacrament without tests or resistance.

As the story works its way out, its theme is not subversive of clerical authority. The conflict begins, after all, because Lidwina wants a consecrated host, and it results in her receiving frequent communion, humbly and piously. According to one of her hagiographers, the moral of the story is that the faithful can always substitute "spiritual communion" (i.e., meditation) if the actual host is not given.[96] But the story has radical implications as well. It suggests that Jesus can come directly to the faithful if priests are negligent or skeptical, that a priest's word may not be authoritative on the difference between demonic possession and sanctity, that visionary women might test priests. Other stories in Lidwina's life have similar implications. She forbade a sinning priest to celebrate mass; she read the heart of another priest and learned of his adultery.[97] Her visions of souls in purgatory especially concerned priests, and she substituted her sufferings for theirs.[98] One Ash Wednesday an angel brought ashes for her forehead before the priest arrived.[99] Even if Lidwina did not reject the clergy, she sometimes quietly bypassed or judged them.

Lidwina focused her love of God on the eucharist. In receiving it, in vision and communion, she became one with the body on the cross. Eating her God, she received his wounds and offered her suffering for the salvation of the world. Denying herself ordinary food, she sent that food to others; and her body gave milk to nurse her friends. Food is the basic theme in Lidwina's story—self as food and God as food. For Lidwina, as for the many Flemish holy women before her, eating and not eating were thus, finally, one theme. Both fasting and eating the broken body of Christ were acts of suffering. And to suffer was to save and be saved.

◆ France and Germany

The various *vitae* of Lidwina of Schiedam do not show the pious woman collecting a large number of disciples, male or female.[100] Indeed, Lidwina had few parallels or imitators in her own region, either in her day or over the next hundred years. But if we turn from the Low Countries to the rest of Europe, we find that food metaphors, food miracles, and food practices characterized the lives of women saints well into the sixteenth century. Despite the suggestion of recent scholars that the nature of female sanctity changed between 1200 and 1500 and displayed different patterns in north and south, the themes found in Low Country spirituality, from Mary of Oignies to Lidwina of Schiedam, echo throughout fourteenth- and fifteenth-century Europe.

Female roles differed, to be sure, according to region and period. Some women, especially Italian laywomen and tertiaries, centered their lives on active charity, whereas others, usually northern nuns or recluses, centered theirs on ecstasy and prayer. But food—as symbol and as fact—remained crucial in both these roles, in all regions and in all periods. To the more contemplative nun, fasting and illness (the two were frequently indistinguishable) were preparation and occasion for mystical union, for being fed by Christ. For those in whose lives serving was more important, fasting and eucharist were the self-denial and self-replenishment that made the feeding of others possible. Moreover, as the life of Lidwina of Schiedam suggests, the two roles were sometimes not so different after all. Alice of Schaerbeke, languishing in her cell with leprosy, and Lutgard of Aywières, fleeing from crowds, were clearly contemplatives, while Mary of Oignies led a more active life, nursing the sick and begging. But Lidwina, lying paralyzed on her bed and often in ecstasy, ordered much food sent to the poor and saw her suffering as service. Even Mary of Oignies and Lutgard combined ecstasy and curing.

Withdrawal and action, prayer and service, thus tended to fuse as values in women's lives, despite their varying institutional frameworks and emphases. And food was a central metaphor for this fusion. To medieval women, "feeding" was a basic religious commitment, a transitive and an intransitive verb. Medieval women fed others (*pascere*); they also fed on God (*pasci*). If we survey some of the many stories of French and German holy women from the thirteenth to the fifteenth century, it is easy to see that food themes are as prominent there as they are in the lives of Mary of Oignies, Lutgard of Aywières, Ida of Louvain, and Lidwina of Schiedam. As prominent, and as complicated. Here, too, eating, feeding, fasting, hungering, and being food fuse into a single theme—a theme that expresses the woman's love of neighbor and love of God.

Eucharistic devotion figures centrally in a wide variety of *vitae* from German- and French-speaking areas, and the ecstasies that either accompanied reception of the host or substituted for it underline its quality as food. For example, Beatrice of Ornacieux, whose Life was probably written by Margaret of Oingt (d. 1310), received many visions of Christ in the host at the elevation.[101] One Christmas, when she had worked herself into an agonized feeling of unworthiness before receiving, a crumb of the bread remained in her mouth and swelled, almost choking her. She was unable to eat for a long time after.[102] The nuns of Töss, Unterlinden, and Engelthal, whose collective biographies or *Nonnenbücher* were composed in the early fourteenth century, repeatedly received eucharistic visions. Christ appeared to a sick nun at Töss on a platter as food, and another sick sister nursed at the breast of the Virgin Mary.[103] A nun at Unterlinden saw Christ in a vision celebrating mass; after the celebration, she and all the sisters of the convent went forward and received the sacrament from the Lord's own hand.[104] A nun at Engelthal addressed the baby Jesus, who appeared in a vision: "If I had you, I'd eat you up, I love you so much."[105] Adelheid Langmann, also of Engelthal, thought she married Jesus with the host rather than with a wedding ring.[106] In an even more startling use of food images, Adelheid also claimed that Jesus said to her in several visions: "Your mouth tastes like roses and your body like violets"; "My sugar sweet and honey sweet love, my tender one, my pure one, you are mine and I am yours."[107]

In many other *vitae* of French and German women from the same period, the eucharist serves as marvelously sustaining food, replacing all other nurture. Jane Mary of Maillé (d. 1414), who fasted and punished her body, is said to have looked rosy, well fed, and happy after communion,[108] while Flora of Beaulieu (d. 1347), after being splashed in a vision with the liquid from a golden chalice, went for days without eating.[109] Flora frequently experienced eucharistic ecstasies that left her unable to walk or to swallow; since she assumed that others were similarly affected by receiving or handling the host, she marveled that any priest could fail to achieve mystical delights when celebrating mass.[110] The mouths of both Flora and Jane Mary of Maillé filled miraculously with Christ. Jane Mary found blood in her mouth when she prayed for a drink from the chalice; Flora received a portion of the host when the priest who was celebrating discovered that it had disappeared from the paten.[111]

The pattern of eucharistic food arriving miraculously and replacing ordinary nurture is found throughout the remarkable *vita* of Lukardis of Oberweimar (d. 1309), whose story, like that of her contemporary, Ida of Louvain, is dominated by motifs of offering and receiving food. In a series of vivid visions, Lukardis was miraculously fed by Christ and Mary. Christ often, we are told, brought her delicious drink when she was thirsty.[112] Once when she was too weak to go to the chapel to meditate, she had herself carried there by two sisters; when the door was closed Mary appeared, nursing Jesus, and said, "Ask for what you desire." "Seeing you is enough," replied Lukardis. But Mary insisted. So Lukardis answered that she wished to be fed from Mary's breast. After she was thus fed, "Lukardis lay in her bed for three days and nights without taking food or drink or seeing the light of the sky. For she lay as if dead, but her face was ruddy."[113]

On another occasion, after Lukardis had fasted severely, Christ appeared as a beautiful youth and blew into her mouth. "She was infused with such sweetness and such inner fruition that she felt as if drunk" and once again could not eat for three days.[114] On yet another occasion, when Lukardis was in the infirmary at Easter, her desire for the eucharist grew and grew. A sister saw her struggle into the choir and stand there, moving her mouth as if chewing. After the mass, when the prior asked her if she wished to communicate, she signed that she had already done so; and she continued to chew all day.[115] From communicating every Sunday and feast day, she progressed, at divine command, to communicating every Friday and every day in Lent as well. When several of her sisters murmured that this was an unheard-of innovation, word came that a nun in another monastery had received a vision vindicating Lukardis's practice.[116]

Not only did Lukardis prepare for God by fasting and suffering, receive him palpably as food, and find ordinary nourishment unnecessary after she was miraculously filled, she also fused with Christ in a frenzy of penitential suffering, and the identification spilled over into both stigmata and feeding miracles. As Christ had fed her with his breath, so Lukardis fed a fellow nun by breathing the eucharist into her mouth.[117] Lukardis also functioned as spiritual adviser to a nun who suffered agonies of indecision about whether she might receive communion.[118] Moreover, Lukardis received Christ's wounds inwardly in a vision, and afterwards she induced visible stigmata by compulsively digging her fingers into her own flesh.[119] When a local Dominican had a vision of Lukardis and two others nailed to crosses, God told him that Lukardis was the one to be identified with Christ. "The one who suffers most [is greatest]," God said, "for my Passion brings redemption to the whole world."[120]

To the nuns of Lukardis's convent, food was so natural a metaphor and means of grace that healing and revelation could be experienced as a host blown from mouth to mouth. Other thirteenth- and fourteenth-century women also considered food and eating basic metaphors—and even more than metaphors—for union with God and service of neighbor. The nuns of the Saxon monastery of Helfta, for example, thought

that many of their sisters drank from Jesus' side or heart in ecstasy; and
Gertrude the Great supposedly took the infant Christ to her own breast
in several visions.[121] The beguine Mechtild of Magdeburg, who took
refuge at Helfta in old age, reflects not only the tendency to describe
union in eating imagery but also the confidence, found in Lukardis and
Lidwina as well, that God will feed his followers directly if humans fail
to do so. When, on one occasion, Mechtild lamented, "Must I be without
mass this day?" she received a vision in which John the Baptist celebrated
mass for her:

> Then the maid [Mechtild] went up to the altar with great love and widely
> opened soul. John the Baptist took the white lamb with the red wounds
> and laid it on the mouth of the maid. Thus the pure Lamb laid itself on
> its own image in the stall of her body and sucked her heart with its tender
> lips.[122]

Mechtild, whose own words survive, although rearranged by trans-
lators, saw herself tasting God in mystical union and feeding others by
her suffering. She wrote of both eucharist and ecstasy as "eating God."[123]
She composed a lovely dialogue between the soul and the senses in which
the senses urged her to rest at Mary's knee, watching the angels drink
Mary's milk; but she refused, turning to Jesus' blood as the higher food.[124]
She spoke of her love and her suffering for souls in purgatory not just
as feeding but as nursing—feeding with her blood: "I must give them
my heart's blood to drink. If I pray for them, because of their great need
and see the bitter fate they must suffer for every sin, then I suffer as a
mother."[125] Over and over again, in such visions, Christ is food, desire is
insatiable hunger or thirst, serving is feeding or nursing, and (however
odd this may seem to modern sensibilities) the mouth is a fundamental
way of meeting God.

In the *Nonnenbücher* and women's *vitae* of the thirteenth to the fifteenth century, fasting (sometimes induced by illness, sometimes leading
to it) was closely intertwined with heavenly feast. Not eating was preparation for eucharist; it was also renunciation of the world and union
with the agony of Christ's redeeming death. Indeed, the author of the
nuns' book of Unterlinden called fasting *imitatio Christi* and the glory
of the martyrs.[126] Saints such as Douceline of Marseilles (d. 1274) and
Jane Mary of Maillé fasted as an aspect of eucharist devotion. Douceline
went into ecstasy every time she received communion, saw prayer as a

substitute for eating, and in a vision entered the tabernacle to "taste" Christ's sweetness.[127] Jane Mary, who convinced her husband on their wedding night to observe chastity, suffered patiently from illness in the early years of her marriage. After her husband's death she cared for the poor "like Martha," sending delicacies from her table to the sick, the old, and the pregnant, and fasted on brown bread and uncooked herbs until her body was pale and skeletal. But Christ himself summoned her to the eucharist, appeared in visions with his wounds all bleeding, changed water into wine for her, and kept her rosy and beautiful with himself as food. (She lived to be eighty-two.) Her charitable feeding of others was rewarded when she fed an angel in disguise.[128]

Many of the French and German *vitae*, like those from the Low Countries, depict women who apparently became unable to eat normally. Alpaïs of Cudot, who supposedly lived forty years on the eucharist alone, began her "fast" during a severe illness (perhaps leprosy), in which she swelled and stank and was left for dead by her family.[129] Cured by Mary, who told her that she would never need to eat or drink again, Alpaïs afterwards took only tiny bits of food, which she chewed for the juice, spitting out the pulp. Her Cistercian hagiographer underlined the inter-dependence in her life of eucharistic feast and bodily fast, of a closed and shriveled earthly body and the "fattening" ecstasies sent from heaven.[130] Alpaïs, who was paralyzed, clearly developed physical difficul-ties in swallowing; at one point she was acutely afraid of taking even a whole host into her throat, until John the Evangelist came in a vision to help her.[131] Although she saw her inedia as an infirmity, she clearly val-ued it as a spiritual gift as well, and she thought it was a temptation of the devil to desire it cured.[132] Her chroniclers emphasize the fact that her body, which earlier ran with stinking sores, closed up; after death her intestines were almost empty.[133]

Despite (and also by means of) her bodily agony, Alpaïs served others with visions, advice, and even food. An interesting addendum to one of the manuscripts of her *vita* says that when the prior of Cudot brought her bits of pork to suck she ate them all and was horrified by her greed, for she usually sent what was left on her table to an old woman in the neighborhood who lacked even the necessities of life. The next day she sent all the pork morsels to the old woman and that night saw a vision of the devil as a cook, bearing food.[134] The suggestion in this story that a saintly abstainer might lose control and slip, almost against her will, into gluttony finds echoes in a few later lives (for example, those of Elsbet Achler of Reute [d. 1420], Catherine of Siena, and Columba of Rieti) that give evidence of surreptitious and compulsive gorging by female fasters.[135]

Behind the lives discussed here, whether sharply individualized like the portrait of Alpaïs or stereotyped like the nuns' book from Töss, we find a common pattern. Like outcroppings of rock that may take differing and sometimes twisted forms but are built on the same crystalline structure, these stories have a unifying theme behind their flamboyant variety of detail. In them, God is food and self is food. The communication of God to humanity and the giving of one self to another through suffering or service is understood as "feeding"—an imparting of flesh that nurtures as it is consumed. Such a complicated exchange of flesh requires fasting from ordinary food as the standard prerequisite. Thus closing and opening, abstaining and eating, are the basic patterns organizing such narratives and such lives.

This common crystalline structure underlies the stories of four of the greatest religious women of the north of Europe—Elizabeth of Hungary or Thuringia, Margaret of Hungary (d. 1270 or 1271), Dorothy of Montau, and Colette of Corbie. To all four, obsessive fasting, accompanied by sleeplessness and frenetic activity, became a focal point of piety. All four struggled for control over their vocations. All four fed others. Yet despite the large amount of scholarship devoted to their lives, the common pattern has gone unnoticed. It will therefore be useful to take a few paragraphs to tell their stories.

The life of Elizabeth of Hungary, married at fourteen to the son of the duke of Thuringia and widowed at twenty, has become so encrusted with legend that it is hard to decipher.[136] The importance of her stern confessor, Conrad of Marburg, in inducing her obsession with food is impossible to assess at this distance.[137] It is clear, however, that she felt intense guilt about her husband's wealth and probably about her love for him as well. It is also clear that she ceased eating the food from her husband's table for fear it had been acquired immorally and that she hid her acute fasting, crumbling her bread to make it appear she had eaten and spending her dowry to buy a little untainted food for herself and her servants. Once she took the habit of a tertiary, she performed extreme fasts while cooking for and serving others. Throughout her life she compulsively gave away food.[138] After death, her body oozed healing oil.[139] The stories and descriptions that accumulated around her—even those that are clearly apocryphal (like the legend of bread turned to roses)—stressed her food distribution to the poor and her motherly "nourishing" of her sons, the friars.[140]

Another royal saint, Margaret of Hungary, a nun from girlhood who ferociously refused offers of marriage,[141] practiced similar food asceticism. She too was frenetic in the service of others, even cleaning latrines and carrying the excrement and vomit from seriously ill nuns.[142] To avoid eating, Margaret several times served her sisters at the beginning of the meal, escaped to the chapel to pray, and returned to serve them again;[143] she frequently covered her face with a cloth during meals.[144] She hid her own illnesses, lest she be sent to the infirmary and offered meat, and her body was so "emaciated and pale" from fasting that all marveled.[145] Yet she insisted on cooking for others, freezing her hands in cold water and cutting them on fish scales, and she went into ecstasy at communion, remaining for hours afterward in the church and refusing ordinary food.[146] Moreover, her body itself, which she refused to wash or care for, cured the sick. Wash water from her hair, when held in the mouth or swallowed, cured ill sisters and even a brother in another monastery.[147]

The laywoman Dorothy of Montau (or Prussia), whose food asceticism began early and brought her into severe conflict with her mother,[148] felt agonies of guilt over enjoying three small fishes, developed nausea at the sight or smell of food, ate so little she ceased excreting, and would have gone without food entirely at one point in her life had not her confessor intervened.[149] She was passionately devoted to the eucharist, around which her most elaborate visions and images clustered, and she developed a kind of mystical pregnancy or swelling in preparation for communion.[150] Anxious to be free of her husband and housework, she enjoyed begging, and one cannot help suspecting that among its attractions was the fact that, like her frequent trances, it relieved her of the job of preparing food.[151] One of her husband's fierce complaints was that while she was in ecstasy she forgot to shop, or cooked the evening meal without scaling the fish or cleaning the vegetables.[152] Her descriptions of eucharistic trances, written down by her confessor, John Marienwerder, not only mention sensible effects such as visions of Christ bleeding on the cross or offering a heavenly banquet,[153] they also make it clear that she saw the agony of actual hunger for the host as a necessary preparation for the proper reception of communion and as the extension, in this life, of the pains of purgatory. She reported that Christ said to her:

> Those people who receive me [in the host] because it is customary to do so or in order to win favor or praise from others receive great damnation in taking me, for they do not have the intense desire of love. Indeed I just said to you that he who does not hunger for my body . . . does not really desire eternal life. For it is necessary that man clamor and labor for me, that he wail aloud either here in this world or in purgatory. And you must have for me, before consuming the sacrament, a great labor and hunger; and after noon [i.e., after the mass], you must have a great hunger and labor for eternal life. . . . He who does not hunger greatly for me will not be filled by me nor have delight in me. For how can anyone have sweetness and delectation in that food who has not hungered for it? And how can he be satiated and contented from food in which he has not placed all his hope of delight?[154]

Of Dorothy's eucharistic craving, John wrote:

> Often, indeed, because of the frenzy [aestus] of this desire she was not able to pray; her heart grieved so that it seemed to her as if she wanted to die if she was not permitted to receive the sacrament on that day. Sometimes . . . she could hardly stand or walk. . . . Often . . . she remained in bed as if oppressed with a grave illness. [So God ordered her confessor to give her communion three times a week.] . . . But her desire was not satisfied by this; for now she hungered in such intense desire and destitution of all strength that it appeared to her that she could never express her hunger or accept into her mouth any corporeal food. . . . And this desire grew night and day.[155]

Indeed, Dorothy frequently toyed with the idea of extending her excruciating fasts to the host itself; for despite her craving for the eucharist, she experienced overwhelming sensations of unworthiness and had to be reassured repeatedly by Christ that he desired her to partake of the precious food of his body.[156]

One final story from the north of Europe underlines how central food motifs had become in women's lives by the fifteenth century. Colette of Corbie was first a hermit and then the influential reformer of the Clares.[157] She traveled from monastery to monastery working for strict observance and even—with male support—dabbled in papal politics. She was an exact contemporary of Lidwina of Schiedam, who died in

1433 at the age of fifty-three, and, as with Lidwina, the several surviving *vitae* seem to be embroidered with certain themes that hagiographers and readers considered appropriate to female saints.[158] Like Lidwina, Colette supposedly went for long periods of time without eating or sleeping. Her hagiographer, Peter of Vaux, comments proudly that she "went beyond the Fathers," for she spent forty days and nights without food or drink, "something that is impossible or against nature . . . but not impossible to or against God."[159] Like Lidwina, Colette experienced eucharistic ecstasies. Like her fasting contemporary, she supposedly received stigmata.[160]

A copy of Colette's own exhortation to her nuns survives. While it mentions fasting among other severe austerities, it lays no particular stress on food asceticism.[161] But in the hagiographical accounts, food is a central theme. Colette supposedly began to fast as a child, giving away her dinner to other schoolchildren, running from the family table to welcome beggars at the door and press them to accept her food. From girlhood she ate no meat. Throughout her life she sent food from her table to those in the surrounding city and countryside, and sometimes she miraculously multiplied food or wine for her monasteries.[162] Moreover, she effected cures with food, putting bread she had chewed into the mouths of two sick sisters or, on another occasion, curing with a crumb of bread.[163] Her kiss healed a leper; she was cured by receiving the Virgin's kiss in a vision; a sick nun once claimed that she recovered because Colette appeared to her in a vision and offered her a "beautiful fruit" to eat.[164] Colette healed another woman by blowing over the woman's cancerous face water she had held in her mouth.[165] During her lifetime she cured a nun who, possessed by the devil, suffered a terrible bout of bodily rigidity and could not eat or drink.[166] After her death water from her relics supposedly healed a woman who had scarcely eaten for thirteen years. (As additional evidence of the importance of food rituals in this culture, we should note that the cured woman herself first accepted the food of the eucharist and then *fasted* in thanksgiving for her recovery.)[167] Colette's biographer stresses that she never menstruated, "a special grace not heard of in others," and that both in life and in death her body gave off only sweet odors.[168]

So important was the eucharist in Colette's piety that she heard mass every day and communicated frequently; but she preferred to do so in private because she could not control her weeping and trances, and a crowd often gathered to gawk. She frequently saw Christ in visions at the elevation and sometimes, out of reverence and frenzy, she was almost unable to swallow the host. She could not eat after mass and often remained rapt in ecstasy for many hours.[169] Once, when the priest filled the chalice with water by mistake, she knew that God was not present at the moment of consecration. On another occasion, when the priest forgot to consecrate a host for her, Christ brought the wafer with his own hand. A miniature of this scene, painted between 1468 and 1477 for Margaret of York, wife of Charles the Bold of Burgundy, shows how such an immediate and individual relationship between God and the soul could seem to bypass clerical authority (see plate 11).[170] On another occasion, Colette saw a vision of the Christ child on a dish, carved up like a piece of meat; afterwards, as she brooded over the horrifying vision, she knew that it represented Christ's reparation for our sins.[171] Imitating this macerated flesh in her own body, she beat and starved herself and sometimes briefly displayed on her body the marks of Christ's Passion.[172]

Thus the active and forceful reformer Colette, like her more passive and pitiful contemporary Lidwina, not only fasted from ordinary food, she also feasted on heavenly food. Indeed, Colette *became* food. In her asceticism and her trances, she was the tortured flesh of Christ's broken body, offered up for sin. And as she moved among her sisters or among the poor, she nurtured them in another way, through her comforting presence. With her own mouth she provided food to heal the ill and needy.

To a modern sensibility, there is a great difference between inner meditation that visualizes God in food images and what psychologists today call *somatization*—that is, manifestations in one's body of emotional and spiritual reactions (such as stigmata, sweet mucus in the mouth, feelings of being filled or stifled, or spontaneous exudings of sweat or milk). But to a Gertrude, a Lukardis, or a Flora of Beaulieu, such experiences were merely differing points on a continuum that was encounter with God. To medieval people, Mechtild of Hackeborn's vision of the communion cup as Christ's heart was not simply a poetic image of a theological tenet,[173] nor was Colette's inability to eat after communion simply a bodily response to mental excitement. What is striking for my purposes therefore is that—whether they are ineffable experiences described in poetic language, visions seen with the eyes of the body, or full bodily manifestations—the meetings with God that medieval women received were often eatings, tastings, and savorings. The mouth (breathing, kissing, spitting, swallowing, and sucking) was a way of uniting with God and serving neighbor. Desire for Christ was felt in mind, soul, and entrails as insatiable hunger or thirst. Abstinence from ordinary sustenance was not so much a goal in itself as a tribute to the overwhelming sweetness, the exhilarating pain, of the meat and drink that God was.

♦ Italy

More *vitae* of women saints come from Italy than from any other region in the later Middle Ages. Perhaps for this very reason, as scholars such as Vauchez, Petroff, Weinstein, and Bell have recently emphasized, Italian lives fall into a consistent and predictable pattern. They place a strong emphasis on charitable activity in the world, laced with miracle. They are also strongly male-oriented: these women saints often simultaneously dominate and are dominated by the confessors who eventually write their biographies. Thus, in contrast with Low Country women of the thirteenth century or German nuns of the early fourteenth, Italian female saints seem to be more isolated from other women, without the support of organized female communities. Yet, as in northern stories, the underlying crystalline structure is there. A few examples will show the prominence of eucharistic devotion, food asceticism, feeding miracles, and food images in these Italian lives.

Eucharistic piety is a significant theme in the *vitae* of Gherardesca of Pisa (d. 1260 or 1267), Margaret of Cortona, Angela of Foligno, Alda of Siena (d. 1310), Agnes of Montepulciano, Catherine of Siena, Rita of Cascia (d. mid-fifteenth century), Columba of Rieti, and Catherine of Genoa. Although earlier Italian *vitae*, such as those of Gherardesca and Umiltà of Faenza (d. 1310) sometimes depict the eucharist as cleansing water more than nourishing blood and stress seeing over eating, women's stories in general make the role of Christ's body and blood as holy food very clear.[174] Margaret of Cortona, Angela of Foligno, Columba of Rieti, and Catherine of Genoa, for example, craved frequent reception and substituted the eucharist quite explicitly for the food they denied themselves in long fasts.[175]

Margaret of Cortona, one of the most interesting of women saints because of her lowly origins, was directed by Christ to center her piety in daily communion; she focused on the host both her agonized sense of unworthiness and her desperate need for Jesus' special love. She craved reception but was often too terrified to go forward to receive.[176] She adored priests. Jesus supposedly said to her in a vision:

> Daughter, I complain to you bitterly about the irreverence of priests who touch me daily in such great numbers without knowing or loving me. For if they truly knew me they would know that there is no beauty in the created world similar to that of those priests who celebrate. And they would not come to touch me with polluted hands.[177]

Margaret was given the gift of detecting by taste unconsecrated hosts or those consecrated by unworthy clerics.[178] Jesus warned her in a vision not only to "cling to the breasts of consolation" but to join with the sorrows of the cross as well. In another vision he said to her: "You wish to be my daughter of milk but you will be my daughter of poison, because of the pains you suffer."[179] She spoke repeatedly of Christ as "living bread" and saw herself as an example to others, both of abstinence from earthly food and of heavenly eating—an eating that was experienced simultaneously as suffering and as joy.[180]

Other Italian women also looked to the eucharist with obsessive concentration of purpose and hope. Angela of Foligno—a contemporary of Margaret who, like Margaret, was released to follow a religious life by the death of a man—described the host as sweeter than any other food. She said she would have liked to keep it on her tongue a great while longer, if she had not heard that one must swallow it instantly:

> She said then that sometimes, when she made communion, the host expanded in her mouth and she tasted neither the bread nor the [ordinary] meat which we know. Certainly it had the savor of meat but with a completely different taste, which "I do not know how to compare to anything else in this world." It went down with great ease and sweetness and not with the difficulty to which she was accustomed. She said that it softened quickly and was not hard as it usually was. And it had such sweetness that "had I not heard it said that a person ought to swallow quickly I would have held it freely in my mouth with great delay. But at such times I remember suddenly that I ought to swallow quickly, and the body of Christ goes down whole with that savor of unknown meat, nor

do I need to drink anything afterwards. But this does not normally happen and so I make a great effort that no crumb of the host remains between my teeth. But when it does descend in this way, it gives me a great feeling of peace. And this is discerned outwardly in my body, because it makes me tremble violently, so that only with great effort am I able to grasp the chalice."[181]

Angela repeatedly referred to Christ as "our food" and "our table," and in a vision saw him put the friars of Foligno, her "sons," into his side, whence they emerged with lips rosy from drinking blood.[182] On another occasion Christ appeared to her all bleeding and gave her his wound to suck; she prayed to be allowed to drink his suffering and death but knew she was not worthy to die a martyr.[183]

The *vita* of Alda (or Aldobrandesca) of Siena, which survives only in a sixteenth-century version, shows a similar concern with the eucharist as nurturing blood. In one of her eucharistic visions, Alda tasted a drop of blood from Christ's side; on another occasion the drop fell onto her girdle and she sucked it out with her mouth. In honor of such visions, Alda had a picture painted that, reversing the usual image of the nursing madonna, showed Mary drinking from Christ's side while holding him in her arms.[184]

Food asceticism is also common in these Italian texts, as self-discipline, as preparation for eucharist, or as union with the cross. Margaret of Cortona, for example, undertook extended fasts and struggled to conquer thirst. She refused to keep for herself more than crumbs from her begging, giving the whole loaves to the poor. She spoke of her efforts to eat less and less as a war against the body in which no treaty of peace was possible.[185] So fixated on food did her greed and guilt become that the devil tortured her with phantasms and odors of delicacies she had never even seen.[186]

Some women, such as Catherine of Siena, Catherine of Genoa, and Columba of Rieti, quickly became unable to eat. Villana de' Botti (d. 1361), like Angela of Foligno, found that she lost her appetite for corporeal food when she was praying.[187] Rita of Cascia, who in her youth tried to tame and expiate the violence of her ill-tempered husband by fasts and service of the poor, ate hardly at all in later life; her religious companions believed she was sustained by frequent communion.[188] But other women found hunger difficult to conquer. Clare Gambacorta of Pisa (d. 1419), who mixed ashes with her food to spoil the taste and ate

PLATES I

1 & 2. In this Swabian retable of about 1440 the emphasis on the eucharist as food is clear. The central panel depicts the so-called mystical mill. In a stunning reversal of ordinary Christian roles, Mary (with the assistance of the four evangelists) serves as miller or celebrant, pouring in the flour, while at the bottom the assembled prelates humbly receive the wafer that is Christ.

On the closed wings, Christ as servant distributes food and washes the feet of the apostles. As it often does in medieval miracle stories, the wafer itself separates the perfidious from the virtuous: a small demon leaps from the mouth of Judas when he receives the holy food. Ulm Museum.

3. According to legend, Christ as bleeding victim appeared to Pope Gregory the Great (d. 604) while he was saying mass. As eucharistic miracles proliferated in the later Middle Ages, the story became a popular iconographic theme. In this *Mass of St. Gregory* from 1486, by the Master of the Holy Kinship, Christ bleeds into the chalice. Museum of the Catherineconvent, Utrecht. Copyright Stichting Het Catharijneconvent.

4. This 1469 painting from the studio of Friedrich Herlin is a striking illustration of the medieval conception of Christ as food. From the wound in Christ's right foot a stalk of wheat grows and pierces his left hand. A grapevine grows from his left foot. Stadtmuseum, Nördlingen.

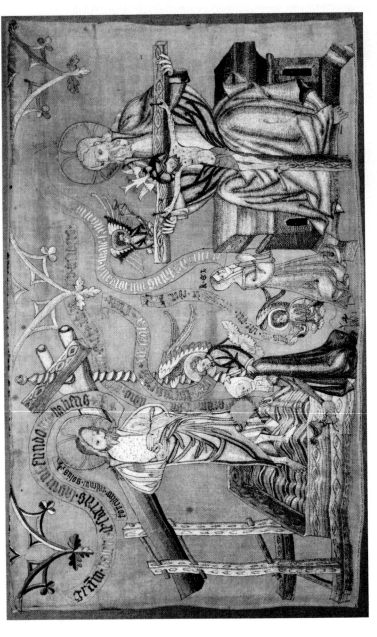

5. This silk embroidery, recently restored and redated to the early fifteenth century, depicts the iconographic motif of Christ in the winepress. Pressed under the crossbeam, Christ points with his bleeding hand to the wound in his side. A nun collects the blood/wine in a chalice. The embroidery illustrates both the close association of blood and wine in miracle and in art and the medieval tendency to emphasize women as recipients of eucharistic favors. Germanisches Nationalmuseum, Nürnberg. Copyright Germanisches Nationalmuseum.

6. According to medieval lore, only a female virgin could
capture the fabled unicorn, who would come and lay his
head in her lap. In this retable of 1506, the beast lies in
Mary's lap, which is depicted as parallel to a central
throne-like altar that holds a crucifix. The woodcarving,
which would itself have been the backdrop against
which a priest elevated the host, thus comes as close as a
medieval artist could come to depicting the very moment of the conception of Christ. The moment of
conception illustrated here, like the moment of transubstantiation that occurred on the altar in front of the
retable, was the moment of the enfleshing of God.
The Cathedral, Lübeck.

7. Medieval artists often associated the eucharist with female saints. In this woodcarving from 1520–1530, we find the Virgin and child flanked by the martyrs Catherine and Barbara. Barbara, here depicted with chalice as well as sword, was the medieval saint most commonly linked to the eucharist, for popular opinion held that her devotees would not die without a chance to receive the sacrament at life's end. Holy Ghost Hospital, Lübeck.

only the scraps left on others' plates, had to inflict pain on herself to divert her attention from her aching, growling stomach.[189]

Abstinence and eucharistic devotion are not merely incidental themes in these texts. We can see how integral they are—and how integrally tied one to the other—in Angela of Foligno's *Book of the Experience of the True Faithful* or *Book of Divine Consolation*, which, although written down by her confessor, frequently includes her own words.[190] The book treats food in part as a symbol of human corruption. When Angela wanted to declare her former hypocrisy publicly, she proposed to parade through the streets with rotting meat and fish tied around her neck.[191] When she began to receive the comfort of God's presence, she found, she tells us, that she scarcely needed to eat at all. Sometimes she wished that she might be released entirely from food in order to revel only in the sweetness of prayer and eucharist.[192]

But food was more to Angela than simply a symbol of human corruption. Food was physicality; and Angela understood Christ to be saying to her in vision after vision that she must fuse with, not flee, the physicality that suffered and bled on the cross. So Angela decided to reject the "temptation" both to exhibit her guilt in the symbolism of rotting food and to cease eating in order to dally with Christ.[193] She came to see her desire to parade through the streets as the sin of despair. She later said of this episode, in one of her few extant letters:

> I wanted to put a cord around my throat and have myself led through public places . . . while people jeered: "See the great miracle of God; he has made manifest all the iniquities and evil deeds, the hypocritical acts and sins, which she kept hidden through her whole life." You know that I was then in such desolation that I despaired completely of God and his gifts and entered into struggle with him.[194]

Angela came through her despair to a vision of true humility. She argued that Christ valued meekness of heart more than the "works" of fasting, abstinence, and poverty. She reported that Jesus said to her in a vision: "Your whole life—your eating and drinking and sleeping and everything you do in living—is pleasing to me [if you love me]," and she wrote:

> Oh my sons, listen. . . . [Christ] did not say: "Learn fasting from me" . . . nor "Learn . . . poverty . . ." nor "Learn to work miracles," . . . but he said only this: "Learn from me for I am meek and humble of heart."

For truly he made this humility of heart and proper comportment of body the foundation and most firm root of all virtues; because neither abstinence nor the harshness of fasting, nor external poverty and vile clothing . . . nor virtuosity in miracles is worth anything without humility of heart. But when founded on this root, blessed are abstinence and harshness and vile clothing; blessed and living are such works.[195]

From a dichotomy in which human food was negative and divine food a replacement, Angela seems to have moved to a notion that one must eat the blood of suffering, a food both earthly and divine. Once the crisis of her conversion was over, food asceticism became less important in her spirituality. Blood and drinking were her dominant images for encounter with God. The eucharist she took came to be not so much a replacement for earthly food as the dying flesh of Jesus, with which she merged in infinite sweetness and infinite suffering.[196] She told her confessor:

Once, when I was at Vespers and was contemplating the crucifix, . . . suddenly my soul was lifted into love, and all the members of my body felt a very great joy. And I saw and felt that Christ, within me, embraced my soul with that arm by which he was crucified . . . and I felt such great security that I could not doubt it was God even if all men told me to doubt. . . . So I rejoice when I see that hand, which he holds out with the signs of the nails, saying to me: "Behold what I bore for you."

Now I can feel no sadness at the Passion . . . for all my joy is in that suffering God-Man. And it seems to my soul that it enters within that wound in the side of Christ and walks there with delight.[197]

She also wrote:

The moment of communion approached. . . . And I was present [with the angels], as I had asked. . . . And I saw him, with the eyes of the spirit, very clearly, first living, full of suffering, bloody and crucified; and then [I saw him] dead on the cross. I felt it; I had so lively a sadness at the pitiful sight that my heart seemed almost to break. But on the other hand I felt great delights and a vast joy at the presence of the angels.[198]

In her day-to-day activities, Angela, like many other Italian tertiaries, came to express this *imitatio crucis* by feeding and caring for the sick.[199] Here too, perhaps because she cared for their bodies as a substitute for Jesus' own, she used metaphors of eating quite literally. Like Catherine of Siena, who drank pus, and Catherine of Genoa, who ate lice, Angela drank water that came from washing the sores of lepers. One of the scabs stuck in her throat, she said, and tasted "as sweet as communion."[200]

In many of the other Italian *vitae*, as in Angela's, abstinence from food and devotion to the eucharist are connected to the feeding and serving of others—either by charity or by miracle. Margaret of Cortona served as adviser to many afflicted like herself with scrupulosity.[201] She cared for the sick. She detected and excoriated corrupt clergy.[202] Christ himself commanded her to be an example of abstinence, fasting, and patience.[203] Umiltà of Faenza—whose piety, like Margaret's, was characterized by eucharistic devotion and abstinence—performed a food multiplication miracle that, according to her hagiographer, she likened to the gospel miracle of the loaves and fishes.[204] Umiltà's disciple Margaret of Faenza (d. 1330) miraculously made watered wine sweet and multiplied loaves for workmen at the monastery.[205] Alda of Siena cured the sick; served the poor, especially in her old age; distributed the produce from her farm to the destitute; and twice changed water into wine.[206] Agnes of Montepulciano saw her prayers rewarded with a rain of manna from heaven, and a similar shower blessed a spring she visited.[207] She frequently multiplied oil, wine, and bread for her sisters and once changed meat into fish to make it more appropriate Lenten fare.[208] Catherine of Siena herself reported that God enabled Agnes and eighteen nuns to survive for three days on greens alone, after which he helped Agnes feed the sisters for two meals on five little rolls.[209] After her death Agnes's body exuded sweet oil from hands and feet, and the oil effected many cures.[210]

The theme of exuding appears in several Italian *vitae*, as it does in those from the Low Countries and Germany. Flemish women were more apt to exude milk, Italian and German women oil or manna; but in *vitae* from all regions the theme is clear. Rita of Cascia, for example, who closed her body to ordinary eating, developed a permanently running sore on her forehead (supposedly made by the crown of thorns); after death she exuded a sweet odor.[211] In a similar story, we are told that Margaret of Città di Castello exuded oil after death; she also supposedly effected cures through three precious stones found in her heart during autopsy.[212] The body of Rose of Viterbo (d. ca. 1252) was found at exhumation to have produced "manna like sweet smelling oil."[213] Whether oil, milk, or manna, the precious substance exuded by the woman's body was usually seen as curing and feeding. Moreover, the exuding of extraordinary fluids was accompanied by extraordinary closure. A woman whose body was communicated to others was usually a woman who herself ate only the special food of God—the eucharist.

In Italy, as in the Low Countries and France, the *vitae* of late fourteenth- and fifteenth-century abstainers are often more elaborate than thirteenth-century texts. Their extravagant details tend to suggest to modern readers either pathology on the part of their subjects or uncontrolled imagination on the part of their authors. Yet it is from these late texts—the lives of Lidwina, Colette, and Columba of Rieti—that we get our clearest sense of the crystalline structure underlying not merely the behavior of saintly women but also the expectations of ordinary women and men, which shaped that behavior. Thus the sixteenth-century *vita* of Columba of Rieti (d. 1501) can serve as a summary of the pattern we have learned to recognize in texts from the preceding period.[214] Struggling to control her environment through fasting, like Rita of Cascia and Dorothy of Montau, consumed with desire for the eucharist, like Margaret of Cortona and Ida of Louvain, giving away everything, like Margaret of Hungary, and afflicted with diabolical visions of food, like Alpaïs, Elsbet Achler, and Angela of Foligno—Columba of Rieti starved herself to death at the age of thirty-four.

Columba's hagiographer begins his story by underlining the theme of food. He suggests that Columba's future sanctity was foreshadowed by her mother's abstinence from all food and drink except greens, vinegar, and wild grapes during her pregnancy. Like Rose of Viterbo's hagiographer, he presents the holy girl as abstaining while still a baby at the breast.[215] At age five, he tells us, Columba made herself a hairshirt and was teased by her mother's friends for refusing to eat.[216]

Columba's food asceticism had apparently led to a conflict of wills with her mother even before her parents decided to find a husband for her. That decision precipitated further conflict, during which, like Clare and Catherine of Siena, Columba cut off her hair.[217] As part of this struggle, she began to fast two days a week and five Lents a year, taking only water and bread or unripe fruit. She also practiced flagellation and sleep deprivation, and she gave away so much family food that her mother came to her once to say that there was nothing to eat, at which point Columba performed a food multiplication miracle. When her mother and her confessor tried to entice her with herbs or vegetables, she mixed ashes, dirt, or water into the food to spoil the taste.[218] She fell into trances while doing housework, once even dropping a baby into the fire.[219] Her harassed mother exclaimed: "You despised a husband, you neglect your household chores, and now you remain at leisure for your own pleasure. Daughter, I say you must work." But Columba saw a vision of Jesus, who said, "Follow me." She returned to her senses with gaiety and pointed out to her mother that God's commands override those of parents.[220] Throughout her life the extravagant self-denial continued, as did the passionate service of others and the stubbornness about deciding for herself. She clearly lost the ability to deal normally with bodily sensations and, although feeling horror of food and drink, sometimes drank vinegar or licked the dirty dishes waiting to be washed, without knowing what she was doing.[221]

Columba's fasting was connected to a craving for the eucharist, which she was eventually permitted to receive daily.[222] Although she could never articulate her joy at receiving God's body, she sometimes cried when she returned to her cell after mass and felt horror when she compared ordinary food with the celestial sweetness.[223] The devil, who came in ugly visions to tempt her with bread and fruit and with a nude male body, even tried to induce in her doubts about transubstantiation. When he told her she was guilty of homicide because she was starving herself, she cried out that she was only disciplining the flesh. "He eats all things who refreshes himself on God," she asserted, "since in him all things are contained." "That's what you think!" replied the devil. "It contains only seeds, like flour and bread." But the next day Columba received comfort in the form of a vision of Jesus hanging on the cross above the chalice. On another occasion, after an exhausting set of visions in which the devil repeatedly forced food to her mouth, she suddenly laughed and cried out, "In the name of Jesus, take it away; *you* eat!"[224]

Columba, like Margaret of Cortona, revered priests for their power over the eucharist and even shed tears of love and awe for her own spiritual father.[225] But her eucharistic visions sometimes bypassed priestly control. One night she was led to communion by the saints in a vision, and the next day, when her confessor accused her of neglecting the eucharist, she said, "Why, father, you gave me communion this morning at the big altar." He denied it, but when he looked for the host, he found it had disappeared.[226]

If we read between the lines of the *vita*, it is clear, in part because of the biographer's defensiveness, that she was much criticized by religious people and did not always submit.[227] A group of nuns once tried to force her to eat, suspecting that she starved herself because of unrequited love.[228] Although she ate a grape and drank water before visitors to disprove rumors that she was subsisting on the eucharist alone, she obeyed immediately when Dominic ordered her in a vision to eat only the sacrament.[229] Her priests could not dissuade her. Receiving nothing beyond the host—not even pure water—she died.

Like other fasting saints, Columba fed and served others, both by miracle and by the work of her hands. She nursed the sick during the plague. She washed her companions' feet at meals. When a poor widow lacked food, Columba told her to go home and look again, and the woman found sustenance. On another occasion Columba caused a little bit of flour to make much bread.[230]

With the clinical detail that tells us we are in the sixteenth century rather than the thirteenth, Columba's hagiographer underlines—as the biographers of Alpaïs, Colette, and Lutgard had done earlier—the drying up of the ascetic's body. Attempting to prove both that Columba was kept healthy by the eucharist and that her body gave no evidence that she had eaten "heavy" food, especially meat, the biographer details her lovely smell, her failure to sweat, the purity of her fingernails, the strength of her limbs and teeth, and the beauty of her countenance. He reports that she told her prioress that she did not menstruate. He also claims that water ran right through her when she drank and that she only occasionally eliminated a tiny bit of yellow fecal matter.[231] But no matter how closed and controlled her body was, the investigators who opened her chest five days after her death discovered around her dry heart a stream of pure and living blood.[232]

Thus in Columba's life, as in many other female lives from all over Europe, eucharistic devotion, charitable food distribution, feeding miracles, abstinence, and self-starvation were major themes. Such *vitae* clearly indicate that fasting and eucharistic piety were central practices in women's search for union with God. Moreover, these lives suggest that hagiographers, those who read their stories, and those who revered their subjects associated fasting, eating, and feeding others with the religiosity of women. Accounts such as the *vitae* of Mary of Oignies, Ida of Louvain, Lukardis of Oberweimar, Angela of Foligno, Dorothy of Montau, Lidwina of Schiedam, Colette of Corbie, and Columba herself are not merely fragments of documentation about asceticism and devotion. They are pieces of literature whose drama and pathos are woven around the central motif of bodies as food: God's body, dying in order that Christians may eat and live, and women's bodies, receiving food, refusing food, becoming food.

Yet hagiography—no matter how elegant its structure—is notoriously stereotypical and exaggerated. The stories of saints sometimes express more clearly the expectations of authors and readers than the hopes and fears in the hearts of their retiring and earnest subjects. We must therefore ask whether women's own writings suggest the same fixation on food that their confessors and biographers often built into their *vitae*. The answer, as we shall see in the next chapter, is that they do.

5

Food in the Writings of Women Mystics

Let him kiss me with the kiss of his mouth: for thy breasts are better than wine,
Smelling sweet of the best ointments. Thy name is as oil poured out: therefore young maidens have loved thee.
Draw me: we will run after thee to the odour of thy ointments. The king hath brought me into his storerooms: we will be glad and rejoice in thee, remembering thy breasts more than wine.
· ·
I sat down under his shadow, whom I desired: and his fruit was sweet to my palate.
He brought me into the cellar of wine: he set in order charity in me.
Stay me up with flowers, compass me about with apples: because I languish with love.   SONG OF SONGS 1:1–3, 2:3–5

I gave you milk to drink, not meat; for you were not able yet. But neither indeed are you now able; for you are yet carnal.
                                                       I CORINTHIANS 3:2

LATE MEDIEVAL mystics borrowed from Scripture, particularly from the Song of Songs, the notion of using images of food and eating to talk about the soul's desire for God. When they thought about eucharist or about mystical union itself, they thought of the sweetness of the bridegroom's breasts, of milk and the honeycomb, of flowing oil, and of the cellar of wine. Moreover, drawing on Paul's words, they conceived of spiritual instruction, even of divine illumination, as milk offered to those not yet grown to adulthood. Thus they sometimes saw Jesus or the apostles and saints as nursing mothers or as a banquet of refreshment and love.[1]

To medieval exegetes and spiritual writers, such themes were not mere metaphors. Intellect, soul, and sensory faculties were not divided, with a separate vocabulary to refer to each. Rather, God was known with senses that were a fusion of all the human being's capacities to experience. When medieval writers spoke of eating or tasting or savoring God, they meant not merely to draw an analogy to a particular bodily pleasure but, rather, to denote directly an experiencing, a feeling/knowing of God into which the entire person was caught up. The mystical writer Rudolph Biberach (d. ca. 1350) pointed out that *sapientia* (wisdom, good taste) and *sapere* (to taste or savor) are related etymologically: "to taste" is "to know."[2] As William of St. Thierry put it in the twelfth century: ". . . gustare, hoc est intelligere."[3]

Thus almost all medieval mystics sometimes speak of "tasting God," and the verb itself is a kind of bridge between the physical act of eating the host and the inner experience of resting in the sweetness (*fruitio*) of mystical union. It is exactly because mystics experienced God with more than intellect, and felt comfortable using sensual language to express the experience, that they and their hagiographers sometimes differed over whether a vision was seen with the eyes of the body or the eyes of the mind. An inner, glorious, wordless moment, described in highly affective language to a sister or a confessor, easily became a vision or an apparition or a miracle as it was retold by one excited hearer after another. Bernard of Clairvaux, for example, said that things come from God without images, and Gertrude of Helfta's biographers quoted Bernard in an effort to explain that Gertrude's visions were merely Christ's way of teaching her what ultimately surpasses all senses. Gertrude's sisters, however, were sure she received Christ's heart as food and drink, hid in it as the dove in the rocks, or nursed from it through his side.[4]

Because of exegetical tradition and because of the central place of the eucharist in the liturgy, verbs such as *manducare* (to chew), *pascere, pasci* (to feed), *sapere* or *gustare* (to taste), *edere* (to devour), *esurire* (to hunger), and *fruor* (to delight in, with connotations of to fructify) came naturally to late medieval spiritual writers. But many other equally sensual verbs were available for expressing the search for and enjoyment of God—verbs of seeing, of hearing, of touching—and these words too reverberate with complex biblical and liturgical resonances. God could be light, water, heat, word, or song, as well as the bread of angels or sweet wine.[5] The Song of Songs suggested metaphors of sexual union and fertility at least as much as metaphors of drunkenness and feasting.[6]

And many highly affective writers, such as Ruysbroeck, Rolle, and Suso, seem to have preferred images of the sea or of melody to imagery of food, despite their eucharistic piety. Yet women mystics in the later Middle Ages were particularly fond not only of images of tasting and devouring but also of extended, elaborate metaphors of hunger and of bread, blood, and food. If handbooks and survey accounts of the history of piety have tended to associate female spirituality with nuptial or erotic metaphors,[7] it appears to be more because modern sensibilities are titillated by such images than because they are women's most common metaphors for union with the divine or because they represent a distinctively female pattern of expression. What does seem more characteristic of women mystics than of men, however, is hungering for God.

In the pages that follow I analyze the words that women themselves wrote or spoke. I might have chosen other figures for detailed consideration—for example, Angela of Foligno or Mechtild of Magdeburg. I have decided to treat Hadewijch, Beatrice of Nazareth, and the two Italian Catherines in part because I can in that way limit myself to two regions, treating two representatives each of northern and southern piety. I have also chosen these four figures because I can, in each section, couple a woman whose own writing survives, articulated in several distinct genres, with a woman whose ideas were partially mediated but by no means entirely masked by those who recorded them.

At first glance this chapter may seem merely to continue explanation and depiction of themes treated in chapter 4. This is not so. The women considered in the previous chapter are seen, so to speak, from the outside. Occasionally their "sayings" have been recorded by hagiographers; sometimes a few letters or direct accounts of visions have survived. But for the most part, their voices are silent. Thus I had to induce their theology from their behavior—an enterprise of uncertain reliability, as medieval inquisitorial records show only too clearly. In contrast, the women I consider in the present chapter tell us how they gave meaning to their experiences. They articulate a mystical theology of considerable power and beauty. And in that theology they tell us that to offer and to become food (i.e., macerated, torn, and nurturing flesh) is to serve and to save. It is necessary to listen with some care to their voices, for although these women have been much studied by scholars, the complexity of their ideas has seldom been understood.[8]

◆ *Hadewijch and Beatrice of Nazareth*

Sometimes we find imagery of eating, devouring, and hungering in mystical writers of whose lives we know little. This is the case with Hadewijch,[9] the first great poet in the Flemish language, who probably wrote between 1220 and 1240, was probably the leader of a beguine group from which she was at some point exiled, and was perhaps actually accused of quietism, a charge she seems to have been anxious to refute.[10] Of her own religious practices we know only what is suggested by obscure autobiographical fragments in her poems, letters, and visions. She warns against gluttony, urging her daughters that they should never have "taste" for anything outside God,[11] and she was clearly deeply devoted to the eucharist, the reception of which is mentioned as providing the occasion for at least four of her thirteen recorded visions.[12] But even though we know little of Hadewijch's spiritual practices, we can see the power of food as an image in her writing. Hungering and devouring, if not her central metaphors, are nonetheless repeatedly used in her poems and letters to talk about the "love" that is her central concern—a love that is both God and the search for God.[13] Moreover, as Paul Mommaers and J. Reynaert have pointed out, the mystical oneness she achieves—not an ecstatic transcending of humanness but a joining with Jesus' "concrete, disconcerting, human Humanity"—is an experience she calls "tasting":

> The Countenance which he there made visible was invisible and inaccessible to the sight for all creatures who never lived human and divine love in one simple Being, and who could not grasp or cherish in the undivided taste the one nature.[14]

> I was chosen [to receive revelations] in order that I might taste Man and God in one knowledge [*dat ic mensche ende god in eenre const smaken soude*].[15]

The union toward which Hadewijch strained with every fiber of her being was best spoken of in paradoxes, she felt, because it was the soul's only goal, yet impossible of more than momentary attainment. Thus it was best articulated in the cries of pain, the images of hell and loneliness, that reflect the mystic's failure to retain it. Hadewijch wrote both some of the most affective, sensual, even erotic descriptions of union with

Christ ever penned and some of the fiercest criticism of affective spirituality, denying that love is ever sweetness, joy, or peace. Exactly because
final rest is never possible in this life, Hadewijch again and again challenged her spiritual daughters to fuse with the humanity of Christ before
attempting to "become God with God" (i.e., to rest in sweetness).[16] The
Hadewijch who could describe her soul melting erotically into the beautiful human Jesus at the moment of eating and drinking his body in
communion also wrote:

> Hell is the seventh name
> Of this Love wherein I suffer.
> For there is nothing Love does not engulf and damn.
> . . . .
>
> As Hell turns everything to ruin,
> In Love nothing else is acquired
> But disgust and torture without pity;
> Forever to be in unrest,
> Forever assault and new persecution;
> To be wholly devoured and engulfed [al verslonden
> . ende al verswolghen]
> In her unfathomable essence,
> To founder unceasingly in heat and cold,
> In the deep, insurmountable darkness of Love.
> This outdoes the torments of hell.[17]

To Hadewijch, one sought union with a human Christ in a frenzy of
suffering that included and transcended pleasure and pain.

. For such union, both hunger and eating were powerful images. Hadewijch wished to express the total incorporation of humanity into hu-
manity-divinity (eating of God by the self and of the self by God), yet
she also felt an aching desire that yearned for a filling beyond satiety. To
hunger and to devour, for her, had clear overtones of physicality joining
physicality. To eat meant both to fuse with, in erotic union of mouth to
mouth, and to become pregnant with, to have grow within one's belly.
Yet such union was union with suffering; for "frenzied devouring" carried with it connotations of failure ever to be filled, ever to stay the
agonized longing that returned and returned and returned.

Hadewijch sometimes speaks of the soul as fed by Christ in the eucharist or in ecstasy. She borrows from William of St. Thierry the image

of the soul reared by Christ, "nursed with motherly care . . . [and] disciplined by the rod of fatherly mercy."[18] She says love "nourishes [the humble] with her food."[19] And she describes the beginnings of her own mystical life in language that uses *devour*, *swallow*, and *drink* to express a sweet engulfing of self in God:

> Since I was ten years old I have been so overwhelmed by intense love that I should have died, during the first two years when I began this, if God had not given me other forms of strength. . . . And through all these tokens with which I met in the intimate exchange of love between him and me—for as it is the custom of friends between themselves to hide little and reveal much, what is most experienced is the close feeling of another, when they relish, devour, drink, swallow up each other [*Ende in doer smakene, Ende in doer etene, Ende in doer drinckene, Ende in verswelghene elc anderen*]—by these tokens that God, my Love, imparted to me . . . he gave me . . . confidence in him. . . . Sometimes Love so enlightens me that I know what is wanting in me—that I do not content my Beloved according to his sublimity; and sometimes the sweet nature of Love blinds me to such a degree that when I can taste and feel her [*te ghesmakene Ende te gheuoelne*] it is enough for me.[20]

Sometimes, drawing on the Songs of Songs, she weaves together language of kissing and eating and flowing oil, expressing a clear sense that the food-body God gives in the eucharist is received by Christians as both erotic and nourishing sweetness:

> He delivered up to death his substance, that is to say his holy Body . . . and he gave himself to be eaten and drunk, as often as we will. . . . Yes, much smaller than an atom compared to the entire world is what we receive from God compared to what we could have from God, if we trusted in him and would receive it from him. Alas, how many souls now remain thus unfed, and how few consume him among those who have the right to eat and drink!
>
> He relaxed time; that is, he is patient to wait for our advance to a good life when we will. We see his mouth brought close to us to kiss him who wishes it. His arms are outstretched: He who wishes to be embraced may throw himself into them.[21]

The union of mouth to mouth she describes is sometimes frankly erotic, underlining the extent to which all the senses are involved in this knowing and experiencing of God:

They penetrate each other in such a way that neither of the two distinguishes himself from the other. But they abide in one another in fruition, mouth in mouth, heart in heart, body in body, soul in soul.[22]

In her poem "Love's Seven Names" she asserts that we do eat God:

> . . . love's most intimate union
> Is through eating, tasting and seeing interiorly.
> He eats us; we think we eat him,
> And we do eat him, of this we can be certain.[23]

In these stanzas, eating is a central metaphor not merely because the eucharist is the place in Christian ritual in which God is most intimately received but also because *to eat* and *to be eaten* express that interpenetration and mutual engulfing, that fusion of fleshly humanness with fleshly humanness, that Hadewijch saw as necessary for uniting with a God-who-is-man. Moreover, in one of her visions Hadewijch herself experienced what she evokes in her poetry. Her account of this meeting with God reads like a description of sexual orgasm (and it is only our modern sensibility that makes the suggestion a shocking one):

> He came in the form and clothing of a Man, as he was on the day when he gave his Body for the first time . . . he gave himself to me in the shape of the Sacrament, in its outward form . . . and then he gave me to drink from the chalice. . . . After that he came himself to me, took me entirely in his arms, and pressed me to him; and all my members felt his in full felicity, in accordance with the desire of my heart and my humanity [*na miere herten begherten. na miere menscheit*]. So I was outwardly satisfied and fully transported. Also then, for a short while, I had the strength to bear this; but soon, after a short time, I lost that manly beauty outwardly in the sight of his form. I saw him completely come to nought and so fade and all at once dissolve that I could no longer distinguish him within me. Then it was to me as if we were one without difference.

Hadewijch goes on to suggest that such inner "dissolving" is one with the "outward" seeing, feeling, and tasting of the sacrament.[24]

Eating or being fed is not, to Hadewijch, merely a union in which God takes the initiative, a swallowing or devouring of the soul by God. The soul too gives food. It "suckles" what it loves. And it reaches out to taste and masticate the sweetness of the Lord. In the poem her editor calls "Were I But Love," Hadewijch speaks of our own loving as a kind of feeding:

> I greet what I love
> With my heart's blood.
> . . . .
> I long, I keep vigil, I taste [*Jc hake, ic wake, ic*
> *smake*]
> . . . .
> I suffer, I strive after the height,
> I suckle with my bood [*Jc soghe met minnen bloede*];
> I greet the sweetness that can
> Alleviate my madness [*orewoede*] of Love.[25]

In her poem "Love's Growth" she speaks of being pregnant with Love, a sweet child, which is carried and nourished in pain and finally "wholly engulfs from within" the mothering soul.[26] Thus, to Hadewijch, biological images for the love offered and received by the self are images of the utmost intimacy. To love is to give one's bodily fluid as food, to carry a foetus within oneself, to chew or to be chewed; it is not merely to kiss but also to feel the other within one's own bowels or heart. To love is to engulf and be engulfed, to masticate and to assimilate, to flow out with nurture so that one's body becomes food for another.

But metaphors of eating are usually to Hadewijch not metaphors of engulfing and incorporating but metaphors of emptiness and hunger. No matter how much one "tastes," one is never full. The more profound the intimacy with God, the greater the unrequited craving. Hadewijch writes:

> When anyone seeks Love and undertakes her service, he must do all things for her glory, for during this time he is human and needy; and then he must work chivalrously in all things, be generous, serve, and show mercy, for everything fails him and leaves him in want.[27]

Thus Hadewijch does not conclude her poem "Love's Seven Names" with assurances of heavenly nurture. She continues:

> And we do eat him, of this we can be certain.
> But because he remains so undevoured,
> And so untouched, and so undesired,
> Each of us remains uneaten by him
> And separated so far from each other.
> But let him who is held captive by these chains
> Not cease to eat his fill,

> If he wishes to know and taste beyond his dreams
> The Godhead and the Manhood![28]

And her poem builds to Love's seventh name:

> He who knows Love and her comings and
>   goings
> Has experienced and can understand
> Why it is truly appropriate
> That Hell should be the highest name of
>   Love.[29]

Ultimately, to Hadewijch, love is most closely approached in paradox. Thus her central food images are images of an eating that leaves one hungry, of an unfulfilled craving that nevertheless is the only food.

> What is sweetest in Love is her tempestuousness,
> Her deepest abyss is her most beautiful form;
> . . . .
> To die of hunger for her is to feed and taste;
> Her despair is assurance;
> Her sorest wounding is all curing;
> To waste away for her sake is to be in repose;
> . . . .
> Her tender care enlarges our wounds;
> . . . .
> Her table is hunger.[30]

To Hadewijch, the deepest danger for the soul would be to try to escape or bypass such frenzy and pain. To her daughters she wrote:

> We all indeed wish to be God with God, but God knows there are few of us who want to live as men with his Humanity, or want to carry his cross with him, or want to hang on the cross. . . . But before Love thus bursts her dikes, and before she ravishes man out of himself . . . , he must offer her noble service and the life of exile.[31]

In a vision, she received a chalice full of blood; when she drank it, she realized it was the chalice of patience.[32] And in the same vision God told her: "Since you are a human being, live in misery as man [mensch]."[33] She spoke of expanding her suffering, her terrible craving for God, into such compassion for others that she would have braved God's condemnation to bring them to love him. Her agony was thus a kind of service, which once even managed to coerce God into releasing souls from their deserved judgment.[34] But she learned that the power of God's awful decision lay beyond even the service of suffering. She wrote:

> I have never experienced Love in any sort of way as repose. . . . For I was a human creature, and Love is terrible and implacable, devouring and burning. . . . Now for persons, my repose lay in loving each of them in what was proper to him. . . . As for persons who failed God and were strangers to him, they weighed heavy on me. For I was so laden with his love and captivated by it that I could scarcely endure that anyone should love him less than I. And charity for others wounded me cruelly, that he should let these souls be such strangers to him. . . . I would gladly have purchased love for them by accepting that he should love them and hate me. . . . But the sovereign power that is actual Love spares no one. . . . This power held me back once again when I had wished to free all men.[35]

Thus, to Hadewijch, the soul should strive not so much to rest in satiety as to suffer a deeper hunger beyond filling. For the truest satiety is the pain of desire; the truest repose is the horror of God's power. And all we attain—fullness or hunger—is the gift of Love.

> For I depend wholly on [Love],
>   If I shall ever ascend clear to her summit.
>   Whatever else I did,
>   My hunger [*hongher*] would remain as strong as ever:
>   Did she not give me full satisfaction in her.
> So I remain on Love's side,
> Whatever may happen to me after that:
> The pain of hunger for her, the joy of satisfaction in her,
>   No to desires, or yes to delight.[36]

Hadewijch's reason for stressing hunger rather than repose is not merely experiential. It does not lie simply in her sense that desire grows ever greater as it tastes more of the ineffable sweetness. For Hadewijch's language reflects doctrine as well. It reflects her conviction that the God we meet is humanity as well as divinity, and nowhere more human than when his flesh becomes food.[37] "Dear child," she wrote to a disciple, "you have much to do if you are to live the Divinity and the Humanity."[38] "[Christ said]: 'If you wish to be like me in my Humanity, as you desire to possess me wholly in my Divinity and Humanity, you shall desire to be poor, miserable, and despised by all men; and all griefs will taste sweeter to you than all earthly pleasures.'"[39] Hunger, then, to Hadewijch, is incorporation with Christ's suffering humanity, which is our path to his divinity. The more we hunger with Christ, the more we are filled. The more we unite with—"eat"—the loneliness, the death, the body of Christ on the cross, the more fully God unites with us, swelling our fullness and our desire.

> Inseparable satiety and hunger
> Are the appanage of lavish Love
> . . . .
>
> Satiety: for Love comes, and they cannot bear her;
> Hunger: for she withdraws, and they complain.
> . . . .
>
> How does Love's coming satiate?
> Filled with wonder, we taste what she is,
> She grants possessing of her sublime throne:
> She imparts the great treasure of her riches.
>
> How does Love's refusal create hunger?
> Because we cannot come at what we wish to know
> Or enjoy what we desire:
> That increases our hunger over and over.
> . . . .
>
> May new light give you new ardor;
> New works, new delights to the full;
> New assaults of Love, new hunger so vast
> That new Love may devour new eternity![40]

Thus we see that the food metaphors in which Hadewijch speaks of her mystical craving express her confidence that we experience God through all our senses. Our knowing is a tasting, a swelling, a being full, a flowing out that engages all our humanity. Such metaphors also express her conviction that the sweetness of God's coming is infinite pain, even madness, for however much we taste, we crave more. The fuller our desire, the hungrier our soul. And, finally, such metaphors of bodily encounter—conjuring up as they do teeth and mouths, bowels and breasts, flesh chewed and swallowed and made into new flesh—reveal how much, to Hadewijch, the God who is the infinite abyss beyond all language and metaphor is also fleshly humanity—a humanity that suffers and feeds.

Hadewijch's sense of union with God as frenzy, like her eucharistic fervor and her passionate images of devouring and desire, finds a parallel in the *vita* of her Flemish contemporary, Beatrice of Nazareth. In Beatrice, the frenzy becomes illness, "insanity," in image and in fact; the eucharist becomes a cascade of blood, with which the woman's body unites itself. About Beatrice's life we know enough to see that asceticism and eucharistic devotion were central to her actual piety, that she sought hysteria as a means of fusing with Christ's cross, and that from this fusion came health, which spilled over into—bled into—service for others.

Beatrice came from a religious family. When she was seven her mother died, and her father committed her to the beguines of Léau to learn her letters. She was later educated at one of the Cistercian monasteries her father had founded, and she made her profession there at sixteen. At about age thirty-seven she became prioress at Nazareth, yet another of her father's foundations, and served in this capacity until her death at sixty-eight.[41] Beatrice wrote down her spiritual experiences, inserting among them short essays on ascetic or mystical topics, at least one of which has survived in the original language. The whole forms a kind of spiritual autobiography. After Beatrice's death, an anonymous confessor of Nazareth translated the autobiography into a Latin that, where we can compare it to her Flemish original, appears both florid and essentially truthful.[42] This autobiography makes it clear that Beatrice tortured her body in extreme asceticism—flagellating herself, sleeping on stones, walking on ice, binding thorns between her breasts and around her loins, and, even in illness, eating only dry bread—and that devotion to the eucharist was at the heart of her piety.[43]

To Beatrice, illness, which is chiefly insanity (*orewoet* in Flemish, *insania amoris* or *aestus* in Latin), is the essential—the *lived*—metaphor for union with Christ.[44] For this illness, however, food/drinking/blood is a major image; and both food/drinking/blood and frenzy/hysteria/insanity are, to Beatrice, images of physicality, of union with the agonized human body of Christ on the cross. Such union came to Beatrice most frequently at reception of communion, a reception that produced illness and health,[45] for it led the body to languish beyond consciousness and yet to pour out in blood for the sisters.[46]

Beatrice's frenzied centering of her life in the eucharist, her vacillation between joy and terror, reflects the ambivalence about communion found in thirteenth-century theology. As we saw in chapter 2 above, theologians of the period both urged and warned against frequent reception. Beatrice—like Gertrude the Great and Margaret of Cortona—responded to such warnings both with agonized feelings of unworthiness, of fear of Christ the judge, and with cravings for the holy food.[47] Beatrice's union with Christ in the eucharist was thus both awe-ful and intimate, intensely erotic and excruciatingly painful—as paradoxical as the images of love in Hadewijch's poems. Once, on the second Sunday in Epiphany, when she proposed to go to communion, she "saw him [i.e., Jesus], the sweetest spouse of the soul, standing on the altar," with his outstretched arms, drawing her to him, and she "desired the saving reception of his body, in marvelous tasting."

> Refreshed by this most health-giving communion, in the marvelous embrace of the same divinity, she suddenly felt her whole soul, diffused through all the members of her body, so violently caught up that the same little body felt itself in all its individual members strongly gathered into the embrace. Indeed, in the union of this sweet embrace, the Lord applied the heart of his chosen one to his own heart, and he absorbed her whole spirit within himself; and the soul of Beatrice tasted there a heavenly flood of charity. . . . At this taste, losing the use of her corporeal senses, she fell to earth and her feet could not hold her. . . . And the nun who cared for her in her sickness went before her holding her by her arms . . . , and [she fell down]. And afterwards, when she came back to herself, the nun put her in her bed where she lay for a whole day inebriated in inestimable sweetness of mind, jubilant and exulting, in tranquil peace of conscience, resting with Christ.[48]

On other occasions her desire for Christ was such torture that she feared to die of it. Drawing on her own description, her hagiographer tells us that she languished more than a year in the following way:

> The fervor of this desire inflamed her mind so much that as often as she remembered [Christ's death and her own exile, she cried]. And her heart, for a long period of time laid open by desire, and her arteries, also opened, frequently brought [to her] a horror of death, since they could not be brought back to their natural condition, because of the impediment of her desire. . . . Indeed such was the wounded devotion [*sauciata deuotio*] of this holy woman, such the desire for celestial joys, such the affection, at once wounded and languishing in love [*vulnerata simul et amors languens*], that, in the fervor of her desire, rivers of copious blood frequently poured from her mouth and nostrils. . . . So finally this violent desire continually dominated in her mind, ever growing, until very often, des-

titute of the obedience of her corporeal senses, she was not able to discern by their services what was outside her. . . . However one great solace remained: . . . the vivifying consolation of the sacrament of the Lord's body and blood. . . . This was the highest solace of the holy woman, this her one and only refuge from all the miseries of the human condition, this at once the nourishment that sustained her [*sustentationis pabulum*], and the saving provision [*viaticum*] on the way of present exile, and a food of medicinal value in her violent seizures and outbursts.[49]

Occasionally Beatrice's desire literally choked her. Once, upon hearing the word preached in the convent, "her heart was shattered." "Deserting its natural place it rose up to her throat and remained there for a long space of time, trembling and palpitating, from which she contracted a great illness."[50] After her first mystical trance, her laughter became so uncontrolled that God had to put out the bedroom lamp by a miracle to hide the contortions of her face from her sisters.[51] A few years later, she began to meditate on "how Christ fed her with the milk of consolation and maternal affection," and she began to think that if the Lord did all those benefits for her, then also he suffered all his pains for her. So she strove "to discover how to shape herself to such torture [or insanity] . . . and so follow perfectly Christ's footsteps." And she consulted her spiritual adviser about the desirability of "molding herself to the way of . . . madness or foolishness" for Christ—i.e., of driving herself mad. But her adviser counseled against it.[52]

According to Beatrice's biographer, she came after many years to a state in which the sacrament cured her from all sickness, in which her inebriation and joy in Christ flowed out into overpowering compassion. She then served the sick and the poor, reading the hearts of those in distress and even arguing the cases of criminals before the local judge.[53] Moreover, Beatrice's own words suggest that she herself saw such a pattern in her life, a movement from sickness to service. In her little treatise on the seven steps of love, which survives in her own version, she describes the stages as: (1) the search for purity, (2) disinterested love, (3) torture because one cannot love enough, (4) the first experience of absorption in God, (5) insanity [*orewoet*], (6) triumphant love, and (7) the violent death of love eternal, the final fusion with Christ. The steps alternate between torture and peace.[54] The final stage is as paradoxical as Hadewijch's notion of love as hell. In it, "the heart becomes crazy within," the mind is "suspended," and the senses "are drawn toward joy." "Love calls [the soul] and dismisses it, sweetens it and tortures it, gives death and offers life, gives health and then wounds again, gives insanity and wisdom."[55] Along the way to ultimate union, however, the soul is described in images of serving. At the second stage it is a serving maid; at the sixth stage, a mother ruling a large family.[56]

Throughout Beatrice's writing, drinking is a central image of union, bleeding a central image of both suffering and joy. Beatrice speaks of the fourth stage of love as a cup brimming over.[57] Of the fifth stage she writes:

> Meanwhile love, which moves so violently and tumultuously in the heart, grows beyond measure and overflows so in the soul that the heart thinks itself much wounded, and these wounds are daily renewed and made more painful. . . . And thus it seems to her that her veins are opened and her blood flows, her marrow is weakened, . . . and her chest burns and her throat dries up. . . . In this time she feels her heart pierced by an arrow up to the throat and finally even to the brain. . . . And by all these [assaults] she is much wounded, and her heart truly rejoices and loses all its strength. And truly her soul is nourished, and her love is fed, and her mind is suspended. . . . And always her soul is more and more excited and lured onward, never saturated or satiated. For the more it is tortured and wounded, the more it is renewed and calmed, and that which profoundly wounds it alone gives to it health.[58]

She frequently saw visions of blood at mass. Once, when she received the sacrament and meditated on Christ's wounds, she "saw that all the blood which flowed from those wounds flooded into her heart . . . so that she was washed perfectly clean. . . . And in this fire of love which burned within her a certain special friend was brought into the sight of her heart and both were united so in Christ that one spirit was made from two."[59] In another set piece, a Christmas meditation on the mysteries of the Incarnation, Beatrice's basic metaphor is drinking Christ, as rivulets, as streams, or as a mighty river. Those who drink rivulets are those who strive for virtues; those who drink streams are those whose compassion grows in memory of the Passion. But highest are those who imitate and fuse with the cross, for they drink Christ himself.[60]

Thus, to Beatrice, insanity-which-is-also-health was both an image of union and a way of life. Drinking Jesus' blood was both a metaphor for *imitatio Christi* and a ritual act (the reception of communion) that lay at the heart of religious practice. Bleeding was a metaphor for pain and loss of self-control; it was also a metaphor for joy and redemption. And it was a bodily function of the woman mystic who lay in bed, out of her senses with inebriation, and who rose to advise troubled sisters and visitors from the world outside the convent.

To Hadewijch, hunger and devouring were powerful and central images for the love that is union. To her contemporary, Beatrice, drinking and bleeding were images for the insanity that is union. Both mystics thus proceed to divinity through a humanity that is intensely physical. Their language expresses a spirituality in which God is not merely described as if he were a body but is eaten and drunk because he is a body. And because the pain of God's bodiliness is the instrument of salvation, imitation of that God is through the wounds, laughter, tears, suffocation, and hunger that occur in the self (body and soul) of the mystic struggling toward ecstasy.

◆ Catherine of Siena and Catherine of Genoa

If we move on a hundred years or more and many miles to the south, we find in the two greatest women writers of medieval Italy, Catherine of Siena (d. 1380) and Catherine of Genoa (d. 1510), a similar concentration on eating and drinking, on bread and blood, as the crucial images for encounter with God. In both cases, we know enough about the women's actual lives to be sure that obsessive fasting and eucharistic piety were key elements in their religious practices. We also know that fasting and feeding became *lived* metaphors for them, as illness and bleeding did for Beatrice of Nazareth. Both Catherines fed the destitute, by ordinary charity and by miracle. Both ate the filth of the sick they tended. Both felt that it was in the excruciating pain of more than earthly hunger that they fused with the agony of Christ on the cross and offered up such agony for the salvation of the world.

Many contemporary and near-contemporary accounts of the life and miracles of Catherine of Siena survive;[61] and we have, in addition, her own writings (dictated but certainly authentic)—i.e., the *Dialogue*, her voluminous correspondence, and some of her prayers.[62] Not surprisingly, these materials sometimes give divergent interpretations, particularly of her miracles and visions. And twentieth-century scholars have debated the dates of certain key events in her life (particularly in her adolescence).[63] Nevertheless, some things are not in doubt. It is clear that not eating was a central element in Catherine's behavior, that eucharistic piety was at the core of her religious practice,[64] that food—especially blood as food—was *the* central metaphor in her prolix metaphorical writing, and that her (predominantly male) advisers and followers saw not eating, eating, and feeding as highly significant aspects of her impact on others.[65]

There is reason to suspect that Raymond of Capua—whose biography of Catherine most scholars have preferred as the basic source for her life—had his own reasons for emphasizing her decidedly odd eating behavior. Raymond himself had poor health and felt much guilt about his own difficulties in fasting. He was, moreover, a propagandist for strict Dominican practice and found Catherine useful as a model of fasting, vigils, and self-abnegation. Raymond himself was clearly less critical of Catherine's inability to eat than her previous confessors had been—in part because of his own distrust of doctors.[66] He enjoyed associating both fasting and miraculous feeding with women saints. He not only wrote a biography of Agnes of Montepulciano, in whose life rains of manna are the characteristic miracle,[67] he also introduced Agnes into his *vita* of Catherine,[68] and he may have been one of the reasons for Catherine's interest in Agnes, which is reflected in her letters, in the *Dialogue*, and in her visits to Agnes's monastery.[69] His Life of Catherine certainly lays more stress on her inability to eat than she herself does in her letters. For example, although Raymond and Catherine agree on the importance to her of Mary Magdalen, Raymond says at least three times that the Magdalen is a model for Catherine because the Magdalen fasted for thirty-three years,[70] whereas Catherine herself always presents Mary Magdalen as a model because she stood under the cross and was inundated with the blood of Christ.[71] Furthermore, Raymond's account may emphasize nursing and feeding miracles and visions somewhat more than other sources. Raymond, for example, places a vision of Christ as nursing mother just after the crucial moment in which Catherine drinks pus from the diseased breast of the tertiary Andrea, whereas the anonymous *Miracoli* (*Miracles*) places at this turning point a vision of marriage with Christ.[72] But, in this case, there is no great need for skepticism; Catherine's own letters are filled with images of nursing from the breast of Christ.[73] Thus, regardless of the interest Raymond and other male advisers may have had in associating images of feeding and nursing with women saints or in revering their self-sacrifice through fasting, both the wide variety of extant sources and Catherine's own words make clear the centrality of food in her spirituality.

If we can trust Raymond's account, Catherine was her mother Lapa's twenty-third child, the only one Lapa nursed at her own breast and later her favorite. Catherine's twin sister, Giovanna, was sent out to a wet nurse and died. The last child, born to Lapa when Catherine was weaned, was given the name of the dead twin. No particularly subtle psychological analysis is necessary to suggest that such a configuration of events (i.e., the death of one's sister because one was chosen for nursing and the constant reminder then of the dead twin in the name of the very child who supplanted one as the youngest) might precondition a favored girl-child to guilt—and guilt associated with food and nursing. Moreover, Raymond reports (and there is no reason to doubt this) that Catherine's older sister Bonaventura starved herself after marriage because of the dissolute behavior of her husband[74]—a fasting that successfully manipulated the young man into reform—and that this same Bonaventura later tempted Catherine into displaying the mild vanity of elegant dress. Shortly after Catherine agreed to make herself pretty, Bonaventura died in childbirth. (Lapa's last child, Giovanna, called Nanna, died about the same time.)[75] Catherine thus had in her beloved sister Bonaventura a graphic illustration of the success that fasting could achieve and of the dangers of marriage and pregnancy. It does not seem surprising that whatever the exact chronology of Catherine's emerging vocation, she rejected marriage and food.[76] Furthermore, since one source reports that there was talk later of marrying her to Bonaventura's widower, we may also suspect that Catherine felt guilt about surviving as a replacement for both her sisters and thus determined to substitute for their suffering rather than for their pleasure.[77]

Catherine clearly began fasting as a child and developed a distaste for meat quite early.[78] She took the Desert Fathers as models. (Several sources tell of her running away to a cave as a little girl.)[79] She then developed an intense adolescent conflict with her family, especially her mother, over her asceticism and her refusal to consider marriage; at the height of this conflict she cut off her hair, she scalded herself at the hot baths to which she was taken on vacation, and she developed a pox from which she made no effort to recover. In the course of the struggle with her family, Catherine went through a period of withdrawal during which she practiced extreme sleep deprivation as well as self-starvation. Both Raymond of Capua and Thomas Antonii de Senis (also known as Caffarini) associate food visions—visions of fruit trees or of nursing from the side of Christ—with this period of her life, although they do not give the same food visions.[80]

Raymond reports that Christ summoned Catherine out of her withdrawal by commanding her to eat again with her family at table, something she was physically unable to do.[81] He says that she spoke of the pain of eating as "dealing out justice [i.e., punishment] to this miserable sinner [i.e., herself]"[82] and that she focused all her hunger on the eucharist.[83] Several eye-witnesses along with Raymond report seeing her shove twigs down her throat to bring up the food she could not bear to have rest in her stomach. Other accounts report spontaneous vomiting. The *Miracoli* describes Catherine, like Alpaïs, chewing and sucking morsels of food which she then spit out.[84] Raymond wrote:

> The habit of receiving communion practically every day struck root in her and became part of her life. . . . Her longing for more and more frequent communion was so intense that when she could not receive it her very body felt the deprivation, and her forces seemed to droop. . . . After the vision just described [i.e., the vision of drinking from the wound in Christ's side], and especially whenever she received Holy Communion, a very torrent of heavenly graces and consolations flooded her soul. These were so abundant that their efforts brimmed over upon her body also, checking the natural flow of its vital juices, and so altering the action of her stomach that it could no longer assimilate food. Indeed, the taking of food became to her not merely unnecessary but actually impossible, except to the accompaniment of great bodily suffering. If food was ever forced down her throat, intense pain followed, no digestion took place, and all that had been violently forced down was violently forced back again.
>
> . . . I myself saw it happen, not once, but again and again, that her emaciated body would be reduced to the last extremity, unable to take anything to restore its forces but a drink of cold water . . . and then suddenly she would seize . . . an opportunity of taking on some work for the honor of God's name or the good of souls, and like a flash, without the help of any other restorative [i.e., without eating], . . . all her forces would revive.[85]

Catherine said in her own letters that she could not eat. The condition was, she said, an "infirmity" (*infermità*).[86] But she also defended herself to an anonymous detractor (probably in 1373 or 1374) by saying that she made an effort to eat once or twice a day and suggesting that God sent the infirmity to cure her "gluttony" (*el vitio della gola*).[87] Rudolph Bell has carefully documented the stages of her inedia. From about age sixteen, she subsisted on bread, water, and raw vegetables. From about twenty-three she gave up bread, surviving on the eucharist, cold water, and bits of food (mostly bitter herbs) that she sucked and then spit out or swallowed and vomited up. (Raymond calls this "eating nothing.") In January, 1380, when she was about thirty-three years old, she gave up water for an entire month, offering her suffering as expiation for the crisis of the church in Italy. Although she ended her total fast in February, she died on April 29, 1380, emaciated and wracked by stomach pains.[88]

Catherine clearly lost the ability to read bodily sensations in what we consider a normal manner. For example, she seems to have seen any hunger pangs as "greed," to have lost the ability to feel "cold," and to have felt panic at the passage of any food down her throat.[89] Sometimes she seems cut loose from any ordinary sense of ego boundaries at all, as when she blames herself for Raymond's cowardice or for all the ills of the world.[90] Her hagiographers comment on her "restless energy" and sleeplessness, which increased as she ate less and less.[91] One might interpret as binge-eating her pattern of long fasts followed by eating several times a day[92] or her practice of forcing herself first to eat and then to vomit. Moreover, she developed a complex casuistry about her self-starvation, arguing to her first confessor and later to Raymond that, since eating caused her torture, it was the sin of suicide for her to eat—a far worse homicide of the self than starving oneself, because it was homicide by greed.[93] Sympathetic scholars have sometimes suggested that she progressed from viewing ascetic practices as an end to seeing them as a means to kill the will, and her letters suggest this.[94] But although she wrote to her anonymous correspondent that she prayed to God to remove her eating infirmity, it was exactly her considered and mature understanding of it *as* an infirmity (rather than a voluntary practice or a delusion of the devil) that allowed her to retain the behavior without any effort to alter it. A passage in the *Dialogue* where she says that Agnes of Montepulciano was able to survive on vegetables alone only because she was "perfect" suggests that Catherine may have seen (and cultivated) her own non-eating as a mark of God's favor, despite her protestations that it was an abnormal physical condition, not a religious practice at all.[95]

After Catherine's period of withdrawal into a cell in her father's house,[96] she rejoined her family and plunged into a combination of fasting, sleeplessness, and hyperactivity, particularly frenetic housework and feeding of others. She did the laundry at night. When the household servant got sick, Catherine carried out the servant's work and nursed her in her illness as well.[97] She gave away great quantities of food, and on one occasion, when she angered her father by giving away the best wine, God miraculously made the cask flow again.[98] The ten years of her extreme inedia were, by all accounts, filled with caring for the poor and sick, often by preparing food for them at odd hours,[99] and her chief and repeated miracles were cures of illness (the chief miracle performed by all saints, of course) and miraculous feedings or food multiplications.[100] Raymond draws the analogy between one of her miracles and the gospel feeding of the five thousand.[101] In the miracle of Alessia's corn, the food multiplication was threefold: first, sour wheat turned sweet; second, the flour made more bread than it should have; finally, the loaves themselves multiplied.[102] Catherine herself in the *Dialogue* reveals her own interest in feeding miracles by recounting those of Dominic and Agnes, although her basic concern in the treatise is spiritual teaching, not miracles.[103] Thomas Antonii de Senis reports two occasions on which she miraculously restored breast milk to women whose breasts had gone dry.[104] Moreover, Catherine often combined healing with feeding. For example, she gave wine to someone she cured, and she diagnosed a possessed man as needing food.[105] In the most vividly described of the miracles that followed her death, Catherine miraculously prepared the family dinner for a woman who had gone to church instead of cooking for her sons.[106] Raymond, in recounting her feeding miracles, underlines both the contrast between her own closed body and her bounty in feeding others, and the fact that feeding is a maternal role parallel to giving birth. He says:

> The whole city was in commotion. Everybody . . . flocked to catch sight of her. "What a woman!" they said. "One who drinks no wine herself, but can by a miracle fill with wine an empty cask!"[107]

> Take note, dear Reader [of this miracle in which bread is multiplied]. How great must have been the merit of this maiden when the Queen of Heaven herself assisted her in making bread for her children. In so doing

the Mother of the Word of God gave us to understand that, as through Catherine she supplied us with such wholesome bread to feed our bodies, so too she purposed by means of her to supply us also with the word of salvation which is the bread that feeds the spirit. And indeed all of us, as if impelled . . . by . . . God, habitually called Catherine "mother." . . . She truly was a mother to us, who continually gave birth to us from the uterus of her mind, enduring for us the groans and pangs of labor [*nos non absque gemitibus et anxietatibus parturiebat ex utero suae mentis*], and fed us [*nos nutriebat*] assiduously on the bread of sound and saving doctrine.[108]

Indeed, Catherine saw her suffering (which included her painful and growing inability to eat) as service. Several sources report her miraculous "death" and "resurrection," and the *Miracoli* says explicitly that she agreed to continue living only because the Virgin Mary promised that God would free souls from purgatory because of her pain.[109] She tried to substitute her own agonies for her father's time in purgatory.[110] On the occasion of her mother's "death" without confession Catherine simply insisted that God bring Lapa back to life because God had already agreed to save Catherine's family as a reward for her suffering.[111] Like Hadewijch, Lutgard, Beatrice of Nazareth, Lukardis of Oberweimar, and Margaret of Cortona, Catherine saw her suffering as quite literally merged both with Christ's agony on the cross and with the pains of purgatory. She therefore knew with utter confidence that her pains *did* save souls.

Serving as well as suffering thus lay at the heart of Catherine's life; both were explictly underlined not only by what she did but also by the males who chronicled her story and corresponded with her. Repeatedly they emphasize her food asceticism, usually admiringly; repeatedly they call her "mamma"; repeatedly they speak of her in nursing metaphors. For example, in his panegyric written soon after her death, William Flete, an English hermit of considerable reputation, reported the sweet odor that came from her clothes during life, the blood that flowed from her mouth in her eucharistic ecstasies, the agony she suffered when she attempted to eat, and the "food" she offered to her "sons" by her holy words.[112]

Accounts of Catherine's life accentuate not only her food abstention and feeding of others; they also underline her substitution of the filth of disease and the blood of Christ's agony for ordinary food. Several of her hagiographers report that she twice forced herself to overcome nausea by thrusting her mouth into the putrifying breast of a dying woman or by drinking pus, and the reports stress these incidents as turning points in her developing inedia, her eucharistic craving, and her growing compulsion to serve others by suffering.[113] She told Raymond: "Never in my life have I tasted any food and drink sweeter or more exquisite [than this pus]."[114]

> [And] on the night following . . . a vision [of Christ with his five wounds] was granted to her as she was at prayer. . . . "My beloved," [Christ] said to her, "you have now gone through many struggles for my sake. . . . Previously you had renounced all that the body takes pleasure in. . . . But yesterday the intensity of your ardent love for me overcame even the instinctive reflexes of your body itself: you forced yourself to swallow without a qualm a drink from which nature recoiled in disgust. . . . As you then went far beyond what mere human nature could ever have achieved, so I today shall give you a drink that transcends in perfection any that human nature can provide. . . . " With that, he tenderly placed his right hand on her neck, and drew her toward the wound in his side. "Drink, daughter, from my side," he said, "and by that draught your soul shall become enraptured with such delight that your very body, which for my sake you have denied, shall be inundated with its overflowing goodness." Drawn close . . . to the outlet of the Fountain of Life, she fastened her lips upon that sacred wound, and still more eagerly the mouth of her soul, and there she slaked her thirst.[115]

From that time on, says Raymond, she could not digest ordinary food.[116] But, although she could swallow no corporeal food, she feasted not only on pus but also on the eucharist.[117]

The various accounts of Catherine's life all stress her eucharistic devotion. Like other fasting women, Catherine substituted frequent communion for ordinary eating, although she encountered criticism for this from confessors, family, and her fellow tertiaries.[118] Like Margaret of Cortona, she detected an unconsecrated host, yet also like Margaret she revered priests passionately for their ability to celebrate mass.[119] Raymond recounts her ecstasies, trances, frenzies, bleedings, and tears at the eucharist, and he associates her craving for Christ's blood, like her drinking of pus, with a nursing Christ.[120] He reports one occasion on which God inspired her confessor to celebrate because of Catherine's desperate need to communicate. Later Catherine supposedly said (in a traditional metaphor, found, for example, in the *Ancrene Riwle* and the Revelations of Gertrude of Helfta):

Father, do you know what the Lord did to my soul that day? He behaved like a mother with her favorite child. She will show it the breast, but hold it away from it until it cries; as soon as it begins to cry, she will laugh for a while and clasp it to her and, covering it with kisses, delightedly give it her full breast. So the Lord behaved with me that day; he showed me his most sacred side from afar and I cried from the intensity of my longing to put my mouth to the sacred wound. After he had laughed for a little while at my tears—at least that is what he seemed to do—he came up to me, clasped my soul in his arms, and put my mouth to where his most sacred wound was, that is to say, the wound in his side. Then with its great longing my soul entered right into that wound and found such sweetness and such knowledge of the Divinity there that if you could ever appreciate it you would marvel that my heart did not break, and wonder how ever I managed to go on living in the body in such an excess of ardour and love.[121]

When we compare Raymond's account of Catherine's words with Catherine's own letters, we find that Raymond has not misled us. The image of the nursing Christ is one of her favorite metaphors and is closely associated with the eucharist.[122] But in Catherine's words there is a different emphasis, one reminiscent of Angela of Foligno's. Much more than in Raymond's paraphrase, Catherine herself stresses service, the drinking of pain as well as comfort, and the active seeking of breast (Christ) by the infant (soul).[123] She writes to a Florentine abbess:

We cannot nourish others unless we nourish ourselves at the breasts of divine charity. . . . Yes, mother, we must do as a little child does who wants milk. It takes the breast of its mother, applies its mouth, and by means of the flesh it draws milk. We must do the same if we would be nourished. We must attach ourselves to the breast of Christ crucified, which is the source of charity, and by means of that flesh we draw milk. The means is Christ's humanity which suffered pain, and we cannot without out pain get that milk that comes from charity.[124]

Again and again in the letters and in the *Dialogue*, Catherine describes the holy soul climbing up Christ's body, seeking the breast, and drinking bitterness as well as comfort, like the medicine a sick child sometimes takes in with its mother's milk.[125] In the *Dialogue* she puts the following words into God's mouth:

Now Adam's sin oozed with a deadly pus, but you were too weakened to drain it yourself. But when the great doctor came (my only-begotten son) he tended that wound, drinking himself the bitter medicine. . . . And he

did as the wet nurse who herself drinks the medicine the baby needs. . . .
My son was your wet nurse, and he joined the bigness and strength of
his divinity with your nature to drink the bitter medicine of his painful
death on the cross so that he might heal and give life to you who were
babies weakened by sin.[126]

In addition to the many eucharistic miracles and visions recounted by
Catherine's hagiographers, we have Catherine's own descriptions of the
centrality of the eucharist. She urges a number of her correspondents to
frequent communion.[127] In the *Dialogue*, she tells, in richly metaphorical
language, of her visions. She speaks of smelling the stench of sin, of
tasting the fragrance of the sacrament; she says that the taste of blood
was "wonderfully present to [her] mouth and bodily taste for several
days" after receiving.[128] She says explicitly that God provides the eucharist
as a substitute for "heavy physical bread," which excites gluttony and
lust. She also says explicitly that ministers, whom she respects and fears
because of their control of the holy food, sometimes deny the soul the
food it craves.[129] And she tells of two miracles in which Christ fed her
directly in visions because servers or celebrants would not.[130]

The visions that Catherine's biographers associated with turning
points in her life all had as their central theme the redemption of humanity as physicality by the substitution of Christ's flesh for human
fleshliness. Raymond reported, for example, that Jesus exchanged hearts
with Catherine and took a tunic out of his side to keep her warm.[131] Just
as Christ enabled Lutgard of Aywières and Douceline of Marseilles to
avoid ordinary bodily contact with others, yet drew them into his own
physicality through the fusion of mouth to mouth and heart to heart, so
Christ enabled Catherine to fuse with his body.[132] Not every vision is
reported by all biographers and not all are emphasized by Catherine
herself,[133] but where we can compare her own descriptions with those of
her hagiographers, the emphasis on redeemed flesh and physicality becomes even more striking. For example, several sources tell us that as a
child she saw a vision of Christ as bridegroom and pope (or bishop), and
that, after she married Christ (an event clearly modeled on Catherine of
Alexandria's mystical marriage), she rejected earthly bridegrooms.[134] In
her hagiographers' accounts, Catherine was married with a ring of silver
or gold and jewels, which Raymond says she could always see. But Cath-

erine herself, in letter after letter, says we do not marry Christ with gold or silver but with the ring of Christ's foreskin, given in the Circumcision and accompanied by pain and the shedding of blood.[135] Thus those who admired Catherine saw her as putting on quite literally the flesh of Christ, which, as holy flesh, protected her from the ordinary bodily sensations of hunger and thirst and cold. But Catherine herself saw that flesh less as substitute and protection than as blood and agony, shed for the sake of the world.

Although Catherine abhorred her own flesh, condemning it as a "dung heap,"[136] she saw the fleshliness of Christ not as some sort of miraculous protection to save us from human vulnerability but as the "way" or "bridge" to lead us to salvation through suffering.[137] She even said that the ring of flesh with which Christ marries us in the Circumcision is a sign that he is the spouse of our humanity.[138] Thus, hateful as body may have been to Catherine, it was *body* that she saw as uniting us to the body of God. And it united us to God by suffering.[139]

The theme of suffering, which rings throughout Catherine's voluminous correspondence, is, of course, a traditional Christian theme. Indeed there is probably not a single original image in all the hundreds of letters. But no one who has read Catherine's work can fail to realize that eating and blood were so prominent in her interpretation of religious experience as to give a unique note to her writing, despite its essentially derivative, even monotonous, content.

Metaphors of eating, drinking, hungering, and vomiting, of food, blood, tables, and servants are central in Catherine's writings.[140] *To eat* to Catherine means *to be* or *to become, to take in* or *to love*. Her standard formulation of Christian obligation is to "eat at the table of the cross the food of the honor of God and the salvation of souls."[141] Most fundamentally, for Catherine *to eat* and *to hunger* have the same meaning: one eats but is never full, desires but is never satiated.[142] Both are active, not passive, images.[143] Both stress pain more than joy.[144] Both mean, most basically, to suffer and to serve—to suffer because in hunger one joins with, "eats," Christ on the cross; to serve because to hunger/suffer is to expiate the sins of the world. For Catherine, the hungering of ordinary Christians is service because it fuses not only with the sufferings of those in purgatory but also with the death throes of Christ that are also the bleeding/feeding of a nursing mother.[145] To a layman Catherine wrote:

> Seat yourself at the table of the cross. . . . There, all inebriated with the precious blood, take the food of souls, suffering pain, opprobrium, curses, villainy, hunger, thirst, and nudity. . . . You must suffer pain and be in shadow. My soul knows it, and it is hungry for your salvation.[146]

To a laywoman she said:

> [Jesus] made of his blood a drink and his flesh a food for all those who wish it. There is no other means for man to be satisfied. He can appease his hunger and thirst only in this blood. . . . A man can possess the whole world and not be satisfied (for the world is less than man) until blood satisfies him, for only that blood is united to the divinity. . . . Eight days after his birth, Christ spilled a little of it in the Circumcision, but it was not enough to cover man. . . . Then on the cross the lance . . . opened his heart. The Holy Spirit tells us to have recourse to the blood. . . .
>
> And then the soul becomes like a drunken man; the more he drinks, the more he wants to drink; the more it bears the cross the more it wants to bear it. And the pains are its refreshment and the tears which it has shed for the memory of the blood are its drink. And the sighs are its food.[147]

To three women of Naples, Catherine wrote:

> Dearest mother and sisters in sweet Jesus Christ, I, Catherine, slave of the slaves of Jesus Christ, write to you in his precious blood, with the desire to see you confirmed in true and perfect charity so that you be true nurses of your souls. For we cannot nourish others if first we do not nourish our own souls with true and real virtues. . . . Do as the child does who, wanting to take milk, takes the mother's breast and places it in his mouth and draws to himself the milk by means of the flesh. So . . . we must attach ourselves to the breast of the crucified Christ, in whom we find the mother of charity, and draw from there by means of his flesh (that is, the humanity) the milk that nourishes our soul. . . . For it is Christ's humanity that suffered, not his divinity; and, without suffering, we cannot nourish ourselves with this milk which we draw from charity.[148]

Catherine repeatedly exhorted the clergy to suffer and to serve.[149] She wrote to Cardinal Peter of Ostia:

> Divine goodness has placed you in the mystical body of the holy church, has nourished you on the breast of this gentle spouse, so that you can eat on the table of the cross the holy food of the honor of God and the salvation of souls. It wants you to be nourished only by the cross, by fatigues of body and anguishes of desire.[150]

To another cardinal she explained: "Give the blood of Christ to your soul that it may be aroused . . . and run to the battle to fight manfully. . . . Let her [your soul] seat herself at the table of the cross and let her there take the food of souls for the honor of God, suffering with patience, bearing the faults of neighbor in great compassion, and accepting all injustice."[151]

Catherine stresses explicitly that one should "eat souls on the table of the cross" in place of ordinary food.[152] She describes her prayers and suffering for Raymond by saying: "Sweetest father, your soul . . . has become food to me and no moment passes in which I do not take this food on the table of the sweet sacrificed Lamb with ardent love."[153] Sometimes the spiritual food of which she speaks is bread or meat. She calls Christ the bread of angels.[154] She even speaks of the eucharistic lamb as "roasted not boiled" on the "spit of the cross."[155] And in several letters she elaborates the unusual Trinity of table (Father), food (Son), and servant (Holy Spirit).[156] But much more frequently in Catherine's usage the soul "eats" liquids—milk or wine or blood. And blood is Catherine's central image. Almost all her letters begin with greetings in the sacred blood, and she screamed out "Blood! blood!" on her deathbed.[157] Although devotion to the blood of Christ had a long history in late medieval Italy and Christ's blood was, to earlier devotees, most fundamentally a symbol of the washing away of sin, blood to Catherine was food or life.[158] Blood "feeds" or "is eaten" in her letters almost as frequently as it "cleanses" or "washes."[159] Two aspects of the religious world of the fourteenth century as Catherine experienced it help explain why blood as food was central to her thought: her reverence for the clergy, and her devotion to the humanity of Christ.

Catherine revered priests as "little christs"; her awe, like Margaret of Cortona's, centered on their control of the eucharist, which she craved.[160] But in Catherine's day the cup was denied to the laity altogether, and Catherine's extravagant respect for priests' authority thus focused on their control of and access to the awesome and taboo chalice. It is significant that she repeatedly referred to clergy as "ministers of the blood," not "of the body."[161] She called the pope "vicar of Christ's blood" and said that he held "the keys of the blood."[162] In eucharistic miracles, it was blood that remained in her mouth or poured from it, although what she actually received was bread (interpreted, of course, as both elements in the theological doctrine of concomitance).[163]

Blood may also have had, to Catherine, other associations with an authority and power she herself wielded only indirectly, through prayer or persuasion. Blood was in general a more public and social symbol than bread, as well as a more ambivalent symbol. Bread symbolized household and charity and support of life, but blood symbolized war, civil strife, and executions. Moreover, it was the support of life even more basically than bread, because it coursed through the veins as life itself.[164] In the famous incident in which Catherine stood beneath the scaffold to receive the head of a young man executed for a political crime, the blood that covered her and smelled so sweet was clearly a symbol of politics and the public arena, of suffering and injustice, and of life itself—all of which could be redeemed only by assimilation to Christ's innocent blood, on which we feed in suffering and service.[165]

Catherine's craving for blood was not merely a craving for encounter in Christ with all that was denied her socially and politically: the chalice, the power of the clergy, the public arena. She also craved blood because she craved identification with the humanity of Christ, and she saw this humanity as physicality. Although scholars have sometimes seen the spirituality of all late medieval women as "erotic" or "nuptial,"[166] Catherine's sense of the flesh is extremely unerotic. She writes, especially to women, of "putting on the nuptial garment," but the phrase means suffering.[167] In her repeated descriptions of climbing up Christ's body from foot to side to mouth, the body is either a female body that nurses or a piece of flesh that one puts on oneself or sinks into.[168] Physicality is the foreskin of the Circumcision—flesh that bleeds.[169] Catherine understood union with Christ not as an erotic fusing with a male figure but as a taking in and a taking on—a becoming—of Christ's flesh itself.

In fact, Catherine clearly associated Christ's physicality with the female body, underlining thereby both her capacity for assimilation to Christ and her capacity, like his, for service. She called humanity "Adam" as well as "Eve," of course.[170] But, adopting both the gender stereotypes of her day and the age-old Christian notion of female weakness, she associated fleshliness and sensuality especially with "woman."[171] She stressed repeatedly that Mary provided in her womb the stuff (i.e., the menstrual matter) from which the Spirit fashioned Christ's human body.[172] And she repeatedly called Christ's wound a breast.[173] Indeed, to Catherine Christ was a nursing mother more often than a bridegroom.

Catherine's image of Christ as maternal, which had a long ancestry in twelfth- and thirteenth-century spirituality, must be understood against the background of contemporary physiological theory.[174] Medieval natural philosophers thought that breast milk was blood. Thus blood was the quintessential food—and it was poured out as food or provided as the basic stuff of life only by female bodies. Therefore, as I shall discuss at greater length in chapter 9, the female body was an obvious image for a God who died to give birth to the world and bled to feed all souls. Catherine herself noted explicitly that the female body is food and therefore an appropriate image for both male and female self-sacrifice. When she wrote to her own natural brother about his obligations to Lapa, she stressed that a mother's body gives flesh to and feeds its child.[175] She continued this theme when she described charity:

> On how sweet a mother is charity! She nourishes on her breast the children [i.e., the virtues] to whom she gives birth. . . . She *is* a food, which nurtures the soul in its hunger. . . . And the soul, consumed in this furnace, wants to eat the food forever, and the more it eats the more it hungers.[176]

She wrote to a cleric: "Be faithful. Run with Mary's desire to honor God and save souls. . . . Guard your own soul and body so you can nourish other souls and give birth to them."[177]

At the heart of Catherine's understanding of "eating," "hungering," and "bleeding," therefore, was identification of serving with suffering. For example, Catherine wrote to the Queen of Hungary about a crusade:

> Truly, noble mother, when the soul beholds the lamb on the wood of the holy cross, because of its ineffable love for creation, she conceives such a great love for the salvation of souls that she would give herself up a hundred thousand times to death to save even one soul from eternal death. And one cannot make a sacrifice more pleasing to God than this. You know that he loves this nourishment so much that he did not fear, in taking it on, bitterness, suffering, death, or outrage. Even our ingratitude did not stop him from running, inebriated and passionate for our salvation, to the opprobrium of the cross. So I invite you . . . to this food. You have found the place where one must take it and the fruit is ripe. . . . The place is the garden of Holy Church, and there is planted the tree on which hangs the fruit, Christ.[178]

To Catherine, suffering was serving because Christ had become flesh—a flesh that, by bleeding and dying, saved the world. Not resurrection then but incarnation was at the center of her theology.[179] It was in suf-

179

fering, not in triumph, that she saw herself becoming Christ—Christ as food and Christ as redemption. Her agonies of starvation, illness, and stigmata *were* the agonies of the cross and of purgatory. Such suffering was fertile and generative, for it was the source of salvation. As she wrote to one of her confessors: "The immaculate lamb [Christ] is food, table, and servant." This table, said Catherine, offered the fruits of true and perfect virtues. "And we who eat at that table become like the food [i.e., Christ], acting not for our own utility but for the honor of God and the salvation of neighbor."[180]

Thus, throughout Catherine's letters, her concern for saving souls through her own agony was expressed in the paired metaphors of feeding and fasting. Feeding and fasting were central practices in her life as well. Catherine rejected food, as she rejected her own flesh; yet she gave food to the poor and hungry. And she ate both pus and the eucharist, confident that the body of God and the bodies of her neighbors were, for herself and for others, the way of salvation. When we turn to the other great Italian Catherine, Catherine of Genoa, the theorist of purgatory, we find a similar conception of suffering as service. To this later Catherine, as to her forerunner, food is the fundamental metaphor—for suffering, for service, and for love.

Three works survive that reflect Catherine of Genoa's teachings, although none was written by her. All three were put together shortly after her death, and two, the *Life* and the *Dialogue*, are partly autobiographical. The *Life* is based on her acts and sayings, taken down after 1495 by her confessor, Marabotto, her spiritual son, Ettore Vernazza, and possibly others. The *Dialogue*, which treats her inner history, is probably a combination of three works. In the last part an unknown author recounts and interprets Catherine's final illness and death in excruciating detail. The first two parts—generally agreed to be of higher literary quality—are also of uncertain authorship. An early tradition attributes the first part to Catherine herself, but some scholars argue that she is unlikely to have dictated such a sophisticated use of dialogue form. All scholars agree that *The Treatise on Purgatory* reflects her own ideas on purgation, at least in its original form (i.e., the first seven chapters). It was probably written down by Vernazza; certain theological glosses were introduced before the official publication in 1551.[181] Thus, although no single sentence of Catherine's work can be trusted as her own language, the treatises taken together give a clear picture of the inner and outer life of a woman in whose piety fasting, eucharist, and suffering were the central foci.[182]

Born in 1447 and refused permission to enter a convent at thirteen, Catherine was plunged into depression by her marriage at age sixteen to a young nobleman, Giuliano Adorno. Her despair at the marriage, into which she was forced for financial and political reasons by an older brother two years after her father's death, was perhaps increased both by the fact that Giuliano's family was an enemy of her own and by what later scholars have called Giuliano's wasteful and dissolute behavior. (Although "dissoluteness" is hard to evaluate across the centuries and might well be exacerbated by a wife's depression, it is certain that Giuliano squandered his family money, for he went bankrupt about 1474, and that he had a mistress and an illegitimate child.) After five years of severe *accidia* and withdrawal, Catherine made an effort to return to social life. She collapsed into even more acute depression at Christmas 1472. A number of things then happened.

Many scholars, wishing to organize mystical and saintly biographies around turning points and into neat stages, see a sudden conversion at her Lenten confession of March, 1473, and her subsequent vision of Christ carrying the cross. It is more accurate, however, to see a period of about three years (or perhaps longer) during which certain external constraints on Catherine's life were removed and she forged for herself, out of a period of severe self-abnegation, a new life pattern in which fasting, eucharistic devotion, serving, and union with Christ were the central motifs.[183] The first months after the confession and vision of 1473 were months of virulent asceticism, including acute food deprivation and illness. Then, between March, 1473, and March, 1476, Catherine's husband went bankrupt and Catherine learned of his mistress and illegitimate child. These events—normally deeply humiliating—were perhaps freeing to a woman who hated her marriage. In any case, they provided for her an opportunity to throw herself into care of the poor and sick and identification with their suffering and destitution. By 1476 Giuliano had agreed to a chaste marriage; by 1478 he joined her in voluntary poverty and in the hospital work in which they spent the rest of their lives. It was during these years that Catherine developed a regular pattern of fasting and eucharistic craving; she was permitted daily communion from 1474 on.[184] This pattern lasted until she was fifty-two years old, at which point she relaxed her rigid fasting behavior simultaneously with relinquishing responsibility for her soul into the hands of a confessor and spiritual director.[185] (She had spent her adult years without one.) She died at sixty-three, in an acute illness that once again made eating impossible.[186]

Like Angela of Foligno and Catherine of Siena, Catherine of Genoa—in the long period between 1476 and 1499—combined periodic inedia with eating both filth and the body of God. Moreover, like her two predecessors, she explicitly connects these forms of eating and not eating. Catherine took in illness and filth by mouth.[187] She kissed a tertiary suffering from plague and caught the disease. She rubbed her nose in pus and ate scabs and lice in order to overcome her nausea at illness.[188] In the initial crisis after March, 1473, she attacked her body ferociously, adulterating her food to kill her sense of taste. She almost completely ceased to eat and she tried to stop sleeping. She was afflicted with atrocious hunger and thirst. After 1476 she settled into a pattern of fasting every Advent and Lent on only water, vinegar, and salt, during which period she was unable to keep food in her stomach without vomiting. She appears to have worried about her inedia, fearing it might be pride or morbid self-punishment, for one version of the *Life* reports in passing that she asked her confessor whether she should force herself to eat.[189] Like Catherine of Siena, she developed what appears to us a bizarre relationship to bodily sensations, experiencing burning or extreme cold, heaviness, convulsions, and invisible stigmata.[190] She sometimes bit or burned herself while in trances.[191] She felt hunger and thirst so extreme she licked the earth in agony, yet she claimed she experienced no desire to eat.[192] She spoke explicitly of the need to destroy what we would call the ego or break its boundaries, insisting on using *we* instead of the pronoun *I* or her name.[193] Yet both the *Life* and the *Dialogue* insist on the centrality to her of eating holy food. She tells us that three days after her confession of 1473 she "felt the pull of Holy Communion, which from that day never left her."[194] One version of the *Life* attributes to her sentiments that, whether authentic or inauthentic for Catherine herself, are typical of late-fifteenth-century religious women:

> When she was at mass she was often so occupied interiorly with her Lord, that she did not hear a word; but when the time came to receive communion she accused herself, and would say: "Oh! my Lord, it seems to me that if I were dead, I should come to life, in order to receive thee, and

if an unconsecrated host were given to me, that I should know it by the taste, as one knows wine from water."[195]

She said repeatedly that she felt hunger only for communion.[196]

The second of Catherine's spiritual dialogues weaves together these themes of eating and not eating in a way that clearly implies that eating pain and eating Christ substitute for eating ordinary food.[197] In this dialogue, the personification Humanity (i.e., human frailty) first attacks its own need for friends and for food. Once it conquers ordinary hunger, it allows itself to desire true nourishment, and God gives communion. Humanity is then so inebriated with sweetness that Soul (another personification) is frightened and asks God to remove the feelings of bliss. Catherine comments that Soul does not want sweetness or reward, but God sends it. She also suggests that God sends service of the sick to give Humanity something to do,[198] and she speaks of serving in food metaphors, as "kneading bread" or "fasting,"[199] just before she tells of eating "lice as big as pearls" "many times."[200] Thus, in Catherine's life, as she herself interprets it in the *Dialogue*, ordinary food is a symbol for inept, rebellious body (which she often calls "humanity" [*umanità*]).[201] But food is also a symbol of God. For food is eucharist, that celestial sweetness through which the soul achieves mystical union. And food is the filth and horror of suffering, through which one also joins God and serves one's fellow creatures. Desire for God is hunger—insatiable hunger.[202] The food that is God and the food that is neighbor are thus the nourishment we crave, inebriated yet unfilled.

At the core of Catherine's spirituality is suffering, that paradoxical suffering which for her, as for Hadewijch and Beatrice, is ultimate pain and the ecstasy beyond. The suffering *is* purgatory, and in a sense, therefore, purgatory itself is both Christ's death agonies on the cross and the agonies of the soul as it is annihilated in the fiery bliss, the devouring mouth, of God.[203] Catherine's purgatory is Christ's love, with which we can never fully join. It is *imitatio Christi*, but an *imitatio* never fully achieved. It expiates our sins and those of others, but it is not so much a place or a time as an *experience* of purging, and we could not wish it a moment shorter, for ourselves or for others. Catherine writes:

> In purgatory, great joy and great suffering do not exclude one another. . . .
> And if the living were to offer alms for the benefit of the souls in purgatory, to shorten the assigned time of their purgation, still those souls

could not turn with affection to watch, but would leave all things to God, who is paid as he wishes. . . . What he wills for them is what gives them joy.[204]

To Catherine, purging is a suffering so vast that in it fuse one's own cleansing, one's neighbor's expiation, and the death agonies of Christ. In suffering one is therefore serving neighbor and hungering for God.

Catherine says explicitly that of all the metaphors one might choose for this moment which is at the heart of the universe, the metaphor she prefers is that of hunger for bread. In the *Treatise on Purgatory* she writes:

> Joy in God . . . is the end of these souls. . . . No image or metaphor can adequately convey this truth. One example, however, comes to mind. Let us imagine that in the whole world there was but one bread and that it could satisfy the hunger of all. Just to look at it would be to nourish oneself. That bread is what a healthy man, with an appetite, would seek; and when he could not find it or eat it, his hunger would increase indefinitely. Aware that that bread alone could assuage his hunger, he would also know that without it his hunger could never abate. Such is the hell of the hungry who, the closer they come to this bread, the more they are aware that they do not as yet have it. Their yearning for that bread increases, because it is their joy. Were they to know that they would never see the bread, that would be perfect hell, the case of the damned souls who no longer hope to see the true bread and the true God. The hungry souls in purgatory, however, though they do not see as much of the bread as they would wish, hope to see it and fully enjoy it one day. This, then, is their suffering, the waiting for the bread that will take away their hunger.[205]

Throughout Catherine's teachings, hunger and fire (reflecting her own bodily experiences of atrocious hunger and burning flashes) are the basic images for desire and for encounter with God. In the *Life* as in the *Purgatory*, we find eating bread as an elaborate spiritual metaphor. In chapter 32 (of the 1551 edition) the annihilation of ordinary food by a devouring body becomes an image for the purification—even annihilation—of the self in mystical union. Here the recorder of Catherine's sayings reports:

> "Take a loaf," said the saint, "and eat it, and after you have eaten it, its substance goes to the nutriment of the body, and what is superfluous

passes away; for if nature retained it, having no need of it, the body would die. Now if that bread should say to the body: Why do you deprive me of my existence, for by my nature I am not satisfied to be thus reduced to nothingness? If I could, I would defend myself from thee, for it is natural for every creature to preserve itself,—the body would answer: Bread, thy being is designed for my support, which is more worthy than thee, and hence thou shouldst be more content with the end for which thou wast created, than with thy own being; for if it were not for thy end, thy being would have no value but to be thrown aside, as something worthless and dead. It is thy end which gives thee a dignity to which thou canst not attain but by means of thy annihilation. If thou wouldst live for thy end, thou wouldst not care for thy being, but wouldst say: Quickly, quickly, take me from myself, and let me attain my end for which I am created."[206]

Christ's blood, both as drink and as cleansing water, was also a key metaphor to Catherine. She received a vision of the bleeding Christ after her traumatic Lenten confession of 1473. And the redactor of her *Life* reports that:

filled with compassion for the blindness of man, she said "If by taking my blood and giving it to man to drink, I could make known to him this truth [about love], I would give it all for love of him. I cannot endure the thought that man, created for the good that I see and know, should lose it. . . . If I knew how, I would leave nothing undone to make known how dreadful a thing is this privation of the love of God."[207]

Thus Catherine of Genoa used hunger as a metaphor for insatiable desire, eating as a metaphor for love, and bread as a symbol of self and of God. She consciously and explicitly chose food as her central image for mystical union. Moreover, Catherine lived these figures of speech. Fasting, feeding others, and feasting on the eucharist were not, to her, occasional practices. They were the way she loved her neighbor and drew near her God.

Not all women writers, of course, made food so central an image as did Hadewijch, Beatrice, and the two Catherines. To the German mystics Hildegard of Bingen, Elizabeth of Schönau, Gertrude the Great, and Mechtild of Hackeborn it was a useful metaphor but not a central one; nor was food a crucial image to Julian of Norwich or Margaret of Oingt. And Margaret Porete, whose *Mirror of Simple Souls* was condemned in the early fourteenth century, rejected the whole tradition of affective spirituality with an attack on "works" (such as fasting and communion) that went far beyond Tauler's or Eckhart's. But, to all these writers (except Margaret Porete), the humanity of Christ, understood as physicality, was crucial; and eucharistic devotion was important to them all.[208] Moreover, there are other women writers from the period, for example Mechtild of Magdeburg, Angela of Foligno, and Margery Kempe, to whom food practices and food images were fundamental.[209] And in the four great writers examined here, food, hunger, eating, and feeding were far more vibrant and complex images than they ever were to male writers, even those such as Ruysbroeck and Tauler who helped elaborate late medieval eucharistic devotion.[210] Furthermore, to each woman the image resonated with its own particular power.

Hadewijch's union with God was erotic and anguished; her basic food metaphor was hunger. Beatrice's union was insane and frantic; her metaphors were drinking and bleeding. Catherine of Siena's encounter with God was in suffering and serving; her rich images revolved most basically around eating and blood. To Catherine of Genoa, union was suffering, even annihilation; the metaphor was eating and being eaten. What ties these distinctive spiritualities together is the same pattern we find in women's lives, as seen by themselves and by male biographers. It is a threefold pattern: women fast, women feed others, and women eat (but never ordinary food). Women fast—and hunger becomes an image for excruciating, never-satiated love of God. Women feed—and their bodies become an image of suffering poured out for others. Women eat—and whether they devour the filth of sick bodies or the blood and flesh of the eucharist, the foods are Christ's suffering and Christ's humanity, with which one must join before approaching triumph, glory, or divinity.

III

THE EXPLANATION

6

Food as control of self

*It is an often discussed question why anorexia nervosa is so conspicu-
ously less frequent in males than in females. It may well be related to
pubescence itself, to the psychological effects of the male sex hor-
mones. . . . It is quite possible that the characteristic slave-like attachment of a child to the mother is more apt to develop in a girl and
efforts to solve psychological problems through manipulation of the
body are also considered characteristically female. It is probable that it
is unusual for a boy to be caught in this developmental impasse. In
addition, male pubescence will flood a boy, even one who has this
type of attachment, with such powerful new sensations of a more ag-
gressive self-awareness that the event of puberty makes a new self-
assertion possible.*

HILDE BRUCH
Eating Disorders
(1973)[1]

WHY IS FOOD so central a theme in the religiosity of medieval
women? The answer is complicated, and it will not do to rush to a single
explanation. Indeed, the remainder of this book provides several answers
and groups them into two kinds. In this chapter and the next, I describe
the various functions food served for women—the manifold ways in
which eating, feeding, and not eating enabled them to control their bodies and their world. In the last three chapters, I treat the symbolic meanings food held for women and the significance, for both sexes, of the
notion that woman is food. If the reasoning in chapters 6 and 7 at times
finds, in words and deeds, import that medieval people would not have
recognized, the final chapters take seriously the significances medieval
women and men attributed to their own experience.

My full explanation, then, is multifaceted. But I can begin simply.
Food is important to women religiously because it is important socially.

It is a fact cross-culturally that food is particularly a woman-con-
trolled resource. In the majority of cultures, food preparation is a wom-

an's role.[2] It was certainly so in medieval Europe. One of the earliest extant French cookbooks, the fourteenth-century *Viandier*, assumes that basic cookery is done by women. The author says he does not describe the preparation of certain items, such as cabbage, leeks, and veal with saffron and pepper sauce, because "women and their mistresses and everyone know how to cook them."[3] But, beyond women, "everyone" did not know. When an elderly Parisian husband wrote a now famous book of housekeeping advice for his young bride about 1392, his book revealed that he himself was not a cook. A recent historian points out that he "describes certain aspects of cookery any working cook would have taken for granted."[4] Although the first cookbooks were written by men and the job of chef in the wealthiest households went to males, everyone agreed that the basic social responsibility for food preparation was woman's.[5]

Indeed, cooking was so much a woman's role that it appeared, to men, not merely arcane but threatening. When medieval men projected their hostility toward women into suspicion of what went on in the women's quarters, they frequently spoke of women's control of food.[6] Men suspected women (especially wives) of manipulating them by adding potions or poisons to their meals. The *Decretum* of Burchard of Worms, compiled between 1008 and 1012, lists the spells and incantations resorted to by women; most of them involve manipulating food—for example, increasing or decreasing the sexual ardor of a husband by adding to his food such things as menstrual blood, semen, or dough kneaded with a woman's buttocks.[7]

There are many reasons for the association of women and food preparation that is found in so many cultures. One reason seems to be the biological analogy. Through lactation, woman is the essential food provider and preparer. As the novelist Elias Canetti expresses it:

> In a *family* the husband contributes food and the wife prepares it for him. The fact that he habitually eats what she has prepared constitutes the strongest link between them.
> The *mother* . . . is the core and very heart of this institution. A mother is one who gives her own body to be eaten. She first nourishes the child in her womb and then gives it her milk. This activity continues in a less concentrated form throughout many years. . . . Her passion is to give food.[8]

Indeed, in a number of cultures (e.g., modern Latin America, Indonesia) women prepare and serve food but do not eat with the family. In most complex societies, even upper-class women who are freed from the task of food preparation still have the responsibility of supervising those who cook. There is certainly reason to think that eating in the European Middle Ages was stereotyped as a male activity and food preparation as a female one. The sexes were often separated at medieval banquets, and women were sometimes relegated to watching from the galleries.[9] The history of Western cooking, as reflected in cookbooks, diaries, and memoirs, suggests that "heavy" food, especially meat, was seen as more appropriate for men and lighter food for women,[10] in part because meat had, for a thousand years, been seen as an aggravator of lust.[11] Cookbooks came increasingly to suggest that women—who prepared the meals—hardly needed to eat at all.[12] We now know that such notions, by the nineteenth century, actually produced dietary deficiencies in women;[13] indeed, the twentieth-century Western craze for female dieting may owe something to this older assumption that women prepare food and men eat it.

This traditional association of women with food preparation *rather than* food consumption helps us to understand certain aspects of the religious significance of food. To prepare food is to control food. Moreover, food is not merely *a* resource that women control; it is *the* resource that women control—both for themselves and for others. In the long course of Western history, economic resources were controlled by husbands, fathers, uncles, or brothers. Yet human beings can renounce, or deny themselves, only that which they control. Thus, in periods such as the later Middle Ages in which world-denial was a favorite religious response, women found it easier to renounce food than anything else (for example, money, sexual activity, or family ties).[14] It was far more difficult to flee one's family, to deny a father's plans for one's betrothal, or to refuse sexual relations to a husband than it was to stop eating. In periods in which charity and service were deeply valued, women found food the easiest thing to give away. Slipping out of the kitchen or banquet hall with food for the poor was the most convenient, the least ostentatious, service. Moreover, both women's food distribution and their fasting appeared culturally acceptable forms of asceticism, because what women ordinarily did most visibly—as housewives, mothers, or the mistresses of great castles—was to prepare and serve food rather than to eat it. Yet if women's food distribution or food avoidance became acute enough to disrupt their role as food preparer, it could wreak havoc with social relations. It could therefore—a point to which I shall return—be an extremely effective form of manipulation.

At the simplest level of explanation, therefore, we can say that medieval women fasted and fed others because preparation and distribution of food were women's special concerns. It is worth noting that in many cultures, fasting as a religious activity is done primarily by women, although fasting as scientific experiment or as political protest is usually performed by men. Among Eskimos, for example, it is customary for the husband to go out fishing while the wife remains at home fasting for a good catch.[15] In Old Testament Judaism, fasting is almost the only religious act for which women (e.g., Judith, Esther, Sarah, the mothers of Samuel and Samson) are prominent models of piety. In India, where the hunger strike was used very effectively by Gandhi and his followers as a *political* weapon, fasting is performed primarily by women when it is offered as a *religious* act for private or familial gains. (The most common pattern is for a woman to fast in order to gain a specific benefit for a male relative.)[16] Gandhi in fact learned fasting from his devout mother, who added fasts to the already strict Hindu schedule.[17] In the European tradition also, the hunger strike has been effectively used by men for political purposes. Its recent popularity with the Irish Republican Army has a long and specific tradition behind it. Medieval Ireland (like medieval India) had an actual legal procedure of "fasting to destrain," in which a creditor fasted against a debtor to gain repayment or a man fasted against his adversary to gain restitution.[18] In Tudor/Stuart England and among the Puritans in the New World, public fasts, proclaimed by the government to expiate or protest particular events, became increasingly political. The 1774 fast of the Massachusetts and Virginia colonists to express dissatisfaction with England was the first modern mass political protest by fasting.[19] But, as we have seen, fasting as an individual act of world renunciation has been more central in the religiosity of European women than of men.[20]

Fasting and charitable food distribution, and their miraculous counterparts—surviving on the eucharist alone, food multiplication miracles, the female body that exudes food or curing liquid—were thus, in one sense, religious expressions of social facts. They manifested in religious behavior the sexual division of labor. Since late medieval spirituality valued both renunciation and service, each gender renounced and distributed what it most effectively controlled: men gave up money, property, and progeny; women gave up food. Moreover, such a division of religious response clearly suited medieval men. Several scholars have pointed out that late twelfth- and early thirteenth-century women (e.g., Clare of Assisi and Mary of Oignies) who wished to follow the new ideal of mendicant poverty—that is, to renounce economic supports—were simply not permitted either by their families or by religious authorities to do so.[21] The older aristocracy and the new urban patriciate might allow or encourage daughters to withdraw into convents or hermit cells or to perform fasts and vigils under their fathers' or uncles' or husbands' roofs, but women wandering and begging and living without servants went too far. So women such as Mary and Clare and Ida of Louvain substituted fasting for other ways of stripping the self of pleasure and support. The thirteenth-century hagiographer Thomas of Cantimpré commented explicitly that Christina the Astonishing gave up food because she had nothing else to give up for Christ.[22] Between the twelfth and the sixteenth century, beguines, tertiaries, devout laywomen who resided in the houses of fathers or spouses, and even nuns whose convent life seemed to them insufficiently austere were able to renounce the world in the midst of abundance by refusing to eat or drink anything that was paid for by family wealth. Margery Kempe fasted at her husband's table; Catherine of Siena and Ida of Louvain refused food provided by their fathers; Elizabeth of Hungary lived among her husband's relatives but refused to eat any food except that purchased with her dowry.[23] Because food preparation was woman's sphere, food asceticism and food distribution were for women obvious modes of imitating the vulnerability and generosity of Christ. Moreover, fasting and feeding were acts of charity and of self-denuding that could be performed even when a woman was unable to determine the framework of institutions or economic supports within which she lived.

The issue of control is, however, much more basic than this analysis suggests. Food-related behavior was central to women socially and religiously not only because food was a resource women controlled but also because by means of food women controlled themselves and their world. Bodily functions, sensations, fertility, and sexuality; husbands, mothers, fathers, and children; religious superiors and confessors; God in his majesty and the boundaries of one's own "self"—all could be manipulated by abstaining from and bestowing food. In order to understand this, we must look closely at women's fasting and feeding behavior. It seems wise to begin with the question I earlier postponed, the question of the applicability of modern psychological or medical models. For in the flood of recent writing on food "disorders," the issue of control has been central. And, as several recent writers have noticed, the fasting behavior of some medieval women clearly fits rather well the modern syndrome known as *anorexia nervosa*. How helpful, then, are modern clinical definitions for our understanding of late medieval piety?

♦ Was Women's Fasting Anorexia Nervosa?

The idea that some saintly or mystical women of the late medieval/early modern period were anorectics is not new. In fact, historians of medicine have vied with each other in finding the earliest cases of eating disorders. One medical historian has argued that it is only in the seventeenth century that we find an account of female fasting sufficiently detailed to fit modern clinical definitions.[24] But some have seen anorectic or anorexia-like behavior in earlier cases.[25] In a bizarre communication to a British medical journal, one doctor recently argued that the legend of the bearded female saint Wilgefortis—which was explained by the great Bollandist scholar Delehaye as springing from misperception of a veiled crucifix—is an early and complete description of the complex of features (including hirsutism) considered by psychologists to characterize anorexia.[26] Earlier in this century Catholic scholars such as Pater and Thurston strove to differentiate "natural" (which sometimes meant pathological, i.e., anorectic or hysterical) and "miraculous" (i.e., supernaturally produced) fasting.[27] And a number of recent scholars have mentioned in passing—sometimes quite defensively—the possibility that prominent medieval saints such as Catherine of Siena and Catherine of Genoa suffered from anorexia nervosa. Rudolph Bell has recently published a careful and detailed study of anorexia among Italian women from the eleventh to the seventeenth century.[28]

Many of these discussions, whether they grant or refuse the label *anorexia nervosa* to early cases of female fasting, seem to assume that we are in the presence of a trend which we can call either the "secularization" or the "medicalization" of behavior.[29] They assume, that is, that medieval people gave theological significance to behavior that psychiatrists and doctors today see in secular terms, whether medical, psychoanalytical, or psychodynamic. Thus they sometimes suggest that medieval women and their confessors attribute not eating to divine or demonic inspiration whereas modern women and their therapists blame it either on psyche or on biochemistry. (This claim can be used either to support the notion that such fasting is anorexia nervosa, because it is the same phenomenon differently interpreted, or to deny the notion that such fasting is anorexia, because "anorexia" is a modern cultural construct.) The argument is related to the idea, which has been much fought over by historians of psychiatry, that late medieval witches and/or their victims were frequently the society's mentally ill—often hysterics and sometimes anorectics—whose behavior was attributed by theologians to both moral failing and demonic possession.[30] But, in order to understand medieval behavior, the first thing we must note is that such a claim is not quite right. It is not quite true (although there are elements of truth in it) to say that fasting was theologized in the Middle Ages and is secularized or medicalized today. As the cases I discuss above make clear, medieval people did not see all refusal to eat as "fasting" (i.e., asceticism) or all extended abstinence as miraculous. And the case of the modern mystic Simone Weil and her many admirers, like the case of the German stigmatic Theresa of Konnersreuth, makes it clear that not all female abstinence in the twentieth century is medically or psychologically interpreted.[31]

Medieval writers had in fact a number of paradigms for explaining extended periods of not eating. Not eating was sometimes seen as supernaturally caused—either miraculous or demonic. It was sometimes seen as naturally caused; as such, it was sometimes but by no means always interpreted as a condition to be cured. (Both miraculous and naturalistic explanations were sometimes used by theologians—as the Council of Trent used the case of Nicholas of Flüe—to prove the doctrine of transubstantiation.) Not eating was sometimes interpreted as deliberate fraud or as self-delusion. We can find all three paradigms even in early saints' lives and chronicles. The notion that refusal to eat can be fraudulent or attention-getting behavior, or illness, was no new discovery in the sixteenth and seventeenth centuries.

Inedia appears in a number of medieval documents as simply a physiological condition. The author of the ninth-century life of Walburga, for example, presents a case of loathing for food as an illness, which the saint cures. A fifteenth-century life of Colette of Corbie also treats inability to eat as an illness.[32] Roger Bacon said of a thirteenth-century Englishwoman that her survival without eating was not miraculous, "but rather a work of nature," and gave a somewhat tortured but ingenious explanation of how the balance of elements in her body might make this possible since nothing came in as food, but nothing went out as excrement. Thomas Netter, in a fifteenth-century theological treatise, argued that Joan the Meatless distinguished consecrated from unconsecrated hosts by a natural skill, because her condition was such that she could not bear any bodily food. Catherine of Siena herself referred to her inability to eat as an "infirmity," not a voluntary religious practice. Lidwina of Schiedam claimed that she deserved no praise for abstinence since she was in fact unable to eat. Alpaïs of Cudot indicated her understanding of her condition as an illness (which was to be patiently borne) by having a vision of the devil as a doctor who offered to cure it. As early as the ninth century, chroniclers were busy collecting stories of freaks and marvels and did not present all cases of women who refused to eat as examples of sanctity or illustrations of God's power. The very fact that supposed saints such as John the Good of Mantua and Columba of Rieti sometimes ate before an audience to demonstrate that they *could* eat—i.e., that their abstinence was voluntary—suggests that medieval interpreters drew a clear distinction between inability to eat and asceticism. Some authors found only the latter a mark of sanctity, although some (for example, Elsbet Achler's hagiographer) did present any surviving without eating as a mark of divine favor.

Medieval people themselves thought that self-starvation was sometimes a delusion and sometimes a carefully orchestrated fraud. When we note the charges against which holy women defended themselves we see quite clearly what a number of their contemporaries suspected. Catherine of Siena was accused of being deluded, even of being a witch. Columba of Rieti was accused of merely wasting away from love-sickness. Both Catherine and Columba defended themselves against the charge that their refusal to eat was a form of suicide and therefore a mortal sin. It was Catherine's own definition of her behavior as an infirmity that enabled her to claim that eating would be an even more grievous suicide. Moreover, if Elsbet Achler did not hide food under her bed, someone else hid it there to create the illusion of the fraud her sisters suspected.[33] And in the fifteenth and sixteenth centuries several fraudulent fasters were unmasked.[34] The fact that there were "frauds" indicates that those who "pretended" expected to gain prestige—whether as freak or as saint. But the rather defensive tone of hagiographers (such as the biographer of Columba of Rieti) who claimed that fasting saints showed no signs of emaciation indicates that "miraculous abstinences" were as regularly doubted as applauded.

It thus appears that medieval writers themselves spoke rather differently of fasting as voluntary penance and of cases of women, especially young girls, who were unable to eat. If they did not treat these latter cases as matters for doctors alone, they also did not see them simply as aspects of penitential asceticism. Medieval people themselves were clear about the difference between choosing to renounce food, one of the pleasures of civilization, and being in the throes of a behavior pattern that made eating impossible. They even occasionally saw saints such as Colette and Walburga, who *chose* not to eat, as patrons and curers of those who suffered from what we would call food disorders. If medieval chroniclers reported certain refusals to eat as freakish behavior not necessarily connected to religiosity, what then is to prevent us from seeing them as cases of anorexia nervosa, having, as some current medical opinion argues, a biochemical basis?

Twentieth-century work on anorexia and the closely related disorder bulimia (binge-eating) offers many explanations of the syndrome. Psychodynamic interpretation relates the behavior to neurosis, generated fundamentally by an overcontrolling parent; behaviorist theory sees bingeing or self-starvation as learned behavior; sociocultural theory relates food disorders to the cultural requirements of slimness and nurturing imposed on women. Biochemical explanations have been particularly popular recently. One current variant sees anorexia-bulimia as a type of biologically caused depression with a pharmacological cure. (In the past few years researchers have had notable success curing binge-eating with drugs long used to treat biochemically caused depression.)[35] Moreover, research on the physiological bases of psychological differences between the sexes suggests that differences in male and female metabolism make it easier for women to fast, and even that men and women crave different types of food (particularly protein and carbohydrates, respectively) because these foods actually taste different to them and are used by their bodies in different ways.[36] There is thus evidence that some eating behavior that departs significantly from the ordinary does in fact have a physiological basis, and nothing one could adduce about medieval people would either confirm or deny this conclusion.[37]

Even for the modern period, however, there are facts that confute a rigidly biochemical explanation. Most researchers agree that the incidence of bulimia and anorexia is increasing rapidly today, although recent talk of an "epidemic" may be journalistic over-reaction.[38] No behavior with a purely biological cause could fluctuate as drastically in incidence as anorexia is agreed to do. The behavior, then, whatever basis it may in some cases have in the physiology and the family history of individuals, is also, in the very particular form it takes, learned; and it is learned from a culture that has complex and long-standing traditions about women, about bodies, and about food. Whatever biological or psychological underpinnings it may have, twentieth-century anorexia has a cultural context.[39]

The same is true for medieval cases of food delusion and miraculous abstinence. Although some medieval women—for example, Alpaïs and Lidwina of Schiedam—were unable to eat for grave physical reasons, there is much evidence to suggest that the virtuoso fasting behavior of women must be explained primarily in a cultural context. The first and most basic argument for a cultural explanation comes from the distribution of medieval cases.

Miraculous abstinence itself is attributed only to men in the patristic period. Several of the Desert Fathers of the third and fourth centuries were said to subsist on the eucharist alone. When such stories are taken up by theologians in the fifteenth century as proof of doctrinal matters they begin once again to be told occasionally of men. But in the long intervening medieval period they are told only of women.[40] No biological cause could possibly explain such discrepancies in distribution. Even if we assume that the incidence of a behavior remains constant and merely the reporting of it changes (an assumption we are hardly entitled to make), then the reporting itself becomes the interesting and retrievable phenomenon. And what is chosen for reporting is clearly culturally conditioned. Moreover, the medieval evidence suggests that cultural models are crucial in producing food-related behavior.

Where extended abstinence is reported for men, the model of the Desert Fathers is clearly at work. The story, told in Lidwina's *vita*, of a certain Gerard who went from Cologne to Egypt, climbed a tree, and lived there miraculously for years on manna from heaven is so obviously a re-telling of patristic material that it deserves little credence as contemporary reporting. And many thirteenth-, fourteenth-, and fifteenth-century women (for example, Mary of Oignies, Catherine of Siena, Colette) were seen by their admirers through lenses shaped by patristic legend. This is a cultural model in the most obvious sense. The ninth-century life of Walburga suggests a far more subtle shaping of behavior by cultural expectation. The stories of Irchinbald and Friderade told there (see above, pp. 89–90) are both stories of individuals who, for reasons that are undoubtedly partly physiological, have uncontrollable food reactions—first hunger, then revulsion. The action of the saint's relics and the expectations of observers produce opposite results in the two cases, however. Walburga "cures" the man; she fails to "cure" the woman, and another interpretation is then placed on the woman's behavior. As the story goes, the man's gluttony is followed by loathing for food, and the saint's relics then enable him to return to normal eating. But the girl's gluttony, which did not end until she confessed it as a terrible guilt, was followed by food revulsion that a sympathetic nun could not cure. Those around the girl then came to see the not eating as a marvel and had it attested to by a priest. It seems likely that the divergent outcomes of the two stories had something to do with the expectations of those who viewed the two afflicted people. Not eating seemed to them a more appropriate story for a woman. As gluttony in a woman was a more terrible guilt, so in her, not eating was less likely to be "cured" or in need of "cure." Thus the prevalence of not eating among women seems to have something to do with which behaviors the culture saw as behaviors "to be cured."

What determines whether an episode is seen as something "to be cured" in a given culture is complex. But for the late Middle Ages there is clear evidence that behavior and occurrences that both we and medieval people see as "illnesses" are less likely to be described as something "to be cured" when they happen to women than when they happen to men. Women's illness was "to be endured," not "cured." Patient suffering of disease or injury was a major way of gaining sanctity for females but not for males. As Weinstein and Bell have demonstrated, women account for only 17.5 percent of those canonized in the later Middle Ages, but they account for 53.2 percent of those saints in whose lives patient bearing of infirmity was the central factor in reputation for sanctity. Ernst Benz has catalogued the prominence of sickness as a theme in women's visions.[41] Indeed, the *vitae* of some women saints, such as Serafina of San Gimignano (d. 1253), have as their sole theme the saint's illness.[42] And many holy women desired to be ill. Villana de' Botti refused prayers for relief of sickness; Gertrude of Helfta embraced headaches as a source of grace; Beatrice of Nazareth, who desired the torments of illness, was healed almost against her wishes; Margaret of Ypres so desired to join with Christ's suffering that she prayed for her infirmities to last beyond the grave.[43] Dauphine of Puimichel (d. 1360) even suggested that if people knew how useful diseases were for self-discipline, they would purchase them in the marketplace.[44] Julian of Norwich asked for and received the grace of sickness and death in literal *imitatio Christi*. In her thirtieth year, she "died" and returned to life, while receiving a vision of the Crucifixion with "the red blood running down . . . , hot and flowing freely and copiously, a living stream."[45]

Not just illness in general but the specific illness of not being able to eat was embraced by medieval women. Alpaïs and Lidwina rejoiced in their inedia and saw the desire to be cured as a temptation. Catherine of Siena refuted charges of suicide or stubbornness by interpreting her eating behavior as infirmity.

Of course, not everyone saw illness as desirable. Lidwina herself hated her illness when she was first afflicted. The heroic embracing of sickness characterized only saints. But it seems to have characterized saintly women far more often than saintly men.

The growing incidence of cases of female abstinence in the later Middle Ages occurs in the context of other new miracles. Miraculous abstinence increases as female eucharistic devotion increases and as such devotion becomes more and more literally the conviction that taking the eucharist is feeding on the body of God. Miraculous abstinence also increases markedly in the centuries in which stigmata and other miracles of bodily manipulation first appear. Between the late twelfth century and the sixteenth, many women were reported to experience the wounds of Christ appearing upon their bodies and bleeding—a miracle never before reported.[46] Francis of Assisi (and the modern figure Padre Pio) are the only males who are believed to have possessed all five of Christ's wounds in visible stigmata; and they are not said to have displayed periodic bleeding.[47] But many cases were reported in the late Middle Ages of women who displayed full stigmata which bled in a rhythmic pattern—most frequently, on Fridays. All cases of red marks (called espousal rings) appearing miraculously around fingers are, not too surprisingly, female. Most cases of bodily elongation are female. And in the medieval and modern periods most stories of sweet-smelling bodies, living and dead, are told about women, although (like tales of surviving on the eucharist) such stories are told of men in antiquity.[48] I shall return to the significance of these new miracles below. My point here is that abstinence becomes an important characteristic of women's piety in the same period that sees an increase in several types of female miracles of bodily manipulation and an increase in the extent and literalism of women's devotion to holy food. Thus cultural as well as biological causes clearly lie behind women's fasting, for fasting is only one aspect of a broad spectrum of behaviors that appear in the later Middle Ages because of changing cultural values and images.

Does it make sense, however, to apply the label *anorexia nervosa* to the fasting behavior of late medieval women if we use a psychological rather than a biochemical understanding of anorexia? The answer depends in part on which definition of *anorexia* we choose. Current psychological definitions differ, and many are so narrow and culture-bound as to be quite obviously inapplicable to women's behavior before the nineteenth century.[49] If anorexia is defined as "the relentless pursuit of thinness" or as "dieting" that has gone out of control, then anorexia can be diagnosed only in cultures that associate thinness with beauty.[50] And dieting was not, of course, a medieval practice, nor thinness a medieval value.[51] But other psychological definitions of anorexia are considerably subtler and more flexible than those that connect it narrowly to twentieth-century notions of female attractiveness.

The German-American psychiatrist Hilde Bruch describes anorexia as "self-inflicted starvation in the absence of recognizable organic disease and in the midst of ample food."[52] The Italian psychiatrist Mara Selvini Palazzoli sees anorexia/bulimia as a deliberate struggle against persistent hunger, although the hunger is usually denied or disguised. The act of eating, says Palazzoli, fills anorectics "with fear and anxiety, and . . . they consider [it] degrading and self-defeating," although they often compulsively urge food on others.[53] These experts agree that the physical symptoms of anorexia, which may be simply the results of starvation, are fatigue, anemia, and amenorrhea. The psychological symptoms are disturbance in body concept, disturbance in perception of bodily functions (often combined with sleeplessness and food-related hyperactivity), and "a paralyzing sense of ineffectiveness." Anorectics typically feel themselves to be puppets, manipulated by others, unable to assert themselves against or to please a controlling parent—usually an energetic and loving mother. Not eating is, for them, an experience of control—control of self, which they substitute for the control of circumstances they are unable to achieve. They tend to see the self as split or to lose all sense of "ego." They are notoriously difficult to treat in psychotherapy because they lie; and the extent of their dishonesty suggests that they are incapable of perceiving their bodily urges and their food-related behavior realistically. They are afraid of touching and being touched, and they fear and dislike their own corporality. The onset of the syndrome comes typically for girls—who are the vast majority of the victims—at puberty. Menstruation, like hunger, is seen as shameful, violating, and threatening; body, like food, is seen as frightening and powerful; sexual maturation is seen as vulnerability, as loss of what little capacity for self-determination the child had possessed. Modern psychodynamic explanations of anorexia/bulimia thus see control as the basic issue. In "typical" anorexia, the woman starves herself as a way of asserting power over—manipulating—her body, which is hated and feared. And primary anorexia is thus distinguished from atypical anorexia (which some writers, for example Bruch, also call "hysteria"), in which the woman is obsessively concerned with food and its significance but manipulation of body size is incidental. Treatment of anorexia, whether in individual or family therapy, focuses on intra-family dynamics, particularly the mother-daughter relationship; it tries to restore to the girl, who has spent her life pleasing others, some sense of setting and meeting her own standards.[54]

How well does this more complex delineation of anorexia nervosa describe medieval behavior? Some medieval *vitae* depict extravagant fasting that appears closer to atypical anorexia (or hysteria) than to primary anorexia. "Hysteria" is no longer recognized by psychiatrists as a diagnosis, and the hysterical behavior so much studied in the nineteenth and early twentieth centuries by Charcot and Freud is, in the late twentieth century, found only in the Third World or in very rural areas of Europe.[55] But some medieval saints in whose lives food was a central obsession seem closer to classic nineteenth-century hysterics than to modern cases of typical anorexia. The term *hysterical* seems to fit at least some of the behavior of Beatrice of Ornacieux and Beatrice of Nazareth, who experienced the kind of choking sensations, known as *globus hystericus*, often characteristic of hysteria or acute anxiety.[56] The term also appears to describe Ida of Louvain and Rita of Cascia, whose bodies broke out in sores (sometimes stigmata) that appeared or disappeared with various levels of religious excitement, as well as Ida of Léau, Christina the Astonishing, and the many other women who experienced trances, "fits," and nosebleeds brought on by mystical desire. The spasms described in the *vita* of Lukardis of Oberweimar, in which her spine was arched and her legs and head drawn back so tightly that her body nearly formed a circle, are a recognized form of hysterical behavior known as *opisthotonos*. (Two famous modern "fasting girls," Margaret Weis and Sarah Jacobs, suffered from similar attacks.)[57] Moreover, in some cases of extended starvation, the inedia appears to be merely one manifestation of general depression. Jane Mary of Maillé, Angela of Foligno, and Catherine of Genoa, for example, themselves connected their inability to eat to what medieval people called *accidia*—a kind of spiritual sloth or despair. And they seem to have recognized marriage as its cause. Such women might perhaps better be labeled depressives than anorectics. But the distinction is unimportant. As I noted above, some recent medical research hypothesizes that anorexia/bulimia is a form of depression.

Despite the fact that some extended starvation seems better described as depression or hysteria, a psychological or psychodynamic definition of anorexia seems at first glance applicable to some medieval women, among them Mary of Oignies, Juliana of Cornillon, Margaret of Ypres, Jane Mary of Maillé, Elizabeth and Margaret of Hungary, Elsbet Achler, Angela of Foligno, Margaret of Cortona, Catherine of Siena, Columba of Rieti, and Catherine of Genoa. These women went through intense periods of inability to eat, often beginning in adolescence. They ate and vomited until they damaged their throats and digestive systems. Some of them (for example, Angela of Foligno and Catherine of Genoa) later "recovered," at least partly, from their fasting; some (for example, Elsbet Achler, Catherine of Siena, and Columba of Rieti) died. Like modern anorectics, many of these saints lost "normal" body concept or perception. They sometimes experienced strange sensations of swelling or flying. Dorothy of Montau and Ida of Louvain, for example, swelled as if pregnant with Christ;[58] Douceline of Marseilles levitated; Beatrice of Ornacieux moved miraculously through or over walls. Both Catherine of Siena and Catherine of Genoa lost the ability to gauge temperature; Catherine of Genoa experienced extreme and mysterious periods of freezing or burning; and on occasion Catherine of Siena, Columba of Rieti, and Lidwina of Schiedam all failed to perceive fire as hot. Many of these women steadfastly denied being hungry although their actions betrayed agonies of greed and thirst, which they focused on the eucharist. Ida of Louvain attacked a locked pyx with her bare hands, desperate for the host.[59] Catherine of Genoa, Columba of Rieti, and Elsbet Achler seem not to have known that they were licking dirty dishes, drinking vinegar, or hoarding food to assuage the hunger they denied feeling.

Many of these women displayed the euphoria, the sleeplessness and hyperactivity, and the casuistry characteristic of present-day anorectics. A number of female saints (for example, Mary of Oignies and Colette) supposedly did not sleep at all, and the town officials of Schiedam testified that Lidwina did not sleep. As we saw in chapter 5, Catherine of Siena prepared food for her family and did their laundry at night; when her mother tried to force her to go to bed, she surreptitiously substituted a board for the mattress. Mary of Oignies, Elizabeth of Hungary, Margaret of Hungary, and Angela of Foligno fed others frantically and obsessively; and Elizabeth, like modern anorectics, riveted attention on her eating behavior by inquiring into the source of every morsel of food. Catherine of Siena and Columba of Rieti developed intense and theologically elaborate defenses of their refusal to eat. Many of these fasting women also combined self-denial with an acute sense of unworthiness and inability to act. Margaret of Cortona, Beatrice of Nazareth, and Juliana of Cornillon, for example, suffered repeated periods of self-doubt; Catherine of Genoa developed the theory that one should destroy the ego so completely that the first-person-singular pronoun would disappear altogether from one's speech.[60]

It thus seems possible to apply to some extended fasting done by medieval women the modern psychological labels *anorexia nervosa* and *bulimia*. There are, however, problems with such application. The first problem is the most obvious: our information about the behavior of these women is often too fragmentary to allow us to "diagnose" (or classify) them properly or to extrapolate from behavior to cause, yet the psychodynamic definition assumes a cause—in family situation and interactions, particularly in the relationship of mother and child. Some of the medieval cases that look most like modern "food disorders" may have origins that have nothing to do with family dynamics. For example, Alpaïs, Lidwina, and Dorothy of Montau refused to eat and felt a guilt over hunger sensations that resembles modern anorectic behavior. All three experienced conflict with their mothers when young. But they clearly suffered from other serious diseases—in Alpaïs's case possibly leprosy, in Lidwina's gangrene, in Dorothy's some sort of defect in the auto-immune system.[61] Thus it is impossible, from the evidence we have, to know to what exactly one should attribute their odd sense of bodily functions, their food craving and vomiting. Moreover, modern researchers have been aware, since the Carnegie Institute experiments of the early years of this century, that starvation or fasting itself produces queer behavior patterns and mental reactions such as exaggerated and exhibitionist claims, paranoia, sleeplessness, inability to gauge body temperature, and euphoria.[62] It is thus possible that some medieval women who *chose* to fast developed, as a *result* of starvation, those psychological characteristics that some recent therapists see as symptoms or even "causes" of the mental disease anorexia nervosa.[63]

The psychodynamic theory of anorexia/bulimia is, moreover, like other diagnostic concepts in modern psychiatry, both reductionist and individualistic in its approach to causation. Just as recent biochemical definitions of anorexia/bulimia display the modern Western tendency to reduce mental and emotional experience to physiological phenomena, so psychodynamic definitions reduce it to dynamics in the psyche or the psyche's personal history. Such definitions assume that the *interpretation* given to behavior by the behaver is an epiphenomenon. What a girl or woman says about her eating behavior is thus labeled "rationalization" or "symptom." According to such interpretation, Catherine of Genoa's notion that her thirst was diabolically induced or Catherine of Siena's argument that eating is suicide can be seen as "casuistry" or "avoidance tactics"—and therefore as further evidence of the inaccurate perception of bodily sensations that characterizes anorectics. Such labeling is, in one sense, quite plausible, of course; the two Catherines do seem occasionally to have used religious categories to distance themselves from their own behavior. But even in these two examples such explanation dismisses ideas (the concepts of *the devil* and *suicide*) that would need historical and cultural explanation if taken seriously. Moreover, the mystical theory advanced by the two Catherines, Beatrice of Nazareth, Mary of Oignies, and Hadewijch (like the theories of the modern mystic Simone Weil) should surely not be treated as (i.e., reduced to) casuistry or loss of ego boundaries. The notion of substituting one's own suffering through illness and starvation for the guilt and destitution of others is not "symptom"—it is theology.

Finally, explanations that work backward from a given behavior to locate its sources in family dynamics can, as critics of psychoanalysis often point out, explain only individual cases. Such explanations can account for the guilt and depression of particular women—for Angela of Foligno's or Margery Kempe's shame over sex in marriage, for example, or Catherine of Siena's guilt about her position as favorite child and survivor.[64] Such explanations cannot, however, account for a widespread pattern of women who refuse to eat, because the explanations do not take seriously enough the symbols involved—"food" and "body"— or see that their meaning *qua* symbols comes from the culture, not from the events of a specific life. The course of an individual life can never explain why the depression or guilt in that life expresses itself in symbols such as "blood" and "hunger" or why a particular theological notion, such as the idea of service through suffering, emerges as a solution. We cannot understand the voluntary starvation of any particular woman unless we understand fully what food means to those among whom she lives. If we take seriously the images and symbols in which guilt, responsibility, joy, and unhappiness manifest themselves, sociological and cultural explanations are necessary. Modern psychodynamic definitions cut a portion of the behavior of medieval women off from its broader and richer context.

Thus whatever physiological and psychodynamic factors may have influenced medieval behavior—and I dismiss neither set of factors— cultural setting was crucial. Biology, psyche, and culture interpenetrated and influenced each other. This means that "medieval anorexia" is not quite the right topic for historical investigation. We should not isolate the rather rare phenomenon called by contemporaries "miraculous abstinence" or "fasting girls" from the broader phenomenon of the overpowering concern with food—with feast as well as fast—that characterizes the lives and writings of medieval women. Not only did medieval women deny themselves food, they also *became* food—in their own eyes and in the eyes of male admirers. And when they ate God, they were not merely focusing their hunger sensations (otherwise unrecognized) on the eucharist. They were also reversing their ordinary cultural role of food preparers and food abstainers. They were "eating" a God whose edible body—a nursing body—was in some sense seen as female and therefore as food. Moreover, women manipulated far more than their own bodies through fasting. They manipulated their families, their religious superiors, and God himself. Fasting was not merely a substitution of pathological and self-defeating control of self for unattainable control of circumstance. It was part of suffering; and suffering was considered an effective activity, which redeemed both individual and cosmos. Women's inedia was therefore not so much bizarre behavior afflicting a few individuals, as part of a broader pattern that included eucharistic devotion, food multiplication miracles, devotion to Christ's humanity, the theology of purgatory, and care of the sick. Such fasting can be understood only if we understand the late medieval notion of *imitatio Christi* as fusion with the suffering physicality of Christ, and late medieval notions of the female as flesh.

Thus it is not particularly helpful to know that Catherine of Siena can be said to be, in the modern sense, anorectic or even bulimic (although the statement is clearly true). The question is: why is food so central to women? Modern definitions of anorexia, while helpful in pointing out that "control" is a key issue in anorectic behavior, obscure our perception of such behavior by glossing over the fact that *food* and *corporality* are at stake. Psychologists today note that anorectics are usually female and that women tend to manipulate their bodies whereas men manipulate their environments.[65] But, as the quotation with which I opened this chapter suggests, they do not know why. Because they do not take seriously the symbols used in women's experience or the ideologies formulated about it, they have cut the phenomenon of refusal to eat off from its context of food-related behavior. Moreover, they have neglected female attitudes toward suffering and generativity. Yet one suspects such attitudes to be part of the context in which modern girls, as well as medieval ones, view both bodies and food.

I will, then, leave aside the fact that some of the fasting behavior of late medieval women can be described by the modern psychological and medical term *anorexia nervosa* and address, rather, the question of why so much of the religious behavior and the religious language of these women revolved around food.

◆ Food as Control of Body:
The Ascetic Context and the Question of Dualism

I suggested above that women used food in a wide variety of ways because food was the basic resource over which they had most control. Women did not merely abstain from food. They also distributed food, both prosaically and miraculously. They merged with Christ through food. In miraculous exuding, they became food. In short, women had many ways of manipulating and controlling self and environment through food-related behavior, for food formed the context and shape of women's world—of their responsibilities and privileges—more fundamentally than it did the world of men. To say this, however, is merely to skim the surface. It almost reduces to saying that women used food, as fact and as symbol, because it was there to be used. Clearly, then, we must probe beyond this. We must ask on a deeper level about both the function and the meaning of eating and not eating.

To do so is to confront directly some extremely difficult problems in historical interpretation. It is ultimately to confront both the question of the nature of asceticism and the question of the basic structures—psychological, social, and religious—of women's lives in the later Middle Ages. In answering these questions, I must propose some very large revisions of what has always been assumed about women and medieval Christianity. To put it very simply, in these last five chapters I argue that the extreme asceticism and literalism of women's spirituality were not, at the deepest level, masochism or dualism but, rather, efforts to gain power and to give meaning. I also argue that although men and women agreed in seeing food as a female concern, the symbol had profoundly different and asymmetrical meanings to the two sexes because men and women had different social, psychological, and religious experiences.

Let me begin, then, with the way women exerted control over their own bodies through fasting, for whatever other function food had for medieval women, it was clearly a means by which they manipulated physicality. The interpretation historians of religion have given to this phenomenon has been monolithic—so much so that it has come to seem common sense. Late medieval women hated their bodies and their sexuality, we are told, and punished them through fasting and other forms of self-mutilation. They internalized a misogyny to which the philosophical, scientific, theological, and folk traditions and the structures of church and society all contributed.[66] Some historians have responded to women's ascetic practices with embarrassment or even anger; others have responded with compassion. Conservative historians of theology have sometimes blamed the women.[67] Historians of medicine or psychiatry have sometimes blamed society.[68] Marxist and feminist historians have often blamed the church.[69] But, whatever its cause, women's asceticism has seemed to modern scholars self-evidently dualistic and pathological—an effort to flee or destroy the flesh so that the spirit might return to God. It has generally met with repugnance or, occasionally, with voyeuristic prurience. Those who have felt it necessary to defend the past (always a risky undertaking) have thus had either to take the offensive and blame institutions or individuals who "oppressed" women or to ignore the full range and extremism of the self-torturing behavior and concentrate on other aspects of women's spirituality.[70] But when we place even the most extravagant fasting and self-mutilation in its medieval context it is not clear that such behavior was rooted either in self-hatred or in dualism.[71]

There is no question that the experiencing of pain was a prominent aspect of the spirituality of both late medieval women and late medieval men. There is no question also that it was more prominent in women's religiosity. I pointed out above the centrality of illness—self-induced or God-given—in women's claims to sanctity. And women who were not ill (for example, Mechtild of Magdeburg and Hadewijch) frequently desired to identify with Christ through loneliness and persecution. Some Italian saints drank pus or scabs from lepers' sores, eating and incorporating disease, and the desire for illness is a common theme in the *Nonnenbücher*, where the sisters expose themselves to bitter cold or pray to be afflicted with leprosy.[72] Moreover, the central theme in women's visions, increasing from the thirteenth to the early fifteenth century, was fusion with the crucified body of Christ. These visions stream with blood. And in the frenzy of trance or ecstasy, pious women sometimes mutilated themselves with knives, as Mary of Oignies did, or, like Beatrice of Nazareth and Elizabeth of Spalbeek, drove themselves to what they and their companions saw as "insanity."[73]

Deliberate and systematic physical punishment was part of the daily routine for many religious women.[74] The sixteenth-century account of the life of Alda of Siena, for example, says that the saint slept on a bed of paving stones, whipped herself with chains, wore a crown of thorns, and carved for herself, as an object of devotion, a wooden nail like the one that pierced Christ's feet.[75] Dorothy of Montau put herself through a pantomime of the Crucifixion that involved praying with her arms extended in the form of a cross and later, in imitation of Christ's burial, lying prostrate with the entire weight of her body supported only by toes, nose, and forehead.[76] Jane Mary of Maillé stuck a thorn into her head in remembrance of Christ's crown of thorns.[77] Reading the lives of fourteenth- and fifteenth-century women saints greatly expands one's knowledge of Latin synonyms for whip, thong, flail, chain, etc. Ascetic practices commonly reported in these *vitae* include wearing hair shirts, binding the flesh tightly with twisted ropes, rubbing lice into self-inflicted wounds, denying oneself sleep, adulterating food and water with ashes or salt, performing thousands of genuflections, thrusting nettles into one's breasts, and praying barefoot in winter. Among the more bizarre female behaviors were rolling in broken glass,[78] jumping into ovens, hanging from a gibbet,[79] and praying upside down. (In the latter case, the nun's skirts clung, modestly and miraculously, around her ankles.)[80] The author of the nuns' book of Unterlinden in the Alsace wrote:

> In Advent and Lent, all the sisters, coming into the chapter house after Matins, or in some other suitable place, hack at themselves cruelly, hostilely lacerating their bodies until the blood flows, with all kinds of whips, so that the sound reverberates all over the monastery and rises to the ears of the Lord of hosts sweeter than all melody.

And she called the results of such discipline *stigmata*.[81]

Thus fasting was part of a broader pattern of conduct that appears to modern eyes to be a systematic attack on the flesh. Moreover, fasting was part of a pattern of piety in which what we would call psychological manipulation of the body is a prominent theme. Whereas extreme penitential asceticism is found in male as well as female saints (for example, Francis of Assisi, Henry Suso, James Oldo, Peter of Luxembourg), psychosomatic manipulation is almost exclusively female. Wounds imitating those on Christ's feet, hands, side, or head or sometimes even the scourge marks on his back appeared on the bodies of many female saints in the thirteenth, fourteenth, and fifteenth centuries.[82] Red marks known as espousal rings sometimes appeared on women's fingers. And women's wounds often appeared, or bled, at the day and hour of the Crucifixion. Stories are even told of miraculous elongation of women's bodies and of women levitating many feet in the air or flying over walls.[83] Even after death the bodies of saintly women were discovered to have been controlled and marked in strange ways. Intestines and stomachs were found to be empty, hearts were discovered to be etched with the signs of Christ. Although some women, for example Gertrude of Helfta, received the wound of love "inwardly," others were thought to become Christ more literally. Clare of Montefalco's spiritual sisters came to believe so intensely that Christ had planted his cross in her heart that at her death in 1308 they threw themselves upon her body, tore out her heart, and found incised upon it the insignia of the Passion.[84]

The bodies of holy women were frequently seen by medieval people as exuding miraculous fluids, substances, or odors. Of the three most famous myroblytes of the Middle Ages, two (Catherine of Alexandria—who supposedly bled milk when beheaded—and Elizabeth of Hungary) were women, and although research remains to be done on the distribution of this phenomenon, a disproportionate number of medieval myroblytes appear to have been women—for example, Walburga, Hedwig of Silesia, Agnes of Montepulciano, and Lutgard.[85] Women also seem to account for the majority of cases of bodies that exuded sweet odors, either from wounds or sores that appeared during life or from bodies (which sometimes also became young and beautiful) after death.[86] Flemish holy women such as Christina the Astonishing, Gertrude van Oosten, and Lidwina fed others with milk that flowed from their virgin breasts, often during meditations on the Nativity, and their Italian counterparts sometimes either exuded or called down clouds of manna.[87] Moreover, hagiographers frequently point out that holy women do not excrete or menstruate. So far does this concern with exuding extraordinary effluvia and repressing ordinary ones go that by the sixteenth century, biographers (such as Columba of Rieti's hagiographer) argue that holy women do not sweat or have sour breath.[88] And, introducing a newly "scientific" note into the growing concern with the closing off of female bodies, an account published in 1603 of Jane Balam of the area around Poitiers states explicitly that this fasting girl excreted neither feces nor urine, did not menstruate, never sweated except from the armpits, discharged no filth or dandruff from her hair, and only occasionally gave forth spittle from her mouth or tears from her eyes.[89]

To medieval people themselves, what modern eyes see as self-punishment or psychosomatic manipulation was *imitatio Christi*—a fusion with

Christ's agony on the cross. Thus medieval writers were often uninterested in certain distinctions that in the early modern and modern periods have fascinated canon lawyers, theologians, and psychiatrists—distinctions, for example, between miraculous and self-induced or between visible and invisible. To Gertrude the Great, Lutgard, Francis of Assisi, Lukardis, or Catherine of Siena, the point was the pain of stigmata or of the wound in the heart, not the visibility of the scars. The point was pain because the pain was Christ's. Visible wounds could be an embarrassment. To Rita of Cascia and Jane Mary of Maillé the thorn wounds they suffered were *imitatio Christi*. The fact that Rita's appeared by autosuggestion and Jane Mary's came from a real thorn was not an important difference. When Beatrice of Ornacieux thrust a nail through her hand, she was said to receive stigmata. Lukardis of Oberweimar's hagiographer says that she drove the middle finger of each hand, hard as a nail, through the palm of the opposite hand, until the room rang with the sound of hammering, and stigmata "miraculously" appeared.[90] Only a few days after a sister nun asked innocently why Lukardis did not also bear the marks of the thorns on her forehead, these, also "miraculously," appeared. Both because medieval people did not divide body and mind so sharply as we do or the senses from one another, and because the significance of "stigmata" was the experience of pain, not its source, accounts of such bodily changes, particularly in the thirteenth and fourteenth centuries, tell us less about what caused them or how they looked than about their meaning.

Thus it is clear that medieval women intended to produce pain when they performed many of their religious practices. It is also clear that they were somewhat more likely than men to inflict injury on themselves systematically with flails or thorns, stones or nettles, and that they were a great deal more likely than men to have their desire for pain result in somatic changes and to have these changes scrutinized and recorded by admirers and biographers of both sexes, who found female bodies fascinating.[91] Does this mean that women wished to eschew physicality and become spirit? Does it mean that female fasting was an effort to punish the flesh, to destroy or deny its urges, to repress its sexuality? There is certainly some evidence to support such an interpretation.

Male biographers (frequently) and women themselves (occasionally) suggest that body should be disciplined, defeated, or even destroyed, in order to release or protect spirit. Some women actually reflect the very old Mediterranean notion of the female body as polluting. In the four-teenth century, for example, Bridget of Sweden prohibited her nuns from touching altar cloths with their bare hands.[92] Several late medieval saints—for example, Douceline of Marseilles and Lutgard of Ay-wières—seem to have developed an obsessive fear of any bodily contact. Clare of Montefalco said she would rather spend days in hell than be touched by a man.[93] Lutgard panicked at an abbot's insistence on giving her the kiss of peace; Jesus had to interpose his hand in a vision so that she was not reached by the abbot's lips. She even asked to have her own gift of healing by touch taken away.[94] Douceline of Marseilles, who per-formed many miracles by touch (sometimes inadvertently),[95] was deeply antagonistic to any bodily contact with a man.[96] When she was a child, Christ had to force her to overcome her abhorrence of the male body by appearing in a vision with a disgusting sickness and demanding that she touch his chest.[97] Although she forced herself and her sisters to care for the repulsively ill, she beat a seven-year-old girl brutally for looking at a workman.[98] Christina of Stommeln (d. 1312), who fell into a latrine while in a trance, awoke in fury because the lay brother who rescued her touched her in order to do so.[99] In the lives of many women, particularly those, like Lutgard, who had experienced physical (especially sexual) brutality, the touch of Christ's body came as a healing experience to replace all other touching, which was abhorrent.[100]

Many holy women were profoundly afraid of the sensations of their bodies—especially hunger and thirst. Mary of Oignies, for example, was so afraid of taking pleasure in food that Christ had to make her unable to taste. In the sad little story of Alpaïs sending away the few morsels of pork given her to suck, we see a bizarre fear that any enjoyment of food might mushroom madly into gluttony or lust. Women such as Ida of Louvain, Elsbet Achler, and Columba of Rieti, who sometimes snatched up food and ate without knowing they were doing so, clearly directed their hunger toward the eucharist partly because it was an ac-ceptable object of craving and partly because it was a self-limiting food. Such women felt desperately vulnerable before bodily needs and used asceticism to destroy them.

It is also possible that some fasting had as a goal other sorts of bodily control. There is some suggestion in the accounts of biographers that fasting women were admired (as are fasting women in India today) for suppressing excretory functions.[101] Several hagiographers comment with approval that holy women who do not eat also cease to excrete, and Roger Bacon used the phenomenon as part of his naturalistic explanation of inedia.[102] Moreover, at least three hagiographers point out explicitly that the menstruation of their saintly heroines ceases.[103] Medieval theology was profoundly ambivalent about menstruation—a point to which I shall return—but natural philosophers and theologians were aware that fasting does in fact suppress menstruation.[104] Albert the Great noted that some holy women ceased to menstruate because of their fasts and austerities and commented that their health did not appear to suffer as a consequence.[105] Although medieval women such as Beatrice of Nazareth, Margaret of Ypres, Lutgard, Ida of Louvain, Lukardis, and Rita of Cascia delighted in the abnormal bleeding from nose, mouth, or stigmatic wounds that accompanied trances and mystical union, it does not seem unreasonable to suggest that they may also have desired cessation of that more ordinary female bleeding that their religion interpreted ambivalently at best. Figures such as Juliana of Cornillon, Mary of Oignies, Catherine of Siena, and Catherine of Genoa, whether married or not, escalated their food asceticism markedly at puberty.

Moreover, in controlling eating and hunger, medieval women were sometimes explicitly controlling sexuality. Ever since Jerome, male writers had warned religious women that food was dangerous because it excited lust; and the medieval authors of theological *summae* and manuals of religious practice for virgins repeated these warnings.[106] Some late medieval hagiographers remarked that women (for example, Alda of Siena) fasted in order to quell sexual desire.[107] This point should not be exaggerated. As Weinstein and Bell point out, male biographers generally overemphasized women's sexual temptations, because cultural stereotypes suggested that women were far more voracious sexually than men were.[108] Women writers actually paid little attention to lust, and even authors of *Mirrors for Virgins* in the high Middle Ages devoted less attention to food as an arouser of lust and to lust itself than one would expect from the interest of modern historians in the subject.[109] But there were women (for example, Margaret of Cortona, Catherine of Sweden) who associated food abstinence with chastity and greed with sexual desire.[110] In Columba of Rieti's painful and graphic visions, food and naked bodies were interwoven temptations, as they had been for Jerome so many centuries earlier. And in a charming story that associates food and sexuality on a deeper level, the baby Catherine of Sweden refused not only the breast of her sinful wet nurse but even the breast of her saintly mother, Bridget, whenever Bridget had had conjugal relations the night before.[111]

Medieval texts thus suggest that women sometimes abstained from food in order to subvert lust. It also seems that some women punished their flesh for enjoying sexual pleasure, and some, for whom sexual activity was a torment, punished the body that was unwillingly subjected to it. Some women (for example, Alda of Siena, Umiltà, Angela of Foligno, Margery Kempe) felt guilty in later life because sexual activity within marriage had been enjoyable, and some saints, such as Elizabeth of Hungary, loved their husbands.[112] But even women in happy marriages often felt guilty about their sexuality. The confessor of Ellen of Udine (d. 1458) records her own explanation of her penitential asceticism:

> I wear a hair shirt because of the silken undergarments and precious stuffs with which I used to clothe myself. . . . Thirty-three stones I put in the soles of my shoes because I have so often offended God with my leaping and dancing. . . . I flagellate my body for the impious and carnal pleasures with which I indulged it during my marriage and out of regard for my Lord who was whipped at the post for me.[113]

Some women, such as Mary of Oignies, Jane Mary of Maillé, Rita of Cascia, Dorothy of Montau, and Catherine of Genoa, hated their marriages. Although the exact reasons are often impossible to retrieve now, dislike of sex was clearly one. Francesca Romana de' Ponziani (d. 1440), for example, vomited whenever she was forced to have sexual relations with her husband. Yvette of Huy (d. 1228) said, after her husband's death, that nothing could compel her to the sexual act again.[114] And medieval marriages were often brutal. For every wife who persuaded her husband to accept continence on the wedding night or after, there is a story of a woman (for example, Clare of Assisi's sister) beaten almost to death by a husband whom she refused to accept.[115] Thus it seems reasonable to suggest that some medieval women renounced food because of overpowering and deeply rooted fears of sexuality. When women such as Margery Kempe and Angela of Foligno fasted, they were disciplining bodies that had previously, they felt, run out of control in hunger and thirst and erotic desire. When girls such as Rita of Cascia and Catherine of Genoa fasted, they were exerting control over flesh because flesh was in fact—whatever its emotional response—acted upon, by the demands of the marital debt, in ways abhorrent to its inhabitor.

The food practices of medieval women thus sometimes appear to be efforts not just to control but even to attack or punish the body. And, as chapter 2 demonstrates, there was clearly an element of dualism in the fasting practices of the Fathers, which medieval women inherited. Although there were many strains in antique fasting, the notion of disciplining or even punishing the body was clearly one. Some of the Fathers explicitly saw the ascetical life as a substitute for martyrdom or as a hurting of the body to force it to virtuous deeds. Gluttony was seen as the cause of more serious sins. As John Climacus put it: the sons of gluttony are fornication, hardening of the heart, and sleep with impure thoughts; its daughters include laziness, loquacity, scurrility, and boldness.[116] Thus fasting, as pseudo-Athanasius says, purifies the body and the mind, drying up bodily humors and putting impure thoughts to flight.[117] The *Sayings of the Fathers* reports the words of a certain Daniel: "As the body waxes fat, the soul grows thin; and as the body grows thin, the soul by so much waxes fat."[118] John Chrysostom related such arguments particularly to women when he said: "Nothing is worse than a dissipated woman; nothing worse than a drunken woman."[119] These notions were repeated by later medieval preachers and spiritual advisers. Peter Damian, for example, writing of a penitent who carried his fasting beyond Lent, said that it was done to "crucify the carnal passions," to "break the taste and extinguish the fervor of concupiscence." Peter the Chanter warned that we must make our bodies pure, "for the stomach and the genitals are close together"; thus "we must bear the stigmata of Christ in our bodies (Gal. 5:6) by abstinence and penitence."[120]

One strain in medieval moral teaching thus associated fasting with a kind of practical (not philosophical) dualism. According to this strain, abstinence was rejection of body. Moreover, there is some reason to argue that women were more drawn to such fasting than men because women were especially associated with the evils of body, which needed to be punished or expiated. Borrowing from Jerome, Augustine, and Gregory the Great, among others, medieval moral teaching saw women as especially afflicted with the weakness of the flesh.

Antique and medieval misogyny and its roots in dualism are phenomena too well known to need much explanation here.[121] From the scientific and philosophical tradition came the notion of woman as an incomplete or inferior male and the idea that, in the process of conception, woman provided the matter from which the foetus was shaped whereas man contributed the shaping or animating form or principle. From the Fathers of the third and fourth century, newly concerned with sexual desire as the paradigm for human evil, came the notion of woman as flesh and man as spirit. It is true, as several recent scholars have stressed, that Augustine believed there was friendship within marriage and spoke of marriage as the redemption of the sexual act.[122] But he also treated sexual desire as the most basic symbol of willfulness and saw the female as the symbol of a flesh that must be subject to the male (spirit or reason). Such views led to the assumption of later medieval theologians that virtue was harder for "weak" women to achieve. The medieval church itself elaborated a kind of functional inferiority of women to complement the physiological and ontological inferiority elaborated by earlier philosophical and theological tradition. Although some (for example, Aquinas) argued that women were unfit for priesthood because of their natural state of subjection and some (for example, Bonaventure) disqualified women because of Christ's male sex, woman's increased exclusion from clerical leadership and from certain new types of evangelical religious life (for example, mendicant poverty) was connected to the notion of her inferiority—i.e., her fleshliness and weakness.[123] Even the folk tradition, in its carnival rituals of reversed sex roles and its lewd tales of cuckolded husbands, expressed a clear sense of the female as disorderly and sexually voracious.[124] It thus seems possible to suggest, as the vast majority of historians have done, that women understood themselves to be symbols of the flesh, saw fasting and other forms of asceticism as weapons for routing that flesh, and therefore adopted extreme starvation and other forms of self-mutilation in an effort to rise to the level of spirit and to become, metaphorically speaking, male.

To make such an argument appears, however, to involve a profound misunderstanding of late medieval religious life. I do not deny that dualism was one element in asceticism or that misogyny was one element in women's self-perception. And a negative sense of the female body clearly underlay behaviors that were directed toward shutting off menstruation, excretion, hunger, sexual response, and even the ordinary sensations of warmth and touch and sleepiness. But late medieval asceticism was not, at its most basic level, dualistic, nor was internalized misogyny the dominant element in women's conception of their religious role. We must go

217

beyond the interpretations that see women's food behavior as primarily punishment or control of body. And we must do this for three reasons. First, women's food behavior—fasting and feeding—was an effective way of manipulating the environment in a world in which food was woman's primary resource. Second, women's radical asceticism was less an internalizing of the church's negative views of flesh and female than a rebellion against the moderation of the high medieval church, which was moving toward a more positive sense of the body. Third, food asceticism, food distribution, and eucharistic devotion did not, to medieval people, mean self-torture; rather, they were ways of fusing with a Christ whose suffering saves the world.

In the next chapter, I consider in detail the first two of these three arguments. I consider, that is, how women controlled and manipulated their environment through their control of food, and why they needed to do so. And I argue that women's radical asceticism was not only a rejection of a world in which they had little control over their bodies and their destinies but also a rejection of a church which, as it touched more and more of life and provided ordinary folk with appropriate ways to be religious, seemed a threat as well as an opportunity to those pious women who wanted, without compromise or moderation, to imitate Christ.

7

FOOD AS CONTROL
OF CIRCUMSTANCE

As they came by a cross, her husband sat down under the cross [and said]: "Margery, grant me my desire, and I will grant you your desire. My first desire is that we shall still lie together in bed as we have done before; the second, that ye shall pay my debts, ere ye go to Jerusalem [on pilgrimage]; and the third, that ye shall eat and drink with me on the Friday as ye were wont to do."

"Nay, sir," said she, "to break the Friday, I will never grant you whilst I live."

"Well," said he, "then I shall meddle with you again."

She prayed him that he would give her leave to say her prayers, and he granted it kindly. . . .

Then Our Lord Jesus Christ with great sweetness spoke to her, commanding her to go to her husband, and pray him to grant her what she desired, "and he shall have what he desireth. For, my dearworthy daughter, this was the cause that I bade thee fast, so that thou shouldst the sooner obtain and get thy desire, and now it is granted to thee. I will no longer that thou fast. Therefore I bid thee in the Name of Jesus, eat and drink as thy husband doth."

Then this creature thanked Our Lord Jesus Christ for his grace, and goodness, and rose up and went to her husband, saying to him:

"Sir, if it please you, ye shall grant me my desire and ye shall have your desire. Grant me that ye will not come into my bed, and I grant you to requite your debts ere I go to Jerusalem. Make my body free to God so that ye never make challenge to me, by asking any debt of matrimony. After this day, whilst ye live, I will eat and drink on the Friday at your bidding."

Then said her husband: "As free may your body be to God, as it hath been to me."

THE BOOK OF MARGERY KEMPE
(1436)[1]

To STRESS women's food practices and concerns as control of body is to focus too narrowly on fasting—on not eating. In fact, as we have seen, women's fasting was part of a broader pattern of behavior in which feeding others and eating God were also central. Women's fasting was explicitly seen, by women themselves and by their confessors and advisers, as preparation both for receiving the eucharist and for almsgiving. Women gave to the poor and sick the food they denied themselves; women cleansed their bodies of prosaic food in order to ready them for the coming of the food that was Christ.

When we look at women's various food practices together, we find that voluntary starvation, charitable food distribution, and eucharistic devotion were all means by which women controlled their social and religious circumstances quite directly and effectively. Far from substituting control of self for control of circumstance or destroying ego and body while attempting to direct the attention of others toward them, women's food practices frequently enabled them to determine the shape of their lives—to reject unwanted marriages, to substitute religious activities for more menial duties within the family, to redirect the use of fathers' or husbands' resources, to change or convert family members, to criticize powerful secular or religious authorities, and to claim for themselves teaching, counseling, and reforming roles for which the religious tradition provided, at best, ambivalent support.

♦ Food and Family

In the stories I told in chapters 4 and 5, it is very clear that women often coerced their families both through fasting and through feeding others.[2] To an aristocratic or rising merchant family of late medieval Europe, the voluntary starvation of a daughter or a spouse could be deeply perplexing and humiliating. The charitable activities of female family members could appear to be rejection of the family's success and of its values. A woman's fasting and food distribution could therefore be effective means of criticizing, manipulating, educating, or converting family members.

Let me begin with a few examples in which food practices had very specific results. One of the most charming, from the autobiography of the fourteenth-century Englishwoman Margery Kempe, is quoted in the epigraph above. In this passage, Margery, speaking of herself in the third person, describes a discussion with Christ about her ascetic practices. The exchange has something of the tone of two housewives gossiping about how to manage a difficult and childish husband. Christ and Margery decide that although Margery wishes to practice both food abstention and sexual continence, she should offer to trade one behavior for the other. The most interesting aspect of the passage, for our purposes, is the fact that the ploy was successful. Margery's husband, who had married her in an effort to rise socially in the town of Lynn and was obviously ashamed of her queer penitential clothes and food practices (as well as being in need of her money), finally agreed to grant her sexual abstinence in private if she would return to normal cooking and eating in front of the neighbors.

Other examples of successful management of family members through food practices are easy to find. Rita of Cascia and Catherine of Siena's sister Bonaventura, who apparently reacted to profligate young husbands by wasting away, were thereby able to tame disorderly male behavior. Mary of Oignies and Catherine of Genoa eventually won over their husbands to lives of chastity and charity by the model of their own behavior—a model made more convincing by the heroic severity of their self-denial. Columba of Rieti and Catherine of Siena rebelled against household tasks (and against the mothers who imposed them) by refusing to eat. Columba, Catherine of Siena, and Ida of Louvain also used trances at what were, to the family, very inconvenient moments in order to avoid domestic roles: both Catherine and Columba supposedly let babies fall into the fire while they were rapt in mystical ecstasy.

Wives as well as daughters used fasting, charity, and ecstasy as means to escape the role of food preparer or nurturer. Dorothy of Montau, like Margery Kempe, made elementary mistakes in cookery (such as failing to scale the fish before frying them) or forgot entirely to cook and shop while she was in mystical trances. The Italian tertiary Margaret of Cortona refused to cook for her illegitimate son (about whom she obviously felt agonizing ambivalence) because, she said, it would distract her from prayer.[3] But she energetically fed the poor and sick both by miracle and by charity. We are told by Raymond of Capua that Catherine of Siena, after her death, miraculously cooked for a woman devotee who had gone to church instead of preparing dinner for her sons. Catherine thus, from beyond the grave, blessed and approved by miracle a woman's escape from the ordinary maternal duty of food preparation.

Since food practices so successfully manipulated and embarrassed families, it is not surprising that voluntary starvation and charitable food distribution often originated or escalated at puberty—the time at which families began negotiations for husbands for their daughters. Female saints such as Catherine of Siena, Columba, Lidwina, Francesca Romana, and Margaret of Hungary sometimes cut off their hair to make themselves ugly, longed for disease as an escape from marriage, or threatened self-mutilation if that was the only way to avoid a husband. Margaret of Hungary, for example, when offered a suitor, threatened to cut off her nose.[4] It thus seems likely that fasting was sometimes an effort to avoid or postpone an unwanted marriage by becoming physically unattractive. From the moment marriage was suggested to her, Lidwina of Schiedam wanted to be ugly, and she may have been cultivating physical problems before her fall on the ice and her miraculous abstinence.

But fasting and giving away family property were not merely ways of appearing ugly and intractable, and thereby presenting oneself as unpromising marital material. They were also ways of defining oneself by choosing a very different life from that of one's family. And they were effective ways. Some girls, such as Christina of Markyate, Lutgard, Mechtild of Magdeburg, and Elsbet Achler, had to flee to hermitages, beguinages, or convents in order to escape family; others, such as Catherine of Siena and Lidwina, created—partly by their extravagant fasting, charity, and eucharistic devotion—an alternative to marriage without ever leaving home.[5] Given the options open to medieval girls, who could hardly pick their husbands or their futures directly, such behaviors were often constructive ways of escaping from unwanted suitors and choosing to serve and influence a broader world than that of the kitchen and the nursery.

We must not forget that avoiding marriage was not easy. Many girls were forced to accept husbands. Francesca Romana, for example, eventually accepted marriage and bore several children, although she had felt a great abhorrence of men since childhood and had suffered from paralysis at puberty when her father refused her permission to enter a convent.[6] Once a girl was married, she often had to wait long years—until death or disaster struck her husband—before she could pursue the religious practices she craved. (One suspects that, without her husband's bankruptcy, Catherine of Genoa's religious genius might never have acquired voice.) A comparison of male and female saints' *vitae* suggests that medieval parents were less willing to accept the religious vocations of daughters than those of sons.[7] Even the religious tradition presented girls with contradictory ideals—that of the dutiful daughter, who patiently accepted the parents' choice of husband, and that of the heroic virgin, who bore any torture rather than surrender her virginity. The fact that the *vitae* of women saints (in contrast to those of men) show a pattern of vocations to virginity emerging in childhood perhaps suggests that girls who managed to define their own statuses—particularly as tertiaries and beguines, set apart by virginity but living in the world— had to start preparing the way early for family acceptance of their vocations.[8] Several scholars have recently suggested that conflict between parents and children over religious vocation increased in the thirteenth and fourteenth centuries.[9] Fasting and charitable food distribution seem to have functioned as weapons girls deployed in the intra-family war.

Indeed, women's food practices were in some sense a rejection of family. As David Herlihy has said, a family is a group of people who reside—and especially *eat*—together. To refuse commensality is both to refuse the meal as symbol of familial bond and to refuse the most basic support that a father's money and a mother's household skill can provide: food.[10] To give away the contents of family cupboards and cellars is to reject the comfort, the security, and the social status that the labors of the family provide; it is also to reject the values of parents who cling to such status and comforts. Many medieval girls seem to have expressed such rejection, both of their own families and of the state of marriage, through fasting and food distribution.[11] Columba of Rieti, for example, once gave away the family's food until there was nothing left to eat. Some families, understanding the message of rejection, responded with rage or ridicule or persecution. Christina the Astonishing, for example, so angered her sisters by her charity and asceticism that they locked her up. Some families, however, gave grudging and puzzled acceptance, even support, to their daughters' desires for religious life, thus manifesting their own ambivalence about marriage and families. Lidwina of Schiedam's mother, for example, although she was annoyed with her daughter's neglect of domestic duties, supported her in her hesitations about marriage. In the life of Catherine of Siena we see food practices as a quite successful device by which a girl avoids becoming an object in the marriage market as her older sisters had done. But Catherine's food practices were more; they were also the girl's self-definition and her intense rejection of parental, especially maternal, values.

Catherine's *vita* shows how constricted life could become for a girl once she came to her parents' attention as marriageable. As a child, Catherine had been permitted to wander around the city and play in the streets so freely that, on one occasion, no one noticed her day-long absence from home.[12] At puberty she suddenly found herself pressured to groom herself to attract men and allowed out of the house only with a chaperone. Small wonder that Catherine and her parents then began to fight over both her physical appearance and her right to privacy. Catherine rejected her parents' ambitions for her by cutting off her hair and starving herself; her parents responded by denying her a room of her own, a space within which she could practice the prayer and asceticism that defined her as religious. When forced to share a bed with her mother because of her refusal to sleep and her busyness all night, Catherine put a board under the mattress or crept out of bed to lie on the floor. When taken against her will on a holiday, Catherine scalded her body in the hot baths of the vacation spot. Thus, by a series of ascetic behaviors, Catherine slowly forged for herself, without ever leaving home, a life whose values were utterly different from those of her wealthy merchant father and her doting, efficient mother with a brood of twenty children. It took a miracle to bring her father to acceptance of her life; and her mother—who understood only too well what it meant—seems never to have been completely reconciled to it.

It is hard not to see intense conflict with family in Catherine's behavior, a conflict in which fasting was crucial. Similarly it is hard not to see, in Elizabeth of Hungary's practice of giving away food from her husband's table, intense rebellion against her husband's family, by whom she had been raised. Her refusal to eat (or feed her servants) any food except that purchased with money from her dowry seems to reflect a deep sense that only property from her own paternal line (i.e., from the family that had not raised her) could be trusted as morally untainted. Although the well-known story that Elizabeth's basket of bread for the poor turned into roses when her husband accosted her is apocryphal and untrue to all we know of Louis's attitude, it is significant that the story, with its implications of intra-family conflict, was told—and told not just of Elizabeth but of at least five women saints in the later Middle Ages.[13]

For Ida of Louvain, whose *vita* is interwoven with food motifs of all kinds, rejecting drink was a rejection of family values in a more specific sense. Ida's extreme fasting, her fascination with the inebriating delights of Christ's blood, her repeated miracles that changed other fluids into wine, her refusal to accept any food or economic support from her family other than the room she lived in, and her obsession with giving away food and drink surely owe something to the fact that her merchant father, whose values she was rejecting, sold wine. Rejection of family authority and values could, moreover, focus on surrogate families as well as biological ones. Juliana of Cornillon, who was raised by a nurse called Sapientia in a small cell dependent on a religious house and was disciplined as a child for what her confessor saw as willful and excessive fasting, returned to self-starvation in adolescence. One suspects that this behavior, and the stubborn, enigmatic responses that she made to her sisters concerning it, were in part expressions of hostility toward the religious "family" that had reared her.

Historians of the modern and early modern world such as Lawrence Stone, Philippe Ariès, and Peter Laslett have long argued that the Middle Ages had little conception of childhood and none of adolescence, that the close-knit affective family was a product of the late-seventeenth and eighteenth-century gentry and bourgeoisie, that medieval families were extended rather than nuclear, and that medieval parents often had little to do with rearing their children.[14] If this were so, one could hardly expect family dynamics to play a role in the food practices of medieval girls. But historians of the Middle Ages have recently objected to this picture.[15] They suggest, partly on the basis of the saints' lives I describe above in chapters 4 and 5, that the nuclear family with tight affective bonds did exist in the Middle Ages, particularly in urban areas in the thirteenth and fourteenth centuries.[16] They also suggest that agnatic or patrilineal principles were replacing the bilineal family in the later Middle Ages, making the situation of daughters more problematic but not eclipsing a family sense of responsibility for them.[17] If daughters were increasingly a problem for families, it stands to reason that family was increasingly a problem for daughters.

Recent research demonstrates the problem very clearly. After 1200, women's life expectancies outran men's. Women became a surplus in the population. The typical age discrepancy between husband and wife increased. (On average, men married at 30, women at 15 to 17.) The dowry—now the daughter's only claim on the family property, as patrilineal principles triumphed—inflated wildly. By the fourteenth century, as Dante tells us, the birth of a daughter could bring despair to a father's heart if he contemplated what it would cost to provide for her.[18] But exactly because he did feel some obligation to his female children, a prosperous father pushed to arrange early marriages for daughters. It thus seems reasonable to suspect that daughters resented the pressure, feeling guilty about the strain their dowries put on family resources and yet angry about the fact that this one large payment bought off their parents' obligation to them. Even in the thirteenth century, Elizabeth of Hungary's refusal to use or consume anything derived from the property of her husband's family, who raised her, can be interpreted as her way of clinging to her dowry—the only thing she retained from the family that had sent her away to be raised in a foreign land. Such social facts suggest that some girls may have seen betrothal and marriage as abandonment by their own families. It is thus not surprising that adolescents such as Francesca Romana, Lidwina of Schiedam, and Catherine of Genoa reacted with a wild anger, which turned inward toward themselves as self-hatred or despair, when suitors were proposed.

Marriage for a woman was a life-threatening undertaking, and some female hesitation needs no more complex explanation than this. Daughters grew up exposed to the drudgery of household tasks and aware, through the experiences of older sisters as well as mothers, of the pain and dangers of childbirth—a point preachers did not fail to refer to in sermons and treatises on virginity.[19] For example, Catherine of Siena's momentary surrender to her sister's insistence that she make herself pretty to attract men was brought to a stunning conclusion when that same sister demonstrated to what it all really led by dying in childbirth. It is thus hardly surprising that some girls rejected marriage and some brides struggled fiercely and desperately for continence. Nor is it surprising that parents and husbands—themselves ambivalent about family and marriage for the same cultural reasons that convinced their daughters and wives—sometimes gave support to women who escaped to religious houses or who lived, under their own roofs, a life set apart. Moreover, as several scholars have underlined, the behavior of medieval merchants often suggests ambivalence, even guilt, about the wealth they so eagerly garnered.[20] Permitting a wife or a daughter to give away this wealth might exacerbate such ambivalence but it might also assuage guilt. Some families and husbands clearly expressed their religious impulses through their daughters' and wives' asceticism. And some husbands, such as Catherine of Genoa's and Mary of Oignies's, even espoused chastity, charity, and fasting in imitation of their pious wives.

Thus women's food practices were effective ways of shaping their lives, of rejecting roles they did not desire, of criticizing and redirecting the values of husbands and parents.[21] But it was not merely family who were influenced by such practices; food behavior manipulated and controlled religious authorities as well. By their eucharistic visions, their charity, their food miracles, and their fasting, medieval women bypassed certain forms of clerical control that stood between them and God. They also forged for themselves roles as healers, teachers, and savers of their fellow Christians that were in explicit contrast to the characteristic forms of male leadership.

◆ Food Practices and Religious Roles

When we turn from the function of food practices within the family to the function of food practices within the church, it is crucial to note that fasting, feasting, and feeding are merely aspects of the same phenomenon: the religious significance of food. These aspects were closely intertwined in the daily lives of holy women. Whether a woman was withdrawn from the world or living in it, whether she saw herself as a contemplative or as a servant of the poor, she tended both to reject food and to see it as a powerful symbol of union. Girls and women who fasted hungered for the eucharist and received, along with it, visions and supernatural signs that bestowed power upon them. Fasting women gave, to the needy, food, alms, and other less tangible but even more significant benefits, such as remission of purgatory or insight into the true state of the soul.

Taken together, the food practices of holy women sometimes bypassed the clergy, sometimes exposed their failures, and sometimes frankly usurped their authority—not so much by claiming priestly office as by simply allowing Christ or the spirit to speak through the "weaker vessel."[22] It is easiest to see the way food practices manipulated religious authorities by looking at eucharistic miracles, especially those miracles, told almost exclusively of women, in which unconsecrated hosts or unchaste celebrants were identified. Such miracles grew directly out of female fasting. Observers agreed that fasting girls generally vomited out any food they were made to receive. The ability of such girls to tolerate eucharistic bread (which sometimes turned to honey or flesh in their mouths) was indeed sometimes used by theologians such as Thomas Netter to prove the doctrine of transubstantiation.[23] If ordinary bread could not be tolerated, then that which was swallowed must be the flesh of Christ; if no other food was ever taken, the weekly or daily morsel that alone sustained life must be the body of God. Whether a pious woman swallowed or vomited thus became a test of the priest who provided the wafer. If a truly holy woman such as Mary of Oignies, Lidwina of Schiedam, or Joan the Meatless vomited out a host, suspicion immediately turned on the priest who had offered it. The faithful assumed that he had given the girl an unconsecrated host, either by mistake or by dishonesty. Going further, they might see the pious woman's rejection of the host as a reason for questioning the priest's act of consecration. However theologically unsound the conclusion might be, they tended to deduce that in some unspecified way he was disqualified by immorality (usually sexual immorality). In the conflict of Lidwina of Schiedam with her priest (discussed above, pp. 128–29), such a miracle proved decisive. Lidwina's gagging on the host was taken by some adherents as proof of the priest's deviousness; he had not in fact offered her the host, they thought, but had attempted to trick her instead. Lidwina herself then presented her ability to swallow a different host as proof of its divine source. And the lesson that this second host arrived directly from Christ to replace the priest's fraudulent offering was not lost on those who flocked to see the miraculous drops of blood which graced it. Lidwina not only achieved, through this drama, the frequent communion she craved; through this and other insights she repeatedly criticized the priest and established a general impression of his dissoluteness.[24]

Women's eucharistic visions, like their sense of taste, were a kind of litmus test for clerical immorality or negligence. Women frequently saw the corruption of the clergy at the moment of consecration or elevation.

Margaret of Cortona, for example, saw the hands of an unchaste priest turn black when he held the host. When the priest brought an unconsecrated wafer by mistake, Margaret vomited it out. Mary of Oignies and Ida of Louvain also knew miraculously when celebrants were unchaste or unauthorized to officiate. Colette of Corbie was aware, as if by miracle, when the priest forgot to fill the chalice with wine during mass.[25] Women sometimes also saw, in eucharistic visions, the failings of their fellow Christians. A nun of Engelthal, for example, saw the host turn into the Christ child, who then came down from the altar and approached her sisters with behavior that varied according to their respective degree of purity.[26]

Clerics were not merely passively manipulated by such visions. They actively sought, in holy women, both a standard of piety and a window open to the divine. Religious women were seen by men as an alternative to and a criticism of wealth, power, and office. In their visions and devotions, women mystics were the point where the powerful male found a reversal and a critique of exactly those things about which he felt greatest ambivalence.[27] Woman, in other words, was "liminal" to men in the technical sense given the term by the anthropologist Victor Turner.[28] Thomas of Cantimpré, James of Vitry, and Tauler, among others, deliberately used stories of the eucharistic devotion of holy women to shame the clergy for lukewarm piety. James and Thomas also spoke of the women whose stories they chronicled as "mothers" to clerics and described their inspiration of men as a form of "preaching."[29] The biographers of the Italian tertiaries Angela of Foligno and Margaret of Cortona saw them as spiritual mothers who had only "sons" (the Franciscan friars). Thirteenth-century heretical groups such as the Guglielmites in Italy and the followers of Bloemardine in the Low Countries, who tried to set up a female church or preach a female God, had male followers and may, as heresies, have been male creations.[30] Inspired criticism of male—especially clerical—corruption was understood, by both men and women, to be a female role. Mechtild of Magdeburg, for example, who did not scruple to hurl abusive epithets at local canons and friars, saw visions in which hell and the lower circles of purgatory were populated entirely by men (with the important exception of princesses—presumably, to Mechtild, the only powerful and therefore dangerous female role).[31] The function of pointing out uncomfortable truths to society was sometimes seen as possession by demons rather than inspiration by Christ, but whether demonic or divine, it issued primarily from women, who were marginal to the roles they criticized.[32]

Women's visions came most frequently in a eucharistic context. And women's special and intimate relationship to the holy food was itself often a way of rejecting or bypassing ecclesiastical control. Late medieval theologians and confessors attempted to inculcate awe as well as craving for the eucharist, and women not only received ambiguous advice about frequent communion, they were also sometimes barred from receiving it at exactly the point at which their fasting and hunger reached fever pitch.[33] In such circumstances, many women simply received in vision what the celebrant or confessor withheld. Alice of Schaerbeke, denied the cup because of leprosy, was reassured by Christ in impeccable thirteenth-century theology that she received both body and blood in the host,[34] but it was far more common for Christ to provide the desired communion in a vision than to reassure the woman about its absence. When Lutgard of Aywières was required by her abbess to omit frequent communion, God engineered events so that the benefit was restored.[35] When little Imelda Lambertini (d. 1333) was denied communion because she was too young, the host flew down from heaven and hovered over her, and the priest was forced to give her the eucharist.[36] When Ida of Léau's Cistercian superiors (in an effort to curb women's devotion) passed legislation denying access to the cup to any nun who went out of her senses, Christ provided Ida with communion.[37] Ida of Louvain, denied communion because she was a novice, had the impression that she slipped (whether bodily or in a vision she never knew) into the ranks of the nuns to receive the host; on another occasion, when there was no service, she was miraculously transported into the tabernacle to taste God.[38] Stories of Christ as a priest bringing the host or the chalice to sick women are very common. The nuns' book of Töss, for example, describes a vision seen by a nun too sick to swallow the eucharist: a tablecloth descended to her with Christ's body on a platter; in a beautiful light, a hand appeared from heaven and gave her "our Lord" "just as if she received him from the altar."[39]

Both the visionary women and their confessors were acutely sensitive to the problematic implications of such visions. Bypassing clerical authority might be taken to imply that priests were unnecessary. Thus James of Vitry, in his *Historia occidentalis*, tells of a fasting woman who received communion from a dove and adds that she received it the next day from a priest at the dove's command, "lest it be believed that she was deprived of the reception of the true sacrament by a phantasm."[40] Stories of women who received either communion or absolution in a vision are frequently glossed with assurances that they had recourse to a priest as soon as they were able. In the vision collections produced by the nuns of Helfta, for example, the vision itself frequently exhorts its recipient to hasten to actual communion.[41] But sometimes the woman who is stricken with fainting fits, paralysis, or nosebleeds at mass and experiences a "filling" by Christ, accompanied by sensations of chewing and sweetness on the tongue, *prefers* the mystical communion. Ida of Louvain and Lukardis of Oberweimar clearly preferred nursing at Mary's breast or resting within the arms of Christ and had no desire afterwards to receive the actual elements.

Some women went even further in their visions: not merely bypassing clerical mediation (and thereby implying it to be unnecessary), they actually claimed a kind of priestly role. We see such a challenge to the priesthood—a challenge that always treads the thin edge of orthodoxy— in some of the visions of the thirteenth-century nun Gertrude the Great. When Gertrude assured her sisters that they were forgiven by Christ and bade them go to communion, a vision informed her that those who followed her advice were closer to Christ than either those who abstained because no confessor was available or those who communicated without consulting Gertrude.[42] When Gertrude worried about her sins, Christ told her that he renewed in her soul "all seven sacraments in one operation more efficaciously than any other priest or pontiff can do by seven separate acts."[43] When Gertrude received the power to discriminate between guilty and innocent, "discerning through Christ's spirit," Christ in a vision called it "the power of binding and loosing" and described it as analogous to ordination.[44] When Christ in a vision told Gertrude that he would bring to pass whatever she promised in his name, he touched her tongue, saying, "Behold, I give my words into your mouth," and explained:

Is not the faith of the universal church that promise once made to Peter: *Whatever you bind on earth will be bound in heaven* [Matt. 16:19]? And firmly she believes this to be carried out by all ecclesiastical ministers. Therefore why do you not equally believe because of this that I can and will perfect that which, moved by love, I promise to you by my divine mouth?[45]

No element in these visions contradicts orthodox teaching on confession or communion, for Gertrude herself or the nuns who wrote of her experiences carefully gloss each incident so that Gertrude merely announces forgiveness, guilt, or innocence, which are free gifts or judgments of God. But the bypassing of sacraments and priest is clear, as is Gertrude's own extraordinary power to give counsel in their stead, and the analogy of female mystic to priest is repeatedly drawn.

It was particularly in their eucharistic visions that mystical women saw themselves in "priestly" images and claimed roles and opportunities otherwise prohibited to them. Some women received, in visions, the power to distribute the eucharist and to touch altar vessels—a power they were forbidden because of their gender.[46] Some received the consecrated chalice, which they were denied because of their lay status. For example, a woman who had loved Juliana of Cornillon very much in her life saw her after death at mass; the friend then received from Christ the high priest a rich and beautiful chalice, and Juliana his handmaiden assisted him with her virgin hands. Mechtild of Hackeborn thought she received from Christ his heart in the form of a cup marvelously chiseled, and he said: "By my heart you will praise me always; go, offer to all the saints the drink of life from my heart that they may be happily inebriated with it." Angela of Foligno, feeling that the celebrant was unworthy, had a vision of Christ bleeding on the cross, and angels said to her: "Oh you who are pleasing and delicious to God, behold, he has been administered to you and you have him present. Moreover, he is given to you in order that you may administer and present him to others." Lukardis of Oberweimar brought the eucharist to a fellow nun by blowing into her mouth.[47] Ida of Louvain, who had been criticized by the chaplain to her convent, was "clothed in sacerdotal clothes or priceless ornaments" and miraculously received the host while he celebrated, unaware of her presence. Moreover, on the following day, she again miraculously received the sacrament during a mass at which "no one was usually admitted to receive the host with the exception only of the minister who celebrated." Benevenuta of Bojano (d. 1292) and Mechtild of Hackeborn both saw visions of the Virgin Mary administering the chalice.[48] Catherine of Siena, like many of her holy predecessors, repeatedly received a sensation of blood in her mouth when she took the wafer.[49] There was nothing theologically incorrect in such miracles, for the faithful were taught in the doctrine of concomitance that body and blood were received together. Furthermore, visions of chalices or flying hosts could always be interpreted as images of grace or charity. But the insistence on receiving blood and on distributing the elements that we find in women's visions appears to reflect a keen desire for that which the woman—because of her gender and because of her lay status—was not permitted to do.

Thus, in their eucharistic visions, women not only received God as holy food, they also sometimes claimed for themselves, at least metaphorically, both the priest's proximity to God and the sacerdotal role of mediator between human and divine. Moreover, the most extreme implications of such female visions were occasionally extrapolated, probably more by male than by female adherents, into heterodox claims—such as those of the followers of Bloemardine or Guglielma—for a female clergy, a female church, or perhaps even a female manifestation of God on earth.[50] Such occurrences were very rare, however. For the most part, women claimed the priesthood only by analogy or in very private and carefully glossed visions. Indeed, holy women such as the nuns of Helfta, Catherine of Siena, and Columba of Rieti often felt extravagant regard for the clergy. Catherine called them "little christs." Some, such as Margaret of Cortona, trembled before the priestly power to consecrate and distribute (and, therefore, withhold) the sacrament. It is thus incorrect to see women's ecstatic religiosity primarily as aping clerical power. Rather, women forged, through charity, miracle, and fasting, an alternative role—an essentially lay and charismatic role—authorized not by ordination but by inspiration, not by identification with Christ the high priest but by imitation of Christ the suffering man. Women's charismatic, prophetic role was an alternative to, and therefore a critique of and a substitute for, the characteristic male form of religious authority: the authority of office.

To women's charismatic role, food was central. The charitable food distribution of aristocratic and bourgeois women such as Ida of Louvain, Elizabeth of Hungary, Lidwina, and Jane Mary was a life-saving gift to the starving poor of town and countryside. And such generosity captured the popular imagination by its courage. To empty family cupboards in defiance of husbands and fathers, to renounce family support, to work or beg in order to feed the poor—these were heroic and sometimes dangerous acts. Moreover, women fed the needy with miraculous food as well. Sometimes, like Umiltà and Margaret of Faenza, they multiplied food both for those within the convent and for those outside its walls; sometimes God rewarded their sanctity, as he did Agnes of Montepulciano's, by rains of food from heaven; sometimes, like Lutgard, Lidwina, or Christina the Astonishing, they were miraculously changed into food itself, feeding, healing, and saving with the liquids from their breasts or fingertips. The teaching, healing, and counseling so powerfully and frequently performed by holy women were often accompanied by food symbolism. Colette of Corbie, for example, cured the sick by placing in their mouths crumbs of food that she had chewed with her own teeth. Ida of Louvain and Lidwina of Schiedam converted the doubting by food miracles.

Moreover, the female fasting that moved fathers and husbands, confessors and bishops, also moved God. Women made demands on God by their abstinence. Catherine of Siena demanded that he return her mother to life, because Catherine had already done the requisite suffering. Mary of Oignies fasted to make a demon leave a possessed nun. Lutgard, at the command of the Virgin Mary, undertook three seven-year fasts against heretics and the enemies of God. Many holy women were granted by Christ the power to remove a specific number of souls from purgatory through fasting and pain. Alice of Schaerbeke, dying in torment from leprosy, was assured by Christ that her suffering, including her suffering at the *loss* of communion, released souls from purgatory.[51] And women undertook the holy eating, for which fasting prepared, as a form of service as well. When the doctrine of vicarious communion— i.e., the notion that one person can receive communion for another— was developed in the thirteenth century, some monasteries of women were especially attracted to it. Although male theologians expressed the doctrine in clerical form, arguing that the priest receives for the church, women asserted the possibility of offering up *their* communions for others. A beguine in Strasbourg in 1317 argued that the communion of a lay person would profit as much for the redemption of a departed soul as the mass of a priest.[52] In a particularly literal-minded version of such a notion, we find Gertrude of Helfta thinking that she should chew the communion wafer into as many crumbs as possible so that Christ would save exactly that many souls from purgatory.[53]

234

Thus holy women fed others not merely through charity and miracle but also through their own fasting and eating. When we listen to the words of mystics such as Hadewijch, Catherine of Siena, and Catherine of Genoa, we see that both fasting and communion (whether the wafer is taken on the tongue or the elevated host is adored with the eyes) are part of a never-filled craving for God. This craving is pain as well as glory. It is pain so vast that it fuses with all pain. It *is* therefore the pain of purgatory.

Purgatory was to these women not primarily a place in the cosmos or a counting house where deeds are measured and exchanged. Imagery of the marketplace—however much it may dominate contemporary male writing—is almost absent from their poetry and visions. Purgatory was, rather, the fact of suffering.[54] For mystics such as Mechtild of Magdeburg, Julian of Norwich, and Catherine of Genoa, purgatory was less punishment than loss or alienation. Purgatory was being without (or, rather, very far away from) God. In this sense life, too, was purgatory. Fasting and disease and eucharistic frenzy were all purgatory. And if the pain was there to be endured, eddying around one whenever the glory faded—as it always did fade—then one might decrease it for others by enduring more oneself. Mystical women substituted not only their communions for the hunger of others but their pain for the punishment of others as well. Hadewijch even wrote that she had been too audacious in her claims for her suffering and her love, for she had wished to snatch from hell itself four whom God had condemned. So tolerant was God of her ignorance, she said, that he actually allowed her to "deliver from despair" and "spiritual death" the four for whom she had endured all manner of agony and alienation.[55]

The saving and serving role that mystical women created for themselves in the later Middle Ages was therefore neither aping of the clergy nor open rebellion against clerical prerogative. It was simply another model—a charismatic model, a lay model. Women saw themselves as authorized to teach, counsel, serve, and heal by mystical experience rather than by office. Despite occasional visions in which they themselves received sacerdotal trappings, female mystics usually saw themselves as laity rather than priests, recipients rather than consecrators. Both Juliana of Cornillon and Mechtild of Magdeburg, for example, inspired by God to lead and to criticize his church, suggested that he should send clerics instead; they both, however, came to accept their prophetic and visionary

role as an alternative.[56] Gertrude of Helfta, tougher and more androgynous in her self-image, envied priests their ability to handle God but said
that it might be more dangerous than useful to their own spiritual state.[57]
Already in the twelfth century the theologian Hildegard of Bingen explained the different and fully complementary roles of men and women,
underlining both their equal and mutual contributions to the biological
process of conception and their paired religious roles as mystic on the
one hand and priest on the other.[58] Gherardesca of Pisa (d. 1269), in one
of her visions, expressed this sense of man as priest, woman as recipient:
"On Sundays, Blessed John [the Evangelist] celebrates the mysteries of
the mass, with all holy clerics of every religious order being present for
the office, and the Blessed Mary receives the eucharist of the Lord seven
times for all sinners. . . . None except Saint John dares to sing mass there
[in heaven], nor does anyone dare to take communion, except the Blessed
Virgin."[59] Catherine of Siena in the fourteenth century was told by Christ
in a vision that she need not dress as a man, for Christ had chosen to
speak through her, the weaker vessel.[60]

Even the distribution of eucharistic miracles makes it clear that both
men and women increasingly viewed the role of recipient, of pious lay
person, as a female role. As I pointed out above, almost all medieval
miracles that specifically concern reception of the eucharist occurred to
women,[61] and almost three-fourths of the lay saints from the later Middle
Ages were women.[62] (It is significant that the occasional male who receives the eucharist directly from Christ or angels or a dove—i.e., whose
act of *receiving* is given special emphasis—is invariably not a priest but
a layman, and a layman of low status. Receiving—i.e., eating, rather
than preparing, holy food—and lay status thus tend to go together, and
neither is associated with powerful and admired males.)[63] The pattern of
miracles, like the pattern of canonizations, underlines the dichotomy:
men are priests, whose act of consecrating God shimmers with unearthly
power; women are recipients, whose act of eating is dignified with the
reassurance that the food they take is really God.

In women's religiosity, however, the role of vessel, of recipient, was
elevated to new significance. Whereas male theologians saw the priest as
divinized in the act of consecration and even attempted to identify priest
with church, women saw their act of receiving, of eating, as pregnant
with salvation. Women substituted their communions for the negligence
of those who did not—or could not—eat; women offered their suffering

in hunger or disease for the suffering of the sinful in purgatory. Indeed, some women's visions elevated the status of recipient above that of priest: Juliana of Cornillon advised a priest to be a recipient; Agnes Blannbekin saw the eucharist depart from a corrupt priest and fly into her own mouth.[64]

Thus women's food practices controlled their religious circumstances as well as their domestic ones. Not only did women successfully avoid marriage or shape it more to their liking by refusing commensality and giving away family food; they also tested clergy by their food miracles, took on direct service of their fellow Christians through food distribution, and bypassed ecclesiastical limitations on their intimacy with God in astonishing encounters with Christ himself as nursing mother, chalice bearer, or bleeding meat. Moreover, elevating their fasting and hunger for God into cosmic significance, women offered their suffering for the salvation of sinners—here on earth and beyond, in the far reaches of purgatory, as well. Food was not merely a device by which women manipulated those—fathers, husbands, confessors, priests—who had greater authority than they; rather, food observances, food miracles, and food metaphors were a means by which women shaped for themselves complex, spiritually effective, and distinctive roles within the medieval church.

◆ Food Practices as Rejection of Moderation

When we see clearly the array of functions that women's food practices performed in late medieval society, we understand how myopic it is to view female fasting as primarily an attack on body. The counseling and healing medieval women practiced through their eucharistic visions and miracles, the criticisms of the church they announced in inspired utterances, the salvation they offered to their fellows through disease and suffering are far more emphasized in women's own words and far more prominent in stories about them than any theme of dualism between body and spirit or any notion of the female as weak or evil.

It is not enough, however, to argue against the conventional interpretation of women's religiosity as internalized dualism or misogyny by pointing out that other, social functions can be found for women's asceticism. There is a deeper problem with the interpretation that states that women's fasting and feasting, their self-punishment, miraculous bodily manipulation, and eucharistic frenzy were internalizations of medieval stereotypes of the flesh and the female as negative. The problem is this. In the period in which this characteristic female spirituality emerges, theology was developing in precisely the opposite direction. The theologians of the twelfth- and thirteenth-century church were busy making an honored place in the scheme of things for the laity, for women, for the female body, and for marriage. It was precisely these theologians who, as I indicated in chapter 2, argued for moderation in asceticism and in eucharistic devotion, warning women against extensive fasts and prohibiting the familiarity of too frequent communion. Thus the extremism of religious women in the later Middle Ages can hardly be an internalizing of the views male theologians held either of food practices or of the female. Yet twelfth- and thirteenth-century theology and religious life supplied the context within which women's extravagant asceticism and eucharistic devotion were forged. It seems likely, therefore, that women's religiosity was a reaction against the moderation urged by church leaders, against new efforts to make a place—but a secondary place—for women and for the laity within a Christian universe. In order to explain this, a little more must be said about the direction of twelfth-and thirteenth-century theology.

Much attention has recently been given to the ways in which preachers of the twelfth to the early fourteenth century expanded the notion of Christian roles within society. Although canon lawyers increasingly defined the clergy as set apart by life style and prerogatives and to a large extent equated the church with the clergy, preachers wrote repeatedly both about and for the variety of what they called "orders" (statuses) in society and devoted much care to explaining how each was religious.[65] The anonymous twelfth-century author of the *Libellus de diversis ordinibus*, for example, argued that God intends a diversity of ways of serving him to exist together, "as a harmony is achieved from different chords."[66] James of Vitry wrote that clerics, priests, married people, widows, virgins, soldiers, merchants, peasants, craftsmen, and "other multiform types of men," each group having its own rules and institutions "according to the diverse types of talents," make up collectively the body of the church under "the abbot Christ."[67] Just as feudal lawyers busied themselves in classifying the many degrees of "freedom"—that is, of

238

privilege and obligation—that characterized the wide variety of roles and statuses in medieval society, so moralists and theologians, from the twelfth century on, busied themselves in saying why these diverse statuses were all valuable (although not, of course, all equal) before God. Corporate metaphors, classical and Pauline in origin ("there are many members but one body"), and paraphrases of John 14:2 ("there are many mansions but one house of God") became increasingly popular.[68]

The growing sense that a worldly role such as craftsman or married woman might have a rule of life defining it and might win for its practitioners merit before God was reflected in what some scholars have called the "rise of lay spirituality."[69] From the later twelfth century on, the church, increasingly organized hierarchically under the papacy, felt a greater and greater responsibility for ordinary layfolk, devoted more attention to defining for them their characteristic forms of devotion, and canonized more and more lay (even married) saints. Theologians defined marriage as a sacrament and did not in this process, as Georges Duby has pointed out, totally spiritualize it; if its basic significance lay in the commitment of the partners, it was a coupling of bodies as well. Preachers romanticized the Holy Family and the marriage of Mary and Joseph.[70] Theologians even debated whether the Virgin Mary menstruated and one group among them decided that she did, giving new and positive significance to a physiological process once considered a curse and a punishment.[71]

These same theologians and canon lawyers, who permitted and even gave (somewhat grudging) spiritual significance to sexuality and childbearing, modified earlier notions of fasting—in part to make it possible for the laity to meet the minimum requirements. In the thirteenth to the fifteenth century, the number of categories of exemption from fasting increased, and the standard fast came to be broken earlier in the day. Fasting was often treated by preachers and exegetes as symbol rather than act. It was seldom spoken of as an attack on the body. Aquinas, for example, saw fasting as a means to curb the demands of the body—not a rejection of matter but a limited renunciation of one of the goods of God's creation. "To starve the body" would be, said Aquinas, to steal from what it should be and offer to God only "stolen goods." To fast into ill-health would destroy one's "dignity" as a person.[72] An early example of the kind of pressure for moderation that characterizes the

medieval church can be found in a late-eleventh-century letter from
Geoffroy, abbot of Vendôme, to a certain brother Robert, who had taken
on himself what Geoffroy considered inappropriate abstinence:

> If you love to fast, I praise this, that you may eat by fasting and abstain
> by eating. For he eats by fasting and abstains by eating who eats thus
> daily what in no way satisfies the stomach. For to abstain one day and on
> another eat fully does not seem laudable. On the days on which people
> eat nothing they murmur much; and then on days when they eat much
> they feel inappropriate joy. Therefore it is better that we recognize need
> and daily sustain ourselves and refrain from vice. . . . For gaining eternal
> life, abstinence of the body is not enough unless the fast of the soul is
> married to abstinence.[73]

The tone of late medieval preachers and theologians often has this note
of rationality, sobriety, and decency, this sort of concern for steady, moderate observance, especially when addressing women. Even those, like
Abelard and Suso, who had reason to know that some women were
capable of great devotion and asceticism, advised that extravagant austerities were "unsuitable to your [i.e., the female] sex and unnecessary
for your disposition."[74]

Georges Duby has recently suggested that those men and women who
turned to heresy in the twelfth and thirteenth centuries were in part
reacting against a church which tried to control and domesticate marriage—a church which made a place in the scheme of things for women
and sexuality, but a secondary place.[75] Whether or not this is a correct
analysis of the impulse to reject the institutional church, it appears to
present a clue to the extravagance of women's spirituality. While preachers were busy formulating sermons *ad ordines* that carefully defined a
place for every sort and condition of person, while lawyers pressed for
canonization of every type of saint in part so that a model might be
available for every type of Christian, while moralists urged moderation
in ascetic practice so that the church might be broad enough for all—
pious women elaborated a religiosity that was in no way moderate, a
sense of self that was in no way secondary. Instead, immoderate and
frantic, women mystics soared beyond all careful gradations and distinctions into the immediate presence of God.

The extent to which women's spirituality was itself a rejection of a
successful and moderate church, with its cozy domestication of women

and of the laity, can be seen in the alarm with which preachers viewed it. Theologians such as Gerson and David of Augsburg, who saw the extravagance of women's religiosity and sometimes themselves described it in extravagant language, were upset by its exuberance and its sensuality.[76] Albert the Great, although he would not allow it to be attacked as heresy, denigrated it as ridiculous. Tauler warned that although God sometimes came to pious women in visions, this was not, and should not be, the normal way of meeting him.[77] In the early fourteenth century, some women mystics who rejected the moderate, decent spirituality of carefully graded works and prayers as "inferior" (and rejected as well the affective religious responses of some of their sister mystics) were condemned or burned.[78]

Moreover, women themselves sometimes suggested, in their strident refusal to accept counsels of moderation, that moderation was exactly what they objected to. Columba of Rieti, who once attempted to pacify criticism by eating, refused to take anything but the sacrament once Dominic appeared in a vision and authorized her behavior. Catherine of Siena, who obediently tried to eat when commanded by her confessor and who defended herself to a male detractor by saying that her inedia was merely an infirmity and without spiritual significance, revealed what was probably her true understanding of asceticism when she said, of Agnes of Montepulciano, that survival without eating is characteristic of "the perfect." Hadewijch, who sometimes in her letters and visions apologized for her audacity, also luxuriated in the power that her agony achieved. She reported that Christ said to her: "Beautiful revelations and miracles have happened to you during your days . . . more than to any person who was born since I died."[79] He also, she tells us, addressed her:

> O strongest of all warriors! You have conquered everything and opened the closed totality [i.e., the union of humanity and divinity in Christ], which was never opened by creatures who did not know, with painfully won and distressed Love, how I am God and Man! O heroine, since you are so heroic, and since you never yield, you are called the greatest heroine! It is right, therefore, that you should know me perfectly.[80]

A more immoderate vision could hardly be imagined.[81]

The immoderateness of women's spirituality is found in their notions of self-abasement as well as in their mystical heights, their sense of being special to God. So tortured did some women become not only with their own awareness of unworthiness but also with their compassion for others who were alienated from God that they offered to go to hell itself. Gertrude the Great claimed that one should be willing to take the eucharist to one's own condemnation if such an act contributed to God's glory.[82] Mechtild of Magdeburg cried out in anguish to ask Christ how he could allow souls to languish in hell, and she repeatedly prayed for their release.[83] Hadewijch, who had confidence that her suffering lifted her to likeness ("God promised me so much suffering for the sake of likeness to himself that I, in preference to all men and more than all men, should suffer this in order to content him and live as a perfect human being"),[84] also used her suffering to beat against God's justice and demand the release of condemned souls.

> In one thing I did wrong in the past, to the living and the dead, whom I with desire would have freed from purgatory and from hell as my right. But for this be you [God] blessed: Without anger against me, you gave me four among the living and the dead who then belonged to hell. Your goodness was tolerant of my ignorance. . . . For I did not then know your perfect justice. . . . Through love I wished to snatch the living and the dead from all debasement of despair and of wrongdoing, and I caused their pain to be lessened, and those dead in hell to be sent into purgatory, and those living in hell to be brought to the heavenly mode of life.[85]

The story that Tauler told as an example of humility to the nuns he advised, rings true as evidence of both the radical self-abnegation and the soaring triumph of contemporary female spirituality:

> You will never gain what you want until you want nothing created, but only the Creator. . . . Children, there is nothing further I want to say to you, except to tell you a little story which illustrates well what I mean. I know a Canaanite woman [cf. Matt. 15:21–28]; let us call her that because the incident I am going to tell you about happened less than four years ago, and she is still alive. She once experienced rapture, and was transported so that she could see God and our Lady and all the saints. At the same time she saw herself placed unutterably far away from God. Then this soul, in such unspeakable torment, turned to our Lady and to all the saints and begged them all to help her. But then she saw that they did not pay the slightest attention to her entreaty; they were in such great joy and bliss that they neither heard nor heeded her prayers. Then, as we mortals do, she invoked the Passion and death and wounds of our Lord Jesus Christ, but for answer she was asked how she could invoke what she had never honored. When she saw that our Lady and the saints and

the blessed Passion of our Lord were of no help to her, she turned to the Lord Himself, and this human soul said: "Oh Lord, since no one will help me, see, my loving God, that I am Your poor creature and You are my God, and then judge me according to Your adorable will. If it is Your will that I should be forever in the deepest torments of hell, I submit to it all, dear Lord, as Your blessed will." And so she utterly abandoned herself for all eternity; but she had hardly made this act of self abandonment when she was at once taken up, far above all intermediaries, and was drawn utterly into God's abyss, truly submerged in His marvelous divinity.[86]

Such exuberance and extremism sometimes carried women into positions that theologians saw as heterodox—as "dualist" or "quietist" or "antinomian." And, despite the convincing efforts of both medieval and modern theologians to spell out the opposing philosophies and theologies behind "heterodox" and "orthodox" positions, the two positions fuse together so closely in actual mystical writing that the same phrase can often be interpreted both ways. In Hadewijch, for example, both religious affectivity and a deep critique of affectivity cry out in the same poetic line—so that quietism and even antinomianism can be suspected in her notion that God, the infinitely lovable and desirable, is beyond all possible effort or desire. In Catherine of Siena's description of Agnes as "perfect" because of her vegetarianism and attack on the body, we find a terminology that might occur in Cathar literature as well. It seems that we as historians should avoid adopting the medieval categories of "heterodox" and "orthodox" as our categories of analysis not only because, as scholars such as Grundmann have argued,[87] the same particular themes frequently occur in both types of religiosity, but also because, behind women's often quite divergent religious practices and ideas, lay a common extremism of reaction that suggests dissatisfaction with clerical advisers and their counsels of sweet reasonableness.

In conclusion, then, we can say that women's food practices functioned as a way of criticizing and controlling those in authority. They also provided a distinctive way for women to serve their fellows and meet their God. But they did more. By their very extravagance, audacity, and majesty, they rejected the success of the late medieval church, rejected—for a wider, more soaring vision—an institution that made a tidy, moderate, decent, second-rate place for women and for the laity.[88] Like the desert ascetics of the fourth century whom they sometimes took as models, women mystics from the twelfth to the fourteenth century were in certain ways reacting against the "triumph" of the church. And, like those early monks and ascetics, women often expressed their dissatisfaction with what they saw as their religion's worldliness and compromise not by leaving the institution but by fulfilling its precepts with a vehemence that frightened and titillated its leaders.

Food practices functioned in all these ways. But function is not meaning. It is time to look at what the wild soaring vision actually meant.

8

THE MEANING OF FOOD:
FOOD AS PHYSICALITY

The immaculate lamb [Christ] is food, table, and servant. And this
table offers the fruits of true and perfect virtues. . . . And the table is
pierced with veins, which run with blood. . . . Oh my son, run to this
table [and drink]. . . . And when [the soul] has drunk, it spits up the
blood on the heads of its brothers [because it is too full with hot and
inebriating wine] and is thus like Christ who continually pours out
his blood not for his utility but for ours. And we who eat at that table
become like the food [i.e., Christ], acting not for our own utility but
for the honor of God and the salvation of neighbor.

CATHERINE OF SIENA (D. 1380),
WRITING TO ONE OF HER CONFESSORS[1]

AS THE WRITINGS of Catherine of Siena make clear, to eat Christ is
to become Christ. The Christ one becomes, in the reception of communion and in the *imitatio* of asceticism, is the bleeding and suffering
Christ of the cross. The flesh of Jesus—both flesh as body and flesh as
food—is at the very center of female piety. And this flesh is simultaneously pleasure and pain.

We cannot understand medieval religiosity until we realize how different such probing and embracing of body as pain-pleasure is from
most modern notions of body, in which pleasure and pain are seen as
opposites and the cultivation of pain is rejected as pathological. In understanding this difference it is helpful to remember how little medieval
people could do to mitigate discomfort of any kind. Thus medieval
metaphors and symbols express the *experiencing* of body more than the
controlling of it.[2] Sensations and senses that we differentiate from one
another tend to be fused in medieval piety, where satiation is described
as "hungry" and discomfort is called "delicious." To deny bodily responses toward the world is often, to a medieval writer, to release torrents

of bodily energy toward God. An approach to the body so alien to our modern one needs further explanation for the twentieth-century reader.

♦ Food and Flesh as Pleasure and Pain

As I explained in chapter 6, the fasting and eucharistic frenzy, charity and self-denial, of pious women frequently brought excruciating pain. Yet women did not ordinarily speak of these practices as punishment or as escape from the body. Angela of Foligno found the taste of pus "as sweet as communion"; Beatrice of Nazareth spoke of Jesus' torment as "healthy wounds"; the author of the nuns' book of Unterlinden described the sound of self-flagellation as melody, rising sweet to the ears of the Lord of Hosts. Women's own view of physicality was not, most basically, dualistic. When women spoke of abstinence, of eucharistic ecstasy, of curing and healing through food, they called it *imitatio Christi*. "Imitation" meant union—fusion—with that ultimate body which is the body of Christ. The goal of religious women was thus to realize the *opportunity* of physicality. They strove not to eradicate body but to merge their own humiliating and painful flesh with that flesh whose agony, espoused by choice, was salvation. Luxuriating in Christ's physicality, they found there the lifting up—the redemption—of their own.

The humanity of Christ, understood as including his full participation in bodiliness, was a central and characteristic theme in the religiosity of late medieval women.[3] Often it had erotic or sensual overtones. For example, Margery Kempe was so intensely attracted to Christ's maleness that she wept whenever she saw a male baby; in her visions she cuddled with Christ in bed and was bold enough to caress his toes.[4] Angela of Foligno, Adelheid Langmann, and Catherine of Siena, among others, married Christ in eucharistic visions. Underlining the extent to which the marriage was a fusion with Christ's physicality, Adelheid received the host as a pledge rather than a wedding ring, while Catherine received, not the ring of gold and jewels that her biographer reports in his bowdlerized version, but the ring of Christ's foreskin. Many late medieval women had visions of bathing or nursing the Christ child. To some (for example, Ida of Louvain, Agnes of Montepulciano, and Margaret of Faenza), the pleasure was so intense that they refused to surrender the baby again to his mother Mary.[5] The beautiful young Christ who appeared to Lutgard, Margaret of Ypres, and Margaret of Oingt, baring his breast, was both nursing mother and sensual male lover.[6] Hadewijch described encounter with this Christ, mouth on mouth, body on body, in language that seems to report the experience of orgasm (see above, p. 156). The twelfth-century author of the story of Christina of Markyate reports a similarly sensual encounter:

> Day and night she knelt in prayer, weeping, and lamenting, and begging to be freed from [sexual] temptation. . . . Then the Son of the Virgin looked kindly down upon the low estate of His handmaid and granted her the consolation of an unheard-of grace. For in the guise of a small child He came to the arms of his sorely tried spouse and remained with her a whole day, not only being felt but also seen. So the maiden took Him in her hands, gave thanks and pressed Him to her bosom. And with immeasurable delight she held Him at one moment to her virginal breast, at another she felt His presence within her even through the barrier of her flesh. Who shall describe the abounding sweetness . . . ? From that moment the fire of lust was so completely extinguished that never afterwards could it be revived.[7]

Margery Kempe thought Christ said to her:

> "Daughter, thou desirest greatly to see Me, and thou mayest boldly, when thou art in thy bed, take Me to thee as thy wedded husband, as thy dearworthy darling, and as thy sweet son, for I will be loved as a son should be loved by the mother, and I will that thou lovest Me, daughter, as a good wife ought to love her husband. Therefore thou mayest boldly take Me in the arms of thy soul and kiss My mouth, My head, and My feet, as sweetly as thou will. And as often as thou thinkest of Me, or wouldst do any good deed to Me, thou shalt have the same reward in Heaven, as if thou didst it to Mine own Precious Body which is in Heaven."[8]

Italian women too report erotic visions. Angela of Foligno burned so in penitence that she stripped before the crucifix and offered herself naked to Christ, pledging perpetual chastity.[9] She described her union with Christ thus:

> Once, during Lent, feeling herself very dry, she asked God to give her something of himself. . . . And her eyes were opened. She saw love, which came sweetly toward her. She saw its beginning but not its end [caput et non finem], but it was continuous. And she did not know how to

compare it to any color. But all at once when it came to her, it seemed to
her that she saw it clearly with the eyes of the soul, more clearly than she
was able to see with bodily eyes, and in touching of her it seemed to take
the form of a sickle [*unius falcis similitudo*]. Not that there was any mea-
surable likeness. Love took the appearance of a sickle, because then at
once love withdrew itself, not conferring itself as much as she expected. . . . Thus it made her languish all the more. . . . and she understood it as the operation of grace.

And then at once she was filled with love and inestimable satiety,
which, although it satiated, generated at the same time inestimable hunger
[*famem inextimabilem*], so that all her members were unstrung and her
soul languished and desired to fly away [*omnia membra tunc disjungebantur
et anima languebat et desiderabat pervenire*]. And she wished neither to see
nor to feel any creature. And she did not speak and did not know whether
she could speak, but within she spoke, clamoring that God not let her
languish in such a death, for she thought life to be death.[10]

Umiltà, in a fragment that supposedly reproduces one of her own sermons, speaks of John the Evangelist in vivid erotic imagery:

In renewing love, you have thrust that knife [of love] in me anew. You
have bound me to you so firmly that it is impossible for me to be pulled
away or carried away from your love. O most beloved John, you have
bound me with chains of gold, and you have married me with a ring.[11]

Scholars have, of course, suggested that such reactions were sublimated
sexual desire, but it seems inappropriate to speak of "sublimation."[12] In
the eucharist and in ecstasy, a male Christ was handled and loved; sexual
feelings were, as certain contemporary commentators (for example,
David of Augsburg) realized, not so much translated into another me-
dium as simply set free.[13]

In women's writing and visions, such images of marriage and sexual
consummation often describe exactly the torment and suffering that
women saw as *imitatio Christi*. In one of the most touching of all thirteenth-century *vitae*, an anonymous biographer describes Alice of
Schaerbeke:

And a little after this, . . . as she surpassed in virtues what could be
expected from the number of her years, God wished to purge her within
. . . from all strife and iniquity of this world, not because of any crime
or defect in her but because she was his spouse. . . . And so that she would
be free to rest with God alone and dally in the cubicle of her mind as in

a bridal chamber and be inebriated with the sweetness of his odor . . . ,
he gave her an incurable disease, leprosy. And the first night when she
was sequestered from the convent because of the fear of contagion, she
was afflicted with such sadness her heart was wounded. . . . [So she cried
and prayed at God's feet] . . . and the tender Lord seeing the humility of
his handmaiden with the eye of his mercy wanted to restore her. . . . And
he filled her with the sweet odor of divinity . . . and so she remained,
visited only by God. . . . And when she had learned from what she experienced to take refuge in the most secure harbor of God, she ran to
Christ's breasts and wounds, in every tribulation or anguish, every depression or dryness, like a little child drinking from its mother's breasts, and
by that liquid she felt her members restored.[14]

Juliana of Cornillon's biographer says (quoting the Song of Songs) that
since she could not literally die with Christ as she wished, she suffered
in spirit with him on the cross and held this pain between her breasts
"like a bundle of myrrh."[15] Margaret of Oingt writes that, meditating on
the crucifix, she took out the nails and carried Christ's body between the
arms of her heart, and kissed and swooned over the wounds.[16] Indeed,
Margaret received a vision that graphically expressed awareness that her
piety implied sensual encounter with Christ: the branches of a dry and
dead tree (presumably Margaret herself) flowered when they were
flooded by a great river of water, and on the branches were written the
words *sight, hearing, taste, smell,* and *touch.*[17] She also reports a vision
of Jesus as a doorway through which the soul must pass and says the
"person" who received the vision then vowed to say fifty Pater Nosters
in memory of Christ's wounds. But when the "person" prayed, she offered five Pater Nosters not only for each of the five wounds but for
other parts of his body as well—head, eyes, ears, nose, and mouth—
bathing and anointing "in spirit" his precious body.[18] The frank sensuality of Margaret's devotion to Jesus' suffering flesh has not escaped modern commentators, who have vehemently disapproved.[19]

Such response to the body of Jesus contained elements of terror as
well as of joy. Some women were driven to what their contemporaries
called insanity and others mutilated themselves while in ecstasy. But
however extravagant some of these reactions may have been, none is
accurately described as flight from matter or as "decadent" or "literal-
minded" symbolism.[20] In a religiosity where wounds are the source of a
mother's milk, fatal disease is a bridal chamber, pain or insanity clings

to the breast like perfume, physicality is hardly rejected or transcended. Rather, it is explored and embraced. Even the abhorrence of touch or warmth or food, which women such as Mary of Oignies, Lutgard, Douceline, Catherine of Siena, and Catherine of Genoa developed after meeting the fire, the kisses, and the flesh of Christ, were not rejection of the body. They were, rather, a numbing of the ordinary senses left by the transfixing encounter with God. In such religiosity, bodily impulses and emotions—the person's full sensuality—were released into new experience. Physicality was freed and transfigured. But it had to be aroused by God.[21]

Women's food images often evoked such transfiguring of body and suggested an almost physical union with the divine. In both the metaphors of poetry and the experiences of trance and vision (and these frequently flowed together), women met God as flesh taken into, *eaten by*, flesh. Thus Hadewijch, Mechtild of Magdeburg, and Ida of Louvain spoke of encounter with God as "eating" him, and Anna Vorchtlin said to the infant Jesus—in the sort of affectionate teasing mothers have used with babies for centuries—"I would eat you up, I love you so much." Catherine of Siena repeatedly spoke of serving and saving others as eating. She described the soul ascending to God as a baby reaching for the maternal breast. And she emphasized the breast as symbol not only of charity but also of the flesh that is our humanness.[22]

Food was a multifaceted symbol in medieval spirituality. Yet, as the sophisticated rhythms of Hadewijch and the theology of Catherine of Siena suggest, food most basically meant flesh; flesh meant suffering (sometimes ecstatic, delicious suffering); and suffering meant redemption. Fasting, feeding, and feasting were thus not so much opposites as synonyms. Fasting was flight not *from* but *into* physicality. Communion was consuming, i.e., becoming, a God who saves through physical, human agony. To feed others was to offer one's own suffering as food. Whether ecstatically and defiantly confident in the glory of divinity, to which physicality was inextricably linked, or tortured in the paradoxical darkness of humanity, which is truer than glory because glory is beyond—medieval women went to God through suffering. They frequently called this journey "eating" or "hungering," because to eat is to join with food—and God is food, which is flesh, which is suffering, which is salvation.

Late medieval theology itself, of course, provided the basic equation:

food equals body. It taught that, at the central moment of Christian ritual, the moment of consecration, God became food-that-is-body. This moment then recapitulates both the Incarnation and the Crucifixion. In becoming flesh, God takes on humanity, and that humanity saves, not by being but by being broken. The food on the altar was thus for all Christians a symbol both of assimilation and of rending. To eat was to consume, to take in, to become God. And to eat was also to rend and tear God. Eating was a horribly audacious act. Yet it was only by bleeding, by being torn and rent, by dying, that God's body redeemed humanity. To become that body by eating was therefore to bleed and to save—to lift one's own physicality into suffering and into glory.

The particular implications that late medieval theology gave to the eucharist were themselves, however, historically conditioned. As we saw in chapter 2, the sacrament itself took on many meanings over the long course of the Middle Ages. It could underline the power of the sacrificing priest and of the propitiated God. It could symbolize the church, either as believers gathered into one body through commensality or as a unity defended against those who would rend it assunder by heresy or apostasy. It could reflect a moment in the cosmic war of good and evil— the moment at which God tricked the devil by offering himself as bait. It could stand for the transformation of suffering into salvation. The eucharist could thus recapitulate either the Incarnation (God becomes humanity), the Crucifixion (God dies for humanity), or the Resurrection (humanity is glorified). In order to understand why the food practices and images of late medieval women were such a consistent probing of and exulting in humanity (understood as full physicality), we must look further at the ways late medieval people of both sexes showed increasing concern with matter and corporality as religious issues. For in the period between 1200 and 1500, physicality came to the forefront as a religious concern.

◆ *The Late Medieval Concern with Physicality*

Notions of the eucharist shifted in fundamental ways from the days of the early church to the later Middle Ages. Although theologians and visionaries never forgot that the bread on the altar was the memorial of a communal, passover meal and of Old Testament sacrifice, they increas-

251

ingly emphasized the eucharist as suffering and bleeding flesh. As the thirteenth and fourteenth centuries wore on, theologians came to place the saving moment of Christian history in the Crucifixion rather than in the Incarnation or Resurrection; visionaries saw Christ in the elevated host or chalice not as regal lord, lavishly robed priest, or warrior against Satan, but as crucified man; poets and saints used *hunger* and *abstinence* less as metaphors for self-control or for dependence on the bounty of God than as images for never-satiated, sensual, and agonized yearning. Behind these shifts in metaphor and in theology lies a heightened concern with matter, with corporality, with sensuality. Although, as we have seen, some ambivalence about matter, some sharp and agonizing dualism, remains in late medieval religiosity, no other period in the history of Christianity has placed so positive (and therefore so complex and ambiguous) a value on the bodiliness of Christ's humanity.

The late medieval concern with matter and physicality was in part an explicit move in Christendom's war on heresy. A more positive significance was given to body in theology because various extreme Christian and quasi-Christian positions seemed to denounce flesh and matter. In the thirteenth century, theologians themselves saw the full philosophical and theological dualism of the Cathars as the major threat to Christian orthodoxy. Starting from the premise of a cosmic dichotomy between spirit and matter, the Cathars rejected the doctrine of the Incarnation, argued that the holy or "perfect" must flee the flesh in this life, and challenged the notions of resurrection of the body and of purgatory. In the fourteenth century, various forms of intense mysticism were defined as heresy because they seemed to ignore or reject the flesh in other ways. In certain quietist forms, mysticism sometimes seemed to deny all spiritual and moral striving by transcending all suffering and alienation— all humanness. In its more antinomian forms, mysticism sometimes threatened to permit the body all license because it took body as fundamentally "unreal." Thus, the various late medieval heterodoxies, diverse though they were, seemed to contemporaries to have in common a denigration of the body, a denial that it might be either a source or a recipient of salvation. Many twelfth-, thirteenth-, and fourteenth-century theologians and preachers (including the first great woman theologian, Hildegard of Bingen) argued explicitly that denial of the eucharist (i.e., of the notion that God becomes flesh and food) was one of the chief dangers of all kinds of heresy.[23]

Modern historians have suggested that the formulation of the doctrine of transubstantiation, the spread of devotion to the host as *corpus Christi*, and the church's enthusiastic encouraging of miracles in which the host turned into flesh were part of a general effort to counter heresy.[24] Medieval authors sometimes said as much. James of Vitry and Thomas of Cantimpré, writing about the female mystical movement of the Low Countries, held up women saints, with their reverence for Christ's body and blood, as an alternative to the Cathar view that the physical is the creation of an evil God.[25] The cardinal legate who helped Juliana of Cornillon propagate the feast of Corpus Christi supported it explicitly as a weapon against dualism.[26] Preachers such as Peter Damian, Eckbert of Schönau, and Alan of Lille chose stories of bleeding hosts to embellish their diatribes against heretics.[27] And, as I explained in chapter 2, eucharistic miracles themselves sometimes denounced superstition, apostasy, or unbelief. It is also quite possible to read the eucharistic devotion of the high Middle Ages as a move to counter heresy by increasing clerical control. Some confessors (for example, Margaret of Cortona's and Dorothy of Montau's) seem to have urged women toward frequent communion not only as an effort to keep their devotional life orthodox but also as a way of tying them more firmly into the ecclesiastical supervision which confession represented.[28]

We must, however, look beyond any conscious efforts at propaganda against Cathar dualism or aberrant mysticism if we are to understand the attention paid to matter and flesh in late medieval spirituality. A concern to give the proper significance to flesh was not so much a concern that characterized orthodox as opposed to heterodox, as it was a concern that bound all religious reactions of the period together (however much they might differ over what the proper significance was). It is sometimes impossible for us, as it was for contemporaries, to draw a line between Cathar and orthodox asceticisms (both stressed fasting and continence, for example) or between quietist and orthodox mysticism (both, for example, valued desire for God more than "works"). This fact indicates that *all* the religiosity of the period was animated in deep ways by the need to take account of (rather than merely to deny) matter, body, and sensual response.

Indeed, wherever we turn in the later Middle Ages we seem to find the theme of body—and of body in all its aspects, pleasure as well as pain. For example, the efforts of theologians and canon lawyers to define marriage as a sacrament, to see in family a source of grace, to accept and even sentimentalize female bodily functions such as lactation, at least in treating Jesus' mother, all indicate a new acceptance of body. The piety of the mendicants, especially the Franciscans, was permeated by attention to the fact of body, both in intense union (through asceticism) with Christ's suffering and in a view of all creation as the traces and footprints of God. Francis of Assisi, as is well known, rejoiced both in punishing what he called "the ass" (his body) in *imitatio Christi* and in finding God's glory in birds, flowers, sun, and moon—in all the creatures of the universe. One of the most important philosophical formulations of the thirteenth century, Thomas Aquinas's statement of the hylomorphic composition of the human person, was a new attempt to come to terms with matter. The doctrine says that what the person *is*, the existing substance *man*, is form and matter, soul and body. To Aquinas, the person *is* his body, not just a soul using a body; the resurrection of the body thus became, for the first time, not merely theologically but also philosophically necessary.[29]

Women were not usually directly in touch with such abstract theological or philosophical speculation as Thomas's idea of hylomorphism, but they nonetheless reflected in their visions a general sense of body as necessary for salvation. The same authors who lifted bodily agony toward the divine through metaphors of love, marriage, sweet tasting, and delight also spoke of the glories of matter and creation. The author of the nuns' book of Unterlinden, who described flagellation as music, commented that *homo* (our humanity) really includes all creatures.[30] Margaret of Oingt, who glorified the self-induced stigmata of Beatrice of Ornacieux and offered to become a leper if God so willed, saw Christ's humanity as a clear mirror in which is reflected all the beauty of creation.[31] Mechtild of Hackeborn, who rolled in broken glass, saw a vision of the celebrating priest in which his vestments were covered with every blade and twig, every hair and scale, of the flora and fauna of the universe. As she looked in surprise, she saw that "the smallest details of creation are reflected in the holy Trinity by means of the humanity of Christ, because it is from the same earth that produced them that Christ drew his humanity."[32] Such visions make it quite clear that "humanity" included not merely senses and agonies but bones and flesh, even sticks and stones, as well. For better or worse, for pain or pleasure, body was becoming more and more of an issue in theology and in piety.

Behind such late medieval ideas, we hear echoing fundamental shifts in devotion that came in the long span of years between antiquity and the twelfth century. More than any other factor, it was the cult of saints that introduced into Christian theology and practice a sense of the power of body.[33] Beginning in a Roman world that feared the dead as polluting and legislated against their removal or dismemberment, a Christian enthusiasm for bodies, especially mutilated dead bodies, as loci of divine power made steady headway throughout the early Middle Ages. Indeed, those (such as Guibert of Nogent in the twelfth century) who opposed the cult understood precisely what was at stake: the cult of relics not only abolished a distinction between spirit and matter; in giving terrifying power to bone and sinew, it forced a new look at what it meant for every human to *be* a body.[34]

This sense of body as locus of the divine had become so powerful by the thirteenth century that the consecrated host was frequently compared to the bodies of the saints and revered as a relic of Christ. Not only did the practice of reserving the host in pyxes or tabernacles spread rapidly after 1200, the host was sometimes actually reserved in a reliquary or displayed, in a pyx, alongside reliquaries. Mobile tabernacles were often modeled on reliquaries. The practice of burning candles or lamps before the host was clearly borrowed from the manner in which relics were treated, and the practice of visiting the host as if it were a relic spread rapidly, probably having begun with female recluses.[35] A particularly vivid example of this parallelism of eucharist and relics is provided in the behavior of Hugh, Bishop of Lincoln, who chewed off a piece of Mary Magdalen's arm while visiting Fécamp and defended himself to the horrified onlookers by replying that if he could touch the body of Christ in the mass, he could certainly apply his teeth to the Magdalen's bones.[36]

This emphasis on the fact that Christ's humanity is truly flesh and blood led to an increasingly literal sense of what "imitation" of Christ meant. By the late twelfth century, *imitatio* as a spiritual theme had moved far beyond the Cistercian notion of affective meditation on the events of the life of Jesus.[37] The greatest spiritual writer of the twelfth century, Bernard of Clairvaux, had taught that we identify with Christ by extending our compassion to his humanity through pitying the suffering humanity of our neighbors.[38] But by 1200 Francis of Assisi and Mary of Oignies actually received in their bodies the wounds of Christ

255

while a seraph looked on. About 1275, Philip of Clairvaux described a recluse, Elizabeth of Spalbeek, who acted out the persecution of Christ every twenty-four hours, dragging herself about, beating herself, and bleeding from stigmatic wounds and from under her fingernails.[39] In the fourteenth century holy women such as Dorothy of Montau, Rita of Cascia, and Julian of Norwich and holy men such as Henry Suso and Robert of Salentino (d. 1341) acted out the Passion in elaborate pantomimes or prayed for literal death in imitation of the Crucifixion.[40]

Some descriptions of holy women stressed explicitly that *imitatio* is fact, *not* memory or imagination. We are told, for example, that Margaret of Cortona and Lukardis of Oberweimar became one with the Crucifixion *rather than* simply remembering or pitying Christ's suffering.[41] Margaret of Ypres's extreme self-flagellation as a means of joining with Christ was called a *recordatio* (remembrance), but in such a passage the meaning of the word *remember* has changed.[42] Beatrice of Nazareth, more theologically sophisticated than many of her fellow women mystics, spoke of three grades of moving toward Christ: turning toward grace; growing in the memory of Christ's Passion; and, finally, inhering in Jesus.[43]

By 1350, preachers were increasingly emphasizing *imitatio* as literally "shaping oneself to."[44] When Ludolf of Saxony, in his *Life of Christ*, explained how Christians should conform themselves to Christ (*actus conformationis*), he said they should not, for example, merely meditate on how Christ was slapped but should instead slap themselves. (The slap should, however, be "moderate.")[45] Suso explained how literal copying of Christ's agonies saved both neighbor and self:

> And I . . . desire from this day forth to stand before your throne as the trusty representative of all sufferers. . . . If suffering brought with it no other gain than that by our griefs and pains we grow in likeness to Christ, our prototype, it would still be a priceless benefit. . . . Even if God should choose to give the same eternal reward to those who suffer and to those who do not, we should nevertheless prefer afflictions as our earthly portion in order to resemble our leader.[46]

This sense of *imitatio* as *becoming* or *being* (not merely feeling or understanding) lay in the background of eucharistic devotion. The eucharist was an especially appropriate vehicle for the effort to become Christ because the eucharist *is* Christ. The doctrine of transubstantiation was crucial. One *became* Christ's crucified body in *eating* Christ's crucified body. Thus the reception of the eucharist led so naturally to stigmata, visible or inward, that contemporaries hardly worried about how to account for their appearance. *Imitatio* was incorporation of flesh into flesh. Both priest and recipient were literally pregnant with Christ. The metaphor of the good soul as Christ's mother, which had an ancestry going back to Mark 3:35, became in the thirteenth century more than metaphor. Caesarius of Heisterbach described a priest who swelled up at the consecration, pregnant with Christ.[47] Christina Ebner dreamed of being pregnant with Jesus. By the fourteenth century Dorothy of Montau was almost required by her confessor to exhibit mystical pregnancy as part of her preparation for communion.[48] In other instances of such literalism, the dying Juliana Falconieri was observed to incorporate the eucharist by having it fade into her chest[49] and Clare of Montefalco's sisters claimed to see the insignia of Christ's Passion etched upon the muscle of her heart after death.[50]

Nothing in late medieval notions of *imitatio* implied that Christ's humanity was merely body or that Christ was merely human. Repeatedly, between the thirteenth and the fifteenth century, mystics stressed that the Christ encountered in the eucharist was fully human, soul as well as flesh, and fully God. Guiard of Laon in his *De eucharistia*, composed in the early thirteenth century, argued that there were three fruits of the eucharist because of its three elements: body, soul, and divinity of Christ.[51] In the late fourteenth century, Catherine of Siena, in her *Dialogue*, put the following words into the mouth of God:

I am that Sun, God eternal, whence proceed the Son and the Holy Spirit. . . . The person of the incarnate Word was penetrated and kneaded into one dough with the light of my Godhead, the divine nature. . . .

What tastes and sees and touches this sacrament? The soul's sensitivity. How does she see it? With her mind's eye. . . . This eye sees in that whiteness [of the bread] the divine nature joined with the human; wholly God, wholly human; the body, soul and blood of Christ, his soul united with his body and his body and soul united with my divine nature, never straying from me.

. . . And at the words of consecration I revealed myself to you. You saw a ray of light coming from my breast, like the ray that comes forth from the sun's circle yet never leaves it. Within this light came a dove, and dove and light were as one and hovered over the host. . . . Your bodily eyes could not endure the light, and only your spiritual vision remained, but there you saw and tasted the depth of the Trinity, wholly God, wholly human, hidden and veiled under that whiteness.[52]

The joy mystics felt in physical union with Christ's humanity was never a denial of Christ's divinity. Becoming Christ physically was, rather, a way of being snatched up into his divinity. The more theologically so-phisticated of mystical writers (for example, the Helfta nuns, Hadewijch, and the two Catherines) insisted repeatedly on the two natures of Christ.[53] But as Hadewijch put it (in her own subtle language which it is so dangerous to quote out of context), we cannot just "be God with God," we must also "be human with Christ."[54] Or as Angela of Foligno put it (in her biographer's paraphrase of her teaching):

[The soul in this present life sees, feels, and knows] the lesser in the greater and the greater in the lesser, for it discovers uncreated God and "humanated" God [*Deum humanatum*], that is divinity and humanity, in Christ, united and conjoined in one person. . . . And sometimes, in this present life, the soul receives greater delight in the lesser than in the greater. For the soul is more conformed and adapted to the lesser which it sees in Christ, the incarnate God, than it is to that which it sees in Christ, the uncreated God; because the soul is a creature who is the life of the flesh and of all the members of its body. Thus it discovers both God "humanated" and God uncreated, Christ the creator and Christ the creature, and in that Christ it discovers soul with flesh and blood and with all the members of his most sacred body. And this is why, when the human intellect discovers, sees, and knows in this mystery Christ the man and Christ-God, ordainer of the mystery, this intellect feels delight and expands in him, because it sees God "humanated" and God uncreated conformed, and made like itself—because, that is, the human soul sees the soul of Christ, his eyes, his flesh, and his body. But, while it looks . . . , it should not forget also to turn to the higher . . . , the divine.[55]

There is nothing specifically female about the late medieval concern with matter and body or about the extravagance of certain fourteenth- and fifteenth-century efforts at *imitatio*. Physicality as problem and op-portunity was a basic theme throughout late medieval religiosity. But this theme was taken up especially intensely in women's lives and wom-en's writing and was expressed there especially in eucharistic devotion and in other sorts of food imagery. For this there are specific cultural as well as psychological and social reasons. To put it simply, the weight of the Western tradition had long told women that physicality was particularly their problem, nurturing particularly their opportunity.

In order to place women's food practices in their full historical context, it is therefore necessary to come at last to the vexed question of the "image of woman." In chapters 9 and 10, I explore how the long-standing association of "woman" with "body" and with "food" contributed to the distinctive emphases in women's piety that are the subject of this book. I also argue that the notion of woman as food and flesh had different implications for medieval women themselves and for their male admirers and detractors.

9

Woman as body and as food

And thus man and woman are dependent on each other so that each is necessary to the other; because man is not called "man" without woman nor is woman named "woman" without man. For woman is necessary to man, and man is the consolation of woman; and neither of them can be without the other. And man truly signifies the divinity of the Son of God, and woman his humanity.

For the same God created man strong and woman weak, and her weakness gave rise to sin. And divinity is strong but the flesh of the Son of God is weak, and through it the world is restored to its first life. For truly that flesh, immaculate and inviolate, like a spouse, proceeds from the virgin womb. HILDEGARD OF BINGEN
(TWELFTH CENTURY)[1]

LATE MEDIEVAL theology and piety emphasized Christ as suffering and Christ's suffering body as food. Recent scholarly work on spirituality has not ignored this emphasis; indeed, it would be impossible to do so. Yet scholars have not always noticed that such concerns were more prominent in women's religiosity than in men's. Where they have noticed the fact, only internalized misogyny has come to mind as an explanation. But serious misunderstandings of medieval religion are involved in such a description of women's piety. I have argued above at length that the nature of medieval families and marriage patterns, the nature of clerical authority, and the sexual division of labor all help to explain why the piety of women had different emphases and themes from that of men and why food practices as well as food metaphors were crucial to women. But in order to understand women's religiosity we must also probe more deeply into the nature of symbol. For it seems likely that women were drawn to identify with Christ's suffering and feeding flesh because both men and women saw the female body as food and the female nature as fleshly. Both men and women described Christ's body in its suffering and its generativity as a birthing and lactating mother and may at some almost unconscious level have felt that woman's suffering was her way of fusing with Christ because Christ's suffering flesh was "woman." The question of what *the female* meant as symbol in late medieval thought must, however, be approached with great care.

◆ *Woman as Symbol of Humanity*

The so-called image of woman has been much and heatedly discussed by recent students of medieval theology.[2] Some of the discussion has been more obfuscating than helpful. Some modern commentators have, for example, deplored the fact that certain patristic figures (such as Tertullian and Augustine) argued that woman *qua* woman was not created in God's image, although woman *qua* human being was. The meaning of such statements in patristic writing is, however, quite complicated.[3] And by the thirteenth century such arguments, used in theological and legal writing, often referred to woman's social role (i.e., her subordination to man in the family) as well as to her anatomical or biological role.[4] Thus to argue that woman as wife (a creature ruled by man) could not be an image of the kingship of God might become not so much a proof of female inferiority as an argument for rebellion against family and a source of confidence for women who retained virginity or aspired to continence. In any case, the notion that woman was "not in God's image" was not absorbed by medieval women, even married women, as a prohibition of their approach to God. On the contrary, the writing of women mystics is full of references to being created in God's image. Gertrude the Great, Margaret of Oingt, Douceline of Marseilles, and Beatrice of Nazareth all rejoiced in their creation in the image and likeness of God and saw this image as the basis on which *imitatio* is built.[5] In a vision, Mechtild of Hackeborn saw Christ place his hands on hers and give her "the imprint of resemblance like a seal in wax."[6] And Catherine of Siena wrote, addressing God: "By the light of understanding within your light I have tasted and seen your depth, eternal Trinity, and the beauty of your creation. Then when I considered myself in you, I saw that I am your image."[7]

Another aspect of medieval theological views of woman has also been deplored by modern scholars, and there is reason to think that this notion did influence medieval women. This is the notion that, allegorically speaking, "woman is to man as matter is to spirit." Thus *woman* or *the feminine* symbolizes the physical, lustful, material, appetitive part of human nature, whereas *man* symbolizes the spiritual, or rational, or mental. As we saw above in chapter 6, the roots of this idea were multiple, scientific as well as theological. Ancient scientists had argued frequently that at conception, woman contributes the stuff (or physical nature) of the foetus, man the soul or form.[8] Patristic exegetes had regularly seen woman (or Eve) as representing the appetites, man (or Adam) as representing soul or intellect.[9] When combined with the negative view of marriage and sexuality that characterized much early Christian thought, such views could and did encourage misogyny. They were subtle views, of course. And often writers such as Tertullian and Augustine who voiced them had in mind primarily the integration of various aspects into a single personality when they spoke of "masculine" and "feminine." These patristic thinkers often rejected marriage more as a way of rejecting family than as a way of rejecting body or woman.[10] But by the later Middle Ages, as we saw in chapter 1, such rhetoric did sometimes justify the suppression of women's religious life simply because women, even chaste women, were seen as a temptation to the clerics who supervised them. It also provided a basis for the witch-hunting theology that labeled elderly women as fleshly and irrational, even diabolical. Moreover, as Weinstein and Bell have pointed out, it led not only theologians but also male hagiographers to comment on women's weakness, to focus on sexual temptation in telling women's stories, and to attribute the failings of men to women rather than to the men themselves.[11]

The notion that woman is to man as matter is to spirit was sometimes used by male theologians and biographers not only to denigrate women but to castigate male failure as well. The argument went thus: if women, who were more vulnerable to sin than men, less rational and strong, could revere Christ in the eucharist or flagellate their bodies into submission and ecstatic union, how heinous by comparison were the crimes of male self-indulgence and clerical corruption! Moreover, men went beyond the use of "the female" as a way to castigate themselves. They were accustomed to invert the image of woman and see her as not only below but also above reason.[12] They somewhat sentimentally saw as an apotheosis of female weakness and un-reason Mary's love for souls and her mercy toward even the wicked who superstitiously revered her. They encouraged women's visions as special, supra-rational contact with the divine and romanticized women's mysticism in exotic rhetoric. Sometimes they even used *woman* as a symbol of the soul cherished by God and called themselves the "brides" of Christ.[13]

Women writers were aware of the idea that woman is to man as flesh is to spirit. The first great female theologian, Hildegard of Bingen, knew the tradition in both its exegetical and scientific forms and, indeed, argued against some of its implications.[14] Some late medieval women (for example, Mechtild of Magdeburg and Catherine of Siena) did fall into a regular pattern of using *man* or *manly* to mean strong, while describing themselves as "weak" or "despised" women, "beggars," "poor maids," "little girls," etc.[15] By and large, however, women did not draw from the traditional notion of a symbolic dichotomy between male and female any sense of incapacity for virtue, for spiritual growth, or for salvation. Women writers tended either to ignore their own gender, using androgynous imagery for the self (as did Gertrude the Great and Hadewijch), or to embrace their femaleness (as did Margery Kempe) as a sign of closeness to Christ. Catherine of Siena, for example, although she urged her male and female correspondents to be men rather than weak women, received a vision from Christ in which he told her that she need not take on male dress as a sign of her power to speak for God.[16] Her usual images for herself were either female or androgynous: she was the bride to Jesus the bridegroom, or a child to Jesus the nursing mother. If anything, women drew from the traditional notion of the female as physical an emphasis on their own redemption by a Christ who was supremely physical because supremely human. Influenced by the growing concern with Christ's humanity as bodiliness, they sometimes even extrapolated from the notion that male is to female as spirit is to flesh the notion that, in Christ, divinity is to humanity as male is to female. Whereas male writers used the traditional dichotomy of male and female to criticize particular women and to differentiate sharply between male and female roles, male and female characteristics, women used the dichotomy differently. To women, the notion of the female as flesh became an argument for women's *imitatio Christi* through physicality. Subsuming the male/female dichotomy into the more cosmic dichotomy divine/human, women saw themselves as the symbol for all humanity.

In making this symbolic equation of *homo* or *humanitas* with Eve, Mary, or *mulier*, women were, of course, aided by the very slipperiness of the notion of *humanity*. A recent translator of Catherine of Genoa has pointed out that, in her work, the allegorical meaning of *umanità* tends to slip back and forth between "humanness" and "flesh" or "fleshly urges."[17] The author of the nuns' book of Unterlinden even used *homo* to mean all creatures.[18] In the erotic passage from Hadewijch quoted above in chapter 5, *humanity* (*menscheit*) clearly implies *body*: "and all my members felt his in full felicity, in accordance with the desire of my heart and my humanity." Such usage tended both to obscure any sharp sense of a body/soul dichotomy (for both body and soul were human) and to imply that humanness intimately involved physicality. It was this sense of humanity as entailing bodiliness (although not reducible to it) that women expressed in expanding the male/female dichotomy from spirit/flesh to divine/human.

From Hildegard of Bingen and Elizabeth of Schönau to Catherine of Siena and Julian of Norwich, women theologians in the later Middle Ages used *woman* to symbolize *humanity*. To Elizabeth of Schönau the humanity of Christ appeared in a vision as a female virgin.[19] To Hildegard of Bingen, Christ's humanity was to Christ's divinity as woman is to man, and *mulier* represented humankind, fallen in Eve, restored in *ecclesia* and *Maria*. In the passage quoted as epigraph to this chapter, Hildegard not only writes explicitly that "man signifies the divinity of the Son of God, and woman his humanity," she also argues that the two are complementary in our salvation as male and female are necessary to each other in religious life and in the biological process of procreation. Repeatedly in her work, Hildegard describes that which is redeemed by Christ—the humanity (including physicality) that comes from Mary— as feminine; and she underlines the association of woman-humanity with fleshliness by arguing that Adam is created from clay but Eve from flesh. Thus Eve's creation not from seed but from flesh (*non ex semine* but *caro de carne*) is a parallel to the Incarnation of Christ.[20] Moreover, the parallel woman-humanity-Christ is enhanced by Hildegard's sense that Christ's body is also *ecclesia* ("church"—a feminine noun invariably symbolized iconographically by a female figure). In a famous eucharistic vision, Hildegard saw what she called the "figure of woman" (*muliebris imago*) receiving from Christ, hanging on the cross, a dowry of his blood, while below the cross stood an altar with the chalice and around the chalice were revealed as in a mirror the events of Christ's earthly life (see plate 12). And Hildegard heard the words: "Eat and drink the body and blood of my Son to abolish the prevarication of Eve and receive your true inheritance." Although the priesthood was, to Hildegard, revered and essential (and limited to men), the priest enters this eucharistic vision only after holy church. The image of both sinful *and saved* humanity is the image of woman.[21]

Moreover, to women writers such as Hildegard, Mechtild of Magdeburg, and Catherine of Siena, Mary was the source and container of Christ's physicality: the flesh Christ put on was in some sense female, because it was his mother's. The roots of such theological interpretation lie partly in scientific theory. Aristotelian physiological doctrine held that the mother provides the stuff of the foetus, the father the form or animating principle, whereas a more Galenic interpretation (which Hildegard, for example, reflected) held that the male and female seeds together produce the infant.[22] But whichever theory of conception a medieval theologian held, Christ (who had no human father) had to be seen as taking his flesh from Mary. This sense that Christ as body is formed from Mary's body led Hildegard to argue that it is exactly *female* flesh—the very weakness of woman—that restores the world. Thus flesh is to her, in her visions and in the theological exegesis they stimulate, symbolized by *woman*. Christ's flesh (his mother's flesh) is his spouse: "truly that flesh, immaculate and inviolate, like a spouse, proceeds from the virgin womb." A century after Hildegard, Mechtild of Magdeburg went further and implied that Mary was a kind of pre-existent humanity of Christ as the Logos was his pre-existent divinity. Mechtild argued that the Incarnation joined the Logos (the pre-existent Son of God) with a pure humanity, created along with Adam but preserved as pure in Mary after the Fall.[23] Other women writers imply the same thing. Catherine of Siena, who usually referred to humanity as "Adam,"[24] sometimes associated it with the flesh of Mary. She wrote, speaking of Mary's sorrow at the Crucifixion:

> Oh sweetest love, which was the sword that pierced the heart and soul of the mother! The Son was broken in body, and the mother similarly, for his flesh was from her. Indeed it is just that she suffered in what befell him for he took his immaculate flesh from her. . . . He had the form of flesh and she, like hot wax, received the imprint of desire and love for our salvation from the sealing of the Holy Spirit, and by means of this seal the divine Word was incarnate.[25]

Margaret of Oingt, like Hildegard, wrote that Mary is the *tunica humanitatis*, the clothing of humanity, that Christ puts on.[26]

In a very unsettling reflection of this emphasis on Christ as assuming Mary's flesh, a fourteenth-century woman from Montaillou said she could not believe in the real presence:

> One day as I was going to the church of the Holy Cross to hear mass, I heard some women . . . saying that a woman had given birth on the roadside. . . . Hearing this, I thought of the disgusting afterbirth that women expel in childbearing and whenever I saw the body of the Lord raised on the altar I kept thinking, because of that afterbirth, that the host was something polluted. That's why I could no longer believe it was the body of Christ.[27]

The agonized skepticism of this woman Aude about the sacraments and even about God sprang from roots so deep we can no more diagnose them than could the inquisitor who examined her for symptoms of Cathar heresy. But it is clear that her obsession with the host as a woman's placenta arose in the context of a spirituality that laid graphic emphasis on the consecrated wafer as a product of, a fragment and exuding of, the female womb.

Such ideas lie in the background of the theology of "God's motherhood," developed by Julian of Norwich in the late fourteenth century and much commented upon by recent scholars.[28] The use of *mothering* as a description for the nurturing and loving (even the disciplining) that the soul receives from God is not new with Julian, nor are Julian's extended images of Jesus as lactating and birthing mother. Jesus' birthpangs had been extensively described by Margaret of Oingt in the thirteenth century, and his nursing of the soul was elaborated by, among others, Guerric of Igny in the twelfth century and Catherine of Siena and the anonymous monk of Farne in the fourteenth.[29] What is new in Julian is the idea that God's motherhood, expressed in Christ, is not merely love and mercy, not merely redemption through the sacrifice of the cross, but also a taking on of our physical humanity in the Incarnation, a kind of *creation* of us, as a mother gives herself to the foetus she bears. In a very difficult passage, Julian explains that the second person of the Trinity is our mother because in him/her we are double, substantial *and* sensual (that is, what we are is human, and this kind of a soul—a human soul—is one that knows and feels *in a body*). "Our substance is the higher part, which we have in our Father, God Almighty; and the second person of the Trinity is our Mother in nature in our substantial creation, in whom we are founded and rooted, and he is our Mother of mercy in taking our sensuality."[30] In other words, the full creature that we are, body as well as soul, is redeemed in Christ because Christ is fully human. This fundamental fact of salvation is appropriately symbolized not by "father," who relates to and is responsible for the soul or reason or spirit of the child, but by "mother," from whom the child's physicality comes and whose existence therefore makes possible its wholeness. So, as Julian puts it, in our mother "our parts are kept undivided." To Julian, therefore, Mary is our mother because her flesh is Christ's; but she is a shadow of the truer mother, Christ himself, who gives to us our humanity by taking it on:

> For in the same time that God joined himself to our body in the maiden's womb, he took our soul, which is sensual, and in taking it, having enclosed us all in himself, he united it to our substance. In this union he was perfect man, for Christ, having joined in himself every man who will be saved, is perfect man.
>
> So our Lady is our mother, in whom we are all enclosed and born of her in Christ, for she who is mother of our Savior is mother of all who are saved in our Savior; and our Savior is our true Mother, in whom we are endlessly born and out of whom we shall never come.[31]

Male writers were most apt to use "male" and "female" as dichotomous images, representing, for example, nurture versus discipline, or weak versus strong, or inspiration versus the authority of office; and male writers saw God's motherhood in his nursing and loving rather than (as Julian did) in the fact of creation.[32] But male writers too associated the flesh of Christ with Mary and therefore with women. Robert Grosseteste (d. 1253) wrote to the monks of Peterborough: "In your monastery continually dwells the King of heaven, not only by his divinity but also, in the sacrament of the eucharist, by the true substance of the flesh, which he took from the Virgin."[33] And male writers occasionally saw *the female* as symbol of Christ's humanity. In a complex passage that equates Adam with all humanity but sees that humanity as the bride of Christ, Ruysbroeck wrote:

> This bridegroom is Christ and man's nature is the bride. . . . [And the devil deceived the man] in whom humanity first existed. And by false counsel he seduced her, Nature, the bride of God. And she was driven out into a strange land. . . . But when God thought it time . . . then he sent his only begotten Son on earth, into a splendid court and into a glorious temple, which was the body of the glorious maiden Mary. There

he espoused this bride, our nature, and united her with His Person by the noble virgin's most pure blood.[34]

Thus human nature, fallen in Adam, is taken on, *married*, and redeemed by Christ the bridegroom in Mary's body. It is the bride; it is symbolized by the female. And if our nature is not Mary herself (the second Eve)— as it appears to be to Mechtild—its marriage to Christ is nonetheless made possible only by the body and blood of woman.[35]

The association of Christ's flesh with woman was reinforced in iconography, where Mary had a place of honor on eucharistic tabernacles. The modern historian Dumoutet has described a number of late medieval instances in which a figure of Mary actually *is* the tabernacle in which the consecrated host is reserved; and, as I explained above, retables tended to associate the consecration with the Incarnation by depicting together the officiating priest and scenes of the Annunciation or of Mary with her baby.[36] In the so-called Vierges ouvrantes (plate 13), statues of Mary opened to reveal the Trinity inside, thus underlining the notion that Mary is the container (i.e., the womb, the tabernacle, the reliquary) within which rests the body of God.[37] William Durandus the Elder in his *Rationale divinorum officiorum* of 1285–1291 said that the reliquary (*capsa*) into which the priest put the consecrated host was, symbolically speaking, the body of Mary.[38] Francis of Assisi, in his "Salutation of the Blessed Virgin," addressed Mary thus:

> Hail, his [i.e., Christ's] Palace.
> Hail, his tabernacle.
> Hail, his robe.
> Hail, his Handmaiden.[39]

And Suso called her the shrine in which Wisdom reposes.[40] In one of Bernard of Clairvaux's sermons on the Purification, the parallel between the child in Mary's womb and the host offered on the altar is explicitly drawn. Bernard suggests that Mary, mother and celebrant, provides and presents to the faithful the body that is their salvation: "Offer your son, sacred Virgin, and present the blessed fruit of your womb to God. Offer the blessed host, pleasing to God, for the reconciliation of us all."[41] Indeed, since woman's body was seen as the place where the Incarnation happens, the consecrating priest was sometimes described as a pregnant woman: Caesarius of Heisterbach described a priest who swelled in mystical pregnancy; an often-quoted twelfth-century text praised the dignity of priests because in their hands Christ is incarnated "as in the Virgin's womb."[42]

The symbolic association of humanity with the female thus derived strength both from the association of humanity with physicality (and *woman* was the symbol of flesh) and from the association of Christ's humanity with his mother. It is in this context that we must understand women's devotion to Mary, for women's devotion was less to Mary's social or religious role as woman than to her physical role as bearer of humanity. This explains a rather curious fact, noted by recent historians.[43] Mary is not really as important as one might expect in women's spirituality.

As the work of Simone Roisin has suggested, Mary was probably more important in men's visions than in women's in the later Middle Ages.[44] Moreover, Weinstein and Bell have demonstrated that the humanity of Christ was a more prominent emphasis in women's piety than was devotion to the Virgin.[45] This is not to say that Mary was unimportant to women. Particularly in southern European saints' *vitae*, the theme of *imitatio Mariae* is strong. The biographer of Douceline of Marseilles, for example, sees her as imitating the poverty of Mary, whereas her beloved Francis imitated the poverty of Christ directly.[46] And Margery Kempe clearly identified with Mary and wished, like her, to take Christ in her arms. But we frequently find that it is male biographers of women who stress the theme of women's imitation of Mary (and of other women).[47] Some women saints do, it is true, see themselves in visions swooning with Mary before the cross. But *all* women saints swoon on the cross with Christ himself.[48] The reverence for Mary that we find in women mystics is less a reverence for a "representative woman" than a reverence for body, for the bearer and conduit of the Incarnation. Thus devotion to Mary tended to be a prelude to devotion to her child. If Mary was important in Hadewijch's mysticism, for example, or in Julian of Norwich's theology, it was because Christ's body was the occasion for human redemption and Mary's body, the source of Christ's body, was the symbol of the bodiliness of us all.[49]

◆ Woman's Body as Food

Medieval people did not simply associate body with woman. They also associated woman's body with food. Woman was food because breast milk was the human being's first nourishment—the one food essential for survival. Medieval writers and artists were fond of the theme, borrowed from antiquity, of lactation offered to a father or other adult male as an act of filial piety.[50] The cult of the Virgin's milk was one of the most extensive in late medieval Europe.[51] A favorite motif in art was the lactating Virgin (see, for example, plates 14, 21, 22, 23, 24). The allegorical figure Charity was frequently depicted as a nursing mother, and sometimes the other virtues also were represented as women with flowing breasts (see plates 15 and 16).[52] The allegorical figure *Ecclesia* was also frequently shown as a nursing mother (see plate 17).[53] Even the bodies of evil women were seen as food. Witches were supposed to have queer marks on their bodies (supernumerary breasts) at which they nursed incubi.[54]

Male and female writers used nursing imagery in differing ways. Men were more likely to use images of being nursed; women, metaphors of nursing. When male writers spoke of God's motherhood, they focused more narrowly on the soul being suckled at Christ's breast, whereas women were apt to associate mothering with punishing, educating, or giving birth as well.[55] Most visions of drinking from the breast of Mary were received by men (the most famous are the visions of Bernard of Clairvaux—see plates 18 and 19—and Henry Suso), although there are at least two cases of German nuns receiving the same vision in the late thirteenth century.[56] In contrast, women (for example, Ida of Louvain and Margery Kempe) sometimes identified with Mary as she suckled Jesus or received visions of taking the Christ child to their breasts.

Both men and women, however, drank from the breast of Christ, in vision and in image. Both men and women wove—from Pauline references to meat and milk and from the rich breast and food images of the Song of Songs—a complex sense of Christ's blood as the nourishment and intoxication of the soul.[57] Both men and women therefore saw the body on the cross, which in dying fed the world, as in some sense female. Again, physiological theory reinforced image. To medieval natural philosophers, breast milk was transmuted blood, and a human mother— like the pelican that also symbolized Christ—fed her children from the fluid of life that coursed through her veins.[58] As early as the second century, Clement of Alexandria had spoken of Christ as mother, drawing out the analogy between a God who feeds humankind with his own blood in the eucharist and a human mother whose blood becomes food for her child.[59] In the twelfth century, nursing imagery often referred to milk and honey, but by the thirteenth and fourteenth centuries the image of the nursing Jesus regularly stressed blood more than milk as the food of the soul.[60] Mechtild of Magdeburg, for example, not only drew a parallel between blood and milk, she also spoke of blood as superior food and saw her own prayer and suffering for other souls as nursing them with blood.[61] When Catherine of Siena spoke of drinking blood from the breast of mother Jesus, she explicitly glossed blood as suffering—both Jesus' suffering and her own.[62]

Such an association of Christ's wounds with woman's body and of woman with the food of the eucharist is also found in late medieval art. Medieval artists explicitly associated the lactating Virgin with the eucharist. The breast of the Virgin was associated visually with the grape and thereby with passages from the Song of Songs that were interpreted as eucharistic references (see plates 20, 21, 22), and the nursing Virgin was also depicted as a table or an oven on which the child (i.e., the body or the food) was offered or baked (see plates 14, 24).[63] In those pictures where the child does not himself nurse but, rather, seems to invite the viewer toward the breast (see plates 14 and 23), some assimilation of Mary's milk and the blood of the eucharist may be intended. Barbara Lane has pointed out, for example, that in a miniature of about 1380–1385 from the Turin-Milan Book of Hours (see plate 23), the child makes no attempt to nurse, and Mary's gesture of pressing milk from her breast is directed toward a kneeling supplicant who seems far more anxious for the food than does the child.[64]

Artists, however, went further than merely associating the breasts of Mary with eucharistic feeding of the soul. There are a few late medieval paintings that suggest (even if they do not directly depict) the lactating Jesus familiar from devotional texts. We find this suggestion most strikingly in an obscure painting over which the great historian Gougaud puzzled a generation ago (see plate 25).[65] The painting (now in the Accademia in Venice) was made in the fifteenth century by a certain Quirizio for the monastery of St. Clare on the island of Murano. Quirizio (one of whose other extant paintings also depicts a eucharistic theme) shows a young, to our eyes somewhat feminine, and very beautiful Christ displaying the wound in his right side, located high up, where a nipple would be.[66] He lifts up and offers the wound with two fingers of his left hand, just as the Virgin offers her breast to the infant Christ in hundreds of medieval paintings. With his right hand he gives the host to a kneeling nun. And around him is written in phrases borrowed from the Song of Songs: "Come to me, dearly beloved friends, and eat my flesh" and "Come to me, most beloved, in the cellar of wine and inebriate yourself with my blood." Quirizio's painting is related iconographically to those depictions that art historians call the "eucharistic Man of Sorrows" (see plates 26, 27, 30), and in at least one of these graphic images of Christ's flowing blood as food the female figure Charity (herself often depicted with flowing breasts) receives the saving liquid in a chalice as the nun in Quirizio's picture receives the wafer.[67] These paintings remind us of the picture (not extant) which a sixteenth-century hagiographer reports Alda of Siena to have commissioned—a picture of a stunning reversal, in which Mary drinks from the breast of Christ while holding him in her arms.[68]

The parallelism of Christ's wound and Mary's breast suggested in Quirizio's painting is sometimes made explicit in medieval art. An image of the Virgin presenting her breast often accompanies the figure of Christ exposing his wound, to form the so-called Double Intercession. For example, in a mid-fifteenth-century miniature from the Turin-Milan Book of Hours, Mary touches her breast, which she does not do in the standard portrayal of the Madonna of Humility (see plate 28).[69] In a Last Judgment by Jan Provost (early sixteenth century), the Virgin and Christ bare and lift up their breasts in exactly parallel gestures (see plate 29).[70] In some such depictions, it is not merely the breast as symbol of compassion or charity (and therefore of intercession) that is offered; it is the breast as food, parallel to the bleeding (i.e., nurturing) wound. In an early-sixteenth-century depiction of Christ as the Man of Sorrows, for example, Christ in the central panel lifts up a bleeding wound while on the right-hand panel the Virgin, standing beside Bernard whom she nursed, lifts up her breast in an identical gesture (see plate 30). The picture reminds us that literary accounts of the miracle of the lactation of Bernard describe Bernard as choosing between the bleeding wound of Christ and the flowing breast of his mother.[71]

Since Christ's body was a body that nursed the hungry, both men and women naturally assimilated the ordinary female body to it. Women mystics such as Mechtild of Magdeburg and Catherine of Siena used the metaphor of the nursing mother to describe their own suffering for others, sometimes clearly implying that their spilling of blood-milk was *imitatio* of Christ's nurturing and inebriating wounds-breasts. Moreover, miraculous lactating, exuding, and feeding were characteristic female miracles in the later Middle Ages. Male hagiographers such as Thomas of Cantimpré saw women saints dripping holy fluid from breasts or fingertips. Several pious virgins from the Low Countries—Christina the Astonishing, Gertrude van Oosten, and Lidwina of Schiedam—supposedly nursed their adherents or cured others with their breast milk. Women mystics themselves had visions of feeding others, including the Christ child. The union of mouth to mouth, which many women (for example, Lutgard, Beatrice of Nazareth, Lukardis, Margaret of Faenza) gained with Christ, became also a way of feeding.[72] Lutgard's saliva cured the sick; Lukardis blew the eucharist into a sister's mouth; Colette of Corbie cured with crumbs she chewed and placed in the mouths of others. In a gesture that seems erotic as well as comforting and nurturing, Margaret of Faenza kissed her friend Benevenuta, who was recovering from a trance induced by the mass, and received consolation.

> Sister Margaret placed her face on her [friend's] face and kissed her: and then she felt such sweetness and consolation go out from her [friend] and enter into her, that it seemed to her that all the consolations of the world could not be equal to this. And this consolation remained in Sister Margaret for many days, with a great abundance of tears.[73]

As noted above, legends of miraculous exuding after death seem to have been attached more frequently to women's bodies than to men's after the eleventh century.[74] And where marvelous effluvia were part of a saint's power (as in the cases, for example, of Nicholas of Myra, Walburga, Agnes of Montepulciano, Elizabeth of Hungary, Margaret of Città di Castello, Rose of Viterbo, and Mary Magdalen de' Pazzi), food and nursing motifs tended to be of striking importance in the saint's story. The legendary Catherine of Alexandria, for example, from whose tomb on Mount Sinai holy oil was carried all over the Western world, was supposed to have bled milk rather than blood from her severed veins when beheaded.[75] Indeed, one suspects that stigmata appeared most frequently on women's bodies because stigmata (like the marks on the bodies of witches and the wounds in the body of Christ) were not merely wounds but also breasts. In this literal becoming of the crucified body, which a female mystic might achieve by ecstasy or by eating the bleeding host which feeds humankind, woman's wounds-breasts recapitulated the wounds-breasts of Christ.

Thus the female body was seen as powerful in its holy or miraculous exuding, whether of breast milk or of blood or of oil. Such extraordinary flowing out was predicated on extraordinary closure. Holy women were often said neither to eat nor to excrete. Stigmatics or myroblytes were often miraculous fasters—for example, Mary of Oignies, Lutgard of Aywières, Christina the Astonishing, Elizabeth of Hungary, Agnes of Montepulciano, Elsbet Achler, Catherine of Siena, Lidwina of Schiedam—and theologians underlined the fact that those who bled or exuded unusual fluids did not excrete in ordinary ways. The emphasis of hagiographers, who pointed out that saints neither excreted nor menstruated, and of early modern pamphleteers, who praised the so-called fasting-girls for not exuding so much as sweat or dandruff, seems based on some notion of balance. In the thirteenth century Roger Bacon tried to explain such phenomena naturalistically by arguing that the matter a fasting woman did not excrete might enable her to survive without eating; but, taken together, the stories of pious women suggest a deeper, symbolic balance: a balance of eating with not eating, exuding with not exuding. Closing herself off to ordinary food yet consuming God in the eucharist, the holy woman became God's body. And that body flowed out, not in the involuntary effluvia of urine or menstrual blood or dandruff, but in a *chosen* suffering, a *chosen* excreting, that washed, fed, and saved the world.

The extreme interest in physicality and the close association of woman with body and food that characterized late medieval culture seem to lie behind not only women's eucharistic piety and food asceticism but also the startling number of women's miracles that involve bodily change. Women's bodies gave off sweet smells as well as healing effluvia, indulged in ecstatic nosebleeds and trances, displayed abrupt changes in size and appearance, and broke out in miraculous physical marks ranging from espousal rings to stigmata. Once we take as seriously as medieval people did the idea that on the altar God becomes food (torn and bleeding meat), we can see as never before how much of such piety was literally *imitatio Christi*. The somatic changes women underwent parallel to a striking extent the savors, aromas, marks, and alterations that occur in the consecrated host. No wonder women manipulated their bodies; in doing so, they became God—a God who feeds and saves.[76]

Many assumptions in the theology and culture of Europe identified woman with flesh and with food. This same theology taught that the redemption of all humanity lay in the fact that Christ was flesh and food. Moreover, both Christ and women were food insofar as they were bodies. God, like woman, fed his children from his own body, and if God did not make his children from his own flesh, he saved them by taking for himself a body from their humanity. Thus women found it very easy to identify with a deity whose flesh, like theirs, was food. In mystical ecstasy, in communion, in ascetic *imitatio*, women ate and became a God who was food and flesh. And in eating a God whose body was meat and drink, women both transfigured and became more fully the flesh and the food that their own bodies were.[77]

An exploration of what *woman* meant to late medieval men and women, of what symbols and assumptions clustered around *the female*, thus helps us to understand why certain metaphors were so prominent in women's spiritual writing and why women not only practiced certain religious behaviors but also occasionally carried those behaviors to extraordinary lengths. I should, however, close this effort to explain why women chose certain images and practices with an obvious but necessary warning. Symbol does not determine behavior. The images I have discussed here were far too complex, too multivalent, to dictate any specific response. Just as women's food practices manipulated their environment with divergent and unpredictable results, so women's attempts to imitate Christ, to *become* the suffering and feeding body on the cross, issued in a wide variety of life stories. Although most religious women seem to have understood their devotional practices as in some sense serving as well as suffering, they acted in very different ways. Some, such as Catherine of Genoa, Elizabeth of Hungary, and Mary of Oignies, expressed their piety in feeding and caring for the poor. Some, such as Alpaïs, Alice of Schaerbeke, and Elsbet Achler, lay rapt in mystical contemplation as their bodies decayed in disease or in self-induced starvation that was offered for the salvation of others. Some, such as Beatrice of Nazareth, grew from a period of withdrawal, insanity, and disease into a later phase of confident leadership; some, such as Margaret of Hungary and Dorothy of Montau, spent their lives in a busy combination of charitable activities and acute, self-punishing asceticism. It is misleading to try to sketch a composite life story for religious women.[78] And it implies a misunderstanding of the fundamental nature of symbols to suggest that they compelled specific behaviors.[79] Instead, symbols enabled women to express and give meaning to certain basic realities that all societies face: the realities of suffering and the realities of service and generativity.

Yet, women chose certain symbols—especially eating and pain—more frequently than did men. And the medieval notion of the female as body and food seems to have suggested that the realities of suffering and service, although universal aspects of the human condition, somehow pressed more heavily on women or that women found in them a special significance. Indeed, the association of woman with body and food was characteristic of texts written by both women and men. This association thus not only helps us to understand the multifaceted behavior of medieval women, it also raises profound questions about whether men and women used symbols in the same way. For, if men and women lived together in a society in which *male* and *female* not only symbolized different things but also had asymmetrical (that is, unequal and non-parallel) values, it is reasonable to ask whether the two sexes made the same use of gender-related images, or indeed of any images. Did the notion of female as food or body, weakness or unreason, mean to a person who *was* female what it meant to a person who was not? In conclusion, therefore, let me turn to the question of how women's images of food and body symbolized self, making the answer more precise by delineating, as comparison, how men's religious behavior and images reflected men's selves.

10

WOMEN'S SYMBOLS

God has nowhere to put his goodness, if not in me . . . no place to put himself entire, if not in me. And by this means I am the exemplar of salvation, and what is more, I am the salvation itself of every crea-ture, and the glory of God. . . . For I am the sum of all evils. For if of my own nature I contain what is evil, then I am all evil. . . . Now if I am all evil, and he is all goodness, and one must give alms to the poorest being, or else one takes away what is hers by right, and God can do no wrong, for otherwise he would undo himself—then I am his goodness because of my neediness. . . . I need to have the whole of his goodness, that my evil may be staunched: my poverty cannot make do with less. And his goodness, being powerful and prevailing, could not endure my begging, and I would perforce have to beg if he did not give me all his goodness. . . . So it is clearly evident that I am the praise of God forever, and the salvation of human creatures—for the salvation of any creature is nothing but knowing the goodness of God. . . . Nor can I ever lose his goodness, since I can never lose my evil.   MARGARET PORETE (D. 1310)[1]

My Me is God.   CATHERINE OF GENOA (D. 1510)[2]

IN WESTERN EUROPE in the Middle Ages, as in many cultures today, women cooked and men ate. One of the strongest social links between male and female lay in the fact that wife or servant cooked what husband and lord provided and in the even more consequential fact that mother's womb and mother's milk guaranteed survival for the next generation. As Elias Canetti says: "A mother is one who gives her own body to be eaten." This is not, of course, to say that women never ate or that only male children were nourished from the female body. It is, rather, to say that social arrangements and cultural symbols stereotyped reception of nurture as a male activity, provision of nurture as a female one.

It is against this background that we must locate the food symbolism of medieval Christianity. And when we understand Christianity's fundamental symbols in such a context, they burst upon us with stunning and unexpected import. For in the mass the priest prepares food, and the food itself is a body that feeds with its own fluids and saves with the fleshly covering it provides. If medieval people turned to the Madonna and child as a symbol that the awfulness and mercy of God have already reached across the abyss created by the sin of humankind, how much more confidently did they turn to God himself, lactating on the cross, bearing the soul in his womb, feeding the faithful from the hands of his special cooks and servants, the clergy? When Catherine of Siena spoke of God as table, Christ as roasted flesh, and the Holy Spirit as waiter and servant, she was not indulging in an odd feminine need to use domestic images; she was expressing a startling reversal at the heart of Christian imagery. When medieval texts and medieval visions spoke of clerics as pregnant with Jesus, they expressed not gender confusion on the part of male authors and worshipers but the polysemous, fertile, paradoxical quality that Christian symbols share with all symbols. In the mass, priest and God are symbolically woman (although they are other things as well)—woman as food preparer, woman as food.

Medieval worshipers knew that women were barred from clerical orders and from places near the altar where God was handled; they knew that one justification for such prohibition was the gender of the human body born of Mary.[3] Increasingly from the twelfth to the fifteenth century, they saw woman as quintessential recipient, man as quintessential celebrant, maker and controller of the body of God. Yet they occasionally saw the New Testament account of the Presentation in the Temple as a moment at which Mary—the vessel that bore God's body—was priest.[4] More than occasionally they saw the celebrant as pregnant with the host. And in the cult of the Sacred Heart, they frequently saw God's body itself lactating, giving birth, clothing our humanness with the spotless humanness of God. In exactly that period of medieval spirituality that scholars have dismissed as "literal" and "degenerate," symbols flowered into a complexity that lifted the full panorama of human experience toward the divine. Priest was king and cook. God was father and mother, power and nurture, sword and breast. If the male monopoly of religious leadership and descriptions of God as male mirrored social hierarchy, descriptions of God as female and the startling reversal at the heart of the mass provided an alternative to and a critique of the asymmetry between the sexes in the ordinary workaday world.

Having said all this, have we, however, said enough? Were the food symbols of medieval religion simply reversals? And were they, as reversals, perceived and used in similar ways by women and men? In particular, did the medieval women whose lives I chronicle here find their most profound self-expression and their most successful access to God through elevation by reversed images into male roles, freedoms, and capacities? The answer is clearly no. However unexpected and profound the reversal at the heart of the mass, that reversal does not express the deepest self-perception of the women whose visions and words form the heart of this book. If Hildegard of Bingen, Hadewijch, Mechtild of Magdeburg, and the two Italian Catherines soared far above the humility suggested by their conventional references to themselves as "poor little women," "unlettered" and "soft," it was not because they claimed male power and authority or found their deepest release in a sense of receiving self waited on by priest as cook, Holy Spirit as waiter, or God as mother. It was because they knew God acted through the lowly. Women's symbols did not reverse social fact, they enhanced it. Thus Hadewijch could conceive of her ignorant self as wrenching souls out of hell; Catherine of Genoa could claim power through suffering when she spoke of her "Me" as "God"; Margaret Porete (burned at the stake for her confidence in the annihilation of souls in divinity) could claim "I—*because* I am lowly—am the exemplar of salvation." Women's symbols expressed the fact that woman *as what she is*—soft, unwise, poor, and human—is loved and saved by God.

In order to understand the import of this observation, some methodological and theoretical background is necessary.

♦ The Meaning of Symbolic Reversal

Anthropologists, who have provided twentieth-century historians with important tools for understanding how symbols "mean," have suggested that in ritual and in narrative, reversal of symbols often marks crucial moments or turning points. These anthropologists have tended to see such symbolic reversals as providing a "liminality"—a moment of escape from role and status, a crossing of boundaries or margins into an opposite role or perhaps into rolelessness—that ultimately reinforces normal social structures.[5] On the other hand, historians such as Natalie Davis have frequently seen a revolutionary potential or at least a powerful social critique in such symbolic reversals.[6]

The analysis of medieval symbols I have given above supports, to some extent, both such interpretations. Medieval women who saw themselves in visions as distributors of the chalice, as preachers, or as hearers of confession were clearly carrying out symbolic inversions, as were medieval laypeople whose visions claimed the cup, the blood of Christ, as their own.[7] And such inversions were, as the story of Lidwina of Schiedam and the miraculous host suggests, *both* effective rebellions against clerical control *and* escape valves, so to speak, that by providing a means of bypassing authority at moments of crisis actually reinforced the normal distribution of authority at non-crisis moments. Thus women's use of symbolic reversals can be seen as a defiance of male authority. But the prevalence of such reversals in medieval religion can also be seen as forming a context within which conventional asymmetries between men and women, clergy and laity, were undergirded and reinforced.

Such interpretations of symbol are helpful in reading medieval experience. But I wish to question them on a deeper level, for my study of food and flesh as symbol in later medieval spiritual writing and practice suggests that symbols as dichotomies, and therefore symbolic reversals, are less important in women's spirituality than in men's.

Let me begin with a clarification. The notion of renunciation of the world—i.e., following the naked and suffering Christ by renouncing status, power, personal comfort, and family—was at the heart of late medieval Christianity. Increasingly, as many historians have noticed, such renunciation was practiced *within* the world. Friars, tertiaries, and even laypeople rejected the wealth and status their families might have provided; they practiced, sometimes even within marriages, not only sexual continence but also a studied ignoring of the special demands of family love and loyalty. Late medieval women, like men, saw a certain rupture with ordinary worldly life as a mark of religious commitment. The miraculous abundance of tears given to Margery Kempe, her white clothes, and her hard-won continence were a lay equivalent of the vows, veils, and convent walls that set nuns apart from society. In arguing that men and women thought differently about a life of religious commitment, and especially that women represented the religiously inspired soul in metaphors that suggest a profound continuity between women's biological and cultural role in the world and women's spiritual vocations, I am not ignoring the fact that for women, as for men, some departure from ordinary social roles was necessary to make a religious life possible. Christina of Markyate and Ida of Louvain, like Francis of Assisi, had to escape from the ordinary expectations the world held for rich merchants' children. The nuns whom Hildegard of Bingen dressed as brides,[8] the virgin souls John Gerson described as pregnant with Christ,[9] were of course able to devote their attention to veneration of the eucharist and prayers for those in purgatory *because* they either never bore children and cooked for husbands or were at last able to escape from doing so. The question that concerns me here is not the practical ways religious roles freed people of both genders from certain worldly burdens and pleasures but the particular symbols that men and women chose to describe this freedom.

Our question is therefore twofold. First, do men and women make the same, or similar, use of symbolic reversal? To ask this is to ask whether men and women mean the same thing by *male* and *female*, whether each sex uses reversed gender imagery, and whether each sex achieves by such use a release from ordinary cultural expectations— women acquiring an image of self as public leader, men acquiring the self-image of nurturer and sufferer. The question also involves a second element: do men and women make equal use of dichotomous symbols? For reversal is predicated upon dichotomy—to reverse or invert one's image of self is to move from one pole to its opposite. Yet not all symbols are dichotomous. Symbols may make use of and refer to contradictions and mutual exclusions, but they may also be paradoxes (in which contradictions occur simultaneously) or syntheses (in which contradictions are themselves negated in fusion).[10] If men make greater use than women of symbolic inversion, this fact may be related to a tendency to construe many aspects of reality in terms of either/or. It is thus now necessary to look at men's use of images as well as women's in order to question the prominence in both usages of reversal and dichotomy. The analysis of male writers in chapter 3 will be useful here, especially since the men considered there are those who, in their sensibilities and in their lives, came closest to a female spirituality.

♦ Men's Use of Female Symbols

When we look at male writing in the later Middle Ages we find that symbolic dichotomies and reversals were at its very heart. Men tended to use the male/female dichotomy to underline male/female differences (father versus mother, teacher and disciplinarian versus nurturer, tough versus soft, etc.) and to castigate or romanticize female weakness. As I have demonstrated elsewhere, men tended to associate a clearly delineated set of social and biological characteristics with each gender, even when they were using gender as a symbol, and they tended to see these sets of characteristics as opposites. For example, Guerric of Igny (d. ca. 1157) wrote: "The Bridegroom [Christ] . . . has breasts, lest he should be lacking any one of all duties and titles of loving kindness. He is a father in virtue of natural creation . . . and also in virtue of the authority with which he instructs. He is a mother, too, in the mildness of his affection, and a nurse."[11] An anonymous Franciscan, describing Francis and Elizabeth of Hungary as parents of the friars minor, wrote: "He was the father . . . and she was their mother. And he guarded them like a father, she fed them like a mother."[12] In their symbolic universe, men tended to use the male/female dichotomy not only as symbol of authority/nurture, spirit/flesh, law/mercy, strong/weak, but in a broader sense as a way of expressing the contrast between God and soul, divinity and humanity, clergy and laity.[13] To medieval men, God was (as he has been to most of the pious throughout the long Christian tradition) metaphorically male—father or judge, bridegroom or friend—and the soul (partly because of the linguistic gender of *anima*) was frequently symbolized or described as female. Moreover, the gender dichotomies we find in men's writings were reinforced by other gender dichotomies that were implicit in the ways people lived. Men were food receivers, women food preparers and generators. Men were priests and women laity. Men were authoritative by office or ordination; women's religious power derived from inspiration, from ecstatic visitation.

Whatever other patterns lie behind these dichotomies, one is clear. If male is to female as spirit is to flesh, food receiver to food generator, clergy to laity, office to inspiration, law to mercy, and divine to human, then that which is symbolized by *male* is in some sense a product of culture, cut off from nature or biology. Thus, although it may at first appear incoherent or even contradictory that *the female* should symbolize *both* inspiration versus office *and* flesh versus spirit, there is a consistent dichotomy behind these pairs. The fundamental contrast seems to be between (a) constructs of laws, patterns, forms, erected at some distance from, if not in opposition to, nature, and (b) a more instinctual, internal, biological "human nature." In this sense, flesh is natural and spirit cultural just as prophetic inspiration is interior, subjective, natural, whereas clerical authority is an external, cultural structure independent of personal moral, experiential qualifications.

Structuralist anthropologists have recently taught us to see such a dichotomy as a basic contrast in human symbol systems. I have been influenced by their formulations, above all by Sherry Ortner's,[14] but I do not mean here what they mean. I agree with Ortner's critics that her theory is universalist in undesirable ways, ignoring the possibility that subgroups in a society, especially women, may hold differing and even disagreeing perspectives on the symbolic dichotomies used by dominant cultural groups.[15] Thus I am not here saying that the culture/nature dichotomy was an objectively true dichotomy between male and female. Nor am I saying that medieval women espoused such a dichotomy. I am merely pointing out that this is the pattern symbols fell into in male writing and religious practice between 1200 and 1500.

Such a symbolic pattern was, to men, profoundly disturbing. For the same male writers who came to see the church as the clergy, to see their gender as the symbol for God's divinity, to argue that male, clerical mediation was the necessary bridge between heaven and earth, knew they partook of fallen humanity. They knew Christ had preached: "Blessed are the meek." Their piety reflected their ambivalence. Increasingly they stressed not God's authority but Jesus' accessibility, not Judgment Day or Resurrection but a man laying down his life for his friends. They had recourse to visionary women for comfort and counsel—and for the direct inspiration they were afraid they no longer received.[16] And they spoke (as a definitely subordinate but nonetheless highly charged theme) of Jesus as mother and of themselves as women.

Sometimes, in calling themselves women, male writers used *woman* as a term of opprobrium. Helinand of Froidmont castigated his brothers: "Behold God compares men to women . . . and not merely to women, but to *menstruating* women!"[17] But more frequently they used *woman* as a symbol of dependence on God—both as a way of describing themselves as cared for by God and as a way of underlining their own renunciation of worldly power and prestige. In his "Letter to all the Faithful" Francis of Assisi said, describing virtuous friars:

> It is they who are the brides, the brothers and the mothers of our Lord Jesus Christ. A person is his bride when his faithful soul is united with Jesus Christ by the Holy Spirit; we are his brothers when *we do the will of* his *Father who is in heaven* [Matt. 12:50], and we are mothers to him when we carry him in our hearts and bodies by love with a pure and sincere conscience, and give him birth by doing good deeds which enlighten others by example.[18]

Speaking of friars who go in groups of three or four to hermitages, he wrote:

> Two of these should act as mothers, with the other two, or the other one, as their children. The mothers are to lead the life of Martha; the other two, the life of Mary Magdalen. . . . The friars who are mothers must be careful to stay away from outsiders. . . . The friars who are sons are not to speak to anyone except their mother or their custos [superior].[19]

Suso saw himself as a maiden picking roses, a baby nuzzling its mother's breast. Ruysbroeck wrote: "Man's nature is the bride [of Christ]."[20]

When a male writer described another man as a woman (for example, Bonaventure speaking of Francis of Assisi) or when a man (for example, Richard Rolle or Suso) described himself that way, he was using symbolic reversal. Man became woman metaphorically or symbolically to express his renunciation or loss of "male" power, authority, and status. He became woman, as Eckhart said, in order to express his fecundity, his ability to conceive God within.[21] Such reversal seemed necessary in a religion at whose heart lay contradiction and Incarnation: God-become-man. When Tauler sought a symbol of the soul's utter self-abasement before God, its utter denuding and emptying, he not only chose the poor Canaanite woman of Matthew 15:21–28, who referred to herself as lower than a dog, he also cited a contemporary woman who received a vision in which she was abandoned by all intermediaries between creation and Creator and who therefore cried aloud to God that she would accept condemnation to hell itself if it was his will.[22] In such a sermon, "woman" is a symbol and an example not only of the utterly contemptible and of the redeemed but also of the great reversal at the heart of the gospel: the fact that it is the contemptible who *are redeemed.*

The food and flesh imagery I examine in this book is, as I have explained above, a particular case of such symbolic inversion. Much about the priest's role and about the theology of *imitatio Christi* in the later Middle Ages involves a reversal of cultural assumptions about gender. On the one hand, of course, given the symbolic patterns, the priest was "male" and the communicant "female"; the priest was God and the recipient human. As is well known, Bonaventure argued that women could not be priests because the priesthood, the authority of God, had to be symbolized by a male.[23] But, in another sense, as I have demonstrated, God's dying body was female—a birthing and lactating mother—and the priest was female too. He was Mary, for in his hands, as in her womb, Christ was incarnate;[24] he was food preparer and distributor to recipients who ate. In the central moment of the mass the male celebrant waited, ready to care for and distribute a heavenly food, a vulnerable body, provided by a father-mother God for the benefit of human children.

Iconographic evidence too suggests that the mass implied gender reversal. Pictures of Christ distributing food and washing the feet of guests at the Last Supper outnumber visual representations of Christ as king or priest in the later Middle Ages. In such paintings Christ is depicted in one of society's most admired *female* roles: the role of food preparer and servant. A fifteenth-century retable from Ulm (plates 1 and 2) shows just such a reversal. On the outer wings (when closed), we find Christ as servant and food distributor, testing Judas with the wafer (as many mystical women tested false priests). When opened, the retable displays the eucharist represented both as a baby in the chalice and as flour ground through a mill. Mary and the four evangelists pour the grain into the funnel (i.e., celebrate). Apostles turn the crank. It is the prelates of the church, garbed in all their splendor, who wait quietly below as recipients.

Thus male writers, artists, worshipers, and priests in the later Middle Ages made use of sharp symbolic dichotomies, and many of their most profound and moving images were symbolic reversals. Moreover, men's own life stories tended to be stories of crisis and conversion. They enacted the reversals they used as symbols, stripping themselves naked (as did Francis of Assisi before his father), putting on the clothing of a child, a beggar, or a woman (as Richard Rolle did in becoming a hermit), suddenly and dramatically renouncing wealth, influence, and wife to take up poverty and chastity (as did John Colombini).[25] As I pointed out in chapter 1, many more medieval men than women underwent abrupt changes of life-style during adolescence. Having greater access to power and family wealth, men were able to abandon them more abruptly and flamboyantly, and medieval boys seem to have been older on average than girls when stricken by the impulse to abandon the world.

Many explanations can be suggested for the fact that men tend to use images, and live lives, of contrast, opposition, and reversal. Structuralist anthropologists have sometimes argued that dichotomous images of hard/soft, male/female, law/mercy, reason/unreason tend to appear in cultures with strongly patrilineal inheritance patterns, because the female (although necessary for procreation) tends in fact to be a disruptive force in such societies, a force outside law and structure.[26] Such explanation, though plausible, appears to reflect none of the subtlety of late medieval imagery, and it does not explain reversal, although it may explain dichotomy. Another way of relating imagery to social structure seems more convincing. This is simply to note that most gradations of status in the later Middle Ages were gradations of male status. The growing consciousness of the multiplicity of statuses and roles that characterizes twelfth- and thirteenth-century writing is predominantly a growing awareness of a variety of male roles. As Georges Duby has pointed out, women were outside the "three orders" of medieval society: those who pray, those who fight, and those who till the soil.[27] Even in the church, although nuns were "clergy" in one sense (that is, they were "regular"; they took vows), in another sense all women were laity—that is, outside orders. Women, as I said in chapter 1, often shied away themselves from highly structured institutional forms, avoiding rules and vows; and male characterization of women was usually according to their marital or sexual status—widow, virgin, married woman—rather than their institutional affiliation. Thus women were not "on" a ladder of roles and statuses in the same sense that men were.[28] It is hardly surprising therefore that complex imagery of role reversal, of inversion of power and status— of fool become king, boy become pope, man become woman or woman become man—appealed more to men, for whom the precise gradations of society were self-definitions that might bear down with a psychological weight that demanded periodic release.

There may also be psychological and theological reasons for men's preference for dichotomy and reversal. As several theorists have recently pointed out, the maturation of a boy (in Western culture, medieval and modern) requires a fundamental break in self-image: a boy must learn that he cannot be the mother who is his first projection of self, his first love, his first model.[29] A boy's growing up is therefore a learning to be other than female—a learning both to reverse his own desires and self-definition and to see the female as "other." Small wonder therefore that reversals and conversions become central in male ways of thinking about and symbolizing spiritual growth.

Moreover, the nature of the symbolic dichotomies men generated contained within itself pressure for reversal. Not only did Christian theology state that the humble, the lowly, "the last," were eventually to come first, thus dictating that men must find reversed symbols to speak of progress toward God (for example, the soul as woman, child, fool).[30] The male symbols themselves, in referring to that which is cut off from nature, that which is cultural construct, forced recognition of their opposites, for men knew themselves to be not merely "divine," "clerical," "spirit," and "authority." Because the symbols associated "the male" with culture, with "more than" and "other than" human nature, these symbols implied that in order to *be* human nature the male must take opposites to himself in symbol. The particular group of cultural activities, responsibilities, and symbols associated with *the male* by men itself implied contrast and reversal. The set of activities, responsibilities, and symbols associated with *the female* did not, in the same way, imply its obverse. That which *the female* symbolized—nurture, body, laity, humanity, inner inspiration—did not require anything else—for example, power, spirit, office, divinity—in order to conjure up person. Nor did it imply that reversal was necessary in order for person, for that-which-is, to be given religious meaning. Woman already *was* that which is, in Christianity, given religious meaning. For woman was, in fact as well as symbolically, human.

Thus the very set of dichotomous symbols that clustered around male/female in the Western tradition suggested that men—powerful, clerical, authoritative, rational, "divine" men—needed to become weak and human, yet spiritual, "women" in order to proceed toward God. And male writers in the later Middle Ages used much such reversed imagery for self. Moreover, they often assumed that reversed imagery and dichotomous symbols were appropriate ways of reflecting on female experience. Male writers urged women to "become male" or "virile" in their rise to God.[31] Male hagiographers and chroniclers were fascinated by stories of women's cross-dressing in order to enter religious houses—probably to the point of fabricating such incidents.[32] Male writers devoted much attention to female weakness, both by underlining women's sexual temptations and by expatiating upon the inappropriateness of asceticism to women's soft, tender, and inconstant bodies. Suso wrote to a spiritual daughter: "You are weaker than Eve in paradise." The compiler of the Life of Ida of Louvain praised her by saying she was "not a woman or lazy, but like a man in constancy."[33]

There is much evidence that religious men in the thirteenth, fourteenth, and fifteenth centuries were fascinated by women—both by the female visionaries who became, through their very lowliness, the mouthpieces of God on high and by the ordinary mothers, housewives, laundresses, and maidservants who were signs of the depths to which Jesus stooped in redeeming humankind. As I suggested in chapter 3 above, male mystics such as Bernard, Francis, Rolle, Suso, Tauler, Eckhart, and Gerson advised women, admired women, and abhorred women. They adopted the image of woman—woman who was more humble and more fleshly than they—to speak of their own approach to God. In describing themselves as nursing mothers or suckling babes, these men were describing the self they became in conversion as the opposite of adult and male. In speaking of their conversions as the espousing of nakedness, poverty, suffering, and weakness, they were, even more generally, renouncing and reversing the prerogatives of wealth, strength, and public power that their world connected to adult male status. If male writers were fond of seeing themselves as brides, mothers, and children, such reversed images were only one set of metaphors in a symbolic world in which the man had to see his basic religious commitment as flight from power and glory—for Jesus himself had fled power, no matter how much kings and prelates might wield it in his name.

◆ Women's Symbols as Continuity

Female writers, expressing their religious desires and fears in the same symbolic tradition as men and worshiping in the same rituals, also in some ways used and reflected the clusters of dichotomies I have just described. Some of women's images of food and flesh were not only expressions of such dichotomies but profound reversals as well. In both eucharist and mystical union, women inverted what the culture assumed them to be. Just as Christ's death on the cross was a symbolic reversal—for he became, not *male* (king or priest or recipient of nurture), but *female* (a lactating and birthing mother, nurturer of others)—so the female communicant experienced gender reversal. She became not nurturer and feeder of others but receiver. In the mass, the roles of clergy and laity reversed ordinary social roles. The celebrant became food preparer, the generator of food, the pregnant mother of the incarnate God; the woman recipient feasted, with eyes and palate, on a food she did *not* prepare or exude. Woman's jubilant, vision-inducing, intoxicated eating of God was the opposite of the ordinary female acts of food preparation and of bearing and nursing children.[34]

Yet, on a deeper level, women's eating of God was not a reversal at all. For in the mass and in mystical ecstasy women became a fuller version of the food and flesh they were assumed by their culture to be. In union with the dying Christ, woman became a fully fleshly and feeding self—at one with the generative suffering of God. Woman's eating, fasting, and feeding others were synonymous acts, because in all three the woman, by suffering, fused with a cosmic suffering that really redeemed the world. And these three synonymous acts and symbols were not finally symbolic reversals but, rather, a transfiguring and becoming of what the female symbolized: the fleshly, the nurturing, the suffering, the human.

Women's food images and food practices thus reflect a larger pattern. For women's way of using symbols and of being religious was different from men's. It appears as a kind of sub-text within a larger text, dominated by dichotomous symbols and symbolic inversions, and it is always aware of male/female oppositions and of images of reversal. But women's sense of religious self seems more continuous with their sense of social and biological self; women's images are most profoundly deepenings, not inversions, of what "woman" is; women's symbols express contradiction and opposition less than synthesis and paradox.[35]

This quality of women's religious writings has been consistently noted by the greatest scholars who have studied them, although it has not been placed in a theoretical framework. Baron von Hügel, commenting on Catherine of Genoa's use of simultaneity of opposites or paradoxes, says, "For it was the element of simultaneity, of organic interpenetration of the God-like *Totum Simul*, which chiefly impressed her in these deepest moments."[36] Brant Pelphrey, in his exposition of the theology of Julian of Norwich, suggests that Julian saw sin as a necessary (if painful) part of being human and that her theory of union with God did not involve "stages" the soul "passed beyond" but, rather, a continuity of self, a becoming fully human with Jesus.[37] Peter Dronke, writing on Margaret Porete and the female heretics of Montaillou, comments both on the originality of women's approach to evil and on the lack of "apriorism" in women's writings, pointing out their avoidance of rules of either/or and their substitution of singular, existentially appropriate solutions.[38]

All this is not to say that male mystics never use paradox (one thinks of Nicholas of Cusa) or that male theologians never push such paradoxical synthesis to the point of reconciling heaven and hell (one thinks of Origen) or that male penitents never substitute continuity of self in Jesus for passage up the hierarchy of the cosmos to God (one thinks of Francis).[39] But the explosion of paradox in a Hadewijch, a Margaret Porete, or a Catherine of Genoa, the agonized rejection of the existence of hell in a Mechtild of Magdeburg or a Julian of Norwich, the delicious groveling in the humiliations of being human that characterizes virtually every religious woman of the later Middle Ages—these form a consistent pattern that is found only infrequently in religious men. And behind the pattern lies a confidence that all is one—all is, as Julian said, a hazelnut held in the palm of God's hand—because it is finally the humanity that we most despicably are that is redeemed.[40] It is our "Me" that becomes God.[41]

To argue this is to argue that religious women saw themselves as human *because* they were women, as redeemable *because* they were women. It may appear a very odd argument in light of certain recent feminist claims. Jo Ann McNamara, Rosemary Ruether, Marie Delcourt, and Marina Warner have, for example, argued that because male was in Western culture superior to female, woman had to take on symbolic maleness (or, at the very least, abandonment of femaleness) in order to signify spiritual advance.[42] They cite not only a few scattered references in the patristic period to women seeing their courage as "male" but also the many (predominantly patristic) stories of transvestite saints—of women masquerading as men, and sometimes even growing beards, in order to escape marriage (or rape) or to enter monasteries. They also cite Joan of Arc. Such work tends to suggest that gender reversal was a powerful symbol to women. Moreover, recent research demonstrates that cross-dressing by males was extremely rare in the Middle Ages (and sometimes persecuted as sexual perversion).[43] Although historians who focus on Joan of Arc have not tended to find parallels to her cross-dressing in the later Middle Ages (thus weakening their case), it is in fact true that late medieval women did adopt male dress, especially in order to run away from their families or to go on pilgrimages.[44] Why, then, do I suggest that reversals, especially gender reversals, were *not* crucial in women's religiosity?

My argument is basically that cross-dressing was for women primarily a practical device, whereas to men it was primarily a religious symbol. Women sometimes put on male clothes in order to escape their families, to avoid the dangers of rape and pillage, or to take on male roles such as soldier, pilgrim, or hermit. But, once freed from the world by convent walls or hermitage, by tertiary status, by the practice of continence, by mystical inspiration, or even by miraculous inedia, women spoke of their lives in female images. They saw themselves, metaphorically speaking, not as warriors for Christ but as brides, as pregnant virgins, as house-wives, as mothers of God. Perhaps exactly *because* cross-dressing was a radical yet practical social step for women, it was not finally their most powerful symbol of self. For men, on the contrary, who did not cross-dress as a practical step and could have gained nothing socially by it except opprobrium, gender reversal was a highly charged, even fright-ening symbol.[45]

In any case, whatever the reason for the fascination felt by medieval men with female cross-dressing—a fascination apparently shared by modern historians of both genders—the evidence concerning imagery is clear. Women's basic images of religious self were *not* inverted images, not male images. Where women used gender as image they usually spoke of themselves as female to a male God or as androgynous. Mechtild of Magdeburg, Hildegard of Bingen, Catherine of Siena, and Margery Kempe referred to themselves as poor women, unlettered and weak. Hildegard actually dressed her nuns as brides when they went to receive communion. Margery gloried in relating to God as wife and mother.[46] Catherine reported that she had wanted, as a child, to imitate one of the early transvestite saints, but as an adult she heard directly from Christ in a vision that such reversal was not necessary: God preferred her to teach and inspire others as a lowly woman.[47]

As I explained in chapter 9, women's use of female images did not express any incapacity for godliness or for approach to God. Indeed,

Peter Dronke has pointed out that the topos of the "poor little woman" was sometimes an ironic claim to divine inspiration, to being the vessel or mouthpiece chosen by God.[48] And some women writers passed beyond even such irony. Julian of Norwich, for example, deleted her reference to female incapacity when she expanded her *Showings* into their longer, more theologically audacious and sophisticated version.[49] Moreover, women's images for self were frequently androgynous, for they frequently included qualities the larger culture stereotyped as male (such as discipline or judgment) in their understanding of "motherly" or "womanly." Gertrude of Helfta, Hadewijch, Catherine of Siena, and Julian of Norwich all mix gender images and personality characteristics (such as tenderness, severity, love, discipline) so thoroughly in describing both the soul and God that one can only intermittently see in their writings the common association of soul with female and God with male. Finally, where women's own symbols did associate with self activities or characteristics that the broader culture saw as female (for example, lactation and food preparation, weakness and fleshliness), women tended to broaden these symbols to refer to all people rather than to underline the opposition of male/female. As we saw above, women's sense of themselves as symbolizing the "humanity of Christ" carried the concept *human* beyond any male/female dichotomy.[50]

Hildegard of Bingen, for example, did write that male and female are different in social, biological, and religious roles (although even here she stressed complementarity more than did the male theologians of her day). But her most profound use of woman as symbol drew no contrast to men at all. "Woman" was what modern writers sometimes call "mankind." In Hildegard's vision of salvation, the "image of woman"—that is, humanity—stands below the cross and receives Christ's blood (see plate 12). Two centuries later, Catherine of Siena did criticize women as weak. But she said, of herself and other women, that they were all children, drawing the milk of suffering from the breast of Christ's humanity. And by suffering she meant Christ's suffering and their own. Thus the soul was a suckling child who became one with a mother whose feeding was suffering, and that suffering saved the world. The child *was* the mother; the eating *was* feeding others; the suffering *was* fertility. Such images go beyond dichotomies, yet they arise from and express ordinary female experiences. Women's images, although informed and made possible by the symbolic oppositions of the dominant theological tradition, are themselves neither dichotomies nor inversions.

Just as men's lives show much actual conversion and reversal, paralleling the strongly dichotomous nature of their symbols, so women's actual life stories show less reversal, paralleling their use of symbols of continuity. As I noted in chapter 1, Weinstein and Bell have demonstrated that the pattern of women's lives shows fewer ruptures; instead, there is gradually dawning vocation, voiced earlier and consolidated far more slowly.[51] This difference does not appear to be entirely a matter of women's greater powerlessness, of the extreme difficulty they sometimes faced in rejecting suitors, husbands, children, or parental dictates if a vocation to chastity or deprivation came to them in adolescence or adulthood. Survey of a large number of medieval saints' lives suggests that girls (unlike boys) often knew before the age of eight that they wished to avoid marriage. To such women, virginity and humble service of family members or of sister nuns was as much a continuation of childhood as it was an escape from the adult status "married woman."

The same sort of explanation I suggested for male use of symbols may explain female usages as well. Girls' more continuous self-development, involving no fundamental need to develop a concept of "other," may help explain women's avoidance of dichotomous imagery and their tendency to elaborate as symbols aspects of life closer to ordinary experience (eating, suffering, lactating). Recent feminist psychological theory has suggested that the profoundly asymmetrical patterns of child-rearing in Western culture may influence female children toward a less acute sense of binary oppositions and of "otherness."[52] Moreover, women's place in some sense outside the *ordines* (statuses) of late medieval Europe may suggest why images of status reversal seemed to them less pertinent and interesting. Structuralist anthropologists have recently shown the ways dichotomous symbols—especially the fundamental dichotomy culture/nature—tend to express *and support* the power of those identified with "culture."[53]

Whatever explanation one proposes, it is clear that women's way of using and living symbols was different from men's. The difference lay not merely in what symbols were chosen but also in how symbols related to self. Where men stressed male/female contrasts and used imagery of reversal to express their dependence on God, women expressed their dependence on God in imagery at least partly drawn from their own gender and avoided symbolic reversals. Although men wrote about the nature of woman, women tended to write, not about gender (male versus female), but about the soul or about humanity. There is thus a sense in which women's use of metaphors and images took a shape of its own, oblique to a male tradition of spiritual writing in which the male/female dichotomy was a symbol for many other oppositions. And yet it is clear that women's sense of self was formed within and influenced by the symbolic dichotomies of the dominant theological tradition. It was from age-old notions that God, mind, and power are male whereas soul, flesh, and weakness are female that women drew inspiration for a spirituality in which their own suffering humanity had cosmic significance.

◆ Conclusion

In exploring the religious significance of food to medieval women, I have touched upon two larger issues: the nature of medieval asceticism, and the significance of gender in medieval religion. Although this book does no more than raise these issues and suggest the direction new interpretation of them might take, it is well to underline them in closing. For, if I am right on these two issues, we must revise some of the received wisdom about the Middle Ages.

I have suggested throughout the discussion in chapters 6, 7, 8, and 9 that medieval asceticism should not be understood as rooted in dualism, in a radical sense of spirit opposed to or entrapped by body. The extravagant penitential practices of the thirteenth to the fifteenth century, the cultivation of pain and patience, the literalism of *imitatio crucis* are, I have argued, not primarily an attempt to escape from body. They are not the products of an epistemology or psychology or theology that sees soul struggling against its opposite, matter. Therefore they are not—as historians have often suggested—a world-denying, self-hating, decadent response of a society wracked by plague, famine, heresy, war, and ecclesiastical corruption. Rather, late medieval asceticism was an effort to plumb and to realize all the possibilities of the flesh. It was a profound expression of the doctrine of the Incarnation: the doctrine that Christ, by becoming human, saves *all* that the human being is. It arose in a religious world whose central ritual was the coming of God into food as macerated flesh, and it was compatible with, not contradictory to, new philosophical notions that located the nature of things not in their abstract definitions but in their individuating matter or particularity. Thus Francis of Assisi telling his disciples that beatings are "perfect happiness," Beatrice of Ornacieux driving nails through her palms, Dorothy of Montau and Lukardis of Oberweimar wrenching their bodies into bizarre pantomimes of the moment of Crucifixion, and Serafina of San Gimignano, revered *because* she was paralyzed, were to their own contemporaries not depressing or horrifying but glorious. They were not rebelling against or torturing their flesh out of guilt over its capabilities so much as using the possibilities of its full sensual and affective range to soar ever closer to God.[54]

Just as I have suggested in the last five chapters that medieval asceticism was not primarily dualism, so I have argued that medieval women are not best understood as creatures constrained and impelled by society's notions of the female as inferior. Women's piety was not, fundamentally, internalized dualism or misogyny. Although misogynist writing did certainly sometimes equate *woman* with sexual temptation and underline the male/female contrast as a dichotomy of superior/inferior, strong/weak, spirit/flesh, I consider it mistaken to take the ideas of male theologians and biographers about women as the notions of women about themselves. Women and men existed, of course, in the same universe of symbols and doctrine and were taught by the same scriptures, the same preaching. Women were clearly aware of their supposed inferiority; some commented upon it or even appropriated it as a way to God. I have shown above how some women castigated themselves for their sexual impulses. But from among the symbols and doctrines available to them, women and men chose different symbols—men renouncing wealth and power, women renouncing food. They used symbols in different ways. Men, who were dominant, used symbols (among them the male/female dichotomy) to renounce their dominance. Reversals and oppositions were at the heart of how symbols worked for men. The image of woman as contrasted to that of man was, in the later Middle Ages, a topic of primary interest to men. To women, however, male/female contrasts were apparently of little interest; symbols of self were in general taken from biological or social experience and expressed not so much reversal or renunciation of worldly advantage as the deepening of ordinary human experience that came when God impinged upon it.

In their symbols women expanded the suffering, giving self they were ascribed by their culture, becoming ever more wonderfully and horribly the body on the cross. They became that body not as flight from but as continuation of self. And because that body was also God, they could sum up their love of God in paradox: "Hell is the highest name of Love," as Hadewijch said, or as Margaret Porete put it, "I am the salvation itself of every creature. . . . For I am the sum of all evils."

In the final analysis, it is wrong to see medieval women as internalizing the idea of their gender as inferior, because contrasts of male/female, superior/inferior, spirit/flesh seem, as *contrasts*, to have been less important to women than to men. If it is inaccurate to see late medieval asceticism as self-hating because it is wrong to think that medieval people saw flesh primarily as opposed to spirit, it is doubly inaccurate to see female asceticism as based in dualism, because all dualities were less important to women. Women saw themselves not as flesh opposed to spirit, female opposed to male, nurture opposed to authority; they saw themselves as human beings—fully spirit and fully flesh. And they saw all humanity as created in God's image, as capable of *imitatio Christi* through body as well as soul. Thus they gloried in the pain, the exudings, the somatic distortions that made their bodies parallel to the consecrated wafer on the altar and the man on the cross. In the blinding light of the ultimate dichotomy between God and humanity, all other dichotomies faded. Men and women might agree that female flesh was more fleshly than male flesh, but such agreement led both sexes to see themselves as in some sense female-human. For it was human beings as *human* (not as symbol of the divine) whom Christ saved in the Incarnation; it was body as flesh (not as spirit) that God became most graphically on the altar; it was human suffering (not human power) that Christ took on to redeem the world. Religious women in the later Middle Ages saw in their own female bodies not only a symbol of the humanness of both genders but also a symbol of—and a means of approach to—the humanity of God.

EPILOGUE

It may be that vice, depravity and crime are nearly always . . . attempts to eat beauty, to eat what we should only look at. Eve began it. If she caused humanity to be lost by eating the fruit, the opposite attitude, looking at the fruit without eating it, should be what is required to save it.

If I grow thin from labour in the fields, my flesh really becomes wheat. If that wheat is used for the host it becomes Christ's flesh. Anyone who labours with this intention should become a saint.

SIMONE WEIL (D. 1943)[1]

If cultural emphasis followed the physiological emphasis, girls' [puberty] ceremonies would be more marked than boys'; but it is not so. The ceremonies emphasize a social fact: the adult prerogatives of men are more far-reaching in every culture than women's, and consequently . . . it is more common for societies to take note of this period in boys than in girls.
RUTH BENEDICT (1934),
QUOTED BY A CONTEMPORARY ANORECTIC,
SHEILA McLEOD (1981)[2]

Theresa Neumann of Konnersreuth, a Bavarian peasant woman who died in 1962, supposedly displayed both stigmata and miraculous abstinence. Like Lidwina of Schiedam, she was observed by a commission which solemnly authenticated her inedia as total and extended.[3] Simone Weil, a philosopher and mystic who died in 1943, undertook fatal self-starvation in an effort to identify with the poor and oppressed of the world. Like Catherine of Genoa, Weil spoke of gluttony as a metaphor for sin and used the notion of self becoming food as an image for personal suffering that fuses with the redemptive suffering of Christ. We still find, in the twentieth century, examples of the female piety that emerged in thirteenth- and fourteenth-century Europe.

Yet for the most part, women's concern with food in our own century occurs in a different context. Women cultivate not closeness to God but physical attractiveness by food abstinence, which they call *dieting*. The recent increase of self-starvation among white, privileged, adolescent females is not called *fasting* or *asceticism* by the medical profession into whose purview it comes, but *anorexia nervosa*. The notion that food and eating are problems to women has become a cliché.[4] When the popular feminist magazine *Ms.* devoted its October, 1983, issue to food, it treated a range of issues from deformities supposedly produced by contaminated meat to bulimia among college students; the joy of cooking or eating was noticeably absent.[5] Late-twentieth-century studies of women and food that go beyond describing the nexus usually associate refusal to eat with the question of control. Cultural interpretations of anorexia nervosa focus on ways the media urge women to control body size; psychodynamic interpretations concentrate on the girl's efforts to rebel against an overcontrolling mother; even biological explanations relate anorexia to female depression, which manifests itself (whatever its cause) in feelings of powerlessness and worthlessness.[6]

Modern attention to the topic "women and food" appears to be very much more one-sided than medieval practice and symbolism. It is therefore not surprising that recent historians have taken little notice of the religious significance of food nor that the small attention that the topic has begun to receive has focused on medieval parallels to the modern disease entities *anorexia nervosa* and *bulimia*. But to study fasting without studying rituals of eating, to consider the pain of asceticism while ignoring the explicit words of its practitioners is not the most fruitful way to approach the history of our European past. For medieval food behavior was service of others as well as rending and sacrifice. Religious ritual centered on eating as well as on abstaining.

As I have shown above, medieval women sometimes rejected both body and family through food practices. Food behaviors helped girls to gain control over self as well as over circumstance. Through fasting, women internalized as well as manipulated and escaped patriarchal familial and religious structures. But the self-starvation of some thirteenth-, fourteenth-, and fifteenth-century women had a resonance and a complexity that are not captured by the analogy to modern disease entities. My purpose in this book has been to put the behavior, the symbols, and the convictions of women and men in the distant past into their *full* context. Only by considering all the meanings and functions of medieval practice and belief can we explain medieval experience without removing its creativity and dignity.

My approach clearly assumes that the practices and symbols of any culture are so embedded in that culture as to be inseparable from it. Thus, just as I have argued that the notion of *anorexia nervosa*, which emerged in the late nineteenth century to describe one type of inedia, should not be wrenched from its modern context and applied to the fourteenth and fifteenth centuries, so I would argue that medieval symbols, behaviors, and doctrines have no direct lessons for the 1980s.[7] They were produced by a world that has vanished. Nor would I want us to return to the Middle Ages. However beautiful the prose of Catherine of Siena or the poetry of Hadewijch, the actual lives of some late medieval women must give us pause. Although we may wish for an enriching of our symbolic universe, it is hard to want, for ourselves or our daughters, a life like Lidwina's or Alpaïs's, or even like Theresa Neumann's or Simone Weil's. No one could wish to return to a society in which the horrors of leprosy, gangrene, or starvation can be mitigated only by symbols that glorify pain and sacrifice. Those recent scholars who have attempted to urge medieval devotions on the modern church run the risk of ignoring the savagery of some medieval asceticism, the sentimentality of much medieval preaching, the sexism of medieval (and modern) society, and the inappropriateness of even the most generous fourteenth-century notions of mother to a world with modern technology.[8] On the other hand, those scholars who have attacked the piety of late medieval women for not meeting modern needs have merely pointed out the obvious, while sometimes making it harder for us to understand the wellsprings of ideas that, in their own context, had great power and beauty.

Are there, then, any implications of my study for twentieth-century culture, in which the association of woman and food is still so striking, yet the meaning of the association is so different? The most basic implication, I think, is this. Although medieval life styles and devotions seem inapplicable (without great revision) to modern problems, the range and richness of medieval symbols have something to teach us about the impoverishment of our own. Compared to the range of meanings in medieval poetry and piety, our use of *body* and *food* as symbols is narrow and negative. And because our understanding of food and flesh is fearful and awkward, our therapies for those who suffer from "eating disorders" are narrow and awkward too. Our answer to those who see no beauty or hope in the fact of embodiment is a concentration on the issue of control.[9] And such a concentration appears to me to reflect exactly the cultural emphasis that produces the problem.

Medieval people saw food and body as sources of life, repositories of sensation. Thus food and body signified generativity and suffering. Food, which must be destroyed in order to give life, and body, which must be torn in order to give birth, became synonymous; in identifying themselves with both, women managed to give meaning to a physical, human existence in which suffering was unavoidable. Religious women in the thirteenth and fourteenth centuries, who withdrew from the tasks of child-bearing and nurturing which the culture assigned to females, nonetheless expressed through their imagery a wide range of positive resonances for both physicality and food.

In contrast, modern people see food and body as resources to be controlled. Thus food and body signify that which threatens human mastery. They signify the untamed, the rebellious, the excessive, the pro-liferating. Messages modern women absorb from the popular culture of magazine advertisements and television urge them to control their bodies with deodorants, tranquilizers, headache remedies, diets, etc. Breasts are not, to modern people, symbols of food. The onset of puberty is not an occasion for rejoicing by an adolescent girl or her parents. Menstruation is less a prelude to creativity and affectivity than a frightening sign of vulnerability. Body and food are thus symbols of the failure of our efforts to control our selves.

Body and food have become such symbols, of course, because we *are* in many ways able to control basic aspects of bodily experience—espe-cially fertility and pain. I would not want to suggest that we relinquish that control. It has brought anesthetics and antiseptics to still bodily suffering, reproductive freedom to open women's lives—and those of men and children—to new forms of creativity and fulfillment, advances in nutrition and fertilizers to make hunger less acute in at least a portion of the globe. But our modern images of food and body, particularly female body, as all that threatens mastery seem to me unattractive and even dangerous in two very different ways.

First, our modern assumptions obscure the fact that food *is* food and body *is* body. Twentieth-century discussions of anorexia nervosa, for ex-ample, seem to have assumed, when Freudian, that body means

300

sexuality[10] and, when non-Freudian, that eating means control. These assumptions are not completely unhelpful. Yet the refusal of female teen-agers to eat seems most obviously related both to the physiological changes of puberty, which signal the possibility of motherhood, and to the basic assumption in our culture that women are food preparers, not food consumers. The method I have followed in this book, of relating various food practices and symbols within a society to each other, sug-gests that modern analysts might gain important insights into modern behavior patterns by seeing food as food and placing it in its cultural context.

Second, our modern use of food and body as symbols of all that we seek to control seems to me a vain effort to hide from ourselves the fact that our control is not—cannot be—total. And I do not refer here merely to the obvious failures of our social policies and our technology that are represented by the starvation of parts of the Third World. I mean that the sort of control we appear to want is impossible unless we can control death itself. For unless we conquer death, suffering must always be a reminder of it—a foretaste of our own death and of the loss of those we love. Unless we conquer death, fertility (however frightening it may be) will be necessary for our survival: new life, issuing from women's bodies, will be our collective immortality.

But we have not conquered death. There is thus bravado, tragic and pathetic bravado, in the assumption that mental health and happiness depend upon suppressing fertility and suffering—the basic reminders that death is ever in our midst. Perhaps, then, our culture cannot afford to consider the issue of women and food merely as a case study in healthy and unhealthy control. Perhaps we cannot afford to see body, especially female body, and nourishment merely as threats to human mastery. In-deed, our very tendency to think in terms of control may encourage violence toward female bodies and callousness toward any pain we can-not manage to assuage. Thus we may, more than we realize, need posi-tive symbols for generativity and suffering. Our culture may finally need something of the medieval sense, reflected so clearly in the use of *birthing* and *nursing* as symbols for salvation, that generativity and suffering can be synonymous.[11] Perhaps we should not turn our backs so resolutely as we have recently done either on the possibility that suffering can be fruitful or on food and female body as positive, complex, resonant sym-bols of love and generosity.

301

♦————————————————————————————————

I said above that medieval lives and rhetoric have no direct relevance to ours. But even medieval symbols are no solution to modern woes. We cannot adopt such symbols as an answer to the impoverishment of twentieth-century images. That is why I have relegated thoughts on the modern world to an epilogue that is in no way a conclusion. But a deeper understanding of what the ideas and lives of medieval women really meant not only helps us explain why they were as they were, it also rescues them from oblivion and illuminates their humanity. And such illumination gives us much to admire as well as much to abhor. By comparison, we may thus see a little more clearly what to admire and abhor about ourselves. In this sense, then, the female lives I have chronicled here *are* relevant to our own. If their images and values cannot become our answers, they can nonetheless teach us that we need richer images and values. Perhaps also they can point the direction in which we should search.

PLATES II

8. Giving food to the poor was a popular charity with female saints and one
to which male relatives sometimes objected. This fourteenth-century picture of the so-called *Miracle of St. Elizabeth* shows Elizabeth of Hungary
accosted by her husband, who supposedly disapproved of her practice of
distributing food. When she defended herself by claiming that her apron
held only roses, a miracle changed the bread she was hiding into flowers.
The story is not found in the early sources concerning Elizabeth, but it was
attached to her and to a number of other female saints throughout the later
Middle Ages. Pinacoteca, Perugia.

9. Artists and writers in the Middle Ages frequently transferred stories from one saint to another. Here an artist accomplishes the transfer by the simple expedient of painting *S. Rosa* over the name of Elizabeth in a fifteenth-century painting by Benozzo di Lese, called Gozzoli. The woman with an apronful of roses thus becomes Rose of Viterbo, a saint who acquired what was, even by medieval standards, a large number of borrowed miracles. Museo di S. Francesco, Montefalco.

Oñ le lieue heer verhoerde haer ghebet eñ ōsocht se met eenre onsprekeliker siecten dat si vlepsce⁓

10. In the fourteenth and fifteenth centuries, medieval women were often revered for their patient suffering of illness and injury. One such suffering
saint was Lidwina of Schiedam, whose long period of paralysis and inedia
began with the skating accident depicted here. This woodcut from the
1498 edition of John Brugman's *vita* of Lidwina is probably the first surviving picture of skates. Museum of the Catherineconvent, Utrecht. Copyright Stichting Het Catharijneconvent.

11. These miniatures from a fifteenth-century manuscript of the Life of Colette of Corbie made for Margaret of York, wife of Charles the Bold, depict miracles typical of female saints. (a) Colette miraculously fills a cask that has become empty through the carelessness of Sister Jeanne Ravardelle. (b) Colette receives visions of the sufferings of Christ. (c) Christ himself comes to administer the host to Colette while the priest, Henry of Baume, says mass.

12. Painted under the visionary's own direction, this
miniature of the sixth vision from the second
part of Hildegard of Bingen's *Scivias* shows
what Hildegard calls the "image of woman"
(that is, Church or Humanity) marrying Christ
and receiving his blood as her dowry.

13. This devotional object from late-thirteenth- or early-fourteenth-century Germany (above) is a small nursing Madonna, made of wood covered with linen, gesso, and gilt. It opens (below) to show the Holy Trinity inside. (The body has been broken off the crucifix.) Such objects depicted for medieval Christians the idea that Mary is the tabernacle that houses God. The Metropolitan Museum of Art, gift of J. Pierpont Morgan, 1917.

14. Late medieval art emphasized Mary both as provider of food to her son Jesus and as provider of Jesus-as-food to all Christians. In this painting by Robert Campin (d. 1444), Mary offers her breast to the viewer, while the child glances toward us as well. She presents the baby in front of a fire and firescreen, thus suggesting a parallel between Jesus and bread. Robert Campin, *Madonna and Child before a Firescreen*. The National Gallery, London. Reproduced by courtesy of the Trustees, The National Gallery, London.

15. In medieval art and devotional literature, lactation was a popular symbol of nourishment, generosity, and love. This small panel, attributed to Lucas Cranach the Elder (1472–1553), depicts Charity and her children. The emphasis on breast as food is underlined by the fruit, which parallels the breast in shape as well as function. Similar or virtually identical paintings can be found in many European museums. Musée d'Histoire et d'Art, Luxembourg.

16. In this sixteenth-century Fountain of the Virtues in Nürnberg, all seven allegorical figures lactate as a symbol of the fertility of virtue. Several of the figures also provide nurture in other ways, by offering fruit, a chalice, or a jug.

17. The church was frequently depicted by medieval writers and artists as a lactating mother. In this detail from a marble pulpit in the cathedral at Pisa, Giovanni Pisano (d. 1314) shows a stern-faced *ecclesia* nursing two tiny Christians at her breasts. The figures below represent the four cardinal virtues. The Cathedral, Pisa.

18. The legend that Bernard of Clairvaux was nursed by the Virgin was told
throughout Europe in the later Middle Ages. It seems to have first become
popular as an iconographic motif in Spain. This detail from the Retable of
St. Bernard, painted about 1290 by the Master of Palma, is an early depiction of the miracle. Sociedad Arqueológica Luliana, Palma de Mallorca.

19. More than one hundred and fifty years later than the previous picture, this Lactation of St. Bernard from the Retable of St. Ildefonso, painted about 1460 by the Master of Osma, shows more sentimentalized figures but the same miracle. The Cathedral, El Burgo de Osma, Soria.

20. In this Flemish painting from about 1510, Mary feeds the Christ
child grapes, symbol both of the breast and of eucharistic wine.
NGA#1937.1.43. *The Rest on the Flight into Egypt*, Gerard David.
National Gallery of Art, Washington, Andrew W. Mellon Collection.
Copyright National Gallery of Art.

21. In this painting from 1544, *Virgin and Child in a Landscape*, Jan van
Hemessen emphasizes the parallelism of breast and grapes (a common
eucharistic symbol) by placing the lactating Virgin in a grape arbor.
The food theme is also underlined by the fruit in the child's hand.
National Museum, Stockholm.

22. In Maerten de Vos's *The Holy Kinship* from 1585, maternal feeding is
emphasized in a multitude of symbols. At the center Mary holds a grape
cluster in front of her breast while the Christ child plucks a grape. On the
right a woman suckles a baby while a second woman points to her own
breast with one hand and toward Mary with the other. On the left another
woman feeds milk soup to a child. Male figures are relegated to a rather
shadowy background. Museum of Fine Arts, Ghent.

23. In *Virgin and Child*, a miniature of about 1380–1385 from the Milan section of the Turin-Milan Book of Hours, Mary presses from her breast a tiny stream of milk, which she directs toward a kneeling petitioner. Somewhat coyly, the Christ child turns aside. The reader of this lavish devotional book was no doubt intended to identify with the suppliant. Museo Civico di Torino.

24. In Jan van Eyck's famous Lucca *Madonna* of about 1436, Mary holds her suckling infant in a setting replete with eucharistic associations. Art historians have suggested that Mary's lap is an altar on which Christ is displayed. The basin in the niche to the right may be intended to evoke the niche south of the altar where a priest washes his hands at mass. Städelsches Kunstinstitut, Frankfurt.

25. *The Savior*, by Quirizio da Murano (fl. 1460–1478), shows a sweet-faced Christ lifting up the wound in his side (positioned where a nipple would be found). With his right hand he offers a eucharistic wafer, which might almost have been taken from the wound, to a kneeling nun of the order of Poor Clares. Angels carry banners bearing those phrases from the Song of Songs that had long been interpreted as referring to the wine of the eucharist. The painting illustrates both the medieval tendency to associate Christ's feeding with female recipients and the close linking of wine and wafer in the doctrine of concomitance. It also evokes the mother Jesus so popular in devotional literature. Accademia, Venice.

26. This picture of the Eucharistic Man of Sorrows with the allegorical figure
Charity was painted about 1470 by a northwest German master and may
depict a vision received by Gertrude of Helfta. Both the purposeful
manner in which Christ fills the cup from his breast and the vividness of
the blood itself are typical of such eucharistic paintings. Wallraf-Richartz-
Museum, Cologne.

27. The pious in the fourteenth and fifteenth centuries felt a passionate yearning for the blood of Christ, perhaps in part because the communion cup was now withheld from the laity. Artists found a variety of ways of emphasizing this saving blood both as suffering and as food. In *The Man of Sorrows*, painted about 1510 by Jacob Cornelisz, a sorrowing Christ pours forth his own life from palm and breast into a eucharistic chalice in order to feed humankind. Mayer van den Bergh Museum, Antwerp. Copyright A.C.L., Brussels.

28. This mid-fifteenth-century miniature from the Turin-Milan Book of
Hours depicts the so-called Double Intercession. Pleading with God the
Father, who here appears enthroned as ruler and judge, Mary lifts up her
breast and Christ exposes his wound. The parallelism of wound and breast
is clearly underlined. Cabinet des Dessins, Musée du Louvre, Paris.

29. Even when handling motifs other than the Double Intercession, late medieval artists emphasized the parallel between Christ's wound and Mary's breast. In this *Last Judgment* of 1525 by Jan Provost, Christ appears as judge and avenger, before whom Mary petitions for souls. The modest motion by which Mary's fingers lift up her breast clearly recapitulates Christ's almost cradling gesture toward the wound that saves the world. Groeningemuseum, Bruges.

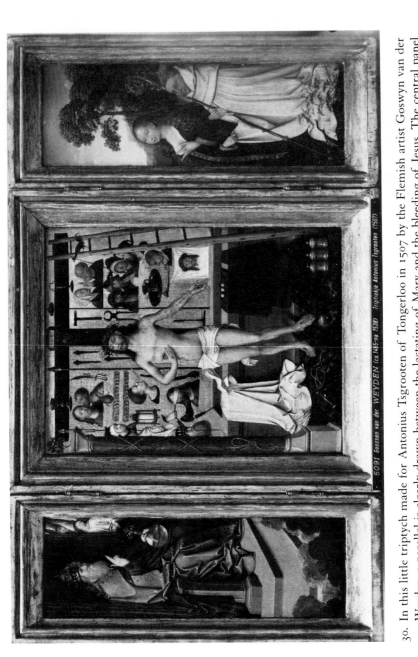

30. In this little triptych made for Antonius Tsgrooten of Tongerloo in 1507 by the Flemish artist Goswyn van der Weyden, a parallel is clearly drawn between the lactating of Mary and the bleeding of Jesus. The central panel shows Christ with the instruments of the Passion. Above on the cross a small heart with its own vivid wound recapitulates the bleeding wound of the man below. To the right, in a gesture that mimics Christ's, Mary displays her breast, which the viewer cannot mistake for a symbol of pity and intercession alone. It is clearly a symbol of food as well, since beside her stands Bernard of Clairvaux, whom she nursed. Koninklijk Museum

ABBREVIATIONS

Sources frequently cited in this work are referred to by the abbreviations listed below. The Index of Secondary Authors directs the reader to the first, full, bibliographic citation of each of the other works mentioned in the Notes.

AASS   J. Bollandus and G. Henschenius, *Acta sanctorum . . . editio novissima*, ed. J. Carnandet et al. (Paris: Palmé, etc., 1863–). Not all the volumes in this series are in their third edition, but the series as a whole is the third edition.

AB   *Analecta Bollandiana* (Brussels: Société des Bollandistes, 1882–).

AF   The Fathers of St. Bonaventure's College, eds., *Analecta franciscana, sive Chronica aliaque varia documenta ad historiam Fratrum minorum spectantia* (Quaracchi: Collegium S. Bonaventurae, 1885–).

Angela of Foligno, ed. Ferré and Baudry   Angela of Foligno, *Le Livre de l'expérience des vrais fidèles: Texte latin publié d'après le manuscrit d'Assise*, ed. and trans. M.-J. Ferré and L. Baudry (Paris: Droz, 1927).

Aquinas, ST   Thomas Aquinas, *Summa theologiae*, Blackfriars ed., 61 vols. (New York: McGraw-Hill, 1964–1981).

Baker, MW   Derek Baker, ed., *Medieval Women: Dedicated and Presented to Professor Rosalind M. T. Hill . . .* , Studies in Church History, Subsidia 1 (Oxford: Blackwell, 1978).

Braun, *Altar*   Joseph Braun, *Der christliche Altar in seiner geschichtlichen Entwicklung*, 2 vols. (Munich: Koch, 1924).

Browe, *Die Wunder*   Peter Browe, *Die Eucharistischen Wunder des Mittelalters*, Breslauer Studien zur historischen Theologie, NF 4 (Breslau: Müller und Seiffert, 1938).

BS   *Bibliotheca sanctorum*, 12 vols. (Rome: Istituto Giovanni XXIII della Pontificia Università Lateranense, 1961–1969).

Bynum, JM   Caroline Walker Bynum, *Jesus as Mother: Studies in the Spirituality of the High Middle Ages*, Publications of the Center for Medieval and Renaissance Studies, UCLA, 16 (Berkeley and Los Angeles: University of California Press, 1982).

◆————————————————————————————————

Bynum, "Women Mystics"   Caroline Walker Bynum, "Women Mystics and Eucharistic Devotion in the Thirteenth Century," *Women's Studies* 11 (1984): 179–214.

Caesarius, *Dialogus*   Caesarius of Heisterbach, *Dialogus miraculorum*, ed. Joseph Strange, 2 vols. (Cologne: Heberle, 1851).

Catherine of Genoa, *Edizione critica*, ed. Umile Bonzi   Umile Bonzi da Genova, ed., *S. Caterina Fieschi Adorno*, vol. 2: *Edizione critica dei manoscritti cateriniani* (Turin: Marietti, 1962).

Catherine of Siena, Dialogue, ed. Cavallini   Catherine of Siena, *Il Dialogo della Divina Provvidenza ovvero Libro della Divino Dottrina*, ed. Giuliana Cavallini (Rome: Edizioni Cateriniane, 1968).

Catherine of Siena, Letters, ed. Misciattelli   Catherine of Siena, *Le Lettere de S. Caterina da Siena, ridotte a miglior lezione, e in ordine nuovo disposte con note di Niccolò Tommaseo a cura di Piero Misciattelli*, 6 vols. (Siena: Giuntini y Bentivoglio, 1913–1922).

DHGE   *Dictionnaire d'histoire et de géographie ecclésiastiques* (Paris: Letouzey et Ané, 1912–).

DMA   *Dictionary of the Middle Ages*, ed. Joseph Strayer (New York: Scribner's, 1982–).

Dronke, WW   Peter Dronke, *Women Writers of the Middle Ages: A Critical Study of Texts from Perpetua (+ 203) to Marguerite Porete (+ 1310)* (Cambridge: Cambridge University Press, 1984).

DS   *Dictionnaire de spiritualité, ascétique et mystique, doctrine et histoire*, ed. M. Viller et al. (Paris: Beauchesne, 1932–).

DTC   *Dictionnaire de théologie catholique*, ed. A. Vacant et al., 15 vols. and *Tables générales* (Paris: Letouzey et Ané, 1909–1950).

Dumoutet, CD   Edouard Dumoutet, *Corpus Domini: Aux sources de la piété eucharistique médiévale* (Paris: Beauchesne, 1942).

Engelthal   Karl Schröder, ed., *Der Nonnen von Engelthal Büchlein von der Genaden Überlast*, Bibliothek des literarischen Vereins in Stuttgart 108 (Tübingen: Literarischer Verein in Stuttgart, 1871).

Goodich, VP   Michael Goodich, *Vita Perfecta: The Ideal of Sainthood in the Thirteenth Century*, Monographien zur Geschichte des Mittelalters 25 (Stuttgart: Hiersemann, 1982).

Gougaud, DAP   Louis Gougaud, *Devotional and Ascetic Practices in the Middle Ages*, trans. G. C. Bateman (London: Burns Oates and Washbourne, 1927).

Grundmann, *Bewegungen*   Herbert Grundmann, *Religiöse Bewegungen im Mittelalter: Untersuchungen über die geschichtlichen Zusammenhänge zwischen der Ketzerei, den Bettelorden und der religiösen Frauenbewegung im 12. und 13. Jahrhundert* . . . (1935; repr. with additions, Hildesheim: Olms, 1961).

Imbert-Gourbeyre, *Stigmatisation*   Antoine Imbert-Gourbeyre, *La Stigmatisa-*

tion: L'Extase divine et les miracles de Lourdes: Réponse aux libres-penseurs, 2 vols. (Clermont-Ferrand: Librairie Catholique, 1894).

John Marienwerder, *Vita latina*, ed. Westpfahl   John Marienwerder, *Vita Dorotheae Montoviensis Magistri Johannis Marienwerder*, ed. Hans Westpfahl, Forschungen und Quellen zur Kirchen- und Kulturgeschichte Ostdeutschlands 1 (Cologne: Böhlau, 1964).

Julian, *Book of Showings*, ed. Colledge and Walsh   Julian of Norwich, *A Book of Showings to the Anchoress Julian of Norwich*, ed. Edmund Colledge and James Walsh, Studies and Texts 35, 2 parts (part 1 contains the Short Text, part 2 the Long Text) (Toronto: Pontifical Institute of Medieval Studies, 1978).

Kieckhefer, UnS   Richard Kieckhefer, *Unquiet Souls: Fourteenth-Century Saints and Their Religious Milieu* (Chicago: University of Chicago Press, 1984).

McDonnell, *Beguines*   Ernest W. McDonnell, *The Beguines and Beghards in Medieval Culture, with Special Emphasis on the Belgian Scene* (New Brunswick, N.J.: Rutgers University Press, 1954; repr. ed. 1969).

MGH.SS   *Monumenta Germaniae historica. Scriptores rerum germanicarum* and *Scriptores . . . nova ser.* (Hannover: Hahnsche Buchhandlung, etc. 1826–   ).

MGH.SSRM   *Monumenta Germaniae historica. Scriptores rerum merovingicarum* (Hannover: Hahnsche Buchhandlung, 1885–   ).

OB   Bernard of Clairvaux, *Sancti Bernardi opera*, ed. J. Leclercq, C. H. Talbot, and H. M. Rochais (Rome: Editiones Cistercienses, 1957–   ).

Oeuvres de Marguerite   Margaret of Oingt, *Les Oeuvres de Marguerite d'Oingt*, ed. and trans. Antonin Duraffour, Pierre Gardette, and Paulette Durdilly, Publications de l'Institut de Linguistique Romane de Lyon 21 (Paris: Belles Lettres, 1965).

Omnibus   Marion A. Habig, ed., *St. Francis of Assisi: Writings and Early Biographies: English Omnibus of Sources*, 3d ed. (Chicago: Franciscan Herald Press, 1973).

Pater, MA   Thomas Pater, *Miraculous Abstinence: A Study of One of the Extraordinary Mystical Phenomena*, Catholic University of America Studies in Sacred Theology 100 (Washington, D.C.: Catholic University of America Press, 1946).

PG   J.-P. Migne, ed., *Patrologiae cursus completus: series graeca*, 162 vols. (Paris: Migne, 1857–1866).

PL   J.-P. Migne, ed., *Patrologiae cursus completus: series latina*, 221 vols. (Paris: Migne, etc., 1841–1864).

Roisin, *L'Hagiographie*   Simone Roisin, *L'Hagiographie cistercienne dans le diocèse de Liège au XIIIᵉ siècle* (Louvain: Bibliothèque de l'Université, 1947).

SC, Sér. mon.   Sources chrétiennes (Paris: Editions du Cerf, 1941–), Série des textes monastiques d'Occident (Paris: Editions du Cerf, 1958–).

Schiller, *Iconography*   Gertrud Schiller, *Iconography of Christian Art*, trans. Janet Seligman, 2 vols. [the first two vols. of *Ikonographie*] (London: Humphries, 1971–1972).

Schiller, *Ikonographie*   Gertrud Schiller, *Ikonographie der christlichen Kunst*, 4 vols. (Gütersloh: Mohn, 1966–1980).

Suso, *Deutsche Schriften*   Henry Suso, *Heinrich Seuse: Deutsche Schriften im Auftrag der Württembergischen Kommission für Landesgeschichte*, ed. Karl Bihlmeyer (Stuttgart: Kohlhammer, 1907).

Tauler, *Die Predigten*   John Tauler, *Die Predigten Taulers: Aus der Engelberger und der Freiburger Handschrift sowie aus Schmidts Abschriften der ehemaligen Strassburger Handschriften*, ed. Ferdinand Vetter (Berlin: Weidmannsche Buchhandlung, 1910).

Thurston, PP   Herbert Thurston, *The Physical Phenomena of Mysticism* (Chicago: Regnery, 1952).

Töss   Elsbet Stagel, *Das Leben der Schwestern zu Töss beschrieben von Elsbet Stagel*, ed. Ferdinand Vetter, Deutsche Texte des Mittelalters 6 (Berlin: Weidmannsche Buchhandlung, 1906).

Tubach, *Index*   Frederic C. Tubach, *Index exemplorum: A Handbook of Medieval Religious Tales*, FF Communications 204 (Helsinki: Finnish Academy of Sciences and Letters, 1969).

"Unterlinden"   Jeanne Ancelet-Hustache, ed., "Les 'Vitae Sororum' d'Unterlinden. Edition critique du Manuscrit 508 de la Bibliothèque de Colmar," *Archives d'histoire doctrinale et littéraire du moyen âge* 5 (1930):317–509.

Vauchez, *La Sainteté*   André Vauchez, *La Sainteté en Occident aux derniers siècles du moyen âge d'après les procès de canonisation et les documents hagiographiques*, Bibliothèque des études françaises d'Athènes et de Rome 241 (Rome: Ecole Française de Rome, 1981).

Vie de Douceline   J.-H. Albanés, ed. and trans., *La Vie de Douceline, fondatrice des béguines de Marseille* (Marseilles: Camoin, 1879).

Vita Beatricis   L. Reypens, ed., *Vita Beatricis: De Autobiografie van de Z. Beatrijs van Tienen O. Cist. 1200–1268* (Antwerp: Ruusbroec-Genootschap, 1964).

Weinstein and Bell, SS   Donald Weinstein and Rudolph M. Bell, *Saints and Society: The Two Worlds of Western Christendom, 1000–1700* (Chicago: University of Chicago Press, 1982).

NOTES

♦ *Introduction*

1. John Tauler, Sermon 31, Second Sermon for Corpus Christi, in Tauler, *Die Predigten*, p. 310; E. Colledge and Sister M. Jane, trans., *Spiritual Conferences* (St. Louis: Herder, 1961), p. 258.

2. For example, Malcolm David Lambert, *Franciscan Poverty: The Doctrine of the Absolute Poverty of Christ and the Apostles in the Franciscan Order, 1210–1323* (London: SPCK, 1961); and Lester K. Little, *Religious Poverty and the Profit Economy in Medieval Europe* (Ithaca: Cornell University Press, 1978). See also John V. Fleming, *An Introduction to the Franciscan Literature of the Middle Ages* (Chicago: Franciscan Herald Press, 1977), pp. 73–109; and below, chap. 3 n. 159.

3. For recent examples, see John Bugge, *Virginitas: An Essay in the History of a Medieval Ideal*, Archives internationales d'histoire des idées, séries minor 17 (The Hague: Nijhoff, 1975); and Weinstein and Bell, SS, pp. 73–99. Leo Steinberg, "The Sexuality of Christ in Renaissance Art and in Modern Oblivion," *October* 25 (Summer 1983): 1–222 (published in book form, New York: Pantheon, 1983), provides a fascinating counterpoint to the argument in this book. Steinberg sees Christ's sexuality (by which he really means Christ's genitality) as a basic symbol of his humanity. He therefore stresses the maleness of Christ in fifteenth-century art and piety, whereas I, beginning with food symbolism, find a Christ whose humanity is symbolized in female as well as male images.

4. Peter Brown, "Response" to Robert M. Grant, "The Problem of Miraculous Feedings in the Graeco-Roman World," *Center for Hermeneutical Studies: Protocol of the Forty-Second Colloquy* (Berkeley: Graduate Theological Union and University of California, 1982), p. 23.

5. As Fernand Braudel points out, poverty was at the heart of the long course of Mediterranean history, and famine was recurrent, the natural outcome of a general shortage of resources. See Fernand Braudel, *The Mediterranean and the Mediterranean World in the Age of Philip II*, trans. Siân Reynolds, 2 vols. (New York: Harper and Row, 1972–73), vol. 1, esp. pp. 241–56. On later medieval economic history, see *The Cambridge Economic History of Europe*, vol. 1, 2d ed., ed. M. M. Postan (Cambridge: Cambridge University Press, 1966), and vols. 2 and 3, ed. M. M. Postan et al. (Cambridge: Cambridge University Press, 1952, 1963); Robert Boutruche, *La Crise d'une société: Seigneurs et paysans du Bordelais pendant la guerre de cent ans* (1947; Paris: Belles Lettres, 1963); Robert

Brenner, "Agrarian Class Structure and Economic Development in Pre-Industrial Europe," *Past and Present* 70 (February 1976): 30–75; and the symposium articles on Brenner's work in *Past and Present* 78–97 (February 1978–November 1982). The extent of the economic crisis of the early (i.e., pre-plague) fourteenth century has been greatly debated, especially for England; see the summary of the debate in Ian Kershaw, "The Great Famine and Agrarian Crisis in England 1315–1322," in R. H. Hilton, ed., *Peasants, Knights and Heretics: Studies in Medieval English Social History* (Cambridge: Cambridge University Press, 1976), pp. 85–132 (repr. from *Past and Present* 59 [May 1973]).

6. See, for example, Fritz Curschmann, *Hungersnöte im Mittelalter: Ein Beitrag zur deutschen Wirtschaftsgeschichte des 8. bis 13. Jahrhunderts* (Leipzig: Teubner, 1900), esp. pp. 59–60, 110, 112, 142; Wilhelm Abel, *Agrarkrisen und Agrarkonjunktur in Mitteleuropa*, 3d ed. (Hamburg: Parey, 1978); Marie-Josèphe Larenaudie, "Les Famines en Languedoc aux XIVᵉ et XVᵉ siècles," *Annales du Midi* 64 (1952): 27–39; Elisabeth Carpentier, "Autour de la peste noire: Famines et épidémies dans l'histoire du XIVᵉ siècle," *Annales: Economies, sociétés, civilisations* 17.5 (1962): 1062–92; H. S. Lucas, "The Great European Famine of 1315, 1316 and 1317," in E. M. Carus-Wilson, ed., *Essays in Economic History*, vol. 2 (London: Arnold, 1962), pp. 49–72 (repr. from *Speculum* 5 [1930]); and Kershaw, "Great Famine." Salimbene's chronicle for 1286 gives a graphic example of a thirteenth-century man who became obsessed with fear of famine and hoarded food. Children, angered by his greed and hypocrisy, exacted revenge on his corpse. See the excerpt from Salimbene's chronicle in G. G. Coulton, *From St. Francis to Dante: Translations from the Chronicle of the Franciscan Salimbene . . .* , 2d ed. (1907; repr. Philadelphia: University of Pennsylvania Press, 1972), pp. 163–64; see also ibid., pp. 190–91. Thomas of Celano's second Life of Francis of Assisi speaks of an early thirteenth-century famine so bad that bread was made from the bark of trees and dead children were eaten; see Thomas of Celano, Second Life of Francis, bk. 2, chap. 23, par. 53, in AF, vol. 10, pp. 163–64. Two saints discussed in chap. 4, below, provide further examples of hardship. Alpaïs's parents, at the urging of her brothers, left her to starve because she was too ill to cart manure; Margaret of Città di Castello, born weak and blind, was abandoned by her family.

7. For an extraordinary example of differences in diet based on class or status differences, see the passage from *Le Despit au villain* quoted in Robert Gottfried, *The Black Death: Natural and Human Disaster in Medieval Europe* (New York: Free Press, 1983), pp. 99–100. On this point, see also Constance B. Hieatt and Sharon Butler, eds., Introduction to *Curye on Inglysh: English Culinary Manuscripts of the Fourteenth Century (Including the "Forme of Cury")*, Early English Text Society (London: Oxford University Press, 1984), pp. 5–6; and Jack Goody, *Cooking, Cuisine and Class: A Study in Comparative Sociology* (Cambridge: Cambridge University Press, 1982), pp. 138–44.

8. See, for example, Mikhail M. Bakhtin, *Rabelais and His World*, trans. H. Iswolsky (Cambridge: M.I.T. Press, 1968); and Piero Camporesi, *Il Pane selvaggio* (Bologna: Il Mulino, 1980), esp. pp. 25–44.

9. See, for example, C. H. Talbot, ed. and trans., *The Life of Christina of Markyate: A Twelfth-Century Recluse* (Oxford: Clarendon Press, 1959), pp. 182–89, where Christina and a certain Margaret feed a mysterious pilgrim (i.e., Christ). One of the signs of his holiness is that he "tastes rather than eats." For a similar story of feeding a mysterious

stranger whose extraordinariness is proven by the fact that he does not really eat, see *Vie de Douceline*, chap. 8, pars. 6–9, pp. 66–69.

10. Life of Margaret of Cortona, chap. 3, par. 51, AASS February, vol. 3 (Paris, 1865), p. 313. Readers should note that I give date of death and identifying information the first time an individual is mentioned. See the General Index for the page where that first reference occurs.

11. Gunther of Pairis, *De oratione, jejunio et eleemosyna libri tredecim*, bk. 12: *De jejunio*, chap. 3, PL 212, col. 210. On Gunther, see *Dictionnaire des auteurs cisterciens*, ed. Emile Brouette, Anselme Dimier, and Eugène Manning, La Documentation cistercienne 16 (Rochefort, Belgium: Abbaye Notre-Dame de St. Remy, 1975–78), vol. 1, fasc. 3, cols. 324–25.

12. Life of Catherine of Sweden, chap. 1, par. 4, AASS March, vol. 3 (Paris, 1865), p. 504.

13. *Tractatus beati Gregorii pape contra religionis simulatores*, chap. 69, in Marvin Colker, ed., *Analecta Dublinensia: Three Medieval Latin Texts in the Library of Trinity College Dublin* (Cambridge: Medieval Academy of America, 1975), p. 47; see also p. 6 for the dating.

14. For a discussion of recent anthropological studies of food practices, see Gillian Feeley-Harnik, *The Lord's Table: Eucharist and Passover in Early Christianity* (Philadelphia: University of Pennsylvania Press, 1981), pp. 6–18; and Goody, *Cooking, Cuisine and Class*, pp. 10–39. For a psychoanalytic interpretation of food ritual, see Mary Ellen Ross and Cheryl Lynn Ross, "Mothers, Infants, and the Psychoanalytic Study of Ritual," *Signs: Journal of Women in Culture and Society* 9.1 (1983): 26–39. Although a useful corrective to Freud, this article does not take us very far in understanding the mass.

15. Mechtild of Magdeburg, *Offenbarungen der Schwester Mechtild von Magdeburg oder Das Fliessende Licht der Gottheit*, ed. Gall Morel (Regensburg: Manz, 1869; repr. Darmstadt, 1963), bk. 2, chap. 22, p. 43; trans. Lucy Menzies, *The Revelations of Mechtild of Magdeburg (1210–1297) or The Flowing Light of the Godhead* (London: Longmans, 1953), p. 48. On Mechtild's death date, see Hans Neumann, "Beiträge zur Textgeschichte des 'Fliessenden Lichts der Gottheit' und zur Lebensgeschichte Mechtilds von Magdeburg," *Nachrichten der Akademie der Wissenschaften in Göttingen, Philologisch-historische Klasse* (1954), p. 70.

16. Hadewijch, *Mengeldichten*, ed. J. Van Mierlo, Leuvense Studiën en Tekstuitgaven (Antwerp: N.V. Standaard Boekhandel, 1954), poem 16, p. 79; trans. Columba Hart, *Hadewijch: The Complete Works* (New York: Paulist Press, 1980), p. 353.

17. John Tauler, Sermon 30, First Sermon for Corpus Christi, in Tauler, *Die Predigten*, p. 293; trans. Colledge and Sister M. Jane, *Spiritual Conferences*, p. 100. In this sermon, Tauler actually moves quickly away from our eating God as an image of union to a discussion of God's eating us ("gnawing at our consciences") as an image of punishment (*Die Predigten*, pp. 294–95).

18. William of St. Thierry, *Exposé sur le Cantique des cantiques*, ed. J. M. Déchanet, SC 82, Sér. mon. 8 (1962), chap. 38, p. 122; trans. Columba Hart, *The Works of William of St. Thierry*, vol. 2: *Exposition on the Song of Songs*, Cistercian Fathers Series 6 (Spencer, Mass.: Cistercian Publications, 1970), p. 30.

19. William of St. Thierry, *Meditativae orationes*, chap. 10, PL 180, col. 236; trans. Sister Penelope, *The Works of William of St. Thierry*, vol. 1: *On Contemplating God . . .* , Cistercian Fathers Series 3 (Spencer, Mass.: Cistercian Publications, 1971), pp. 152–53. For other examples of food imagery, see J. Huizinga, *The Waning of the Middle Ages: A Study of the Forms of Life, Thought and Art in France and the Netherlands in the XIVth and XVth Centuries*, trans. F. Hopman (1924; repr. Garden City: Doubleday, 1956), pp. 197–200.

20. All five of the important recent works on medieval saints deal with this issue. See Pierre Delooz, *Sociologie et Canonisations* (Liège: Faculté de droit, 1969), which is summarized in idem, "Towards a Sociological Study of Canonized Sainthood in the Catholic Church," in Stephen Wilson, ed., *Saints and Their Cults: Studies in Religious Sociology, Folklore and History* (Cambridge: Cambridge University Press, 1983), pp. 189–216; Vauchez, *La Sainteté*; Weinstein and Bell, SS; Goodich, VP; and Kieckhefer, UnS. On the way in which a holy person serves as an exemplar or model for a society, see also Peter Brown, "The Saint as Exemplar in Late Antiquity," *Representations* 1.2 (Spring 1983): 1–25. For a bibliography of recent works on sanctity and hagiography, see Wilson, *Saints and Their Cults*, pp. 309–417. For basic biographical and bibliographical information on individual saints, the best reference work is now *Bibliotheca sanctorum*. The standard guide to editions is the Bollandists, eds., *Bibliotheca hagiographica latina antiquae et mediae aetatis*, Subsidia hagiographica 6, 2 vols. (1898–1901; repr. Brussels: Société des Bollandistes, 1949).

21. Hagiography, by its nature, is more reliable as evidence for what people believed than as evidence for the details (especially the chronology) of individual lives. Indeed, the process of applying modern psychological or medical models to medieval lives often tempts historians to trust the particulars of medieval accounts more than is wise. Understanding this should not, however, lead one to fall into the opposite error of ignoring the distinction between clearly legendary material, on the one hand, and fairly trustworthy contemporary accounts, on the other. See below, chap. 6 n. 82. For a splendid discussion of these methodological problems, see Siegfried Ringler, "Die Rezeption mittelalterlicher Frauenmystik als wissenschaftliches Problem, dargestellt am Werk der Christine Ebner," in Peter Dinzelbacher and Dieter R. Bauer, eds., *Frauenmystik im Mittelalter*, Wissenschaftliche Studientagung der Akademie der Diözese Rottenburg-Stuttgart, 22.–25. Februar 1984, in Weingarten (Ostfildern bei Stuttgart: Schwabenverlag, 1985), pp. 178–200.

22. A few minor details of format follow from this approach. First, in order to aid scholars who wish to track down references and may have to resort to different editions from those I use, I cite medieval works by chapter and paragraph (where these are available) as well as by page number. Second, when I give additional material in the footnotes, I usually cite the texts in the original language. These further examples are intended for scholars, but it may interest the general reader as well to see the variety of vernacular languages in which women's ideas survive. Third, I provide in the notes some historiographical comment on the differences between my interpretations and those of other scholars, some discussion of methodology, and an occasional suggestion for further research. Except for the treatment of anorexia nervosa in chapter 6, however, I have refrained from cluttering the text with discussion of modern interpretations. One other

matter of format is also worth mentioning. I occasionally repeat an example when it serves to demonstrate two very different analytical points. In such cases, I do not repeat the documentation, but readers can find the first occurrence of the example by using the General Index. In cross-references, a note number standing alone refers to the same chapter; when a cross-reference is to a different chapter, the chapter number is given as well.

◆ *1. Religious Women in the Later Middle Ages*

1. James of Vitry, Life of Mary of Oignies, prologue, pars. 6–8, AASS June, vol. 5 (Paris, 1867), p. 548; translation adapted in part from translations by Henry Osborn Taylor, *The Medieval Mind: A History of the Development of Thought and Emotion in the Middle Ages*, 2 vols., 4th ed. (London: Macmillan, 1925), vol. 1, pp. 477–78; and Mc-Donnell, *Beguines*, p. 330.

2. Much of chapter 1 will appear under the same title but in somewhat different form in *The Encyclopedia of World Spirituality*, vol. 17: *Christian Spirituality: High Middle Ages and Reformation*, ed. Jill Raitt (New York: Crossroad, 1987). It appears here with permission of the Crossroad Publishing Company.

3. Suzanne F. Wemple, *Women in Frankish Society: Marriage and the Cloister, 500 to 900* (Philadelphia: University of Pennsylvania Press, 1981).

4. Richard W. Southern, *Western Society and the Church in the Middle Ages*, Pelican History of the Church 2 (Harmondsworth: Penguin, 1970), pp. 318–31.

5. See Rosalind B. Brooke and Christopher N. L. Brooke, "St. Clare," in Baker, MW, p. 276; Christopher N. L. Brooke and Wim Swaan, *The Monastic World* (London: Elek, 1974), pp. 167, 177–78, 254 n. 2.

6. In the modern world there are roughly three women in religious orders to every man (Brooke and Brooke, "St. Clare," p. 276), though recently the number of nuns in the United States has sharply declined (see "Vows of Defiance," *Newsweek*, 19 March 1984, pp. 97–100). The change from women as a minority of those in religious orders to a large female majority seems to have come in the later Middle Ages.

7. On religious women, the basic works are Karl Bücher, *Die Frauenfrage im Mittelalter*, 2d ed. (Tübingen: Laupp, 1910); Joseph Greven, *Die Anfänge der Beginen: Ein Beitrag zur Geschichte der Volksfrömmigkeit und des Ordenswesens im Hochmittelalter*, Vorreformationsgeschichtliche Forschungen 8 (Münster: Aschendorff, 1912); Grundmann, *Bewegungen*; Philibert Schmitz, *Histoire de l'ordre de saint Benoît*, 7 vols. (Maredsous: Editions de Maredsous, 1942–1956), vol. 7: *Les Moniales*; Stephanus Hilpisch, *Die Doppelklöster: Enstehung und Organisation* (Münster: Aschendorff, 1928); idem, *Geschichte der Benediktinerinnen*, Benediktinisches Geistesleben 3 (St. Ottilien: Eos Verlag der Erzabtei, 1951); Micheline Pontenay de Fontette, *Les Religieuses à l'âge classique du droit canon: Recherches sur les structures juridiques des branches féminines des ordres* (Paris: Vrin, 1967); and Robert E. Lerner, "Beguines and Beghards," DMA, vol. 2 (1983), pp. 157–62. For further bibliography, see C. Erickson and K. Casey, "Women in the Middle Ages: A

Working Bibliography," *Medieval Studies* 37 (1975): 340–59; and Bynum, JM, pp. 9–16, 182 n. 33.

8. See AASS March, vol. 3 (Paris, 1865), pp. 361–63; the Benedictines of Paris, *Vies des saints et des bienheureux* . . . , vol. 3 for March (Paris: Letouzey et Ané, 1941), p. 481.

9. For other examples of women who founded orders, see Goodich, VP, p. 174.

10. The Conrad of Marchtal text is quoted by Southern, *Western Society and the Church*, p. 314; and by A. Erens, "Les Soeurs dans l'ordre de Prémontré,' *Analecta Praemonstratensia* 5 (1929): 10 n. 20. There is no manuscript copy of this condemnation, which first appears in a sixteenth-century work of dubious reliability. See Norbert Backmund, *Monasticon Praemonstratense; id est, Historia circariarum atque canoniarum candidi et canonici Ordinis Praemonstratensis*, 3 vols. (Straubing: Attenkofer, 1949–1956), vol. 1, p. 85 n. 5; and Carol Neel, "Women's Roles in Medieval Monastic Life: Double Monasteries and the Twelfth-Century Reform," paper delivered to the Sixth Berkshire Conference on the History of Women, 1–3 June 1984, n. 4 of typescript. For the quotation from Bernard, see *Sermones super Cantica canticorum*, Sermon 65, par. 4, in OB, vol. 2 (1958), pp. 174–75. (Bernard often, however, wrote to individual women with tact and graciousness.) See also Giles Constable, "Aelred of Rievaulx and the Nun of Watton: An Episode in the Early History of the Gilbertine Order," in Baker, MW, pp. 205–26.

11. John B. Freed, "Urban Development and the 'Cura Monialium' in Thirteenth-Century Germany," *Viator* 3 (1972): 311–27; idem, *The Friars and German Society in the Thirteenth Century*, Medieval Academy of America Publications 86 (Cambridge: Medieval Academy of America, 1977); and Frederick Stein, "The Religious Women of Cologne, 1120–1320" (Ph.D. dissertation, Yale University, 1977). See also maps and index to Frédéric Van der Meer, *Atlas de l'ordre cistercien* (Amsterdam: Elsevier, 1965); and Brooke and Brooke, "St. Clare," p. 276 n. 2.

12. See Neel, "Double Monasteries." Premonstratensian double houses did, however, disappear in western Europe.

13. Freed, "Urban Development."

14. Michael Goodich, "Contours of Female Piety in Later Medieval Hagiography," *Church History* 50 (1981): 20–32; idem, VP, pp. 173–85; Brenda M. Bolton, "*Vitae Matrum*: A Further Aspect of the *Frauenfrage*," in Baker, MW, pp. 253–73; Roisin, *L'Hagiographie*, pp. 113, 129.

15. See, for example, Richard C. Trexler, "Le Célibat à la fin du moyen âge: Les Religieuses de Florence," *Annales: Economies, sociétés, civilisations* 27 (1972): 1329–50; Freed, "Urban Development." Regional variations in the types of religious structures available to women are currently being explored in a major research project conducted by Mary Martin McLaughlin and Suzanne Wemple at Barnard College. A study of the extent to which women were over-represented as witnesses and adherents in canonization proceedings, regardless of the sex of the saint, would be instructive as another index of female religiosity. Some of the material in Goodich, VP (esp. pp. 163, 209) suggests that they were in fact over-represented, although Goodich does not pursue the point.

16. Gottfried Koch, *Frauenfrage und Ketzertum im Mittelalter: Die Frauenbewegung im Rahmen des Katharismus und des Waldensertums und ihre sozialen Wurzeln: 12.–14. Jahrhundert*, Forschungen zur mittelalterlichen Geschichte 9 (Berlin: Akademie-Verlag, 1962); Eleanor C. McLaughlin, "Les Femmes et l'hérésie médiévale: Un Problème dans

l'histoire de la spiritualité," *Concilium* 111 (1976): 73–90; Richard Abels and Ellen Harrison, "The Position of Women in Languedocian Catharism," *Medieval Studies* 41 (1979): 215–51.

17. There is a very large literature on twelfth- and thirteenth-century heresy. For two recent interpretations, see Malcolm Lambert, *Medieval Heresy: Popular Movements from Bogomil to Hus* (New York: Holmes and Meier, 1977); and R. I. Moore, *The Origins of European Dissent* (New York: St. Martin's Press, 1977).

18. See Robert E. Lerner, *The Heresy of the Free Spirit in the Later Middle Ages* (Berkeley and Los Angeles: University of California Press, 1972); Eleanor C. McLaughlin, "The Heresy of the Free Spirit and Late Medieval Mysticism," *Medievalia et Humanistica* n.s. 4 (1973): 37–54.

19. This was basically Grundmann's interpretation; see *Bewegungen*.

20. In addition to the works cited in n. 11 above, see McDonnell, *Beguines*; Brenda M. Bolton, "*Mulieres sanctae*," in *Studies in Church History*, vol. 10: Derek Baker, ed., *Sanctity and Secularity: The Church and the World* (1973), pp. 77–95; and Kaspar Elm, "Die Stellung der Frau in Ordenswesen, Semireligiosentum und Häresie zur Zeit der heiligen Elisabeth," in University of Marburg, ed., *Sankt Elisabeth: Fürstin, Dienerin, Heilige: Aufsätze, Dokumentation, Katalog* (Sigmaringen: Thorbecke, 1981), pp. 7–28.

21. Lerner, "Beguines and Beghards," p. 160; Stein, "Religious Women of Cologne."

22. See Bücher, *Frauenfrage*; and Greven's summary of earlier literature in *Anfänge*, pp. 1–27. For more recent economic and social interpretations, see Dayton Phillips, *Beguines in Medieval Strasburg: A Study of the Social Aspect of Beguine Life* (Stanford: Stanford University Press, 1941); and Ernst Werner and Martin Erbstösser, *Ideologische Probleme des mittelalterlichen Plebejertums. Die freigeistige Häresie und ihre sozialen Wurzeln* (Berlin: Akademie-Verlag, 1960).

23. See Werner and Erbstösser, *Ideologische Probleme*; Eva G. Neumann, *Rheinisches Beginen- und Begardenwesen: Ein Mainzer Beitrag zur religiösen Bewegung am Rhein*, Mainzer Abhandlungen zur mittleren und neueren Geschichte 4 (Meisenheim am Glan: Hain, 1960); Freed, "Urban Development." See also Lerner, *Heresy of the Free Spirit*, p. 231.

24. See, for example, Bücher, *Frauenfrage*; and David Herlihy, "Women in Medieval Society," repr. in *The Social History of Italy and Western Europe, 700–1500*, Variorum reprints (London, 1978).

25. For the religious surplus explanation, see Greven, *Anfänge*; Grundmann, *Bewegungen*; Southern, *Western Society and the Church*, pp. 318–31; Bolton, "*Mulieres sanctae*."

26. Ghent memorial of 1328, in Paul Fredericq, *Corpus documentorum Inquisitionis haereticae pravitatis Neerlandicae*, vol. 1 (Ghent: Nijhoff, 1889), p. 176; trans. adapted in part from McDonnell, *Beguines*, p. 83.

27. See above, n. 10. On misogyny generally, see Diane Bornstein, "Antifeminism," DMA, vol. 1 (1982), pp. 322–25.

28. Freed, "Urban Development"; idem, *Friars and German Society*; Stein, "Religious Women of Cologne."

29. Alice A. Hentsch, *De la littérature didactique du moyen âge s'adressant spécialement aux femmes* (Cahors: Coueslant, 1903); and Matthäus Bernards, *Speculum Virginum: Geistigkeit und Seelenleben der Frau im Hochmittelalter* (Cologne: Böhlau, 1955). See also

Clarissa Atkinson, "'Precious Balsam in a Fragile Glass': The Ideology of Virginity in the Later Middle Ages," *Journal of Family History* 8.2 (Summer 1983): 131–43; and Peter Brown, *Virginity and Society: Men, Women and Renunciation in Late Antiquity*, forthcoming.

30. Vauchez, *La Sainteté*, pp. 216–18. If one considers all kinds of saints together, men account for 81.7 percent of the proceedings and 85.7 percent of the canonizations; women account for 18.3 percent of the proceedings and 14.3 percent of the canonizations. Only in the category of lay saints did women fare slightly better than men. Between 1198 and 1431, women account for 41.2 percent of the proceedings and 44.5 percent of the canonizations, men for 58.8 percent of the proceedings and 55.5 percent of the canonizations.

31. Weinstein and Bell, SS, pp. 220–21. See also Vauchez, *La Sainteté*, pp. 243–49, 316–18, 402–10; Jane Tibbetts Schulenberg, "Sexism and the Celestial Gynaeceum from 500 to 1200," *Journal of Medieval History* 4 (1978): 117–33; and Goodich, VP, p. 173. Schulenberg, using the *Bibliotheca sanctorum*, estimates 15 percent by 1250, 24 percent by 1300. Vauchez, using canonization proceedings, calculates that 16.3 percent of saints in the thirteenth century and 27.3 percent in the period from 1305 to 1431 were women.

32. Marc Glasser, "Marriage in Medieval Hagiography," *Studies in Medieval and Renaissance History* n.s. 4 (1981): 3–34, esp. p. 32 n. 58; Vauchez, *La Sainteté*, p. 442. Weinstein and Bell's tables (SS, pp. 123–37) indicate that a higher percentage of female than of male saints were married—a fact that partly explains the larger percentage of holy women who experienced conflict arising from their sexual lives (ibid., p. 97).

33. Weinstein and Bell, SS, pp. 97–99, 225–27; Vauchez, *La Sainteté*, p. 440–45.

34. Weinstein and Bell, SS, pp. 194–219, 221 (table); Vauchez, *La Sainteté*, pp. 243–49, 317. According to Vauchez, women account for 21.4 percent of the proceedings among mendicants but for only 12.5 percent of the canonizations.

35. Vauchez, *La Sainteté*, p. 317.

36. I have discussed this trend in Bynum, JM, pp. 9–21, 250–54. Vauchez, *La Sainteté*, pp. 243–60, 402–10, discusses the feminization of lay piety, especially under mendicant auspices, and the clericalization of male piety.

37. See Bynum, JM, p. 15; Jean Leclercq, "Medieval Feminine Monasticism: Reality vs. Romantic Images," *Benedictus: Studies in Honor of St. Benedict of Nursia*, Studies in Medieval Cistercian History 8 (Kalamazoo: Cistercian Publications, 1981), p. 61; and Josef Jungmann, *The Mass of the Roman Rite: Its Origins and Development (Missarum Sollemnia)*, trans. F. A. Brunner, 2 vols. (New York: Benziger, 1951, 1955), vol. 2, p. 386 n. 95.

38. Quoted in Francine Cardman, "The Medieval Question of Women and Orders," *The Thomist* 42 (1978): 596. See also Ida Raming, *The Exclusion of Women from the Priesthood: Divine Law or Sex Discrimination?* trans. N. R. Adams (Metuchen, N.J.: Scarecrow Press, 1976), pp. 81–82.

39. According to the tables in Goodich, VP, pp. 211–40, 144 of 518 saints who flourished between 1215 and 1334 were women. Of these female saints, most were religious or quasi-religious. (Goodich lists 131 as being affiliated with an order, but this number is probably too high [see at n. 48 below].) Only 36, however, are listed as either abbesses or prioresses; another 5 are described as founders of orders. See also Bynum,

JM, pp. 247–62, esp. p. 249; Weinstein and Bell, SS, pp. 221–38. The most extravagant practitioners of penitential asceticism and ecstasies were almost by definition disqualified from major administrative positions.

40. See Eileen Power, "The Position of Women," in G. C. Crump and E. F. Jacobs, eds., *The Legacy of the Middle Ages* (Oxford: Clarendon Press, 1926), pp. 401–34; Jo Ann McNamara and Suzanne Wemple, "The Power of Women through the Family in Medieval Europe, 500–1100," *Feminist Studies* 1 (1973): 126–41; idem, "Sanctity and Power: The Dual Pursuit of Medieval Women," in Renate Bridenthal and C. Koonz, eds., *Becoming Visible: Women in European History* (Boston: Houghton-Mifflin, 1977), pp. 90–118; and the various articles in Herlihy, *Social History of Italy*.

41. For recent, convincing critiques of the notion of *a* "status" of women, see Martin King Whyte, *The Status of Women in Preindustrial Societies* (Princeton: Princeton University Press, 1978), esp. pp. 116–17; Michelle Zimbalist Rosaldo, "The Use and Abuse of Anthropology: Reflections on Feminism and Cross-Cultural Understanding," *Signs: Journal of Women in Culture and Society* 5 (1980): 401; Naomi Quinn, "Anthropological Studies on Women's Status," *Annual Review of Anthropology* 6 (1977): 181–83; and Penny Schine Gold, *The Lady and the Virgin: Image, Attitude and Experience in Twelfth-Century France* (Chicago: University of Chicago Press, 1985), preface.

42. For examples of these collective biographies, see "Unterlinden"; *Töss*; *Engelthal*; Anna von Munzingen, "Chronik des Klosters Adelhausen," ed. J. König, *Freiburger Diözesan-Archiv* 13 (1880): 131–93; A. Birlinger, ed., "Leben heiliger alemannischer Frauen des 14./15. Jahrhunderts, 4: Die Nonnen von Kirchberg bei Hagerloch," *Alemannia* 11 (1883): 1–20; F. W. E. Roth, ed., "Aufzeichnungen über das mystische Leben der Nonnen von Kirchberg bei Sulz," *Alemannia* 21 (1893): 103–48; H. Zeller-Werdmüller and J. Bächtold, eds., "Die Stiftung des Klosters Ötenbach und das Leben der seligen Schwestern daselbst," *Zürcher Taschenbuch* N.F. 12 (1889): 213–76; A. Birlinger, ed., "Leben heiliger alemannischer Frauen des 14./15. Jahrhunderts, 5: Die Nonnen von St. Katharinenthal bei Dieszenhofen," *Alemannia* 15 (1887): 150–84; and Karl Bihlmeyer, ed., "Mystisches Leben in dem Dominikanerinnenkloster Weiler bei Esslingen im 13. und 14. Jahrhundert," *Württembergische Vierteljahrshefte für Landesgeschichte* N.F. 25 (1916): 61–93. Some of these works are cited and discussed in Browe, *Die Wunder*; Walter Muschg, *Die Mystik in der Schweiz, 1200–1500* (Frauenfeld: Huber, 1935), pp. 205–41; and Louis Cognet, *Introduction aux mystiques rhéno-flamands* (Paris: Desclée de Brouwer, 1968), pp. 196–201 and passim.

43. Dumoutet, CD, p. 125. Gerson, a central figure in the fourteenth- and fifteenth-century debate over women's visions, was suspicious of Bridget of Sweden but sympathetic to Joan of Arc. In general, he felt that women's religious enthusiasm was excessive and suspect; see John Gerson, *De examinatione doctrinarum*, pt.1. considerations 2a and 3a, in John Gerson, *Joannis Gersonii . . . omnia opera*, ed. Louis Ellies-Dupin, 5 vols. (Antwerp, 1706), vol. 1, pp. 14–26; quoted in Julian, *Book of Showings*, ed. Colledge and Walsh, vol. 1, p. 151. But Gerson's *De probatione spiritum* provided tests for authenticating visions.

44. Lerner, *Heresy of the Free Spirit*; Vauchez, *La Sainteté*, pp. 439–48; Weinstein and Bell, SS, pp. 228–32. On male suspicion of visionary women, see also Otto Langer, "Zur dominikanischen Frauenmystik im spätmittelalterlichen Deutschland," and Dieter

R. Bauer, "Diskussionüberblick," in Dinzelbacher and Bauer, *Frauenmystik*, pp. 341–46, 373.

45. On medieval misogyny see Hentsch, *La Littérature didactique*; August Wulff, *Die frauenfeindlichen Dichtungen in den Romanischen Literaturen des Mittelalters bis zum Ende des XIII. Jahrhunderts*, Romanische Arbeiten, ed. Carl Voretzsch, vol. 4 (Halle: Niemeyer, 1914); Vern L. Bullough, "Medieval Medical and Scientific Views of Women," *Viator* 4 (1973): 487–93; Eleanor C. McLaughlin, "Equality of Souls, Inequality of Sexes: Women in Medieval Theology," in Rosemary Ruether, ed., *Religion and Sexism: Images of Women in the Jewish and Christian Traditions* (New York: Simon and Schuster, 1974), pp. 213–66; Marie-Thérèse d'Alverny, "Comment les théologiens et les philosophes voient la femme?" *La Femme dans les civilisations des Xᵉ–XIIIᵉ siècles: Actes du colloque tenu à Poitiers les 23–25 septembre 1976, Cahiers de civilisation médiévale* 20 (1977): 105–29; and Bornstein, "Antifeminism." The recent bibliography on witchcraft is enormous: see H. C. Erik Midelfort, "Witchcraft, Magic and the Occult," in Stephen Ozment, ed., *Reformation Europe: A Guide to Research* (St. Louis: Center for Reformation Research, 1982), pp. 183–209. For the theory that the romanticization of women (in the cult of the Virgin and in courtly love) may be causally linked to the persecution of women, see Jeffrey B. Russell, *Witchcraft in the Middle Ages* (Ithaca: Cornell University Press, 1972), p. 284; but see also E. W. Monter, "The Pedestal and the Stake: Courtly Love and Witchcraft," in Bridenthal and Koonz, *Becoming Visible*, pp. 119–36. For a discussion of the witch as an image of disorder or "misrule" (i.e., an inversion of ordinary social structures and values), see Stuart Clark, "Inversion, Misrule and the Meaning of Witchcraft," *Past and Present* 87 (May 1980): 98–127. Responsible scholarship on witchcraft has paid surprisingly little attention to the images of woman entailed in both witch belief and witch persecution. For two works that do treat this topic, see Thomas Forbes, *The Midwife and the Witch* (New Haven: Yale University Press, 1966); and Christina Larner, *Enemies of God: The Witch-Hunt in Scotland* (London: Chatto and Windus, 1981), esp. pp. 3–4. On the *Malleus maleficarum* itself, the most extreme example of medieval misogyny, see Sydney Anglo, "Evident Authority and Authoritative Evidence: The *Malleus Maleficarum*," in S. Anglo, ed., *The Damned Art: Essays in the Literature of Witchcraft* (London: Routledge and Kegan Paul, 1977), pp. 1–31.

46. A number of women saints were suspected of witchcraft or demonic possession— e.g., Catherine of Siena, Lidwina of Schiedam, and Columba of Rieti, all discussed in chapters 4 and 5 below.

47. Twentieth-century scholarship has been in agreement on the basic characteristics of women's spirituality. See, for example, Taylor, *Medieval Mind*, vol. 1, pp. 458–86; Leclercq, "Medieval Feminine Monasticism," pp. 65–66; and the works cited in Bynum, JM, pp. 14–19, 170–73, 247–62. The quantitative work of Vauchez, *La Sainteté*, and Weinstein and Bell, SS, pp. 220–38, basically supports these earlier interpretations. Weinstein and Bell argue (SS, p. 237) that there was a "masculine type" of saint (a holder of temporal or ecclesiastical power, a missionary or preacher, a heroic public figure), called *masculine* because such a pattern was limited to men. But they call the contrasting type of saint (characterized by penitential asceticism, mystical ecstasy, and supernatural signs, especially visions and miraculous bodily changes) "androgynous" rather than "feminine" because such spiritual concerns, although more prominent in women's lives, are found

in men's also. If, however, a piety can be characteristic of women only if it is limited to them by canon law or social convention, there can be no piety characteristic of women because there is no religious role exclusive to them (nun being only a female version of monk and beguine having a male counterpart, beghard). It seems better, therefore, to speak of a women's piety when we find, as we do in the thirteenth to the fifteenth century, certain devotional emphases (for example, suffering) significantly more popular with women, especially if these emphases are (as I argue in chapter 9 below) closely tied to cultural stereotypes of "the female." The composite picture of women mystics in Elizabeth Petroff, *Consolation of the Blessed* (New York: Alta Gaia Society, 1979), pp. 1–82, overinterprets the evidence in its theory of "seven stages" and overemphasizes the "feminine" element in visions, but it has brilliant insights. On the general question, see the wise words of Dronke, WW, pp. x–xi. See also Peter Dinzelbacher, "Europäische Frauenmystik des Mittelalters. Ein Überblick," in Dinzelbacher and Bauer, *Frauenmystik*, pp. 11–23.

48. Bolton makes this point in *"Vitae Matrum,"* p. 260.

49. See below, chap. 4; and Simone Roisin, "La Méthode hagiographique de Thomas de Cantimpré," *Miscellanea historica in honorem Alberti de Meyer*, 2 vols. (Louvain: Bibliothèque de l'Université, 1946), vol. 1, p. 552.

50. Weinstein and Bell, SS, pp. 19–47. The tables on pp. 123–37 indicate that of the 646 male saints surveyed, 357 (55 percent) converted as teenagers and only 96 (15 percent) as children; of 172 female saints, 55 (31 percent) converted as children and 58 (34 percent) as adolescents. I have discussed the significance of this finding at greater length in Caroline W. Bynum, "Women's Stories, Women's Symbols: A Critique of Victor Turner's Theory of Liminality," in Frank Reynolds and Robert Moore, eds., *Anthropology and the Study of Religion* (Chicago: Center for the Scientific Study of Religion, 1984), pp. 105–25. See also below, chap. 10 n. 51.

51. See below, chap. 4. On Umiliana dei Cerchi, see Vauchez, *La Sainteté*, p. 244.

52. See, for example, the case of Francesca de' Ponziani of Rome, in Weinstein and Bell, SS, pp. 39–40.

53. See Bynum, "Women's Stories, Women's Symbols."

54. Weinstein and Bell, SS, pp. 220–38; Vauchez, *La Sainteté*, pp. 243–56.

55. See below, pp. 76–77, 200–201, and 210–11.

56. At the prayers of Tiedala of Nivelles, a monk of Villers received the Christ child at his breast; see McDonnell, *Beguines*, p. 328; and Browe, *Die Wunder*, p. 106. Elizabeth Petroff (*Consolation*, p. 74) points out that the Italian women saints she has studied nursed only from Christ, never from Mary, in their visions. A nun of Töss, however, received the "pure, tender breast" of Mary into her mouth to suck because she helped Mary rear the Christ child (*Töss*, pp. 54–55). And Lukardis of Oberweimar had a vision of Mary nursing Jesus; upon asking, she received Mary's breast to drink from and tasted "great delight beyond human sweetness" (Life of Lukardis, AB 18 [1899]: 318–19). For men who nursed from Mary, see below, chap. 9 n. 56.

57. See above, n. 47; Ernst Benz, *Die Vision: Erfahrungsformen und Bilderwelt* (Stuttgart: Klett, 1969); and Peter Dinzelbacher, *Vision und Visionsliteratur im Mittelalter* (Stuttgart: Hiersemann, 1981), pp. 226–28. On the basis of the tables on pp. 123–37 of Weinstein and Bell, SS, it appears that women saints, who were about 18 percent of

those canonized, account for about half of the saints who were especially devoted to Jesus but for only about a third of the saints characterized by devotion to Mary. Such a statistic does not support the notion that women turned especially to female figures as mediators. Insofar as these women did display somewhat more attachment to Mary than did men, the fact seems accounted for by the greater affectivity of female piety generally: women were more interested in all members of the Holy Family (including Joseph, Anne, and Joachim) than were men. Roisin, *L'Hagiographie*, pp. 108, 111–120, has found that in thirteenth-century Cistercian visions from the north of Europe, the Virgin is more important to men. The humanity of Christ is, however, more important to women.

58. Weinstein and Bell, SS, p. 216.

59. Vauchez, *La Sainteté*; Weinstein and Bell, SS; Kieckhefer, UnS; Goodich, "Contours of Female Piety." On recluses and the eremitical life, see Louis Gougaud, *Ermites et reclus: Etudes sur d'anciennes formes de vie religieuse* (Ligugé: Abbaye Saint-Martin de Ligugé, 1928), and *L'Eremitismo in Occidente nei Secoli XI e XII*, Pubblicazioni dell'Università cattolica del Sacro Cuore, Miscellanea del Centro di Studi Medioevali 4 Contributi 3 ser., Varia 4 (Milan: Società Editrice Vita e Pensiero, 1965).

60. On Angela, see below, chap. 4; on Mechtild, see Bynum, JM, pp. 228–47; on Christina, see Talbot, *Life of Christina of Markyate*, and Christopher J. Holdsworth, "Christina of Markyate," in Baker, MW, pp. 185–204; on Catherine of Siena, see below, chap. 5.

61. See Bynum, JM, pp. 240–47, 252–55; Goodich, "Contours of Female Piety"; Roisin, *L'Hagiographie*, pp. 113, 129.

62. See Columba Hart, Introduction to Hart, *Hadewijch: Works*, p. 4. On Hadewijch, see below, chap. 5.

63. Vauchez indeed admits this (*La Sainteté*, pp. 255–56).

64. See below, chap. 4, for the Flemish saints, especially Lidwina of Schiedam, and chap. 5 for the two Italian Catherines, of Siena and of Genoa, and for Beatrice of Nazareth.

65. Homey images are very common in women's visions. See, for example, my discussion of the nuns of Helfta in Bynum, JM, pp. 170–262; Elsbet Stagel's account of the visions of the nuns of Töss in *Töss*; the visions of the laywoman Margery Kempe, in S. B. Meech and Hope Emily Allen, eds., *The Book of Margery Kempe*, Early English Text Society 212 (London: Oxford University Press, 1940); and Petroff's discussion of Italian nuns and tertiaries in *Consolation*. For examples of women's visions of Jesus as baby, see Bynum, "Women Mystics," p. 189. Men also used homey imagery; see, for example, the discussion of Suso in chap. 3 below.

66. On Gertrude of Helfta, see Bynum, JM, pp. 186–209; on Gertrude van Oosten, see below, chap. 3, and on Margery Kempe, below, chap. 7.

67. See below, pp. 263–67 and 290–93.

68. For examples of male writers who saw women as weak and urged them to spiritual virility, see John Tauler, Sermon 33, Fourth Sermon for Corpus Christi, in Tauler, *Die Predigten*, pp. 129–30; Life of Ida of Louvain, AASS April, vol. 2 (Paris, 1865), p. 159, where the anonymous (almost certainly male) compiler, working from material provided by Ida's confessor, says that Ida "was not a woman or lazy but like a

strong man in constancy" and that the devil was frustrated by her "manly boldness"; Life of Juliana of Cornillon, AASS April, vol. 1 (Paris, 1866), p. 442, where a male author writes that Juliana hastened to perfection, "her sex forgotten," although she "had corporeal fragility behind which many hide their cowardice and lukewarmness"; Life of Ida of Léau, AASS October, vol. 13 (Paris, 1883), p. 112, where a male author says Ida "was like a man seizing weapons" and fought the devil "virilely, not in a womanly way." Thomas of Celano, in his prefatory letter (addressed to Pope Alexander IV) to the Life of Clare of Assisi (in Francesco Pennacchi, ed., *Legenda sanctae Clarae virginis*, Società internazionale di studi Francescani in Assisi [Assisi: Tipografia metastasio, 1910], pp. 1–3), calls Clare a "model for the weaker sex" and stresses her *imitatio Mariae* (in contrast to Francis's imitation of Jesus), although Clare's own writings, edited in the same volume, stress *imitatio Christi*. See also chap. 5 below on Catherine of Siena and Umberto Mattioli, "La Tipologia 'virile' nella biografia e nella letteratura cateriniana," *Atti, Congresso Internazionale di Studi Cateriniani, Siena–Roma, 24–29 Aprile 1980* (Rome: Curia Generalizia O.P., 1981), pp. 198–222.

69. Caesarius, *Dialogus*, Distinctio 8, chaps. 71–78, vol. 2, pp. 141–48, are on confessors; Dist. 8, chaps. 79–89, vol. 2, pp. 148–56, are about virgins.

70. See above, n. 1, and below, chap. 2 at n. 119.

71. See above, n. 68; and Weinstein and Bell, SS, pp. 235–36.

72. John Anson, "The Female Transvestite in Early Monasticism: The Origin and Development of a Motif," *Viator* 5 (1974): 1–32.

73. See, for example, the works on the question of ordination cited in n. 38 above; McNamara and Wemple, "Power of Women"; idem, "Sanctity and Power"; E. McLaughlin, "Equality of Souls"; Rosemary Ruether, "Misogynism and Virginal Feminism in the Fathers of the Church," in Ruether, *Religion and Sexism*, pp. 150–83; Marina Warner, *Alone of All Her Sex: The Myth and the Cult of the Virgin Mary* (New York: Knopf, 1976); idem, *Joan of Arc: The Image of Female Heroism* (New York: Knopf, 1981); Carol P. Christ, "Heretics and Outsiders: The Struggle over Female Power in Western Religion," *Soundings* 61.3 (1978): 260–80; and Petroff, *Consolation*.

74. A related problem is the tendency of recent writers on spirituality to ignore women's perspective. Vauchez, *La Sainteté*, and Weinstein and Bell, SS, for example, treat the notion of woman as sexual temptation, found in misogynist writing, as the key religious concern bearing down on women. Georges Duby, *The Knight, the Lady and the Priest: The Making of Modern Marriage in Medieval France*, trans. Barbara Bray (New York: Pantheon, 1983), treats marriage as the exchange of women by men. All three authors, although animated by a rhetorically heightened concern for women's suffering, treat woman as object, viewed by, manipulated by, subjugated by, or admired by men, rather than as subject, generating her own spirituality.

75. For a psychoanalytic interpretation of why food is a symbol of mutilation and aggression, see Lillian Malcove, "Bodily Mutilation and Learning to Eat," *Psychoanalytic Quarterly* 2 (1933): 557–61. See also Peggy Reeves Sanday, *Divine Hunger and Cannibal Monsters: Cannibalism as a Cultural System* (Cambridge: Cambridge University Press, forthcoming). Sanday shows the connection, in a number of cultures, between cannibalism (actual or metaphorical) and widespread use of symbols taken from physiological

processes. For a startling evocation of the eucharist as cannibalism, see Francine du Plessix Gray, *World without End* (New York: PBJ, 1982), pp. 136–37.

♦ 2. Fast and Feast: The Historical Background

1. Pope Leo the Great, Sermon 20, Ninth Sermon for the December Fast, pars. 2–3, PL 54, cols. 189–90. On Leo's notion of fasting, see Alexandre Guillaume, *Jeûne et charité dans l'église latine des origines au XIIe siècle en particulier chez saint Léon le Grand* (Paris: Editions S.O.S., 1954). For the same sentiment, see Peter Chrysologus (d. 450), Sermon 41, PL 52, col. 317: "Fratres, sint deliciae pauperum nostra jejunia, ut temporale jejunium nostrum in aeternas possit nobis delicias immutari."

2. See above, pp. 1 and 3–4.

3. Augustine, *City of God*, bk. 10, chap. 6, PL 41, col. 284C; Hilary, *Tractatus in CXXV psalmum*, par. 6, PL 9, col. 688B–C; idem, *De Trinitate*, bk. 8, chaps. 13–14, PL 10, cols. 246–47, esp. col. 246: "Eos nunc, qui inter Patrem et Filium voluntatis ingerunt unitatem, interrogo utrumne per naturae veritatem hodie Christus in nobis sit, an per concordiam voluntatis? Si enim vere Verbum caro factum est, et vere nos Verbum carnem cibo dominico sumimus; quomodo non naturaliter manere in nobis existimandus est, qui et naturam carnis nostrae jam inseparabilem sibi homo natus assumpsit, et naturam carnis suae ad naturam aeternitatis sub sacramento nobis communicandae carnis admiscuit? Ita enim omnes unum sumus, quia et in Christo Pater est, et Christus in nobis est. Quisquis ergo naturaliter Patrem in Christo negabit, neget prius non naturaliter vel se in Christo, vel Christum sibi inesse; quia in Christo Pater, et Christus in nobis, unum in his esse nos faciunt. Si vere igitur carnem corporis nostri Christus assumpsit, et vero homo ille, qui ex Maria natus fuit, Christus est, nosque vere sub mysterio carnem corporis sui sumimus (et per hoc unum erimus, quia Pater in eo est, et ille in nobis); quomodo voluntatis unitas asseritur, cum naturalis per sacramentum proprietas, perfectae sacramentum sit unitatis."

4. Alan of Lille, *Summa de arte praedicatoria*, chap. 34: *De jejunio*, PL 210, col. 177D.

5. Aquinas, ST, II, IIae, q. 148: *De gula*, art. 3, vol. 43, pp. 122–24. For the patristic notion that Adam's sin was gluttony, see Herbert Musurillo, "The Problem of Ascetical Fasting in the Greek Patristic Writers," *Traditio* 12 (1956); 17 n. 43.

6. Ambrose, Hymn 3: *Splendor paternae gloriae*, in A. S. Walpole, *Early Latin Hymns* (London: Cambridge University Press, 1922), p. 38. Because Latin hymns lose so much in literal translation and may be familiar to many readers, I have cited them in the original.

7. Clemens Blume, ed., *Analecta hymnica medii aevi*, vol. 54 (Leipzig: Reisland, 1915), p. 257; trans. adapted from Joseph Connelly, *Hymns of the Roman Liturgy* (Westminster, Md.: Newman Press, 1957), p. 130. For other eucharistic sequences of the thirteenth and fourteenth centuries, see Blume, *Analecta hymnica*, vol. 54, pp. 258ff.

8. Cyprian, Letter 63, PL 4, cols. 372–89, esp. 384B: "Quo et ipso sacramento populus noster ostenditur adunatus; ut, quemadmodum grana multa in unum collecta et commolita et commista panem unum faciunt, sic in Christo, qui est panis coelestis, unum

sciamus esse corpus, cui conjunctus sit noster numerus et adunatus." See also Adalbert Hamman, "Mystère eucharistique," in DS, vol. 4, pt. 2 (1961), cols. 1570–71.

9. For Cyprian, see above, n. 8; Gregory the Great, *40 homiliarum in Evangelia*, Homily 15, par. 5, PL 76, col. 1137. Aquinas quotes Gregory in ST, II, IIae, q. 147, art. 2, vol. 43, p. 94.

10. For Leo, see above, n. 1; and see Guillaume, *Jeûne*, p. 83.

11. See J. A. MacCullough, "Fasting," *Encyclopedia of Religion and Ethics*, ed. James Hastings et al., 13 vols. (New York: Scribner's, 1908–1927), vol. 5, pp. 759–65; Henri Leclercq, "Jeûnes," *Dictionnaire d'archéologie chrétienne et de liturgie*, ed. Fernand Cabrol and Henri Leclercq, vol. 7, pt. 2 (Paris: Letouzey et Ané, 1927), cols. 2481–504; A. Villien, "Abstinence," in *Dictionnaire de droit canonique*, vol. 1 (Paris: Letouzey et Ané, 1935), cols. 129–35; Placide Deseille, "Jeûne," in DS, vol. 8, pt. 2 (1974), cols. 1164–79; F. Mugnier, "Abstinence," in DS, vol. 1, cols. 112–33; Rudolph Arbesmann, "Fasting and Prophecy in Pagan and Christian Antiquity," *Traditio* 7 (1949–1951): 1–72; Goody, *Cooking, Cuisine and Class*, pp. 116–19; and Eric N. Rogers, *Fasting: The Phenomenon of Self-Denial* (Nashville: Nelson, 1976), an interesting popular account that, unfortunately, lacks adequate documentation.

12. MacCullough, "Fasting," p. 760; Deseille, "Jeûne," col. 1165; Arbesmann, "Fasting and Prophecy," pp. 7–8.

13. See works cited in n. 11 above, and Musurillo, "Ascetical Fasting," pp. 1–64.

14. See esp. Musurillo, "Ascetical Fasting," p. 62. Of course, the early Christians were also reacting against Jewish food prohibitions and, therefore, against food prohibitions as a means of group definition. Marcel Simon ("De l'observance rituelle à l'ascèse," *Revue de l'histoire des religions* 193 [1978]: 77) suggests that free access to food was bought by the renunciation of marriage. But compare Goody, *Cooking, Cuisine and Class*, pp. 144–45.

15. Augustine, Sermon 207, Third Sermon for Lent, par. 1, PL 38, col. 1043.

16. Augustine, Sermon 210, Sixth Sermon for Lent, chap. 10, par. 12, PL 38, col. 1053. On the new awareness of the poor in the late antique world, see Evelyne Patlagean, *Pauvreté économique et pauvreté sociale à Byzance: 4ᵉ–7ᵉ siècles* (Paris: Mouton, 1977).

17. Maximus, Sermon 50a, par. 3, ed. Almut Mutzenbecher, Corpus christianorum, series latina 23 (Turnhout: Brepols, 1962), p. 203.

18. Walpole, *Hymns*, pp. 320–21.

19. Isidore of Seville, *De ecclesiasticis officiis*, bk. 1, chap. 44, PL 83, col. 776B.

20. Arbesmann, "Fasting and Prophecy," p. 3.

21. Clement of Alexandria, *Eclogae propheticae*, 14.2, *Clemens Alexandrinus*, ed. Otto Stählin, vol. 3, Die griechischen christlichen Schriftsteller der ersten Jahrhunderte 17 (Berlin: Akademie-Verlag, 1970), p. 140; quoted and trans. by Musurillo, "Ascetical Fasting," p. 13.

22. Abbot Nilus, *Tractatus de octo spiritibus malitiae*, chap. 1, PG 79, col. 1145B; quoted and trans. by Musurillo, "Ascetical Fasting," p. 16.

23. [Pseudo-]Athanasius, *De virginitate*, chap. 7, ed. Eduard F. von der Goltz, Texte und Untersuchungen zur Geschichte der altchristlichen Literatur N.F. 14 (Leipzig: Hinrichs, 1905), p. 41; quoted and trans. by Musurillo, "Ascetical Fasting," p. 17.

24. Aline Rousselle, "Abstinence et continence dans les monastères de Gaule méri-

dionale à la fin de l'antiquité et au début du moyen âge: Etude d'un régime alimentaire et de sa fonction," *Hommage à André Dupont: Etudes médiévales languedociennes* (Montpellier: Fédération Historique du Languedoc Mediterranéen et du Rousillon, Université Paul-Valery, 1974), pp. 239–54.

25. John Cassian, *Institutions cénobitiques*, bk. 5, chap. 11, ed. Jean-Claude Guy, SC 109, Sér. mon. 17 (1965), p. 206. Cassian even attributed Sodom's fall to gluttony; see John Boswell, *Christianity, Social Tolerance and Homosexuality: Gay People in Western Europe from the Beginnings of the Christian Era to the Fourteenth Century* (Chicago: University of Chicago Press, 1980), p. 98.

26. Jerome, Letter 54, par. 9, *Sancti Eusebii Hieronymi epistulae*, pt. 1, ed. Isidore Hilberg, Corpus scriptorum ecclesiasticorum latinorum 54 (Vienna: Tempsky und Freytag, 1910), p. 476.

27. See works cited above, n. 11, and F. Cabrol, "Carême," in *Dictionnaire de droit canonique*, vol. 2 (1937), cols. 1345–54.

28. Ember Days were Wednesday, Friday, and Saturday fasts, observed in the fourth, seventh, and tenth months of the year. See Arbesmann, "Fasting and Prophecy," p. 44.

29. Arbesmann, "Fasting and Prophecy," pp. 3–5, 34–37.

30. See Mugnier, "Abstinence." On Irish practice, see Louis Gougaud, *Christianity in Celtic Lands: A History of the Churches of the Celts, Their Origin, Their Development . . .* , trans. Maud Joynt (London: Sheed and Ward, 1932), pp. 96–99; and John Ryan, *Irish Monasticism: Origins and Early Development* (London: Longmans, Green, 1931), pp. 386–97. Ryan (p. 392) tells of three Irish monks who died from fasting.

31. Rule of St. Benedict, chaps. 39–41, 43, 49, in Timothy Fry et al., eds., *RB 1980* (Collegeville, Minn.: Liturgical Press, 1981), pp. 238–40, 242–44, 252. (See also p. 433.) In addition to the fasts prescribed by the church, Benedict also prescribes fasts—i.e., days on which the brothers do not eat until after None (about 3:00 P.M.)—on Wednesdays and Fridays from Pentecost to September 14 and on every weekday thereafter until Lent. See David Knowles, "The Diet of Black Monks," *Downside Review* 52, n.s. 33 (1934): 273–90, esp. p. 276; reprinted in idem, *The Monastic Order in England: A History of Its Development from the Times of St. Dunstan to the Fourth Lateran Council, 940–1216* (1940; 2d ed., Cambridge: Cambridge University Press, 1963), pp. 456–65. The dietary regime of Western monks before Benedict was more severe: see Rousselle, "Abstinence," p. 246.

32. Mugnier, "Abstinence," col. 122.

33. John Chrysostom, Homily on Matthew 46–47, PG 58, col. 480; quoted and trans. by Musurillo, "Ascetical Fasting," p. 41. John goes on to say that he does not wish to denigrate or trivialize fasting but, rather, to point out that fasting is not sufficient for salvation if other practices and virtues are neglected.

34. Gregory of Nyssa, *De virginitate*, chap. 21, PG 46, col. 401C; quoted by Musurillo, "Ascetical Fasting," p. 40.

35. Musurillo, "Ascetical Fasting," pp. 50–51.

36. Cuthbert Butler, ed., *The Lausiac History of Palladius . . .* , 2 vols. (Cambridge: Cambridge University Press, 1898–1904), vol. 2, p. 52. See Arbesmann, "Fasting and Prophecy," p. 34

37. John Chrysostom, *De studio praesentium*, Homily 5, PG 63, col. 489; quoted and

trans. by Musurillo, "Ascetical Fasting," p. 7. Chrysostom goes on to point out that these women cared for the sick and prepared food for others. Women also advised food asceticism. In the *Sayings of the Fathers*, a certain Syncletica is reported as urging her followers not to be seduced by the delights of the world. She admonishes: "Others hold as valuable the art of cooking; but you, through fasts and vile food, go beyond them in abundance of nourishment" (*Apophthegmata Patrum*, sayings of Syncletica, par. 5 [87], PG 65, col. 422C).

38. Romanos Melodes, *Hymnes*, ed. José Grosdidier de Matons, 5 vols., SC 99, 110, 114, 128, 283 (1964–1981), vol. 1, pp. 328–37.

39. Ibid., pp. 364–403.

40. Ibid., p. 390.

41. Ibid., pp. 392–94.

42. Ibid., vol. 3, pp. 110–31.

43. Ibid., vol. 4, p. 550.

44. Ibid., p. 556.

45. Ibid., vol. 3, p. 168.

46. For a modern statement of this sensibility, see Alexandre Schmemann, "Jeûne et liturgie," *Irenikon* 27 (1954): 292–301.

47. In general, Western Christians throughout the Middle Ages were required both to fast (that is, to refrain from eating until evening or midafternoon) and to abstain from meat and, usually, from other food of animal origin on all Fridays and Saturdays, on the quarter days, on the vigils of a few great feasts (e.g., Christmas), and on all the days of Lent except Sundays. Complete fast was required before reception of communion. For a brief discussion, see P. M. J. Clancy, "Fast and Abstinence," *New Catholic Encyclopedia* (New York: McGraw-Hill, 1967), vol. 5, pp. 846–50. On abstinence, see Aquinas, ST, II, IIae, q. 147, art. 8, vol. 43, pp. 114–16. As Aquinas notes, there was local variation in whether abstinence from eggs, milk, and milk products was required.

48. Lambert, *History of the Counts of Guines*, chap. 113, MGH.SS, vol. 24 (1879; repr. ed. New York: Kraus Reprint, 1964), p. 615; cited in Duby, *The Knight, the Lady and the Priest*, p. 263.

49. Barbara Ketcham Wheaton, *Savoring the Past: The French Kitchen and Table from 1300 to 1789* (Philadelphia: University of Pennsylvania Press, 1983), pp. 12–14; and Bridget Ann Henisch, *Fast and Feast: Food in Medieval Society* (University Park: Pennsylvania State University Press, 1976), pp. 28–58. For a description of medieval treatments of food from a medical point of view, see Lynn Thorndike, "Three Tracts on Food in Basel Manuscripts," *Bulletin of the History of Medicine* 8 (1940): 355–56.

50. Mugnier, "Abstinence," cols. 123–29; E. Vacandard, "Carême, jeûne de," in DTC, vol. 2, cols. 1737–44; Guillaume, *Jeûne*, pp. 155–63; Gerd Zimmermann, *Ordensleben und Lebensstandard. Die "Cura Corporis" in den Ordensvorschriften des abendländischen Hochmittelalters*, Beiträge zur Geschichte des alten Mönchtums und des Benediktinerordens 32 (Münster: Aschendorff, 1973), pp. 40–51.

51. Aquinas, ST, II, IIae, q. 147, art. 4, vol. 43, pp. 98–104.

52. Wheaton, *Savoring the Past*, p. 12. See also below, n. 124.

53. See Colker, *Analecta Dublinensia*, p. 57; and Knowles, "Diet," pp. 280–82.

54. Aquinas, ST, II, IIae, q. 148, arts. 4-6, vol. 43, pp. 124–34.

55. Zimmermann, *Ordensleben*, pp. 40–41.

56. Mugnier, "Abstinence," cols. 123–29. See also Peter Damian's accounts of Saints Romuald, Venerius, and Rudolph, PL 144, cols. 961–62, 974–75, 1011; and idem, *De Quadragesima et Quadraginta duabus Hebraeorum mansionibus*, PL 145, cols. 543–45.

57. On this point see Giles Constable, *Attitudes toward Self-Inflicted Suffering in the Middle Ages*, Ninth Stephen J. Brademas, Sr., Lecture (Brookline, Mass.: Hellenic College Press, 1982), pp. 21–22.

58. Bonaventure, *Vitis mystica*, additamentum 5, chap. 42, par. 135, *Opera omnia*, vol. 8 (Quaracchi: Collegium S. Bonaventurae, 1898), pp. 216–17. The concern for "circumstances" here reflects a desire to avoid scandalizing others.

59. Peter of Celle, Sermon 15, PL 202, col. 681C–D. See also the Lenten Sermons of Isaac of Stella, PL 194, cols. 1787ff., esp. col. 1791.

60. Peter the Chanter, *Verbum abbreviatum: Opus morale*, chap. 133, PL 205, col. 328.

61. Bernard of Clairvaux, Sermon 3 for Lent, pars. 2–4, PL 183, cols. 175C–76C.

62. Quoted from Suso's letter to Elsbet Stagel in Life of Suso, in Suso, *Deutsche Schriften*, p. 107; trans. M. Ann Edward in *The Exemplar: Life and Writings of Blessed Henry Suso, O.P.*, ed. Nicholas Heller, 2 vols. (Dubuque: Priory Press, 1962), vol. 1, p. 103.

63. Alan of Lille, *Summa*, chap. 34, PL 210, cols. 176–78; quoted passages at 176D–77A, 178A–C.

64. Aquinas, ST, II, IIae, qq. 146–47, vol. 43, pp. 82–117, esp. pp. 92, 106.

65. See below at nn. 103–4.

66. Quoted, respectively, from the "Pange, lingua": "Observata lege plene / Cibus in legalibus, / Cibum turbae duodenae / Se dat suis manibus" (Aquinas Byrnes, ed., *The Hymns of the Dominican Missal and Breviary* [St. Louis: Herder, 1943], p. 168); and "Sacris solemniis": "Noctis recolitur / Cena novissima, / Qua Christus creditur / Agnum et azyma / Dedisse fratribus / Juxta legitima / Priscis indulta patribus" (ibid., p. 172).

67. Ibid., p. 174. See also "Lauda, Sion, Salvatorem" in ibid., pp. 180–88.

68. Tubach, *Index*. See entries for "abstinence," "fasting," "bread," "loaves and fishes," "meat," "host," and "chalice."

69. On early monasticism, see Derwas J. Chitty, *The Desert a City: An Introduction to the Study of Egyptian and Palestinian Monasticism under the Christian Empire* (1966; repr. London: Mowbray, 1977). For a psychoanalytic interpretation of monasticism as a substitute for martyrdom, see Carl A. Mounter, "Guilt, Martyrdom and Monasticism," *Journal of Psychohistory: A Quarterly Journal of Childhood and Psychohistory*, 9.2 (Fall 1981): 145–71.

70. See P. Brown, "Response to Grant."

71. See Victor Saxer, *Morts, martyrs, reliques en Afrique chrétienne aux premiers siècles: Les Témoignages de Tertullien, Cyprien et Augustin à la lumière de l'archéologie africaine*, Théologie historique 55 (Paris: Beauchesne, 1980), pp. 141–49.

72. See, for example, Bede's account of Pope Gregory's letter of 601 to the missionary Mellitus; Bede, *A History of the English Church and People*, bk. 1, chap. 30, trans. Leo Sherley-Price and R. E. Latham (rev. ed., Harmondsworth: Penguin, 1968), p. 87. See also Ronald C. Finucane, *Miracles and Pilgrims: Popular Beliefs in Medieval England* (Totowa: Rowman and Littlefield, 1977), pp. 31–32.

73. Wayne A. Meeks (*The First Urban Christians: The Social World of the Apostle Paul* [New Haven: Yale University Press, 1983], p. 158) points out that festive meals were common in the voluntary associations of the Mediterranean world and that our earliest evidence about Christianity suggests that outsiders saw the eucharist in this way.

74. A. Hamman, E. Longpré, E. Bertaud, et al., "Eucharistie," in DS, vol. 4, pt. 2 (1961), cols. 1553–1648, esp. cols. 1568–96.

75. Robert Murray, *Symbols of Church and Kingdom: A Study in Early Syriac Tradition* (London: Cambridge University Press, 1975), pp. 76–79, quoted passages on pp. 77 and 76, respectively. On Cyprian and Romanos, see above, nn. 8, 38–45.

76. Feeley-Harnik, *Lord's Table*, pp. 139–64. Meeks (*First Urban Christians*, pp. 157–63) also stresses the extent to which "the single loaf used in the ritual symbolizes the unity . . . of the community." He emphasizes that "Paul uses the symbolism of the Supper ritual not only to enhance the internal coherence, unity, and equality of the Christian group, but also to protect its boundaries vis-à-vis other kinds of cultic association" (p. 159).

77. See Hamman, "Mystère eucharistique," cols. 1553–86, and J. H. Strawley, "Eucharist," *Encyclopedia of Religion and Ethics*, vol. 5, pp. 540–63.

78. Walpole, *Hymns*, pp. 350–51.

79. Ibid., pp. 345–46. The "Sancti, uenite" is the oldest eucharistic hymn in existence.

80. Dumoutet, CD; F. Baix and C. Lambot, *La Dévotion à l'eucharistie et le VIIe centenaire de la Fête-Dieu* (Gembloux: Duculot, 1964); Peter Browe, *Die Verehrung der Eucharistie im Mittelalter* (Munich: Hueber, 1933); Jules Corblet, *Histoire dogmatique, liturgique et archéologique du sacrement de l'eucharistie*, 2 vols. (Paris: Société Générale de Librairie Catholique, 1885–1886).

81. Decrees of the Fourth Lateran Council, in Henry Denzinger, *Enchiridion symbolorum: Definitionum et declarationum de rebus fidei et morum*, 34th ed., ed. A. Schönmetzer (Freiburg: Herder, 1967), document 802, p. 260. Note the close connection between the notion of the unity and exclusivity of the church and the doctrine that the eucharist *is* God's body and blood.

82. See Browe, *Die Wunder*; Dumoutet, CD. See also Edouard Dumoutet, *Le Désir de voir l'hostie et les origines de la dévotion au Saint-Sacrement*, Université de Strasbourg (Paris: Beauchesne, 1926).

83. Dumoutet, CD, pp. 109–10.

84. See Aquinas, ST, III, qq. 75–76, vol. 58, pp. 52–122. See also Dumoutet, CD.

85. "Pange, lingua" in Stephen Gaselee, ed., *The Oxford Book of Medieval Latin Verse* (repr. Oxford: Clarendon Press, 1937), p. 144; and Byrnes, *Hymns*, p. 168; trans. adapted from Connelly, *Hymns*, p. 120. In writing the office for Corpus Christi, Thomas borrowed from an earlier office. The extent of his "authorship" of these hymns is in doubt; see Baix and Lambot, *La Dévotion*, pp. 89–91. See also F. T. E. Raby, *A History of Christian Latin Poetry from the Beginnings to the Close of the Middle Ages*, 2d ed. (Oxford: Clarendon Press, 1953), pp. 402–14.

86. "Sacris solemniis," in Byrnes, *Hymns*, p. 172; trans. adapted from Connelly, *Hymns*, pp. 121–23.

87. "Verbum supernum prodiens," in Gaselee, *Medieval Latin Verse*, p. 145; trans. adapted from Connelly, *Hymns*, p. 123.

88. "Lauda, Sion, Salvatorem," in Gaselee, *Medieval Latin Verse*, pp. 146–47; and Byrnes, *Hymns*, pp. 180–88; trans. adapted from Connelly, *Hymns*, p. 126.

89. Dumoutet, CD, pp. 1–50.

90. See the works cited in nn. 74 and 80, above, esp. Emile Bertaud, "Dévotion eucharistique: Esquisse historique," DS, vol. 4, pt. 2, cols. 1621ff.

91. Lionel Rothkrug, "Popular Religion and Holy Shrines: Their Influence on the Origins of the German Reformation and Their Role in German Cultural Development," in James Obelkevich, ed., *Religion and the People, 800–1700* (Chapel Hill: University of North Carolina Press, 1979), pp. 30–32.

92. Louis Gougaud, "Etude sur la réclusion religieuse," *Revue Mabillon* 13 (1923): 86–87.

93. See Baix and Lambot, *La Dévotion*, p. 67. In his synodal statutes, Odo of Sully, bishop of Paris (1196–1208), required his priests to elevate the host. The practice existed in the Cistercian order before 1210; see McDonnell, *Beguines*, p. 311. See also Browe, *Die Verehrung*, p. 35; M. Camille Hontoir, "La Dévotion au saint Sacrement chez les premiers cisterciens (XIIᵉ–XIIIᵉ siècles)," *Studia eucharistica DCC anni a condito festo sanctissimi Corporis Christi* (Antwerp: De Nederlandsche Boekhandel, 1946), pp. 132–56; and Anton L. Mayer, "Die heilbringende Schau in Sitte und Kult," in Odo Casel, ed., *Heilige Überlieferung: Ausschnitte aus der Geschichte des Mönchtums und des heiligen Kultes: . . . [für] Ildefons Herwegen*, Beiträge zur Geschichte des Alten Mönchtums und des Benediktinerordens, Supplementband (Münster: Aschendorff, 1938).

94. Browe, *Die Verehrung*; Jungmann, *Mass of the Roman Rite*, vol. 1, pp. 119–21, and vol. 2, pp. 206ff.

95. The incident is cited by Rothkrug, "Popular Religion," p. 36, and by Anton Mayer, *Die Liturgie in der europäischen Geistesgeschichte: Gesammelte Aufsätze*, ed. E. von Severus (Darmstadt: Wissenschaftliche Buchgesellschaft, 1971), p. 45, referring to Edouard Dumoutet, *L'Iconographie de l'introit du Iᵉʳ dimanche de l'avent . . .* (1925), pp. 34–36, which I have been unable to consult.

96. See John Marienwerder, *Septililium B. Dorotheae*, treatise 3: *De eucharistia*, chap. 2, ed. Franciscus Hipler, in AB 3 (1884): 409. In his work on the life of Christ, Ludolf of Saxony assimilated "eating" to "seeing": "Venias et nihilominus quotidie ut videas Jesus in praesepio spirituali, scilicet in altari, ut carnis suae frumento merearis cum animalibus sanctis refici" (quoted in Mary Immaculate Bodenstedt, *The "Vita Christi" of Ludolphus the Carthusian*, Catholic University of America Studies in Medieval and Renaissance Latin Language and Literature 16 [Washington, D.C.: Catholic University of America Press, 1944], p. 133 n. 94).

97. See esp. Baix and Lambot, *La Dévotion*, pp. 75ff.; and Bertaud, "Dévotion eucharistique," cols. 1621–37.

98. Bertaud, "Dévotion eucharistique," col. 1632.

99. Baix and Lambot, *La Dévotion*, pp. 113–23; Gougaud, DAP, pp. 75–130; and Bynum, JM, pp. 132–33, 173 n. 12, 191–93.

100. Theodor Klauser, *A Short History of the Western Liturgy: An Account and Some Reflections*, trans. John Halliburton (2d ed., Oxford: Oxford University Press, 1979), pp. 98–103, 120; Jungmann, *Mass of the Roman Rite*, vol. 2, pp. 374–80; C. N. L. Brooke,

"Religious Sentiment and Church Design in the Later Middle Ages," *Bulletin of the John Rylands Library*, 50.1 (Autumn 1967): 13–33.

101. Klauser, *Western Liturgy*, p. 110; Jungmann, *Mass of the Roman Rite*, vol. 2, pp. 381–82; Baix and Lambot, *La Dévotion*, pp. 40–41; Corblet, *Histoire dogmatique*, vol. 1, pp. 188–91; Browe, *Die Wunder*, pp. 97–98.

102. Jungmann, *Mass of the Roman Rite*, vol. 2, pp. 381–85, 412–14. Among Cistercians and Dominicans, an ablutions cup was given to communicants (usually after mass was over), and its use continued after the chalice was withdrawn in the later thirteenth century. See Archdale King, *Liturgies of the Religious Orders* (London: Longmans, 1955), pp. 129–30, 372.

103. Aquinas, ST, III, q. 80, art. 12, reply obj. 3, vol. 59, pp. 84–85. See also III, q. 76, art. 2, vol. 58, pp. 96–100.

104. Jungmann, *Mass of the Roman Rite*, vol. 2, p. 364.

105. Quoted in Yves Congar, "Modèle monastique et modèle sacerdotal en Occident de Grégoire VII (1073–1085) à Innocent III (1198)," *Etudes de civilisation médiévale (IXᵉ-XIIᵉ siècles): Mélanges offerts à Edmond-René Labande* (Poitiers: C.E.S.C.M., 1973), p. 159.

106. Quoted in ibid.

107. Francis of Assisi, "Letter to a General Chapter," in Francis, *Opuscula sancti patris Francisci Assisiensis*, ed. the Fathers of St. Bonaventure's College, Bibliotheca Franciscana Ascetica Medii Aevi 1, 2d ed. (Quaracchi: Collegium S. Bonaventurae, 1949), pp. 102–3; trans. B. Fahy in *Omnibus*, p. 105.

108. Brooke, "Religious Sentiment."

109. Joseph Duhr, "Communion fréquente," DS, vol. 2 (1953), cols. 1234–92, esp. cols. 1236–71.

110. Albert the Great, *Commentarii in IV Sententiarum*, dist. 13, art. 27, in Albert, *Opera omnia*, ed. August Borgnet, vol. 29 (Paris: Ludovicus Vivès, 1894), pp. 378–80; and *Liber de sacramento Eucharistiae*, Dist. 4, tract. 4, chap. 3, in *Opera omnia*, vol. 38 (1899), p. 432: "De his autem qui mulieres omni die communicant, videtur mihi quod acriter reprehendendi sunt: quia nimio usu vilescere faciunt sacramentum, vel potius ex levitate mulierum putatur esse desiderium quam ex devotione causatum." See also Duhr, "Communion fréquente," col. 1260.

111. The crucial text from Augustine, quoted over and over in the discussions of frequent communion, is "Crede et manducasti," Tractate 25 on the Gospel of John, chap. 12, PL 35, col. 1602. Albert the Great, for example, cites it in his commentary on the Fourth Book of the Sentences, Dist. 9, *Opera omnia*, vol. 29, p. 212. In the Middle Ages, it was often used to argue for substituting "spiritual communion" (i.e., inner meditation) for reception. See Duhr, "Communion fréquente," col. 1246.

112. Life of Margaret of Cortona, AASS February, vol. 3, pp. 341, 344. Desire for the eucharist and obsessive fear of receiving it unworthily are themes throughout Margaret's *vita* (see pp. 304–63 passim).

113. Gertrude the Great, *Oeuvres spirituelles*, ed. Pierre Doyere, vol. 2: *Le Héraut*, SC 139, Sér. mon. 25 (1968), pp. 303–7.

114. Ibid.

115. See below, chap. 4, for the cases of Margaret of Cortona, Ida of Louvain, Lid-

wina of Schiedam, Dorothy of Montau, Alpäis of Cudot, and Colette of Corbie. See also Duhr, "Communion fréquente," cols. 1262–63, 1268, for examples of late medieval women who obtained frequent communion or were denied it.

116. Ida of Léau was denied the cup when the Cistercians passed legislation forbidding it to nuns who went into ecstasy at communion (Life of Ida of Léau, AASS October, vol. 13, pp. 113–14); see McDonnell, *Beguines*, p. 315 n. 140. See also Life of Juliana of Cornillon, AASS April, vol. 1, pp. 445–46.

117. See the case of Dorothy of Montau, discussed by Kieckhefer, UnS, pp. 22–23.

118. John Marienwerder comments that Dorothy of Montau's hunger for the eucharist was so vast that, if she had been permitted, she would have snatched the host from the hands of the priest with her teeth (*Septililium B. Dorotheae*, treatise 3, chap. 2, in AB 3, p. 409).

119. James of Vitry, Life of Mary of Oignies, AASS June, vol. 5, p. 568. See also epigraph to chap. 1; and Bynum, "Women Mystics."

120. Browe, *Die Wunder*; Bynum, "Women Mystics."

121. The new emphasis on "seeing" God is reflected in the increasing number of miracles connected with elevation rather than reception. In orders (e.g., Franciscan nuns or tertiaries) where communion was infrequent, ecstasies tended to come at the elevation. Eucharistic miracles could even involve knowing whether "Christ" (i.e., the consecrated host) was present on the altar, or being transported, when there was no service, into the tabernacle to taste Christ. See Life of Juliana of Cornillon, AASS April, vol. 1, p. 450; *Vie de Douceline*, pp. 133–35; Life of Ida of Louvain, AASS April, vol. 2, p. 172. Ida also knew miraculously the exact moment of consecration, even if the elements were not elevated (ibid., p. 173).

122. Wheaton, *Savoring the Past*, pp. 1–26; Reay Tannahill, *Food in History* (New York: Stein and Day, 1973), pp. 209–33.

123. Wheaton, *Savoring the Past*, pp. 1–2, 15–16, 21. On sotelties, see also Constance B. Hieatt and Sharon Butler, *Pleyn Delit: Medieval Cookery for Modern Cooks* (Toronto: University of Toronto Press, 1976), p. 156; Henisch, *Fast and Feast*, pp. 206–36. For examples of medieval foods and feasts see Lynn Thorndike, "A Medieval Sauce-Book," *Speculum* 9 (1934): 183–90; and Hieatt and Butler, *Curye on Inglysch*.

124. Wheaton, *Savoring the Past*, p. 13; Henisch, *Fast and Feast*, pp. 48–49. A Basel manuscript in a fifteenth-century hand, described by Thorndike ("Three Tracts on Food," p. 364), gives a description of food for Fridays and Lent that makes it clear that the absence of flesh meat did not necessarily mean a reduction in the variety or elegance of meals. For a catalogue of miracles in which one kind of food turns into another, see C. Grant Loomis, *White Magic: An Introduction of the Folklore of Christian Legend*, Medieval Academy of America Publication 52 (Cambridge: Medieval Academy of America, 1948), p. 57.

125. See, for example, Duhr, "Communion fréquente," cols. 1254–59; C. W. Dugmore, *The Mass and the English Reformers* (London: Macmillan, 1958); Strawley, "Eucharist"; Brooke, "Religious Sentiment."

126. On Hildegard's vision, see below, pp. 264–65 and plate 12.

127. Rupert of Deutz, *De divinis officiis*, bk. 2, chap. 11, PL 170, col. 43. On Rupert's eucharistic teaching generally, see Ursmer Berlière, *L'Ascèse bénédictine des origines à la*

fin du XIIe siècle: Essai historique (Paris: Desclée de Brouwer, 1927), pp. 86–91. See also John H. Van Engen, *Rupert of Deutz* (Berkeley and Los Angeles: University of California Press, 1983).

128. *Revelationes Gertrudianae ac Mechtildianae*, vol. 2: Mechtild of Hackeborn, *Sanctae Mechtildis virginis ordinis sancti Benedicti Liber specialis gratiae* (Paris: Oudin, 1877), bk. 1, chap. 1, pp. 7–10.

129. *Revelationes Gertrudianae ac Mechtildianae*, vol. 1: Gertrude the Great, *Sanctae Gertrudis magnae virginis ordinis sancti Benedicti Legatus divinae pietatis* . . . (Paris: Oudin, 1875), bk. 4, chap. 1, p. 286. But this spirituality is also very individualistic: we are assured that each sister who reposed on Christ's breast enjoyed him so fully that he might have been given to her alone (ibid., p. 287).

130. See Hontoir, "La Dévotion," pp. 134–35, 137. See also Rothkrug, "Popular Religion," p. 41.

131. Jean Leclercq, "Les Méditations eucharistiques d'Arnauld de Bonneval," *Recherches de théologie ancienne et médiévale* 13 (1946): 53.

132. Tubach, *Index*, pp. 59, 75–76, 207–12, 401–2.

133. Browe, *Die Wunder*, p. 104. On body symbolism generally, see Mary Douglas, *Natural Symbols: Explorations in Cosmology*, with new intro. (New York: Pantheon, 1982).

134. Browe, *Die Wunder*, p. 124.

135. Ibid., p. 119. For another, somewhat threatening blood miracle, see Adam of Eynsham, *The Life of St. Hugh of Lincoln*, ed. and trans. Decima L. Douie and Hugh Farmer, 2 vols. (London: Nelson, 1961), bk. 5, chap. 4, vol. 2, pp. 93–94. In this case a priest recounts to Hugh how, when he celebrated after committing a mortal sin, the host turned into flesh and blood, freezing him with fear. Other boundary-reinforcing blood miracles can be found in Corblet, *Histoire dogmatique*, vol. 1, pp. 447–515 passim.

136. Caesarius of Heisterbach, *Die Fragmente der Libri VIII Miraculorum des Caesarius von Heisterbach*, bk. 1, chap. 1, ed. Aloys Meister, Römische Quartalschrift für christliche Alterthumskunde und für Kirchengeschichte, Supplement, vol. 13 (Rome: Spithöver, 1901), pp. 4–6. For the use of the host as a magical charm, see Peter Browe, "Die Eucharistie als Zaubermittel im Mittelalter," *Archiv für Kulturgeschichte* 20 (1930): 134–54.

137. Rothkrug, "Popular Religion," p. 29. See also Browe, *Die Wunder*, pp. 128ff.

138. Browe, *Die Wunder*, pp. 115–16; Jungmann, *Mass of the Roman Rite*, vol. 1, pp. 119ff., and vol. 2, p. 210. For another example of blood avenging desecration, see Henry of Huntingdon's chronicle, bk. 8, chap. 22, *Henrici Archidiaconi Huntendunensis Historia Anglorum*, ed. Thomas Arnold, Rerum Britannicarum Medii Aevi Scriptores 74 (London: Longman, 1879), p. 277, where he reports that blood bubbled out of the walls of a church being held as a castle and says that he saw the phenomenon with his own eyes. Yet another example occurs in a story added to the *Little Flowers of St. Francis*, pt. 3, chap. 5, trans. Raphael Brown, in *Omnibus*, pp. 1481–82. A well-known passage from Froissart's chronicle that describes the flagellants and associates the collecting of their "miraculous blood" with "foolish women" is quoted in Gottfried, *Black Death*, p. 70.

139. See James of Vitry, Life of Mary of Oignies, AASS June, vol. 5, pp. 547–50, 562–63, 565–66. For eucharistic devotion as a counter to heresy, see McDonnell, *Beguines*, pp. 310, 315, 330, 415; and Bolton, "*Vitae Matrum*," pp. 267–68.

140. Thomas of Cantimpré, Life of Lutgard of Aywières, AASS June, vol. 4 (Paris, 1867), pp. 196, 197, 205.

141. Gertrude the Great, Oeuvres, vol. 3: Le Héraut, SC 143, Sér. mon. 27, bk. 3, chap. 18, pp. 102–4. See also above at nn. 113–14.

142. Thomas of Celano, Second Life of Francis, bk. 2, chap. 159, par. 209, AF 10, pp. 250–51. Bread is sometimes simply a symbol of blessing and unity (see ibid., chap. 163, par. 217, p. 255).

143. On Catherine, see below, pp. 175–80.

144. On medieval medical theory, which argued that breast milk is processed blood, see Mary M. McLaughlin, "Survivors and Surrogates: Children and Parents from the Ninth to the Thirteenth Centuries," in L. DeMause, ed., The History of Childhood (New York: Psychohistory Press, 1974), pp. 115–18; Michael Goodich, "Bartholomaeus Anglicus on Child-Rearing," History of Childhood Quarterly: The Journal of Psychohistory 3 (1975): 80; and Charles T. Wood, "The Doctors' Dilemma: Sin, Salvation and the Menstrual Cycle in Medieval Thought," Speculum 56.4 (October 1981): 719.

145. Gertrude the Great, Oeuvres, 3: Le Héraut, bk. 3, chap. 30, p. 142.

146. "Dulcis Jesu memoria," in Gaselee, Medieval Latin Verse, pp. 111–13. On this hymn see André Wilmart, "Le 'Jubilus' sur le nom de Jésus dit de saint Bernard," Ephemerides liturgicae: Analecta historico-ascetica 57, n.s. 27 (1943): 3–285, which gives a slightly different version of some lines. See also Raby, Christian Latin Poetry, pp. 326–31.

147. Ivo, letter, chap. 2, pars. 14–15, in Ives: Epître à Séverin sur la charité. Richard de saint-Victor: Les quatre degrés de la violente charité, ed. Gervais Dumeige, Textes philosophiques du moyen âge 3 (Paris: Vrin, 1955), pp. 61–63.

148. See below, chap. 5 n. 30.

149. Peter of Vaux, Life of Colette of Corbie, trans. Stephen Juliacus, chap. 10, par. 84, AASS March, vol. 1 (Paris, 1865), p. 558.

150. Life of Ida of Louvain, chap. 4, pars. 23–24, AASS April, vol. 2, p. 164.

151. On these metaphors in monastic texts, see Jean Leclercq, Etudes sur le vocabulaire monastique du moyen âge, Studia Anselmiana 48 (Rome: Herder, 1961), pp. 134–38; and idem, The Love of Learning and the Desire for God: A Study of Monastic Culture, 3d ed., trans. Catherine Misrahi (New York: Fordham University Press, 1982), p. 73.

152. See Schiller, Ikonographie, vol. 4, pt. 1: Die Kirche (1976), p. 62. This motif is related to the motif of Christ in the winepress. For example, in plate 5, a silk embroidery from the early fifteenth century, we see Jesus with his breast bare and his wound bleeding under his clothes into the press. A kneeling nun receives the blood in a chalice. See Schiller, Iconography (1972), vol. 2: The Passion of Jesus Christ, pp. 228–29. As James H. Marrow points out, medieval depictions of the winepress shifted from the twelfth-century image of Christ treading the grapes in the press to the fourteenth- and fifteenth-century motif of Christ as victim pressed beneath the cross-beam (Passion Iconography in Northern European Art of the Late Middle Ages and Early Renaissance: A Study of the Transformation of Sacred Metaphor into Descriptive Narrative [Kortrijk: Van Ghemmert, 1979], p. 85). Similarly, early depictions of the mystical mill show Christ or God as miller: Schiller, Ikonographie, vol. 4, pt. 1: Die Kirche, p. 62. See also Braun, Altar, vol. 2, plate 336.

153. For a medieval vision that parallels the mass of St. Gregory and makes it perfectly clear that the blood is food, see the vision of John of Alverna discussed below, chap. 7 n. 49. See also Schiller, *Iconography*, vol. 2: *Passion*, pp. 226–28; and Braun, *Altar*, vol. 2, plate 269.

154. Schiller, *Iconography*, vol. 2: *Passion*, p. 206.

155. It is not certain that there are, in patristic writings, any claims to receive Christ's body sensually; see E. Longpré, "Eucharistie et expérience mystique . . . ," DS, vol. 4, pt. 2, col. 1596.

◆ 3. Food as a Female Concern: The Complexity of the Evidence

1. Life of Alpaïs of Cudot, bk. 1, chaps. 2–3, AASS November, vol. 2, pt. 1 (Brussels, 1894), pp. 178, 180; see below, n. 77.

2. See E. Cobham Brewer, *A Dictionary of Miracles: Imitative, Realistic and Dogmatic* (Philadelphia: Lippincott [1896]), pp. 145–50; Tubach, *Index*, entries 766–67, 1732, 2566, pp. 63–64, 141, 202; and Thurston, PP, pp. 385ff.

3. Bernard of Clairvaux was supposedly nursed by Mary in a vision; see Léon Dewez and Albert van Iterson, "La Lactation de saint Bernard: Légende et iconographie," *Cîteaux in de Nederlanden* 7 (1956): 165–89. Clare of Assisi supposedly nursed from Francis's breast in a vision; see below at n. 186. For other lactation visions, see below, chap. 9 n. 56. For legends that both Paul and Catherine of Alexandria bled milk when beheaded, see Bynum, JM, p. 132 n. 76.

4. For lists of cases of "miraculous" or extended inedia, see Thurston, PP, passim, esp. pp. 363ff.; Pater, MA; W. B. Gerish, intro. to *The Hartfordshire Wonder or Strange News from Ware: Being an Exact and True Relation of one Jane Stretton . . .* , Hertfordshire Folklore 5 (London: J. Clark, 1669; repr. with Gerish's intro., Bishop's Stortford, 1908), pp. 5–8; Hyder E. Rollins, "Notes on Some English Accounts of Miraculous Fasts," *Journal of American Folk-lore* 34.134 (October–December 1921): 357–76; Rogers, *Fasting*, pp. 9–32; and H. Schadewaldt, "Medizingeschichtliche Betrachtungen zum Anorexie-Problem," *Anorexia Nervosa: Symposium 24./25. April 1965 in Göttingen*, ed. J.-E. Meyer and H. Feldmann (Stuttgart: Thieme, 1965), pp. 1–14.

5. Benedict XIV, *De servorum Dei beatificatione et beatorum canonizatione*, bk. 4, pt. 1, chap. 26, and app. by J. B. Beccari to bk. 4, pt. 1 (new ed., Naples: Johannis-Franciscus Pacus, 1773–1775), vol. 8, pp. 219–29, and vol. 15, pp. 89–127.

6. See Jérôme Ribet, *La Mystique divine, distinguée des contrefaçons diaboliques et des analogies humaines*, 2 vols., new ed. (Paris: Poussielgue, 1895), esp. vol. 2, p. 510; and Imbert-Gourbeyre, *Stigmatisation*.

7. See Thurston, PP; and Pater, MA.

8. William A. Hammond, *Fasting Girls: Their Physiology and Pathology* (New York: Putnam, 1876); Robert Fowler, *A Complete History of the Case of the Welsh Fasting-Girl (Sarah Jacob) with . . . Observations on Death from Starvation* (London: Renshaw, 1871). On this literature see Joan J. Brumberg, " 'Fasting Girls': Reflections on Writing the History of Anorexia Nervosa," in *History and Research in Child Development*, ed. Alice

B. Smuts and John W. Hagen, Monographs of the Society for Research in Child Development (Chicago: University of Chicago Press, 1986), pp. 93–104.

9. Rogers, *Fasting*, pp. 107–32.

10. See below, chap. 6.

11. See, for example, Duhr, "Communion fréquente," cols. 1256–68; and Gougaud, DAP, pp. 113–14. See also my discussion in Bynum, JM, pp. 170–72, 193 n. 58, 257.

12. Hontoir, "La Dévotion," pp. 132–56; idem, "Le Septième Centenaire de la Fête-Dieu: Sainte Julienne et les cisterciennes," *Collectanea ordinis Cisterciensis reformatorum* 8 (1946): 109–16; Browe, *Die Wunder*, passim, esp. pp. 23–24; Rothkrug, "Popular Religion," p. 28.

13. See the works cited above, n. 12; McDonnell, *Beguines*, pp. 299–330; and Roisin, *L'Hagiographie*, pp. 106–22.

14. See Baix and Lambot, *La Dévotion*, p. 70; Bertaud, "Dévotion eucharistique," cols. 1623–24, for the claim that eucharistic devotion appealed especially to nuns and recluses. For the claim that it appealed to beguines, see Greven, *Anfänge*, p. 69; Herbert Grundmann, "Zur Geschichte der Beginen im 13. Jahrhundert," *Archiv für Kulturgeschichte* 21 (1931): 314; E. Neumann, *Beginen- und Begardenwesen*, p. 91. Bolton ("*Vitae Matrum*," p. 267) has pointed out that the devotion cannot be identified with any particular style of life, and Vauchez (*La Sainteté*, p. 427) points to lay interest in the eucharist.

15. On this point, see André Vauchez, *La Spiritualité du moyen âge occidental VIIIᵉ–XIIᵉ siècles*, Collection SUP (Paris: Presses Universitaires de France, 1975), pp. 5–8; and Bynum, JM, p. 4.

16. This is true of Kieckhefer, UnS, and, to a lesser extent, of Vauchez, *La Sainteté*; Weinstein and Bell, SS; and Goodich, VP.

17. Kieckhefer's *Unquiet Souls*, which emphasizes religious concerns, is a welcome corrective to this tendency.

18. Weinstein and Bell, SS, table 18, p. 234.

19. Kieckhefer, UnS, p. 172. Ruysbroeck also received ecstasies (if not actual visions) while celebrating; see below, nn. 24 and 240. All sorts of visions were more common with women than with men in this period; see Dinzelbacher, *Vision und Visionsliteratur*, pp. 151–55, 226–28.

20. Vauchez, *La Sainteté*, pp. 224–26, 347–48, 405–6, 450–51.

21. Thurston, PP, pp. 385–91. Thurston, who includes modern saints as well, lists twenty-three men and twenty women. On the common hagiographical motif of women's distribution of bread that turns into roses, see below, chap. 7 n. 13.

22. The following paragraph is based on Browe, *Die Wunder*. For other miracles, see Corblet, *Histoire dogmatique*, vol. 1, pp. 447–515.

23. Browe, *Die Wunder* p. 23.

24. For an early example of the kind of eucharistic miracle that supports priestly authority, see the early-ninth-century Life of Evurtius in *Catalogus codicum hagiographicorum latinorum Bibliotheca nationali Parisiensi*, Subsidia hagiographica 2, vol. 2 (Brussels: The Bollandists, 1890), pp. 317–18; and the later version in the *Liber sancti Jacobi*, ed. Jeanne Vielliard, in *Le Guide du pèlerin de Saint-Jacques de Compostelle* (Mâcon: Protat, 1938), pp. 58–60. In this miracle the hand of God appeared over the head of the celebrating priest, imitating his actions (and thereby demonstrating that Christ offers the

sacrifice in every mass). For a fourteenth-century example, see the Life of Jan van Ruysbroeck by Henry Uten Boghaerde (Henry Pomer), which is bk. 2 of "De origine monasterii Viridisvallis una cum vitis B. Joannis Rusbrochii primi prioris hujus monasterii et aliquot coaetaneorum ejus" (AB 4 [1885], chap. 28, pp. 302–3). In this account we are told that Ruysbroeck, old and blind, was forbidden by his superior to celebrate because of his feebleness. Ruysbroek defended himself, claiming that the feebleness was ecstasy and that Jesus had come to him to say, "Tu es meus et ego tuus."

25. See McDonnell, *Beguines*, pp. 305–15; Hontoir, "Sainte Julienne"; Baix and Lambot, *La Dévotion*, pp. 75–80; and the Life of Juliana of Cornillon, AASS April, vol. 1, pp. 442–75.

26. Cyprien Vagaggini, "La Dévotion au Sacré-Coeur chez sainte Mechtilde et sainte Gertrude," *Cor Jesu: Commentationes in litteras encyclicas Pii PP. XII 'Haurietis aquas,'* 2 vols. (Rome: Herder, 1959), vol. 2, pp. 31–48; Ursmer Berlière, *La Dévotion au Sacré-Coeur dans l'ordre de saint Benoît*, Collection Pax 10 (Paris: Lethielleux, 1923); Gougaud, DAP, pp. 75–130.

27. McDonnell, *Beguines*, p. 313. On Agnes Blannbekin and the scandal caused by the publication of her revelations in 1731, see G. Allmang, "Agnès Blannbekin," DHGE, vol. 1 (1912), col. 977; and Peter Dinzelbacher, "Die 'Vita et Revelationes' der Wiener Begine Agnes Blannbekin (†1315) im Rahmen der Viten- und Offenbarungsliteratur ihrer Zeit," in Dinzelbacher and Bauer, *Frauenmystik*, pp. 152–77.

28. Jungmann, *Mass of the Roman Rite*, vol. 2, pp. 20–21; Vauchez, *La Sainteté*, pp. 431–32; Duhr, "Communion fréquente," cols. 1256–68.

29. Imbert-Gourbeyre, *Stigmatisation*, vol. 2, pp. 183, 408–9. For criticisms of Imbert-Gourbeyre, see Pierre Debongnie, "Essai critique sur l'histoire des stigmatisations au moyen âge," *Etudes carmélitaines*, 21.2 (October 1936): 22–59; and E. Amann, "Stigmatisation," DTC, vol. 14, pt. 1 (1939), cols. 2617–19.

30. Caesarius, *Dialogus*. Bk. 11 concerns dying; bk. 12 concerns the punishment of the dead. In bk. 8 (visions), there are three appearances of the Christ child to women (chaps. 3, 7, 8) and two to men (chaps. 2, 5); eight appearances of the crucifix to men (chaps. 11, 13, 14, 17, 18, 20, 21, 23) and four to women (chaps 10, 15, 16, 22; one might also count chap. 9). The opening and closing chapters of bk. 9 (on the eucharist) deal with celebrants and the proof of transubstantiation and are about males; chaps. 33–51 (which deal with the laity) have nine visions to women (chaps. 33, 34, 35, 36, 39, 40, 46, 47, 50) and ten to men (chaps. 37, 38, 41, 42, 43, 44, 45, 48, 49, 51); of the scattered remaining chapters on recipients, three are about males (chaps. 24, 63, 64) and one about a female (chap. 25).

31. Conrad of Eberbach, *Exordium magnum cisterciense*, ed. Bruno Griesser, Series scriptorum s. ordinis cisterciensis 2 (Rome: Editiones Cistercienses, 1961); Peter the Venerable, *Liber de miraculis*, PL 189, cols. 851–954; Gerald of Wales, *Gemma ecclesiastica* in Gerald of Wales, *Opera*, ed. J. S. Brewer, vol. 2 (London: Longman, 1862).

32. See James of Vitry, *The Historia occidentalis of Jacques de Vitry: A Critical Edition*, ed. John F. Hinnebusch, Spicilegium Friburgense 17 (Fribourg, Switzerland: University Press, 1972); and Thomas of Cantimpré, *Liber qui dicitur bonum universale de proprietatibus apum* (Cologne: Johan Koelhoff, ca. 1479). The eucharist is, however, unimportant in James's *sermones vulgares*; see James of Vitry, *The Exempla or Illustrative Stories*

from the Sermones Vulgares of Jacques de Vitry, ed. Thomas F. Crane, Publications of the Folk-lore Society 26 (London: Nutt, 1890).

33. Tubach, *Index*, pp. 207–12.

34. Women's stories are a higher percentage of those about cloistered religious. Of 252 stories concerning monks and nuns, 61 (or 24 percent) are about women.

35. Tubach, *Index*: stories of males are told in entries 32–37, 2058; stories of females in entries 33, 38, 40 (two stories).

36. Ibid. Entries 33 and 38 urge moderation. Entry 40 concerns two women tricked by the devil.

37. Ibid. Women's stories are told in entries 1176, 1983, 1990, 3198, 3718.

38. Ibid. Entry 1983 tells of a woman who fasted three years. Entry 3198 says Mary Magdalen fasted thirty years. The monk in entry 1982 fasted seventy-eight weeks.

39. Ibid., entries 1990, 3718.

40. Jerome, Letter 54, *Ad Furia de viduitate servanda*, in *Sancti Eusebii Hieronymi epistulae*, pt. 1, ed. Hilberg, pp. 466–85; and idem, Letter 22, *Ad Eustochium*, chaps. 17–18, PL 22, cols. 404–5. Jerome's other major discussion of fasting, food, and lust is in *Contra Jovinianum*, bk. 2, chaps. 5–17, PL 23, cols. 290–312. Jerome also urged women to avoid excessive abstinence; see Arbesmann, "Fasting and Prophecy," pp. 38–39.

41. Fulgentius of Ruspe, Letter 3, chap. 13, PL 65, col. 332. See also PL 65, col. 132.

42. Peter the Chanter, chapter on fasting from *Verbum abbreviatum*, PL 205, cols. 327–28.

43. See A. George Rigg, "'Metra de Monachis Carnalibus': The Three Versions," *Mittellateinisches Jahrbuch* 15 (1980): 134–42.

44. See Colker, *Analecta Dublinensia*, pp. 47, 57, and the passage cited in n. 13 of my intro. The twelfth-century monk of Evesham, who received a vision of those suffering in purgatory, showed no special concern with food abuses, however. See below, n. 130.

45. See Knowles, "Diet," and above, chap. 2 n. 53.

46. Eileen Power, *Medieval English Nunneries, c. 1275 to 1535*, Cambridge Studies in Medieval Life and Thought (Cambridge: Cambridge University Press, 1922), pp. 161–236.

47. See above, chap. 2 nn. 110, 139; and Browe, *Die Wunder*, pp. 110–11.

48. John Gerson, *Collectorium super Magnificat*, Treatise 9, in John Gerson, *Oeuvres complètes*, ed. Palémon Glorieux, vol. 8: *L'Oeuvre spirituelle et pastorale* (Paris: Desclée, 1971), pp. 397–98; and see Longpré, "Eucharistie et expérience mystique," cols. 1602–4.

49. Richard Rolle's *Form of Living*, like his two other English epistles, was written for a woman. Henry Suso's *Little Book of Eternal Wisdom*, the heart of which is meditations on Christ's death, is addressed chiefly to nuns, as is his *Book of Letters*. The second part of Ruysbroeck's *Mirror of Eternal Salvation* is a treatise on the eucharist that was probably written for Margaret of Meerbeke. He also addressed his *Book of the Seven Cloisters* to her. Dionysius the Carthusian wrote six sermons on the eucharist for Mechtild of Nimègue and other ecstatics.

50. On Guiard, see P. C. Boeren, *La Vie et les oeuvres de Guiard de Laon, 1170 env.–1248* (The Hague: Nijhoff, 1956), pp. 157–58. Tauler preached most of his sermons, which stress mysticism and frequent communion, in German to nuns; see Karl Boeckl, *Eucharistie-Lehre der deutschen Mystiker des Mittelalters* (Freiburg: Herder, 1924), pp. 74–122.

51. Baix and Lambot, *La Dévotion*, pp. 48–52.

52. Corblet, *Histoire dogmatique*, vol. 2, passim, esp. pp. 513–51.

53. Dumoutet, CD, pp. 77–80. Agnes, Catherine, and Dorothy were also common figures on retables; see Braun, *Altar*, vol. 2, p. 493.

54. Dumoutet, CD, p. 80; and Corblet, *Histoire dogmatique*, vol. 2, p. 550.

55. Victor Saxer, *Le Culte de Marie Madeleine en Occident des origines à la fin du moyen âge*, Cahiers d'archéologie et d'histoire 3, 2 vols. (Auxerre: Société des Fouilles Archéologiques et des Monuments Historiques de l'Yonne, 1959).

56. Hontoir, "La Dévotion," p. 152; and Corblet, *Histoire dogmatique*, vol. 1, pp. 557, 563. See also Braun, *Altar*, vol. 2, p. 624, for an eleventh-century miniature from Prague that associates the Annunciation with a pyx, thus suggesting that reservation of the sacrament recapitulates the moment of the Incarnation.

57. Dumoutet, CD, p. 79.

58. William Durandus the Elder, *Rationale divinorum officiorum*, bk. 1, chap. 3, sect. 25 (Venice: Mattheus Valentinus, 1580), fol. 11r; see also plate 13.

59. Dumoutet, CD, p. 79.

60. See Braun, *Altar*, vol. 2, plates 329, 333, 334, 336, 346, 360, 361. On the Mary Altar in plate 7 see Carl Georg Heise, *Lübecker Plastik* (Bonn: Cohen, 1926), pp. 11–12.

61. See above, p. 68, and below, pp. 271–72 and 285.

62. See above, nn. 40–41, and chap. 2 nn. 25–26; and Musurillo, "Ascetical Fasting," pp. 13–19.

63. Musurillo, "Ascetical Fasting," pp. 25–39; Arbesmann, "Fasting and Prophecy," pp. 34–38; Browe, *Die Wunder*, pp. 49–50.

64. See above, chap. 2 n. 56.

65. James of Vitry (Life of Mary of Oignies, bk. 1, chap. 5, AASS June, vol. 5, p. 552), says, speaking of Mary's stigmata and fasting, that those who admire Simeon Stylites and Anthony should admire such asceticism in "the weaker sex." Raymond of Capua (Life of Catherine of Siena, pt. 1, chap. 3, pars. 63–65, AASS April [Paris, 1866], vol. 3, pp. 877–78) mentions Paul, Anthony, and other fasters, and says that although Catherine lived in her own home, not in a monastery or in the desert, she nonetheless surpassed these saints "in the matter of abstinence." See also Raymond, Life of Catherine, pt. 2, chap. 5, p. 905.

66. Peter of Vaux (Life of Colette of Corbie, chap. 17, par. 166, AASS March, vol. 1, p. 573) compares Colette to the Fathers who "lived in caves and practiced austerities." But, he adds, Colette "went beyond the Fathers."

67. Life of Suso, chaps. 20, 35 in Suso, *Deutsche Schriften*, pp. 60, 103–7. Among the aphorisms included by Suso are: "The first duty of a spiritual beginner is to show. himself firm in the fight against gluttony (Anthony)"; "Pale features, a lean body and a humble bearing are the best ornaments of a spiritual person (Helias)"; "An unchaste body, like an unruly horse, must be tamed by depriving it of food (Hilarion)." Trans. Edward, *Exemplar*, vol. 1, pp. 100–3.

68. Vauchez, *La Sainteté*, pp. 347–413; and T. E. Bridgett, *History of the Holy Eucharist in Great Britain*, 2 vols. (London: Kegan Paul, 1881), vol. 2, pp. 177ff.

69. See below, pp. 107–9.

70. Vauchez, *La Sainteté*, pp. 347–48.

71. Raymond of Capua, Life of Catherine of Siena, pt. 2, chap. 5, par. 170, AASS

April, vol. 3, p. 905; Letter of Stefano Maconi in Catherine of Siena, *L'Opere della serafica santa Caterina da Siena*, ed. Girolamo Gigli, vol. 1 (Siena: Bonetti, 1707), pp. 460–89, esp. p. 473; and Augusta Theodosia Drane, *The History of St. Catherine of Siena and Her Companions* . . . , 4th ed., 2 vols. (London: Burns, Oates and Washbourne, 1915), vol. 1, pp. 199–202, for a summary of various contemporary accounts of her eating and vomiting.

72. See the epigraph to this chapter.

73. In many cultures "not eating" is more a description of an emotional state than a factual claim. Anthropologist Karen Brown of Drew University tells me, for example, that in Haiti "I haven't eaten today" means "I am depressed" and that in both Haiti and Nigeria "Have you eaten?" is a greeting that means "How are you?"

74. For what follows see Goodich, "Contours of Female Piety"; Roisin, *L'Hagiographie*, pp. 113, 129; and above, chap. 1 n. 42.

75. Felix Vernet, *Medieval Spirituality*, trans. the Benedictines of Talacre (London: Sands and Co., 1930), p. 61.

76. The Life of Columba of Rieti, written by her confessor, Sebastian Perusinus, suggests both that Columba consciously imitated Catherine of Siena from childhood and that her biographer underlined parallels to Catherine as he wrote Columba's *vita*. See, for example, AASS May, vol. 5 (Paris, 1866), pp. 155*–59*. On female saints who modeled themselves on Catherine of Siena, see Gabriella Zarri, "Le Sante Vive. Per una tipologia della santità femminile nel primo cinquecento," *Annali dell' Istituto Storico Italo-Germanico in Trento* 6 (1980): 371–445.

77. Alpaïs's *vita* was written after 1180 by a Cistercian of Echarlis; she is also mentioned by Robert of Auxerre, Ralph Coggeshall, Caesarius of Heisterbach, James of Vitry, and Stephen of Bourbon. These latter references all focus on the miraculous inedia; James and Caesarius both associate her with other cases of miraculous abstinence. See James of Vitry, *Historia occidentalis*, ed. Hinnebusch, pp. 87–88; Caesarius, *Dialogus*, bk. 7, chap. 20, and bk. 9, chap. 47, vol. 2, pp. 25, 201–2; and AASS November, vol. 2, pt. 1 (Brussels, 1894), pp. 167–209, which prints all the early references.

78. See Bynum, JM, pp. 199–201.

79. Roisin, *L'Hagiographie*.

80. See, for example, Constable, *Self-Inflicted Suffering*.

81. Kieckhefer, UnS, pp. 12–14.

82. James of Vitry (Life of Mary of Oignies, bk. 1, chap. 1, AASS June, vol. 5, p. 550) says that we should "admire the fervor not imitate the works." The author of the Life of James of Porto (in AF, vol. 3 [1897], p. 620) says James's austere life is "magis admirandam quam imitandam." Raymond of Capua (in the Life of Catherine of Siena, pt. 2, chap. 16, par. 310, p. 939) underlines the same contrast. Speaking of a miracle in which God first multiplied wine and then turned it sour, he says the first event shows how highly God thought of Catherine, the second how humbly she thought of herself. The first teaches us to honor her, the second to imitate her: "in primo dedit nobis materiam ipsam honorandi, in secundo ipsam imitandi." It was more common, however, for biographers to urge readers to imitate the saints. See, for example, Life of Juliana of Cornillon, prologue, AASS April, vol. 1, p. 442; and below, chap. 8 n. 43. Bonaventure's Life of Francis of Assisi gives an interesting twist to the theme. Bonaventure suggests

that spectators at one of Francis's extravagant displays of self-abasement dismissed his behavior as "magis admirabilem quam imitabilem" (Bonaventure, *Legenda maior*, pt. 1, chap. 6, par. 2, in AF, vol. 10, p. 583).

83. *Legatus*, bk. 5, chap. 7, *Revelationes Gertrudianae ac Mechtildianae*, vol. 1, p. 543.

84. On Abelard's view of women, see Mary M. McLaughlin, "Peter Abelard and the Dignity of Women: Twelfth-Century 'Feminism' in Theory and Practice," in *Pierre Abelard, Pierre le Venerable: Les courants* . . . , Colloques internationaux du Centre National de la Recherche Scientifique 546 (Paris: Editions du Centre National de la Recherche Scientifique, 1975), pp. 287–333; John Benton, "Fraud, Fiction and Borrowing in the Correspondence of Abelard and Heloise," in ibid., pp. 469–506; and d'Alverny, "Comment les théologiens . . . voient la femme."

85. Life of Suso, chap. 35, in Suso, *Deutsche Schriften*, p. 107; trans. Edward, *Exemplar*, vol. 1, pp. xxxiv, 103. Presumably Suso is not implying that *mensch* refers only to males but suggesting that different individuals have different crosses to bear.

86. Thomas of Celano, Life of Clare of Assisi, chap. 11, par. 18, in Pennacchi, *Legenda*, pp. 26–27.

87. See above, chap. 2 n. 110; and Grundmann, *Bewegungen*, p. 414. Albert said that the claim of a nun to nurse Jesus "fatuitas est verberibus potius quam verbis corrigenda" (ibid., p. 414 n. 128).

88. Ibid., p. 413.

89. For example, Peter of Luxembourg, who tried to live on bread and water alone and to sit at table without eating, was on one occasion commanded by the pope to eat and did so obediently. (His health was, however, already ruined.) See Life of Peter, chap. 4, pars. 22–23, AASS July, vol. 1 (Paris, 1867), p. 451; Process of canonization, chap. 4, in ibid., pp. 470–75.

90. Weinstein and Bell, SS, pp. 235–36.

91. Walter Seton, ed., "The Letters from Saint Clare to Blessed Agnes of Bohemia," *Archivum Franciscanum historicum* 17 (1924): 516–17.

92. Angela of Foligno, ed. Ferré and Baudry, par. 21, p. 24: "Postea habui sentimenta Dei, et habebam tantam delectationem in oratione, quod non recordabar de comestione. Et voluissem quod non opportuisset me comedere, ut possem stare in illa oratione. Et intermiscebat se hic quedam temptatio, scilicet quod non comederem, vel, si comedebam, quod comederem in parvo pondere valde; set cognovi esse temptationem." See also the inadequate edition in AASS January, vol. 1 (Paris, 1863), chap. 1, par. 34, p. 190. Christ himself supposedly told Angela that sleeping, eating, and drinking are acceptable if done in love for him: "Et dixerat michi per viam in eundo A[s]sisium ita: 'Tota vita tua, comedere et bibere, dormire et omne tuum vivere michi placet'" (Angela of Foligno, ed. Ferré and Baudry, par. 35, p. 54). Angela herself wrote that a humble heart was more important than fasting or poverty (ibid., par. 180, p. 418).

93. *Vita Beatricis*, bk. 2, chap. 15, pp. 103–4. Life of Columba of Rieti, chap. 5, par. 31, AASS May, vol. 5, p. 162*.

94. Thomas of Cantimpré, Life of Lutgard, bk. 2, chap. 14, AASS June, vol. 4, p. 198. Raymond of Capua, Life of Catherine of Siena, pt. 2, chap. 5. pars. 168–69, AASS April, vol. 3, p. 904; all of pt. 2, chap. 5, deals with Catherine's detractors.

95. See above, chap. 2 n. 112.

96. *Legatus*, bk. 4, chap. 14, pp. 343–44.

97. See below, chap. 5.

98. Raymond of Capua, (Life of Catherine of Siena, pt. 2, chap. 5, par. 173, p. 905), mentions Mary Magdalen and the Fathers as examples of extreme fasting, adding that "sanctity depends on charity not fasting." For Raymond's own difficulties with fasting, see Drane, *History of St. Catherine*, vol. 1, p. 223; Hyacinthe-Marie Cormier, *Le Bien-heureux Raymond de Capoue . . . sa vie, ses virtues, son action*, 2d ed. (Rome: Imprimerie Vaticane, 1902), pp. 113–16; and Coneth Kearns, trans., *The Life of Catherine of Siena* (Wilmington, Del.: Glazier, 1980), p. xv. In a letter to Philip of Alençon, Cardinal of Ostia, Raymond somewhat guiltily defended himself from the charge that he was a hypocrite because he urged others to fast but failed to fast himself. His shortcoming, he argued, was due to physical incapacity; at least, he added, he assisted the saints who provided many worthy examples. He also suggested that the criticism of his eating was deflecting the unfair attacks that had been made on abstainers (H. M. Cormier, *B. Raymundi Capuani . . . opuscula et litterae* [Rome: Ex Typographia Polyglotta S.C. de Propaganda Fide, 1899], pp. 66–68). For Raymond's Life of Catherine as propaganda for Observant reform, see Robert Fawtier, *Sainte Catherine de Sienne: Essai de critique des sources: Sources hagiographiques*, Bibliothèque des Ecoles Françaises d'Athènes et de Rome 121 (Paris: de Boccard, 1921), pp. 118–30. Although Fawtier is excessively skeptical about some of the details in Raymond's account, his picture of Raymond's motives is useful. On the controversy over the Catherine legend generated by Fawtier, see Kearns in *Life of Catherine of Siena*, pp. lx–lxx.

99. See John of Mantua, Process of canonization, AASS October, vol. 9 (Brussels, 1858), pp. 816, 840.

100. Life of Columba of Rieti, chap. 12, par. 110, AASS May, vol. 5, p. 184*.

101. See Gregory of Tours, *Liber vitae Patrum*, prologue, MGH.SSRM, vol. 1, pt. 2, ed. W. Arndt and B. Krusch (1885), pp. 662–63. On this point, see H. Delehaye, *The Legends of the Saints: An Introduction to Hagiography*, trans. Mrs. V. M. Crawford (London: Longmans, 1907); and René Aigrain, *L'Hagiographie: Ses Sources, ses méthodes, son histoire* (Paris: Bloud et Gay, 1953). Plate 9 above illustrates the point by showing how artists transferred iconographical motifs from one saint to another simply by changing the name.

102. Weinstein and Bell, SS, p. 46.

103. Aelred of Rievaulx, *Genealogia regum Anglorum*, PL 195, col. 715. Suso learned penitential asceticism from his mother (Life of Suso, chap. 42, in Suso, *Deutsche Schriften*, pp. 142–43). Ida of Louvain was taken to mass by her mother (Life, bk. 1, chap. 1, AASS April, vol. 2, p. 159). Her hagiographer, who worked from records kept by her confessor, stresses her reaction against her father's wealth.

104. Peter of Luxembourg, Process of canonization, chap. 1, arts. 2–10, and chap. 4, and Life of Peter, chap. 3, par. 19, and chap. 4, par. 29, AASS July, vol. 1, pp. 464–65, 470–75, 457, 459. Peter's father fasted and gave away money; his mother gave away food. Both parents died when Peter was quite young.

105. Peter of Vaux, Life of Colette, chap. 1, par. 10, AASS March, vol. 1, p. 542.

106. John Marienwerder, *Vita Lindana*, chap. 1, pars. 15, 17, AASS October, vol. 13 (Paris, 1883), pp. 505–6; see also chap. 2, par. 44, p. 515. See Kieckhefer, UnS, pp. 25–26.

Lidwina of Schiedam, however, had a model of fasting in her grandfather; see *Vita prior*, chap. 1, par. 5, AASS April, vol. 2 (Paris, 1865), p. 271.

107. Life of Juliana, bk. 1, chap. 1, AASS April, vol. 1, pp. 443–44.

108. According to Ancelet-Hustache, there is no reason to believe the tradition that Sophia, who was pious, persecuted Elizabeth (see Jeanne Ancelet-Hustache, *Sainte Elisabeth de Hongrie* [Paris: Editions franciscaines, 1946], pp. 123–24).

109. Raymond of Capua, Life of Catherine of Siena, pt. 1, chap. 1, par. 25, AASS April, vol. 3, p. 869.

110. See below, epigraph to chap. 7.

111. Browe, *Die Wunder*, p. 50.

112. Einhard, *Annales* for 825, in MGH.SS, vol. 1, ed. G.H. Pertz (1826; repr. New York: Kraus Reprint, 1963), p. 214. Cited in Sigibert, *Chronica*, for year 823, in MGH.SS, vol. 6, ed. Pertz (1844), p. 338; and in Hugh, *Chronicon* for year 823, in MGH.SS, vol. 8, ed. Pertz (1848), p. 353.

113. AASS February, vol. 3 (Paris, 1865), pp. 529–77, gives six short *vitae* of Walburga; that by Wolfhard is on pp. 529–48. See also Francesca M. Steele, *The Life of St. Walburga* (London: Heath Cranton, 1921).

114. Wolfhard, Life of Walburga, chap. 1, pars. 3–4, p. 530.

115. Steele, *Life of Walburga*, pp. 133–36. One of Walburga's later hagiographers, Bishop Philip of Eichstätt, claimed (in 1306) to have been cured by the oil and also asserted that it flowed more copiously during mass; see Philip, Life of Walburga, chap. 7, pars. 37–38, AASS February, vol. 3 (Paris, 1865), pp. 567–68.

116. See Steele, *Life of Walburga*, p. 151; and Herbert Thurston, ed., *Butler's Lives of the Saints*, vol. 2 (London: Burns, Oates and Washbourne, 1930), pp. 338–39.

117. The stories of Irchinbald and Friderade are found in Wolfhard, Life of Walburga, bk. 1, chap. 6, par. 23, p. 534 and bk. 4, chap. 3, pp. 546–48, respectively.

118. See Agnes B.C. Dunbar, *A Dictionary of Saintly Women*, vol. 1 (London: Bell, 1904), pp. 132–35. (Dunbar's work, though quite uncritical, is useful for summarizing legends.)

119. Lawrence of Durham, Life of Bridget of Kildare, chap. 3, par. 14, AASS February, vol. 1 (Paris, 1863), p. 174.

120. Matthew Paris, *Historia major juxta exemplar Londinense 1571 verbatim recusa*, ed. William Wats (London: Richard Hodgkinson, 1640), p. 327. For this period, Matthew draws mostly from Roger of Wendover's *Flowers of History*.

121. James of Vitry, *Historia occidentalis*, ed. Hinnebusch, pp. 87–88.

122. Caesarius, *Dialogus*, bk. 9, chap. 47, vol. 2, pp. 201–2; cf. bk. 7, chap. 20, vol. 2, pp. 25–28.

123. Roger Bacon, *Opus minor*, in *Fr. Rogeri Bacon opera quaedam hactenus inedita*, ed. J.S. Brewer, vol. 1 (London: Longman, Green, Longman and Roberts, 1859), pp. 373–74.

124. Thomas Netter [Waldensis], *Opus de sacramentis, in quo doctrinae antiquitatum fidei Ecclesiae catholicae contra Witclevistas, Hussitas et eorum asseclas Lutheranos aliosque haereticos continentur* (Salamanca: Apud Ioannem Mariam da Terranova et Iacobum Archarium, 1557), fols. 111v–112r. The story of Joan is followed by an account of Lidwina of Schiedam that emphasizes her inedia and severe medical problems.

125. For the fraudulent faster, see Flaminio Maria Annibali da Latere, *Vita della Vergine Santa Coleta* . . . (Rome: Antonio Fulgoni, 1805), p. 87. For the cure, see *Miracula* (compiled 1471), par. 7, AASS March, vol. 1 (Paris, 1865), p. 594.

126. See Pater, MA; Rollins, "Notes on Some English Accounts"; Schadewaldt, "Medizingeschichtliche Betrachtungen"; and Gerish, intro. to *The Hartfordshire Wonder*, p. 6.

127. Schadewaldt, "Medizingeschichtliche Betrachtungen," p. 7; and Gregory Zilboorg with George M. Henry, *A History of Medical Psychology* (New York: Norton, 1941), pp. 207–10.

128. See Browe, *Die Wunder*, p. 50. The story of a hermit who lived in a tree and was fed on manna from heaven, told in the *vita* of Lidwina of Schiedam, is so clearly a bit of romantic fiction that I have not counted it; see below, p. 126. Nor have I counted the fourteenth-century story of Francis of Assisi fasting for forty days; see below, n. 140.

129. On Peter of Luxembourg, see above, n. 89. Life of James Oldo, chap. 2, pars. 14–15, AASS April, vol. 2 (Paris, 1865), p. 603–4.

130. Edward Arber, ed., *The Revelation to the Monk of Evesham: 1196, Carefully Edited from the Unique Copy now in the British Museum of the Edition [of]* . . . *William de Machlinia about 1482* (London: 5 Queen Square, Bloomsbury, n.d.), pp. 19, 27; modern English trans. by Valerian Paget, *The Revelation to the Monk of Evesham Abbey* (New York: John McBride, 1909), pp. 35, 61. The monk's refusal to eat is treated as illness rather than asceticism. It is also pertinent to note that the monk's own vision of souls in purgatory shows no interest in food abuses. Greed is mentioned in passing as one of the sins of religious men (*Revelation*, ed. Arber, chap. 3, p. 73).

131. See Walter Daniel, Life of Aelred, in *The Life of Aelred of Rievaulx by Walter Daniel*, ed. and trans. F. M. Powicke (New York: Oxford University Press, 1951), pp. 48ff. Walter stresses Aelred's food asceticism for the four years before his death: "Nec mirum, siquidem parum comedens et minus bibens ciborum appetitum abstinencie inedia incredibilis extinxit omnino in seipso." He also says that Aelred took medicines out of his mouth and threw them on the ground (p. 48) and ate no food at all for several days before his death (p. 59). This does not quite amount to a claim to miraculous abstinence.

132. *Chronica pontificum et imperatorum Mantuana* for year 1256, MGH.SS, vol. 24 (Hannover, 1879), p. 216. On Facio of Cremona, see André Vauchez, "Sainteté laïque au XIIIᵉ siècle: La Vie du bienheureux Facio de Crémone (v. 1196–1272)," *Mélanges de l'Ecole Française de Rome: Moyen âge; temps modernes* 84.1 (1972): 13–53.

133. See Gerish, introduction to *The Hartfordshire Wonder*, p. 5.

134. See, for example, Raymond of Capua, Life of Catherine of Siena, pt. 1, chap. 1, pars. 27, 31, 33, 38 (as a child, Catherine imitated the Fathers by retreating to a cave, and thought of imitating Euphrosyne, one of the transvestite saints); chap. 3, pars. 57, 63–64 (she imitated Dominic by scourging herself, and the Desert Fathers by fasting); chap. 7, pars. 114–17 (Jesus married her with a ring; the parallel to Catherine of Alexandria is explicitly drawn); pt. 2, chap. 5, pars. 172–73 (her fasting is seen as parallel to both Mary Magdalen's and that of the Desert Fathers) (AASS April, vol. 3, pp. 869–72, 876–78, 890–91, 905). See also above, nn. 65–67 and chap. 1 n. 68.

135. Bynum, JM, pp. 126, 128.

136. Ibid., pp. 113–25.

137. See Bernard of Clairvaux, *Sermones super Cantica Canticorum*, Sermon 71, OB, vol. 2 (1958), pp. 214–24. Wolfgang Riehle (*The Middle English Mystics*, trans. B. Standring [London: Routledge and Kegan Paul, 1981], pp. 107–10) seems to suggest that such metaphors figure more prominently in women's writings.

138. See Vauchez, *La Sainteté*, pp. 381–83; and Kieckhefer, UnS, pp. 40–41, 141. On Peter of Luxembourg and James Oldo, see above, n. 129. See also Constable, *Self-Inflicted Suffering*.

139. Francis calls himself a "mother" in his letter to Leo; see The Fathers of St. Bonaventure's College, ed., *Opuscula sancti patris Francisci Assisiensis*, Bibliotheca Franciscana Ascetica Medii Aevi 1, 2d. ed., (Quaracchi: Collegium S. Bonaventurae, 1949), p. 116; trans. Fahy in *Omnibus*, p. 118. For examples of Francis's repeated description of the good friar as mother, see below, chap. 10, nn. 18–19. Thomas of Celano also quotes both Francis himself and his friars as calling Francis "mother"; see Thomas, Second Life of Francis, bk. 2, par. 137, in AF, vol. 10, p. 209; and chap. 136, par. 180, in ibid., p. 233. Francis does not seem to refer to himself as "father," although Thomas does so repeatedly. Bonaventure also describes Francis as "mother"; see *Legenda minor*, chap. 3, seventh and eighth lessons, in AF, vol. 10, pp. 664–65. Odo of Cheriton, in a sermon recorded in 1219, attributed to Francis the claim that "he was a woman whom the Lord impregnated by his word and thus he brought forth spiritual children"; see Cajetan Esser, *Origins of the Franciscan Order*, trans. Acedan Daly and I. Lynch (Chicago: Franciscan Herald Press, 1970), pp. 11, 208.

140. I have not here considered the fourteenth-century material, but it is worth noting that the *Little Flowers of St. Francis* (chap. 7) claims that Francis passed one Lent eating only half a loaf. The *Flowers* also attributes (chap. 33) a food miracle to Clare and tells (chap. 15) of a meal Clare and Francis shared at which neither one ate (*I Fioretti di San Francesco*, ed. Fausta Casolini [Milan: Giacomo Agnelli, 1926], pp. 29–32, 133–34, 56–59). See below, chap. 10 n. 7. There is a useful concordance of the early Francis material, compiled by T. Desbonnets and D. Vorreux and trans. by M. A. Habig in *Omnibus*, pp. 1619–65.

141. On Francis's food asceticism, see Thomas of Celano, First Life of Francis of Assisi, bk. 1, chap. 19, par. 51, AF, vol. 10, pp. 39–40; Bonaventure, *Legenda maior*, pt. 1, chap. 5, par. 1, p. 577; and idem, *Legenda minor*, chap. 3, first lesson, p. 662. See also Jordan Joseph Sullivan, *Fast and Abstinence in the First Order of St. Francis: A Historical Synopsis and a Commentary*, Catholic University of America Canon Law Series 374 (Washington, D.C.: Catholic University of America Press, 1957).

142. Life of Francis of Fabriano, chap. 1, par. 6, AASS April, vol. 3 (Paris, 1866), p. 993; see also ibid., p. 90.

143. See, for example, Thomas of Celano, Second Life of Francis, bk. 2, chap. 80, par. 114, p. 198, and chap. 160, pp. 251–52. See also the Leo material, chaps. 3 and 9, in Rosalind B. Brooke, *Scripta Leonis, Rufini et Angeli Sociorum S. Francisci: The Writings of Leo* . . . (Oxford: Clarendon Press, 1970), pp. 92, 102.

144. Thomas of Celano, First Life of Francis, bk. 1, chap. 19, par. 51, pp. 39–40.

145. Francis of Assisi, Rule of 1223, chap. 3, *Opuscula*, p. 66; trans. Fahy, *Omnibus*, pp. 59–60.

146. Francis of Assisi, Rule of 1221, chap. 9, *Opuscula*, pp. 36–38; trans. Fahy, *Omnibus*, pp. 39–40.

147. Francis of Assisi, Rule of 1221, chap. 9, *Opuscula*, p. 38, and Rule of 1223, chap. 3, *Opuscula*, p. 67, respectively.

148. Francis of Assisi, Letter to All the Faithful, *Opuscula*, p. 91; trans. Fahy, *Omnibus*, p. 95. Sullivan (*Fast in the First Order of Francis*, p. 6) points out that fasting was relaxed in the order during Francis's lifetime.

149. Brooke, *Scripta Leonis*, chap. 2, p. 90. Sullivan (*Fast in the First Order of Francis*, p. 6) comments that Francis required much less fasting than did many contemporary religious orders.

150. Brooke, *Scripta Leonis*, chap. 1, pp. 88–90. See also Bonaventure, *Legenda maior*, pt. 1, chap. 5, par. 7, pp. 579–80.

151. Brooke, *Scripta Leonis*, chap. 5, p. 94; Thomas of Celano, Second Life of Francis, bk. 2, chap. 133, par. 176, p. 231.

152. Brooke, *Scripta Leonis*, chap. 26, pp. 134–36; Thomas of Celano, Second Life of Francis, bk. 2, chap. 15, par. 44, p. 158.

153. Brooke, *Scripta Leonis*, chaps. 29, 101, pp. 140, 266–68; see also story 4 in Brooke's appendix, pp. 296–98. Thomas of Celano, Second Life of Francis, bk. 2, chap. 23, pp. 162–64; and Treatise on the Miracles of Francis, chap. 5, AF, vol. 10, pp. 284–86. Bonaventure, *Legenda maior*, pt. 1, chap. 5, par. 10, p. 581, and pt. 1, chap. 7, par. 12, ibid., p. 591.

154. Brooke, *Scripta Leonis*, chaps. 39–40, pp. 156–60. Thomas of Celano, First Life of Francis, bk. 1, chap. 19, par. 52, p. 40; Thomas, Second Life of Francis, bk. 2, chaps. 48, 94, pp. 177–78, 207. Bonaventure, *Legenda maior*, pt. 1, chap. 6, par. 2, pp. 582–83.

155. Thomas of Celano, Second Life of Francis, bk. 2, chap. 138, par. 183, p. 235; trans. Placid Hermann, *Omnibus*, p. 508. See also Thomas, Second Life of Francis, bk. 2, chap. 139, par. 186, pp. 236–37.

156. Thomas of Celano, Second Life of Francis, bk. 2, chap. 151, par. 199, p. 244.

157. See above, n. 154; and Bonaventure, *Legenda maior*, pt. 1, chap. 4, par. 8, pp. 574–75.

158. Bonaventure, *Legenda maior*, pt. 1, chap. 4, par. 11, p. 576, and chap. 4, par. 1, pp. 571–72.

159. See Lambert, *Franciscan Poverty*; Fleming, *Introduction to Franciscan Literature*; and Little, *Religious Poverty*. Lambert is especially useful for explaining how Francis thought in images or stories, not legal categories. Much recent work, emanating from M. Mollat's seminar at the Sorbonne, has stressed the importance of poverty as a religious concern against its social background; see, for example, Michel Mollat, ed., *Etudes sur l'histoire de la pauvreté (moyen âge-XVIᵉ siècle)*, 2 vols. (Paris: Publications de la Sorbonne, 1974).

160. Thomas of Celano, Second Life of Francis, bk. 2, chap. 60, par. 93, pp. 185–86; Bonaventure, *Legenda maior*, pt. 1, chap. 7, par. 6, p. 589.

161. See Thomas of Celano, First Life of Francis, bk. 1, chap. 6, par. 15, pp. 14–15; Second Life of Francis, bk. 2, chaps. 162–63, pp. 253–56. Bonaventure, *Legenda maior*, pt. 1, chap. 2, par. 4, and chap. 14, par. 3, pp. 564–65, 621–22.

162. Brooke, *Scripta Leonis*, chap. 39 and appendix, chap. 3, pp. 156–58, 294–96.

163. Thomas of Celano, Second Life of Francis, bk. 2, chap. 137, par. 181, pp. 233–34.

164. Thomas of Celano, First Life of Francis, bk. 3, chap. 2, pars. 127–50, pp. 104–14. Only in par. 133 (p. 106) is food an instrument of healing.

165. Thomas of Celano, Second Life of Francis, bk. 2, chaps. 53–57, 59, 137, pp. 182–85, 233–34.

166. In early accounts, Francis simply kisses a leper, ashamed because he has earlier scorned their foul smell (Thomas of Celano, First Life of Francis, bk. 1, chap. 7, par. 17, p. 16), or eats with them (Brooke, *Scripta Leonis*, chap. 22, pp. 124–26). In Thomas's Second Life of Francis (bk. 1, chap. 5, par. 9, pp. 135–36), Francis kisses the leper and gives him alms. In Bonaventure's *Legenda maior* (pt. 1, chap. 1, pars. 5–6, pp. 562–63), Francis kisses and gives alms to lepers and tears off his clothes for beggars. Only in Bonaventure's *Legenda minor* do we begin to find an emphasis on the placing of the mouth on the pus of lepers' sores (chap. 1, eighth lesson, pp. 657–58)—the aspect of Francis's asceticism that Italian women would later not only echo but also heighten considerably.

167. Bonaventure, *Legenda maior*, pt. 1, chap. 1, par. 6, pp. 562–63; trans. Fahy, *Omnibus*, p. 639.

168. Thomas of Celano, Second Life of Francis, bk. 2, chap. 152, par. 201, p. 245; Bonaventure, *Legenda maior*, pt. 1, chap. 9, par. 2, p. 598. Francis's eucharistic devotion is not stressed in the earliest material.

169. Francis of Assisi, Admonitions, number 1 on the Body of Christ, *Opuscula*, pp. 3–5; and Letter 2, *Opuscula*, p. 103.

170. See above, n. 169; also Francis of Assisi, Concerning Reverence for the Body of Christ and Cleanliness of the Altar, *Opuscula*, pp. 22–23; and Letter 5 to All Superiors of the Friars Minor, *Opuscula*, pp. 113–15. Francis writes: "Et, si in aliquo loco sanctissimum corpus Domini fuerit pauperrime collocatum, iuxta mandatum Ecclesiae in loco pretioso ab eis ponatur et consignetur et cum magna veneratione portetur et cum discretione aliis ministretur. Nomina etiam et verba Domini scripta, ubicumque inveniantur in locis immundis, colligantur et in loco honesto debeant collocari" (p. 114). Such an attitude makes the host and the Bible parallel and treats both as holy objects; the stance reflects no sensitivity to eucharist as food.

171. P. Hilarion, "S. Francis et l'eucharistie," *Etudes Franciscaines* 34 (1922): 520–37.

172. On the early documents concerning Clare, see Maria Fassbinder, "Untersuchungen über die Quellen zum Leben der hl. Klara von Assisi," *Franziskanische Studien* 23.3 (1936): 296–335.

173. Thomas of Celano, Life of Clare of Assisi, chap. 11, par. 18, in Pennacchi, *Legenda*, pp. 26–27; trans. in *The Legend and Writings of Saint Clare of Assisi* (St. Bonaventure, N.Y.: Franciscan Institute, 1953), pp. 31–32. See also Bull of canonization, pars. 53–54, AASS August, vol. 2 (Paris, 1867), p. 750, and Thomas, First Life of Francis, bk. 1, chap. 8, pars. 19–20, pp. 17–18; Thomas lists poor food and clothing, and abstinence from food and speech, as two of the six virtues of Clare's followers.

174. Clare of Assisi, Rule, chap. 3, par. 10, in *Seraphicae legislationis textus originales* . . . (Quaracchi: Collegium S. Bonaventurae, 1897), p. 56.

175. Clare of Assisi, Third Letter to Agnes, in Seton, "Letters from Saint Clare," p. 517.

176. Clare of Assisi, Rule, chap. 3, par. 6, *Seraphicae legislationis textus*, p. 56.

177. Clare, Third Letter to Agnes in Seton, "Letters from Saint Clare," p. 517.

178. Ibid.

179. Thomas of Celano, Life of Clare of Assisi, chap. 17, par. 28, in Pennacchi, *Legenda*, pp. 39–40.

180. Ibid., chap. 13, par. 21, pp. 30–31.

181. Donald Attwater, ed., *The Penguin Dictionary of Saints* (Harmondsworth: Penguin, 1965), p. 87; and Corblet, *Histoire dogmatique*, vol. 2, p. 551.

182. Thomas of Celano, Life of Clare of Assisi, chaps. 9–10, pars.15–16, in Pennacchi, *Legenda*, pp. 23–26. See also Bull of canonization, par. 56, p. 750.

183. Thomas of Celano, Life of Clare of Assisi, chap. 7, par. 12, pp. 19–20. See also ibid., chap. 24, par. 38, pp. 52–53.

184. Ibid., chap. 8, par. 14, p. 23.

185. Ibid., chap. 23, par. 37, pp. 50–52.

186. Zeffirino Lazzeri, ed., "Il Processo di canonizzazione di S. Chiara d'Assisi," in *Archivum Franciscanum Historicum* 13 (1920), 3d witness, par. 29, p. 458. See also 6th witness, par. 13, p. 466.

187. See Bynum, JM, pp. 110–69; and above, n. 139.

188. Albert Huyskens, *Quellenstudien zur Geschichte der hl. Elisabeth Landgräfin von Thüringen* (Marburg: Elwert, 1908), p. 70 n. 3.

189. See above, n. 19.

190. Henry Suso, *Büchlein der Ewigen Weisheit*, chap. 13, in Suso, *Deutsche Schriften*, pp. 251–52.

191. Life of Suso, chap. 42, in Suso, *Deutsche Schriften*, pp. 142–43. Suso bore his mother's name rather than his father's; the prologue of the 1512 edition of his works suggests that he made this choice in order to imitate her virtues more easily. See Heller, introduction to Edward, trans., *Exemplar*, vol. 1, pp. xxxvii–xxxviii.

192. Suso's *vita* seems to have been compiled by someone who reworked Elsbet Stagel's notes; it incorporates some of Suso's correspondence, but that also can be demonstrated to have been reworked; see Heller, intro. to Edward, trans., *Exemplar*, vol. 1, pp. xviii–xli; and Aigrain, *L'Hagiographie*, p. 314.

193. See, for example, Life of Suso, chaps. 28, 37–38, in Suso, *Deutsche Schriften*, pp. 82–83, 114–30.

194. Ibid., chap. 29, pp. 84–85; trans. Edward, *Exemplar*, vol. 1, pp. 80–81. Life of Suso (chap. 22, p. 63) reports that a certain Anna received a vision of Suso with children hanging onto his clothing; chap. 33 (p. 99) reports Elsbet's own words to Suso, comparing him to a pelican who feeds her young with her own blood. While these two passages might indicate that Suso's two female followers suggested the feminine metaphors in the *vita*, Suso's own visions contain other, far more explicitly maternal images.

195. Ibid., chap. 20, pp. 55–56. Suso, meditating on Job 7:1, saw a vision of a young man offering him knightly garb. Once clothed in this military attire, Suso complained: "Wafen got! wie ist es mir ergangen, waz ist uss mir worden! Sol ich nu riten sin? Ich pflege hinnan fúr vil lieber mins gemaches." He agreed to accept the knightly role when he understood that it meant struggle and pain, not glory.

196. Suso, *Büchlein*, chap. 2, in *Deutsche Schriften*, p. 204; trans. Edward, *Exemplar*, vol. 2, p. 9.

344

197. Life of Suso, chap. 20, pp. 58–59.

198. Suso, *Büchlein*, chap. 5, pp. 211–12; trans. Edward, *Exemplar*, vol. 2, pp. 17–18. In Life of Suso (chap. 10, p. 30) he receives the Christ child to cuddle from Mary but is described as Simeon.

199. Life of Suso, chap. 3, p. 15; and Suso, *Büchlein*, chap. 6, p. 216. In the latter passage, Suso speaks of the soul as a fawn that has left the mother doe.

200. Life of Suso, chap. 3, p. 15; trans. Edward, *Exemplar*, vol. 1, p. 12. Suso rather liked the image of God as mother; see Suso, Sermon 1 in Suso, *Deutsche Schriften*, p. 498.

201. Life of Suso, chap. 18, pp. 49–50. Although the passage does not explicitly say Suso nursed, it draws an analogy both to a sick cleric described by Vincent of Beauvais and to John Chrysostom, who did.

202. Ibid., chap. 35, p. 107. See also above, n. 85.

203. Indeed, Suso once used *woman* as a term of disapprobation when describing himself; see ibid., chap. 44, pp. 149–52.

204. Suso, *Briefbüchlein*, Letter 4 in Suso, *Deutsche Schriften*, p. 369. We should not forget that the compiler of the *Exemplar*—perhaps a nun—reworked these letters.

205. Ibid., p. 370. Suso also used female images for the holy soul when he addressed women. See, for example, Suso, Letter 14 (*Grosses Briefbuch*, in Suso, *Deutsche Schriften*, pp. 447–48), where Suso says God has taught us to practice austerity and has raised us from kitchen servants into queens.

206. See esp. Life of Suso, chaps. 4, 13–18, 29, 31, pp. 15–17, 34–53, 84–86, 90–92.

207. Suso's food visions and metaphors mostly involve fruit. See ibid., chaps. 7, 11, pp. 24–25, 31–32. In *Büchlein* (chap. 23, p. 303), he addresses the eucharist as fruit, jewel, pomegranate, and grape; in chap. 19 (p. 276) he sees Christ lying dead under the cross as fruit: "Herr, . . . alle min sinne werdent gespiset von dieser sůzen vruht under disem lebenden bǒme des Krúzes." The prominence of fruit as an image reflects not only Suso's personal taste but also his awareness that humankind first fell through eating fruit; see ibid., chap. 16, pp. 265–66, where Mary, the second Eve, is seen as a paradise in which the saving fruit grows.

208. Life of Suso, chap. 20, p. 61. Chap. 7 (p. 25) also points out that his hunger and thirst sometimes got out of control.

209. Ibid., pp. 24–25.

210. To Suso, food was just one of many images of God's goodness. For example, in *Büchlein* (chap. 5, pp. 211–16), Wisdom says to soul: "I am your Brother, your Spouse. . . . Bathe yourself in my blood. . . . I will give you the ring of betrothal and new garments. . . . I will give you medicine," etc. In chap. 23 (pp. 290–303), where eucharist and therefore food is emphasized, the soul is seen as bathed and clad as well as fed.

211. Suso, *Briefbüchlein*, Letter 8, pp. 385–86.

212. Life of Suso, chap. 7, pp. 24–25. See Huizinga, *Waning*, p. 152.

213. See Mary Felicitas Madigan, *The "Passio Domini" Theme in the Works of Richard Rolle: His Personal Contribution in its Religious, Cultural, and Literary Context*, Salzburg Studies in English Literature, Elizabethan and Renaissance Studies 79 (Salzburg: Institut

für englische Sprache und Literatur, Universität Salzburg, 1978); and Kieckhefer, UnS, pp. 89–121.

214. Henry Pomer, Life of Jan van Ruysbroeck, "De origine monasterii Viridisvallis . . . ," bk. 2, chap. 3, AB 4, 284–85.

215. See above, n. 50; and Eric Colledge, intro. to Colledge and M. Jane, *Spiritual Conferences*, pp. 4–12.

216. On Rolle, see Hope Emily Allen, *Writings Ascribed to Richard Rolle, Hermit of Hampole, and Materials for His Biography*, Modern Language Association of America monograph series 3 (New York: Heath, 1927); Frances M. M. Comper, *The Life of Richard Rolle Together with an Edition of His English Lyrics* (London: Dent, 1928); and Nicole Marzac, *Richard Rolle de Hampole (1300–1349): Vie et oeuvres et édition critique . . . du Tractàtus super Apocalypsim*, Thèse pour . . . Université de Paris: Faculté des Lettres et Sciences Humaines (Paris: Vrin, 1968). The Office prepared for Rolle is in S. W. Lawley, ed., *Breviarium ad usum insignis ecclesie Eboracensis*, vol. 2, Publications of the Surtees Society 75 (Durham: Andrews, 1883), cols. 785–820. On the miracles, see the table in Comper, *Life of Rolle*, pp. 311–14. All the miracles are cures. Of those for adults, 13 are for women, 7 for men. Of the seven miracles concerning children, six are for male children and one for a female child, but some of those for boys are performed at a mother's behest.

217. David Knowles, *The English Mystical Tradition* (London: Burns and Oates, 1961), p. 62. The conjecture about the reason for Rolle's misogyny is Knowles'.

218. John Tauler, Sermon 12 for Tuesday in Passion Week, in Tauler, *Die Predigten*, p. 58; trans. Colledge and M. Jane, *Spiritual Conferences*, p. 64. (The various editions of Tauler number the sermons differently. I have used Vetter's numbering. There is a concordance to the editions in Georg Hofmann, ed., *Johannes Tauler: Predigten* [Freiburg: Herder, 1961], pp. 628–34).

219. Tauler, Sermon 49 for the Nativity of Mary, in Tauler, *Die Predigten*, p. 220. In Sermon 37 (p. 142), commenting on Luke 15:8, he sees the woman who searches for a lost kid as a symbol of God's divinity and the lamp she holds as Christ's humanity.

220. Tauler, Sermon 31: Second Sermon for Corpus Christi, in Tauler, *Die Predigten*, pp. 310–11; for a translation see below, p. 111.

221. Tauler, Sermon 33: Fourth Sermon for Corpus Christi, in Tauler, *Die Predigten*, p. 130; trans. Colledge and M. Jane, *Spiritual Conferences*, p. 274.

222. Tauler, Sermon 81: First Sermon for Triduum of St. Cordula, *Die Predigten*, pp. 431–32.

223. Tauler, Sermon 27: Third Sermon for Pentecost, in Tauler, *Die Predigten*, pp. 110–14. For harsher images, see the end of Sermon 37 (pp. 144–47), where Tauler sees God as a stiff broom threshing us and scrubbing us clean (cf. n. 219 above). In Sermon 11 for Monday in Passion Week (ibid., pp. 53–54), Tauler speaks of God as a father thrashing his children with a good stout stick.

224. See Tauler, Sermon 9 for Second Sunday in Lent, in Tauler, *Die Predigten*, pp. 40–46. I shall return to the significance of this sermon below, pp. 242–43.

225. Office of Rolle, Reading 5, in *Breviarium*, vol. 2, cols. 795–96; trans. Comper, *Life of Rolle*, p. 304.

226. Richard Rolle, *Le Chant d'amour (Melos amoris)*, ed. E. J. F. Arnould and trans.

the nuns of Wisques, 2 vols., SC 168–69, Sér mon. 32–33 (1971), chap. 34, vol. 2, pp. 24–26. See also ibid., chap. 42, pp. 92–100.

227. Richard Rolle, *Incendium amoris*, chap. 11, in Richard Rolle, *The "Incendium Amoris" of Richard Rolle of Hampole*, ed., Margaret Deanesly, Publications of the University of Manchester, Historical Series 26 (Manchester: University Press, 1915), p. 175; trans. and ed. by F. Comper from Richard Misyn's text in *The Fire of Love or Melody of Love and the Mending of Life . . . translated by Richard Misyn . . .* (London: Methuen, 1914), pp. 53–54. See also E. J. Arnould, "Richard Rolle of Hampole," in James Walsh, ed., *Pre-Reformation English Spirituality* (Bronx, N.Y.: Fordham University Press, n.d.), p. 143; and the table of themes cited below, n. 248.

228. Rolle, *Incendium amoris*, chap. 39, pp. 265–66; trans. Comper from Misyn in *Fire of Love*, p. 176.

229. Rolle, *Chant d'amour*, chap. 40, vol. 2, pp. 78–80.

230. Tauler, Sermon 3 for Epiphany, in Tauler, *Die Predigten*, pp. 18–19; trans. Colledge and M. Jane, *Spiritual Conferences*, pp. 82–83.

231. Tauler, Sermon 31: Second Sermon for Corpus Christi, in Tauler, *Die Predigten*, p. 313: "Und dise wise, wie man sich alle creaturen sol lossen jagen und daz liden rechter gelossenheit und swiglicheit, das got über alle übunge, vasten oder wachen oder betten oder halsberge tragen oder tusent rûten uf dir zerslagen."

232. Tauler, Sermon 27: Third Sermon for Pentecost, in Tauler, *Die Predigten*, p. 112.

233. Tauler, Sermon 65: Fourth Sermon for the Exaltation of the Holy Cross, in Tauler, *Die Predigten*, p. 355; trans. Colledge and M. Jane, *Spiritual Conferences*, p. 104.

234. Tauler, Sermon 49 for the Nativity of the Virgin, in Tauler, *Die Predigten*, pp. 220–21; trans. Colledge and M. Jane, *Spiritual Conferences*, p. 170.

235. See Tauler, Sermon 40: First Sermon for the Nativity of John the Baptist, in Tauler, *Die Predigten*, p. 166.

236. Tauler, Sermon 21: Fourth Sermon for Ascension, in Tauler, *Die Predigten*, pp. 86–87; trans. Colledge and M. Jane, *Spiritual Conferences*, pp. 97–98.

237. See Jan van Ruysbroeck, *The Spiritual Espousals*, trans. Eric Colledge, Classics of the Contemplative Life (New York: Harper, n.d.), bk. 2, chap. 17, p. 135, and chap. 43, pp. 171–72. The standard editions of Ruysbroeck are *Jan van Ruusbroec: Werken naar het standaardhandschrift van Groenendaal*, ed. J. B. Poukens et al., 4 vols., Het Ruusbroec-Genootschap te Antwerpen (Amsterdam and Mechlin: De Spieghel and Het Kompas, 1932), and Jan van Ruysbroeck, *Opera omnia*, ed. J. Alaerts et al., 10 vols., Studiën en tekstuitgaven van ons geestelijk erf 20 (Tielt: Lannoo, 1981–). See also Stephen Axters, *La Spiritualité des Pays-Bas: L'Evolution d'une doctrine mystique*, Bibliotheca Mechliniensis, 2d ser., vol. 1 (Louvain and Paris: Nauwelaerts and Vrin, 1948), pp. 41–60.

238. Jan van Ruysbroeck, "Les Sept Clôtures," chap. 8, *Oeuvres de Ruysbroeck l'Admirable*, trans. the Benedictines of St.-Paul de Wisques, vol. 3, 3d ed. (Brussels: Vromant, 1921), pp. 169–72.

239. Henry Pomer (in his Life of Ruysbroeck, chap. 22, p. 299) cites as evidence of Ruysbroeck's great obedience his acceptance of his superior's command that he not drink while gravely ill. On this occasion he clearly craved a drink, and there is no suggestion that he normally practiced food asceticism. The statement of Loomis (in *White Magic*, pp. 23, 141 n. 102) that Ruysbroeck fasted from the breast as a child is a mistake. The

parallel Pomer draws to St. Nicholas (in chap. 1, p. 283) is not to fasting but to another miracle.

240. Life of Ruysbroeck, chap. 29, pp. 303–4. Ruysbroeck made a point of celebrating mass daily; he was loath to relinquish this practice even in ill health and old age (chaps. 27–28, pp. 302–3).

241. See Jean-Baptiste Porion, "Hadewijch, mystique flamande et poétesse, 13ᶜ siècle," DS, vol. 7, pt. 1 (1969), cols. 18–22; Eric Colledge, intro. to Ruysbroeck, *Spiritual Espousals*, pp. 10–11; and Columba Hart, intro. to *Hadewijch: Works*, pp. 14–16.

242. See esp. Ruysbroeck, *Spiritual Espousals* (bk. 2, chaps. 9–20, pp. 96–143) for images of water and heat. Chap. 17 (pp. 126–34) discusses the sacrament, with very little eating imagery. In bk. 2 (chap. 21, pp. 139–42) Ruysbroeck uses unquenchable hunger as an image of desire, but the passage quickly returns to images of touch and fire. Ruysbroeck does stress the importance of Christ's humanity as the redemption of our own, and he usually symbolizes this humanity in female images (see prologue, p. 43).

243. Ruysbroeck, "Le Miroir du salut éternel," chap. 3, *Oeuvres*, pp. 65–66.

244. Ibid., chap. 7, pp. 79–80.

245. Ruysbroeck, *Le Livre des XII béguines*, trans. Paul Cuylits (Brussels: Librairie Spéciale des Beaux-Arts, 1900), pp. 75–76, 99.

246. Ibid., p. 80.

247. See *Ruusbroec: Werken*, vol. 4, p. 4 nn. 2, 7, and p. 5 n. 6. In Ruysbroeck's first work, *The Kingdom of Lovers*, he borrowed one of Hadewijch's most extended food metaphors (Poems in Couplets, number 16, lines 31–40; see Hart in *Hadewijch: Works*, p. 14.

248. See François Vandenbroucke, Table of themes, in Rolle, *Chant d'amour*, vol. 2, pp. 277–321, esp. pp. 287, 295, 307–9. Riehle (*Mystics*, pp. 107–8) has pointed out the absence of a eucharistic emphasis in Rolle, as has Vandenbroucke in *Chant d'amour*, vol. 2, p. 308.

249. Rolle, *Incendium amoris*, chap. 32, p. 237. For an extended example of eating imagery becoming imagery of song, see Rolle, *Chant d'amour*, chap. 43, p. 110. See also Vandenbroucke (*Chant d'amour*, vol. 2, p. 285), who points out that sensory experiences are interchangeable in Rolle's vocabulary; and Riehle, *Mystics*, p. 120.

250. See Tauler, Sermons 30–33 for Corpus Christi, in Tauler, *Die Predigten*, pp. 118–31, 292–98, 310–16. For quotations see above, pp. 1 and 4.

251. Tauler, Sermon 30: First Sermon for Corpus Christi, in Tauler, *Die Predigten*, p. 293; trans. Colledge and M. Jane, *Spiritual Conferences*, p. 258.

252. Tauler, Sermon 32: Third Sermon for Corpus Christi, in Tauler, *Die Predigten*, p. 118; trans. Colledge and M. Jane, *Spiritual Conferences*, p. 264.

253. Tauler, Sermon 32, p. 119, trans. Colledge and M. Jane, *Spiritual Conferences*, p. 265.

254. Tauler, Sermon 11 for Monday in Passion Week, in Tauler, *Die Predigten*, pp. 50–56.

255. Tauler, Sermon 24: Second Sermon for the Sunday after Ascension, in Tauler, *Die Predigten*, pp. 97–101; and Sermon 7 for Septuagesima, pp. 30–31.

256. Tauler, Sermon 31: Second Sermon for Corpus Christi, in Tauler, *Die Predigten*, pp. 310–11; trans. Colledge and M. Jane, *Spiritual Conferences*, p. 259. See also Sermon

33 (pp. 125–26), where Tauler warns that spiritual communion may be preferable to actual reception if the reception is automatic or hurried.

257. Suso, at least once, calls tears "womanly" when he means something negative by *tears*—i.e., whining and weakness; see Life of Suso, chap. 44, in Suso, *Deutsche Schriften* pp. 149–52.

258. Cf. Raymond of Capua, who was more unambiguous in admiring an asceticism in women that he was unable to attain; see above, n. 98.

◆ 4. Food in the Lives of Women Saints

1. Life of Lukardis of Oberweimar, AB 18, pp. 337–38.

2. Bolton, "*Mulieres sanctae*," pp. 77–95; idem, "*Vitae matrum*," pp. 253–73; Mc-Donnell, *Beguines*; Roisin, *L'Hagiographie*; idem, "L'Efflorescence cistercienne et le courant féminin de piété au XIIIe siècle," *Revue d'histoire ecclésiastique* 39 (1943): 342–78; R. De Ganck, "The Cistercian Nuns of Belgium in the Thirteenth Century," *Cistercian Studies* 5 (1970): 169–87; and Bynum, "Women Mystics." To the group of Low Country women I treat below one might add Yvette of Huy (d. 1228); see Albert D'Haenens, "Ivetta," BS, vol. 7, cols. 992–93.

3. There is reason to think that hagiographers, in revising earlier material or writing up their personal knowledge of a subject, were especially careful to preserve the sayings, or *logia*, of holy people exactly as they heard or read them. Therefore the words attributed to women may be especially trustworthy evidence. See Martinus Cawley, "The Life and Journal of Lutgard of Aywières . . . ," *Vox Benedictina* 1.1 (January 1984): 20–22. The author of the Life of Ida of Léau, for example, preserves some of her phrases in the vernacular; the *Vita prior* of Lidwina of Schiedam also preserves a few vernacular words.

4. James of Vitry, Life of Mary of Oignies, bk.1, chap. 4 (AASS June, vol. 5, p. 556) says that Mary sometimes heard the words of others "as if honey was in her mouth"; she once received such consolation from spiritual advice that she could not eat material food for a whole day. Bk. 2, chap. 10 (p. 566) speaks of Mary's spiritual communion as "eating," "drinking," and "being filled." See also p. 59 above.

5. Ibid., bk. 1, chap. 1, p. 551. James was aware that fasting normally produces headaches; see ibid., chap. 2, p. 552.

6. Thomas of Cantimpré, Life of Lutgard of Aywières, bk. 1, chap. 1, AASS June, vol. 4, p. 192. The story is a graphic one. Although Lutgard managed to escape, the man's servants accused him of rape and Lutgard was jeered as a rape victim when she rode into the town of St. Trond. For earlier versions of the life of Lutgard, see G. Hendrix, "Primitive Versions of Thomas of Cantimpré's *Vita Lutgardis*," *Cîteaux: Commentarii cistercienses* 29 (1978): 153–206. (This incident is recorded on pp. 162–63 and 177–78.) Hendrix argues convincingly that both the shorter Latin text (VA) and a second Latin text on which the French text (FL) is based are older than Thomas's life. On the other hand, Martinus Cawley ("Life and Journal of Lutgard," pp. 20–22) has argued that Thomas's text gives us better access to Lutgard's life because VA tends to omit any

references to survivors. I have cited Thomas's *vita* below unless differences among the texts make it necessary to cite all three.

7. Thomas of Cantimpré, Life of Lutgard, bk. 1, chap. 1, p. 191.

8. Ibid., bk. 3, chap. 6, p. 205.

9. Life of Ida of Louvain, bk. 1, chap. 4, AASS April, vol. 2, pp. 164–65. The passage not only calls reading "eating," it also draws a parallel between eating and being pregnant. The *vita* of Ida, of uncertain date and written by an anonymous author who claims to be drawing on earlier manuscripts, is not a very reliable historical account. For exactly this reason, it is a useful indication of what miracles and bodily manifestations confessors and church officials considered typical of and appropriate to female saints. See below, n. 32.

10. Ibid., bk. 1, chap. 6, p. 168.

11. Life of Juliana of Cornillon, bk. 1, chap. 2, AASS April, vol. 1, p. 445. According to Juliana's hagiographer, she ate so little material food that her sisters insisted no human creature could subsist on so little, but she lived from the sweetness of prayer and eucharistic desire. On the *vita* of Juliana, see C. Lambot, "Un Précieux Manuscrit de la vie de sainte Julienne du Mont-Cornillon," in *Miscellanea historica in honorem Alberti de Meyer*, Université de Louvain, Recueil de travaux d'histoire et de philologie, 3ᵉ sér., 22 fasc., vol. 1 (Louvain: Bibliothèque de l'Université, 1946), pp. 603–12.

12. James of Vitry, Life of Mary of Oignies, bk. 2, chap. 10, pp. 566–68.

13. Life of Margaret of Ypres, chap. 24, ed. G. G. Meersseman, in "Frères prêcheurs et mouvement dévot en Flandre au XIIIᵉ siècle," *Archivum Fratrum Praedicatorum* 18 (1948): 118–19.

14. Life of Alice of Schaerbeke, chap. 2, pars. 9–11, AASS June, vol. 2 (Paris, 1867), pp. 473–74.

15. Ibid., chap. 2, par. 12, p. 474.

16. Life of Gertrude van Oosten ("of the West") or of Delft, chap. 2, par. 7, AASS January, vol. 1 (Paris, 1863), p. 350. On Gertrude's food asceticism, see ibid., par. 9, p. 350.

17. James of Vitry, Life of Mary of Oignies, bk. 2, chap. 12, p. 571. Cf. James of Vitry, *Historia occidentalis*, ed. Hinnebusch, chap. 38, p. 207, which refers to the same incident.

18. Life of Ida of Léau, chap. 2, pars. 19–20, pp. 113–14.

19. Ibid., chap. 2, par. 18 through chap. 3, par. 26, pp. 112–15.

20. Life of Margaret of Ypres, chap. 40, in Meersseman, "Frères prêcheurs," p. 122.

21. Life of Ida of Louvain, bk. 1, chap. 3, AASS April, vol. 2, pp. 162–63. Life of Christina the Astonishing, chap. 2, par. 17, AASS July, vol. 5 (Paris, 1868), p. 653.

22. Life of Ida of Louvain, bk. 1, chap. 6, p. 163.

23. In some cases eucharistic devotion began very young. Margaret of Ypres experienced extraordinary desire for the host and sweet smells accompanying it at age five; see her Life, chap. 2, in Meersseman, "Frères prêcheurs," p. 107. A male child saint from the same period and geographical area also expressed extraordinary eucharistic piety: Acher (or Archas) of Turnhout (d. ca. 1222); see Thomas of Cantimpré, *Bonum Universale*, bk. 2, chap. 27 (not foliated).

24. Life of Alice, chap. 2, pars. 9–10, AASS June, vol. 2, 473–74; Life of Ida of

Léau, chap. 2, pars. 19–20, AASS October, vol. 13, pp. 113–14. See also Life of Juliana, chap. 2, AASS April, vol. 1, pp. 445–46.

25. Life of Ida of Louvain, bk. 1, chap. 4, and bk. 3, chap. 1, AASS April, vol. 2, pp. 164, 182–83.

26. Thomas of Cantimpré, Life of Lutgard, bk. 2, chap. 1, par. 14, AASS June, vol. 4, pp. 198–99; cf. VA in Hendrix, "Primitive Versions," p. 168. The vindictive note in the story may not be a later addition by Brother Bernard, as the Bollandists suggest: see Hendrix, "Primitive Versions," p. 161. According to all the early lives, Lutgard said, "I shall obey . . . but Christ will vindicate this injury in your body." The abbess was afflicted with pain until she relaxed the prohibition.

27. Life of Ida of Louvain, bk. 2, chap. 3, p. 173; Thomas of Cantimpré, Life of Lutgard, bk. 1, chaps. 1–2, pp. 192–94.

28. Thomas of Cantimpré, Life of Lutgard, bk. 1, chaps. 1–2, pp. 192–94. The French *vita* (ed. Hendrix, "Primitive Versions," p. 181) has Lutgard sucking the song from the lamb's lips. These experiences of comfort tended to come after periods of trial. Lutgard's nursing visions came after she had experienced attempted rape and humiliation. Ida of Louvain received an extended vision of Christ as a baby after she was accused of having been made pregnant by a local friar; see Life of Ida, bk. 2, chaps. 4–5, pp. 175–77.

29. Thomas of Cantimpré, Life of Lutgard, bk. 1, chap. 2, par. 15, p. 194. The French life describes the vision more graphically; see Hendrix, "Primitive Versions," p. 180. On the importance of the mouth in this *vita*, see Cawley, "Life and Journal of Lutgard," pp. 40–44.

30. Life of Ida of Léau, chap. 2, par. 20, AASS October, vol. 13, pp. 113–14.

31. Life of Mary of Oignies, bk. 1, chap. 2, pp. 551–52.

32. Life of Ida of Louvain, bk. 1, chap. 3, pp. 162–63. A later Low Country woman, Gertrude van Oosten, supposedly received all five stigmata in 1340 when she prayed before a crucifix. The wounds bled seven times a day while Gertrude experienced ecstasy. She later asked God to take away the bleeding, but the scars remained. See Life of Gertrude van Oosten, AASS January, vol. 1, pp. 349–53; and *Vies des saints et des bienheureux . . .* , vol. 1 (1935), pp. 128–30. For doubts, partly historical and partly theological, about these cases, see Debongnie, "Stigmatisations," pp. 34, 49–50.

33. Philip of Clairvaux, Life of Elizabeth [of Spalbeek], "nun of Herkenrode," in the Bollandists, eds., *Catalogus codicum hagiographicorum Bibliothecae regiae Bruxellensis*, Subsidia hagiographica 1, vol. 1, pt. 1 (Brussels: Typis Polleunis, Ceuterick and Lefébure, 1886), pp. 363, 378. Despite the reference to her as a nun, Elizabeth appears to have been a recluse in her paternal home: see Debongnie, "Stigmatisations," pp. 30–31.

34. On Lutgard's three seven-year fasts for the sake of others, see Thomas of Cantimpré, Life of Lutgard, bk. 2, chap. 1, pars. 1, 9, and bk. 3, chap. 4, pp. 196, 198, 205. There are references to Lutgard's food asceticism throughout the *vita*. On the saving effects of Alice's suffering, see Life of Alice, AASS June, vol. 2, pp. 471–77.

35. Life of Mary of Oignies, bk. 1, chaps. 2–4, pp. 551–56; Life of Ida of Louvain, bk. 1, chap. 2, pp. 160–62; Life of Juliana, bk. 1, chaps. 1–3, pp. 443–47; Life of Ida of Léau, chap. 4, par. 136, and chap. 6, par. 54, pp. 118, 123; and Life of Margaret of Ypres, chaps. 3, 16, 40, in Meersseman, "Frères prêcheurs," pp. 108, 114, 122. Juliana's biogra-

pher reports that once, in an effort to achieve peace with her sisters, she put food into her mouth, tore it with her teeth, and turned it over in her mouth, but "she was not able to swallow a morsel of it" (bk. 1, chap. 3, p. 447).

36. Thomas of Cantimpré, Life of Lutgard, bk. 2, chap. 1, par. 2, p. 196. The author of the Life of Ida of Léau explained such phenomena thus: "Should we marvel that, to someone who was fed by prayer and meditation, eating earthly food in the refectory would be odious?" (chap. 3, par. 26, p. 115).

37. Philip of Clairvaux, Life of Elizabeth [of Spalbeek], *Cat. cod. hag. Bruxellensis,* vol. 1, pt. 1, p. 378. See Debongnie, "Stigmatisations," p. 33 n. 1.

38. Life of Christina, chap. 2, par. 22, AASS July, vol. 5, p. 654.

39. See above, chap. 3 n. 65.

40. Life of Margaret of Ypres, chaps. 43, 48, in Meersseman, "Frères prêcheurs," pp. 123, 125.

41. Thomas of Cantimpré, Life of Lutgard, bk. 3, chap. 1, p. 204.

42. Life of Alice, chap. 2, pars. 22–23, and chap. 3, par. 27, pp. 475–76.

43. See above, n. 34.

44. Life of Mary of Oignies, bk. 1, chap. 3, p. 553.

45. Life of Alice, chap. 3, par. 26, p. 476.

46. Life of Mary of Oignies, bk. 1, chap. 4, p. 555. See also Bolton, *"Vitae Matrum,"* pp. 257–59.

47. Life of Christina, chap. 2, par. 22, p. 654.

48. Life of Juliana, bk. 1, chap. 1, pp. 444–45.

49. Life of Ida of Louvain, bk. 1, chap. 5, p. 167. We can often see, in accounts of fasting women, that food was readily available if the woman wanted it.

50. Ibid., bk. 1, chap. 5, pp. 165–66, and bk. 2, chap. 5, p. 178.

51. Thomas of Cantimpré, Life of Lutgard, bk. 2, chap. 2, pars. 19–20, 25, pp. 200–201.

52. Life of Juliana, bk. 1, chap. 6, p. 451.

53. Thomas of Cantimpré, Life of Lutgard, bk. 2, chap. 2, par. 21, p. 200. The earlier versions speak merely of a hemorrhage from which she suffered.

54. Ibid., bk. 1, chap. 1, par. 23, p. 193.

55. Philip of Clairvaux, Life of Elizabeth [of Spalbeek], *Cat. cod. hag. Bruxellensis,* vol. 1, pt. 1, p. 378: "de ore ipsius nec saliva nec sputum, nec de naribus ejus alique emunctionis materia aut humor aliquis emanavit."

56. The concern is not, however, a peculiarity of Thomas's, for it is already present in the earlier version or versions of Lutgard's *vita.* See the texts in Hendrix, "Primitive Versions."

57. Life of Christina, chap. 1, par. 9, and chap. 2, par. 19, pp. 652, 653–54.

58. Thomas of Cantimpré, Life of Lutgard, bk. 1, chap. 1, par. 13 through chap. 2, par. 19, pp. 193–94.

59. Ibid., bk. 1, chap. 1, par. 12, p. 193.

60. Life of Mary of Oignies, bk. 2, chap. 10, p. 567. On Nicholas, see Charles W. Jones, *Saint Nicolas of Myra, Bari, and Manhattan: Biography of a Legend* (Chicago: University of Chicago Press, 1978).

61. Life of Gertrude van Oosten, chap. 3, par. 14, p. 350; the lactation supposedly

lasted from Christmas to the feast of the Purification (Feb. 2). For her love of children and her temptation by the devil in the form of a baby, see chap. 2, par. 11, p. 350.

62. Thomas of Cantimpré, Life of Lutgard, bk. 2, chap. 2, par. 23, p. 200.

63. Life of Mary of Oignies, bk. 2, chap. 12, p. 572.

64. Life of Juliana, bk. 2, chap. 9, p. 475.

65. Thomas of Cantimpré, for example, emphasizes the importance of Lutgard as "mother and nurse of the friars." But many of her miracles during life and all of her miracles after death were performed for women; see Thomas, Life of Lutgard, pp. 189–210.

66. As her hagiographers point out, Lidwina's very name, taken from *lyd* and *wyt* (i.e., *patere late*) meant "to suffer profusely."

67. John Gerlach, Lidwina's relative and sacristan of the monastery at Windesheim, wrote her *vita* in Dutch. A second Life (the *Vita prior*) in Latin is based on Gerlach's and augmented with information furnished by John Walter of Leiden, Lidwina's last confessor, and others. This *vita*, with the additions indicated in brackets, is given in AASS April, vol. 2 (Paris, 1865), pp. 271–301, along with a second, longer Life by John Brugman (*Vita posterior*), ibid., pp. 302–60. The Bollandists attributed both the *Vita prior* and the *Vita posterior* to Brugman, but the more recent editor of the *Vita posterior* disagrees, basing his argument on the divergences of style between the two accounts. See John Brugman, *Iohannis Brugman O.F.M. Vita Alme Virginis Lidwine*, ed. A. de Meijer, Rijksuniversiteit te Utrecht teksten en documenten 2 (Groningen: Wolters, 1963), pp. v–xiii. A fourth *vita*, by Thomas à Kempis, is an abridgement of Brugman with some added details that Thomas culled at Schiedam; see Thomas à Kempis, Life of Lidwina, in Thomas à Kempis, *Opere omnia*, ed. H. Sommalius, vol. 3 (1600–1601; new ed. Cologne: Krakamp, 1759), pp. 114–64. See also J.-K. Huysmans, *Sainte Lydwine de Schiedam*, 16th ed. (Paris: Plon, 1909), which must be used with caution; and Debongnie, "Stigmatisations," pp. 55–56. Much of the following discussion has appeared in Caroline Bynum, "Fast, Feast, and Flesh: The Religious Significance of Food to Medieval Women," *Representations* 11 (August 1985): 1–25. I have cited the *Vita posterior* in both the AASS edition and the de Meijer edition.

68. For the document, see AASS April, vol. 2 (Paris, 1865), pp. 304–5.

69. Brugman, *Vita posterior*, pt. 3, chap. 6, pars. 225–26, AASS April, vol. 2, pp. 347–48 (de Meijer ed., pp. 131–35).

70. Brugman, *Vita posterior*, pt. 3, chap. 6, pars. 218–21, p. 346 (de Meijer ed., pp. 130–31).

71. Brugman, *Vita posterior*, pt. 1, chap. 2, par. 19, p. 308 (de Meijer ed., pp. 20–21). Cf. Thomas à Kempis, Life of Lidwina, pt. 1, chap. 5, pp. 118–19.

72. *Vita prior*, chap. 1, par. 9, AASS April, vol. 2, p. 272; see also Thomas à Kempis, Life of Lidwina, pt. 1, chap. 2, pp. 116–17.

73. *Vita prior*, chaps. 1–2, pp. 272–75; Brugman, *Vita posterior*, pt. 1, chaps. 1–2, pp. 305–9 (de Meijer ed., pp. 12–21). See also plate 10, an early illustration of Lidwina's life, which may be the first picture of skates from the Netherlands.

74. See the document cited in n. 68 above; and *Vita prior*, chaps. 2–3, pp. 273–77, and chap. 7, par. 76, p. 286. The authors of both the *Vita prior* and *Vita posterior* give extensive and horrifying medical details.

75. Brugman, *Vita posterior*, pt. 2, chap. 1, par. 72, p. 319; see also ibid., pt. 1, chap. 4, par. 33, p. 311 (de Meijer ed., pp. 29, 52). It is also important to note that Lidwina at first responded to her terrible illness with anger and despair and had to be convinced that it was a saving imitation of the Passion; see *Vita prior*, chap. 5, pp. 279–81; and Thomas à Kempis, Life of Lidwina, pt. 2, chap. 1, pp. 132–33.

76. *Vita prior*, chap. 9, pars. 99–103, pp. 290–91.

77. Brugman, *Vita posterior*, pt. 3, chap. 1, par. 152, p. 334 (de Meijer ed., p. 97).

78. *Vita prior*, chap. 7, par. 77, p. 286: "usque ad mortem, nec ullo utebatur vel cibo vel potu vel somno, sed nec naturalia superflua corporis emittebat, praeterquam per vomitum."

79. *Vita prior*, chap. 11, pars. 121–22, pp. 294–95; Brugman, *Vita posterior*, pt. 2, chap. 8, pp. 329–31 (de Meijer ed., pp. 82–85); see also below, n. 94.

80. Brugman, *Vita posterior*, pt. 2, chap. 10, par. 146, p. 133 (de Meijer ed., pp. 92–93). Brugman (*Vita posterior*, pt. 3, chap. 1, par. 157, p. 335; de Meijer ed., p. 99) points out that a child was healed merely by being placed on Lidwina's bed.

81. *Vita prior*, chap. 10, pars. 107–9, p. 292.

82. Brugman (*Vita posterior*, pt. 3, chap. 4, par. 194, p. 342; de Meijer ed., p. 118) underlines the power of devotion to Mary that brings sweet milk from a rotting body and food from a virgin.

83. *Vita prior*, chap. 6, pars. 58–60, p. 282; Brugman, *Vita posterior*, pt. 3, chap. 4, pars. 193–94, pp. 341–42 (de Meijer ed., pp. 117–18); Thomas à Kempis, Life of Lidwina, pt. 2, chap. 4, pp. 135–36. Both the author of the *Vita prior* and Thomas à Kempis comment that the lactating means that all the virgins were worthy to nurse the baby Jesus.

84. Brugman, *Vita posterior*, pt. 3, chap. 4, par. 194, p. 342 (de Meijer ed., p. 118). Cf. the other two accounts cited in n. 83, above. It may be that two different confessors are referred to.

85. See Thomas à Kempis, Life of Lidwina, pt. 1, chaps. 19, 22, pp. 128, 130–31.

86. *Vita prior*, chap. 7, par. 74, p. 285, and chap. 8, pars. 80–86, pp. 287–88; Brugman, *Vita posterior*, pt. 2, chaps. 2–3, pp. 320–23 (de Meijer ed., pp. 55–63); Thomas à Kempis, Life of Lidwina, pt. 1, chaps. 19–23, pp. 128–31.

87. Thomas à Kempis, Life of Lidwina, pt. 1, chap. 23, p. 131.

88. Brugman, *Vita posterior*, pt. 2, chaps. 8, 10, pp. 329–31, 333–34 (de Meijer ed., pp. 82–85, 91–94). See Debongnie, "Stigmatisations," pp. 55–56. The reference to stigmata, which seems to be Brugman's embroidery on the story, should not be taken literally. But it is important as a reflection of what some contemporaries expected of holy women.

89. Brugman, *Vita posterior*, pt. 2, chap. 10, par. 145, p. 333 (de Meijer ed., p. 92).

90. *Vita prior*, chap. 3, par. 29, p. 276, and chap. 11, par. 128, p. 296. We are told that her relatives and friends especially benefited. The author says explicitly (p. 296): "Ab hinc [1421] autem usque ad mortem suam [1433], communiter patiebatur febres quartanas, et interdum quotidianas, pro sublevatione animarum in purgatorio."

91. Brugman, *Vita posterior*, pt. 3, chap. 1, pars. 153–55, pp. 334–35 (de Meijer ed., pp. 97–99).

92. Brugman, *Vita posterior*, pt. 3, chap. 1, par. 156, p. 335 (de Meijer ed., p. 99).

93. See *Vita prior*, chap. 11, par. 128, p. 296. See also ibid., chap. 5, pars. 42–45, pp. 279–80; and Thomas à Kempis, Life of Lidwina, pt. 2, chap. 22, pp. 155–56.

94. *Vita prior*, chap. 11, pp. 294–97; Brugman, *Vita posterior*, pt. 2, chaps. 7–10, pp. 328–34 (de Meijer ed., pp. 77–94); Thomas à Kempis, Life of Lidwina, pt. 2, chap. 22, pp. 155–56. Thomas gives a very short version, in which Lidwina first sees a crucified boy, then a wounded host; the host descends, and finally Lidwina receives it from the priest. See also Huysmans, *Lydwine*, chap. 7.

95. Different people supposedly saw different patterns in the host, depending on their degree of holiness.

96. Brugman, *Vita posterior*, pt. 2, chap. 7, par. 121, p. 328 (de Meijer ed., p. 79).

97. *Vita prior*, chap. 10, pars. 107–9, p. 292; Brugman, *Vita posterior*, pt. 2, chap. 5, pars. 106–7, and note c, pp. 325–26 (de Meijer ed., pp. 70–71).

98. See *Vita prior*, chaps. 9–10 and 12 passim, pp. 289–98; Brugman, *Vita posterior*, pt. 2, chaps. 4–6, pp. 323–27, and pt. 3, chap. 2, pp. 336–38 (de Meijer ed., pp. 64–77, 101–7). She was also able to spot hypocrisy in religious women; see Brugman, *Vita posterior*, pt. 2, chap. 3, pars. 92–93, pp. 322–23 (de Meijer ed., pp. 62–63).

99. *Vita prior*, chap. 7, par. 73, p. 285; Thomas à Kempis, Life of Lidwina, pt. 1, chap. 18, p. 128.

100. Although Lidwina's small group of followers does not seem to have been predominantly female, she did perform miracles for other women, some of them pathetic victims of cruel husbands or grinding poverty. See *Vita prior*, chap. 9, par. 106, pp. 291–92. See esp. Brugman, *Vita posterior*, pt. 3, chap. 5, pars. 200–201, p. 343 (de Meijer ed., pp. 121–22), where Lidwina persuades a woman, married to a brute of a man, not to commit suicide from despair and converts the man to tenderness by her prayers.

101. Margaret of Oingt, Life of Beatrice of Ornacieux, esp. chaps. 6–7, in *Oeuvres de Marguerite*, pp. 118–23. The biographer tells us that for a long period Beatrice saw the body of Christ "like a little child" every day at the elevation of the host.

102. Ibid., chap. 7, pars. 89–98, pp. 120–23. On another occasion Beatrice prayed before a pyx or portable tabernacle and, in her anguish, asked God for death. A voice spoke to her from the tabernacle and she realized that her illness, particularly the terrible headaches from which she suffered, could contribute to her service of Christ (ibid., chap. 3, pars. 62–66, pp. 110–11).

103. *Töss*, pp. 32, 53–54. Agnes Blannbekin of Vienna spoke of drinking a "refreshing spiritual drink" from the wound in Jesus' side; see Gougaud, DAP, p. 107.

104. "Unterlinden," p. 440. Another nun was given a white lamb by John the Baptist when she had to interrupt her devotions and leave the choir on convent business, and she received the eucharist directly from Christ when she was ill (ibid., pp. 449–50). This same nun inflicted great cross-shaped wounds on her chest with a piece of wood "in order to retain a memory of Christ's passion." The nuns also received many visions of Christ as a bleeding young man or as a baby. In one particularly touching case, a woman who had abandoned her two young children "scarcely out of the cradle" to enter the monastery had a vision of Christ as a newborn baby crying before her (ibid., p. 403).

105. *Engelthal*, p. 36: "Und het ich dich, ich gez dich vor rehter lieb!"

106. Adelheid Langmann, *Die Offenbarungen der Adelheid Langmann, Klosterfrau zu*

Engelthal, ed. Philipp Strauch, Quellen und Forschungen zur Sprach- und Kulturgeschichte der germanischen Völker 26 (Strasbourg: Trübner, 1878), pp. 11–12.

107. Ibid., pp. 26, 47: "dein munt smekt noch rosen und dein leip noch viol"; "mein
zukersüezzez und mein honigsüezzez lip, mein zarte, mein reine, du pist mein und ich
pin dein." Cited by Browe, *Die Wunder*, pp. 109–10. The imagery comes from the Song
of Songs.

108. Life of Jane Mary of Maillé by her confessor, Martin of Bosco-Gualteri, chap.
2, par. 14, and chap. 4, esp. par. 28, AASS March, vol. 3 (Paris, 1865), pp. 737, 739–40.
A witness in the canonization proceedings testified that Jane Mary's body was like skin
and bones from mortification when she died, but then became beautiful (Process of
canonization, chap. 2, par. 14, ibid., p. 747).

109. Life of Flora of Beaulieu, chap. 2, par. 24, AASS June, vol. 2 (Paris, 1867), app.
p. 46*. See also C. Brunel, ed., "Vida e miracles de Sancta Flor," AB 64 (1946), Vida,
chap. 8, pp. 19–20.

110. Life of Flora, chap. 2, par. 25, AASS June, vol. 2, p. 46*, and chap. 3, par. 47,
p. 50*, and passim. See also Vida, ed. Brunel, chaps. 9, 19, pp. 20, 27.

111. Life of Flora, chap. 3, par. 48, AASS June, vol. 2, p. 50*; Process of canonization
for Jane Mary of Maillé, chap. 5, par. 54, AASS March, vol. 3, pp. 754–55. Christina
Ebner received a vision during mass in which she sucked from the wounds in Christ's
divine heart as a bee sucks from flowers (Kieckhefer, UnS, p. 173).

112. Life of Lukardis, chap. 6, AB 18, p. 313. Cf. chap. 45, p. 334, where she experiences the eucharist as a sweet smell.

113. Ibid., chap. 16, pp. 318–19.

114. Ibid., chap. 28, p. 324.

115. Ibid., chap. 29, p. 324. On two other occasions (chap. 19, p. 320, and chap. 26, p.
323), we are told, Lukardis recovered on Easter from a condition resembling hysterical
paralysis, in order to take the eucharist.

116. Ibid., chap. 14, p. 317.

117. Ibid., chap. 51, pp. 337–38.

118. Ibid., chap. 88, p. 360. Once Lukardis comforted the sister, her sadness left and
she did not feel it necessary to return to her confessor.

119. Ibid., chaps. 7–12, pp. 313–15. After one of the nuns asked Lukardis why she
did not have the wounds of the crown of thorns, she acquired them (ibid., chap. 72, p.
353).

120. Ibid., chap. 55, p. 340. In a similar incident, a nun at a convent five miles away
had a vision of Christ with a stern face. He told her that he exhibited this stern face to
all those who did not believe in the miracles he did through Lukardis, whom he had
signed with stigmata (ibid., chap. 63, p. 347).

121. Gertrude, *Oeuvres*: vol. 2: *Le Héraut*, bk. 2, chap. 6, pp. 256–58; ibid., chap. 16,
pp. 290–96 passim. See also Bynum, JM, p. 192 n. 57; Gertrude, *Oeuvres*: vol. 3: *Le
Héraut*, bk. 3, chaps. 18, 73; pp. 102–4, 302; and *Legatus*, bk. 4, chap. 21, pp. 361–64.
Another Helfta nun, Mechtild of Hackeborn, received Christ's heart as a cup at communion and felt herself urged not only to drink but also to offer the saving draft to her
sister nuns; see Mechtild of Hackeborn, *Liber specialis gratiae*, bk. 1, chap. 1, pp. 7–10.

122. Mechtild of Magdeburg, *Licht*, bk. 6, chap. 36, p. 210; trans. Menzies, *Light*, p.

199. On this vision, see Bynum, JM, p. 237. There are excerpts from Mechtild, well translated by John Howard, in Katharina M. Wilson, ed., *Medieval Women Writers* (Athens, Ga.: University of Georgia Press, 1984), pp. 153-85.

123. "Das si nút denne got essen mag" (quoted in Riehle, *Mystics*, p. 107). See also Mechtild of Magdeburg, *Licht*, bk. 2, chap. 4, pp. 30-33, and bk. 2, chap. 22, p. 43.

124. Mechtild of Magdeburg, *Licht*, bk. 1, chap. 44, pp. 21-22.

125. Ibid., bk. 5, chap. 8, p. 136; trans. Menzies, *Light*, p. 133. See also Mechtild of Magdeburg, *Licht*, bk. 3, chap. 10, p. 72; and Bynum, JM, p. 236.

126. "Unterlinden," chap. 5, pp. 341-42. The description also refers to flagellation and other austerities.

127. *Vie de Douceline*, chap. 9, pp. 85-91, on her ecstasies; chap. 10, pp. 133-34, on tasting God in the tabernacle; chaps. 6, 9, pp. 57, 71, 101, 105 on her inability to eat. In Douceline's case, the not eating, the fear of touch, and the ecstasies were also preparation for healing miracles. For a food multiplication miracle by the saint, see ibid., chap. 12, p. 183.

128. Life of Jane Mary, AASS March, vol. 3, pp. 734-44; and Process of canonization, pp. 744-62 passim. Life of Jane Mary (chap. 2, par. 13, p. 736) contains the story of the angel, who is identified as such by the editors of the *vita* but not in the text.

129. For accounts of Alpaïs, see above, chap. 3 n. 77.

130. See above, epigraph to chap. 3.

131. Life of Alpaïs, bk. 4, chap. 2, AASS November, vol. 2, pt. 1, p. 200. On her eating difficulties, see also bk. 2, chap. 1, pp. 182-83.

132. At least twice Alpaïs saw the devil in a vision as a doctor offering medicine. He told her that if she would take it "like ordinary women" she would be cured and would be able to eat ordinary food (see ibid., bk. 3, chap. 4, pp. 196-97, and bk. 4, chap. 1, p. 198).

133. See, for example, the account in the chronicle of Robert of Auxerre (AASS November, vol. 2, pt. 1, p. 167), which emphasizes the emptiness of Alpaïs's intestines, and the account by Ralph Coggeshall (ibid., p. 168), which stresses proof of her inedia.

134. Addenda, chap. 4, AASS November, vol. 2, pt. 1, p. 208.

135. See the discussions of Columba of Rieti and Catherine of Siena below, pp. 147 and 167-70. The clearest case of food stealing by a miraculous faster is Elsbet Achler. Elsbet's *vita* is edited by Karl Bihlmeyer in "Die Schwäbische Mystikerin Elsbeth Achler von Reute (†1420) und die Überlieferung ihrer Vita," in Georg Baesecke and Ferdinand Joseph Schneider, eds., *Festgabe Philipp Strauch zum 80. Geburtstag am 23. September 1932*, Hermaea Ausgewählte Arbeiten aus dem Deutschen Seminar zu Halle 31 (Halle: Niemeyer, 1932), pp. 88-109; and by Anton Birlinger in "Leben heiliger alemannischer Frauen des XIV-XV Jahrhunderts, 1: Dit erst Büchlyn ist von der Seligen Kluseneryn von Rüthy, die genant waz Elizabeth," *Alemannia* 9 (1881): 275-92. See also C. Schmitt, "Elisabeth de Reute," DHGE, vol. 15 (1963), cols. 220-21. Prodded by her confessor into adolescent self-righteousness, Elsbet became a recluse after conflict with her parents, who disowned her. Given permission both by her confessor-hagiographer and by an elderly female recluse, Elsbet passed three years "without eating." If we read between the lines of her *vita*, it seems likely that she became a compulsive secret eater, vomiting up stolen food. A sister who worked in the kitchen even joked, when meat disappeared:

"It was stolen by the cat with two legs." Several incidents suggest surreptitious gorging. We are told, for example, that the devil disguised himself as her spiritual mother and gave her food that made her violently ill. On another occasion the devil supposedly hid meat and salt under her bed, making it look as if she had secreted them there (see esp. Life of Elsbet in Birlinger, "Kluseneryn von Rüthy," p. 280).

136. The basic texts are in Huyskens, *Quellenstudien*. See Ancelet-Hustache, *Elisabeth*, pp. 17–29, and Paul G. Schmidt, "Die zeitgenössische Überlieferung zum Leben und zur Heiligsprechung der heiligen Elisabeth," in University of Marburg, *Sankt Elisabeth*, pp. 1–6. For an excellent survey of the background to Elizabeth's experience, see Kaspar Elm, "Die Stellung der Frau," pp. 7–28.

137. Ancelet-Hustache, *Elisabeth*, passim, esp. pp. 201–6, 314–18; and Mattias Werner, "Die heilige Elisabeth und Konrad von Marburg," in University of Marburg, *Sankt Elisabeth*, pp. 45–69. It was Conrad who ordered her not to eat food gained by exploitation of the poor; at times he also, to break her will, forbade her to distribute alms or bread.

138. See the depositions of 1235 in Huyskens, *Quellenstudien*, pp. 112–40, esp. pp. 115–16, 119–21, 127–29, 137; and Conrad of Marburg's letter (1233) concerning her life, in ibid., pp. 155–60.

139. Huyskens, *Quellenstudien*, pp. 51–52. Elizabeth, Nicholas of Myra, and Catherine of Alexandria were the three most famous myroblytes (oil-exuding saints). It is also worth noting that a woman dreamed of oil flowing from Douceline of Marseilles, although Douceline did not actually become a myroblyte; see *Vie de Douceline*, p. 131.

140. Huyskens, *Quellenstudien*, p. 70 n. 3; and see below, chap. 7 n. 13.

141. Garin of Guy-l'Evêque, Life of Margaret of Hungary (written in 1340), chap. 4, AASS January, vol. 3 (Paris, 1866), p. 518. See also Process of canonization of 1276 in Vilmos Fraknói, ed., *Monumenta Romana episcopatus vesprimiensis (1103–1526)*, vol. 1 (Budapest: Collegium Historicorum Hungarorum Romanum, 1896), pp. 214, 220, 247.

142. Life of Margaret of Hungary, chaps. 1–4, pp. 516–18; Process of canonization, ed. Fraknói, passim, esp. pp. 167–68, 219, 240.

143. Life of Margaret of Hungary, chap. 3, p. 517; Process of canonization, ed. Fraknói, p. 227.

144. Process of canonization, ed. Fraknói, p. 171; Life of Margaret of Hungary; chap. 3, p. 517. One sister deposed (ed. Fraknói, p. 263) that Margaret gave her food to others and rose, fasting, from the table.

145. Life of Margaret of Hungary, chap. 3, p. 517.

146. Ibid., chap. 1, p. 516; Process of canonization, ed. Fraknói, pp. 213, 260, 264.

147. In one very interesting deposition, a sister claimed that she was healed from a serious illness when Margaret appeared by her bed and said, "Get up, sister, and eat something." She also claimed to have benefited when washwater from Margaret's hair was placed in her mouth (Process of canonization, ed. Fraknói, pp. 237–38). Cf. ibid., pp. 267, 288, which suggests that water from Margaret's hair was regularly used for healing. Its efficacy may have been perceived as derived from the fact that Margaret refused to wash either her hair or her body frequently, saying "I want the worms to punish my body" (ibid., p. 266).

148. See above, chap. 3 n. 106. For a discussion of the voluminous material on Dor-

othy, perhaps the best-documented saint of the thirteenth and fourteenth centuries, see Kieckhefer, UnS, p. 210 n. 2.

149. See John Marienwerder, *Vita Lindana*, chap. 1, par. 15; chap. 2, par. 44; chap. 3, par. 72; and chap. 4 passim, AASS October, vol. 13, pp. 505, 515, 527, 535–43; John Marienwerder, *Vita latina*, ed. Westpfahl, bk. 5, chaps. 16–21, pp. 236–45.

150. See Richard Stachnik et al., eds., *Akten des Kanonisationsprozesses Dorotheas von Montau von 1394 bis 1521*, Forschungen und Quellen zur Kirchen- und Kulturgeschichte Ostdeutschlands 15 (Cologne: Böhlau, 1978), pp. 214, 277; and John Marienwerder, *Vita latina*, ed. Westpfahl, bk. 6, chap. 21, pp. 318–20. I have been influenced by a fine unpublished paper ("A Cult of the Maternal: Dorothy of Prussia [1347–94],") by Stephen P. Bensch of the University of California at Berkeley. Bensch stresses not only Dorothy's spiritual pregnancy but also the importance of pregnancy and birthing as images to her.

151. John Marienwerder, *Vita Lindana*, chap. 2, par. 40, and chap. 3, par. 69, AASS October, vol. 13, pp. 514, 525–26.

152. Ibid., chap. 3, par. 63, p. 523. For a fuller discussion, see Kieckhefer, UnS, pp. 27–28.

153. *Septililium B. Dorotheae*, treatise 3: *De eucharistia*, chaps. 25–26, AB 3, pp. 439–41.

154. Ibid., chap. 6, p. 418.

155. Ibid., chap. 3, pp. 410–11.

156. Ibid., chap. 10, p. 425. Christ clearly understood Dorothy. He told her, "I don't want you to abstain, for if you abstain you will just be more anxious than before." On her frenzy for the eucharist at death, see John Marienwerder, *Vita latina*, ed. Westpfahl, bk. 7, chaps. 26–27, pp. 364–68.

157. AASS March, vol. 1 (Paris, 1865), gives a Latin translation of the *vitae* by Peter of Vaux (pp. 538–88), and Petrina of Balme (pp. 600–618). I have been unable to consult Ubald d'Alençon, *Les Vies de Ste Colette Boylet de Corbie . . . écrites par ses contemporains le P. Pierre de Reims, dit de Vaux, et Soeur Perrine de la Roche et de Baume*, Archives franciscaines 4 (Paris: Picard, 1911).

158. In neither case, for example, is the claim to stigmata well documented.

159. Peter of Vaux, Life of Colette, chap. 17, par. 166, p. 573.

160. There are also parallels between Colette and another exact contemporary, Elsbet Achler, who died in 1420 at the age of thirty-four (see above, n. 135). After Elsbet's three years of total fast, she was unable to keep food in her stomach. As she became sick and bedridden, her body broke out in sores that paralleled Christ's wounds. The wounds oozed blood every Friday. See Life of Elsbet in Birlinger, "Kluseneryn von Rüthy," pp. 281–83.

161. Colette's exhortation is in app. 2 to E. Sainte-Marie Perrin, *La Belle Vie de sainte Colette de Corbie (1381–1447)* (Paris: Plon, 1921), pp. 274–77. A brief letter of Colette's is in ibid., pp. 273–74.

162. Peter of Vaux, Life of Colette, chap. 13, pp. 563–65; see also chap. 11, par. 105, p. 562, and chap. 17, par. 166, p. 573.

163. Ibid., chap. 20 ("De miraculis"), par. 232, p. 584, and chap. 11, par. 104, p. 562. See also chap. 20, addenda, par. 257, p. 587.

164. On the leper, see ibid., chap. 20, par. 228, p. 584. On the Virgin's kiss, which

cured Colette of severe pain in the tongue, see chap. 14, par. 127, pp. 566–67. On the sick nun's vision, see chap. 20, par. 227, p. 584.

165. Ibid., chap. 20, par. 233, p. 584.

166. Ibid., chap. 17, par. 175, p. 575.

167. Account of miracles performed after her death in the convent of Ghent, pars. 8–10, AASS March, vol. 1, pp. 593–94.

168. Peter of Vaux, Life of Colette, chap. 9, par. 61, pp. 554–55. Peter tells us that bad smells bothered Colette greatly because of her purity, but that she bore them patiently, as Christ had done. He also tells us that she went for a year without sleep (chap. 17, p. 573) and was greatly afflicted by heat and cold (chap. 14, par. 123, pp. 565–66).

169. Ibid., chap. 12, pp. 562–63; Petrina of Balme, Life of Colette, chap. 6, pars. 61–62, p. 612.

170. See Peter of Vaux, Life of Colette, chap. 12, pars. 109, 113, pp. 565–63; and Ubald d'Alençon, *Miniatures et documents artistiques du moyen âge relatifs à Sainte Colette de Corbie*, Archives franciscaines 5 (Paris: Picard, 1912), plate 13 (reproduced above as plate 11c). For a painting with a similar iconographic motif, see Peter Meller, "La Beata Colomba da Rieti in un Dipinto di Bernardino di Mariotto," *Antichità Viva* 2.9–10 (1963): 24–30.

171. Peter of Vaux, Life of Colette, chap. 10, par. 84, p. 558.

172. Ibid., chap. 11, pp. 560–62; Petrina of Balme, Life of Colette, chap. 4, pars. 38, 42, pp. 607–8.

173. See above, n. 121.

174. For Gherardesca's visions concerning the eucharist, see Life of Gherardesca of Pisa, chap. 3, par. 27; chap. 4, par. 36; and chap. 6, par. 57, AASS May, vol. 7 (Paris, 1867), pp. 166–67, 169, 173. Her hagiographer reports a vision of water flowing from Christ's breast (chap. 7, par. 66, p. 175). There is one vision that stresses blood and mouths (chap. 6, par. 56, p. 173): Gherardesca wanted to pull the nail from Christ's bleeding foot with her teeth and put it into her own body. For Umiltà's eucharistic piety, which is not much emphasized, see Life of Umiltà of Faenza, chap. 1, par. 10, AASS May, vol. 5 (Paris, 1866), pp. 208–9. Her hagiographer reports that her cell was constructed so that she could look into the church and see and receive the sacrament. We find an emphasis on seeing Christ in the pathetic life of the blind girl Margaret of Città di Castello, who supposedly "saw" Christ incarnate quite clearly (as a baby with his parents) whenever the host was elevated; see her *vita*, chap. 6, AB 19 (1900), p. 26; AASS April, vol. 2 (Paris, 1865), p. 191; and M.-H. Laurent, "La Plus Ancienne Légende de la B. Marguerite de Città di Castello," *Archivum Fratrum Praedicatorum* 10 (1940): 125–26.

175. On Columba, see below, pp. 146–48; Catherine of Siena and Catherine of Genoa are treated in chapter 5 below. The lives and the food practices of Margaret of Cortona and Angela of Foligno have now been treated in much greater detail than I attempt here by Rudolph Bell in *Holy Anorexia* (Chicago: University of Chicago Press, 1985). His treatment of Italian women is fuller than mine and in some cases based on editions not available to me; I refer readers to it. I discuss the differences between Bell's method and mine in chap. 6, below.

176. Life of Margaret of Cortona, by her confessor, Juncta Bevegnati, AASS February, vol. 3, pp. 304–63, esp. chap. 7, pp. 338–45. In answering her need for reassurance,

Christ supposedly said to her (chap. 4, par. 63, p. 315): "Tu es filia mea, quia mihi obedis: tu es sponsa mea, quia me solum diligis: tu es mater mea, quia volutatem Patris mei, in quantum vires sufficiunt, imples." So uncertain was Margaret that she feared even her eucharistic craving might offend Christ (see chap. 4, par. 65, p. 316): "Et quia fervorem saepe communicandi prae reverentia illius inaccessibilis lucis interponere nec retardare valebat, dixit: Offendo te, Domine mi, in illa siti avidissima, quam de frequenti communione Corporis et Sanguinis tui concepi. Respondit Dominus dicens: . . . valde mihi de ipsa places." Angela of Foligno also feared communion; see Angelo of Foligno, ed. Ferré and Baudry, par. 63, p. 126.

177. Life of Margaret of Cortona, chap. 7, par. 179, p. 340.

178. In ibid., chap. 7, par. 187, p. 341, Margaret sees a vision of a priest with black (i.e., sinful) hands holding a baby boy. In par. 197, p. 343, she recognizes an unconsecrated host because she feels no sweetness upon receiving.

179. Ibid., chap. 5, par. 135, p. 330, and par. 106, p. 325, respectively.

180. Ibid., chap. 7 passim, esp. pp. 339, 342, 345. On Margaret see also John Moorman, *A History of the Franciscan Order from Its Origins to the Year 1517* (Oxford: Oxford University Press, 1968), p. 223; Father Cuthbert, *A Tuscan Penitent: The Life and Legend of Margaret of Cortona* (London: Burns and Oates, n.d.); and the somewhat fuller version of Juncta Bevegnati's Life of Margaret given in Lodovico da Pelago, ed., *Leggenda della vita e dei miracoli di S. Margherita di Cortona scritta in lingua latina dal di lei confessore Fr. Giunta Bevegnati . . . e traduzione Italiana . . .* (Rome: Tipografia Monaldi, 1858).

181. Angela of Foligno, ed. Ferré and Baudry, par. 80, p. 166; see also Angela of Foligno, *L'Autobiografia e gli scritti della beata Angela da Foligno*, ed. and trans. M. Faloci Pulignani and Maria C. Humani (Città di Castello: "Il Solco," 1932), pp. 140–42. A different version of the passage is found in par. 118 of the Life of Angela of Foligno in AASS January, vol. 1 (Paris, 1863) p. 205. In par. 50 (pp. 90–94 of the Ferré and Baudry edition), Angela describes her ecstasy at the elevation of the host and says that her joints became unstrung (cf. Life of Angela, AASS, p. 205). In par. 41 (Ferré and Baudry edition, pp. 64–66), she explains how she saw Christ in the host and was unable to kneel. So great was her delight that she did not know whether she ran forward or remained still (cf. Life of Angela, AASS, p. 204). Pars. 166–71 (Ferré and Baudry edition, pp. 380–92) give what purports to be Angela's teaching on the eucharist, preserved in Italian (Angela's own language) in the Assisi and Subiaco manuscripts but presented in a scholastic mode unlikely to be hers. The passage stresses the real presence of the physical human Christ and refers several times to the power of the hands of the priest. Pars. 113–16 (Ferré and Baudry edition, pp. 224–26) report more eucharistic visions. There is no critical edition of Angela's writings, which she dictated to her confessor but which often seem to retain her own words. I have used the Ferré and Baudry and the Pulignani and Humani editions. The AASS edition is unreliable, but where the relevant passages are present, I have given references to them to aid readers who do not have access to the rarer editions. I have been unable to consult the edition by Paul Doncoeur, *Le Livre de la Bienheureuse Angèle de Foligno: Texte Latin* (Paris: Art Catholique, 1925). Mary G. Steegman has published an extremely misleading English translation of a sixteenth-century Italian translation of Angela's life, titled *The Book of Divine Consolation of the Blessed Angela of Foligno* (repr. ed., New York: Cooper Square Publishers, 1966).

182. Par. 135, ed. Ferré and Baudry, pp. 290–94 (cf. Life of Angela, par. 127, AASS, p. 206); see also par. 147, Ferré and Baudry ed., pp. 320–22; and pars. 51–52, ibid., pp. 96–102. A fragment cited in the Pulignani and Humani edition (par. 204[3], pp. 330–32) says: "Deus habens amorem evisceratum animae, dat ei blanditias, idest dulcedines, sentimenta et huiusmodi, quae ego voco blanditias, quas anima non deberet appetere: non tamen sunt spernendae quia faciunt animam currere, *et sunt cibus eius*: et ex hiis anima ascendit ad amandum Deum, et innititur transformari in Amatum" (emphasis added).

183. Par. 17, ed. Ferré and Baudry, p. 16: "et tunc [Christus] vocavit me et dixit michi quod ego ponerem os meum in plagam lateris sui. Et videbatur michi quod ego viderem et biberem sanguinem ejus fluentem recenter ex latere suo. . . . Et rogavi Dominum quod faceret me totum sanguinem meum propter amorem suum, sicut feceret ipse pro me, spargere. Et disposui me propter amorem suum quod volebam quod omnia membra mea paterentur mortem aliam passione sua, scilicet magis vilem." Cf. Pulignani and Humani edition, p. 16, and par. 28, AASS, p. 189. See also par. 66, Ferré and Baudry edition, p. 138: "Et tota letitia est modo in isto Deo homine passionato. Et aliquando videtur anime, quod cum tanta letitia et delectatione intret intus in illud latus Christi et cum tanta letitia vadit intus in latus Christi, quod nullo modo posset dici vel narrari."

184. Life of Alda of Siena, chap. 2, par. 21, AASS April, vol. 3 (Paris, 1866), p. 474. In another incident, which reveals a similar devotion to Christ's blood, Alda saw a priest spill a drop of "the sacred blood of Christ" onto the paten. When she screamed out to him, "Lick it up," it began to glow and cured an eye infection she had suffered from (chap. 2, par. 15, p. 474). For other eucharistic ecstasies see chap. 2, par. 14, p. 474. (The Latin text in AASS is translated from a sixteenth-century Italian life based on thirteenth-century documents.)

185. Life of Margaret of Cortona, chaps. 2–3, AASS February, vol. 3, pp. 305–13. See esp. chap. 3, par. 51, where Margaret's confessor quotes her as saying: "Pater mi, cum foedus pacis inter animam meam et corpus habitura non sim, nec unquam sibi parcere velim, sinatis me sine ciborum mutatione ipsum atterere, quia toto tempore vitae meae, donec deficiat, non quiescam: nec ipsum credatis ita mortificatum et debile, ut apparet: quia hoc agit, ut extinguam debitum, quod contraxit in seculo, dum vacavit delicis et voluptatibus suis."

186. Ibid., chap. 5, par. 82, pp. 319–20. There are many other examples of such behavior. Umiltà of Faenza ate only one meal a day and limited that to water and three ounces of bread (Life of Umiltà, chap. 1, par. 11, AASS May, vol. 5, p. 209). (On feast days she expanded her diet to include a few cooked bitter herbs.) Agnes of Montepulciano deprived herself of food and sleep for years and received communion from an angel (see Raymond of Capua, Life of Agnes of Montepulciano, chap. 2, par. 17; chap. 3, par. 26; and chap. 6, par. 54, AASS April, vol. 2 [Paris, 1865], pp. 793, 795, 801). Alda of Siena ate only once a day, sometimes taking only grasses and beans and abstaining even from bread; she drank only water. On Fridays she sometimes ate only vinegar and gall or myrrh to imitate Christ. Her biographer attributes this asceticism to remorse for sexual temptation. See Life of Alda, chap. 2, pars. 10–12, p. 473. Clare of Montefalco (d. 1308) carried out prolonged fasts (see Vauchez, *La Sainteté*, p. 405). Margaret of Città di Castello also punished herself with fasts (see Life of Margaret of Città

di Castello, chap. 2, AB 19, p. 24; and Laurent, "Légende de la B. Marguerite," p. 121). And see Life of Gherardesca, chap. 1, par. 2, AASS May, vol. 7, p. 162.

187. Life of Villana de' Botti, chap. 1, pars. 3, 8, AASS August, vol. 5 (Paris, 1868), pp. 865–66. She supposedly said to her confessor: "Ego cum epistolas Pauli lego, aut divinis assisto eloquiis, mente sic reficior, ut omnis illico diffugiat cibi corporalis appetitus: ita Christi crucifixi meditatione absorbeor, ut nulla omnino sit asperitas tam dura, quae non mihi amoenissima videatur." See also Stefano Orlandi, *La Beata Villana, terziaria domenicana fiorentina del sec. XIV* (Florence: "Il Rosario," 1955). And cf. Angela of Foligno, par. 21, ed. Ferré and Baudry, p. 24 (Life of Angela, par. 34, AASS, p. 190).

188. No contemporary *vita* of Rita survives. See Life of Rita of Cascia, AASS May, vol. 5 (Paris, 1866), pp. 226–28.

189. Life of Clare Gambacorta of Pisa, chap. 1, par. 3, AASS April, vol. 2 (Paris, 1865), p. 507. Clare imposed such strict fasting on herself that she refused fruit even when it was in abundant supply (ibid., par. 5, p. 507); she ate the garbage left over from meals and, like Francis, sprinkled ashes on her food (ibid., chap. 2, par. 21, p. 510). Clare's *vita* was written by a sister of her convent.

190. For editions of Angela's book, see above, n. 181. We know few details of Angela's biography; she seems to have undergone a conversion at about age forty after a life as a married woman and mother. See M.-J. Ferré, "Les Principales Dates de la vie d'Angèle de Foligno," *Revue d'histoire franciscaine* 2 (1925): 21–34; Paul Doncoeur, "Angèle de Foligno (Bienheureuse)," DS, vol. 1 (1932), cols. 570–71; Dronke, WW, pp. 215–17; and chap. 7 n. 11, below.

191. Third letter, in Angela of Foligno, ed. Ferré and Baudry, pp. 494–98: "Ista est quedam humilitas in qua sum inabyssata. . . . Set gaudebam imaginari aliquem modum ut eas simulationes et iniquitates et peccata mea possem manifestare. Et vellem ire per plateas et civitates nuda, et appendere ad collum meum pisces et carnes dicendo: 'Hec est illa vilissima mulier.'" See also ibid., par. 101, p. 200, where Angela describes a period during which she was tortured by feelings of unworthiness and was unable to eat.

192. See Angela of Foligno, par. 21, ed. Ferré and Baudry, p. 24, and par. 108, p. 218.

193. See above, chap. 3 n. 92.

194. Third letter, in Angela of Foligno, ed. Ferré and Baudry, p. 498.

195. See ibid., par. 180, pp. 418–20, and par. 35, p. 54.

196. See ibid., par. 35, pp. 52–54: Angela wished to remain with Christ in ecstasy but he withdrew, and she felt terrible pain. So he gave her a sign of his love—the cross—which she felt both in her body as a real cross and in her soul. See also the passages cited in nn. 181–82 above.

197. Ibid., par. 66, pp. 138–40. But Angela also stresses Christ's suffering; see ibid., pars. 127–29, pp. 250–60; par. 140, pp. 312–14; and par. 179, pp. 412–16.

198. Ibid., par. 151, p. 326.

199. Ibid., par. 53, pp. 104–6; see also Pulignani and Humani edition, pp. 90–92; and Life of Angela, par. 137, AASS, p. 208.

200. Angela of Foligno, par. 53, ed. Ferré and Baudry, p. 106: "et bibimus de illa lotura. Et tantam dulcedinem sensimus quod per totam viam venimus in magna suavitate ac si communicavissemus. Et videbatur michi recte quod ego communicassem; quia

sauvitatem maximam sentiebam, sicut si cummunicassem [*sic*]. Et quia quedam scarpula illarum plagarum erat interposita in gutture, ego conabar ad glutiendum eam, et reprehendebat me conscientia expuere sicut si communicassem, quamvis non expuerem ad ej[i]ciendum set ad deponendum eam de gutture." The shock value of such behavior may have been increased by the fact that eating blood, scabs, etc., was taboo; see Burchard of Worms, *Decretum*, bk. 19, chaps. 84, 91, PL 140, cols. 1002–3.

201. See, for example, Life of Margaret of Cortona, chap. 9, par. 226, 241, AASS February, vol. 3, pp. 349, 352.

202. See above, n. 178, and Life of Margaret of Cortona, chap. 9, AASS, pp. 349–56.

203. Life of Margaret of Cortona, chap. 7, par. 190, AASS, p. 342. Christ called Margaret a "mother of sinners" and a "ladder for sinners": "Cui Christus dixit: 'Scalam peccatorum te feci, ut per exempla vitae tuae pergant ad me.' Et Margarita respondit: 'In quo virtutis exemplo peccatores imitari me possunt?' Et Dominus ad eam: 'Imitabuntur abstinentias tuas, jejunia tua, humilitatem, et tribulationes, quas amore mei alacriter recepisti.'"

204. Life of Umiltà, chap. 3, par. 24, AASS May, vol. 5, pp. 212–13. According to the hagiographer, pieces of a loaf of bread multiplied in the nuns' mouths after Umiltà blessed it, and more pieces were left over than had originally been placed in front of the sisters.

205. John of Faenza, Revelations and Miracles of Margaret of Faenza, chap. 2, par. 7 (xii–xiii), AASS August, vol. 5 (Paris, 1868), p. 853. Both *vitae* of Margaret use food metaphors to describe her ecstasies. John (Revelations, chap. 1, par. 3[v], p. 852) describes Jesus touching her tongue with the kiss of peace. In the *vita* by Peter the Florentine (chap. 2, pars. 8–10 [xii–xiv], p. 849), she is described as receiving invisible stigmata.

206. Life of Alda, chap. 2, par. 16, p. 474, and chap. 3, pp. 474–76.

207. Raymond of Capua, Life of Agnes of Montepulciano, chap. 2, pars. 17–18, and chap. 6, pars. 56–57, pp. 793–94, 801–2. On Raymond's description of Agnes in his Life of Catherine of Siena, see chap. 5 n. 68, below.

208. Raymond of Capua, Life of Agnes of Montepulciano, chap. 3; chap. 4, par. 38; and chap. 7, pars. 60–61, pp. 795–98, 802.

209. Catherine of Siena, Dialogue, ed. Cavallini, chap. 149, pp. 428–29; see also Letter 58, in Catherine of Siena, Letters, ed. Misciattelli, vol. 1 (1913), pp. 265–67, which discusses Agnes as an example to other nuns.

210. Raymond of Capua, Life of Agnes of Montepulciano, chap. 9, pars. 78–81, p. 806.

211. On Rita see above, n. 188.

212. Life of Margaret of Città di Castello, chap. 8, AB 19, pp. 27–28; see also M.-H. Laurent, "Légende de la B. Marguerite," pp. 127–28. It is interesting to note that the nail Alda of Siena had carved as a devotional object supposedly exuded sap three hundred years after it was carved (Life of Alda, chap. 2, par. 17, p. 474).

213. Life of Rose of Viterbo, AASS September, vol. 2 (Paris, 1868), pp. 433–39. For a recent critical examination of Rose's life, see Giuseppe Abate, "S. Rosa da Viterbo, terziaria Francescana (1233–1251): Fonti storiche della vita e loro revisione critica," *Miscellanea Francescana* 52, fasc. 1–2 (January–June 1952): 112–278. The *vita* in AASS,

composed two centuries after Rose's death as part of the Process of canonization, is a compendium of feeding themes borrowed—in some instances explicitly—from the lives of other saints. Of little value as a source of information about Rose herself, it is an important index of fifteenth-century sensibility. We are told that baby Rose fasted from the breast for two days each week (like Nicholas of Myra), that while still a child, she began to macerate her body in severe fasts in order to give food to the poor, that the bread in her apron turned (like Elizabeth of Hungary's) into roses when her father accused her of wasting family goods, that she fed the birds with her own hands (like Francis of Assisi), and that her body (like Elizabeth's and Agnes's) produced manna. See also plates 8 and 9.

214. In the Life of Columba of Rieti by her confessor, Sebastian Perusinus (chap. 13, par. 128, AASS May, vol. 5, p. 190*), Sebastian draws parallels not only between Columba and Catherine of Siena—whom she was obviously aware of imitating (see ibid., chap. 1, par. 8, p. 155*)—but also between Columba and Margaret of Hungary, Agnes of Montepulciano, Joan of Orvieto, and Margaret of Città di Castello. All the women, he says, experienced ecstasies in which they left their senses, levitated, and mirrored in their bodies the Passion of Christ, with their arms stretched out and their necks extended. On Joan of Orvieto, see Antonino Silli, "Giovanna (Vanna) di Orvieto," BS, vol. 6 (1965), cols. 556–57. On Catherine of Siena as model, see above, chap. 3 n. 76.

215. Life of Columba of Rieti, chap. 1, par. 1, p. 153*, and par. 6, p. 154*. Her hagiographer says: "Tempore autem infantilis innocentiae pia Columba, Spiritus Sancti dona sortita, adversum carnem indicit bellum, et pugnum aggreditur." On Columba, see also Baleoneus Astur [Astorre Baglioni], *Colomba da Rieti: "La seconda Caterina da Siena" 1467–1501* (Rome: Edizioni Cateriniane, 1967), which uses a vernacular version of Sebastian's life of Columba.

216. Sebastian Perusinus, Life of Columba, chap. 1, par. 7, p. 154*. The excerpts from the Process of canonization (par. 2, AASS May, vol. 5 [Paris, 1866], p. 223*) also emphasize her penitence, her extended abstinence, and her eucharistic fervor.

217. Life of Columba of Rieti, chaps. 1–4, pp. 153*–61*. It is interesting to note that the hagiographer says the struggle turned her mother into a "harsh mother-in-law" and left Columba "an orphan" (par. 14, p. 157*).

218. Ibid., chap. 2, pars. 10, 12, p. 156*.

219. Ibid., chap. 4, par. 27, p. 161*.

220. Ibid., par. 28, p. 161*.

221. Ibid., chap. 17, par. 162, p. 200*.

222. Ibid., chap. 4, pars. 21–22, p. 159*: her hagiographer points out that she tried to give up all food but green fruit, bread and water (and sometimes even bread), but she yearned avidly for "that true bread, the eucharist," which sustains celibacy, comforts the soul, excites us to war, repels demons, and gives us a foretaste of glory. See also chap. 5, pp. 162*–64*, and chap. 13, par. 119, p. 187*.

223. Ibid., chap. 20, par. 189, p. 208*.

224. Ibid., chap. 5, par. 31, p. 162*. See also chap. 3, pars. 19–20, p. 159*.

225. Ibid., chap. 5, par. 31, p. 162*. See also chap. 20, pars. 187–89, p. 208*.

226. Ibid., chap. 5, par. 32, p. 162*.

227. Ibid., chap. 13, pp. 186*–90*, and chap. 15, pars. 151–52, p. 197*.

228. Ibid., chap. 8, par. 71, p. 171*.
229. Ibid., chap. 12, par. 110, p. 184*; and chap. 20, pars. 191ff., pp. 209*–12*.
230. Ibid., chap. 17, par. 163, p. 200*; and chap. 7, pars. 49 and 51, p. 167*.
231. Ibid., chap. 13, par. 122, p. 188*.
232. Ibid., chap. 22, par. 217, p. 217*.

◆ 5. Food in the Writings of Women Mystics

1. See above, chap. 2 nn. 138–40, 151, 155.
2. See Riehle, *Mystics*, pp. 104–10 and passim. Riehle says (pp. 109–10): "For the mystic affective contemplation implies receiving wisdom and savouring divine love at the same time. The idea of knowledge and wisdom which are sensual and which can be savoured was widely accepted and completely taken for granted until the seventeenth century, and is something which we today, who are so used to the idea of the 'dissociation of sensibility'—to use Eliot's famous phrase—have long since lost." For a useful warning against reading literary images as direct evidence of life situation, see Lillian Herlands Hornstein, "Analysis of Imagery: A Critique of Literary Method," *Publications of the Modern Language Association of America* 57.3 (1942): 638–53.
3. William of St. Thierry, *De natura et dignitate amoris*, chap. 10, par. 31, PL 184, col. 399: "*Haec est*, inquit, *vita aeterna, ut cognoscant te solum verum Deum* . . . (John 17:3). Beata scientia, in qua continetur vita aeterna. Vita ista ex illo gustu est, quia gustare, hoc est intelligere. Ex hoc gustu per hunc saporem in hac sapientia minimus ille Apostolorum satiatus, exhilaratus, confirmatus, *Mihi*, inquit, . . . *data est haec gratia* . . . (Ephes. 3:8–18)." And see above, chap. 2 at nn. 146–47.
4. See Bynum, JM, pp. 186–209, esp. p. 200 n. 91.
5. See Riehle, *Mystics*, passim, and above, pp. 102–12.
6. Rosemary Herde, "Das Hohelied in der lateinischen Literatur des Mittelalters bis zum 12. Jahrhundert," *Studi medievali* 3.8.2 (1967): 957–1073; Jean Leclercq, *Monks and Love in Twelfth-Century France: Psycho-Historical Essays* (Oxford: Oxford University Press, 1979).
7. See Bynum, JM, pp. 170–74.
8. For exceptions, see below, chap. 10 nn. 36–38.
9. There is very little good recent work on Hadewijch except in Dutch. The best discussions in other languages are J. Van Mierlo, "Hadewijch, une mystique flamande du 13ᵉ siècle," *Revue d'ascétique et de mystique* 5 (1924): 269–89, 380–404; Porion, "Hadewijch," DS, vol. 7, cols. 13–23; Paul Mommaers, Preface, and Columba Hart, introduction to Hart, *Hadewijch: Works*, pp. xiii–42. For recent Dutch bibliography, see Hart, *Hadewijch: Works*, and J. Reynaert, *De Beeldspraak van Hadewijch*, Studiën en tekstuitgaven van ons geestelijk erf 21 (Tielt: Ruusbroec-Genootschap, 1981).
10. See Letter 17 in Hart, *Hadewijch: Works*, pp. 82–84.
11. Letter 15 in Hart, *Hadewijch: Works*, ll. 75–81, p. 79: "The fourth point [of nine points for the pilgrim traveling toward God] is: You must keep yourself from gluttony,

that is, from any worldly self-satisfaction: let nothing outside of God ever suffice you or have any taste for you, before you have tasted how wonderfully sweet he is (Ps. 33:9). Oh, remember this, and bear it always in mind: Whatever anyone takes pleasure in, other than God Alone, is all gluttony." See Hadewijch, *Brieven*, ed. Jan Van Mierlo, vol. 1 (Antwerp: N.V. Standaard-Boekhandel, 1947), p. 127. Hadewijch clearly uses *gluttony* primarily metaphorically.

12. Hart, *Hadewijch: Works*, pp. 263-305. Vision 1 comes when the sacrament is brought to her bedside; vision 3 comes after reception (Hadewijch's characteristic way of expressing this is "I had gone to God"); vision 4 comes at mass, during the epistle; vision 6 comes as she feels great desire to receive; in vision 7 she experiences full physical union with Christ when he gives her communion in both kinds in a vision (the vision, however, comes at Matins); vision 12 comes during mass.

13. For recent debate over what exactly *minne* (love) means to Hadewijch, see Norbert De Paepe, *Hadewijch Strofische Gedichten: Een studie van de minne in het kader der 12e en 13e eeuwse mystiek en profane minnelyriek* (Ghent: Koninklijke Vlaamse Academie, 1967), and Hart, Introduction to Hart, *Hadewijch: Works*, p. 8. For images of tasting, hungering, and inner sweetness in Hadewijch, see Reynaert, *Beeldspraak*, pp. 202-20.

14. See Reynaert, *Beeldspraak*, pp. 208-10, and Mommaers, Preface, in Hart, *Hadewijch: Works*, pp. xxiii-xiv. Mommaers's translation differs somewhat from Hart's; see ibid., p. 303. For the text, see Paul Mommaers, ed., *De Visioenen van Hadewijch: Middelnederlandse tekst . . .* , Spiritualiteit 15, supplement (Nijmegen: B. Gottmer, 1979), vision 14, ll. 72-73: "in ere naturen smake onghesceden metter gheheelre godheit" (edition not paginated).

15. Vision 14, Hart, *Hadewijch: Works*, p. 305; Mommaers, *De Visioenen*, supplement, vision 14, ll. 141-43.

16. See, for example, Letter 6 in Hart, *Hadewijch: Works*, ll. 227-35, p. 61: "Nowadays this is the way everyone loves himself; people wish to live with God in consolation and repose, in wealth and power, and to share the fruition of his glory. We all indeed wish to be God with God, but God knows there are few of us who want to live as men with his Humanity, or want to carry his cross." See Van Mierlo, *Brieven*, vol. 1, p. 64. See also Hart, *Hadewijch: Works*, vision 1, ll. 288ff. and 341ff., pp. 268 and 269: "He [Christ] continued: '. . . If you wish to be like me in my Humanity, as you desire to possess me wholly in my Divinity and Humanity, you shall desire to be poor, miserable and despised by all men; and all griefs will taste sweeter to you than all earthly pleasures. . . .' 'Since, then, you are a human being, live in misery as man. . . . Feel yourself as man in all the hardships proper to the human condition, except sin alone.'" See Mommaers, *De Visioenen*, supplement, vision 1, ll. 254-60 and 311-18.

17. Poems In Couplets, poem 16: Love's Seven Names, Hart, *Hadewijch: Works*, p. 356; Hadewijch, *Mengeldichten*, p. 83.

18. Letter 18, pp. 103-11, in Hart, *Hadewijch: Works*, p. 87; and in Van Mierlo, *Brieven*, vol. 1, p. 156. See ibid., vol. 2, pp. 22-25, for the borrowings from William of St. Thierry.

19. Poems in Stanzas, poem 39: Love's Blows, l. 18, Hart, *Hadewijch: Works*, p. 240; see E. Rombauts and N. De Paepe, eds., *Hadewijch: Strofische Gedichten: Middelneder-*

landse tekst en moderne bewerking . . . , Klassieken uit de Nederlandse Letterkunde . . . (Zwolle: W. E. J. Tjeenk Willink, 1961), p. 274. See also Letter 22, in Hart, *Hadewijch: Works*, ll. 224–26, p. 99.

20. Letter 11, in Hart, *Hadewijch: Works*, ll. 10–45, p. 69; Van Mierlo, *Brieven*, vol. 1, pp. 93–95.

21. Letter 22, in Hart, *Hadewijch: Works*, ll. 143–59, p. 97; Van Mierlo, *Brieven*, vol. 1, 193–94. Both here and at ll. 251–63, Hadewijch quotes Song of Songs 1:1–2.

22. Letter 9, in Hart, *Hadewijch: Works*, ll. 7–11, p. 66; Van Mierlo, *Brieven*, vol. 1, pp. 79–80.

23. Poems in Couplets, poem 16: Love's Seven Names, Hart, *Hadewijch: Works*, ll. 37–40, p. 353; Hadewijch, *Mengeldichten*, p. 79. But see below, nn. 28 and 29.

24. Vision 7, in Hart, *Hadewijch: Works*, pp. 281–82; see Mommaers, *De Visioenen*, supplement.

25. Poems in Couplets, poem 15, Hart, *Hadewijch: Works*, ll. 1–2, 33, 37–40, pp. 350–52; Hadewijch, *Mengeldichten*, pp. 72–74.

26. Poems in Couplets, poem 14, esp. ll. 132–34, Hart, *Hadewijch: Works*, pp. 345–50; Hadewijch, *Mengeldichten*, pp. 65–71.

27. Letter 17, Hart, *Hadewijch: Works*, p. 84; Van Mierlo, *Brieven*, vol. 1, pp. 143–44.

28. Poems in Couplets, poem 16, Hart, *Hadewijch: Works*, ll. 40–48, p. 353; Hadewijch, *Mengeldichten*, p. 79.

29. Poems in Couplets, poem 16, Hart, *Hadewijch: Works*, ll. 165–68, p. 357; Hadewijch, *Mengeldichten*, pp. 83–84.

30. Poems in Couplets, poem 13: The Paradoxes of Love, Hart, *Hadewijch: Works*, ll. 1–2, 4–7, 27, 29, p. 344; Hadewijch, *Mengeldichten*, pp. 61–62.

31. See n. 16 above.

32. Vision 1, Hart, *Hadewijch: Works*, p. 266.

33. Ibid., p. 269; Mommaers, *De Visioenen*, supplement, vision 1, ll. 309–10: "Na dien dattu mensche best Soe leve ellendech als mensche."

34. See vision 5, Hart, *Hadewijch: Works*, pp. 276–77.

35. Vision 11, ibid., pp. 291–92. There remains throughout, however, a strong emphasis on Hadewijch's service of others. In vision 13, ibid., p. 301, Christ tells her he sends her back into her body after fruition "for the sake of those whom you have chosen to become full-grown with you in this, but who are not yet full-grown."

36. Poems in Stanzas, poem 39: Love's Blows, Hart, *Hadewijch: Works*, verses 9 and 10, p. 242; Rombauts and De Paepe, *Strofische Gedichten*, p. 280.

37. She even had a vision in which Christ, as a young child, gave her "his Body" (i.e., the host) to eat: vision 7, Hart, *Hadewijch: Works*, p. 281; the vision occurs just before the vision of Christ as a man described in n. 24 above.

38. Letter 18, ibid., ll. 1–10, p. 85; Van Mierlo, *Brieven*, vol. 1, pp. 151–52.

39. See n. 16 above.

40. Poems in Stanzas, poem 33, Hart, *Hadewijch: Works*, pp. 221–23; Rombauts and De Paepe, *Strofische Gedichten*, pp. 234–38.

41. On Beatrice, see Jan Van Mierlo, "Béatrice de Nazareth," DS, vol. 1 (1932), cols. 1310–14, and *Vita Beatricis*, Latin summary of Dutch intro., pp. 3–9.

42. *Vita Beatricis*, pp. 157–79, gives a literal Latin translation of Beatrice's vernacular text of the *Seven Steps of Love* alongside her translator's version of it. For the vernacular text see L. Reypens and J. Van Mierlo, eds., *Beatrijs van Nazareth seven manieren van Minne* (Louvain: Vlaamsche Booekenhalle, 1926).

43. On her asceticism, see *Vita Beatricis*, bk. 1, chaps. 4–7, pp. 26–35; on her eucharistic devotion, see bk. 1, chaps. 13–14, 18, bk. 2, chaps. 15–16, and bk. 3, chaps. 2, 5, pp. 52–57, 63–64, 103–7, 126–27, 133–34.

44. See Van Mierlo, "Béatrice," col. 1311; and *Vita Beatricis*, bk. 1, chap. 11, p. 48, bk. 3, chap. 6, pp. 134–36, bk. 3, chap. 14 (which gives Beatrice's own treatise on the seven steps), pp. 168–70. In this last passage, Beatrice says, speaking of the fifth step of love: "Hoc ipsum quod magis eam cruciat atque vulnerat, idipsum magis integrat et lenit, et quod eam profundis vulnerat, hoc solum dat ei sanitatem." In bk. 3, chap. 6, p. 136, Beatrice is called *insana* or *fatua* (foolish) for love. Hadewijch also speaks of ecstasy as insanity (*orewoet*); see above, n. 25. Philip of Clairvaux in the Life of Elizabeth of Spalbeek (*Cat. cod. hag. Bruxellensis*, vol. 1, pt. 1, p. 364) calls Elizabeth's ecstasy *imbecillitas*.

45. Beatrice's biographer comments at the end of bk. 1, chap. 18, pp. 63–64, that in early life she was liquified and made ill by the delights of the sacrament but later she was cured from all sickness by it, and this should not, he says, surprise the reader, for the same sacrament is "milk and meat."

46. In *Vita Beatricis*, bk. 3, chap. 15, pp. 180–83, the biographer emphasizes her love and service of others through prayer, advice, and compassion.

47. See above, pp. 58, 138–39, and 141–42. In *Vita Beatricis*, bk. 2, chap. 15, pp. 103–4, the hagiographer provides a theological gloss on the subject of frequent communion, saying both devotion [*spiritualis affectio*] and fear [*timor*] are necessary. He also reports the efforts of the devil to convince Beatrice that because of her sordid thoughts she is unworthy to receive frequently.

48. *Vita Beatricis*, bk. 3, chap. 2, pp. 126–27. There is a similar description in bk. 3, chap. 5, p. 133.

49. Ibid., bk. 2, chap. 16, pp. 105–7.

50. Ibid., bk. 3, chap. 13, pp. 154–55.

51. Ibid., bk. 1, chap. 11, pp. 45–49. The previous chapter makes it perfectly clear that the sisters discussed such experiences together and desired them and that older nuns taught younger sisters to expect them. The hagiographer frequently describes Beatrice's reactions to the visitation of the spirit as immoderate laughter (as well as immoderate weeping); see bk. 1, chap. 18, ll. 16–17, p. 63, and bk. 2, chap. 13, l. 54, p. 99.

52. Ibid., bk. 2, chap. 6, pp. 134–36. Her adviser told her that he did not, however, think it was a suggestion of the devil.

53. Ibid., bk. 3, chap. 15, pp. 180–83.

54. Ibid., bk. 3, chap. 14, pp. 157–79.

55. Ibid., p. 174. The paradoxical language, especially the notion of "healthy wounding," is more prominent in Beatrice's own text than in her translator's version. Similar language is used to describe step five, p. 170; see below.

56. Ibid., the "second step of love," p. 161, and the "sixth step," p. 171.

57. Ibid., p. 166.

58. Ibid., pp. 169–70.

59. Ibid., bk. 3, chap. 12, pp. 152–53.

60. Ibid., bk. 3, chap. 7, pp. 137–40.

61. The basic source for Catherine is the *Legenda maior* by her confessor, Raymond of Capua, in AASS April, vol. 3, pp. 861–967. There is a recent English translation by Conleth Kearns, *Life of Catherine*. A contemporary account which Raymond probably did not know is the anonymous *I Miracoli di Caterina di Jacopo da Siena di Anonimo Fiorentino a cura di Franceso Valli* (Siena: R. Università di Siena, Cattedra Cateriniana, 1936). Other major sources, which were influenced by Raymond's work, are the *Legenda minor* (an abridgment of Raymond) and the *Supplementum*, by Thomas Antonii de Senis (also called Caffarini and Tommaso Nacci da Siena), and the Process of canonization, begun in 1411, known as the Castellano Process or the Process of Venice. See Thomas Antonii de Senis, *Leggenda minore di S. Caterina da Siena (e lettere dei suoi discepoli)*, ed. Francesco Grottanelli (Bologna: Presso Gaetano Romagnoli, 1868); idem, *Libellus de supplemento: Legende prolixe Virginis Beate Catherine de Senis*, ed. Giuliana Cavallini and Imelda Foralosso (Rome: Edizioni Cateriniane, 1974); and M. Hyacinthe Laurent, ed., *Il Processo Castellano . . . con appendice di documenti . . .* , Fontes vitae S. Catharinae Senensis historici 9 (Milan: Fratelli Bocca Editori, 1942). The controversy launched by Robert Fawtier in 1921 over the reliability of the surviving sources on Catherine has produced a flood of painstaking research; see Robert Fawtier, *Sainte Catherine: Essai de critique: Sources hagiographiques*, and idem, *Sainte Catherine: Essai de critique: Les oeuvres*, Bibliothèque des Ecoles Françaises d'Athènes et de Rome 121 and 135 (Paris: de Boccard, 1921 and 1930); and, on the controversy, see Kearns, *Life of Catherine*, pp. lx–lxx, and Bell, *Holy Anorexia*, chap. 2 n. 3. For a fairly recent bibliography see Lina Zanini, *Bibliografia analitica di S. Caterina da Siena, 1901–1950* (Rome: Edizioni Cateriniane, 1971). For a fuller treatment of the chronology of Catherine's "eating disorders," see Bell, *Holy Anorexia*, pp. 23–53. Where Bell has been interested in Catherine's behavior, I have been more interested in Catherine's symbols and theology. Neither of us has treated at much length her important public role toward the end of her life. Useful biographies of Catherine include Innocenzo M. Taurisano, *Santa Caterina da Siena: Patrona d'Italia* (Rome: F. Ferrari, 1940), and Arrigo Levasti, *My Servant, Catherine*, trans. Dorothy M. White (London: Blackfriars, 1954), unfortunately without footnotes.

62. Catherine of Siena, Dialogue, ed. Cavallini; Engl. trans. Suzanne Noffke, *Catherine of Siena: The Dialogue* (New York: Paulist Press, 1980). For the letters, see the incomplete edition by Eugenio Dupré Theseider, *Epistolario di Santa Caterina da Siena*, vol. 1, Fonti per la storia d'Italia, pubblicate dal R. Istituto Storico Italiano per il Medio Evo (Epistolari: Secolo XIV) (Rome: Sede dell'Istituto, 1940), and Catherine of Siena, Letters, ed. Misciattelli (Siena, 1913–1922) (the Florence 1939–40 reprint has different pagination). For the prayers, see Catherine of Siena, *Le Orazioni*, ed. Giuliana Cavallini (Rome: Edizioni Cateriniane, 1978); translated by Suzanne Noffke as *The Prayers of Catherine of Siena* (New York: Paulist Press, 1983).

63. See Francesco Valli, *L'Infanzia e la puerizia di santa Caterina da Siena: esame critico delle fonti*, Biblioteca di "Studi Cateriniani" (Siena: Istituto di Studi Cateriniani nella Regia Università di Siena, 1931). I have been unable to consult idem, *L'Adolescenza di Santa Caterina da Siena: esame critico delle fonti* (Siena, 1934).

64. For Catherine's inedia, see especially Raymond of Capua, Life of Catherine of Siena, pt. 1, chap. 3, par. 38, p. 872, and chap. 6, pars. 58–60, pp. 876–77; pt. 2, chap. 4, par. 164, p. 903; pt. 2, chap. 5, pars. 165–77, pp. 903–7; pt. 3, chap. 6, par. 400, p. 960; and *I Miracoli*, chaps. 4–9, 28–29, pp. 5–9, 23–25. On her eucharistic devotion, see Raymond, Life of Catherine, pt. 2, chap. 5, pars. 170–71, pp. 904–5, and pt. 2, chap. 6, pars. 181, 187–92, pp. 907, 909; Thomas Antonii de Senis, *Libellus de supplemento*, pt. 2, tract. 6, pp. 75–120; and *I Miracoli*, chaps 12, 13, pp. 11–12.

65. Rudolph Bell has collected a number of contemporary references to Catherine's inedia; see *Holy Anorexia*, p. 195 n. 10.

66. See above, chap. 3 n. 98. In the Life of Catherine of Siena, pt. 1, chap. 6, par. 60, p. 877, Raymond seems also to be reflecting on his own experience with fasting.

67. See above, chap. 4 nn. 186, 207, 208, and 210.

68. Raymond, Life of Catherine, pt. 2, chap. 12, pars. 324–28, pp. 942–44. Raymond reports that when Catherine visited Agnes's body, she received a rain of manna as a miracle, and, he says, "there was a reason why this particular kind of miracle should happen there. For while Agnes was alive, a rain of manna falling on her was a usual thing."

69. See above, chap. 4 n. 209.

70. Raymond of Capua, Life of Catherine, pt. 1, chap. 3, par. 64, pp. 877–78; pt. 2, chap. 5, par. 173, pp. 905–6; pt. 2, chap. 6, pars. 183–84, p. 908.

71. See, for example, Letter 61, Catherine of Siena, Letters, ed. Misciattelli, vol. 1, pp. 274–77, and Letter 163, ibid., vol. 3, p. 43. On this point see Kearns, *Life of Catherine*, p. 177 n. 23.

72. Raymond of Capua, Life of Catherine of Siena, pt. 2, chap. 4, pars. 162–63, pp. 902–3 and pt. 3, chap. 6, par. 414, p. 963; *I Miracoli*, chap. 29, pp. 24–25. Fawtier, *Catherine: Sources hagiographiques*, p. 97, points out that visions of Christ or the angels feeding Catherine are less common in *I Miracoli* than in Raymond's account. It is also worth noting that Raymond is more apt to call the wound in Christ's side a "fountain" whereas Catherine's own words stress it as a "breast"; cf. pars. 163 and 191. See also Robert Fawtier and Louis Canet, *La Double Expérience de Catherine Benincasa (sainte Catherine de Sienne)* (Paris: Gallimard, 1948), p. 38.

73. *I Miracoli* and Raymond of Capua's Life of Catherine of Siena give independent accounts of her increasing inedia (see n. 64 above) and a number of her contemporaries noticed it (see n. 65 above). The papal bull of 1461 authorizing her canonization makes explicit mention of her extraordinary fasting; see AASS April, vol. 3 (Paris, 1866), p. 983.

74. Raymond of Capua, Life of Catherine of Siena, pt. 1, chap. 1, par. 25, p. 869. The incident is mentioned only in passing.

75. Ibid., pt. 1, chap. 4, pars. 41–45, pp. 873–74. See also Bell, *Holy Anorexia*, chap. 2.

76. Bell, *Holy Anorexia*, pp. 38–52, makes a convincing case for Catherine's sense of guilt as a survivor forming a major (subconscious) motive for her theology of suffering and her increasing self-starvation.

77. *I Miracoli*, chap. 6, p. 6; cf. Raymond of Capua, Life of Catherine of Siena, pt. 1, chap. 4, par. 46, p. 874.

78. Raymond of Capua, Life of Catherine of Siena, pt. 1, chap. 3, par. 38, p. 872.

79. Ibid., pt. 1, chap. 2, pars. 33–34, pp. 870–71; *I Miracoli*, chap. 3, pp. 3–4; see also Valli, *L'Infanzia*, pp. 48–49, 73–76. One should perhaps point out that many of the incidents of childish piety that Raymond reports strike the modern reader as exactly the sort of play and fantasizing children do engage in.

80. Raymond of Capua, Life of Catherine of Siena, pt. 1, chap. 9, pars. 89ff., pp. 884ff.; Thomas Antonii de Senis, *Libellus de supplemento*, pt. 1, tract. 1, sect. 5, pp. 14–15.

81. Raymond of Capua, Life of Catherine of Siena, pt. 2, chap. 1, pars. 119–24, pp. 892–93, and pt. 2, chap. 5, pp. 903–7.

82. Ibid., pt. 2, chap. 5, par. 177, pp. 906–7.

83. See below, n. 85, and see Life of Catherine of Siena, pt. 2, chap. 12, par. 315, p. 940, where Catherine cries out to Raymond (about her desire for the eucharist): "O si scieretis Pater quantum esurio!"

84. *I Miracoli*, chaps. 4–9, 28–29, pp. 5–9, 23–25; Letter of Stefano Maconi cited above, chap. 3 n. 71; Thomas Antonii de Senis, *Libellus de supplemento*, pt. 2, tract. 2, sect. 6, pp. 34–35, and pt. 2, tract. 6, sects. 42, 43, pp. 101–3; Bell, *Holy Anorexia*, chap. 2; and Drane, *History of St. Catherine*, vol. 1, pp. 199ff.

85. Raymond of Capua, Life of Catherine of Siena, pt. 2, chap. 5, pars. 166–67, 171, pp. 903–4, 905; trans. Kearns, *Life of Catherine*, pp. 160–61 and 164. In Catherine of Siena, Dialogue, ed. Cavallini, chap. 142, pp. 394–99, Catherine writes of desire for the eucharist as intense hunger.

86. Letter 19 (number 92 in Tommaseo numbering), Dupré Theseider, *Epistolario*, vol. 1, pp. 80–82. See also Raymond of Capua, Life of Catherine of Siena, pt. 2, chap. 5, par. 174, p. 906, where he reports that Catherine said: "Deus propter peccata mea percussit me singulari *quadam passione sive infirmitate*, per quam a cibi sumptione sum totaliter impedita: et ego libentissime vellem comedere, sed non possum" (emphasis added).

87. Letter 19, Dupré Theseider, *Epistolario*, vol. 1, pp. 81–82: "Mandastimi dicendo che singularmente io pregassi Dio ch'io mangiassi. E io vi dico, padre mio, e dicovelo nel cospetto di Dio, che in tutti quanti e' modi ch'io ò potuti tenere, sempre mi so' sforzata, una volta o due el dì, di prendare el cibo; e ò pregato continovamente e prego Dio e pregarò che mi dia gratia, che in questo atto del mangiare io viva come l'altre creature, s'egli è sua volontà, però che la mia ci è. E dicovi che assai volte, —quand'io ò fatto ciò ch'io ò potuto, e io entro dentro da me a conosciare la mia infermità e Idio, che per singularissima gratia m'abi fatto correggiare el vitio della gola, —dogliomi molto ch'io, per la mia miseria, non l'ò corretta per amore."

88. Bell, *Holy Anorexia*, chap. 2. In Life of Catherine of Siena, pt. 2, chap. 12, par. 311, p. 939, Raymond reports that some said Catherine communicated daily and lived on the eucharist alone; but this was "not quite true."

89. See above, nn. 85, 87; *I Miracoli*, chap. 8, p. 9; and Raymond of Capua, Life of Catherine of Siena, pt. 2, chap. 3, par. 137, p. 896.

90. See, for example, Letter 267, Catherine of Siena, Letters, ed. Misciattelli, vol. 4, pp. 178–84, and Letter 214, vol. 3, pp. 288–92. See also Raymond of Capua, Life of Catherine of Siena, pt. 2, chap. 4, par. 149, pp. 899–900, where we find her blaming on her own sins the pettiness of the sick woman Palmerina.

91. See Raymond of Capua, Life of Catherine of Siena, pt. 2, chap. 5, par. 171, p. 905.

92. See ibid., pt. 2, chap. 5, par. 170, pp. 904–5, and Drane, *History of St. Catherine*, vol. 1, p. 203.

93. Raymond of Capua, Life of Catherine of Siena, pt. 2, chap. 5, par. 167, p. 904. It is pertinent to note that, with a more sympathetic confessor—one in fact in awe of her prowess at fasting—Catherine became somewhat more tractable, more willing at least to make a pretense of eating; see ibid., pt. 2, chap. 5, pars. 176–77, pp. 906–7. In other words, she was somewhat more willing to modify her behavior (at least superficially) if the interpretation of its significance remained in her control, but she still managed things so that she received little real nourishment.

94. See Canet, pt. 2, in Fawtier and Canet, *Double Expérience*, pp. 311–12, comparing her letters of the early 1370s with her letters of 1378 to 1380. See especially Letter 64 to the hermit William Flete, Catherine of Siena, Letters, ed. Misciattelli, vol. 1, pp. 286–94, where she says: "Pèrdono loro medesimi, spogliandosi, dell'uomo vecchio, cioè della propria sensualità; e vestonsi dell'uomo nuovo Cristo dolce Gesù seguitandolo virilmente. Questi sono che si pascono alla mensa del santo desiderio, e che hanno posto più la sollicitudine in uccidere la propria volontà, che in uccidere o in mortificare il corpo" (pp. 291–92).

95. Catherine of Siena, Dialogue, ed. Cavallini, chap. 149, pp. 426–29.

96. The sources seem to differ somewhat about the length of her retreat. *I Miracoli*, chap. 6, p. 7, says seven years (probably 1362–1370); Raymond of Capua, Life of Catherine of Siena, pt. 1, chap. 6, pars. 57–63, pp. 876–77, and chap. 9, pars. 82–83, pp. 882–83, suggests it was three years. But there may be no conflict in fact, for the retreat was not total, and Raymond is simply giving a more detailed account of its various aspects.

97. We can see something of the problem her behavior posed for her family in pt. 2, chap. 2, pars. 135–37, pp. 896–97, where we have a story of Catherine giving away other people's clothes and the passing remark that her family had to keep everything locked up to prevent her from giving it away.

98. Deposition of Brother Bartholomew Dominici in Laurent, *Il Processo*, pp. 290–92. Another version of the story or another story is told by Raymond of Capua in Life of Catherine of Siena, pt. 2, chap. 3, pars. 140–41, pp. 897–98. Drane, *History of St. Catherine*, vol. 1, p. 82, reports that citizens of Siena still call something that never comes to an end "a cask of St. Catherine." See also Raymond, Life of Catherine of Siena, pt. 2, chap. 16, pars. 298–310, pp. 936–39, on miraculous food multiplications.

99. Catherine became a tertiary in her late teens (probably in 1364 or 65). Her father died in August, 1368, and after this the family home as Catherine had known it came to an end and the family fortunes declined. Catherine, as is well known, took on an increasingly public role as adviser and exhorter of ecclesiastics; historians have differed in their estimates of her success.

100. Raymond of Capua, Life of Catherine of Siena, pt. 2, chaps. 2–4, 6–17, pp. 895–903, 907–39.

101. Ibid., pt. 2, chap. 16, par. 303, p. 937.

102. Ibid., pt. 2, chap. 16, pars. 298–99, p. 936.

103. Catherine of Siena, Dialogue, ed. Cavallini, chap. 149, pp. 425–29. Raymond

himself draws the parallel between Dominic's food multiplication miracles and Catherine's; Life of Catherine of Siena, pt. 2, chap. 16, par. 305, pp. 937–38.

104. Thomas Antonii de Senis, *Libellus de supplemento*, pt. 2, tract. 4, sects. 13–14, pp. 62–64.

105. See deposition of Francesco Malavolti in Laurent, *Il Processo*, pp. 394–96; and Drane, *History of St. Catherine*, vol. 2, pp. 61–64. See also Raymond of Capua, Life of Catherine of Siena, pt. 2, chap. 13, par. 276, p. 930.

106. Raymond of Capua, Life of Catherine of Siena, pt. 3, chap. 4, pars. 370–76, pp. 954–56. Semia, for whom Catherine performs the miracle, cries out: "O mater mea dilecta! Venisti ad domum meam clausis januis ad faciendum mihi coquinam. Nunc scio vere quia sancta es." It is worth noting that Catherine sometimes herself escaped domestic chores through ecstasies, although at other times she insisted on doing more than her share of the housework. See Life of Catherine of Siena, pt. 2, chap. 2, pars. 126–27, pp. 893–94, where her sister-in-law Lisa finds her in ecstasy when she ought to be turning the spit to roast meat. "Quod advertens . . . Lysa . . . sciens modum virginis, coepit ipsa vertere veru, et permisit eam coelestis sponsi frui amplexibus. Cumque coctis carnibus illis et facta coena cunctorum domesticorum, adhuc illa in extasi permaneret; Lysa praefata, perfectis cunctis quae virgo sacra facere solebat servitiis, ipsam permisit ad libitum divinis potiri solatiis."

107. Ibid., pt. 2, chap. 16, par. 308, p. 938; trans. Kearns, *Life of Catherine*, p. 285.

108. Raymond of Capua, Life of Catherine of Siena, pt. 2, chap. 16, par. 300, pp. 936–37; trans. Kearns, *Life of Catherine*, pp. 278–79, with my changes.

109. Raymond of Capua, Life of Catherine of Siena, pt. 2, chap. 8, pars. 212–18, pp. 914–16; *I Miracoli*, chap. 27, pp. 22–23; and see Canet in Fawtier and Canet, *Double Expérience*, pp. 337ff., esp. pp. 354–55.

110. Raymond of Capua, Life of Catherine of Siena, pt. 2, chap. 9, pars. 220–23, pp. 916–17; pt. 3, chap. 7, par. 417, p. 964.

111. Ibid., pt. 2, chap. 11, pars. 241–44, pp. 922–23; see also Fawtier, *Catherine: Sources hagiographiques*, p. 135.

112. See, for example, above, n. 108; Letter of Stefano Maconi in Catherine of Siena, Letters, ed. Misciattelli, vol. 6, Letters of disciples, Letter 12, p. 81 ("però ch'io credo veramente e così confesso, che la Mamma nostra benignissima è mamma; e ò ferma speranza che ogni dì con più chiaro lume credarò e confessarò con maggiore efficacia, lei essere mamma"); and the panegyric of William Flete, quoted in Drane, *History of St. Catherine*, vol. 2, p. 214, and vol. 1, pp. 176–79. (On William Flete see also Fawtier, *Catherine: Sources hagiographiques*, pp. 53–81.) See also Bell, *Holy Anorexia*, chap. 2.

113. Raymond of Capua, Life of Catherine of Siena, pt. 2, chap. 4, pars. 155, 162–63, pp. 901, 902–3, and pt. 3, chap. 7, pars. 412, 414, p. 963; *I Miracoli*, chaps. 32–33, pp. 28–29; Thomas Antonii de Senis, *Libellus de supplemento*, pt. 2, tract. 2, sect. 4, p. 34.

114. Raymond of Capua, Life of Catherine of Siena, pt. 2, chap. 4, par. 162, p. 902.

115. Ibid., par. 163, p. 903; trans. Kearns, *Life of Catherine*, pp. 155–56.

116. Raymond of Capua, Life of Catherine of Siena, pt. 3, chap. 7, par. 414, p. 963.

117. Catherine also experienced what Raymond calls an exchange of hearts with Christ, and from thenceforth she felt as if she lived without her heart; see ibid., pt. 2,

chap. 6, par. 179, p. 907. (Lutgard of Aywières in the thirteenth century supposedly experienced a similar sensation.).

118. See above, nn. 64, 72, 85, 88.

119. Deposition of Brother Franceso of Lucca in Laurent, *Il Processo*, pp. 368–69. For Catherine's respect for priests, whom she calls "christs," see Catherine of Siena, Dialogue, ed. Cavallini, chaps. 14, 23, 113–18, pp. 37–42, 51–54, 274–86 and passim, and Thomas Antonii de Senis, *Libellus de supplemento*, pt. 2, tract. 6, sects. 1–26 passim, pp. 76–88.

120. For the theme of drinking from Christ's side in Raymond's account, see Life of Catherine of Siena, pars. 162–63 (the vision discussed above), pp. 902–3; par. 187 (another vision of drinking from Christ's breast), p. 909; par. 191 (vision discussed below, n. 121), p. 909; and par. 199 (a vision supposedly reported by her earlier confessor, Thomas della Fonte, of Catherine nursed at the breasts of the Virgin), p. 911. See also above, n. 72.

121. Raymond of Capua, Life of Catherine of Siena, pt. 2, chap. 6, pars. 188–91, p. 909; trans. George Lamb, *The Life of St. Catherine of Siena by Blessed Raymond of Capua* (London: Harvill Press, 1960), p. 173, with minor changes. (Lamb's translation is much harder to obtain than Kearns' but is often more literal and accurate.) For the history of the metaphor, see André Cabassut, "Une Dévotion médiévale peu connue: La dévotion à 'Jésus notre Mère,'" *Mélanges Marcel Viller, Revue d'ascétique et de mystique* 25 (1949): 234–45; Bynum, JM, pp. 110–69; Eleanor C. McLaughlin, "'Christ My Mother': Feminine Naming and Metaphor in Medieval Spirituality," *Nashota Review* 15 (1975): 226–48; Julian, *Book of Showings*, ed. Colledge and Walsh; preface and intro. to *Julian of Norwich: Showings*, trans. Colledge and Walsh, introduction by Jean Leclercq (New York: Paulist Press, 1978); and Valerie Lagorio, "Variations on the Theme of God's Motherhood in Medieval English Mystical and Devotional Writings," *Studia mystica* 8 (1985): 15–37. See also Gabriella Anadol, "Le Immagini del linguaggio cateriniano e le lore fonti: La Madre," *Rassegna di ascetica e mistica* 22 (1971): 337–43. In his psychological portrait of Catherine, Rudolph Bell (*Holy Anorexia*, chapter 2) makes much of her picture of nursing and weaning as including bitterness and pain. He cites this passage and especially Letter 81 (Tommaseo number 239) to Pope Gregory XI (Dupré Theseider, *Epistolario*, pp. 332–33) and calls attention to Lapa's inexperience at weaning, which he documents by reference to Raymond, Life of Catherine of Siena, par. 26, p. 869. It may be that Catherine's personal experience of weaning was a painful one (although one must point out that we have no evidence of this), but we should also note that many medieval writers speak of mothers as teasing and disciplining their babies.

122. See Catherine of Siena, Dialogue, ed. Cavallini, chaps. 14 (both priests and Christ seen as nursing mothers), 96 (Christ as nursing mother), 141 (the Holy Spirit as mother—not an extended image), and 151 (God speaks as a nursing mother), pp. 37–42, 225–30, 392–93, 440; and see Letter 1*, Catherine of Siena, Letters, ed. Misciattelli, vol. 6, pp. 1–4 (charity is a mother who nurses her children; she is also a food that nurtures the soul); Letter 86, ibid., vol. 2, pp. 81–88 (we must nurse at the breast of charity; the soul must feed on the pains of the cross, which are sweet); Letter 260, ibid., vol. 4, pp. 137–41, esp. 139–40 (Christ is the nurse who drinks bitter medicine in order to feed the child); and Letter 2*, ibid., vol. 6, pp. 5–9 (Christ is the nurse of the soul). See also the

letter to Gregory XI cited above, n. 121, in which the pope is urged not to turn away from the breast because the milk is bitter (i.e, because the virtuous path is a painful one). Because Catherine's letters in Letters, ed. Misciattelli, vol. 6, are numbered separately, I have used a star (*) after the numbering for that series.

123. Canet in Fawtier and Canet, *Double Expérience*, pp. 304–6, makes this point.

124. Letter 86, Catherine of Siena, Letters, ed. Misciattelli, vol. 2, pp. 81–82. In translating Catherine's Italian I have been aided by the French translation of E. Cartier, *Lettres de sainte Catherine de Sienne*, 4 vols., Bibliothèque Dominicaine, 2d ed. (Paris: Editions Téqui, 1886). I am also grateful to Rachel Jacoff of Wellesley College for assistance.

125. See Letter 81, Dupré Theseider, *Epistolario*, pp. 332–33; Catherine of Siena, Dialogue, ed. Cavallini, chap. 96, pp. 225–30, and chap. 151, p. 440; Canet in Fawtier and Canet, *Double Expérience*, pp. 332, 304–6; and above, n. 122.

126. Catherine of Siena, Dialogue, ed. Cavallini, chap. 14, pp. 40–41, trans. Noffke, *Catherine: The Dialogue*, p. 52.

127. See, for example, Letter 184, Catherine of Siena, Letters, ed. Misciattelli, vol. 3, p. 146 (here she describes Christ on the cross as "arrostito in su la croce al fuoco dell' ardentissima carità"); Letter 358, vol. 5, p. 284.

128. Catherine of Siena, Dialogue, ed. Cavallini, chap. 124, p. 314; trans. Noffke, *Catherine: The Dialogue*, p. 239.

129. Catherine of Siena, Dialogue, ed. Cavallini, chap. 142, pp. 394–400, esp. p. 394; see also chaps. 128–29, pp. 332–45, where Catherine discusses priests who only pretend to consecrate or who say the words of consecration incorrectly.

130. Ibid., chap. 142, pp. 396–99.

131. See Raymond of Capua, Life of Catherine of Siena, pt. 2, chap. 6, pars. 179–82 (Catherine and Christ exchange hearts), pp. 907–8, and pt. 2, chap. 2, pars. 135–37, pp. 896–97 (Christ clothes Catherine with a tunic taken out of his side to keep her warm). And see above, n. 120, for visions in which Catherine joins with Christ's body by nursing at his breast.

132. In the Dialogue one of Catherine's dominant images is Christ's body as a bridge up which we climb. When she speaks of the soul reaching Christ's mouth, however, she implies not primarily that we repose there in a kiss (as the Song of Songs suggests) but that we eat with Christ—we *become* his mouth—and what we eat is suffering (i.e., rejection of our physicality and salvation of our neighbors by vicarious suffering). See, for example, Catherine of Siena, Dialogue, ed. Cavallini, chaps. 26, 51–55, and esp. 76, pp. 57–59, 114–25, 168–71; see below, n. 141, for a quotation.

133. It is significant that Catherine herself chooses to report two kinds of food miracles in the Dialogue—the eucharistic miracles referred to above, n. 130, and the food multiplication miracles mentioned above, n. 103—although she does not report other miracles.

134. *I Miracoli*, chaps. 3–6, 29, pp. 3–7, 24–25; Raymond of Capua, Life of Catherine of Siena, pt. 1, chap. 1, par. 29, p. 870, and chap. 7, pars. 114–17, pp. 890–91. See also Fawtier in Fawtier and Canet, *Double Expérience*, p. 38.

135. Letter 221, Catherine of Siena, Letters, ed. Misciattelli, vol. 3, p. 337: "Ben vedi tu che tu sei sposa, e che egli t'ha sposata, e te e ogni creatura; e non con anello d'argento,

ma con anello della carne sua." Letter 50, vol. 1, p. 236: "Vedi bene, che il Figliuolo di Dio tutti ci sposò nella circoncisione, quando si tagliò la carne sua, dandoci quanto una stremità d'anello, in segno che voleva sposare l'umana generazione." Letter 261, vol. 4, p. 146: "E questo fa l'anima che, essendo liberata dalla servitudine del dimonio, ricomperata del sangue di Cristo crocifisso, non d'oro ne d'argento, ma di sangue . . . e, avendola Dio fatta sposa del Verbo del suo Figliuolo, il quale dolce Gesù la sposò con la carne sua (perocchè, quand'egli fu circonciso, tanta carne si levò nella circoncisione quanta è una estremità d'uno anello, in segno che come sposo voleva sposare l'umana generazione); ed ella amando alcuna cosa fuora di lui, o padre o madre, o sorella o fratelli o congiunti; o ricchezze o stati del mondo, diventa adultera, e non sposa leale nè fedele al sposo suo." And see Letter 143, vol. 2, pp. 337–38. See also Prayer 25: "you [God] espouse our souls to you with the ring of your flesh [or charity]." Noffke, *Prayers*, ll. 50–52, pp. 215, 219 n. 8; the Italian text has "charity," the Latin has "flesh." On Raymond's bowdlerization, see Canet in Fawtier and Canet, *Double Expérience*, pp. 245–46, who points out that Catherine, like Bridget of Sweden, was devoted to the relic of the Circumcision. The Viennese beguine Agnes Blannbekin was also devoted to the foreskin, a fact that created scandal when her revelations were published in the eighteenth century; see Allmang, "Agnès Blannbekin," col. 977.

136. See Catherine of Siena, Dialogue, ed. Cavallini, chap. 13, p. 37 (trans. Noffke, *Catherine: The Dialogue*, p. 50), where she says God's Incarnation is "veiling" his divinity in "the wretched dung heap of Adam." See also chap. 98, p. 234, and chap. 123, p. 307, where she speaks of sensuality as "filth."

137. Catherine of Siena, Dialogue, ed. Cavallini, chap. 96, p. 226; trans. Noffke, *Catherine: The Dialogue*, p. 179: "The soul who has reached this final stage [of union with God] rests on the breast of my [i.e., God's] divine charity and takes into the mouth of her holy desire the flesh of Christ crucified. In other words, she follows his teaching and his footsteps, because she had learned in the third stage that she could not follow after me, the Father. For no pain can befall me, the eternal Father, but it can befall my beloved Son. . . . And you cannot walk without pain, but must achieve proven virtue through suffering." See also below, n. 142.

138. See the passages quoted above, n. 135.

139. Catherine also lays much emphasis on our creation in the image of God and stresses that this image is the basis of our possibility of returning to God; Catherine of Siena, Dialogue, Cavallini, chap. 12, pp. 31–33. Moreover, the image is in some sense humanity, because *that* is what we and Christ have in common. "I [God] gifted you with my image and likeness. And when you lost the life of grace through sin, to restore it to you I united my nature with you, hiding it in your humanity. I had made you in my image; now I took your image by assuming human form" (trans. Noffke, *Catherine: The Dialogue*, p. 46).

140. Vomiting, for example, is to Catherine not only a basic image for purging or emptying but a positive image as well, for the soul that vomits is ready again to hunger for (desire) God. See Catherine of Siena, Dialogue, ed. Cavallini, chaps. 95, 151, pp. 222–23, 437; and Letter 208, Catherine of Siena, Letters, ed. Misciattelli, vol. 3, p. 256: "Adempite il mio desiderio in voi, sicchè io faccia la Pasqua, come detto è. E fate come colui che molto beve che inebbria e perde sè medesimo, e non si vede. E se 'l vino molto

gli diletta, anco ne beve più; in tanto che, riscaldato lo stomaco dal vino, nol può tenere, e si 'l vomica fuore. Veramente, figliuolo, che in su questa mensa noi troviamo questo vino; cioè l' costato aperto del Figliuolo di Dio." The letter also calls Christ "food, table, and servant," discusses hunger for Christ as insatiable, and concludes that, by eating Christ, we too become food and bleed for others.

141. See, for example, Catherine of Siena, Dialogue, ed. Cavallini, chap. 76, pp. 168–69; trans. Noffke, *Catherine: The Dialogue*, p. 140: "[The soul] runs on to the third stair [of Christ], that is, to his mouth, where it is clear that she has arrived at perfection. . . . Now she has arrived at his mouth, and she shows this by fulfilling the mouth's functions. The mouth speaks with its tongue and tastes flavors. The mouth takes what is offered to the stomach, and the teeth chew it. . . . So it is with the soul. First she speaks to me with the tongue of holy and constant prayer that is in the mouth of her holy desire. This tongue has an external and an interior language. Interiorly, the soul offers me tender loving desires for the salvation of souls. Externally, she proclaims the teaching of my Truth. . . . She eats the food of souls for my honor at the table of the most holy cross. . . . And she chews it . . . with hatred and love, the two rows of teeth in the mouth of holy desire. There she takes this food and chews it with hatred for herself and love for virtue in herself and in others." See also Letter 208, Catherine of Siena, Letters, ed. Misciattelli, vol. 3, pp. 255–58; Letter 11, vol. 1, p. 44; Letter 340, vol. 5, pp. 158–66; and below at nn. 146, 150.

142. See, for example, Catherine of Siena, Dialogue, ed. Cavallini, chap. 92, p. 213; trans. Noffke, *Catherine: The Dialogue*, p. 170: "The more she [the soul] hungers, the more she is filled, and the more she is sated, the more she hungers." And Catherine of Siena, Dialogue, ed. Cavallini, chap. 101, pp. 244–45; trans. Noffke, *Catherine: The Dialogue*, pp. 192–93: "The soul [which has been offered the pledge of eternal life] begins to hunger for . . . God . . . And because she is hungry she feasts on that charity for her neighbors which she so hungers and longs for. . . . She remains insatiably and continually hungry. Thus, like a pledge, this hunger is a beginning of the certainty I give the soul. . . . When I say that this pledge is not perfect, I mean that the soul who enjoys it has not yet reached the sort of perfection that will know no suffering in herself or in others. . . . My servants [in this life] find their nourishment at the table of holy desire, and they are at once both happy and sorrowful, just as my only-begotton Son was on the wood of the most holy cross."

143. See Letter 208, Catherine of Siena, Letters, ed. Misciattelli, vol. 3, pp. 255–58; Letter 34, vol. 1, p. 157; Letter 8, pp. 34–38; and Letter 75, vol. 2, pp. 21–24, which makes it clear that, to Catherine, hunger and thirst are infinite and insatiable and that they represent reaching out and grasping, not waiting passively.

144. See, for example, Letter 227, ibid., vol. 3, p. 364.

145. In Catherine of Siena, Dialogue, ed. Cavallini, chap. 131, p. 352, Catherine says explicitly that to eat is to serve, explaining that priests administer the blood and take care of souls and this *is* "the task of eating souls."

146. Letter 329, Catherine of Siena, Letters, ed. Misciattelli, vol. 5, pp. 106–7.

147. Letter 87, ibid., vol. 2, pp. 90–92.

148. Letter 2*, ibid., vol. 6, pp. 5–6.

149. See, for example, Catherine of Siena, Dialogue, ed. Cavallini, chaps. 14, 23,

113ff., pp. 37–42, 51–54, 274ff. See also Letter 270, Catherine of Siena, Letters, ed. Misciattelli, vol. 4, pp. 192–93, in which she urges the pope to be a mother to souls.

150. Letter 11, Catherine of Siena, Letters, ed. Misciattelli, vol. 1, p. 44.

151. Letter 293, ibid., vol. 4, pp. 291–92.

152. See Letter 242, ibid., vol. 4, pp. 50–51, and Letter 296, vol. 4, pp. 305–10. This latter letter actually uses the metaphor of cannibalism to describe hunger for souls: "E pregovi che pigliate questi figliuoli, morti, in su la mensa della santissima croce, e ine mangiate questo cibo, bagnati nel sangue di Cristo crocifisso" (p. 309).

153. Letter 273, ibid., vol. 4, pp. 217–18: "Dolcissimo padre, l'anima vostra, la quale mi s'è fatta cibo (e non passa punto di tempo, che io non prenda questo cibo alla mensa del dolce Agnello svenato con tanto ardentissimo amore)." This letter goes on to mix together images of washing and drinking (or eating) as descriptions of the effects of Christ's sacrifice.

154. See, for example, Letter 262, ibid., vol. 4, p. 148, and Catherine of Siena, Dialogue, ed. Cavallini, chap. 110, p. 265; trans. Noffke, Catherine: The Dialogue, p. 206: "The person of the Incarnate Word was penetrated and kneaded into one dough with the light of my Godhead. . . . And to whom have I entrusted it? To my ministers . . . so that you might have life when they give you his body as food and his blood as drink." See also Catherine of Siena, Dialogue, ed. Cavallini, chap. 135, p. 373.

155. Letter 266, Catherine of Siena, Letters, ed. Misciattelli, vol. 4, p. 175, and Letter 52, ibid., vol. 1, pp. 242–43. The phrase also occurs in a letter from Francesco Malavolti to Neri di Landoccio—a proof both that Catherine's language influenced others and that such graphic descriptions were not offensive to fourteenth-century readers; see Canet in Fawtier and Canet, Double Expérience, p. 244, and Letter 40, Catherine of Siena, Letters, ed. Misciattelli, vol. 6, Letters of disciples, p. 145 ("Pace, gaudio e letizia nel Signore, con desiderio di lavare le macule delle nostre iniquità nel sangue dello isvenato Agnello, arrostito per noi sul legno della santissima croce"). Huizinga cites a similar phrase in a work by one Jean Berthelemy; see J. Huizinga, Herfsttij der Middeleeuwen . . . (Haarlem: Tjeenk Willink and Zoon, 1921), p. 293, citing a manuscript work (1912) by Ch. Oulmont.

156. Letter 75, Catherine of Siena, Letters, ed. Misciattelli, vol. 2, p. 23; and Letter 73, p. 14. And see Catherine of Siena, Dialogue, ed. Cavallini, chap. 78, p. 177.

157. See Drane, History of St. Catherine, vol. 2, p. 271; and Fawtier and Canet, Double Expérience, pp. 230–32, 268.

158. Fawtier and Canet, Double Expérience, pp. 268–73; Gougaud, DAP, pp. 75–130; and M.-D. Chenu, "Sang du Christ," DTC, vol. 14 (1939), cols. 1094–97.

159. See, for example, Letter 143, Catherine of Siena, Letters, ed. Misciattelli, vol. 2, pp. 337–38, where Christ marries humankind with the ring of flesh of the Circumcision, and the blood Christ shed on the cross is said both to wash away sin and to provide a wedding feast from God's own body. See also above, n. 153.

160. See above, n. 119; Letter 28, Catherine of Siena, Letters, ed. Misciattelli, vol. 1, pp. 115–24; and Letter 2, ibid., vol. 1, pp. 5–11.

161. For example, Catherine of Siena, Dialogue, ed. Cavallini, chap. 14, pp. 37–38 (ministers drink from the breasts of the church and serve up "the milk and blood of the bride"); chap. 23, pp. 51–53 (they shepherd souls by administering the blood); chap. 115,

pp. 276–78 (the church is the wine cellar, which contains the blood, and from the blood all the sacraments derive); chap. 131, pp. 352–54 (priests are especially entrusted with the task of "eating souls" because they have the "ministry of the blood"). Drane, *History of St. Catherine*, vol. 1, p. 261, points out how often she refers to priests as "chalices."

162. For example, Catherine of Siena, Dialogue, ed. Cavallini, chap. 115, p. 278, where she says: "Christ on earth [i.e., the pope], then, has the keys to the blood" (trans. Noffke, *Catherine: The Dialogue*, p. 215). And see Letter 346 (to Urban VI), Catherine of Siena, Letters, ed. Misciattelli, vol. 5, p. 202.

163. Catherine of Siena, Dialogue, ed. Cavallini, chap. 124, pp. 313–14. Her long discussion in chap. 110, pp. 263–69, of the doctrine of concomitance appears to reveal some anxiety about the crumbliness of the host. Her interest in the doctrine seems to stem from her desire to be sure she receives the blood (which is denied her) along with the wafer she is regularly given.

164. See, for example, ibid., chaps. 23–24, pp. 51–56.

165. Catherine herself describes the incident in a letter to Raymond; Letter 273, Catherine of Siena, Letters, ed. Misciattelli, vol. 4, pp. 217–23. See also Thomas Antonii de Senis, *Legenda minore*, pt. 2, chap. 7, p. 94.

166. See Bynum, JM, p. 18 n. 25.

167. Letter 215, Catherine of Siena, Letters, ed. Misciattelli, vol. 3, pp. 292–97; Letter 54, vol. 1, pp. 249–51; Letter 262, vol. 4, pp. 145–50 (see esp. p. 148, where the nuptial chamber is the wound in Christ's side). We should also note that in Letter 112 (vol. 2, pp. 197–202), where she offers Christ as a substitute to a married woman who has lost two husbands, she offers him not as bridegroom but as *food*.

168. See above, nn. 122, 125, 141, 143.

169. See above, n. 135.

170. See above, n. 136.

171. See, for example, Letter 205, Catherine of Siena, Letters, ed. Misciattelli, vol. 3, pp. 242–43, and Noffke, introduction to *Catherine: The Dialogue*, p. 21. See also below, pp. 216–17 and 261–69. We should not forget that although Catherine thinks *feminine* means *weak*, and *virile, strong*, she applies both adjectives to both sexes and exhorts women as well as men to boldness (clearly assuming it to be attainable). In Letter 215, Catherine, Letters, ed. Misciattelli, vol. 3, p. 296, for example, she exhorts women to be "knights" in strength and determination.

172. Letter 30, Catherine of Siena, Letters, ed. Misciattelli, vol. 1, pp. 135–42; see also Letter 144, vol. 2, pp. 341–42.

173. See above, at nn. 124–26.

174. See below, pp. 265, 270.

175. Letter 18, Catherine of Siena, Letters, ed. Misciattelli, vol. 1, p. 75.

176. Letter 1*, ibid., vol. 6, pp. 1–2.

177. Letter 342, ibid., vol. 3, p. 174.

178. Letter 145, ibid., vol. 2, pp. 348–49.

179. Many commentators note this; see, for example, Noffke, *Catherine: The Dialogue*, p. 206 n. 3.

180. Letter 208, Catherine of Siena, Letters, ed. Misciattelli, vol. 3, pp. 255–57: "Questa è la Pasqua ch'io voglio che noi facciamo; cioè di vederci alla mensa dell'Agnello

immancolato, il quale è cibo, mensa e servitore. In su questa mensa sono e' frutti delle vere e reali virtù. . . . Questa è una mensa forata, piena di vene che germinano sangue; e tra gli altri vi ha uno canale, che gitta sangue e acqua mescolato con fuoco. . . . O figliuolo dolcissimo in Cristo Gesù, corriamo con sollicitudine a questa mensa. . . . E quando egli ha bene bevuto; ed egli 'l gitta sopra 'l capo de' fratelli suoi: ed ha imparato da colui che continuamente in mensa versa non per sua utilità, ma per nostra. Noi dunque, che mangiamo alla mensa predetta, conformandoci col cibo, facciamo quello medesimo non per nostra utilità, ma per onore di Dio, e per la salute del prossimo." For a fuller translation of the passage see below, epigraph to chapter 8, and see above, n. 140.

181. The fundamental work on Catherine of Genoa remains Friedrich von Hügel, *The Mystical Element of Religion as Studied in Saint Catherine of Genoa and Her Friends*, 2 vols. (London: Dent, 1908), although von Hügel was misled by his opinion that the 1551 edition (of Manuscript A plus additions) of the saint's works was the most trustworthy text. For manuscripts D and D*, today considered the best manuscripts, see Umile Bonzi da Genova, *S. Caterina Fieschi Adorno*, vol. 1: *Teologia mistica de S. Caterina da Genova* and vol. 2: *Edizione critica dei manoscritti cateriniani* (Turin: Marietti, 1961–1962). On Catherine's life and on the controversy surrounding the authorship of her works, see also Umile Bonzi da Genova, "L'Opus Catharinianum et ses auteurs. Etude critique sur la biographie et les écrits de sainte Catherine de Gênes," *Revue d'ascétique et de mystique* 16 (1935): 351–80; P. Debongnie, "Catherine de Gênes (sainte)," DHGE, vol. 11 (1949), cols. 1506–15; idem, "Sainte Catherine de Gênes, vie et doctrine, d'après des travaux récents," *Revue d'ascétique et de mystique* 38 (1962): 409–46; Umile Bonzi da Genova and Marcel Viller, "Catherine de Gênes (sainte)," DS, vol. 2 (1953), cols. 290–325; and Benedict Groeschel, introduction to *Catherine of Genoa: Purgation and Purgatory* . . . , trans. Serge Hughes (New York: Paulist Press, 1979), pp. 1–67.

182. The most I claim below therefore is that the image of Catherine held by those close to her included both extravagant food practices and theological sayings in which metaphors of food and hunger were prominent. The early printed *vita*, which I have cited in the 1568 Florence edition (see below, n. 189), differs greatly from the various manuscripts (see Catherine of Genoa, ed. Umile Bonzi, *Edizione critica*); on the correlations and lacunae of the various versions, see von Hügel, *Mystical Element*, vol. 1, pp. 388–90, 449–51.

183. *Vita*, chaps. 1–5, Catherine of Genoa, *Edizione critica*, ed. Umile Bonzi, pp. 107–20; on her conversion, fasts, and eucharistic devotion, see von Hügel, *Mystical Element*, vol. 1, pp. 104–9, 113–16, 135–37, and vol. 2, pp. 28–40. See also Debongnie, "Sainte Catherine," pp. 427–28.

184. Scholars have differed somewhat on the beginning and end dates of this period of fasting and daily communion; see Groeschel, intro., in Hughes, *Catherine of Genoa*; *Purgation*, pp. 5–7; Debongnie, "Sainte Catherine," pp. 431–33; von Hügel, *Mystical Element*, vol. 1, pp. 109–13, 135–37; Umile Bonzi, *S. Caterina*, vol. 1: *Teologia*, pp. 30–33. It is important to note that, whether Catherine was twenty-six or twenty-nine at the onset of this behavior pattern, it was *not* an adolescent development.

185. It is significant that she experienced spontaneous remission of her extravagant inedia (i.e., of her efforts at extraordinary control of body) at about the same time as she accepted a spiritual director (i.e., spiritual control exercised by another ego).

186. Debongnie, "Sainte Catherine," pp. 440–41, discusses whether the illness was "supernatural," psychosomatic, or some kind of cancer. A diagnosis is not possible at this distance. Contemporaries were, however, fascinated by the fact that she could swallow only the eucharist; see *Il Dialogo spirituale*, in Catherine of Genoa, *Edizione critica*, ed. Umile Bonzi, pp. 433–67.

187. In *Vita*, chap. 5, Catherine of Genoa, *Edizione critica*, ed. Umile Bonzi, p. 120, there is language that suggests that Catherine joined with Christ's breast and mouth in a vision. Debongnie, "Sainte Catherine," pp. 430–31, suggests that this is not Catherine's spirituality, for she ordinarily insists on bypassing the "humanity" of Christ, except for reception of the eucharist. Van Hügel (*Mystical Element*, vol. 2, pp. 39–40) makes a similar point when he suggests that Catherine did not receive stigmata, despite her psychological disposition toward paramystical phenomena, because she did not display great devotion to the humanity of Christ.

188. See *Il Dialogo sprituale*, in Catherine of Genoa, *Edizione critica*, ed. Umile Bonzi, pp. 422–27; trans. Hughes, *Catherine of Genoa: Purgation*, pp. 129–32. And *Vita*, chap. 12, Catherine of Genoa, *Edizione critica*, ed. Umile Bonzi, pp. 140–41.

189. *Vita mirabile et doctrina santa della beata Caterina da Genova . . .* [hereafter *Vita mirabile*] (Florence: Giunti, 1568; repr. 1580), chap. 41, p. 137 (this edition reproduces the 1551 Genoese edition except for correcting certain dialect forms). In reply her confessor criticized her for worrying about practices and motives and urged her to surrender completely to God: "Chi e quello, che si impaccia, et parla di mangiare, o non mangiare sotto specie di stimolo; taci, taci, che ti conosco, et non mi puoi ingannare."

190. *Vita*, chaps. 7–11, Catherine of Genoa, *Edizione critica*, ed. Umile Bonzi, pp. 122–40, and *Il Dialogo spirituale*, in ibid., pp. 400, 402–3, 406–11.

191. *Vita mirabile*, chap. 42, p. 143.

192. See *Vita*, chap. 5, Catherine of Genoa, *Edizione critica*, ed. Umile Bonzi, p. 119, and below, n. 196.

193. See *Vita*, chap. 10, Catherine of Genoa, *Edizione critica*, p. 135, and *Il Dialogo spirituale*, in ibid., pp. 402–3. On her famous statement "in Dio è il mio essere, il mio ME," usually rendered "My Me is God," see below, chap. 10 n. 2.

194. *Il Dialogo spirituale*, Catherine of Genoa, *Edizione critica*, ed. Umile Bonzi, p. 389.

195. *Vita mirabile*, chap. 3, p. 11; trans. by Mrs. G. Ripley, *Life and Doctrine of Saint Catherine of Genoa* (New York: Catholic Publication Society, 1875), p. 31. But see *Vita*, Catherine of Genoa, *Edizione critica*, ed. Umile Bonzi, pp. 62–63, 121–22.

196. *Il Dialogo spirituale*, Catherine of Genoa, *Edizione critica*, ed. Umile Bonzi, p. 432, describing her last illness ("e quando essa non si communicava, restava tutto quel giorno affamata, e pareva che non potesse vivere senza questo sacramento"), and pp. 406–11, where we have a description, in dialogue form, of her response to the vision of the bleeding Jesus. Here she stops eating, acquires a frantic need for communion, and begs God to take away all feelings. But at the reception of communion, her humanity cries out: "Hor a questo modo io potrò vivere!"

197. The Spiritual Dialogue, pt. 2, in Hughes, *Catherine of Genoa: Purgation*, pp. 115–33. Here Catherine's depression before her conversion is described as a period in which she could not eat; after her conversion she is described as having no taste for

anything but love of God. In this condition her humanity cries out that it must have food, but it has trouble finding nourishment in that which satisfies the soul. The communion comes as food for both, although Soul is worried about the bliss that accompanies it and asks God to take "feelings" away. "O Signore, o Signore, io non voglio prova alcuna di te, perché non cerco sentimenti, ma li fuggo come demonij, perché sono cose molto impeditive al puro amore; perché l'huomo se le può attachare con lo spirito e con l'humanità sotto specie di perfettione. E perché l'amore deve essere nudo, perciò ti prego, o Signore, a non mi dare più simil cose, perché non fanno per me" (*Il Dialogo spirituale*, Catherine of Genoa, *Edizione critica*, ed. Umile Bonzi, p. 411).

198. *Il Dialogo spirituale*, Catherine of Genoa, *Edizione critica*, ed. Umile Bonzi, pp. 420–21: "E così fu fatto, perché la mise in tanta povertà, che non poteva vivere se Dio non le havesse proveduto per via di elemosine. E le disse: Accioché tu ti possi esercitare, tu lavorerai per vivere. . . . Non voglio che tu mai habbia propria elettione, ma sempre farai la volutà d'altri."

199. Spiritual Dialogue, pt. 2, in Hughes, *Catherine of Genoa: Purgation*, p. 130; *Il Dialogo spirituale*, Catherine of Genoa, *Edizione Critica*, ed. Umile Bonzi, p. 424.

200. See above, n. 188.

201. On Catherine's use of *umanità*, see Hughes, "Notes on the translation," *Catherine of Genoa: Purgation*, p. 49, and Pierre Debongnie, trans., *La Grande Dame du pur amour: Sainte Catherine de Gênes, 1447–1510, vie et doctrine* . . . , Les Etudes Carmélitaines (Paris: Desclée de Brouwer, 1960), p. xxii. For her close association of food and body, see *Il Dialogo spirituale*, Catherine of Genoa, *Edizione critica*, ed. Umile Bonzi, p. 370, where she describes the capitulation of Body to Soul as turning to the food of pigs and other animals: "e si andava ancora lei pascendo de cibi de porci e bestiali, come il corpo."

202. See above, n. 196. It is also worth noting that in the opening pages of the Dialogue *food* is Catherine's ordinary word for *goal*, i.e., for that which is desired, and *hunger* or *taste* her usual synonym for desire; *Il Dialogo spirituale*, Catherine of Genoa, *Edizione critica*, ed. Umile Bonzi, pp. 355–75. See, for example, p. 357 (Soul to Body: "Se trovassemo cibo che ci pascesse tutti due, come faremo?" And Body to Soul: "Ma sarebbe troppo gran cosa che si trovasse cibo che contentasse due che havessero gusti contrarij") and p. 363 (Soul to Body: "perché gustando queste cose terrene, dubito che mi alenterò il gusto delle cose spirituali").

203. Hughes, *Catherine of Genoa: Purgation*, pp. 81–82; *Trattato del Purgatorio*, in Catherine of Genoa, *Edizione critica*, ed. Umile Bonzi, pp. 343–44: "L'amore di Dio che ridonda nell'anima (secondo che io vedo), le dà un contento che non si può esprimere; ma questo contento a quell'anime che sono nel Purgatorio, non leva una stilla di pena; ma più presto questo amore che si trova ritardato, è quello che le fa la pena, tanto grande quanto è la perfettione di esso amore, del quale Dio l'ha fatta capace. Sì che l'anime nel Purgatorio hanno contento grandissimo e pena grandissima, e l'uno non impedisce l'altro."

204. Hughes, *Catherine of Genoa: Purgation*, pp. 82–83; *Trattato del Purgatorio*, in Catherine of Genoa, *Edizione critica*, ed. Umile Bonzi, pp. 344–45.

205. Hughes, *Catherine of Genoa: Purgation*, pp. 76–77; *Trattato del Purgatorio*, in Catherine of Genoa, *Edizione critica*, ed. Umile Bonzi, pp. 332–33.

206. *Vita mirabile*, chap. 32, pp. 106–7; trans. Ripley, *Life and Doctrine*, chap. 28, pp.

129-30. Von Hügel says of this chapter: "[it] is now one long Discourse which incorporates some short but important authentic sayings" (Von Hügel, *Mystical Element*, vol. 1, p. 450). The lengthy discourse is not in the earliest manuscript. It is impossible to know how much of it is Catherine's own language, but the evidence of the *Trattato del Purgatorio* (above, nn. 203–205) suggests that the basic metaphor is authentic.

207. *Vita*, chap. 27, Catherine of Genoa, *Edizione critica*, ed. Umile Bonzi, p. 297, and in *Vita mirabile*, chap. 43, pp. 146–47; trans. Ripley, *Life and Doctrine*, chap. 33, pp. 143–44.

208. It is true, as von Hügel suggests (see above, n. 187), that Catherine of Genoa showed no special devotion to Christ's humanity—either an erotic attachment to his body (like Hadewijch's) or a sentimental identification with his life story (like Margaret of Oingt's)—but her attachment to the eucharist was a devotion to God encountered through physicality: body and blood, bread and wine. And she was deeply devoted to the suffering of Christ's earthly body. Moreover, some of the most affective of women mystics (like Hadewijch) saw clearly the dangers of mere sentimentality. The dark side of the spirituality of a Hadewijch or a Catherine of Genoa—i.e., its emphasis on suffering—is in part an effort to keep the approach to divinity through humanity from becoming mere indulgence in pleasant feelings.

209. Even Margaret Porete, in *rejecting* this spirituality, nonetheless *describes* it accurately. Elaborating a "freedom" beyond all categories—insanity and wisdom, illness and health, fast and feast, love and loss—Margaret describes as a lower way (the religiosity of the "marred") a spirituality of affectivity and eroticism, fasting and works, prayers and eucharist. See Romana Guarnieri, "Il 'Miroir des simples âmes' di Margherita Porete," *Archivio italiano per la storia della pietà* 4 (1965): 513–635.

210. For male writing in which "eating" is an important image, see above, pp. 1, 4, 66–67, 74, and n. 155, and Guigo II the Carthusian, *Epistola de vita contemplativa (Scala claustralium)*, chap. 13, and *Meditatio* 4, in E. Colledge and J. Walsh, eds., *Lettre sur la vie contemplative . . . Douze Méditations*, SC 163, Sér. mon. 29 (1970), pp. 110–12, 142–46.

♦ *6. Food as Control of Self*

1. Hilde Bruch, *Eating Disorders: Obesity, Anorexia Nervosa and the Person Within* (New York: Basic Books, 1973), p. 304.

2. See Peggy Reeves Sanday, *Female Power and Male Dominance: On the Origins of Sexual Inequality* (Cambridge: Cambridge University Press, 1981), passim, esp. pp. 76–77, and Goody, *Cooking, Cuisine and Class*, p. 193.

3. Wheaton, *Savoring the Past*, p. 22.

4. Ibid.

5. Ibid., pp. 95–111, 124, 163, 209. On this point see also Philippa Pullar, *Consuming Passions: Being an Historic Inquiry into Certain English Appetites* (Boston: Little, Brown, 1970), pp. 136–40. For cookbooks addressed to women before 1746, see Wheaton, *Savoring the Past*, p. 299 n. 49.

6. Duby, *The Knight, the Lady and the Priest*, pp. 70–72, 106.

7. See ibid. and Burchard of Worms, *Decretum*, bk. 20, chap. 152, PL 140, cols. 1012–13.

8. Elias Canetti, *Crowds and Power*, trans. Carol Stewart (New York: Viking, 1962), p. 221. Canetti goes on to stress the mother's feeding as power, which he calls "domination."

9. Wheaton, *Savoring the Past*, p. 2.

10. Nicolas de Bonnefous, *Le Jardinier françois* (1651), suggests that women are particularly drawn to fruit; see Wheaton, *Savoring the Past*, p. 123. Rousseau in *Emile* lists as "tastes proper for [the female] sex" dairy products and sweets, especially desserts, but not meat, wine, or strong liquors; see Wheaton, *Savoring the Past*, p. 226.

11. For this view of meat, see John Chrysostom, Homily 27 on Acts, par. 2, PG 60, col. 207 (which warns women against wine and meat); Aquinas, ST, II, IIae, q. 147, art. 8, vol. 43, pp. 114–17; and above, chap. 2 nn. 24–26 and chap. 3 n. 40. It may actually be true that, for reasons of differences in metabolism, women need more carbohydrates and men more protein; see below, n. 36.

12. See Laura Shapiro, *Perfection Salad: Women and Cooking at the Turn of the Century* (New York: Farrar, Straus and Giroux, 1986).

13. Joan Jacobs Brumberg, "Chlorotic Girls, 1870–1920: A Historical Perspective on Female Adolescence," *Child Development* 53.6 (December 1982): 1468–77.

14. I am in general suspicious of theories of religion that see it as evolving through various stages, but one such evolutionary interpretation, Robert N. Bellah's "Religious Evolution" (*American Sociological Review* 29 [1964]: 358–74), is useful in presenting a brief and clear statement of the idea that the Middle Ages was the period of Western religion in which world-rejection as a value was at its height.

15. MacCullough, "Fasting," p. 763.

16. See Barron Holland, comp., *Popular Hinduism and Hindu Mythology: An Annotated Bibliography* (Westport, Conn.: Greenwood, 1979), pp. 120–21. I am grateful to John S. Hawley of the University of Washington for this information and reference.

17. Rogers, *Fasting*, p. 77. Goody, *Cooking, Cuisine and Class*, p. 118, says, "whereas men's fasts are mostly directed toward improving or upholding their own purity and spiritual status, the fasts of women are largely aimed at enhancing and maintaining auspiciousness for 'the social collective,' that is, for the family."

18. Gougaud, DAP, pp. 147–58; Loomis, *White Magic*, p. 130; Fred Norris Robinson, "Notes on the Irish Practice of Fasting as a Means of Distraint," *Putnam Anniversary Volume* (Cedar Rapids, Iowa: Torch Press, 1909), pp. 567–83 (catalogued separately in Widener Library). The Irish tradition also shows cases of fasting "upon" or "against" both God and devil; see ibid., pp. 578–80.

19. Rogers, *Fasting*, passim, esp. pp. 71–76.

20. The fasting of the suffragettes (see ibid., pp. 83–88) was, of course, a self-conscious use of the hunger strike by women for political goals. But before the modern period organized, self-conscious group starvation by women seems not to have been used as a weapon to gain power over others. The sources, however, do provide occasional suggestions of rebellion against authorities by refusal to eat. See, for example, Clare of Assisi's threat that she and her sisters will not eat if the pope refuses to provide preaching (above, chap. 3 at n. 185) and the case of Cecily Ridgeway, who in 1357 fasted and

remained mute for forty days to avoid pleading in a murder trial; Gerish, introduction to *The Hartfordshire Wonder*, p. 5, and Rollins, "Notes on Some English Accounts," p. 360. A particularly interesting example occurs in the Life of Umiltà, chap. 2, par. 13, AASS May, vol. 5, p. 210, where Umiltà imprisons one of her nuns for not doing her assigned job properly, and the woman refuses to eat.

21. On Mary, see Bolton, "*Vitae Matrum*," pp. 257–59; on Clare, see Brooke and Brooke, "St. Clare," pp. 275–87. And on this point generally see Bynum, "Women's Stories, Women's Symbols."

22. Life of Christina the Astonishing, chap. 2, par. 22, AASS July, vol. 5, p. 654.

23. Much of the evidence to which I shall make passing reference in chapters 6 to 8 has been extensively explored in chapters 3 to 5 above; I have not repeated documentation that has been provided elsewhere. Hence, if no footnote is given, the reader may expect to find specific references by turning to the earlier discussion of the saint in question or by using the index. On Margery Kempe, see below, chap. 7 n. 1.

24. Schadewaldt, "Medizingeschichtliche Betrachtungen," pp. 1–14, esp. p. 10. The modern clinical definition of *anorexia nervosa* was framed in the nineteenth century; see Brumberg, "'Fasting Girls.'" Schadewaldt discusses earlier German literature on the history of extended inedia that is not readily available in this country.

25. John Putnam Demos, *Entertaining Satan: Witchcraft and the Culture of Early New England* (New York: Oxford University Press, 1982), pp. 164–65, has argued that some witches' victims at Salem were anorectic. Thurston, PP, passim, suggests modern psychiatric diagnoses of a number of early miraculous abstainers, stigmatics, etc. Weinstein and Bell, SS, p. 235, call the sixteenth-century Florentine visionary Mary Magdalen de' Pazzi an anorectic.

26. J. Hubert Lacey, "Anorexia Nervosa and a Bearded Female Saint," *British Medical Journal* 285 (18–25 December 1982): 1816–17. See also Delehaye, *Legends*, pp. 109–10.

27. See above, chap. 3 at nn. 4–10. Thurston, who defends as at least possibly supernaturally caused certain very bizarre phenomena, says (PP, p. 365): "Just as I should like to hear of a stigmatic who had no bad family history and had always herself been a thoroughly healthy subject, free from neuroses of any kind, so in the considerable list of those holy people who are reported to have lived for long periods with no other nourishment but the Blessed Sacrament, one looks, but looks in vain, for the name of one who was free from strange inhibitions in the matter of diet and whom the neuropath specialist would have pronounced to be perfectly sound and normal."

28. See, for example, Benedict J. Groeschel, introduction to Hughes, *Catherine of Genoa: Purgation*, p. 11, and Petroff, *Consolation*, p. 41. Rudolph Bell, *Holy Anorexia*, argues for an anorectic type of female saint in the later Middle Ages; Bell uses modern psychological models, although he is careful to point out differences between the late Middle Ages and the twentieth century. See above, Preface and chap. 5 n. 61.

29. Brumberg, "'Fasting Girls,'" and Zilboorg, *Medical Psychology*.

30. Ilza Veith, *Hysteria: The History of a Disease* (Chicago: University of Chicago Press, 1965), passim, esp. pp. 56–75; Gregory Zilboorg, *The Medical Man and the Witch during the Renaissance* (Baltimore: Johns Hopkins, 1935), p. 58; Thomas S. Szasz, *The Manufacture of Madness: A Comparative Study of the Inquisition and the Mental Health Movement* (New York: Harper and Row, 1970), pp. 68ff.

31. See below, Epilogue.

32. The opposite kind of case is presented in the *vitae* of Lutgard of Aywières and Juliana of Cornillon, where the saints cure women who cannot *fast*; see Thomas of Cantimpré, Life of Lutgard, bk. 2, chap. 2, pars. 19–20, 25, AASS June, vol. 4, pp. 200–201; Life of Juliana, bk. 2, chap. 9, AASS April, vol. 1, p. 475.

33. See above, chap. 4 nn. 135, 160.

34. See above, chap. 3 at nn. 125–27. Browe, *Die Wunder*, p. 54 n. 23, describes a woman in the diocese of Metz in the mid-thirteenth century who claimed stigmata and miraculous inedia and was unmasked as a fraud.

35. See Harrison G. Pope and James Hudson, *New Hope for Binge Eaters: Advances in the Understanding and Treatment of Bulimia* (New York: Harper and Row, 1984). For a good summary of the various theories, see Elissa Ely, "Rx for Bulimia," *Harvard Magazine* (November–December 1983): 53ff. Recent popular books on anorexia nervosa include Kim Chernin, *The Obsession: Reflections on the Tyranny of Slenderness* (New York: Harper and Row, 1981); Janice Cauwels, *Bulimia: The Binge-Purge Compulsion* (Garden City, N.Y.: Doubleday, 1983); Marlene Boskind-White and William C. White, Jr., *Bulimarexia: The Binge-Purge Cycle* (New York: Norton, 1983); R. L. Palmer, *Anorexia Nervosa* (New York: Pelican, 1981); and Susie Orbach, *Fat Is a Feminist Issue* (New York: Berkley, 1980).

36. See "Appendix B: Sex Differences in Death, Disease and Diet," in Katharine B. Hoyenga and K. T. Hoyenga, *The Question of Sex Differences: Psychological, Cultural and Biological Issues* (Boston: Little, Brown, 1979), pp. 372–90, and Anne Scott Beller, *Fat and Thin: A Natural History of Obesity* (New York: Farrar, Straus and Giroux, 1977). Already in the twelfth century, Heloise argued that "Nature herself has protected our sex with a greater power of sobriety. It is indeed known that women can be sustained with less nourishment, and at much less expense, than men." See Dronke, WW, p. 132.

37. Anne Waltner of the University of Utah, in her unpublished paper "T'an Yang-tzu: A Ming Dynasty Avatar of the Queen Mother of the West," has uncovered important evidence of anorexia-like behavior in sixteenth-century China. And present-day India presents parallel cases; see below, n. 101. I suspect that as more work is done on female piety in various religious traditions, cross-cultural evidence for the greater propensity of women for self-starvation will grow. Such evidence strengthens the case for some physiological basis to eating behavior but does not prove it, because certain predisposing cultural factors are also present in the societies in question, especially the assumption that woman is food preparer and nurturer.

38. On the spread of anorexia, see A. H. Crisp et al. "How Common Is Anorexia Nervosa? A Prevalence Study," *British Journal of Psychiatry* 128 (1976): 549–54; May Duddle, "An Increase in Anorexia Nervosa in the University Population," *British Journal of Psychiatry* 123 (1973): 711–12; Hilde Bruch, "Anorexia Nervosa: Therapy and Theory," *American Journal of Psychiatry* 139.12 (December 1982): 1531–38. Recent journalistic accounts include "Anorexia: The Starving Disease Epidemic," *U.S. News and World Report* (August 30, 1982): 47–48; and "A Deadly Feast and Famine," *Newsweek* (March 7, 1983): 59ff. See also below, Epilogue, n. 5. For further discussion, see Brumberg, "'Fasting Girls.'"

39. The cultural interpretation presented by recent authors such as Chernin and

Orbach (see above, n. 35) is, however, much too limited, focusing as it does almost exclusively on messages provided by the media and on cultural notions of female thinness as beauty rather than on broader values such as notions of women's role and of family. See below, n. 51.

40. See above, chap. 3 at nn. 128–133.

41. Weinstein and Bell, SS, pp. 234–35; Benz, *Die Vision*, pp. 17–34.

42. Life of Serafina or Fina of San Gimignano, AASS March, vol. 2 (Paris, 1865), pp. 232–38; see also Adone Terziariol, "Fina di San Gimignano," BS, vol. 5, cols. 810–11.

43. Life of Villana, AASS August, vol. 5, chap. 1, pars. 11–12, pp. 866–67; *Vita Beatricis*, passim, esp. p. 64; Life of Margaret of Ypres, in Meersseman, "Frères prêcheurs," pp. 125–26. On Gertrude, see Bynum, JM, pp. 192, 253 n. 295. See also Life of Mary of Oignies, bk. 1, chap. 4, par. 40, AASS June, vol. 5, p. 556, and below, n. 72. For Margaret of Oingt's offer to become a leper if God so willed, see below, chap. 8 n. 31. On the patient bearing of illness by male and female saints in the fourteenth century, see Kieckhefer, UnS, pp. 57–58.

44. Process of canonization, art. 33, in Jacques Cambell, ed., *Enquête pour le procès de canonisation de Dauphine de Puimichel, comtesse d'Ariano (†26–XI–1360)* (Turin: Erasmo, 1978), p. 52: "ac eciam dicebat, et dicere consuevit, quod si gentes huius mundi considerarent quantum corporales infirmitates sunt *utiles* et quantum scparant animum ab amore terrenorum, ipsas infirmitates corporeas, si esset possibile, in foro emerent sicut emunt res alias necessarias ad vivendum." On Dauphine, see also Jacques Cambell, ed., *Vies occitanes de saint Auzias et de sainte Dauphine, avec traduction française, introduction et notes* (Rome: Pontificium Athenaeum Antonianum, 1963); and Kieckhefer, UnS.

45. Julian, long text, chaps. 2–4, *Book of Showings*, ed. Colledge and Walsh, vol. 2, pp. 285–98; trans. Colledge and Walsh, *Julian of Norwich: Showings*, p. 181.

46. See below at nn. 81–90.

47. Thurston, PP, pp. 69, 95–99, 123.

48. Ibid., pp. 135–39, 202, 222–32. On myroblytes, see below, n. 85, and chap. 9 n. 75.

49. For the emergence of *anorexia nervosa* as a diagnosis in the nineteenth century, see Brumberg, "'Fasting Girls.'" For a sophisticated discussion of disease categories as cultural constructs, see Cheryl Ritenbaugh, "Obesity as a Culture-Bound Syndrome," *Culture, Medicine and Psychiatry* 6 (1982): 23–36, esp. 27.

50. For anorexia nervosa as the "relentless pursuit of thinness," see Hilde Bruch, "The Psychiatric Differential Diagnosis of Anorexia Nervosa," in Meyer and Feldmann, eds., *Anorexia nervosa*, pp. 70, 75, and Bruch, *Eating Disorders*, pp. 238, 267.

51. Thinness and paleness were sometimes valued as signs of ascetic practice (see Vauchez, *La Sainteté*, p. 226, and above, chap. 3 n. 67), although hagiographers were also sometimes concerned to demonstrate that the bodies of saints were *not* emaciated because they were truly fed by the eucharist (see above, chap. 4 at n. 108). In any case, such references to body size and skin color had nothing to do with norms of beauty. See, for example, Robert of Auxerre's description of Alpaïs of Cudot in his chronicle account for the year 1180, which says that her body was "withered and thin" "but she was still fat and beautiful in her face" (AASS November, vol. 2, pt. 1 [Brussels, 1894], p. 167). Thus Schadewaldt, "Medizingeschichtliche Betrachtungen," p. 11, seems to oversimplify when he suggests that late medieval people desired to be thin as a sign of sanctity.

52. Bruch, "Differential Diagnosis," p. 70.

53. Mara Selvini Palazzoli, *Self-Starvation: From Individual to Family Therapy in the Treatment of Anorexia Nervosa*, trans. A. Pomerans (New York: Aronson, 1978), p. 86. See also Bruch, *Eating Disorders*, p. 267. For a more Freudian approach, see Helmut Thomä, *Anorexia Nervosa*, trans. G. Brydone (New York: International Universities Press, 1967).

54. See Palazzoli, *Self-Starvation*; Bruch, *Eating Disorders*; idem, *The Golden Cage: The Enigma of Anorexia Nervosa* (Cambridge, Mass.: Harvard University Press, 1978); Salvador Minuchin, Bernice L. Rosman, and Lester Baker, *Psychosomatic Families: Anorexia Nervosa in Context* (Cambridge, Mass.: Harvard University Press, 1978). Bruch says, for example: "Though anorexic patients may die from their condition, it is not death they are after but the urgent need to be in control of their own lives and have a sense of identity" (*Eating Disorders*, p. 269).

55. Veith, *Hysteria*, esp. p. viii; and Wen-Shing Tseng and John F. McDermott, Jr., *Culture, Mind and Therapy: An Introduction to Cultural Psychiatry* (New York: Brunner/Mazel, 1981), pp. 23, 276.

56. See above, chap. 4 at n. 102, chap. 5 at n. 50. On Lukardis of Oberweimar, see chap. 4 at n. 115. The editor of Beatrice of Nazareth's life points out the parallel (*Vita Beatricis*, p. 154). The modern fasting girl Sarah Jacobs experienced similar sensations; see Fowler, *Welsh Fasting-Girl*, p. 32.

57. Thurston, PP, pp. 124–25; Rogers, *Fasting*, p. 15; Fowler, *Welsh Fasting-Girl*, pp. 5–6.

58. See below, chap. 8 nn. 47, 48.

59. Life of Ida of Louvain, bk. 2, chap. 6, AASS April, vol. 2, p. 178. In bk. 2, chap. 2, p. 172, the hagiographer reports an occasion on which she grabbed the hand of a priest holding the host and covered it with kisses. The priest, says the hagiographer, feared she was insane, but he acquiesced. Ida of Léau showed similar eucharistic madness; see, for example, her *vita*, chap. 4, par. 31, AASS October, vol. 13, pp. 116–17. Her hagiographer calls her behavior insanity; see chap. 3, par. 24, p. 114. Ludolf of Saxony, *Vita Jesu Christi* . . . , ed. L.-M. Rigollot, 4 vols. (Paris: Palmé, 1870), pt. 2, chap. 58, par. 1, vol. 4, p. 456, tells of a nun who fell to the ground whenever she heard the Passion story. Philip of Clairvaux calls Elizabeth of Spalbeek's ecstasies *imbecillitas*; Life of Elizabeth, *Cod. cat. hag. Bruxellensis*, vol. 1, pt. 1, p. 364.

60. We should note, however, that these women, like the twentieth-century mystic and anorectic Simone Weil, often developed moving and sophisticated theories that go far beyond the food-related and self-absorbed casuistry of modern "patients." Mary of Oignies, Lutgard of Aywières, Hadewijch, Beatrice of Nazareth, Angela of Foligno, Mechtild of Magdeburg, Catherine of Siena, and Catherine of Genoa seem to have elaborated out of their own self-doubt and hunger both a complex theology of substitution in which their sufferings redeemed the evil of a world for which they felt responsible and a mystical doctrine of annihilation of self in the blinding love of God.

61. This diagnosis of Dorothy's persistent sores is suggested by Kieckhefer, UnS, p. 27 n. 14, after consultation with Dr. Ann Johnston, M.D.

62. On the Carnegie Institute tests, see Rogers, *Fasting*, pp. 125–32. Joan Jacobs Brumberg in her unpublished paper "Nineteenth-Century Medicine and the Public Debate over 'Anorexia,'" delivered at the Sixth Berkshire Conference on the History of

Women, June 1–3, 1984, pointed out the difficulty of distinguishing, in early case reports, between the secondary results of starvation or of disease and a disease-entity itself.

63. Considerations such as these have led Brumberg to argue against the use of the term *anorexia nervosa* before the late nineteenth century, when doctors defined it as a diagnostic category. She suggests that the most the historian is entitled to speak of before that date is "anorexia-like" behavior. See "'Fasting Girls.'"

64. Individualistic explanations can, however, be misleading if they obscure the extent to which a particular behavior is copied or learned from others as part of appropriate conduct rather than welling up from inner springs of trauma. For example, Hope Weissman's recent effort to characterize Margery Kempe's weeping as "hysteria" seems less convincing when one realizes how very common, in the behavior of both men and women, such weeping was in the fourteenth century; "Margery Kempe in Jerusalem: *Hysteria Compassio* in the Late Middle Ages," in M. J. Carruthers and E. D. Kirk, eds., *Acts of Interpretation: The Text in Its Context, 700–1600, Essays . . . in Honor of E. Talbot Donaldson* (Norman, Okla.: Pilgrim, 1982), pp. 201–17. See also above, chap. 5 n. 121.

65. See above, epigraph.

66. It is hard to think of a major recent work that takes women's experience seriously that does not assume this. See, for example, Vauchez, *La Sainteté*; Weinstein and Bell, SS, and Duby, *The Knight, the Lady and the Priest*. Renée Watkins in "Two Women Visionaries and Death: Catherine of Siena and Julian of Norwich," *Numen* 30.2 (1983): 174–98, says, "It is disturbing to notice that, in content, the line of development to which women contributed was even more dualistic and anti-intellectual than medieval Christianity in general" (p. 183). But see below, Epilogue n. 11.

67. For example, such a judgmental tone toward women's spirituality mars the fine introduction in Julian, *Book of Showings*, ed. Colledge and Walsh. Even Kieckhefer, UnS, sometimes feels impelled to 'judge' his subjects as balanced or unbalanced.

68. See the works cited in n. 30 above, esp. Szasz, *Manufacture*.

69. See, for example, Koch, *Frauenfrage*; Sheila Delany, "Sexual Economics, Chaucer's Wife of Bath, and *The Book of Margery Kempe*," *Minnesota Review* n.s. 5 (Fall 1975): 104–15; and above, chap. 2 n. 72.

70. For the latter tendency, see Leclercq, "Medieval Feminine Monasticism," pp. 65–66; E. McLaughlin, "'Christ My Mother'"; and idem, "Women, Power and the Pursuit of Holiness in Medieval Christianity," in *Women of Spirit: Female Leadership in the Jewish and Christian Traditions*, ed. Rosemary Ruether and Eleanor McLaughlin (New York: Simon and Schuster, 1979), pp. 100–30.

71. It is not, of course, merely women's asceticism that has been seen as masochism. For example, Carl Mounter ("Guilt, Martyrdom," p. 145) claims that martyrs and ascetics generally exhibit "atavistic forms of aggression, exhibitionism and self-hatred."

72. See, for example, *Töss*, pp. 37, 50–51. One of the sisters composed a poem that said: "Ie siecher du bist, ie lieber du mir bist" (p. 37).

73. For insanity, see above, n. 59. For self-mutilation see chap. 4 at nn. 35, 119, and see below, n. 77.

74. On women's asceticism as more virulent than men's, see Weinstein and Bell, SS, pp. 233–35.

75. Life of Alda, chap. 2, AASS April, vol. 3, pp. 473–74.

76. John Marienwerder, *Vita latina*, ed. Westpfahl, bk. 2, chap. 5, pp. 68–71; see Kieckhefer, UnS, p. 26.

77. Life of Jane Mary of Maillé, chap. 5, par. 34, AASS March, vol. 3, p. 741. Clare of Rimini (d. 1346) had herself bound to a pillar and beaten on Holy Thursday; see Vauchez, *La Sainteté*, p. 231. Christina of Spoleto (d. 1458) perforated her foot with a nail; see Life of Christina of Spoleto, chap. 1, par. 14–15, AASS February, vol. 2 (Paris, 1864), p. 801. For the extreme asceticism and *imitatio crucis* of Hedwig of Silesia, see Vauchez, *La Sainteté*, pp. 432–33.

78. Mechtild of Hackeborn, *Liber specialis gratiae*, bk. 5, chap. 30, pp. 365–66.

79. Life of Christina the Astonishing, AASS July, vol. 5, pp. 637–60; and see Bolton, "*Vitae Matrum*," p. 263.

80. Life of Lukardis, AB 18, p. 312.

81. "Unterlinden," pp. 340–42.

82. Ida of Louvain, Lukardis, Gertrude van Oosten, and Elsbet Achler, for example, supposedly received stigmata which appeared and disappeared periodically. Rita of Cascia received a running sore on her forehead (supposedly imitating Christ's wound from the crown of thorns) which healed when she wished to travel to Rome and reappeared on her return. Jane Mary of Maillé's self-inflicted thorn wound healed after long duration and left no scar. These particular women are discussed above. On stigmata, see Thurston, PP, passim; Imbert-Gourbeyre, *Stigmatisation*; Debongnie, "Stigmatisations"; and Amann, "Stigmatisation." Thurston, Amann, and Debongnie have been very critical of Imbert-Gourbeyre, who stands convicted of inaccuracy and credulity; but I am more interested in the types of stories medieval people were willing to tell (to which Imbert-Gourbeyre is a good guide) than in the physical or historical basis of the story. This does not mean I wish to ignore the distinction, raised by scholars such as Thurston, between cases well documented enough to suggest that physical marks actually appeared and cases of interior (or virtually undocumented) "stigmata"; nor do I ignore the distinction between the cases for which we can, at the present moment, suggest a physical or emotional cause (i.e., self-induced wounds or hysteria) and cases for which we cannot. In some instances, however, it seems to me that scholars have introduced anachronistic categories in worrying about the distinction between natural and supernatural causation. When Debongnie, for example, expresses scorn at Dorothy of Montau's stigmata because she was afflicted with a disease that produced sores on her body, he ignores the fact that *stigmata* meant wound or mark. See above at nn. 74–81 and see n. 61.

83. A red circle with a red lozenge in the center appeared and disappeared on the finger of Catherine de Ricci (d. 1589). Catherine of Genoa's arm was miraculously lengthened, and Douceline of Marseilles floated many feet off the ground in ecstasy. See Thurston, PP, passim, esp. pp. 139, 200.

84. On Gertrude, see Bynum, JM, p. 192; on Clare, see below, chap. 8 n. 50. Three precious stones, with images of the Holy Family on them, were supposedly found in the heart of Margaret of Città di Castello after autopsy; see above, chap. 4 n. 212. According to Weinstein and Bell, SS, p. 229, women provide 27 percent of wonder-working relics from the medieval period, although only 18 percent of the saints were female.

85. For lists of myroblytes, see Thurston, PP, pp. 268–70; Jones, *Saint Nicolas of Myra*, pp. 144–53; Huysmans, *Lydwine*, pp. 288–91 (which, however, provides no docu-

mentation); and Nicole Hermann-Mascard, *Les Reliques des saints: Formation coutumière d'un droit*, Société d'Histoire du Droit: collection d'histoire institutionnelle et sociale 6 (Paris: Editions Klincksieck, 1975), pp. 68–69. (I have been unable to consult the list in M. D. Marchand, "Aspects économiques du culte des reliques du XIᵉ au XIIIᵉ siècle," Mémoire de maîtrise déposé à la Sorbonne en 1969, p. 18.) Female saints from before 1600 who were believed to exude oil or curing liquid in life or after death are: Catherine of Alexandria, Walburga, Lutgard of Aywières, Christina the Astonishing, Hedwig of Silesia, Elizabeth of Hungary, Agnes of Montepulciano, Margaret of Città di Castello, Rose of Viterbo, Matthia of Nazarei (d. 1300?), and Eustochia of Padua (d. 1469). Male myroblytes are: the apostle Andrew, Nicholas of Myra, John the Almoner (d. 612), Bercharius (d. 685), Willibrord (d. 739), Wunebald (d. 761), King Richard (d. 722), Gundechar (d. 1075), Bishop Hugh of Lincoln, William of York (d. 1154), John of Beverly (d. 721) and Robert Grosseteste. The tomb of Lambert of Vence (d. 1154) supposedly exuded curing water; see AASS May, vol. 6 (Paris, 1866), p. 455. Although I can claim no completeness for this list, it is interesting that women are almost 50 percent, although of course we have information about fewer holy women than holy men. It is also worth noting that many of the male myroblytes come from an early period, in which virtually all saints were male. In some cases (for example, those of Catherine of Alexandria, Nicolas of Myra, John of Beverly), the prodigy is reported for the first time hundreds of years after the death date.

86. See Thurston, PP, pp. 222–32. It appears, however, that there is no preponderance of females among saints whose bodies display blood prodigies after death: pp. 283–93. See also above, n. 84. The interest of late medieval hagiographers in incorruptibility as a sign of saintliness was certainly heightened by the plague pandemic of the fourteenth and fifteenth centuries. Periodic outbursts of plague (between five and twelve years apart) meant that every generation experienced times when the smell and sight of rotting corpses were ubiquitous. People therefore needed to be able to give some religious significance to the fact of putrefaction, but they did this in complex ways. See Gottfried, *Black Death*, pp. 91–92, and my brief discussion in "Disease and Death in the Middle Ages," *Culture, Medicine and Psychiatry* 8 (1985): 97–102.

87. The large number of cures supposedly effected by the wash water of saints is a phenomenon closely related to these holy exudings. Water in which a living holy person or a saint's relics had been washed was often both used as a medicine and held in awe almost as if it were a relic itself; see Hermann-Mascard, *Les Reliques*, p. 274 n. 21. In a case like that of Margaret of Hungary (see above, chap. 4 n. 147), the fact that the saint's skin, dandruff, and lice floated in the water may have been seen as increasing its efficacy; this would suggest that the water was viewed as an extension of the body.

88. See above, chap. 4 n. 231.

89. Rollins, "Notes on Some English Accounts," pp. 363–64.

90. Life of Lukardis, chaps. 7–12, 27, AB 18, pp. 314–17, 353.

91. See above, nn. 82, 84, 85, 87.

92. See Bridgett, *History of the Holy Eucharist*, vol. 1, pp. 181–82. In Gaul, from the early Middle Ages on, women were prohibited from receiving the host with bare hands; see Joseph A. Jungmann, *The Mass of the Roman Rite: Its Origins and Development*

(Missarum Sollemnia), trans. Brunner and Riepe, one vol. abridged ed. (New York: Benziger, 1959), p. 510.

93. Vauchez, *La Sainteté*, p. 406. And see Weinstein and Bell, SS, pp. 33–36.

94. Thomas of Cantimpré, Life of Lutgard, bk. 1, chap. 2, par. 21, pp. 194–95, and bk. 1, chap. 1, par. 12, p. 193.

95. See, for example, *Vie de Douceline*, chap. 9, pars. 9–10, p. 76.

96. In a very perceptive article, Claude Carozzi, "Douceline et les autres," *La Religion populaire en Languedoc du XIIIᵉ siècle à la moitié du XIVᵉ siècle*, Cahiers de Fanjeaux 11 (Toulouse: Privat, 1976), pp. 251–67, has pointed out that popular piety and Douceline's own psychology tended both to make her into a body (i.e., a healing relic) while still alive and to induce in her an extraordinary fear of bodiliness.

97. *Vie de Douceline*, chap. 1, par. 6, pp. 6–8. The text makes it quite clear that his maleness is the problem: "E le malautz reques li per gran necessitat que li era, li menes la man per las costas. E illi adoncs cant ho auzi, enferezi tota de gran vergonha e de gran honestat, e estet en si de lueinh, pensan si ho faria: car era homs."

98. Ibid., chap. 6, pars. 4–5, p. 50.

99. McDonnell, *Beguines*, pp. 354–55.

100. It is hardly surprising that Lutgard, a victim of attempted rape, should feel anesthetized when kissed, over her protests, by a man (even if he were an abbot). Nor is it surprising that the "mouth" and "breast" of Christ should figure centrally in her visions, providing partial healing for her painful experiences of the mouths of men. On touch in Lutgard's Life see Cawley, "Life and Journal of Lutgard," pp. 20–48. Carozzi, "Douceline," points out how touching Christ transformed Douceline's fear of bodily contact into almost obsessive concern for healing the sick, to which activity she aggressively (and sometimes repressively) forced her followers. For an example of "erotic" contact with Christ substituting for and curing ordinary lust, see the passage from the Life of Christina of Markyate cited below, chap. 8 n. 7. Columba of Rieti, like Lutgard, experienced attempted rape and her body went rigid in response; see Life of Columba, chap. 8, AASS May, vol. 5, pp. 169*–170*. She later experienced both trances in which her body became rigid and acute sexual temptation; see above, chap. 4 n. 224, and Bell, *Holy Anorexia*, chap. 6.

101. See, for example, the account of the contemporary holy woman "Sati Mata" by Gabriele Venzky, "Wenn Indiens Frauen Sati machen," *Die Zeit*, October 29, 1982, p. 64.

102. See above, chap. 3 n. 123.

103. Thomas of Cantimpré, Life of Lutgard, bk. 2, chap. 2, par. 21, p. 200; Peter of Vaux, Life of Colette of Corbie, chap. 9, par. 61, AASS March, vol. 1, pp. 554–55; Life of Columba of Rieti, chap. 13, par. 122, p. 188*. See also Philip of Clairvaux's comments on Elizabeth of Spalbeek, above, chap. 4 n. 55.

104. See Wood, "Doctors' Dilemma," pp. 710–27. And see below, chap. 7 at nn. 69–71.

105. Albert the Great, *De animalibus libri XXVI nach der Cölner Urschrift*, vol. 1, Beiträge zur Geschichte der Philosophie des Mittelalters: Texte und Untersuchungen 15 (Münster: Aschendorff, 1916), bk. 9, tract. 1, chap. 2, p. 682. Hildegard of Bingen,

Hildegardis causae et curae, ed. P. Kaiser, Bibliotheca scriptorum graecorum et romanorum Teubneriana (Leipzig: Teubner, 1903), bk. 2, pp. 102–3, comments that the menstrual flow of virgins is less than that of non-virgins. She does not relate this to diet; it may, however, have been an empirically sound observation because of the effects of restricted food intake on the nuns she observed.

106. See above, chap. 2 at nn. 21–26, chap. 3 at nn. 40–42, and below at nn. 116–20.

107. Life of Alda, chap. 2, pars. 10–14, pp. 473–74.

108. Weinstein and Bell, SS, pp. 234–36.

109. See, for example, the *Speculum virginum* discussed in Matthäus Bernards, *Speculum Virginum*, p. 129.

110. See above, introduction at nn. 10, 12, and chap. 4 at n. 185.

111. See Weinstein and Bell, SS, pp. 24–25.

112. Vauchez, *La Sainteté*, p. 445, argues that the attitude of hagiographers and prelates toward marriage became more negative after the thirteenth century.

113. Weinstein and Bell, SS, pp. 93–94.

114. Ibid., pp. 39–40, 88–89; Vauchez, *La Sainteté*, p. 445 n. 506.

115. When Clare's sister Agnes tried to flee her family, she was badly beaten by her kinsmen: Thomas of Celano, Life of Clare of Assisi, pars. 24–26, in Pennacchi, *Legenda*, pp. 33–37. The author of the nuns' book of Unterlinden tells an even more gruesome story of a woman tortured by her husband: "Unterlinden," pp. 374–75.

116. John Climacus, *Scala paradisi*, gradus 14, PG 88, col. 869 (see also cols. 871–72).

117. See above, chap. 2 n. 23.

118. *Apophthegmata Patrum*, Sayings of Daniel, par. 4 (95), PG 65, col. 155b; quoted and trans. Musurillo, "Ascetical Fasting," p. 31.

119. John Chrysostom, Homily 27 on Acts, par. 2, PG 60, col. 207. And see above, n. 11.

120. Peter Damian, Opusculum 32: *De Quadragesima et Quadraginta duabus Hebraeorum mansionibus*, PL 145, cols. 543–44; Peter the Chanter, *Verbum abbreviatum*, chap. 134, PL 205, col. 329.

121. See Kari Elisabeth Børresen, *Subordination and Equivalence: The Nature and Role of Women in Augustine and Thomas Aquinas*, trans. Charles H. Talbot (Washington, D.C.: University Press of America, 1981); Julia O'Faolain and Lauro Martines, eds., *Not in God's Image* (New York: Harper and Row, 1973), which sometimes misleads by quoting out of context; Bullough, "Medical and Scientific Views"; Rosemary Ruether, "Misogyny and Virginal Feminism"; McLaughlin, "Equality of Souls"; Jo Ann McNamara, "Sexual Equality and the Cult of Virginity in Early Christian Thought," *Feminist Studies* 3.3/4 (1976): 145–58; M.–Th. d'Alverny, "Comment les théologiens . . . voient la femme."

122. See Duby, *The Knight, the Lady and the Priest*, pp. 23–29; P. Brown, *Virginity and Society*; see also F. Forrester Church, "Sex and Salvation in Tertullian," *Harvard Theological Review* 68.2 (1975):83–101.

123. See Cardman, "Women and Orders," esp. p. 596, and Bynum, JM, pp. 9–21, 142–45.

124. See Natalie Z. Davis, *Society and Culture in Early Modern France* (Stanford: Stanford University Press, 1975), pp. 124–31.

◆ 7. Food as Control of Circumstance

1. Meech and Allen, *Book of Margery Kempe*, chap. 11, pp. 23–25; trans. Butler-Bowdon, *The Book of Margery Kempe, 1436* (London: Cape, 1936), pp. 48–49. On Margery, see Anthony Goodman, "The Piety of John Brunham's Daughter, of Lynn," in Baker, MW, pp. 347–58; Clarissa W. Atkinson, *Mystic and Pilgrim: The "Book" and the World of Margery Kempe* (Ithaca: Cornell University Press, 1983); Kieckhefer, UnS, passim, esp. 182–90; and Susan Dickman, "The Devout Imagination: Julian of Norwich and Margery Kempe," unpublished manuscript.

2. As in chapter 6 above, so in this chapter I provide footnotes only to those incidents that have not been referred to before.

3. Life of Margaret of Cortona, chap. 2, pars. 16–17, AASS February, vol. 3, p. 307. Margaret was criticized for not talking with her son "ut nihil ei coquere vellet, ne tempus impediretur orandi." She said to him: "Fili mi, cum ad cellam redieras, sicut cibum crudum inveneris, ita sume, tenendo silentium; quia tempus divinis laudibus impendendum, in te nulla ratione distribuam." See also Cuthbert, *Tuscan Penitent*, pp. 22–23, 93–95.

4. Process of canonization, *Monumenta . . . vesprimiensis*, ed. Fraknói, pp. 214, 220.

5. For Christina, see Talbot, *Life of Christina of Markyate*, and Holdsworth, "Christina of Markyate."

6. See Placido Tommaso Lugano, ed., *I Processi inediti per Francesca Bussa dei Ponziani (Santa Francesca Romana) 1440–1453* (Vatican City: Biblioteca Apostolica Vaticana, 1945), and John Mattiotti's account of her life, visions, and conflicts with demons in AASS March, vol. 2 (Paris, 1865), pp. 93–178. And see above, chap. 6 at n. 114.

7. Weinstein and Bell, SS, p. 46.

8. See above, chap. 1 at nn. 50–53, and below, chap. 10 at nn. 51–53.

9. David Herlihy, "Alienation in Medieval Culture and Society," reprinted in *Social History of Italy*; idem, "The Making of the Medieval Family: Symmetry, Structure and Sentiment," *Journal of Family History* 8.2 (1983): pp. 116–30; Michael Goodich, "Childhood and Adolescence among the Thirteenth-Century Saints," *History of Childhood Quarterly* 1 (1974): 285–309; Diane Owen Hughes, "From Brideprice to Dowry in Mediterranean Europe," *Journal of Family History* 3 (1978): 262–96; Weinstein and Bell, SS, passim, esp. pp. 67–72; and Goodich, VP, pp. 82, 100–123, 208.

10. See Herlihy, "Making of Medieval Family," p. 116.

11. Ascetic renunciation of family could also be a rejection of children; see above, n. 3. See also the case of Angela of Foligno who says, at the opening of her *Book*, that she prayed to God that her mother, husband, and children would die, and took great consolation when they did; she says, however, later in the *Book* that the loss of her mother and children was a terrible sorrow (Angela of Foligno, ed. Ferré and Baudry, par. 12, pp. 10–12; par. 35, p. 54). Note that the second reference does not mention her husband. It seems permissible to see some of Angela's grief for her children appearing, transmuted, both in her love for her spiritual sons, the friars, and in her yearning for the baby Jesus (see par. 154, pp. 334–36).

12. Raymond of Capua, Life of Catherine of Siena, pt. 1, chap. 2, pars. 33–34, AASS April, vol. 3, pp. 870–71.

13. See Schmidt, "Leben der heiligen Elisabeth," pp. 1, 5; Ancelet-Hustache, *Elisabeth*, pp. 39–42; and Aigrain, *L'Hagiographie*, p. 205. We owe the story to an anonymous Tuscan Franciscan of the thirteenth century. Later, when Elizabeth joined a convent, her confessor forbade her to give away more than morsels of bread and had her beaten for urging her sisters to charity; see Ancelet-Hustache, *Elisabeth*, pp. 315–16. The story of bread and roses is told of Rose of Viterbo and Elizabeth of Portugal (see Ancelet-Hustache, *Elisabeth*, pp. 39–42 n. 1), Margaret of Fontana (d. 1513) (see Life of Margaret of Fontana, chap. 2, par. 9, AASS September, vol. 4 [Paris, 1868], p. 137), and Flora of Beaulieu (see Clovis Brunel, "Vida de Flor," AB 64, p. 8 n. 4). See also plates 8 and 9.

14. The classic statement is Philippe Ariès, *Centuries of Childhood: A Social History of Family Life*, trans. Robert Baldick (New York: Knopf, 1962); see also Lawrence Stone, *The Family, Sex and Marriage in England, 1500–1800*, abridged ed. (New York: Harper and Row, 1977), and Peter Laslett, *The World We Have Lost* (London: Methuen, 1965), chap. 4.

15. Medieval childhood has recently been the subject of much research, which has tended radically to modify Ariès's picture. Among the best work is M. M. McLaughlin, "Survivors and Surrogates"; Pierre Riché, *De l'éducation antique à l'éducation chevaleresque*, Questions d'histoire 3 (Paris: Flammarion, 1968), pp. 30–39; and David Herlihy, "Medieval Children," in Richard E. Sullivan et al., *Essays on Medieval Civilization: The Walter Prescott Webb Memorial Lectures*, ed. Bede K. Lackner and Kenneth R. Philp (Austin: University of Texas Press, 1978), pp. 109–41.

16. See Herlihy, "Making of Medieval Family," pp. 125–30; Weinstein and Bell, SS, pp. 46–47; and Goodich, VP, passim, esp. p. 207.

17. See Herlihy, "Making of Medieval Family," and Hughes, "Brideprice to Dowry." The work of Georges Duby has also contributed fundamentally to our changing conception of the medieval family. See Duby, *The Chivalrous Society*, trans. Cynthia Postan (London: Arnold, 1977), chaps. 1, 3, 6, 9, 10; idem, *Medieval Marriage: Two Models from Twelfth-Century France*, trans. E. Forster (Baltimore: Johns Hopkins, 1978); and idem, *The Knight, the Lady and the Priest*.

18. See David Herlihy, "Life Expectancies for Women in Medieval Society," p. 16, reprinted in *Social History of Italy*. See also idem, "The Generation in Medieval History," also reprinted in *Social History of Italy*, and J. Hajnal, "European Marriage Patterns in Perspective," in D. V. Glass and D. E. C. Eversley, eds., *Population in History: Essays in Historical Demography* (London: Arnold, 1965), pp. 101–43.

19. On this point, see M. M. McLaughlin, "Survivors and Surrogates," pp. 124–39; Hentsch, *Littérature didactique*; Philippe Delhaye, "Le Dossier antimatrimonial de l'*Adversus Jovinianum* et son influence sur quelques écrits latins du XIIe siècle," *Medieval Studies* 13 (1951):65–86; Bullough, "Medical and Scientific Views," pp. 485–501.

20. See Little, *Religious Poverty*; and Goodich, VP, passim, esp. pp. 123, 208.

21. Religious life and religious community were also very important substitutes for family. Petroff, *Consolation*, pp. 61–62, points this out, giving as an example the visions of the Holy Family received by Umiliana dei Cerchi, whose relations with her own family were unhappy. (On Umiliana, see also Weinstein and Bell, SS, pp. 52–53.) Many other examples could be cited. Margery Kempe (see below, chap. 8 nn. 4, 8) was explicit about substituting Christ for her unsatisfactory husband. Gertrude van Oosten, who

yearned with a deep love toward children, in a vision received Jesus at her flowing breasts (see above, chap. 4 n. 61). The handicapped Margaret of Città di Castello, abandoned as a baby by her parents, was especially fond of children and saw visions of the Holy Family, including Joseph, at the elevation of the host. After death she was found to have three precious stones in her heart and on one of them she and Joseph were etched (see above, chap. 4 nn. 174, 212). When Jane Mary of Maillé was six years old and watching by the body of her dead mother, she received a vision of Mary; Process of canonization, chap. 5, par. 56, AASS March, vol. 3 (Paris, 1865), p. 755. (It is important to note that the witness says *not* that the saint was henceforth devoted to Mary but that she was henceforth devoted to the Passion of Christ.) Jesus was sometimes a child for the childless, a good lover to the unmarried or the unhappily married. The Holy Family was sometimes family to those abandoned or persecuted by their own parents. See also above, chap. 4 n. 28.

22. This is a point I have discussed in JM, chapter 5, and in "Women Mystics," pp. 192–96. In my emphasis on the combination of serving and asceticism in the lives of holy women, I differ from Bell, who argues in his *Holy Anorexia* that the prominence of "holy anorexia" in women's behavior resulted in part from the absence of opportunities for service. I also differ from Vauchez, *La Sainteté*, Kieckhefer, UnS, and Weinstein and Bell, SS, all of which argue for a sharper dichotomy between contemplative and active (serving) roles than I feel the evidence warrants.

23. See above, chap. 3 at n. 124.

24. In an interesting variation on the theme of detecting immorality by taste, Christina of Markyate was able to tell by tasting that a salad had been made from ingredients collected from a forbidden garden. (It is worth noting that she prohibited her servants from using the garden because the man who owned it had denied her a sprig of greens.) See Talbot, *Life of Christina of Markyate*, pp. 190–91.

25. See above, chap. 4 nn. 178, 170; Life of Mary of Oignies, chap. 9, par. 86, AASS June, vol. 5, p. 566; and Life of Ida of Louvain, chap. 6, par. 28, AASS April, vol. 2, pp. 178–79. And seen Browe, *Die Wunder*, pp. 31–49. Women's eucharistic miracles also involved knowing whether the consecrated host was present in the tabernacle, or identifying the exact moment of the consecration; see *Vie de Douceline*, pp. 133–35; Life of Juliana, chap. 5, par. 22, AASS April, vol. 1, p. 450; and Life of Ida of Louvain, chap. 2, par. 9, p. 173.

26. Browe, *Die Wunder*, p. 42.

27. See John Coakley, "The Representation of Sanctity in Late Medieval Hagiography: Evidence from *Lives* of Saints of the Dominican Order," Ph.D. diss., Harvard, 1980, who finds, in fifteenth-century saints' lives, this pattern of women viewed as inspiration and refuge for males.

28. See Victor Turner, *Dramas, Fields and Metaphors: Symbolic Action in Human Society* (Ithaca: Cornell University Press, 1974); idem, "Social Dramas and Stories about Them," in W. J. T. Mitchell, ed., *On Narrative* (Chicago: University of Chicago Press, 1981), pp. 137–64; Victor and Edith Turner, *Image and Pilgrimage in Christian Culture: Anthropological Perspectives* (Oxford: Blackwell, 1978); and Bynum, "Women's Stories, Women's Symbols."

29. For example, Thomas of Cantimpré, in his Life of Lutgard, bk. 3, chaps. 3–16,

AASS June, vol. 4, pp. 204–8, calls Lutgard "mother and nurse of the whole order of preachers" (p. 205), describes a friar relating to her "as to his own mother" (p. 207), and says that his order is left "orphaned" by her death (p. 208). He calls her "mother," however, only in her relationships to males, although many of her miracles are for women. (See above, chap. 4 n. 65, and below, chap. 10 n. 16.) James of Vitry, in the Life of Mary of Oignies, bk. 2, chap. 7, AASS June, vol. 5, pp. 562–63, sees Mary as the inspiration of preachers and says that "with tears, prayers and fasts to God," she prayed that "the merit and office of preaching which she could not exercise in herself" would be lodged in others and that God would give to her a preacher "as a great gift." But James is careful to underline her acceptance of limitation, for he reports in the same chapter that the devil tempted her by appearing to her as a pastor but she replied: "No one is a pastor save our master who preaches the word of God and feeds our souls."

30. Stephen E. Wessley, "The Thirteenth-Century Guglielmites: Salvation through Women," in Baker, MW, pp. 289–303; McDonnell, Beguines, pp. 492–96; Marjorie Reeves, The Influence of Prophecy in the Later Middle Ages: A Study in Joachimism (Oxford: Clarendon Press, 1969), pp. 248–50; William Harold May, "The Confessions of Prous Boneta, Heretic and Heresiarch," in J. H. Mundy et al., eds., Essays in Medieval Life and Thought Presented in Honor of Austin Patterson Evans (New York: Columbia University Press, 1955), pp. 3–30.

31. See Bynum, JM, pp. 240–42, 245.

32. See Mark Reuel Silk, "Scientia Rerum: The Place of Example in Later Medieval Thought," Ph.D. diss., Harvard, 1982, pp. 213–42; I. M. Lewis, Ecstatic Religion: An Anthropological Study of Spirit Possession and Shamanism (Harmondsworth: Penguin, 1971), pp. 85–99.

33. See Duhr, "Communion fréquente," and above, pp. 57–59.

34. Life of Alice, chap. 2, par. 15, AASS June, vol. 2, p. 474.

35. Thomas of Cantimpré, Life of Lutgard, bk. 2, chap. 1, par. 14, p. 199: "Prohibita est pia Lutgardis a Domina Agnete . . . sumere omni die Dominico sacramenta. . . . Nec mora: in vindictam facti, in tantum a Domino per intolerabilem infirmitatem afflicta est, quod ecclesiam ingredi non valeret; nec cessavit dolor per momenta concrescens, donec reatum indiscretionis agnosceret, et prohibitionem in pia Lutgarde poenitens relaxaret."

36. Browe, Die Wunder, pp. 27–28.

37. Life of Ida of Léau, chaps. 2–3, AASS October, vol. 13, pp. 112–15. And see Life of Juliana, chap. 2, AASS April, vol. 1, pp. 445–46.

38. Life of Ida of Louvain, bk. 3, chap. 1, and bk. 2, chap. 2, pp. 182–84 and 172–73. For the miraculous communions of Colette and Columba, see above, chap. 4 nn. 170, 226.

39. Töss, pp. 32–33. For other examples see "Unterlinden," pp. 442–44.

40. James of Vitry, Historia occidentalis, ed. Hinnebusch, p. 88.

41. See Bynum, JM, pp. 203–9, and Browe, Die Wunder, pp. 20–30, on distribution miracles.

42. Gertrude, Legatus, bk. 4, chap. 7, pp. 319–21. See also Bynum, JM, pp. 196–209.

43. Gertrude, Oeuvres, vol. 3: Le Héraut, bk. 3, chap. 60, pp. 244–46.

44. Gertrude, Legatus, bk. 4, chap. 32, pp. 394–95; this passage and the one cited in n. 45 below are translated at length in Bynum, JM, pp. 205–6.

45. Gertrude, *Oeuvres*, vol. 2: *Le Héraut*, bk. 1, chap. 14, pp. 196–98.

46. On this prohibition see Bynum, JM, pp. 15–16, 135–36.

47. For Juliana and Lukardis, see above, chap. 4 nn. 64, 1. For Mechtild, see Mechtild of Hackeborn, *Liber specialis gratiae*, bk. 1, chap. 1, pp. 7–10. For Angela, see Angela of Foligno, ed. Ferré and Baudry, par. 151, p. 326 (cf. AASS, par. 113, p. 204).

48. Life of Ida of Louvain, bk. 3, chap. 1, pp. 182–84; Life of Benevenuta of Bojano, chap. 6, par. 51, AASS October, vol. 13 (Paris, 1883), pp. 163; Mechtild of Hackeborn, *Liber specialis gratiae*, bk. 1, chap. 27, p. 96. For the iconographic motif of Mary as priest, see below, chap. 9 n. 41. It is important to note that the theme is not a claim to priestly office for women but a symbol of the parallelism of the consecration and the Incarnation. The theme of the priesthood of Mary is an extrapolation, not a reversal, of the notion of woman as humanity.

49. On Catherine's perceiving of the host as blood, see above, chap. 5 at n. 163. For a vision received by a man (indeed, by a priest) in which the host and the blood are assimilated to one another, see the Life of John of Alverna (d. 1322), in AF, vol. 3 (1897), p. 445. In a striking parallel to the iconographic motif of the mass of St. Gregory, John, while celebrating mass, saw a wounded Christ appear and bleed into the chalice. When the apparition faded, John saw the form of the bread. See also Acta and Acta alia, in AASS August, vol. 2 (Paris, 1867), pp. 466–67, 469–74, esp. Acta, chap. 4, par. 36, p. 466.

50. See above, nn. 30, 48.

51. See above, chap. 4 at nn. 15, 24, 45.

52. See Jungmann, *Mass of the Roman Rite*, vol. 2, pp. 364–65; and above, chap. 2 at n. 104.

53. See above, chap. 2 at n. 141.

54. For economic imagery in male writing, see Barbara H. Rosenwein and Lester K. Little, "Social Meaning in the Monastic and Mendicant Spiritualities," *Past and Present* 63 (May 1974): 20–32; and Little, *Religious Poverty*. My argument that purgatory is more a pool of suffering than a place takes partial exception to the important recent book by Jacques Le Goff, *La Naissance du Purgatoire* (Paris: Gallimard, 1981). My position implies that the key question to consider in explaining the evolution of the notion of purgatory is not the opposition of heaven and hell but, rather, the role of suffering in Christianity.

55. Vision 5, Hart, *Hadewijch: Works*, pp. 276–77; Mommaers, *De Visioenen*, supplement, vision 5, ll. 27–45.

56. See Life of Juliana, bk. 2, chap. 2, pp. 457–58. On Mechtild, see Bynum, JM, pp. 235–45, where I point out that Mechtild sees the female who is submissive, humble, lowly, and without power and learning as the complement to male priesthood and authority.

57. Gertrude, *Oeuvres*, vol. 3: *Le Héraut*, bk. 3, chap. 36, p. 176. On the respect for the priesthood felt by Gertrude, Mechtild of Hackeborn, and Mechtild of Magdeburg, see Bynum, JM, p. 256 n. 298.

58. Hildegard of Bingen, *Scivias*, ed. Adelgundis Führkötter and Angela Carlevaris, Corpus christianorum: continuatio medievalis 43, 2 vols. (Turnhout: Brepols, 1978), vol. 1, pp. 19–21, 147–48, 290–91. I find the emphasis in Bernhard W. Scholz, "Hildegard von Bingen on the Nature of Woman," *American Benedictine Review* 31 (1980): 361–83, somewhat misleading.

59. Life of Gherardesca, chap. 4, par. 36, AASS May, vol. 7, p. 169; trans. Petroff, *Consolation*, p. 103.

60. See below, chap. 9 n. 16.

61. See above, chap. 2 at nn. 22, 29. For a typical miracle in which a whole convent receives, see "Unterlinden," p. 442.

62. See above, chap. 1 at n. 35, and Vauchez, *La Sainteté*, pp. 249, 317–18, 419–27. In a similar argument, Rothkrug, "Popular Religion," pp. 70–79, points out that, in north Germany, women became the major representatives of lay piety.

63. See Browe, *Die Wunder*, pp. 20–30.

64. Life of Juliana, chap. 5, par. 33, p. 453; Browe, *Die Wunder*, p. 34.

65. I have discussed this trend in my article, "Did the Twelfth Century Discover the Individual?" *Journal of Ecclesiastical History* 31 (1980): 1–17, which is reprinted in an expanded version as chap. 3 of JM, pp. 82–109. See also Yves Congar, "Les Laïcs et l'ecclésiologie des 'ordines' chez les théologiens des XIᵉ et XIIᵉ siècles," *I Laici nella "societas christiana" dei secoli XI e XII: Atti della terza Settimana Internazionale di Studio: Mendola, 21–27 agosto 1965*, Pubblicazioni dell'Università Cattolica del Sacro Cuore 3.5, Miscellanea del Centro di Studi Medioevali 5 (Milan, 1968), pp. 83–117; Giles Constable, introduction to Constable and B. Smith, eds., *Libellus de diversis ordinibus et professionibus qui sunt in aecclesia* (Oxford: Oxford University Press, 1972), pp. xi–xxvii; and Giles Constable, "Renewal and Reform in Religious Life: Concepts and Realities," in Robert L. Benson and Giles Constable, eds., *Renaissance and Renewal in the Twelfth Century* (Cambridge, Mass.: Harvard University Press, 1982), pp. 37–67.

66. *Libellus de diversis ordinibus*, ed. Constable and Smith, pp. 15–17. The remark concerns types of hermits.

67. James of Vitry, *Historia occidentalis*, ed. Hinnebusch, chap. 34, pp. 165–66. See also Anselm of Havelberg, *Dialogues*, ed. Gaston Salet, SC 118, Sér. mon. 18 (1966), bk. 1, chaps. 1–2, pp. 34–35.

68. See Bynum, JM, pp. 93–95; and Alan E. Bernstein, "Political Anatomy," *University Publishing* (Winter 1978): pp. 8–9.

69. See, for example, Vauchez, *La Spiritualité du moyen âge*.

70. Duby, *The Knight, the Lady and the Priest*, esp. pp. 186–90. See also Penny S. Gold, "The Marriage of Mary and Joseph in the Twelfth-Century Ideology of Marriage," in Vern L. Bullough and James Brundage, eds., *Sexual Practices and the Medieval Church* (Buffalo: Prometheus Books, 1982), pp. 102–17; and Herlihy, "Making of Medieval Family," pp. 126–28.

71. Wood, "Doctors' Dilemma."

72. See above, chap. 2 at n. 64.

73. Letter 28, PL 157, col. 170. For another example, see Adam of Eynsham, *Life of Hugh of Lincoln*, bk. 5, chap. 16, vol. 2, pp. 195–97.

74. See above, chap. 3 at nn. 84, 85. A good example of the double bind in which this attitude placed women is discussed by Duby, *The Knight, the Lady and the Priest*, p. 161. A certain Ermengarde, repudiated by one husband and desiring to have her second marriage annulled, was told by the reformer Robert of Arbrissel to be obedient in marriage. Robert urged her to practice much almsgiving but not too much prayer or mortification, since her body should be kept healthy for marriage.

75. Duby, *The Knight, the Lady and the Priest*, esp. chap. 6.

76. See above, chap. 3 nn. 87, 88.

77. See above, chap. 3 at n. 256.

78. On women mystics who were condemned for quietism or antinomianism see the works cited above, chap. 1 n. 18, and Dronke, WW, pp. 202–28. See also below, chap. 8 n. 28.

79. Vision 1, Hart, *Hadewijch: Works*, p. 270; Mommaers, *De Visioenen*, supplement, vision 1 ll. 327–33. God goes on to say that she refused exterior gifts and miracles.

80. Vision 14, Hart, *Hadewijch: Works*, p. 305; Mommaers, *De Visioenen*, supplement, vision 14, ll. 150–57: "die niet en bekinde met ghearbeider minnen ende met gheanxender hoe ic god ende mensche ben Ende want du coene. dus coene best ende dus niet ne bughes soe heetti coenste. ende soe eest recht dattu mi te vollen kins."

81. Immoderate too is Mechtild of Magdeburg's confidence that her suffering with Christ saves 70,000 souls from purgatory. See Mechtild of Magdeburg, *Licht*, bk. 2, chap. 8, p. 35, and bk. 3, chap. 15, pp. 76–78. Moreover, Hildegard of Bingen, despite disclaimers, sometimes alleges that she knows the future or the condition of departed souls; see Dronke, WW, pp. 192–93.

82. See above, chap. 2 n. 113.

83. Mechtild of Magdeburg, *Licht*, bk. 3, chaps. 10, 21–22, and bk. 5, chap. 8, pp. 72, 85–87, 135–36. In bk. 1, chap. 5, p. 7, she offers to go to hell if it will bring God praise. It is out of this kind of anguish that Julian of Norwich forges her organic sense that all of existence is given meaning by God; see below, chap. 10 nn. 37, 40, 49.

84. Vision 14, Hart, *Hadewijch: Works*, pp. 302–3; Mommaers, *De Visioenen*, supplement, vision 14, ll. 32–37. For Angela of Foligno's sense of being special to Christ, see Angela of Foligno, ed. Ferré and Baudry, par. 45, pp. 78–80.

85. Vision 5, Hart, *Hadewijch: Works*, pp. 276–77; Mommaers, *De Visioenen*, supplement, ll. 27–45.

86. Tauler, Sermon 9 for Second Sunday in Lent, in Tauler, *Die Predigten*, pp. 45–46; trans. Colledge and M. Jane, *Spiritual Conferences*, pp. 86–87.

87. On this point see Grundmann, *Bewegungen*; E. McLaughlin, "Free Spirit"; and R. Lerner, *Heresy of the Free Spirit*.

88. To say this is not to deny that, as Vauchez has pointed out (*La Sainteté*, p. 446), hagiographers and preachers in the fourteenth and fifteenth centuries came increasingly to encourage those aspects of women's spirituality that seem to the twentieth-century reader most psychologically disturbed. Watkins, "Two Women Visionaries," p. 187, makes the same point.

◆ 8. *The Meaning of Food: Food as Physicality*

1. See above, chap. 5 n. 180.

2. See above, pp. 151–52 and below, Epilogue. For other recent writers who point out that such spirituality is, in its authors' own terms, not "morbid sentimentality" but,

rather, delight in God's love, see Madigan, *"Passio Domini" Theme*, p. 100, and Kieckhefer, UnS, chap. 4, esp. p. 104.

3. On women's devotion to the humanity of Christ, see Kieckhefer, UnS, esp. chap. 4, and Bynum, "Women Mystics." Pain comes increasingly to be emphasized over pleasure in fourteenth- and fifteenth-century piety. Iconographic evidence is particularly important for showing the increasing devotion to Christ's pain in the Passion. See generally Schiller, *Iconography*, vol. 2: *The Passion of Jesus Christ*; and Marrow, *Passion Iconography*. Browe, *Die Wunder*, pt. 2, chaps. 1–3, discusses the fact that visions of the Christ child in the eucharist are most common in the twelfth and thirteenth centuries, with visions of the bleeding and tortured man gaining steadily in the fourteenth and fifteenth centuries.

4. See Meech and Allen, *Book of Margery Kempe*, passim, esp. chap. 35, pp. 86–89.

5. See Life of Margaret of Faenza, chap. 2, par. 7 (xi), AASS August, vol. 5 (Paris, 1868), p. 849, and Petroff, *Consolation*, p. 62. For other examples, see Gertrude, *Oeuvres*, vol. 2: *Le Héraut*, bk. 2, chaps. 6, 16, pp. 256–58, 290–300; idem, *Legatus*, bk. 4, chap. 3, pp. 300–301; Angela of Foligno, ed. Ferré and Baudry, par. 154, pp. 332–34 (see also Pulignani and Humani ed., par. 245, pp. 386–88, and AASS January, vol. 1, pp. 205–6); and see Ferré and Baudry ed., par. 41, p. 64; Life of Mary of Oignies, passim, esp. bk. 2, chap. 7, par. 72, chap. 10, par. 91, AASS June, vol. 5, pp. 563, 567; Margaret of Oingt, Life of Beatrice of Ornacieux, in *Oeuvres de Marguerite*, pp. 119–21; *Töss*, pp. 36, 38–39, 45, 47, 87–88; and *Engelthal*, pp. 26–27, 31, 36, 39. The Life of Ida of Louvain, bk. 2, chap. 5, pars. 22–23, AASS April, vol. 2, p. 177, describes a vision, which lasted from the reading of the Epistle until the moment of elevation, in which Ida bathes the Christ child (with the help of Elizabeth, mother of John the Baptist), hugs him to her breast, and at first refuses to return him to Mary.

6. Thomas of Cantimpré, Life of Lutgard, bk. 1, chap. 1, par. 2, AASS June, vol. 4, pp. 191–92 (Christ shows the wound in his side to woo her away from a suitor); Life of Margaret of Ypres, ed. Meersseman, "Frères prêcheurs," pp. 107–9, 117–18, 120; and Margaret of Oingt, *Speculum*, in *Oeuvres de Marguerite*, pp. 98–99. See also Life of Lukardis of Oberweimar, AB 18, p. 324 (Christ, as a beautiful youth, breathes into her mouth); Life of Ida of Louvain, bk. 2, chap. 3, par. 11, AASS April, vol. 2, pp. 173–74 (Ida drinks a saving drink from Christ's naked chest); and "Unterlinden," pp. 442–44.

7. Talbot, *Life of Christina of Markyate*, pp. 116–19.

8. Meech and Allen, *Book of Margery Kempe*, chap. 36, p. 90; trans. Butler-Bowdon, *Book of Margery Kempe*, pp. 354–55.

9. Angela of Foligno, ed. Ferré and Baudry, par. 11, pp. 8–10: "Set in ista cognitione crucis dabatur michi tantus ignis, quod stando juxta crucem ex[s]poliavi me omnia vestimenta mea, et totam me optuli ei." (Cf. Pulignani and Humani ed., par. 12, p. 12, which treats the nudity more as a metaphor for renunciation of the world.)

10. Angela of Foligno, ed. Ferré and Baudry, par. 75, pp. 156–58 (cf. Pulignani and Humani ed., par. 75, pp. 132–34, and AASS January, vol. 1, p. 196); discussed by Petroff, *Consolation*, p. 68 (but on the basis of an inadequate text). Note that the desire is described as hunger. Other erotic passages in Angela include (Ferré and Baudry ed.) par. 36, pp. 54–56 (Christ gives her the ring of love); par. 41, pp. 64–66; and par. 45, pp. 78–80.

11. Umiltà, Analecta, chap. 1, par. 7, AASS May, vol. 5 (Paris, 1866), p. 216, trans. Petroff, *Consolation*, p. 143, and see also pp. 66–82.

12. Petroff (*Consolation*, pp. 66–75) makes this point nicely.

13. Browe, *Die Wunder*, pp. 110–11. On the question of women's attitudes toward body, see the perceptive discussion of Hildegard of Bingen in Dronke, WW, pp. 176–77. I do not quite agree that "Manichean" is the most useful description of Hildegard's discussion of sexuality, although she is more negative about body than many women writers. (Her description of sexual intercourse as the male pounding the female like a threshing floor and her clear sense of virginity as protection and even liberation suggest to me that she was less concerned with body as tainting and more concerned with male control as worldly control than Dronke suggests.) I agree, however, with Dronke in seeing many of Hildegard's attitudes toward body as "naturalistic."

14. Life of Alice, chap. 2, pars. 9–10, AASS June, vol. 2, pp. 473–74.

15. Life of Juliana, bk. 1, chap. 4, par. 18, AASS April, vol. 1, p. 449.

16. Margaret of Oingt, Letters, in *Oeuvres de Marguerite*, p. 139.

17. Ibid., p. 147.

18. Ibid., pp. 149–51.

19. See the discussion of her piety in ibid., pp. 164–66. For an unfortunately judgmental tone on the whole affective tradition, see Colledge and Walsh, introduction to Julian, *Book of Showings*, vol. 1, pp. 153, 159, 169, 172, 174, 185.

20. Although it is late in the day to join battle with an interpretation as old as Huizinga's and ungracious to quarrel with one of the great books of the twentieth century, I should point out that my interpretation runs counter to that presented in Johan Huizinga, *Waning*, where Huizinga sees something decadent about the fourteenth- and fifteenth-century proliferation of symbols and allegories and holds that increasingly the categories simply generated other categories without much regard for their referents in "reality." I see this piety as deeply experiential.

21. It should hardly be necessary to point out that in rejecting anachronistic categorizations of such piety I am neither advocating a return to medieval religiosity nor denying that some elements of this spirituality are deeply offensive to modern sensibilities (see below, Epilogue). We should, however, note that modern reactions, based in post-Freudian assumptions that "normal" sexuality is genital and oriented toward a human, adult, heterosexual object, make a more polymorphous sensuality oriented toward the divine by definition "abnormal." Simone Weil, in a modern defense of such "abnormal" sensibility, has written: "To reproach mystics with loving God by means of the faculty of sexual love is as though one were to reproach a painter with making pictures by means of colors composed of material substances. We haven't anything else with which to love. . . ." (*The Notebooks of Simone Weil*, 2 vols., trans. Arthur Wills [London: Routledge and Kegan Paul, 1956; repr. 1976], vol. 2, p. 472). And see above, chap. 5 n. 208.

22. For a particularly erotic use of eating metaphors see above, chap. 4 n. 107.

23. McDonnell, *Beguines*, p. 310.

24. Ibid., pp. 310, 315, 330, 415; Bolton, "*Vitae Matrum*," pp. 267–68; Moore, *European Dissent*, pp. 168–69. Heresy as the context within which thirteenth-century ideas of sanctity must be understood is one of the themes of Goodich, VP.

25. See, for example, James of Vitry, Life of Mary of Oignies, prologue and bk. 2, chaps. 7 and 9, pp. 547–50, 562–63, 565–66.

26. Life of Juliana, bk. 2, chap. 3, pp. 461–62.

27. See above, chap. 2 n. 138.

28. Some women were, after all, attracted to the Cathars and to antinomian or quietist mysticism, in part for reasons I characterized above as "the rejection of moderation." And one is struck by the coincidence that the feast of Corpus Christi, for which several devout women worked long years without success, was suddenly promulgated and preached with great enthusiasm in exactly those years around 1317 in which women's quasi-religious communities and antinomian mysticism (the "Free Spirit") were condemned.

29. The bibliography on Thomas Aquinas's philosophy is mammoth. On his theory of the person, the nonspecialist can consult Frederick C. Copleston, Aquinas (Harmondsworth: Penguin, 1955), or Anthony J. P. Kenny, Aquinas (New York: Hill and Wang, 1980), two very different approaches. On the increasingly positive sense of body in the later Middle Ages, see Bernstein, "Political Anatomy." On the sense of body in Francis of Assisi see the excellent discussion by Jaroslav Pelikan in *Jesus through the Centuries: His Place in the History of Culture* (New Haven: Yale University Press, 1985), pp. 133–44, esp. 138–39.

30. "Unterlinden," p. 352.

31. On the life of Beatrice, probably by Margaret, see above, chap. 4 nn. 101, 102. In Margaret's *Pagina meditationum*, pars. 56–58, in *Oeuvres de Marguerite*, p. 81, she says she is ready to suffer any pain or persecution for Christ—hanging, burning, becoming a leper, etc. (See also pp. 26–27.) For the remark about Christ's humanity, see Margaret, *Speculum*, in *Oeuvres de Marguerite*, p. 101. For a similar sense of the glory of matter, see Gherardesca of Pisa, who worshiped God's majesty in a piece of straw: Life of Gherardesca, chap. 7, par. 69, AASS May, vol. 7, pp. 175–76.

32. Mechtild of Hackeborn, *Liber specialis gratiae*, bk. 4, chap. 3, p. 260. In another vision, John the Evangelist told Mechtild that those who are married and own property are no further from Christ than those who renounce such things "because the Word is made flesh" (chap. 8, p. 265). In Bynum, JM, pp. 170–262 passim, I have stressed the extent to which the nuns of Helfta use regal and joyful images, avoiding the extravagant emphasis on suffering found in Low Country women of the thirteenth century and in fourteenth-century mystics generally, both male and female.

33. See Peter Brown, *The Cult of the Saints: Its Rise and Function in Latin Christianity* (Chicago: University of Chicago Press, 1981). For a fascinating discussion of the twelfth- and thirteenth-century practice of dividing up the dead body so that parts could be buried close to several saints, see Elizabeth A. R. Brown, "Death and the Human Body in the Later Middle Ages: The Legislation of Boniface VIII on the Division of the Corpse," *Viator* 12 (1981): 221–70. Brown comments: "The belief in the importance of the division of the body was rooted in a profound conviction of the significance of the material and an equally profound uncertainty regarding the nature of the hereafter. . . . The practice of division reveals a general unwillingness to admit that, after death, earthly ties with family and friends did not endure" (pp. 266–67).

34. Guibert of Nogent, *De pignoribus sanctorum*, PL 154, cols. 607–85. On Guibert's

fear of the body, see John F. Benton, introduction to *Self and Society in Medieval France: The Memoirs of Abbot Guibert of Nogent (1064?–c. 1125)* (New York: Harper and Row, 1970), pp. 7–33; and Georges Duby, *The Knight, the Lady and the Priest*, pp. 148–49.

35. Dumoutet, CD, pp. 51–100, esp. pp. 59–61, 88–96; E. Bertaud, "Dévotion eucharistique"; Finucane, *Miracles and Pilgrims*, pp. 197–98; Benedicta Ward, *Miracles and the Medieval Mind: Record and Event, 1000–1215* (Philadelphia: University of Pennsylvania Press, 1982), pp. 15–18; and Gary Macy, *The Theologies of the Eucharist in the Early Scholastic Period: A Study of the Salvific Function of the Sacrament according to the Theologians, c. 1080–c. 1220* (Oxford: Oxford University Press, 1984), pp. 87–95.

36. Adam of Eynsham, *Life of Hugh of Lincoln*, bk. 5, chap. 14, vol. 2, p. 170; and see Finucane, *Miracles and Pilgrims*, p. 28.

37. On the distinction between inner "compassion" and outward "imitation," which is at times paralleled by the distinction between *affectus* and *effectus*, see Martin Elze, "Das Verständnis der Passion Jesu im ausgehenden Mittelalter und bei Luther," in Heinz Liebing and Klaus Scholder, eds., *Geist und Geschichte der Reformation: Festgabe Hanns Rückert zum 65. Geburtstag dargebracht von Freunden, Kollegen und Schülern* (Berlin: de Gruyter, 1966), pp. 127–51; Kieckhefer, UnS, p. 105; and Bynum, JM, pp. 82–109. On changes in the notion of *imitatio* and exemplar between antiquity and the high Middle Ages, see P. Brown, "Saint as Exemplar."

38. Bernard of Clairvaux, *De gradibus humilitatis*, chap. 3, in OB, vol. 3, pp. 20–21.

39. Life of Elizabeth of Spalbeek, *Cat. cod. hag. Bruxellensis*, vol. 1, pt. 1, pp. 362–72. See also above, chap. 4 n. 33.

40. Robert actually suspended himself from a cross-shaped tree; see Life of Robert of Salentino, chap. 2, pars. 21–22, and chap. 6, par. 64 (54), AASS July, vol. 4 (Paris, 1868), pp. 499, 507.

41. Life of Margaret of Cortona, chap. 5, esp. pars. 130–31, AASS February, vol. 3, p. 330. Life of Lukardis, AB 18, p. 314; see also pp. 340–41.

42. Life of Margaret of Ypres, ed. Meersseman, "Frères prêcheurs," p. 108. For an instance in which self-mutilation is described as a "memory" of the Passion, see above, chap. 4 n. 104.

43. *Vita Beatricis*, pp. 138–39. The author also sees Beatrice as a model to be "imprinted" on her sisters (p. 185). And see Life of Ida of Louvain, bk. 1, chap. 3, pars. 13–17, pp. 162–63. Throughout the discussion the hagiographer emphasizes "non tam in memoria retinenda, quam in suo corpore perferenda."

44. See Kieckhefer, UnS, chap. 4.

45. Ludolf of Saxony, *Vita Jesu Christi* . . . , pt. 2, chap. 60, par. 3, vol. 4, p. 497. Ludolf says we must, first, learn that Christ suffered such indignity for us: second, we must imitate him by having patience in contumely; third, "quod consilia evangelica non semper oportet servare ad litteram, sed aliquando secundum animi praeparationem, et maxime ubi de hoc ex factis Christi et Sanctorum informationem habemus et auctoritatem. Ad conformandum se huic articulo, poterit homo sibi ipsi dare alapam moderatam ad repraesentandum alapam Christi, pro omnibus verbis suis otiosis, vel etiam pravis et mendosis." Ludolf holds generally that meditation on the events of Christ's life should lead one upward to contemplation. See Mary Immaculate Bodenstedt, *The "Vita Christi" of Ludolphus the Carthusian*, Catholic University of America Studies in Medieval and

Renaissance Latin Language and Literature 16 (Washington, D.C.: Catholic University of America Press, 1944), p. 116.

46. Life of Suso, chap. 31, in Suso, *Deutsche Schriften*, pp. 91–92; trans. Edward, *Exemplar*, pp. 87–88.

47. Caesarius, *Dialogus*, bk. 9, chap. 32, vol. 2, p. 189. And see above, chap. 2 n. 105. For Guerric of Igny's use of the metaphor of the soul as Christ's mother, see Bynum, JM, pp. 120–22.

48. See above, chap. 4 nn. 9, 150. In the Life of Ida of Louvain, pp. 164–65, Ida's "eating" of both communion and scripture is described as parallel to Mary's bearing Christ in her uterus. On Christina's dream, see Georg Wolfgang Karl Lochner, *Leben und Geschichte der Christina Ebnerin, Klosterfrau zu Engelthal* (Nürnberg: Schmid, 1872), pp. 15–16; and Kieckhefer, UnS, p. 156. Hadewijch, *Mengeldichten*, pp. 65–71, trans. Hart, *Hadewijch: Works*, pp. 345–49, works out an extended allegory of the soul pregnant with Christ.

49. Browe, *Die Wunder*, p. 30. Thurston, PP, pp. 159–60, cites an earlier miraculous tale on which this story was based.

50. Vauchez, *La Sainteté*, p. 408. We should note that a Franciscan friar who had been her confessor denounced the discovery as a fraud (ibid., p. 4).

51. Boeren, *Guiard de Laon*, pp. 320–27.

52. Catherine of Siena, Dialogue, ed. Cavallini, chaps. 110–11, pp. 265, 270–71; trans. Noffke, *Catherine: The Dialogue*, pp. 206, 210.

53. For this point *re* the Helfta nuns, see Bynum, JM, p. 191 n. 52.

54. See above, chap. 5 nn. 31–34.

55. Angela of Foligno, ed. Ferré and Baudry, par. 167, pp. 382–84; see also Pulignani and Humani ed., par. 192, pp. 314–16, and AASS January, vol. 1, par. 245, p. 231.

♦ 9. Woman as Body and as Food

1. From, respectively, Hildegard of Bingen, *Liber divinorum operum*, bk. 1, chap. 4, par. 100, PL 197, col. 885b–c; idem, *Liber vitae meritorum*, bk. 4, chap. 32, in J.-B. Pitra, ed., *Analecta sacra*, vol. 8: *Analecta sanctae Hildegardis opera spicilegio Solesmensi parata* (Monte Cassino, 1882; repr. Farnborough: Gregg Press, 1966), p. 158. See Barbara Jane Newman, "*O Feminea Forma*: God and Woman in the Works of St. Hildegard (1098–1179)," Ph.D. diss., Yale, 1981, passim, esp. p. 132. The interpretation in this chapter owes a great deal to Newman's splendid work, the implications of which extend far beyond Hildegard. See also the humane and perceptive interpretation of Hildegard in Dronke, WW, pp. 144–201, and in Elisabeth Gössmann, "Das Menschenbild der Hildegard von Bingen und Elisabeth von Schönau vor dem Hintergrund der frühscholastischen Anthropologie," in Dinzelbacher and Bauer, *Frauenmystik*, pp. 24–47.

2. See above, chap. 6 n. 121.

3. See above, chap. 6 n. 122.

4. See, for example, E. Friedberg, ed., *Corpus iuris canonici*, 2 vols. (Leipzig: Tauchnitz, 1879–1881), vol. 1, pt. 2, causa 33, q. 5, chaps. 12–17, cols. 1254–55; Thomas Aqui-

nas, ST, I, q. 92, arts. 1–2, vol. 13, pp. 34–41, and q. 93, art. 4, vol. 13, pp. 58–61. Theologians agreed that, as Aquinas puts it: "tam in viro quam in muliere invenitur Dei imago quantum ad id in quo principaliter ratio imaginis consistit, scilicet quantum ad intellectualem naturam" (p. 60).

5. On Gertrude the Great, see Bynum, JM, p. 194 n. 65. See also Margaret of Oingt, *Pagina meditationum*, in *Oeuvres de Marguerite*, p. 73, and idem, *Speculum*, in *Oeuvres de Marguerite*, p. 101; *Vie de Douceline*, p. 91 ("Ques es arma? *Speculum divine majestatis*; en la qual Dieus a pauzat son sagell"); and *Vita Beatricis*, pp. 71, 99–100, 110–11.

6. See Bynum, JM, p. 210.

7. Catherine of Siena, Dialogue, ed. Cavallini, chap. 167, p. 499; trans. Noffke, *Catherine: The Dialogue*, p. 365. See also Dialogue, chap. 1, p. 2, where Catherine writes that the soul, created in God's image and likeness and clothed with the "wedding garment of charity," becomes "another Christ," and chap. 13, p. 37, where Catherine writes: "We are your image, and now by making yourself one with us you have become our image, veiling your eternal divinity in the . . . dung heap of Adam" (trans. Noffke, *Catherine: The Dialogue*, p. 50).

8. Bullough, "Medical and Scientific Views," pp. 487–93; Wood, "Doctors' Dilemma"; John F. Benton, "Clio and Venus: An Historical View of Medieval Love," in F. X. Newman, ed., *The Meaning of Courtly Love* (Albany: State University of New York Press, 1969), p. 32; Joseph Needham, *A History of Embryology*, 2d ed. (Cambridge: Cambridge University Press, 1959), pp. 37–74; and Anthony Preus, "Galen's Criticism of Aristotle's Conception Theory," *Journal of the History of Biology* 10 (1977): 65–85. I have learned a great deal from reading the work in progress by Thomas Laqueur, *The Female Orgasm and the Body Politic*.

9. See above, chap. 6 n. 121. In a very influential article, Sherry Ortner ("Is Female to Male as Nature Is to Culture?" in Michelle Rosaldo and Louise Lamphere, eds., *Women, Culture and Society* [Stanford: Stanford University Press, 1974], pp. 67–87) has suggested that the identification of women with "the natural" or "the physical" exists cross-culturally; see below, chap. 10 at nn. 14, 15.

10. On this point, see P. Brown, *Virginity and Society*.

11. Weinstein and Bell, SS, passim, esp. pp. 235–36. For male writers who urged women to "maleness," see above, chap. 1 n. 68.

12. On this point, see Vauchez, *La Sainteté*, p. 445.

13. See above, chap. 3 at nn. 187, 194, 197, 198, 222, and below, p. 282.

14. See d'Alverny, "Comment les théologiens . . . voient la femme," pp. 122–24; Bynum, JM, pp. 91–94; and Gössmann, "Hildegard und Elisabeth," pp. 24–47.

15. On Catherine, see above, chap. 5 n. 171, and below, n. 16; on Mechtild, see Bynum, JM, p. 241. One of the points made by Peter Dronke about a number of writers is that a woman's use of the topos of female weakness can be an assertion of self, a slightly ironic yet totally serious claim of authorial originality, effectiveness, and accomplishment; see Dronke, WW, passim, esp. chap. 3.

16. Raymond of Capua, Life of Catherine of Siena, pt. 2, chap. 1, pars. 121–22, AASS April, vol. 3, p. 892; Catherine tells us that as a child she had been influenced by stories of the transvestite women saints and had thought male dress was necessary. It is important to contrast Catherine's own vision of a Christ who tells her that gender reversal is

not necessary with Raymond's vision of Catherine as male or as Christ himself, ibid., pt. 1, chap. 5, par. 90, p. 884. I have discussed this point in "Women's Stories, Women's Symbols."

17. Serge Hughes, "Notes on the Translation," in Hughes, *Catherine of Genoa: Purgation*, p. 49.

18. See above, chap. 8 n. 30.

19. F. W. E. Roth, ed., *Die Visionen der hl. Elisabeth und die Schriften der Aebte Ekbert und Emecho von Schönau* (Brünn: "Studien aus dem Benedictiner- und Cistercienser-Orden," 1884), p. 60. See also Gössman, "Hildegard und Elisabeth," pp. 41–42.

20. See Hildegard, *Scivias*, pt. 1, vision 2, chaps. 11–12, vol. 1, pp. 19–21; pt. 2, vision 3, chap. 22, vol. 1, pp. 147–48; pt. 2, vision 6, chaps. 76–77, vol. 1, pp. 290–91; and esp. Gössmann, "Hildegard und Elisabeth," pp. 35–36.

21. See Hildegard, *Scivias*, pt. 2, vision 6, vol. 1, pp. 225–306, esp. p. 231. For the context of Hildegard's idea of *ecclesia-Eva-Maria*, see Schiller, *Ikonographie*, vol. 4, pt. 1: *Die Kirche*; B. Newman, "*O Feminea Forma*"; and Dronke, WW, pp. 169–171. For problems with the Corpus christianorum text of the *Scivias*, see Peter Dronke, "Problemata Hildegardiana," *Mittellateinisches Jahrbuch* 16 (1981): 95–131.

22. See above, n. 8.

23. For this interpretation of Mechtild, see Bynum, JM, pp. 229, 233–34, 244.

24. For example, see above, chap. 5 nn. 126, 136.

25. Catherine of Siena, Letter 30, Letters, ed. Misciattelli, vol. 1, p. 137. See also Letter 144, ibid., vol. 2, pp. 341–42.

26. Margaret of Oingt, *Speculum*, in *Oeuvres de Marguerite*, pp. 98–99. And see B. Newman, "*O Feminea Forma*," pp. 131–34.

27. See Dronke, WW, p. 214. Dronke's discussion of the female heretics (pp. 202–15) is superb.

28. A great deal has been written about Julian recently; by far the best study is Brant Pelphrey, *Love Was His Meaning: The Theology and Mysticism of Julian of Norwich*, Salzburg Studies in English Literature, Elizabethan and Renaissance Studies 92.4 (Salzburg: Institut für Anglistik und Amerikanistik, Universität Salzburg, 1982).

29. See Ritamary Bradley, "The Motherhood Theme in Julian of Norwich," *Fourteenth-Century English Mystics Newsletter* 2.4 (1976): 25–30; E. McLaughlin, " 'Christ My Mother' "; Colledge and Walsh, introduction to Julian, *Book of Showings*; Kari Elizabeth Børresen, "Christ notre Mère, la théologie de Julienne de Norwich," *Mitteilungen und Forschungsbeiträge der Cusanus-Gesellschaft* 13 (1978): 320–29; Bynum, JM, chap. 4; and Paula S. D. Barker, "The Motherhood of God in Julian of Norwich's Theology," *Downside Review* 100 (1982): 290–304.

30. Julian, *Book of Showings*, ed. Colledge and Walsh, The Long Text, chap. 58, revelation 14; pt. 2, pp. 585–86; trans. Colledge and Walsh, *Julian of Norwich: Showings*, p. 294.

31. *Book of Showings*, ed. Colledge and Walsh, The Long Text, chap. 57, revelation 14; pt. 2, pp. 579–80; trans. Colledge and Walsh, *Julian of Norwich: Showings*, p. 292.

32. See Bynum, JM, chap. 4, and idem," '. . . And Woman His Humanity': Female Imagery in the Religious Writing of the Later Middle Ages," in C. Bynum, S. Harrell,

and P. Richman, eds., *Gender and Religion: On the Complexity of Symbols* (Boston: Beacon Press, 1986).

33. Robert Grosseteste, Letter 57, *Epistolae*, ed. Henry Richard Luard, Rerum Britannicarum medii aevi scriptores or Chronicles and Memorials . . . 25 (London: Longman, Green, Longman, and Roberts, 1861), p. 178; quoted in Bridgett, *History of the Holy Eucharist*, vol. 2, p. 171.

34. Ruysbroeck, *Spiritual Espousals*, p. 43. Cf. idem, "Le Miroir du salut éternel," chap. 7, in *Oeuvres*, vol. 3, pp. 82–83.

35. For a male writer who sees humanity as Eve, see Juliana of Cornillon's hagiographer, bk. 1, chap. 5, par. 22, AASS April, vol. 1, p. 450, and see below, chap. 10 n. 17.

36. See above, chap. 2 at nn. 56–60, and plate 6.

37. See Barbara G. Lane, *The Altar and the Altarpiece: Sacramental Themes in Early Netherlandish Painting* (New York: Harper and Row, 1984), pp. 12–35, esp. pp. 27–28; see also Christoph Baumer, "Die Schreinmadonna," *Marian Library Studies* 9 (1977): 239–72.

38. See above, chap. 3 n. 58.

39. Francis of Assisi, *Opuscula*, p. 123; trans. Fahy, *Omnibus*, pp. 135–36.

40. Henry Suso, *Büchlein*, chap. 16, in Suso, *Deutsche Schriften*, p. 264: "einen schrin, in dem die Ewig Wisheit sûzelich gerûwet hat." For other literary texts treating Mary as a vessel containing Christ, see Lane, *Altar and Altarpiece*, pp. 27–32.

41. Bernard of Clairvaux, Sermon 3 on the Purification of Mary, par. 2, PL 183, col. 370c; quoted in Lane, *Altar and Altarpiece*, p. 71. The notion of Mary as the place where the enfleshing of Christ happens suggests that Mary may be a symbol of priesthood—a highly controversial idea but one that finds some iconographic support; see pp. 68–72. In plate 47, p. 72, Lane gives a French panel of 1437 (now at the Louvre) that depicts Mary in priestly garb. It should be emphasized that this theme has nothing to do with claiming sacerdotal office for women. Another iconographic motif that suggests Mary as celebrant (because she is the vessel, the place, of Incarnation) is the Mystical Mill; see above chap. 2 n. 152, and plate 1. See also Carol J. Purtle, *The Marian Paintings of Jan van Eyck* (Princeton: Princeton University Press, 1982), passim, esp. pp. 13–15, 27–29.

42. See above, chap. 2 at n. 105, for a fuller quotation.

43. Much more work needs to be done on devotion to the Virgin in the later Middle Ages. The emphasis of Marina Warner, *Alone of All Her Sex*, on Mary as primarily representative woman and model for women seems wrong. For an interpretation that agrees with my own, see Tore Nyberg, "Birgitta von Schweden—Die aktive Gottesschau," in Dinzelbacher and Bauer, *Frauenmystik*, p. 283.

44. Roisin, *L'Hagiographie*, pp. 108, 111–13.

45. According to the tables in Weinstein and Bell, SS, pp. 123–37, women (who were about 18 percent of those canonized) account for about half of the saints who were especially devoted to Jesus but only about a third of the saints especially characterized by devotion to Mary. Women are, by this index, somewhat more devoted to Mary than are men, but this fact does not necessarily reflect a female need for female saints (although it may). See above, chap. 1 n. 57.

46. *Vie de Douceline,* passim, esp. pp. 19 and 43. Margaret of Oingt identifies with both Christ and his mother; see *Pagina meditationum* in *Oeuvres de Marguerite,* passim, esp. p. 77. For devotion to Mary in Italian women saints, see Petroff, *Consolation,* pp. 59–66.

47. For Thomas of Celano's notion of Clare as a model for women, see above, chap. 1 n. 68. Similarly, the author of the Life of Beatrice of Nazareth sees Beatrice as a model for her sisters; see above, chap. 8 n. 43. Women writers tended to assume that saints of both genders were models for both genders; see Mechtild of Magdeburg, *Licht,* bk. 5, chap. 34, pp. 166–67, who associates various male and female saints with various religious statuses. And see below, chap. 10 n. 22.

48. Indeed, as Catherine of Siena makes perfectly clear, in suffering with Mary we are suffering with Christ, for the humanity Mary bears is Christ's; see the passage quoted at n. 25 above. See also above, chap. 7 n. 21, where Jane Mary of Maillé, receiving a vision of the Virgin upon the death of her own mother, becomes devoted for life to the Passion of Christ.

49. Børresen, "Christ notre Mère," points out that neither nuptial mysticism nor devotion to Mary is central to Julian; Colledge and Walsh, introduction in *Book of Showings,* ed. Colledge and Walsh, pt. 1, p. 155, suggest the same conclusion when they comment perceptively that Marian commentaries on the Song of Songs in the later Middle Ages probably competed with rather than enhanced a theology of God's motherhood. For an interpretation of Hadewijch that sees Mary as pivotal in her visions, see C. Hart, introduction to *Hadewijch: Works,* pp. 27–28, 38–39.

50. Adolphe de Ceuleneer, "La Charité romaine dans la littérature et dans l'art," *Annales de l'Académie Royale d'archéologie de Belgique* 67 (Antwerp, 1919), pp. 175–206.

51. P. V. Bétérous, "A propos d'une des légendes mariales les plus répandues: le 'lait de la Vierge,'" *Bullétin de l'Association Guillaume Budé* 4 (1975): 403–11.

52. For representations of Charity distributing bread or a cup, see Adolf Katzenellenbogen, *Allegories of the Virtues and Vices in Medieval Art* (1939; repr. with new bibliographical references, New York: Norton, 1964), p. 48 n. 2, p. 56, and figure 53.

53. Schiller, *Ikonographie,* vol. 4, pt. 1: *Die Kirche,* pp. 84–89, 276–78.

54. Veith, *Hysteria,* pp. 65–71.

55. See Bynum, JM, chap. 4; and Bynum, "'. . . And Woman His Humanity.'"

56. On Suso, see above, chap. 3 n. 201. On Bernard, see E. Vacandard, *Vie de saint Bernard abbé de Clairvaux,* 2 vols. (1895; repr. Paris: Librairie Victor Lecoffre, 1920), vol. 2, p. 78; Dewez and van Iterson, "La Lactation"; and, for the iconography, Rafael M. Durán, *Iconografiá española de San Bernardo* (Monasterio de Poblet, 1953), passim. Alanus de Rupe or Alan de la Roche (d. 1475), founder of modern rosary devotion, tells a similar story of himself in his Revelations: "Post multa divina colloquia, Virgo Lacte suo purissimo lethalia daemonum vulnera plurima perfudit et mox integerrime consanavit" (quoted in Heribert Holzapfel, *St. Dominikus und der Rosenkranz* [Munich: Lentnerische Buchhandlung, 1903], p. 21). Vincent of Beauvais, *Speculum historiale,* bk. 7, chap. 84 (Venice, 1494), fol. 80r, tells of a sick cleric who nursed from the Virgin. See also Alb. Poncelet, "Index miraculorum B. V. Mariae quae saec. VI–XV latine conscripta sunt," AB 21 (1902), p. 359, which lists four stories (numbers 184, 461, 514, and 667) of sick men healed by the Virgin's milk. By the seventeenth century, lactation legends were

attached as well to Dominic (d. 1221), founder of the Dominicans, and to Peter Nolasco (d. ca. 1256), one of the founders of the Mercedarians.

57. The most important biblical roots are Song of Songs 1:2, 1 Cor. 3:1–2, Heb. 5:12, and 1 Peter 2:2. See also Isa. 49:1, 49:15, and 66:11–13, Ecclus. 24:24–26, and Matt. 23:37.

58. M. McLaughlin, "Survivors and Surrogates," pp. 115–18; and Michael Goodich, "Batholomaeus Anglicus," p. 80.

59. Clement of Alexandria, *Paedagogus*, bk. 1, chap. 6, Otto Stählin, ed., *Clemens Alexandrinus*, 2 vols., Die griechischen christlichen Schriftsteller der ersten drei Jahrhunderte 12 and 15 (Leipzig: Hinrichs, 1936–1939), vol. 1, pp. 104–21.

60. See Bynum, JM, pp. 151–54.

61. Mechtild of Magdeburg, *Licht*, bk. 1, chap. 22, and bk. 2, chap. 3, pp. 11–13, 29–30, treats Mary and Christ as parallel figures, each nursing the soul (with milk and blood, respectively). In bk. 1, chap. 44, p. 21, she treats Mary's succor as a lower kind of nurture. In bk. 5, chap. 8, p. 136, Mechtild speaks of herself as mother to souls in purgatory and says: "I must give them my heart's blood to drink. If I pray for them because of their great need and see the bitter fate they must suffer for every sin, then I suffer as a mother" (trans. Menzies, *Light*, p. 133).

62. See also Julian, *Book of Showings*, ed. Colledge and Walsh, The Long Text, chap. 60, revelation 14; pt. 2, pp. 596–98: "The moder may geue her chylde sucke hyr mylke, but oure precyous moder Jhesu, he may fede vs with hym selfe, and doth full curtesly and full tendyrly with the blessyd sacrament. . . . The moder may ley hyr chylde tenderly to hyr brest, but oure tender mother Jhesu, he may homely lede vs in to his blessyd brest by his swet opyn syde."

63. E. James Mundy, "Gerard David's *Rest on the Flight into Egypt*: Further Additions to Grape Symbolism," *Simiolus: Netherlands Quarterly for the History of Art* 12.4 (1981–1982): 211–22; and Lane, *Altar and Altarpiece*, passim, esp. pp. 21–23.

64. Lane, *Altar and Altarpiece*, p. 6. See also her discussion of the Campin Madonna, pp. 2–8 (plate 14 above). And see Carra Ferguson O'Meara, "'In the Hearth of the Virginal Womb': The Iconography of the Holocaust in Late Medieval Art," *Art Bulletin* 63.1 (1981): 75–88; and Purtle, *Marian Paintings*, pp. 98–126.

65. Gougaud, DAP, pp. 104–10. The study of the iconographic tradition of a female Christ by Rudolph Berliner, "God Is Love," in E. Gombrich, J. S. Held, and O. Kurz, eds., *Essays in Honor of Hans Tietze 1880–1954* (Paris: Gazette des Beaux-Arts, 1958), pp. 143–60, does not, unfortunately, contribute anything new to the question.

66. On Quirizio, see Luigi Coletti, *Pittura Veneta del Quattrocento* (Novara: Istituto Geografico De Agostini, 1953), pp. xlvii–xlix, 100–101; Sandra Moschini Marconi, ed., *Gallerie dell' Accademia, Opere d'Arte dei Secoli XIV e XV* (Rome: Istituto Poligrafico dello Stato, Libreria dello Stato, 1955), p. 148; Laudedeo Testi, *La Storia della Pittura Veneziana*, pt. 2: *Il Divenire* (Bergamo: Istituto Italiano d'Arti Grafiche, 1915), pp. 521–24; and Gougaud, DAP, pp. 104–10.

67. On this theme see Schiller, *Iconography*, vol. 2: *Passion*, pp. 205–6. And see above, chap. 3 at n. 61, and esp. plate 5, where a kneeling nun receives Christ's blood from the winepress. See also Katzenellenbogen, *Virtues and Vices*, figure 41.

68. For the passage see above, chap. 4 n. 184.

69. See Barbara Lane, "The 'Symbolic Crucifixion' in the Hours of Catherine of

Cleves," *Oud-Holland* 86 (1973): 4–26, esp. pp. 10–11; idem, *Altar and Altarpiece*, pp. 7–8.

70. See Max J. Friedländer, *Early Netherlandish Painting*, vol. 9, pt. 2, trans. H. Norden with notes by H. Pauwels and M. Gierts (Leyden: Sijthoff, 1973), plate 156. For another example, see Schiller, *Iconography*, vol. 2: *Passion*, p. 225 and plate 802. In this painting of 1508 by Hans Holbein the Elder, the theme of intercession is represented in words as well as pictures. Above Christ as the Man of Sorrows is written: "Father, see my red wounds, help men in their need, through my bitter death." And above Mary: "Lord, sheathe thy sword that thou has drawn, and see my breast, where the Son has sucked." Other examples can be found in Richard C. Trexler, *Public Life in Renaissance Florence*, Studies in Social Discontinuity (New York: Academic Press, 1980), plate 8, p. 26, and in the Hereford Mappa Mundi; see A. L. Moir and Malcolm Letts, *The World Map in Hereford Cathedral and the Pictures in the Hereford Mappa Mundi* (7th ed. Hereford: The Cathedral, 1975), pp. 11, 19.

71. Dewez and van Iterson, "La Lactation." Plate 30 is a triptych made for abbot Antonius Tsgrooten of Tongerloo by Goswyn van der Weyden and authenticated by a document of 1507; see Friedländer, *Early Netherlandish Painting*, vol. 11, p. 107, and A. Monballieu, "Het Antonius Tsgrooten-triptiekje (1507) uit Tongerloo van Goossen van der Weyden," *Jaarboek van het Koninklijk Museum voor Schone Kunsten Antwerpen* (1967): 13–36.

72. Life of Margaret of Faenza, chap. 3, par. 15 (xx), AASS August, vol. 5, p. 851: "et, his dictis, Christus amplexatus est eam, et sibi dedit osculum pacis, ubi tantae suavitatis saporem gustavit, ut putaret se beatitudinis seculum commutasse." For other examples of such kisses, see Petroff, *Consolation*, pp. 70–73.

73. Life of Benevenuta, chap. 10, par. 82, AASS Oct., vol. 13, p. 172.

74. See above, chap. 6, nn. 85–89.

75. Walburga supposedly cured "food disorders," and details of her cult are borrowed from an earlier fertility goddess. Agnes of Montepulciano miraculously multiplied food, practiced extended abstinence, and was blessed by marvelous rains of manna from heaven. Even the great male myroblyte Nicholas of Myra is said to have fasted as a baby by regularly refusing the breast and is revered as the patron saint of children. Douceline of Marseilles, who was not in fact a myroblyte, nonetheless displayed extraordinary emanations while alive (coupled with an extraordinary concern for avoiding bodily contact). And a countess who admired Douceline dreamed of oil flowing from her. See Carozzi, "Douceline," and *Vie de Douceline*, p. 131. On Mary Magdalen de' Pazzi, miraculous abstainer and myroblyte who died in 1607, see Weinstein and Bell, SS, p. 235, and Bell, *Holy Anorexia*, pp. 171–75.

76. It is striking to note that not only did hosts and bodily relics ooze oil, blood, or milk as signs of their sacrality, other devotional objects did so as well. The nail Alda of Siena had carved to aid her meditations oozed sap three hundred years later; see above, chap. 4 n. 212. When Jane Mary of Maillé had a relic of the true cross cut in two, blood flowed out; Process of canonization, chap. 3, par. 24, AASS March, vol. 3, p. 749.

77. The process of becoming God by eating God that I discuss here is, of course, a sort of cannibalism, and it is worth noting that anthropological studies of cannibalism regularly stress it as a way of incorporating the power of what is eaten. Peggy Reeves

Sanday (*Divine Hunger*) shows that in many cultures there is a connection between cannibalism and the use of the female body as symbol. Her analysis indicates that there may be an intrinsic connection between the coming to the fore of female bodily images for Christ in the later Middle Ages and the greater emphasis in the same period on the cannibalistic aspects of the mass.

78. Petroff, *Consolation*, seems to me to have gone too far in this direction.

79. See the warning of Natalie Z. Davis, "Anthropology and History in the 1980s," *Journal of Interdisciplinary History* 12.2 (1981): 267–75.

◆ 10. Women's Symbols

1. Margaret Porete, "'Miroir,'" ed. Guarnieri, chap. 117, pp. 608–9; trans. Dronke, WW, pp. 221–22. On the historical background of the text, the author, and the translations of the text, see Kurt Ruh, "*Le Miroir des Simples Ames* der Marguerite Porete," *Verbum et Signum* 2 (1975): 365–87.

2. "In Dio è il mio essere, il mio ME," *Vita*, chap. 15, Catherine of Genoa, *Edizione Critica*, ed. Umile Bonzi, p. 171. See also D.C. Nugent, "The Annihilation of St. Catherine of Genoa," *Mystics Quarterly* 10.4 (1984): 185.

3. See below, n. 23.

4. See above, chap. 9 n. 41.

5. See above, chap. 7 n. 28.

6. See Davis, "Anthropology and History"; idem, *Society and Culture*, pp. 97–151. For what follows, see also Bynum, "Women's Stories, Women's Symbols."

7. Such a reversal is clearly reflected in the story, told in chap. 33 of the *Little Flowers of St. Francis*, of the pope commanding Clare to bless bread in his presence (Casolini, *I Fioretti*, pp. 133–34). Clare refused, saying a "vile woman" should not bless bread in the presence of the pope, but the pope insisted; upon Clare's act, crosses appeared on the loaves. Although some manuscripts interpolate this story into the Life of Clare (see AASS August, vol. 2 [Paris, 1867], p. 763), there is no evidence that it is early or emanates from Clare herself.

8. Letter 116, from abbess T[engswindis] to Hildegard, PL 197, col. 336c. On this, see Dronke, WW, pp. 165–71. An obvious parallel exists between renouncing marriage in order to become a "bride of Christ" and renouncing food in order to eat God.

9. See above, chap. 3 n. 48. We should also note that women often carried the maternal roles of secular society over into the liturgy, using life-sized dolls and cradles in their Christmas worship; see Elisabeth Vavra, "Bildmotiv und Frauenmystik—Funktion und Rezeption," in Dinzelbacher and Bauer, *Frauenmystik*, pp. 201–30, esp. the reproductions on pp. 212, 213, 215.

10. On this point, see Bynum, "The Complexity of Symbols," in Bynum et al., *Gender and Religion*, and Stephen N. Dunning, "History and Phenomenology: Dialectical Structure in Ricoeur's *The Symbolism of Evil*," *Harvard Theological Review* 76.3 (1983): 1–21.

11. Guerric of Igny, Second Sermon for SS Peter and Paul, chap. 2, in *Sermons*, vol. 2, ed. J. Morson and H. Costello, SC 202, Sér. mon. 43 (1973), p. 384; trans. the monks

of Mount St. Bernard Abbey, in Guerric of Igny, *Liturgical Sermons*, vol. 1, Cistercian Fathers Series 32 (Spencer, Mass.: Cistercian Publications, 1971), p. 155. See also Bynum, JM, p. 122.

12. See above, chap. 3 n. 188. It is worth noting that the only passage in which Hadewijch employs a clear distinction between *father* as an image of authority and discipline and *mother* as an image of nurture and affection is one that borrows the dichotomy in question from a male author, William of St. Thierry. See above, chap. 5 n. 18.

13. I have demonstrated this in twelfth-century Cistercian writing in Bynum, JM, chap. 4. I have suggested that the pattern extends into the thirteenth and fourteenth centuries in "'. . . And Woman His Humanity.'" Some of the evidence given above, chap. 3, pp. 94–112, further supports the generalization.

14. Ortner, "Female to Male." For a somewhat similar argument, see Edwin Ardener, "Belief and the Problem of Women," and "The Problem Revisited," in Shirley Ardener, ed., *Perceiving Women* (New York: Wiley, 1975), pp. 1–28. See also Michelle Rosaldo, introduction and "Women, Culture and Society: A Theoretical Overview," in Rosaldo and Lamphere, *Women, Culture and Society*, pp. 1–42; and Eric Wolf, "Society and Symbols in Latin Europe and in the Islamic Near East," *Anthropological Quarterly* 42 (July 1968): 287–301.

15. See Eleanor Leacock and June Nash, "Ideologies of Sex: Archetypes and Stereotypes," *Issues in Cross-Cultural Research*, Annals of the New York Academy of Sciences 285 (New York: New York Academy of Sciences, 1977), pp. 618–45; Carol P. MacCormack and M. Strathern, eds., *Nature, Culture and Gender* (Cambridge: Cambridge University Press, 1980); and Judith Shapiro, "Anthropology and the Study of Gender," *Soundings* 64.4 (1981): 446–65. Ortner has attempted to deal with some of this criticism in Sherry Ortner and Harriet Whitehead, introduction to Ortner and Whitehead, eds., *Sexual Meanings: The Cultural Construction of Gender and Sexuality* (Cambridge: Cambridge University Press, 1981), pp. 1–27; see esp. preface, p. x. See also Bynum, "Complexity of Symbols."

16. See above, pp. 22–23, 229–30, chap. 4 n. 65, and chap. 7 n. 29; and Vauchez, *La Sainteté*, pp. 439–41. Thomas of Cantimpré's Life of Lutgard is a particularly good example of male recourse to visionary women. Thomas repeatedly describes Lutgard as "mother" and "nurse" to himself, to secular men, and to friars (AASS June, vol. 4, pp. 202–3, 205, 207). He reports that Lutgard, a frequent recipient of visions, enables a priest to have a vision by praying that he be granted one (p. 202). He also reports that a certain man brought to Lutgard by the abbot of Afflighem was struck with horror at his sin when he looked into her face "as if into the face of God's majesty" (p. 201).

17. See Helinand of Froidmont, Sermon 27, PL 212, col. 622b. See also Sermon 20, cols. 646–52, and Helinand of Froidmont, *Epistola ad Galterum*, col. 753b. For other male writers who use *woman* to mean physically or morally weak, see Bynum, JM, pp. 148–49, and Duby, *The Knight, the Lady and the Priest*, passim, esp. pp. 22, 45–46.

18. Francis of Assisi, "Letter to All the Faithful," *Opuscula*, pp. 93–94; trans. Fahy, *Omnibus*, p. 96, with my changes. The concern for giving birth to others by example is typically Franciscan; see Bynum, JM, pp. 105–6.

19. Francis of Assisi, "Religious Life in Hermitages," *Opuscula*, pp. 83–84; trans.

Fahy, *Omnibus*, pp. 71–72. Francis repeatedly refers to the love of friars for each other as maternal. See, for example, Rule of 1221, chap. 9: "Begging alms," in *Opuscula*, p. 38: "Et quilibet diligat et nutriat fratrem suum, sicut mater diligit et nutrit filium suum."

20. See above, chap. 3 nn. 197, 200, and chap. 9 n. 34.

21. See Vauchez, *La Sainteté*, p. 446 n. 511; and Eckhart, Sermon 2, in *Meister Eckhart: The Essential Sermons, Commentaries, Treatises, and Defense*, trans. Edmund Colledge and Bernard McGinn (New York: Paulist Press, 1981), pp. 177–79.

22. Tauler, Sermon 9 for Second Sunday in Lent, in Tauler, *Die Predigten*, pp. 40–46. For a lengthy quotation of this passage, see above, chap. 7 n. 86. Men also took female saints as models of penitence; see Acta alia, chap. 2, of John of Alverna, AASS August, vol. 2 (Paris, 1867), pp. 471–72, where John is seen as another Magdalen.

23. Cardman, "Women and Orders"; J. Rézette, "Le Sacerdoce et la femme chez saint Bonaventure," *Antonianum* 51 (1976): 520–27.

24. See above, chap. 8 n. 47 and chap. 2 n. 105.

25. See Weinstein and Bell, SS, pp. 114–19; see also Giovanni Battista Proja, "Colombini, Giovanni, da Siena," BS, vol. 4, cols. 122–23.

26. See, for example, Victor and Edith Turner, *Image and Pilgrimage*, pp. 161, 199.

27. Georges Duby, *The Three Orders: Feudal Society Imagined*, trans. Goldhammer (Chicago: University of Chicago Press, 1980), pp. 89, 95, 131–33, 145, 209.

28. For example, when Francis of Assisi in chap. 23 of his Rule of 1221 lists "everyone" who should persevere in faith and penance, he writes as follows: "We beseech . . . all those who serve our Lord and God within the holy, catholic, and apostolic Church, together with the whole hierarchy, priests, deacons, subdeacons, acolytes, exorcists, lectors, porters, and all clerics and religious, male or female; we beg all children, big or small, the poor and needy, kings and princes, labourers and farmers, servants and masters; we beg all virgins and all other women, married or unmarried; we beg all lay folk, men and women, infants and adolescents, young and old, the healthy and the sick, the little and the great, all people, tribes, families, and languages, all nations and all men everywhere, present and to come" (*Opuscula*, pp. 59–60; trans. Fahy, *Omnibus*, p. 51). Although it is sometimes unclear how generic the categories are, it *is* clear that all religious women are lumped into the category "religious," that the statuses that reflect occupations are male (kings, princes, laborers, farmers, masters, possibly even servants), that women are categorized by sexual or marital status whereas men are not, and that only "lay folk" includes male and female equally.

29. Nancy Chodorow, *The Reproduction of Mothering: Psychoanalysis and the Sociology of Gender* (Berkeley and Los Angeles: University of California Press, 1978). See also Carol Gilligan, *In a Different Voice: Psychological Theory and Women's Development* (Cambridge, Mass.: Harvard University Press, 1982), chaps. 1, 2, 6. Chodorow's theories have been creatively applied to women saints in India in A. K. Ramanujan, "On Women Saints," J. Hawley and D. M. Wulff, eds., *The Divine Consort: Rādhā and the Goddesses of India* (Berkeley: Berkeley Religious Studies Series, 1982), pp. 316–24. For a different version of this argument, found in the research of John and Beatrice Whiting, see Sanday, *Female Power and Male Dominance*, pp. 182–85. There has been much criticism of the essentialist overtones of Gilligan's work, however. See Judy Auerbach et al., "Commentary on Gilligan's *In a Different Voice*," *Feminist Studies* 11.1 (Spring 1985): 149–61;

Debra Nails et al., eds., *Women and Morality*, special issue of *Social Research* 50.3 (Autumn 1983); Joan W. Scott, "Is Gender a Useful Category of Historical Analysis?" *American Historical Review* (forthcoming).

30. For New Testament passages that require reversal, see, among others, 1 Cor. 1:20 ("Hath not God made foolish the wisdom of this world?") and Mark 10:31 ("But many that are first shall be last").

31. See above, chap. 1 n. 68. For secular histories by male authors that depict virtuous women as "virile," see Duby, *The Knight, the Lady and the Priest*, pp. 234–35. Even male biographers do not always see the spiritual progress of women as increasing "virility"; the hagiographer of Umiltà of Faenza says (chap. 1, par. 5, AASS May, vol. 5, p. 208), that after her conversion she was transformed into "another woman."

32. Anson, "Female Transvestite." See also Vern Bullough, "Transvestites in the Middle Ages," *American Journal of Sociology* 79 (1974): 1381–94.

33. See above, chap. 3 nn. 85, 204, and chap. 1 n. 68. Needless to say, women writers did not generalize about the nature of "man" (used non-generically), although they did both revere and castigate the clergy as a group; see above, chap. 7 at n. 56.

34. Iconographic evidence supports this point, but ambiguously. Of the four plates above that (perhaps) illustrate women's visions (whether or not they were painted by women), all depict woman as recipient: Colette's vision (plate 11c); Hildegard's vision of woman as *humanitas* (plate 12); the picture of Christ with charity, which may represent a vision received by Gertrude of Helfta (plate 26); and Quirizio's depiction of Christ feeding a nun, which Gougaud felt must represent a woman's vision (plate 25, and see above, chap. 9 n. 65). Even here, however, the emphasis on woman's receiving undoubtedly arises more from her status as lay (as opposed to clerical) than from any reversal of her social role as cook.

35. See above at n. 10. Although French feminist writing has been determinedly atheistical and some French feminists will no doubt reject the subject of this book as uninteresting, what I suggest about the continuity of woman's sense of self into her symbolic language in medieval texts could be explained very much as Luce Irigaray has explained present feminist discourse in "The Sex Which Is Not One," trans. Claudia Reeder, in Elaine Marks and Isabelle de Courtivron, eds., *New French Feminisms: An Anthology* (Amherst: University of Massachusetts Press, 1980), pp. 99–106.

36. Von Hügel, *Mystical Element*, vol. 1, p. 238; see also Nugent, "Annihilation of Catherine of Genoa," p. 185. On paradox in Beatrice of Nazareth, see above, chap. 5 n. 55.

37. Brant Pelphrey, *Love Was His Meaning*. This reading of Julian makes her *Showings* a more conceptually and theologically subtle statement of the kind of "continuity of self" I find in other women's writing from the period. On this point see also Susan Dickman, "Devout Imagination."

38. See Dronke, WW, p. x. For further comments on the significance of Dronke's observations, see my review of his book in *Modern Language Quarterly* (forthcoming).

39. But Francis, of course, achieves such an emphasis on his self as human through a series of extravagant reversals, seeing himself as poor, naked, female, leprous, etc.

40. Julian, *Book of Showings*, ed. Colledge and Walsh, The Long Text, chap. 5, revelation 1; pt. 2, p. 299.

41. The French feminist Julia Kristeva, in a brilliant discussion of women's discourse, suggests that women's language "traverses"—it expresses process—whereas man's bifurcates and opposes. She also writes of woman's movement beyond "I" in language—her sense of self as a "subject-in-the-making"—in ways that echo Catherine of Genoa's rejection of the "I" (for very different reasons). See interview with Kristeva by Xavière Gauthier, "Oscillation du 'pouvoir' au 'refus,'" trans. Marilyn August, in Marks and de Courtivron, *New French Feminisms*, pp. 165–67.

42. Jo Ann McNamara, "Sexual Equality"; Ruether, "Misogyny"; Marie Delcourt, "Le Complexe de Diane dans l'hagiographie chrétienne," *Revue de l'histoire des religions* 153 (1958): 1–33; and Warner, *Joan of Arc*. For a sensitive criticism of the approach of these articles, see Evelyne Patlagean, "L'Histoire de la femme déguisée en moine et l'évolution de la sainteté féminine à Byzance," *Studi medievali*, 3rd ser., 17, fasc. 2 (1976): 597–623. Both Delcourt and Patlagean contain references to the important early work by Usener and Delehaye on transvestite saints.

43. Bullough, "Transvestites." John Boswell, *Christianity and Homosexuality*, has little to say about cross-dressing. The fifth-century translator of Soranus, Caelius Aurelianus, sees male cross-dressing as a sign of homosexuality; see Helen R. Lemay, "William of Saliceto on Human Sexuality," *Viator* 12 (1981): 179.

44. Caesarius of Heisterbach tells a few such stories from the late twelfth century, but they are imitated from patristic tales. See Caesarius, *Dialogus*, Distinctio 1, chaps. 40–43, vol. 1, pp. 47–54. For three other examples, see Goodich, "Contours of Female Piety," p. 25, and Matthew Paris, *Historia major*, for the year 1225, pp. 325–27 (adapted from the chronicle of Roger of Wendover). Other examples are Christina of Markyate, who escaped her family in male garb, and Margery Kempe, who wore male clothes on pilgrimage. The girl described by Matthew Paris, who took refuge with the friars, used the opportunity provided by male clothing to preach: "et Evangelium pacis per civitates et castella, et praecipue sexui muliebri praedicare studuerat" (p. 326). For a fifteenth-century story of a woman who disguised herself as a man in order to attend university, see Martin of Leibitz (or of Zips) (d. 1461?), "Senatorium sive dialogus historicus Martini abbatis Scotorum Viennae Austriae," in Hieronymus Pez, ed., *Scriptores rerum Austriacarum veteres ac genuini* . . . , 2 vols. (Leipzig, 1725), vol. 2, col. 629ff., cited in Michael H. Shank, "A Female University Student in Medieval Cracow," *Signs* (forthcoming).

45. In the popular festivals of late medieval Europe, men sometimes masqueraded as women (see Davis, *Society and Culture*, pp. 124–31), and such practices were frequently disapproved of by moralists and theologians. (For an example of disapproval, see Salimbene's chronicle in Coulton, *Francis to Dante*, p. 220.) Moreover, the idea of female cross-dressing was a threatening symbol to men; and there is reason to suspect that the tales of transvestite women that circulated in monastic circles were sometimes expressions of male anxiety and prurience without basis in historical fact (see Anson, "Female Transvestite").

46. See above, n. 8, chap. 8 at n. 8, chap. 9 at n. 15.

47. See above, chap. 9 n. 16. We should not forget that although Catherine spoke of men as courageous and women as weak, she applied the adjectives *manly* and *womanly* to people of both genders; see above, chap. 5 n. 171.

48. Dronke, WW, passim, esp. pp. 66, 82.

49. Julian, *Book of Showings*, ed. Colledge and Walsh, The Short Text, chap. 6; pt. 1, p. 222; the reference is deleted in The Long Text.

50. See above, pp. 179, 261–67, chap. 5 n. 171, and Bynum, JM, chap. 5.

51. See above, pp. 24–25. Dinzelbacher, *Vision und Visionsliteratur*, p. 229, sums up differences between early medieval visions, characteristic of men, and later visions, characteristic of women, in a way that underlines this point. Women's visions were expected and sought for; men's occurred suddenly. Women's visions confirmed them in an already chosen way of life; men's marked the onset of a new life.

52. See above, n. 29. See also Judith Van Herik, "The Feminist Critique of Classical Psychoanalysis," in David Tracy and Steven Kepnes, eds., *The Challenge of Psychology to Faith* [*Concilium: Revue internationale de théologie* 156] (Edinborough: Clark, 1982), pp. 83–86.

53. See above, nn. 14, 15.

54. If I am correct in this admittedly controversial interpretation, the insight should help us see how Christianity is different from the other world religions—none of which has quite this emphasis on the glory and salvific potential of suffering flesh (both ours and God's). My interpretation calls attention to the characteristically Christian idea that the bodily suffering of one person can be substituted for the suffering of another through prayer, purgatory, vicarious communion, etc., and suggests that this idea should not be taken for granted as an implication of the Crucifixion. Rather, it should be explored as one of the most puzzling, characteristic, glorious, and horrifying features of Christianity. See above, chap. 7 n. 54.

♦ Epilogue

1. The quotations come, respectively, from "Forms of the Implicit Love of God," in Simone Weil, *Waiting for God*, trans. Emma Craufurd (New York: Harper and Row reprint of 1951 Putnam ed.), p. 166, and idem, *First and Last Notebooks*, trans. Richard Rees (London: Oxford University Press, 1970), p. 96. On Weil, see Elizabeth Hardwick, "Reflections on Simone Weil," *Signs* 1.1 (Autumn 1975): 83–91, and Judith Van Herik, "Looking, Eating and Waiting in Simone Weil," in T. A. Idinopulos and J. Z. Knopp, eds., *Mysticism, Nihilism, Feminism: New Critical Essays on the Anti-Theology of Simone Weil* (Johnson City, Tenn.: Institute of Social Sciences and the Arts, 1984), pp. 57–90.

2. Ruth Benedict, *Patterns of Culture* (Boston: Houghton Mifflin, 1934), p. 26; quoted in Sheila McLeod, *The Art of Starvation: A Story of Anorexia and Survival* (New York: Schocken, 1982), p. 39. McLeod, whose book is, in my opinion, the best of the recent spate of confessional literature about anorexia, states that she was "horrified and disgusted" by menstruation, that she felt herself to be a "source of pollution," and that she "perhaps sensed" the secrecy surrounding menstruation as "an indication of the inferior status of women" (pp. 39–40). For other autobiographical accounts of anorexia, see Cherry Boone O'Neill, *Starving for Attention* (New York: Continuum, 1982); Aimee Liu, *Solitaire: A Narrative* (New York: Harper and Row, 1979); and Katherine Havekamp, *Love Comes in Buckets* (London: M. Boyars, 1978).

3. See "Neumann, Theresa," in *New Catholic Encyclopedia*, vol. 10 (New York: McGraw-Hill, 1967), pp. 365–66. There is much discussion of Theresa Neumann and other nineteenth-century Catholic cases, especially Louise Lateau (d. 1883) and Domenica Lazzari (d. 1848), in Thurston, PP.

4. See above, chap. 6 n. 38.

5. *Ms.* magazine (October 1983): 41–46, 92ff. The sensationalist headline to Susan Squire's "Is the Binge-Purge Cycle Catching?" reads: "At least half of the women on campus today suffer from some kind of eating disorder."

6. See above, chap. 6 at nn. 35–37.

7. The first English-language definition of anorexia nervosa was provided by Sir William Gull in 1874; see Brumberg, "'Fasting Girls.'"

8. On this point see Rachel Jacoff, "God as Mother: Julian of Norwich's Theology of Love," *Denver Quarterly* 18.4 (Winter 1984), pp. 134–39.

9. See above, pp. 201–2 and chap. 6 n. 8, for recent approaches to "eating" that concentrate on "control." For a modern, unorthodox, and very beautiful evocation of the medieval sense of body—God's body and ours—see the short story by Andre Dubus, "Adultery," in Dubus, *Adultery and Other Choices* (Boston: Godine, 1979), pp. 129–78.

10. See Thomä, *Anorexia nervosa*. The point against the Freudians is made nicely in a modern novel about Jungian analysis by Robertson Davies, *The Manticore* (Harmondsworth: Penguin, 1976), pp. 70–71. The words are put into the mouth of a female psychoanalyst speaking to a male patient: "Sex is very important, but if it were the single most important thing in life it would all be much simpler. . . . It is a popular delusion, you know, that people who live very close to nature are great ones for sex. Not a bit. You live with primitives . . . and you find out the truth. People wander around naked and nobody cares. . . . Their important daily concern is with food. You know, you can go for a lifetime without sex and come to no special harm. Hundreds of people do so. But you go for a day without food and the matter becomes imperative. In our society food is just a start for our craving. We want all kinds of things—money, a big place in the world, objects of beauty, learning, sainthood, oh, a very long list."

11. A recent book that suggests that I am not alone in my concern is Elaine Scarry, *The Body in Pain: The Making and Unmaking of the World* (Oxford: Oxford University Press, 1985). While Scarry's argument is very different from my own, her concern with the relationship between creativity, on the one hand, and pain as experienced in the body, on the other, treats body not as that which we should reject or control but as that of which we must take account.

GENERAL INDEX

Abelard, Peter, 85, 240
Abstinence, 37–38, 41, 46, 78, 140,
    323n.47 (see also Fasting); miraculous
    abstinence, see Fasting, extended or
    miraculous
Accidia, 181, 203
Acher of Turnhout, 350n.23
Adelhausen, 315n.42
Adelheid Langmann of Engelthal, 130,
    246
Adelheid of Katharinental, 77
Adorno, Giuliano, 181
Aelred of Rievaulx, 87–88, 92
Affective piety, 105, 112, 255; erotic
    themes in, see Mysticism, nuptial or
    erotic themes in; importance to
    women, 26, 105, 153–61, 246–51,
    261–96
Agnes Blannbekin, 77, 237, 333n.27,
    355n.103, 377n.135
Agnes of Montepulciano, 246, 273,
    365n.213; Catherine of Siena writes
    about, 169, 170, 241, 243; eucharistic
    piety of, 140, 362n.186; fasting, 169,
    241, 243, 362n.186; myroblyte, 211,
    274, 392n.85; rains of manna, 74,
    145, 166, 234, 273, 371n.68, 412n.75;
    Raymond of Capua's life of, 166
Agnes of Oberweimar, 113–14
Agnes of Prague, 86, 100
Alan de la Roche, 410n.56
Alan of Lille, 31, 44, 45, 64, 253
Albert the Great, 58, 80, 85, 214,
    327n.111

Albigensians. *See* Heresy, dualist
Alda (Aldobrandesca) of Siena, 140,
    142, 145, 209, 214, 272, 362n.186,
    364n.212, 412n.76
Alice of Schaerbeke, 115, 116, 117,
    119, 121, 130, 230, 234, 248, 275,
    351n.34
Almsgiving, 31, 33, 35
Alpaïs of Cudot, 91, 146, 168, 213, 275,
    299; abstinence, 73, 83, 84, 200; food
    distribution and service, 134–35; ha-
    giographers' descriptions of her, 73,
    84, 148, 388n.51; illness, 196, 198,
    200, 205, 308n.6
Ambrose, 32
Anchoresses, 15, 75, 255. *See also*
    Recluses
Ancrene Riwle, 172
Andrew the Apostle, 392n.85
Androgynous imagery, 28, 236, 263, 291,
    292
Angela of Foligno, 146, 148, 152, 186;
    eucharistic piety of, 140, 141–42, 232,
    246, 361nn.176, 181; fasting, 86, 142,
    143–44, 203, 337n.92, 363n.187; food
    as symbol, 86, 143–45, 186; on the
    humanity of Christ, 232, 246, 247–
    48, 258; as "mother" to friars, 27,
    229; relation to her family, 24, 206,
    215, 363n.190, 395n.11; sense of self,
    143–45, 206, 401n.84; service of sick,
    144–45, 182, 204
Anna von Munzingen, 315n.42
Anna Vorchtlin, 250

421

Margaret of Ypres, 24, 115, 116, 117,
119, 120, 200, 203, 214, 247, 256,
351n.35
Margaret Porete, 22, 185–86, 277, 279,
290, 296, 384n.208
Margery Kempe, 7, 206, 221, 280, 291,
318n.65, 390n.64, 417n.44; erotic or
maternal yearnings toward Christ,
28, 246, 247, 263, 396n.21; fasting,
88, 193, 219; identification with Virgin Mary, 269, 270; relationship to
husband, 88, 193, 206, 215, 219, 221,
396n.21
Marriage, 19, 20, 120, 125, 136, 167, 203,
214–16, 220, 222–23, 226–27, 237,
394n.112; of Mary and Joseph, 239;
mystical, 131, 174–75, 246, 248; as a
theme in saints' lives, 24–25, 181,
226, 395n.11; theology of, 238, 254;
women's rebellion against, 222–26,
261, 293, 395n.11
Martha, 134, 284
Martin of Bosco-Gualteri, 356n.108
Martin of Leibitz, 417n.44
Mary, mother of Jesus. See Virgin Mary
Mary Magdalen, 81, 94, 166, 255, 284,
334n.38, 338n.98, 340n.134, 415n.22
Mary Magdalen de' Pazzi, 273, 386n.25,
412n.75
Mary of Oignies, 7, 112, 124, 199, 250,
388n.43, 398n.29; concern with
fluids, 123, 274; desire for poverty,
24, 121, 193; ecstasies, 115–16, 209,
255, 402n.5; eucharistic piety of, 59,
119, 228; fasting and other austerities, 117, 119, 121, 203, 204, 213, 214,
234, 274; James of Vitry's treatment
of her, see James of Vitry; service,
121, 124, 130, 221, 275; stigmata,
119, 274; struggle with family, 120,
193, 215, 227; tears, 115; tests priests,
117, 228, 229
Mary the Egyptian, 81
Mass of St. Gregory, iconographic
theme, 68, 331n.153, 399n.40, plate 3

Matthew Paris, 90, 417n.44
Matthia of Nazarei, 392n.85
Mattiotti, John, 395n.6
Maximus of Turin, 35
Mechtild of Hackeborn, 62, 139, 185,
232, 254, 261, 356n.121, 391n.78,
404n.32
Mechtild of Magdeburg, 209, 222, 263,
279, 291, 401n.81, 410n.47; criticizes
clergy, 27, 229, 235–36; eating metaphors, 3, 31, 106, 133, 186, 250, 271;
eucharistic piety of, 3, 133; on evil,
242, 290; on the Virgin Mary, 133,
265; visions, 133
Mechtild of Nimègue, 334n.49
Menstruation, 122, 123, 138, 148, 190,
202, 211, 214, 217, 239, 274, 283, 300,
394n.105, 418n.2
Miracles: anti-Semitic overtones of, 64;
of blood, 329nn.135, 138; as denun-
ciation of heresy or superstition, 63–
64, 253; of eucharistic distribution,
77, 78, 117–19, 127–29, 130–32, 140–
42, 230, 236–37, 398nn.37, 38, 41,
400n.61, plate 11; of food multiplication or feeding, 76, 90, 122, 126–
27, 138, 145, 146, 148, 170, 192, 233–
34, 357n.127, 396n.13, plates 8, 9 (see
also Lactation, miraculous); interpretation of, 8, 82, 83–84, 87, 151, 194,
391n.82; concerning nature of eucharist, 51, 59–60, 63–64, 76–77, 78,
140–42, 228–33, 274–75, 328n.121,
332n.24, 397n.25
Mirrors for Virgins, 214
Misogyny, 6, 15, 22–23, 27, 86, 208–9,
214, 216–17, 237–38, 262–63, 288,
295, 313n.27, 315nn.43–44, 316n.45,
319n.74. See also Quasi-clerical roles
of women, decline of
Monstrance, 55, 101
Montaillou, 266, 290
Ms. Magazine, 298
Myroblytes, 89, 93, 123, 136, 145–46,
211, 274, 339n.115, 358n.139, 391n.85

INDEX OF SECONDARY AUTHORS

Editors are indexed for the first citation of their names only, unless they are authors as well.

435